EXISTENTIAL PHILOSOPHERS:
KIERKEGAARD TO MERLEAU-PONTY

EXISTENTIAL PHILOSOPHERS:
KIERKEGAARD TO MERLEAU-PONTY

EDITED BY **GEORGE ALFRED SCHRADER, JR.**
PROFESSOR OF PHILOSOPHY, YALE UNIVERSITY

McGRAW-HILL BOOK COMPANY
NEW YORK   ST. LOUIS   SAN FRANCISCO   TORONTO   LONDON   SYDNEY

The cover drawing is a lithograph titled "Negro"
by the Venezuelan artist Gégo.
Courtesy of the Weyhe Gallery

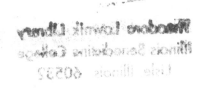

PREFACE

Existential philosophy has played a dominant role in European thought for at least two decades, but it is only within the past few years that it has attracted the attention of American Philosophers. Kierkegaard had been intensively studied by American theologians as early as the 1930s, and, to a lesser extent, Nietzsche. Thus the impact of existentialist thought was felt much earlier in the field of religion than in philosophy. This was due in part to the fact that Kierkegaard was a religiously oriented thinker. But it was due, also, to the absence of naturalistic and positivistic inhibitions on the part of American theologians. The ground had thus been prepared on the American scene for the appropriation of Kierkegaard's philosophical views and a sympathetic reading of those philosophers who have been influenced by him.

The version of existentialist thought that has been best known in this country is that of Jean-Paul Sartre. His plays have been widely read and some of them have been produced in the United States. His book, *Being and Nothingness*, was the first major existentialist work of the twentieth century to be made available in a complete English edition. A few of Karl Jaspers' lectures and minor writings have been made available in English, but as yet only brief sections of his most important philosophical works, such as *Die Philosophie* or *Von der Wahrheit*, have been translated into English. And it was only three years ago that an English translation of Heidegger's most important work, *Being and Time*, made its appearance. Camus has, of course, been translated and widely read. But, like Sartre, he has been better known through his novels than through his philosophical essays. Only during the past year have the books of the late Merleau-Ponty begun to appear in English. Fortunately, they are now being translated in rapid succession.

Until quite recently, therefore, language has constituted a formidable barrier to the study of existentialist writings. It is still a serious limiting factor and will remain so until more translations of the basic materials are made availabile. This explains the fact that it has been more a popular than an explicitly philosophical version of existentialism with which we have been acquainted. Those readers who, in addition to Sartre's plays and the novels of Camus, read *Being and Nothingness*, Heidegger's *Being and Time*, Jaspers' *Die Philosophie*, or Merleau-Ponty's *The Phenomenology of Perception* are certain to be surprised at the subtlety and complexity of existential philosophy. The authors contributing to this volume have made use of the complete writings of the thinker whose philosophy is expounded. They have not only consulted these works in the original language but, in many instances, made their own translations of quoted passages. Our effort has been to offer a critical exposition of the major existentialist writers in the complete context of their writings. We hope, thereby, to refer the reader to materials which might not otherwise have come to his attention.

In recent years there have been a number of accounts of existential philosophy published in English and other languages. But they have tended to fall into two classes. For the most part they have been devoted either to a detailed exposition of a single writer or to a survey of existentialist thought. The conception which underlies the present volume is to present an exposition of existentialism that will neither limit itself to a single writer nor attempt a survey. Each of the existentialists considered has been treated in depth by an author who has devoted major attention to his writings. This procedure has the merit of allowing fairly definitive monographs on each philosopher. In addition, it permits greater diversity in the presentation and critical appraisal of existentialist thought. No attempt has been made to provide a survey of existentialist thought or even to make a comparative evaluation of existentialist writings. As will be evident to the reader, the authors differ widely among themselves as to what they consider important and unimportant, valid and invalid, in existential philosophy. The reader has been deliberately left with the opportunity and necessity of making his own estimate not only of existential philosophy but of the interpretations of it that are offered. We have sought to avoid the impression that there is a single and uniform version of "existential philosophy."

It may strike some readers as surprising that Nietzsche has not been included in this volume. He might well have been included, since he shares a great deal with Kierkegaard and has had an important influence on contemporary existentialist thought. He has not been included for two reasons. First, we have sought to concentrate on contemporary versions of existentialism, and hence have favored more recent thinkers. Second, of the two nineteenth-century representatives of existentialism, Kierkegaard has been more directly influential for subsequent developments than Nietzsche. This judgment could be debated, so I should not wish to put too much stress on it. The scope of the volume required that some limitation be imposed, and of the two, Kierkegaard seemed to be more at the center of contemporary existentialist thought than Nietzsche.

Since Heidegger, existential philosophy and phenomenology have been so intertwined that it is extremely difficult to separate them. Heidegger, Sartre, and Merleau-Ponty are all quite self-conscious about using a phenomenological method and could be legitimately counted as phenomenologists. Still, it is an existentially oriented phenomenology that they have pursued. If we had chosen to emphasize the phenomenological rather than the existential contribution of these writers, it would have been important, also, to include Husserl in our discussion. Husserl has made important contributions to existentialism and could not be ignored in any account of the history of existentialist thought. He has been omitted from this volume because he was not and did not consider himself to be an existentialist. Moreover, in important respects existentialist thought is basically incompatible with the Husserlian attempt to offer a purely descriptive analysis of essential structures. Still, if space had permitted, it would have been desirable to include an exposition of Husserl's philosophy among these essays.

The authors have not directed their essays to any one particular audience. It is hoped that they will prove illuminating to readers with no special background in the subject, as well as to those with an extensive knowledge of it. Because of the existentialists' concern with analysis of the concrete human situation, no reader should have difficulty in gaining access to or following the main drift of the exposition. Here and there the full appreciation of a point may require some degree of philosophical sophistication, but even such passages should not prove unintelligible to the reflective reader.

The immediate objective of these essays is to acquaint the reader with the main versions of current existentialist philosophy. Its ultimate purpose it to provide stimulation and provocation for thought along whatever lines it may take. The problems which have concerned the existentialist writers are both timely and perennial. We may hope to be instructed by them even where we most violently disagree with their conclusions.

GEORGE ALFRED SCHRADER, JR.

CONTENTS

CHAPTER ONE

EXISTENTIAL PHILOSOPHY
RESURGENT HUMANISM

GEORGE ALFRED SCHRADER, JR.

GEORGE ALFRED SCHRADER, JR. *is a professor of philosophy at Yale University, where he was master of Branford College from 1959 until 1966. He received his A.B. from Park College and his B.D. and Ph.D. from Yale. In addition to teaching, he serves as a member of the editorial boards of Kantstudien, The Journal of Existentialism, American Philosophical Quarterly, and Supplementa Kantiana. His publications include "The Thing-in-Itself in Kantian Philosophy"* (Review of Metaphysics, *March, 1949); "Kant's Presumed Repudiation of the 'Moral Argument' in the opus postumum: an Examination of Adickes' Interpretation"* (Philosophy, *July, 1951); "The Status of Teleological Judgment in the Kantian Philosophy"* (Kantstudien, *1953–1954); "Value and Valuation"* in Faith and Ethics *(ed. Paul Ramsey, Harper's, October, 1957); "Existence, Truth, and Subjectivity"* (Journal of Philosophy, *December, 1956); "Responsibility and Existence"* (in Nomos, *Vol. III (The Liberal Arts Press, 1960); "Ontology and the Categories of Existence"* (Kantstudien, *1963); "Emil Brunner's Conception of Philosophy"* in The Library of Living Theology, *Vol. III (The Macmillan Company, 1962); "Autonomy, Heteronomy, and Moral Imperatives"* (Journal of Philosophy, *January, 1963); and "Basic Problems of Philosophical Ethics"* (Archiv für Geschichte der Philosophie, *1964).*

1. The Crisis
in American Philosophy

Attempts to define philosophy by explicating those doctrines and procedures which are held in common by all philosophers are condemned
from the start to a trivial result. To speak interestingly about philosophy is necessarily to speak from a philosophical point of view—even
where one wishes to speak about the whole of it. By the same token
it would be unrewarding to attempt a statement of existential philosophy in terms of a set of shared doctrines. Like any so-called "school"
of philosophy, the existentialist thinkers are characterized as much by
their vigorous differences as by their agreements. Moreover it is not
simply with respect to secondary theses that they disagree, but on
those basic issues the treatment of which sets them apart from other
thinkers. As might be expected from thinkers who stress the importance of the individual, their writings bear the unmistakable mark of
their own individuality. If it makes sense to speak at all of "existential philosophy," it is only because of those shared concerns and
problems which, in spite of considerable diversity, constitute a distinctive philosophical orientation. In writing about "existential philosophy" I shall, therefore, make no pretense to have fitted a diverse set
of thinkers into a common mold nor to have filtered out a set of
doctrines on which they are in implicit if not explicit agreement. I
shall concentrate rather on those questions which have been at the
center of existentialist thought, hoping thereby to set in relief some
of the distinctive categories of this philosophical "point of view."
Although nothing of importance in the exposition will be original in
the sense that it has not been first asserted by one or more of the
thinkers considered in this volume, it would be vain to pretend that
the exposition is anything other than my own. Nothing could be
more comical than a discussion of existentialist philosophy which
claimed to be purely "objective." The expositer necessarily evaluates
and interprets in the way that he selects, presents, and analyzes the
materials with which he works. Both in deciding what to argue for
and how to argue for it, the author is forced to commit himself
philosophically. I shall hope to accept that responsibility in the
modest sketch that follows.

The criticism has been frequently leveled against existential philosophy that
it is essentially a "philosophy of crisis," a despairing response to the
disillusionment of the two World Wars. This criticism is a curious one
for two reasons. In the first place, the two main progenitors of
existentialist thought both wrote during the nineteenth century.
Søren Kierkegaard died in 1855 and Nietzsche in 1900. In view of
the heavy indebtedness of contemporary existentialism to these two
thinkers, the criticism simply misconstrues the historical context
within which existentialist thought was first developed. But more
interesting is the fact that this should be conceived of as a serious
philosophical criticism at all. There can be no doubt that each of the
existentialist thinkers from Kierkegaard to Camus was responding to
what he took to be a critical turn in human history. The criticism

mentioned above is obviously predicated on the assumption that philosophy should have nothing to do with such crises. The question then is not merely whether existential philosophy is a "philosophy of crisis" and thus historically conditioned, but whether philosophy is ever justified in addressing itself to the concrete human situation. It is by no means self-evident that philosophy is legitimately concerned only with a-temporal being or that philosophical truth is a-historical. Nor can the assumption be left unquestioned that philosophy should be oblivious of and irrelevant to the particularities of the human condition. Indeed, much of the appeal of existential philosophy derives from the fact that it has concerned itself with human existence in its cultural and historical context. This is not to say that it has not been concerned about those factors which are constitutive of what Kierkegaard termed the "universally human." It is to confess that the existentialist philosophers have deliberately and self-consciously addressed themselves to the human situation as they themselves have been involved in it.

Eschewing the traditional objective of locating man within an a-temporal cosmos, the existentialist writers have sought to illume those everyday activities and concerns which characterize man's temporal existence. Although they have sought to analyze and describe forms of existence which are unique to twentieth-century man, they have appealed to a logic and an ontology which permits transcendence of this and other historical epochs. The fact that the existentialist thinkers have insisted on human temporality does not entail the rejection of categories which are constitutive of human existence as such. Fortunately we are not forced to choose between an essentialist analysis of man and his world which articulates an objective and a-temporal metaphysics, and a completely parochial and time-bound analysis of a limited phase of human existence. To understand the actuality of man's present situation we must grasp those general possibilities which account for the more ultimate and persistent forms of human motivation. Existentialist philosophers have been no less concerned with such universal and a priori conditions than their classical forebears. It is only that they have insisted on holding the universal and the particular in intimate association at every point in their investigations. If man is intrinsically a finite and temporal being for whom the category of becoming is fundamental, the categories of human existence must themselves participate in temporality. To be universally valid they need not be timeless, but only necessary conditions of human becoming at all times. It is a long-standing though unwarranted philosophical prejudice that for concepts and categories to be universal they cannot change over time. So long as a concept provides a continuous theme to unify temporal process, it need not itself be immune to change. As a matter of fact, all of the fundamental categories of philosophy have been altered in meaning during the course of Western history. If they could not change over time, philosophy itself would be incapable of genuine development. As is evident from the fact that existentialist thought poses something of a crisis for philosophy, the conception of philosophy itself is subject to

constant change.   As in the case of art, the phenomena of the past
can never provide sufficient guidance for determining what is to be
counted as genuine for the future.   There is, of course, a philosophical tradition which provides general guidelines for future experimentation.   But is it not sufficiently closed or definite to determine uniquely
the course of future developments.

To see how existentialist philosophy poses an issue for contemporary
American philosophy it may be useful to review briefly the American
philosophical tradition and, within that context, to consider the viable
present-day alternatives.   The first autonomous philosophy in America
was Hegelian.   Promulgated by members of the "Kant Society," it
gained widespread adherence during the second half of the nineteenth
century and virtually dominated the American scene for over fifty
years.   Josiah Royce was the most original and powerfully systematic
among American neo-Hegelians, but Hegelianism left its mark on
James, Dewey, and Peirce as well.   The most interesting feature of
Hegelian philosophy was its comprehensive relevance to all facets of
human life.   For better or for worse it had implications for religion,
education, art, and politics which were readily appropriated.   Broadly
humanistic in orientation, it prepared the ground for the pragmatism
of James and Dewey.   In many respects Dewey's instrumentalism was
a naturalized version of the prevailing idealism.   Although Dewey
sought to develop a rigorously "scientific" philosophy, he was no less
concerned about human affairs in their fullest scope than his idealist
predecessors.   Dewey's passionate concern for education was symp-
tomatic of his larger ambition to make philosophy relevant to human
experience.   To adopt Dewey's pragmatic naturalism required that one
alter the style of his existence.   Understandably enough, the influence
of Dewey's philosophy reached far beyond the narrow circle of
academic philosophers.

2. The
Positivistic Reaction

But Dewey's pragmatism was avowedly tentative and made a virtue of
vagueness and indeterminacy.   It failed to satisfy what Dewey himself
had diagnosed as the perennial "quest for certainty" among philosophers.   By the end of the Second World War, a good many American
philosophers were eager for a philosophy that would hold greater
promise for certainty and scientific exactitude.   Carrying Dewey's commitment to scientific methodology one step further, they embraced
logical positivism, which sailed under the banner of exact verification.
Experience was no longer the all-embracing affair that it was for
Dewey and the Hegelians, but the atomic deliverances of sensation
alone.   The positivists reverted to Hume in their effort to make experience the basis for verifiable knowledge.   Unlike Hume, however, the
positivists regarded the exact sciences as having a virtual monopoly
on the organization of empirical data.   In effect they regarded Dewey's
hope of making philosophy itself a "scientific" discipline as naïve.   As
they saw it, philosophy must be content to analyze the logic and

method of the exact sciences. Philosophy thus became for them essentially logic and the philosophy of science. The temper of logical positivism was basically different from and in many respects fundamentally opposed to that of Dewey's naturalism. The positivists simply had no concern at all with everyday human experience. Only negatively, in their attempt to establish that unverifiable propositions are essentially meaningless, did they concern themselves with religion or even metaphysics and ethics. Surrendering almost completely any notion of the autonomy of philosophy, they were prepared to take their standard of meaning and truth from the sciences.

Logical positivism was a purely academic and professional version of philosophy. The positivists not only turned their backs on ordinary experience, but advocated the adoption of an artificial language as philosophically ideal. Needless to say, they neither exercised nor sought to exercise any significant influence on general affairs. Although they were caught up within their own cultural epoch, as evidenced by their concern for objective certainty and their repudiation of what they regarded as "meaningless" affirmations, they took no explicit account of time or history. There can be little doubt, however, that positivitism was and is supported by a pervasive mood which defines its concerns both positively and negatively. Why the passion for certainty, objectivity, and verification? Why the impatience with ambiguity, tentativeness, and speculation? It is apparent that there were deep-seated and ultimate motivations intrinsic to positivism which lent urgency to its efforts. If one is to understand positivism as a philosophical movement, one must consider not only the explicit principles and doctrines it professed, but why it took precisely the form it did as a response to the philosophical situation within which it arose and developed. And not merely the philosophical situation, but the human situation in general. Since philosophy does not of itself dictate a specific attitude with respect to meaning and certainty, one must understand the posture of the positivists as expressive of an even more basic human concern for a satisfactory world-orientation. If limited to its own express procedures, positivism could neither understand nor criticize itself as a philosophical movement. Existential in its passion and subjective in its concern for certainty, positivism was more than an academic philosophy. In principle it sought to answer the ultimate questions as to the meaningful and meaningless, and hence to provide guidance for human affairs. If nothing more, it provided a license for free decision where strict verification is not feasible. With Hume it tended to recommend custom as the principal counsel for practical affairs.

Logical positivism is frequently subsumed under the more general rubric "analytic philosophy." The implication is that it shares basically the same orientation as other versions of current analytic philosophy such as linguistic analysis. Actually the two varieties of philosophy have relatively little in common. The term "analytic" suggests, on the one hand, a neutral mode of philosophical reflection which aspires to a pure description of phenomena. Both Husserlian phenomenology and linguistic analysis are "analytical" in that sense of the term. Logical positivism, however, cannot be regarded as "analytic" in that sense. The term "analytic" may refer, also, to a theory of concepts and propositions which regards concepts as logical constructs and necessary propositions as analytically true. In addition, it may designate a version of empiricism which holds that sense impressions can be "analyzed" into atomic units. Logical positivism may be regarded as "analytic" in so far as it espoused both of these doctrines. It is apparent that if the positivists assumed a neutral consciousness for the appropriation of sense data, they required a synthetic faculty to organize them into empirical objects. In their epistemology the positivists were modified Kantians.

Far from being neutral, the positivists committed themselves in highly partisan spirit as to the sort of data which may contribute to genuine cognition and the methods by which it must be organized. Modern science was taken to be the paradigm of empirical knowledge; the problem was simply to determine the criteria which science employs in verifying its claims. This is not to say, of course, that the positivists did not hope to add to the clarity and elegance of science. It is only to emphasize that they accepted the criteria of science as their own standard. Or so they believed. It can be questioned whether practicing scientists were ever so concerned with certainty or even with verification as the logical positivists themselves. If, as many philosophers and scientists have believed, science is nourished by an incurable speculative concern, to limit science to clear and distinct data would be to remove the tantalizing mystery which provokes the scientist to propound new theories. Logical positivism could formulate its own principles of verification only after the fact. Lacking an appreciation for the bolder and less orderly phases of scientific inquiry, it could offer no heuristic principles for a logic of discovery.

But even if one accepts the positivists' interpretation, scientific verification could represent only one method of validating truth claims. It is unpardonably dogmatic to equate scientific meaning with meaning itself or scientific truth with the whole of truth. That the positivists themselves could not altogether avoid the problem of self-reference is indicated by their difficulties in justifying the verification principle. In the end they were forced either to defend their conception of scientific truth on philosophical grounds or to admit that it was arbitrary. Yet their whole program was designed to show that scientific (verifiable) truth is the only legitimate mode of truth. The attempt to solve the basic questions of philosophy by appeal to the standards and criteria of science thus turned out to be a failure. One may continue to embrace logical positivism for methodological or personal reasons, but not, surely, for the reasons that were originally advanced in its support. It simply fails to settle the questions of meaning and truth about which it was so sanguine at its inception. We are left not only with those issues but the further question: Why should philosophy assert itself in so militant a form of positivism? It might seem at first reading that logical positivism is the perfect embodiment of what Kierkegaard termed "objective thought," but precisely the opposite is the case. In their passionate affirmation of their philosophical doctrines, they satisfied Kierkegaard's canon of subjective thinking, namely that one must "exist in his thought." It is because of their rigorous consistency that we are able to determine the strengths and weaknesses of positivism as a philosophical movement. If they failed to relate their philosophy adequately to themselves as men it was not because of objective detachment. They were personally serious in the best sense of the term about such matters as meaning, truth, and certainty. The inadequacy of their philosophical position on existential grounds derives from their programmatic reduction of the scope of philosophy, together with their refusal to offer a reflexive justification of their own first principles.

3. Linguistic Analysis

More recently, however, another form of "analytic philosophy" has come upon the scene, namely, linguistic analysis. It has very little in common with logical positivism, save, perhaps, a common disposition to atomism and a shared distaste for speculation. So far as I can see, however, linguistic analysis is in no way doctrinally committed to any form of atomism, nor is it in principle precluded from considering the language of speculation. Indeed, some linguistic analysts are contextualists in their interpretation of language, and others are not averse to analyzing the language of religion and metaphysics. They profess, however, to be analysts in a perfectly straightforward sense of the term, namely, that they simply assess those meanings which are intrinsic to language without modifying, improving, or even appraising it. For the linguistic analyst, therefore, analysis tends to be a neutral and uninvolved mode of reflection. It attempts to assess only those meanings that are intrinsic to language as used. The reflective analysis thus presumably occurs at a higher (meta-) level than the language analyzed. The goal is to achieve a pure descriptive result. Any statements which the philosopher makes as philosopher are only statements about language as used by others or oneself in one's extra-philosophical capacity. If such a program were possible, it is evident that the philosopher would thus be relieved of all responsibility for meaning and truth at the primary level. He would not even be required to define meaning and truth, but only to indicate how these notions function in ordinary usage.

But is such a program possible? And why "ordinary usage?" Is there really an "ordinary man" whose language is not infected with theological, political, and metaphysical conceptions of some sort? Is not the ordinary man a Christian, a Jew, or an atheist? Does he not accept or reject Marxism and generally with supporting reasons? How does one understand theological or metaphysical concepts as they occur in ordinary usage? Must one not undertake the study of Christian theology or Marxist metaphysics if one is to understand the views that are invoked with linguistic tokens? Or, one may be a Platonist, a Humean, or a Kantian. How is one to understand the term "impression" or "cause" when used by someone imbued with such philosophical notions? And, particularly, how can one tell when such terms are being used correctly or even sensibly? Is not the very notion of ordinary language misleading insofar as it implies a language that is free of highly sophisticated concepts and theories? The language of science, theology, and metaphysics has a way of filtering down into ordinary speech in such a way that our discourse is seriously influenced by fairly comprehensive theories. Freudian terms, for example, are bandied about these days in ordinary discourse with little or no detailed knowledge of Freud's theories. Will common speech reveal what the term "libido" means in Freud's theories? Can one reconstruct Marx's theory of economic determinism from the fragments of his views that occur in daily speech? It seems very hard to believe that reading the daily newspaper or talking with people on the street could ever serve as an adequate substitute for the reading of Freud or Marx. Is it not the other way round, namely, that to understand ordinary discourse we must make explicit appeal to those developed theories which supply many of the terms for common discourse? The answer might be given that we can reconstruct popular Marxism or popular Freudianism from ordinary language. True. But would not that entail a considerable measure of extrapolation on the part of the analyst and hence a major synthetic endeavor? Is that not in fact the sort of skill required of the cultural anthropologist? Is there any reason to believe that a philosopher, simply by being clear-headed and reflective, can achieve the same sort of result?

But there is a second difficulty with a mode of analysis that professes to remain neutral with respect to the contents analyzed. To analyze language the philosopher must determine for himself what language means in its everyday use. Thus to reflect on usage he must play two roles, namely, that of participant in ordinary usage and reflective analyst. He must therefore make appeal to his own primary and experiential understanding of language in carrying out his philosophical project. Since his analytical conclusions necessarily reflect and presuppose his initial understanding of usage, the former cannot be neutral with respect to the latter. If the analysis of language appears to be purely neutral, it can only be because many of the decisions as to meaning have already been made. If one is ever to challenge linguistic meanings as reflectively assessed, one must be able to call into question the primary meanings themselves. It is not possible, therefore, for two philosophers to settle a point of difference about language at the level of meta-reflection alone. If, for example, one of them is a Kantian he will mean something different when using the word "duty" from his utilitarian colleague. Language in use and language as analyzed simply cannot be separated. Not only do the analytical conclusions inevitably reflect decisions as to the primary meaning of language, but reflective conclusions influence ordinary usage itself. A purely neutral description of linguistic meaning is impossible.

I should hasten to point out that there is no reason why this should constitute an embarrassment to the linguistic analyst. He need not surrender his claim as to the importance of language nor even his techniques of analysis. If he frankly recognizes that in analyzing language he must lay down rules as well as assess them, he may proceed without encumbrance. It is, in fact, the reflexive character of such an undertaking that makes it philosophically important. Philosophical reflection is all the more interesting because it cannot successfully adopt a position of neutrality. If objectivity actually required that philosophical reflection be neutral to its materials, it would thereby be rendered largely irrelevant as well. Ordinary language and ordinary experience are in need of philosophical insight not only to clarify them but to improve them. Language reveals the way in which we understand ourselves and our world. Without language our understanding would be both mute and primitive. But ordinary language may be enriched rather than impoverished by the addition of explicit philosophical categories. Adherence to the principles of objectivity and empiricism does not require such modesty as the linguistic analyst frequently professes.

I have referred to linguistic analysis because it stands in competition with existential philosophy on the present American scene. Since existential philosophy professes to be dialectical and involved in its reflections on the human situation, the two appear to stand in the sharpest sort of opposition to one another. As we have seen, the issue turns in part on the status of ordinary language. If philosophy is precluded from introducing categories of its own or, for that matter, from the consideration of language in all of its ramifications, linguistic analysis can claim a legitimate monopoly on philosophical inquiry. But surely even the existentialist thinkers deserve to be read. Yet, how are they to be read or philosophically understood if we are confined to ordinary language? It is one thing to emphasize that philosophical conceptions may be intrinsic to ordinary usage and quite another to limit philosophy to the clarification of ordinary language.

A second and more important issue is that concerning the nature of philosophical reflection as such. If philosophical reflection is intrinsically neutral, any form of existential reflection must be judged a-philosophical. And it is precisely this criticism that some analytic philosophers are prepared to level against it. Against this contention it can be argued that philosophy since the time of Plato has been characterized by its reflexivity. It has not taken the deliverances of the so-called "common man" at face value nor has it hesitated to instruct him. Although from time to time appeal has been made to pure intuition, and hence to a reflecting consciousness that might simply appropriate what is transparently given, this project has had only limited success. The drive toward certainty in philosophy has provided strong motivation for such a program. But the difficulty with the claim to pure intuition—or pure analysis—is that the certainty of the reflective conclusion can never have better credentials than the original datum. If, for purposes of an objective reflection, the datum is left unquestioned —as is required for any pure intuition—it is impossible to provide it with a philosophical pedigree. It is for this reason that such doctrines as sense certainty have been subjected to continual philosophical

scrutiny. If one is to question and justify the original data of reflection, the task for philosophy is made more difficult, but at the same
time, it promises a far more satisfactory result. Philosophical reflection can remain neutral and aloof from its materials only if it fails to
be self-critical and self-justifying. Whether or not the linguistic analyst wishes to undertake the task of self-referential justification, it is
a problem to be dealt with and one that by long-standing tradition has
been assigned to philosophy. It is a mistake, however, to believe that
to become involved with the problem of self-reference precludes
genuine objectivity. On the contrary, it is only when philosophical
principles and procedures are themselves subjected to reflective
scrutiny that true objectivity can be achieved. All inquiry has a
reflexive aspect and philosophical inquiry an explicit reflexive task.
There is and can be no ultimate dichotomy or opposition between
objective reflection and existential inquiry.

The crisis facing American philosophy and American culture today is whether
philosophy is to concern itself directly with all facets of human
experience, not only for the sake of clarifying language and practice,
but to question, modify, and inform it. Whereas analytic philosophy
seeks to remain aloof and uninvolved, existential philosophy begins at
the point of direct personal concern and develops that concern in
formulating its own philosophical theses. Whatever may be one's
tastes and predilections in doing philosophy—and there is adequate
room for variety—the examination of human existence is an objective
which philosophy cannot eschew without seriously impoverishing
itself. If objective truth must be irrelevant to practice, and if eternal
truth is unattainable, a temporal truth that illumines human existence
as it struggles with everyday problems is not to be despised. Philosophy cannot really afford to be too respectable or too academic. Nor
can it afford to surrender the ancient ideal of a wisdom that marries
theory to practice. Existential and analytic philosophy are both essential to the larger task of reflective inquiry. They stand in opposition
only where their proponents take a dogmatic stance and claim a
finality and completeness to which they are not entitled.

In view of the American philosophical tradition, it should not appear surprising that existential philosophy should claim adherents among
American philosophers. It has been, after all, only two decades since
Dewey's pragmatism dominated American thought. Moreover, since
the middle of the last century European ideas have played a crucial
role in shaping American philosophy. It is thus not at all strange that
at the present time American philosophers should be interested in
Heidegger as well as Wittgenstein, in Husserl as well as Russell.
There is no reason to believe that the deeply rooted humanistic tradition of American thought could be permanently displaced by any form
of positivism. Indeed, one of the primary attractions of linguistic
analysis for American philosophers is due to the fact that analysis
involves a radical turn toward concrete experience. Up to the present
time Europe has had a virtual monopoly on existential philosophy.
A good many books have been written *about* existentialism in England

and America, but it has yet to receive a systematic and original expression in either country. What may be hoped for is that existential philosophy will provide a fresh and provocative resource for a new turn in American philosophy. One of the most important lessons we stand to learn from this type of philosophy is that an authentic philosophy must be developed out of our own living tradition. This is not to recommend that American philosophy should become chauvinistic or parochial, or even that it should try to be American. It is only to urge that there are no better materials for philosophical reflection than those supplied by the total situation within which we are presently immersed. Language doubtless has a special significance for the British in that for them it represents the sedimentation of a distinctive way of life. In the United States we simply cannot speak of "ordinary language" in the same way. The situations of the American and the Britisher are different in a great many respects and these differences are philosophically important. If existential philosophy is essentially European in origin and temper, analytic philosophy is peculiarly British. We have much to learn from both traditions and need not hesitate to expound and emulate them as we develop those forms which will be peculiarly our own. Ultimately, however, there can be no substitute for autonomy.

4. The Concern
about Existence

Existential philosophy takes its name from its concern about human existence. Although the term "existence" had been used in Danish and in German to designate things generally, after Kierkegaard it came to have a special and restricted reference. Existence came by stipulation to connote human existence as distinguished from all other sorts of beings. Some expositors of existential philosophy have mistakenly concluded that the distinctive feature of existentialism is its repudiation of fixed essences. They thus construe the concern about existence as a general concern about all existent beings and the stress on existence as a reaction against essentialism. Certain statements of Sartre may have given currency to this interpretation, as also Heidegger's claim that "the essence of man is his existence." But neither Heidegger nor Sartre were concerned about existent beings generally. Nor, for that matter, did either of them or any of the existentialist philosophers advocate a general doctrine of the priority of existence to essence. The status of essential structures has been a long-standing issue in philosophy. In some important respects existential philosophy has a bearing on this issue. But it is by no means the central issue posed by existential philosophers, nor does it reflect their particular concern about existence. Existential philosophy from Kierkegaard to the present has been especially concerned to analyze the peculiar conditions and structures of *human* existence. It is this concern rather than any general metaphysical or epistemological interest in the substance/essence issue that lies at the center of their reflections.

By virtue of its restriction to man, the term "existence" came to have a
special and somewhat technical meaning in existentialist thought. In
everyday speech and not infrequently when talking metaphysics we
speak of any actual entity as existing. In referring to its existence
we mean only to indicate that it is an actual being of some sort
discernible within the empirical world. And we speak even of the
existence of God, meaning that He is an actual rather than a merely
possible being. As soon, however, as we limit the term existence to
human beings it begins to take on special meaning. It then refers
to those special conditions which pertain to the human situation.
Thus from an existentialist point of view to say that a man *exists* is
not merely to say that he is actual in the way that all things are
actual, but to refer to the unique *way* in which he is present in the
world. Just to say that human existence is unique is, of course,
uninformative and of no philosophical significance. As soon, however, as the distinctive features of man's existence are specified, the
term existence begins to take on philosophical import. It is not quite
fair, perhaps, to preempt the term existence for man, since we need
the term to indicate the reality of the great variety of beings copresent with him in the world. But it is tempting to use the single
term "existence" rather than the more complete expression "human
existence" to refer to human beings. Thus Heidegger has used the
German expression *"Dasein"* as a technical term to refer to human
existence. The term *"Dasein"* in standard German usage is as general in connotation as the English term "existence." It is simply that
within Heidegger's philosophical program it has acquired a highly
technical meaning that is carried over into translations of his writings.
And yet in another sense it is not technical at all, since it is defined
initially by Heidegger as designating "that being which I myself am."

Actually it makes little difference whether we understand the term existence
to mean human existence or use the more complete expression. In
either case the important point is that we understand those conditions
which are unique to the being of man. It is surely preferable to
translate the German term *"Dasein"* as either existence or human
existence than to leave it untranslated—especially since in German
it is such a perfectly ordinary word. I have referred to this semantic
problem for two reasons. First, as indicated above, it is important
not to interpret existential philosophy as anti-essentialist and hence
as taking its departure from a general theory of existence. If anything, existentialist thinkers have been too little concerned about
existent things in general, and some of them at least would deny
that existence precedes essence with respect to all entities. Even for
Heidegger existence does not precede essence; it *is* the essence of
man. In the second place, it is important to distinguish between
existence in general and the special mode of human existence. So
long as these distinctions are noted, it makes little difference whether
we regard existential philosophy as concerned about existence or
human existence. It would simply be a bit cumbersome, if not somewhat odd, to speak of "human existentialism."

5. The Dialectic of Spirit:
Hegel and Kierkegaard

Everyone who has read even a smattering of existential philosophy knows that existentialist thinkers make a great deal of such phenomena as dread, anxiety, and despair. Some readers have concluded that to be an existentialist one needs simply to accentuate in a rather brooding way the darker side of life and cosmologize his anguish. Why should dread and the encounter with nothingness have played such an important role in existential philosophy? And why should a philosophy which lays such stress on the negative and even nauseous and demonic side of human life be attractive to anyone at all? Why indeed? Why not rather talk about human happiness and the possibilities of man's adjustment to his natural environment? Is not the job of philosophy more to make man feel at home in his universe than to underscore his alienation from it? If existential philosophy is fundamentally a philosophy of alienation, should we not diagnose the malady and find a suitable remedy?

In considering these questions it is important to note that the existentialists were not the first to introduce the categories of alienation and negativity into philosophy. Although these notions have a history that reaches back into antiquity with antecedents both in Hebraic and Hellenic thought, they were explicit working notions of the Hegelian dialectic. The most distinctive feature of Hegel's conception of man was his employment of spirit as the ultimate category. For Hegel, man is first and foremost a being who functions within the context of history and culture. "Spirit is freedom," as Hegel puts it, and freedom is dialectical process. As constituted by spirit, man is a being who exists not only in himself but for himself and for others. In so far as he exists in these disparate modes he is intrinsically self-alienated. The self-in-itself is not immediately identical with the self-for-itself nor the self-for-others. Negativity is thus an essential determinant of the self as spirit. It is precisely this negativity which motivates and makes possible the dialectic of individual development. By virtue of that original negativity which it harbors within itself, finite spirit dirempts itself and posits itself in a state of disequilibrium. The ultimate task of the self is to achieve an integration of these diverse modes without losing the distinctions which provide it with articulation and content. Spirit for Hegel was not restricted to man, but served as the basic category of his metaphysics. Mediation, conceived of as the reconciliation of dialectical tension, was the chief positive principle of his dialectic. The final mediation occurs through the activity of absolute spirit as it works through the totality of human culture and history.

As Hegel conceived it, spirit is not a simple self-identical substance, but a dialectical unity of tensed factors. It is thus radically different from the Greek conception of soul and in important respects from the notion of the self or ego as it had been developed in modern philosophy. If one looks primarily to the Hegel of the *Phenomenology*, one may agree with Richard Kroner that Hegel was the first of the existentialists. It is no accident that Kierkegaard worked out many of his views through his polemical attack on Hegel, and that in the process, he incorporated many of the Hegelian categories in his own writings. The notions of spirit, dialectic, alienation, and historicity which are so important for Kierkegaard and subsequent existentialists stem pretty directly from the philosophy of Hegel. It is thus not at all surprising that Heidegger should seem to have an ever greater affinity with Hegel in his later essays or that both Sartre and Merleau-Ponty should turn to Hegel for many of their insights. As existential philosophy gradually modified its original stress on the individual and devoted more attention to the encompassing world, it was more or less inevitable that it should move in the direction of the broader Hegelian dialectic. Kierkegaard was able to oppose Hegel with such passion only because he stood on the same ground with him and shared far more with him than he rejected.

But there were important differences between Kierkegaard and Hegel which continue to be reflected in existential philosophy. Although Hegel looked upon man as a dialectical creature whose being is bound up with temporal process, he viewed human becoming as dominated by world history. Thus for Hegel, history is the ultimate mediator. The particular form of alienation experienced by an individual depends upon his situation in world history and cannot be overcome save as historical-cultural processes follow out the logic of their development. Moreover for Hegel there is a necessity governing the dialectic such that each step in the process is dictated by what has gone before and what is yet to happen. The immanent logic of world history prescribes a teleological pattern of development that permits no radical alternatives and only provisional failures and deviations. His optimism was guaranteed by the power of absolute spirit to achieve its ends in the process of its self-unfolding. It was to these two theses of Hegel's philosophy that Kierkegaard was most violently opposed. In his opposition he set the direction for the development of existential philosophy along quite different lines.

It is not the case, as some of his interpreters have concluded, that Kierkegaard dispensed with logical principles in his analysis of the dialectic of finite spirit. Indeed, a great deal of his writing was devoted to the explication of those categories and principles which condition human existence. But whereas Hegel's logic dictated a unique result, Kierkegaard sought to allow for radical alternatives at each step in the dialectical process. In many respects, therefore, Kierkegaard returned to the Kantian notion of freedom as permitting radical choice. At the same time he retained the Hegelian notion of a dialectic that informs every moment of choice and rigorously structures alternative courses of action. But even here the difference between Hegel and Kierkegaard is extremely subtle. For both Hegel and Kierkegaard there is a rational motivation implicit in every choice and every action. To put it in terms that would be congenial to both thinkers, spirit is operative in every human action. There is, therefore, no dichotomy between body and spirit, or between man's animal nature and his intellect and will. But the two thinkers analyze this motivation differently. In spite of his stress on freedom, Hegel was a determinist. He saw every action as uniquely conditioned by its antecedents and moving toward a predetermined *telos*. An adequate explanation of history thus requires that one understand why events have occurred in precisely this way rather than some alternative fashion. There were, in other words, no hypothetical possibilities functioning within the Hegelian scheme.

But it was precisely such hypotheticals that Kierkegaard wanted to introduce. He was perfectly willing to grant that every choice and every development is circumscribed by a logic which prescribes the alternatives. He felt it important to insist, however, that the alternatives are always genuine and that at any point any one of several possibilities could be chosen. Thus Kierkegaard's logic of existence requires that as much attention be paid to the possibilities of failure as to those of success. Human life, as Kierkegaard saw it, is characterized far more by failure than by success. If Kierkegaard emphasized the darker side of life and particularly the possibility of radical failure in achieving genuine selfhood, it was not because he was an irrationalist, but rather because he sought to do greater justice to the facts of human freedom. From Kierkegaard's perspective Hegel's logic was far too tight and left far too little room for the trials of human decision. For the sake of his comprehensive logic of world history, Hegel simply lost the individual as an autonomous being who holds his destiny in his own hands. Kierkegaard doubtless overreacted to the Hegelian stress on the role of world history, and hence tended to isolate the individual from his world situation. Still he offered a genuine alternative to the logic of Hegel so far as the interpretation of human existence is concerned. On many counts Kierkegaard's modification of the Hegelian scheme is superior to the original dialectic and able to dispose of many of the criticisms which have been leveled aginst the Hegelian metaphysics.

Some interpreters of Kierkegaard might not agree with me, but I think it is not putting the matter too strongly to say that for both Hegel and Kierkegaard there is always an optimum goal dictated by the concreteness of a given human situation. They differ, I believe, on two points. In the first place, Hegel would regard the optimum choice as much more highly determinate than Kierkegaard. It would thus be typical for Hegel to regard the choice of a particular career and even where and how that career is to be carried out as implicit in the situation of the agent. Any apparent failure or mistake in choice would thus have to be explained in terms of a larger purpose that is indirectly served by the apparent error. The teleology of history does not move in a straight course for Hegel, but takes many twists, turns, and returns along the route. But it stays always on the right path and inevitably must arrive at its goal. Kierkegaard, on the other hand, denies both that there is a specific course of action that is optimally prescribed by a situation, and further, that any choice at all must be made or carried out. There is thus no basis at all for optimism about world history apart from the leap of faith which places absolute trust in the wisdom, power, and goodness of God.   Whereas for Hegel in the last analysis choice is completely rational and completely warranted, for Kierkegaard no human choice is either fully rational or perfectly justified.   One man may, for example, decide to become a monk and another man to be married.   Although we can perfectly well understand how and why a man may become either a monk or get married and thus subsume either choice under rational categories, we cannot in any way deduce the choice from antecedent conditions, however predisposing they may be.   It is only the fact of alternatives that makes a genuine choice possible and thus lends ethical and religious significance to human action.   It would simply be ridiculous to argue either that every man should be married or even that any particular man should be married.   The married state is but one concrete way of fulfilling one's possibilities as a man.

We can understand the possibility of the two choices, marriage or monasticism.   There are fundamental motives involved in both cases which inform the choice and prescribe further goals.   Moreover, we can understand what a man commits himself to in making either choice. A man may flee from himself into marriage or monasticism, or he may adopt either course as a way of achieving the highest possible self-fulfillment.   There is a logic of marriage, and a logic of monasticism, and a supervening logic which makes the two alternatives intelligible. But if no predisposing factors are sufficient to necessitate either choice, neither are any empirical factors adequate to guarantee consistency and persistence in the choice that is made.   But in spite of this important difference with Hegel, Kierkegaard preserves an important element of the Hegelian dialectic.   Marriage and monasticism are themselves dialectically related in that both are ways of responding to human sexuality.   Moreover, success and failure in marriage must be understood under a common set of principles.   The unfaithful husband is just that, namely, one who has failed to abide by the demands of the marriage contract.   No one understands the unfaithful man better than the man who aspires to be faithful, for he appreciates the sacrifices that must be made and the temptations to be foresworn.

The difference between Hegel and Kierkegaard is thus due in part to their different ways of treating possibility.   Whereas for Hegel every possibility is relative to a historical situation and bound eventually to be realized, for Kierkegaard no concrete possibility need be actualized. But here again we must be careful, for the two thinkers do not interpret possibility in quite the same way.   Hence, to characterize the difference between them as I have just done may be misleading.   A possibility for Kierkegaard is always somewhat abstract; only through choice does it become specific and concrete.   Kierkegaard is far more a Platonist and a Kantian in his interpretation of possibility than is Hegel.   A possibility for Kierkegaard is rather like a Kantian category in that it structures experience while never losing its abstract universality.   Although possibility always conditions actuality, it is never exhausted by embodiment in the latter.   Because the principles involved are always general and at least partially abstract, human motivation can never be fully rationalized.   The price for guaranteeing genuine freedom of choice is that failure must be placed on precisely the same footing as success. Consideration of the possibilities of failure and hence of "despairing" choices serves in the writings of Kierkegaard to highlight the contingent path of a freedom that may also choose adequately. The function of dread is to reveal to the individual the fact of his contingent freedom. He must choose within the limits defined by his situation. And he must choose among incompatible alternatives. Although he may know formally and in general that he has chosen a self-affirming rather than a despairing route, he must improvise at every moment on the theme he has selected. Antecedent to his choice there is or can be no complete warrant for it. Though it can be measured by formal and a *priori* standards, in the last analysis it must be self-justifying. If this makes the ethical and religious life of man more hazardous, it makes it, also, more exhilarating.

6. Essence and Existence

In the post-Freudian world we have become acutely aware of human anxiety and spend millions of dollars trying to eliminate or ameliorate it. We are familiar with dozens of types of neuroses and phychoses, each of which expresses some form of anxiety. Aware of the possibility of "traumatic" experiences, we carefully scrutinize the upbringing of our children and all of our relations with other persons to avoid disturbing complications. And we spend even greater sums to avoid the boredom of what would appear to be an objectively happy and abundant life. Long before Freud, Kierkegaard recognized the possibility of anxiety as response to the dread that stems from human contingency. Whereas Freud and many of his followers have represented anxiety as an abnormal state of mind due to a displacement of libidinal energies, Kierkegaard regarded it as an altogether normal response to the potentially terrifying uncertainty of the human condition. He characterized despair as "anxious dread" and hence as a deficient way of responding to the universal phenomenon of dread. He thus agrees with Freud in viewing anxiety as a pathological state. For Kierkegaard, however, anxiety is a sickness of the human spirit rather than of the psyche alone. Freud himself came to recognize the role of anxiety in all facets of human life and the possibility of applying his psychoanalytic theory to social as well as personal phenomena. The primary difference between Freud and Kierkegaard is that for Freud anxiety is rooted in man's biological nature and can be explained in terms of natural cause and effect processes, whereas for Kierkegaard it is a manifestation of human freedom.

Freud had a splendid clinical grasp of the phenomena of anxiety. He succeeded in demonstrating that human motivation is far more complex than anyone before his time had imagined. He showed conclusively that the apparent reason for behavior is not always if ever the sole or decisive motivation. Thus Freud, too, regarded human behavior as involving elaborate dialectical patterns. The fact that Freud did not use the term "dialectical" and that he felt it necessary to explain the phenomena of anxiety by reference to an essentially biological model of the human psyche should not cause us to lose sight of the true scope of his findings.   His clinical discoveries pointed to possibilities in man that had hardly been dreamed of before his time.   Earlier philosophical and psychological theories of man were simply inadequate to account for such phenomena.   The sole exception, perhaps, was Søren Kierkegaard himself, who not only devoted a book to an analysis of dread but another to "anxious dread" or despair, in which he diagnosed several familiar patterns of neurotic and psychotic behavior and explicitly discussed the role of what he termed "unconscious despair."

It should be apparent from what has been said that existential philosophers attribute an essence to man, if by the term "essence" we mean those intrinsic formal characteristics which limit and define him as the kind of being that he is.   Kierkegaard elaborated a whole set of categories which characterize man as an existent being and attempted to show how human life can be interpreted by the use of these categories.   As I have suggested earlier, such categories are conceived of in the manner of the Kantian categories in that they are *a priori* rules governing the activities of a free being.   In his analysis of man Heidegger specifies what he terms "existentials."   These are *a priori* forms or rules which govern all human activity.   For the existentialists, therefore, man has an essence in the same sense that in Kant's analysis reason and freedom are essential characteristics of man.   This did not mean for Kant that all men must be rational in their conduct, since they may choose to negate their own rational capacity and hence act irrationally.   In the same way, none of the categories delineated by Kierkegaard, Heidegger, or other of the existentialists prescribe in detail how man must act, even though they limit and inform his action.   They function, in other words, much in the same way as general logical principles which are necessarily illustrated in the construction of all logical systems, while not deductively implying a single one of the systems in which they are incorporated.

It is important, therefore, to distinguish between two ways in which the concept of essential form may be interpreted.   One might conceive of it on the Aristotelian model as a determinate nature which is originally present to man at birth and needs only to develop through the various stages of human life to become fully explicit.   Although their natures are different, a man becomes a man in much the same way that an oak tree becomes an oak tree.   In both cases the development represents the unfolding of an essential form ingredient in the original substance.   The nature or essence of man is thus no more problematic to him than the nature of the oak tree is to the tree.   We need not be concerned here about the accuracy of this statement as a precise account of Aristotle's theory of man.   There are complex features of Aristotle's theory, the consideration of which would require detailed and lengthy treatment.   Suffice it to say that a standard view of essential form and one that has been commonly attributed to Aristotle is of the sort just outlined.   Indeed, it is the failure of the existentialists to abide by such a model in analyzing human existence that has prompted widespread criticism from many quarters. The existentialists have certainly rejected any such view of human nature. The question is whether they have substituted for this classical view a model which does justice to the facts of human life while serving to make them equally intelligible.

The case for the classical doctrine of an essential nature is prima facie highly convincing. Is it not evident that the offspring of human parents always turn out to be men, however impaired they may be? We simply never find a case of an offspring of human parents becoming a dog anymore than we find such bizarre switchovers among other creatures of nature. Is it not somewhat ridiculous therefore for anyone to claim that "man's being is problematic" or that he is unique in that he "must choose what he is to be?" It is by no means immediately apparent that a man has any more cause to choose what he is to be essentially than a dog or a monkey. But if that is the case, is not much of the talk of the existentialists simply a poetic fiction designed to give human existence the semblance of grandeur?

Insofar as man is a natural being with an organic body, there is no doubt whatever that he possesses an essential form more complex but basically similar to the essence of other creatures. The question then is not whether the human individual begins his career with a highly determinate nature and, even more, in a highly determinate natural and cultural situation. The issue bears rather upon the significance of his natural potentialities for the achievement of reality as a person. As Aristotle pointed out, man has a rational soul. If he were not originally endowed with reason as a native capacity, he would be unable to acquire it by even the most strenuous effort. No existentialist thinker has intended to deny that man has such native capacities or that they play a decisive enabling and limiting role in all human development. The question posed by the existentialists is: Just how are such capacities used and developed? Precisely what does it mean to say that man is "essentially" rational? Does man possess rationality in the same way that a bird enjoys the capacity for flying? If there is anything peculiar about essential capacities as they pertain to man, we must be able to show with decisive clarity precisely how their status differs from those characteristics which are constitutive of plants and animals.

We have noted previously in our reference to Kant—to whom the existentialists are heavily indebted for their conception of man—that man may either live according to the dictates of reason or attempt to subvert his reason. The fact that man has the capacity for reasoning does not guarantee that he will lead a rationally ordered life. This is not only a fundamental assumption of the Kantian ethics, but a fact about human life that can be confirmed by the most casual observation. If we assume that basic human nature has remained fundamentally unchanged for several thousand years at least, we must take note of the strange fact that creatures possessed of the same essential characteristics have comported themselves in the most diverse ways. We are confronted with a range of human behavior from primitive savagery to the most effete civilized forms. But even if we look at the contemporary world we find enormous variation in the style and manner of human life. Whatever may be said about the constancy of basic human capacities—a question that is not here in dispute—Hegel would appear to be correct in maintaining that human capacities are and can be developed only within the context of history and culture. Hegel's thesis, however, went far beyond the Kantian claim that moral character is an achievement of human freedom. Kant saw that the use a man makes of his talents is ultimately far more important than the sheer fact of having the talents. Since, as Kant analyzed human existence, moral character is an essential condition of selfhood and since, further, character is an achievement of freedom rather than a natural endowment, it follows that in an important respect man must create his own essence. It might be objected, of course, that man is essentially a moral being in that he has the capacity for moral self-determination. And Kant would certainly agree with the thesis asserted in the objection. But there is all the difference in the world between a moral capacity which may or may not be exercised and may be abused even if employed, and a natural essence which necessarily develops under favorable conditions. The human body grows if properly nourished and nurtured and takes the general form and shape it was originally destined to have. But moral character can be developed only through the deliberate exercise of will on the part of the individual. As Socrates pointed out long ago in considering why honorable men sometimes have profligate sons, virtue cannot be transmitted in the same way as biological characteristics. There is no way at all in which it can be guaranteed even by the best of teaching or the most favorable external conditions.

A capacity such as reason or the ability to give one's conduct a law may be regarded as an essential human property. In so regarding it, however, we must recognize that such capacities require freedom for their use and development. Moral categories are, as Kant insisted, categories of freedom rather than of nature. It is this fact which accounts for the basic difference between the essential properties constitutive of plants and animals and the intrinsic capacities of men. Even the fact that man has a body does not dictate how the body is to be used nor what it is to mean. Nothing is more problematic, for example, than human sexuality. The fact that man is a sexual being follows from his biological nature; yet to know that man is sexual in the biological sense is to have only the most elementary knowledge of human sexuality. The human significance of sexuality depends on the way in which man's biological capacity for sexuality is exercised. Kant was interested primarily in the moral significance of human conduct, and thus limited his doctrine of freedom to the moral use of intrinsic talents. For him man's being is problematic only with respect to moral character. Yet, Kant's whole philosophy could be viewed as a philosophy of freedom and all of his categories as categories of freedom. One needs only to generalize Kant's notion of freedom to conceive of man as problematic in every aspect of his existence, not excepting the body itself. When Hegel introduced the notion of spirit as a category which encompasses the totality of human existence and thus supervenes upon all natural potentialities, he both generalized Kant's doctrine of human freedom and prepared the ground for the existentialist conception of man.

Kant was enough of a Platonist to believe that man's empirical nature is basically independent of intellect and will. Thus Kant assumed that we are endowed with inclinations and desires which may be governed and controlled by reason and will, but which are neither penetrated nor constituted by the latter. Although Kierkegaard followed Kant in his conception of freedom, he subscribed to the Hegelian conception of spirit as encompassing the totality of man's being. This entails that no dichotomy can be allowed between natural capacities and moral capacities. If spirit is characterized by freedom and all human activities are subsumed under spirit, it is apparent that all human categories must be viewed as categories of freedom. But if freedom is construed as involving radical options, then every aspect of human existence must be viewed as problematic. It is thus by an extension of the Kantian doctrine of moral freedom as modified by Hegel that we arrive at the existentialist conception of man as, in the words of Heidegger, "a being who in his being is concerned about his being." This sounds like a terribly abstruse statement, but it can easily be given empirical meaning and made intuitively clear. For one thing, the fact that a man is aware of existing does not settle the question whether he is to continue to exist or, if he continues in existence, what he is to do or to be. A man may choose to commit suicide—as thousands of men do every year. Suicide, as the refusal to accept the responsibility of existing, is one of the more radical, perhaps the most radical of all, options available to a man. It is sufficiently radical to qualify every aspect of his existence. He exists with a physical body—but he may refuse this fact. And even if he choses to accept it, he is confronted with the further question what significance he is to attach to his physical existence. Dozens of metaphysical and theological theories have been generated in the attempt to answer this question.

7. Sexuality

Or, to take a less dramatic and more everyday phenomenon, we may relate Heidegger's thesis to human sexuality. Man is born sexual in that he is originally endowed with natural sexual capacities. Yet, nothing is more problematic than his sexuality. We need not accept Freud's theories uncritically to be persuaded that sexual themes are pervasively illustrated throughout human life. They are not only pervasive, but highly complex. One of the lessons we have learned from Freud is how tangled the skein of sexual themes may be over the course of a human life. It is not just a question of sexual aberrations or even of neuroses, but of the great variety of possible variations on the theme of sexuality. Sexuality as it may be present to what Freud termed the "id" is important as providing essential material contents. But it is what happens to these materials in the life of the ego and the superego that determines the patterns of adult sexuality. Although Freud saw more than anyone before him how plastic and variable the expression of sexuality could be, he attempted to analyze it in causal terms. He assumed, in other words, that there is a constant natural mode of sexuality that may be thwarted or distorted through the imposition of cultural forms. Freud failed to see that sexuality can serve as a vehicle for the expression of general human concerns in both its physical and cultural manifestations. Lacking a satisfactory concept to embrace the totality of the self as id, ego, and superego, he could not offer a unified theory of sexuality. Where he appealed to instinct and a blind libido, he might well have invoked those concerns which eventually come to play an explicit and decisive role in adult sexuality. In insisting upon a unified conception of the being of man, the existentialists reject both the Kantian and the Freudian dichotomy between natural processes and their personal/cultural expression.

If nothing is finally settled by the fact of existing, neither is very much settled by virtue of the more specific fact that one is a male sexual being. One has to decide not only what it means to be a male, but how one is to be related to others through one's sexuality—since sexuality carries with it an intrinsic reference to other persons. Man is essentially a being with and for other persons. Because he is a sexual being, all of his relations with other persons involve his sexuality in one way or another. Moreover, the problematic character of his sexuality entails that his existence itself is problematic. We might thus paraphrase Heidegger's statement as follows: As a sexual being man is concerned about his sexuality. This is to say, while existing under the category of sexuality he must determine what form and style to give to his sexual life. Yet, it is not simply about his sexuality that he is concerned, since sexuality can never be isolated from the total context of his life. His concern about his sexuality involves his total existence, and hence a concern about the general style of his life. It is after all, only as one chooses the style of his sexuality and other concrete activities that he chooses a form for his existence. In choosing what it means to be a male, a man thus chooses how he is to be himself.

One of the paradoxes of twentieth-century American culture is that a great many people seek to find intrinsic satisfaction through sexuality while continuing to regard it as a naturalistic component of their existence that is transcendent to their own consciousness. Viewing it in this fashion they are forced to look upon their sexual life as a process which can serve only as a cause of pleasure. They thus seek to manipulate their sexual activity by the employment of carefully studied techniques to produce maximum enjoyment. The paradox is that when sex is viewed in that light it cannot be enjoyed at all; for it is regarded as alien rather than integral to the participating subject. To regard sexual activity as important primarily as a potential cause of pleasure is to deprive oneself of the possibility of enjoying it as an essential expression of one's personal reality. The alienation which seems to vitiate so much of sexual activity today is due not to inhibitions nor to a lack of adequate techniques, but to a reduction of the sexual to a mere physical process extraneous to consciousness. If our sexuality is crippled, it is because we take too dim rather than too exalted a view of the body. Unless we can recover the sense of identification with our own bodies and hence with the physical component of our sexuality, there is no prospect that we will be able to experience immediate satisfaction in our sexual life. The immediacy of a pleasure that is caused by the physical processes of sexuality is radically different from that immediacy which participates in the physical expression itself.

For reasons that have been indicated, the existentialist conception of man is anti-dualistic. As was noted earlier, the existentialists regard existence as dialectical and hence as involving tension and polarity. But they refuse to regard any one feature of human reality as more essential than any other. However unstable and incomplete, man is basically a unitary being. This means that all existential categories apply to the totality of man's being rather than to a particular aspect such as the body or the ego. Although Kierkegaard is the only one of the existentialist writers to employ the notion of spirit as the most basic existential category, the other existentialist writers interpret man in a way that is fully compatible with that category. Again, I should not wish to suggest that there is a single existentialist conception of man on which all writers agree. Nor should I wish to argue that their theories of existence are free of serious problems of a systematic nature. Sartre, in particular, lacks a concept in terms of which to refer to the totality of man's existence and thus has difficulty in relating the various dialectical modes of existence. It remains true, however, that for each of them the being of man is inclusive and any polarities are intrinsic rather than extrinsic to existence. This is not to say that they regard man as isolated from other beings or view such relatedness as unessential. It is simply that in his relatedness to others as in his reflexivity, the whole of his being is involved. Thus he never has any purely "natural" relations to others any more than to himself. To see how such polarities are incorporated within a unitary conception of man it will be useful to consider one such polar tension in some detail.

8. Facticity

Existentialist writers use alternative categories, and hence do not describe the dialectical features of existence in a uniform manner. But they are in agreement that man is an empirically determinate being who yet transcends his determinacy. Both Heidegger and Sartre refer to this polarity by use of the twin terms "facticity" and "transcendence." It will be convenient to adopt this terminology in discussing the basic polarity which permeates human existence. Existentialist writers are noted for their stress on human freedom and the necessity for man to choose what he is to be. If taken by itself the stress on freedom seems to ignore those concrete limiting factors which circumscribe the exercise of choice. In fact, existentialist writers from Kierkegaard to the present have put at least equal stress on the sheer factuality of the human situation. To distinguish their conception of empirical determinacy from other theories of man, Heidegger and Sartre use the term "facticity" to designate the finite determinacy of existence. Man is, as Heidegger expresses it, a "being-in-the-world." Before he ever comes to reflect on himself or to make any deliberate choices he finds himself already involved in a complex and highly determinate everyday world. Far from being a pure disembodied ego, he finds himself to be a creature living at a particular time and place with a particular job, friends, neighbors, etc., within a closely knit social environment. Any deliberate choices he is ever to make must begin with these factual materials and must make use of them in the exercise of choice. No man can do more ultimately than to modify the world within which he finds himself originally situated. As Kierkegaard puts it, man is characterized by necessity and finitude. He has to be the concrete self that he is rather than an abstract or imaginary self.

One of the most difficult and pressing responsibilities confronting a man is to accept himself with his particular body, talents, family, social class, etc. If man is free to be himself, it is not just any self at all, but the particular self that he happens to be. Frequently he is unwilling to accept this restriction and wills not to be himself in his facticity but to be another self. Cinderella dreams of being a princess—and magically becomes one. The waitress dreams of becoming a movie star. Vicariously, millions of people enjoy lives of excitement and adventure through their identification with the heroes and heroines of the movies and television. The housewife flees from herself as one who submits to the drudgery of ironing clothes and cooking meals by participating in the soap opera that she listens to on the radio. Nor is there anything deplorable about such dreaming or vicarious identification save in so far as it represents a flight from oneself. One may forget oneself and temporarily identify with the hero of one's dreams. But not for long can one escape from the realities of his existence.

If the man who desires suicide represents the most extreme repudiation of existence, the flight from facticity is an everyday refusal to accept the concrete determinacy of one's situation. The human situation is not always a happy one and it is generally easier to flee from it than to accept responsibility for it. It is partly for this reason that none of the existentialists accept happiness as a realistic ideal for man. There are other difficulties with happiness as an ideal which we must consider presently. Suffice it to say at this point that the existentialists are unqualifiedly realistic in their appraisal of human facticity. As even their most vehement critics must allow, they have not failed to take account of the darker side of human life—including the direst possibilities of human failure. An indispensable condition of authentic existence is that the individual assume unqualified responsibility for himself as the being he is in fact. The category of facticity thus serves to delineate an inescapable dimension of existence as well as to specify an inexorable demand. It is as a finite being that the indiviual must choose and out of the determinacy of his finite situation. To pretend otherwise is to delude oneself. Every human choice is thus indefinitely if not infinitely corrigible in that every item in man's factual situation bears upon it. The category of facticity thus has crucial implications for the existentialist interpretation of ethics.

Kierkegaard has been accused—even by some of his most sympathetic interpreters—of having cut the individual off from his world. Thus Heidegger's stress upon the fact of man's "worldliness" appears to be a corrective to a serious one-sidedness in Kierkegaard's thought. There is some truth to this contention, but it would be grossly unfair to accuse Kierkegaard of neglecting to stress human finitude. Not only did he regard finitude as an existential category, but he put great stress on the importance of the concrete situation for ethical and religious choice. As represented by the Judge in *Either/Or*, the ethical man relativizes the empirical content of the aesthetic life, and by taking it up within his ethical vocation, makes it essential to his existence. Anything short of this represents a flight from his factical nature. Nor can a man be related to God in a vacuum. If God speaks to man, He addresses him in his particular situation. And if he is summoned by God it is to obedience out of that same situation. Kierkegaard was concerned about the individual in his solitary uniqueness. But he knew full well that no one can become an individual save as he moves inward from the world in the development of his subjectivity. The situation of the individual within world history had received sufficient stress at the hands of Hegel and his followers to require no defense on the part of Kierkegaard. He may well have carried his concept of solitariness to the point where effective communication with the world is seriously threatened. That Kierkegaard himself never lost touch with the world is sufficiently attested by the effectiveness with which he analyzed the everyday phenomena of human life. Kierkegaard is always worth reading, if only for the marvelous jokes with which he reveals in a few strokes the high comedy of creatures who are tensed between time and eternity.

9. Transcendence

But there is another fundamental pole to human existence which pulls in quite another direction. If man is finite, concrete, and determinate in his particular situation and decisively located within the space-time world, he transcends that world in its every detail. By nature a dreamer, his imagination tugs at the moorings of his finitude to project for him a fascinating array of possibilities. As we have seen, the servant girl leads a double life—one of fact and one of fancy. Yet, the life of fancy is no less real in its own way than the one which we sometimes identify with reality. A man is not only the self that he appears to be in fact, but the one he aspires to be. Human life, as Kierkegaard described it, is constituted of actuality and possibility. As he lives, the individual weaves the two threads together, as it were, to constitute a fabric of actualized possibility or, conversely, idealized actuality. In his consciousness of himself and his world the human individual transcends his situation and thus is free within limits to choose the meaning of his life. He may, of course, merely dream of a life that is projected beyond what is actual. If so, he does nothing more than wish for an existence that he does not in fact enjoy. But he may also act and thus seek to translate his aspirations into the language of concrete existence. Authentic existence demands a synthesis of the two polarities and thus a dialectical resolution of the opposition. Yet, no matter how fully human life is idealized, it never loses the aspect of sheer facticity. Too much has been said, perhaps, about dread and anxiety in existentialist writings and not enough about humor—which for Kierkegaard at least was a category of the highest order. If we are unable to make ribald jokes about sex, for example, it must be because we are either indifferent to it or else have taken it too seriously. Humor liberates man from the impossible task of having to fuse the finite and the eternal. Unless we are always on the point of laughter we cannot be truly serious about anything.

Sartre has written a number of existentialist tragedies; his characters move with an exceedingly heavy tread. Fundamentally a moralist bent upon instructing his listeners in the lesson of freedom, Sartre is far too tense to enjoy the comedy of existence. In this respect Kierkegaard has a clear advantage over Sartre as over all of the subsequent existentialists. Because Kierkegaard had carried resignation through to the ultimate point where the alternatives are nihilism/faith, he was able to appreciate the humor which is present even in man's most desperate striving. Camus experimented with comedy, but could never really succeed with it. He, too, was essentially a moralist in the quest of a categorical imperative. Perhaps the critics of existentialism have a sound point after all in their claim that the existentialists are too preoccupied with the darker side of life. Still, if what is needed is a sense of comedy, existentialist categories are well equipped to provide it. Edward Albee's play, *Who's Afraid of Virginia Woolf?* especially the first act, suggests the form that an existentialist comedy might take. He achieves much of his dramatic effect in the play through the contrast between the hilariously funny opening scenes and the disturbing bitterness of the ensuing conflict. Humor feeds on dread and anxiety and, as has long been recognized, provides one of the most satisfying releases from them.

It may appear to be only a highly speculative thesis to assert that all of human life is characterized by transcendence. And highly abstruse to suggest with existentialist writers that through the experience of dread man discovers that he cannot be perfectly at home in his world. Yet, this assertion is based upon one of the most commonplace of human experiences, namely boredom. One may become bored about anything at all and at any time. There are no intrinsically boring experience; any activity is potentially boring. It all depends upon the way in which the individual is related to what he does. To be bored with an activity is to experience it as tedious and without point. One talks to a friend but cares little about what is said on either side. Or one goes to a play but fails to become absorbed in the action. To experience boredom one must have the paradoxical capacity to engage in an activity while in some fashion not being present to it. Or, put in more positive terms, one must be able to transcend an activity even while performing it. Boredom is, in other words, a form of negative transcendence which leaves us with a sense of emptiness.

It is not simply the actual occurrence of boredom that is to be explained—since it occurs only sporadically—but the possibility of boredom. The question why boredom tends to afflict people at particular times and under particular circumstances is an empirical question to be investigated by the social scientist. But the question how it is possible for a creature like man to have such an experience under any circumstances is a philosophical one. The answer given by the existentialists is simple and straightforward. Because man is not only conscious of what he does, in the sense that his awareness animates his activity, but is capable of reflecting on that activity, he has always the power to escape the confinement of the moment. To be a human self is to be aware of oneself and hence to be reflexively self-related in one's consciousness. And not only in one's consciousness but in one's being. As Heidegger describes existence, man is an "ecstatic" being, namely, one who stands at a distance from himself. In the experience of boredom the individual experiences this reflexive polarity in himself. He comes to the recognition that, in the language of Sartre, he is a being not only "in himself" (as immediately present to what he does) but "for himself" (as transcending his own actuality).

When one is confronted with boredom he may respond to it in a variety of ways. He may attempt to reduce the consciousness which introduces the negative quality into his experience in order to reinsert himself once more into the cocoon of immediacy. To be successful he must nullify the incipient transcendence in himself. Refusing to develop a newly awakened capacity and assume responsibility for providing a new basis for meaning, he flees from himself toward his facticity. He wills to be himself but without those complications which call into question the meaning of his everyday activities. The trouble is, however, that he has outgrown himself, and can never succeed in squeezing himself back into an earlier form of existence. In the development of the self there can be no turning back. One may seek to arrest development and refuse to go farther. But once a new stage has been reached, there is no reverse access to a more immediate stage. We are all somewhat nostalgic for our own childhood, when life was more immediate and far simpler. Yet, we know that it is a stage beyond our recovery. Every new moment of self-consciousness brings with it new responsibilities for decision which we understandably dread. Boredom does not imply that life is meaningless, but only that for us it carries no ultimate meaning in its immediate form. It is for this reason that man is forced perennially to turn to philosophy, religion, and art to find an answer to the riddles of existence. In itself boredom is nothing more than an intimation of human transcen-

dence and more to be applauded than deplored. It is only if we refuse
to step beyond immediacy that boredom threatens to reduce everything to universal apathy.

Happiness, if conceived of as a state of perfect equilibrium in which there
is neither tension nor stress, is too simple an ideal for man. As we
most commonly think of it, happiness is a state of contentment
where, as Kant described it, "everything goes according to wish and
will." For happiness to be a realistic ideal for man he would have to
be capable of being completely at home in his world, freed of all
discontent, and perfectly integrated in every aspect of his being.
Since man is at best a fragile synthesis of opposites who inevitably
transcends any situation in which he seeks to contain himself, these
conditions cannot be met. This is not to say, of course, that men
cannot be and are not happy. It is only to insist that the more self-
conscious a man is about the goal of his life, the less he can afford
to aspire to happiness as his ultimate ideal. For happiness is a form
of immediacy which comports only with an immediate self. Because
of the dialectical nature of the human self, any moment of happiness
contains within it the seeds of its own dissolution. Life is not all
tension and struggle and there are periods of relative integration and
stability when the self can simply enjoy itself. Once, however, it
has discovered the contingency of happiness as well as the difficulty
of holding oneself within it, a more sophisticated and comprehensive
ideal must be formulated. There is something pallid and unsatisfying
about those Hollywood dramas in which everything always turns out
for the best. They represent a sentimentalized version of human life
which reduces it to a single uniform dimension. Their image of man
is far too restricted to be able to portray either the tragic or the
comic possibilities of human existence. For suffering they substitute
pathos, and for humor they offer only the amusing.

As the pervasive boredom and apathy of contemporary American life indicate
only too well, a life of immediate enjoyment cannot be ultimately
satisfying for man. For too long we have persuaded ourselves that if
only we could rid ourselves of our repressions and inhibitions, we
should be free to enjoy life as it comes. The Puritan Ethic has been
displaced by the Freudian Ethic. Attempting to discount the injunc-
tions and taboos of our own childhood, we have instructed our
children in the art of immediate self-fulfillment. And we are amazed
and shocked to see their hedonism take a violent and destructive
turn. Yet, if pleasure is to be the medium, it must bear all the
motivations of which men are capable. If it is to be an absolute and
ultimate end, then it must be sought with abandon. And if at the
bottom of the pleasurable moment one fails to find the self for which
he is seeking, he must confront the abyss which lies beyond immediacy. Our conception of man is far too naïve if we cannot understand how the unconditioned quest for pleasure can result in nihilism.
If one is enough of a self to will only pleasure and thus to value
objects only as the means to enjoyment, he has will enough to destroy
the ornaments of his world. When the individual can no longer enjoy
objects in an immediate way and yet can assign them meaning only

in relation to enjoyment, he may become enraged and seek to destroy them.

We simply cannot interpret all manifestations of violent destructiveness as due to frustration—at least not to a frustration which prevents pleasurable activity. We must be subtle enough to recognize that peculiar frustration which stems from the consummation of pleasure. As Kierkegaard expresses it, it is precisely the infinite quality of the will to pleasure which occasions its destructiveness and permits the transition to nihilism. It is dangerous to forget that man is not only a creature of sensuous desires but is possessed of a will which yearns for the unconditioned. If pleasurable activity cannot itself be unconditioned, it can at least be negated by an unconditioned act. To explain the nihilism which hovers over all human endeavour we need not appeal to a "death instinct." We need only take into account the transcendence of a consciousness which cannot in principle receive full satisfaction in sensuous immediacy.

10. Ethics and Existence

Another criticism which has been made of existential philosophy is that no one of the existentialist writers has contributed an ethical theory. A possible exception would be Simone de Beauvoir's *The Ethics of Ambiguity*, which is hardly sufficient to meet the objection. Kierkegaard offered an extensive treatment of the ethical life in his *Either/Or*. But this again was less a treatise on ethics than a descriptive analysis of a mode of life that is governed by ethical categories. Ethics in this instance is nothing more than a metaphysical account of a possible way of existing. The criticism must, therefore, be met head on, since it takes account of a salient characteristic of existentialist thought, namely, that it makes no attempt to deal with ethics in any standard way. In fact, if not by design, it challenges the validity of ethics as a distinct and autonomous discipline. Sartre promised a volume on ethics to follow *Being and Nothingness*. But it has not followed nor could it follow. Whatever Sartre has to say of importance for ethics must be presented in his analysis of the human condition. Nor is there any room left for an ethics in Heidegger's philosophy. Whether this is a serious limitation in existential philosophy or a laudable reorientation in the understanding of ethics can only be decided after one considers how the existentialists dispose of ethical problems. Only if their account of existence is so purely descriptive that it carries with it no normative implications is the lack of an explicit ethics to be counted as a major shortcoming. By the same token, if a normative ethical theory which lacks a satisfactory descriptive analysis of existence fails to illumine ordinary life and even, in some instances, to be relevant to it, the whole project of an autonomous ethics may be misguided.

Since Heidegger, existential philosophy has been inextricably related to another contemporary philosophical school known as "phenomenology." Although Edmund Husserl is generaly credited as the father of contemporary phenomenology, its roots actually go back to Hegel and even to Descartes. Hegel's first major book was entitled *The Phenomenology of Spirit.* In this book Hegel sought to offer a descriptive account of human experience in its broadest compass. Husserlian phenomenology is more Kantian and Cartesian than Hegelian, but later phenomenology, especially in Heidegger, Sartre, and Merleau-Ponty, is more after the fashion of Hegel. It would only divert us from our present concerns to consider in any detail the history of modern phenomenology or even to take note of the principal variations. Without severe distortion we may simply observe that phenomenology since Hegel has been concerned to offer a descriptive account of human experience as it is directly encountered. It may be viewed, therefore, as a particularly inclusive type of empiricism. Hegel never thought of experience as static, nor did he hope to carry out a neutral or uninvolved analysis of experience. As Hegel viewed it, experience is a constantly moving process which never pauses to accommodate our reflection. Even as we look back upon the past we are having to make decisions with respect to the future. Our descriptions always have a temporal reach, therefore, and serve at once to capture the determinacy of the past and to structure the future. There can thus be no descriptive analysis which fails to have normative import, since concepts are essentially temporal and serve as the rational form of highly plastic empirical themes. The existentialists follow Hegel in refusing the dichotomy between descriptive and normative concepts, and hence cannot allow a bifurcation between metaphysics and ethics.

Since he wrote more than a century before Husserl, Kierkegaard could not be regarded as a phenomenologist in the current sense of that term. Still, as we have noted earlier, he was strongly influenced by Hegel with respect to many of his categories and equally so in his method of descriptive analysis. To the extent that Kierkegaard derived his categories from his reflections on existence and sought to justify them by showing how they are illustrated in existence, he employed a phenomenological procedure of sorts. Heidegger, Sartre, and Merleau-Ponty were directly influenced by Husserl, and hence are more programmatic in their use of a phenomenological method. For each of them, therefore, the descriptive analysis of the human situation is the first task to be undertaken by the philosopher. Before we are in any position to know explicitly what we should do in an ethical sense we must understand those concerns which motivate our everyday life. Once we have this understanding, it may be that we have all the guidance we require for the formulation of norms.

It is commonplace these days to attempt to understand deviant behavior by appeal to the psychological world of the agent. So far have we pressed the psychological analysis of human motivation that we are in danger of reducing criminality to the psychotic. But this approach to human behavior is highly instructive in that it enables us to understand human action within a fairly inclusive context. Instead of asking simply for the ethical motivation of deviant behavior we ask how it fits into the total world within which the agent functions. We seek, in other words, first to grasp the meaning of the action from the agent's perspective before attempting to judge it morally. We could, of course, continue to judge it exclusively by moral canons. But our judgment would have to be external to the action and possibly quite irrelevant to it, if we ignored the motivations actually prompting the action. Hannah Arendt has, I believe, made a substantial contribution to our understanding of Nazism in her analysis of the circumstances surrounding Eichmann. It is easy enough to regard Eichmann as an evil man who conspired to destroy thousands and hundreds of thousands of his fellow men. To say that, however, does not help us to understand Eichmann's motivation or even the particular form of his evil action. The difficulty with moralistic analyses of human action is that they are addressed to an abstract entity—namely, man as a purely moral being. The notion of man as a "moral agent" or a "moral being" is useful for purposes of analysis, but seriously misleading if taken as an unqualified fact. Eichmann was not a "moral agent" who, in addition to all of his other motivations, determined his moral will—in this case to radical evil. He was a unitary being of great complexity whose behavior reflected his situation within an encompassing world. We can understand Eichmann's action only if we can understand the tragically abstract and detached way in which he was related both to himself and to other men. That his action was morally evil there cannot be the slightest doubt. But neither is there any doubt that it was evil in a far more inclusive sense of that term. To read about the woman in New York who was recently murdered under the very eyes of neighbors who merely pulled their shades is disturbing. It prompts us to wonder whether there may not be pervasive conditions operating in our civilization which have the dehumanizing effect of transforming our neighbor into an indifferent object. It is not simply to the "world" of the psychotic that we must make appeal for our understanding of human behavior, but to the "world" of the normal and average man.

Existential philosophy, and Heidegger's analysis of existence in particular, has recommended itself as a context for analyzing the world of the emotionally disturbed individual. It has, in fact, occasioned a new school of psychiatry and psychoanalysis known as "existential analysis." This has been possible because the existentialist writers have attempted to offer a categorical analysis of human passion and emotion, including those factors which complicate and disturb man's emotional life. One need not claim that existential philosophy has in any of its expressions said the last word about human motivation to take note of its descriptive usefulness. No competing philosophical perspective during the past twenty-five years has so deeply affected our understanding of ourselves. If the seminal quality of a philosophy can be measured by the extent to which it fertilizes thought in other fields, existential philosophy must be given a high mark. Of late, of course, it has had virtually no competitors, save Marxism and Freudianism, since other schools of academic philosophy have remained studiedly aloof from the human scene. The existentialists, on the other hand, have sought to describe the human situation in such a way that the most ordinary man could find his own experience made

more intelligible.   The ultimate test of the theses of existential philosophy must, therefore, be empirical, namely, whether they faithfully
assess those factors which are operative in the daily life of man.
This does not mean that existential philosophy is simply a codifica-
tion of common sense nor even that it eschews highly technical
formulations.   It is only to say that the existential philosophers have
attempted to understand and describe human life as it is lived.

11. The Rejection
of Dualism

If it is possible to understand the curious behavior of the psychotic individual by appeal to the context of his world, it should be possible to
understand the behavior of the normal man by reference to those
organized meanings which provide the context for his activity. We are
reluctant to attempt such explanation these days because we commonly separate the world of nature from the world of human concerns.   Since Descartes, we despair of the possibility of locating
ourselves as conscious subjects within the natural world as described
by the physical sciences, and hence do not expect to be able to
understand our subjective existence in terms of it.   We appeal to
physical processes in explaining human action, but only in a causal
way.   We thus make use of trans-empirical cause-effect processes to
explain those activities of which we are directly aware.   The experiences of the ego are accounted for by reference to a physical-natural
world which it does not inhabit.   When so regarded the ego is an
epi-phenomenon restricted to the subjective world of its own ephemeral consciousness.

Existential philosophy has challenged both the priority assigned to the
objective world of nature and the bifurcation itself.   Heidegger and
Merleau-Ponty especially have attempted to overturn the Cartesian
dualism of a material-natural and a subjective-mental world.   Whereas
Kierkegaard was content to deal with man's subjectivity, Heidegger
was from the first concerned about the meaning of being and turned
existentialist thought in the direction of ontology.   For Kierkegaard
dread was significant primarily for disclosing human freedom; for
Heidegger, it serves to reveal the mystery of being.   Although
Heidegger began with an analysis of existence, he conceived of it
even in *Being and Time* as a propaedeutic to a general ontology.   His
ontological analysis of existence was designated as "fundamental
ontology," indicating that it was but a first step of foundation for a
more comprehensive theory of being.

In turning to man as the focal point for his initial inquiry into being,
Heidegger did not intend to make the analysis of existence an end in
itself.   He sought rather to gain a secure foothold for dealing with
the more general question as to the meaning of being.   From the
first he had been puzzled about the question that had first been
posed by Leibniz and reiterated by Kant: Why is there something
rather than nothing at all?   But why should Heidegger have started
with the investigation of man?   What possibility did this approach

offer for a movement beyond subjectivity? Is there any connection between Heidegger's later concern about the meaning of beings other than man and his original existential ontology? Some of Heidegger's interpreters have charged that his later essays represent a repudiation of his earlier position, and hence that there is no continuous development in his writings. In his essay in this volume Karsten Harries has shown, I believe, that Heidegger's writings manifest a continuing ontological concern which developed progressively in the course of his reflections. The question about man tacitly involves the larger question as to the meaning of being.

12. Phenomenological Ontology

As Western philosophy became more and more self-conscious about its own procedures, it became increasingly evident that human knowledge is such as to preclude our grasp of reality as it is in itself. Because we can make the world intelligible only through the employment of concepts and categories which stem from our own reason, we can comprehend objects only as we have analyzed and interpreted them. In arguing that we can have no secure knowledge of "things in themselves" Immanuel Kant was only drawing together the threads of a line of inquiry starting with Descartes. It seemed altogether impossible to regard the world view of modern physics as an intuitive awareness of the intrinsic structure of independent reality. A good many philosophers since Kant—among them Heidegger and the other existentialists—have been persuaded that metaphysics and ontology based upon intellectual intuition are impossible. Knowledge is itself an elaborate medium which stands between the inquirer and the object about which he inquires. We can neither dispense with this medium nor leap over it. If ontology is to be possible it must be predicated on a foundation which takes the Kantian critique into account. Hegel was the first philosopher after Kant to attempt a new sort of ontology. Although his metaphysics is generally out of fashion these days, it was astoundingly successful for a time and continues to reverberate even in our day. As has been indicated, Hegel adopted a phenomenological procedure which instead of attempting to leap over experience, exploited it to obtain ontological categories. Thus Hegel's was, by profession at least, an empirically founded ontology which justified its categories in the process of deriving them. This doubtless accounted for the fact that, in spite of the eventual abstractness of the Hegelian logic, his philosophy had a pervasive impact upon all facets of Western culture. By no means restricted to the academic forum, it had a transforming effect upon theology, philosophy of history, and art. Not least of all, it provided a strong impetus for the development of the social sciences. Both Marxism and existentialism are heavily indebted to Hegel's philosophy and for similar reasons, namely, that it offered a method for attempting a philosophical analysis of human experience in its concrete historical manifestations. To a considerable degree both Marxism and existentialism have attempted to fill the void that was left with the departure of the

Hegelian metaphysics. Man simply cannot exist without a philosophical vision of some sort. If he cannot obtain it from the academic philosopher, he will seek it from the novelist, the theologian, or the speculative psychologist. It is unfortunate that the disappointment of our quest for certainty has occasioned a profound despair as to the possibility of making our world intelligible.

But where then does one begin if he dares to undertake ontological inquiry in the light of the devasting critiques to which it has been subjected? Heidegger's answer to this question is clear and simple. The only sensible place to begin is with our own being and the understanding of being that is intrinsic to our situation. The concern about our own being is privileged for two reasons: First, we are that being, and hence an identity of the being that inquires and is inquired about. Thus the identity of the phenomenal object and the thing in itself is guaranteed from the outset. Second, we have an understanding of our own being prior to any reflection upon it. Thus ontological truth is not something to be produced from whole cloth by ontological reflection; it is implicit in our most everyday and ordinary activities. This is, perhaps, Heidegger's most important insight and his most significant philosophical contribution to existentialist thought and philosophy generally.

Jaspers and Heidegger appear to differ radically at this point, in that Jaspers vigorously denies the possibility of a constructive ontology. In this regard their respective versions of existentialism take radically different turns. Before the Second World War, while Jaspers was a professor of philosophy at Heidelberg, Heidegger visited Jaspers frequently. They were in intimate communication as they wrestled with common problems about existence. But their paths eventually diverged as Jaspers remained a confirmed Kantian and thus developed his account of existence within the general framework of Kant's critical philosophy, whereas Heidegger adopted a phenomenological approach which sought to undercut the Kantian distinction between phenomena and things-in-themselves. Still, the difference can be exaggerated as can Heidegger's departure from Kant. For Heidegger insisted on a negative relation interior to the phenomenon, which preserves the distinction between the appearance (*Erscheinung*) and the thing-in-itself as a modality within the phenomenal object. It was at precisely this point, in fact, that Heidegger departed from Husserl's phenomenological program, which viewed the phenomenon as fully immanent to consciousness. Heidegger not only insisted upon the principle of "ontological difference"—the distinction between beings and their being—but made the ontic-ontological distinction the fundamental working principle of his ontology. Heidegger and Jaspers thus offer alternative versions of existentialism. According to Jaspers, existential truth can be experienced only through the encounter with a limit, and hence in the experience of what he terms disruption (*Scheitern*). The transcendence of being is thus experienced in a manner that is primarily negative. A procedure, such as Heidegger's, which acknowledges the distinction between being as transcendence and being as appearance while regarding the latter as a positive disclosure of the former, offers greater promise for philosophy. The chief difficulty with Jaspers' metaphysics is that once it has been formulated there is little more to do than keep oneself open for the experience of transcendence. Jaspers' philosophy lacks the seminal quality of Heidegger's phenomenological ontology. It is understandable, therefore, that it has been Heidegger rather than Jaspers who has had the greater influence on subsequent existentialist inquiry.

To say as Heidegger does that when man inquires about himself he is the identity of subject and object appears to assert only the obvious and trivial thesis that man is a self-identical being. If true at all, it appears to be logically rather than ontologically true, in that the object is simply stipulated to be the subject in this particular case. To make of this something more than a formal but empty truth, it is necessary for Heidegger to show how man can and does inquire about his own being and thus can achieve genuine ontological self-understanding. At the very outset of his inquiry Heidegger attempts to shift the level of the question from the abstract philosophical to the commonplace and everyday. If there is both a concern about and an understanding of our own being implicit in our everyday life, the philosophical thesis can be warranted by appeal to experience and phenomenologically justified. As Heidegger analyzes the matter, it is not simply from the perspective of philosophical reflection that man is concerned about his existence; it is intrinsic to the nature of man that he should be concerned about his being. His concern is not merely intellectual and reflective but emotional and practical. If he is ontologically concerned about his being, it is only because his being is intrinsically problematic to him. We have discussed much the same point earlier in considering freedom and transcendence. Because man is the kind of being who must decide who and what he is to be, he can never regard his existence as a mere substance which follows its course independently of his concerns. Although he has a body, his body is a constant problem to him in that he must decide what to do with and about it. He must, in other words, determine what it means to exist in bodily form in a space-time world. It may appear that the concern about such meaning occurs only at the level of philosophical reflection. But if so it is only because we are insensitive to those concerns which are involved in such simple and elementary acts as deciding what to eat, what clothes to wear, what sort of work to do, how to speak, etc. We have, in other words, answered the question as to the meaning of our being in large part long before we are in a position to formulate it abstractly.

Heidegger rejects not only the dichotomy between the world of physical nature and the world of our subjective consciousness, but the common assumption that physical objects have human meaning only as our subjective values are assigned to them. He insists that the world of objects which is originally disclosed to man is itself a system of reference and meaning structured by our concerns. Objects can initially appear within the horizon of our world only as the terminus of some interest. Only when that interest is neutralized or displaced does the object become a mere thing to which meaning must be arbitrarily assigned. The objective world as scientifically described is not the primordial world of experience, but a modification of that world which reflects highly specialized human interests. Being as we initially encounter it is not, therefore, a meaningless substance or even a physical substance that is devoid of all human significance. On the contrary, it is that with which we are most intimately concerned in our everyday life and which we understand through our ability to relate ourselves to it. This sounds admittedly like the most extreme subjectivism to the modern ear, because we have learned to view the world in a precisely opposite manner. The final test whether it is subjective or objective must be whether it accords with our pre-reflective experience.

Heidegger's account of the world has much in common with Dewey's pragmatism. Like Dewey, Heidegger relates understanding intimately to practice. In the classical sense of that term, Heidegger is a pragmatist, since, for him, to have an understanding of being and to be able to relate oneself effectively to being are inseparable. The difference between them is, of course, that Dewey's pragmatism was naturalistic whereas Heidegger's is not—at least not in the same sense. Because Heidegger does not rule out ontological themes, he is able to describe a good many features of human experience, such as anxiety and dread, which Dewey could not acknowledge. It can be argued, therefore, that Heidegger's is a more open-ended and inclusive empiricism than was Dewey's. Granted, however, the different ways in which they conceive of man's being, both Dewey and Heidegger would, I think, be in agreement on two basic points: First, they would agree, as stated above, that understanding is intrinsic to practice inasmuch as to know how we behave is instructive for knowing how we construe our world. Thus, experience is prior to reflective theory and the primary source for the latter. Second, they would agree, I believe, that even our most highly developed theories, if they mean anything at all, make a difference in practice. Thus to understand our world differently is necessarily to be different in oneself and to be related to objects in a different way. For Heidegger, the explicitly reflective or theoretical dimension of our understanding is never more than the uppermost part of the iceberg. A man understands himself and the world not simply with his mind but with his entire being.

We tend to believe that the mind operates independently of the body and has little to do with the emotions. We have carried this view to the point where we deny even that we have any cognitive apprehension of the world through our volition, emotions, or our action. Yet, we have been forced to recognize that an "emotional" disturbance can shake the foundations of the most elegant intellectual edifice. An otherwise highly intelligent person may be unable to follow a sequence of numbers beyond five, or he may be completely incapable of causal reasoning. A despairing mood may remove all motivation for thought and render his entire world meaningless. We have, I think, far too thin an understanding of science these days because we take the fundamental motivations of scientific inquiry too much for granted. We understand the logic and method of science, but often fail to understand science as a humanly important quest. Existential philosophy is evidently supported by a deeply-seated concern on the part of twentieth-century man. It is thus historically and culturally relative. But what of the rest of philosophy? Have positivism and analysis been developed in a cultural vacuum by minds that are totally abstracted from their situation? It is only honest to recognize that philosophy, like science and all other human pursuits, is motivated by man's fundamental concern to orient himself in the world in which he has to exist. Plato offered a mythical account of human inquiry by reference to a finite soul which has been abandoned in a world where it must sojourn as an alien. The relevance of the myth is immediately apparent and expresses the same basic truth as Heidegger's assertion that man finds himself thrown (*geworfen*) into a world within which he must work out his destiny. The quest for knowledge and certainty is the manifestation of an urgent and deeply seated human need. It is supported by an existential concern and subject to the paralyzing effects of anxiety.

Freud has taught us to look for "unconscious" motives in our behavior which place it in a new and highly interesting dimension. One need not agree with Freud's account of motivation to recognize that the apparent reasons for our actions are not necessarily the complete or ultimate reasons for performing them. It is quite easy to make the transition from Freud's psychoanalytic theory of human behavior to Heidegger's fundamental ontology. We need only expand our analysis in order to grasp the basic principles of his ontology. Stated in its most general terms, Heidegger's thesis is that ontological concerns are operative in all ontic (empirically manifest) human activity. If Heidegger is correct, not only philosophy but ontology is relevant to the most commonplace features of our experience. The ontological themes do not have to be invented or supplied, for they are already there as constitutive elements in the activity itself. For the most part we are so absorbed in the world of everyday practice that we have little awareness of being as such. Initially and for the most part we understand ourselves and our world ontically rather than ontologically. Still, the awareness of being itself is always there however much it may be concealed by the familiar disguises of the practical world. We need only to experience the contingency of our world and the tenuousness of our grasp of it for it to be called radically into question. Dread as the experience of the contingency of being is an ever-present possibility for awakening in man a sense of transcendence. To experience the being of a thing is to be aware of the possibility of its not being. Thus to be aware of one's own being is to have some intimation of death as the possibility of not being. Although Heidegger has stressed the fact of death as revealing the contingency of man's being, birth or any moment of existence would do as well. To be aware of the ontological meaning of any being is to apprehend it as something more than an item within an established context. It is to be aware of its sheer presence as such and to marvel at the fact that it is something rather than nothing at all. It is with the sense of awe, wonder, and mystery that all inquiry begins, and especially, that the inquiry about being takes its origin.   Much of the writing of Heidegger, and, even more, of Marcel has been devoted to reawakening and reenlivening our sense of the mysterious presence of being—not as a substance transcending our world, but as that which stands at the center of appearance.   Being for Heidegger is the being of that which is— and nothing more.

12. Normative and Descriptive Meaning

After what must appear an extended digression, we are now in a position to take up once more the question about the role of ethics in existential philosophy.   The reason for considering Heidegger's existential ontology was to provide a suitable context for clarifying the existentialist approach to ethics.   If we can follow Kierkegaard and Heidegger, all human endeavor is motivated by a basic concern about one's contingent existence.   It is not the sole concern of man, else we should all be incurable egoists, but it is a universal and necessary concern for all men.   In every question that he asks and in every action that he performs, a man puts his own being in question.   He determines with his every gesture and movement how he is to exist, and hence who he is to be.   But what, then, are the implications of such a conception of man for ethics?   It implies, in the first place, that the responsibility for existing is the original and most important task confronting the individual.   Thus, as Camus recognized, the question of suicide is always an ultimate question for man.   To go on to the ethical as commonly understood, namely to ask what one should do as a morally good man, presupposes that an answer to the former question has been given.   To project for oneself ethical goals is one way, ultimately a necessary way, for the individual to assume the positive responsibility for existing.   But if there is no meaning to existence, there can be no meaning to an ethically structured existence.   The choice of an ethical life is a response, therefore, to the basic ontological question: What does it mean to be?

It is altogether mistaken to conceive of ethical choice as the choice only of an ideal self.   In one's ethical aspiration one aspires to be oneself as conceived of in a particular way.   It is to be a real and full-bodied self whose existence will conform to certain prescriptions.   As Kant recognized, the ethically good life is essentially a mode of life in which the individual strives to be responsible for his actions.   Every man is responsible for his actions in a variety of ways—naturally, socially, legally, etc.   To escape responsibility altogether would be to escape from the basic requirements of existence.   But a man is morally responsible only if he gives a law to his own freedom.   In other words, no man is ontologically required to be morally responsible for his conduct.   Yet, that is the only way in which he can render his freedom consistent with his existence. The individual can develop his own reality as a person only through the exercise of intellect and will.   The choice, therefore, whether or not to assume moral responsibility for one's conduct is part and parcel of the larger question whether one is to assume responsibility for one's existence. Moral responsibility must be understood, therefore, as a modification of the basic ontological responsibility which is entailed by existence itself. As Kierkegaard demonstrated in his *Either/Or*, the ethical life serves to provide focus and integration for a mode of life that would otherwise be subject only to the vicissitudes of desire.

There is thus a place for ethics even of the Kantian variety within the existentialist scheme, but only if it is understood as a modification of the basic task of becoming onself. As the existentialists view it, the whole of human life is a search for meaning. Thus in a broader sense of the term existential philosophy is an ethical or, in the eighteenth-century sense of it, "moral" philosophy. Ethics as a special concern is but the self-conscious and deliberate effort to discipline the will to the task of achieving the optimum meaning for human existence. But what then are the guidelines in the search for meaning? If the ethically good life is but a component within the more compressive projection of an optimum mode of existence, precisely what are the norms to be followed?

If one were to follow Sartre's analysis of existence, it would be difficult to avoid a radically pessimistic answer—at least if one considers only what Sartre says explicitly about the justification of choice. As Sartre represents it, all values and principles of action are the products of a freedom which has no appeal beyond itself. When a man has taken a stand, therefore, and defined his principles, he has nothing beyond those principles with which to justify them. And he cannot use the principles themselves, since that would be only to reassert them. One might conclude, therefore, that man is the kind of being who must make choices and that some choices must operate in *a priori* fashion. There would then be something like the Kantian categorical imperative, only it would be potentially different for every man and without rational justification. It is, to be sure, not only Sartre who has seen this dilemma. Other philosophers have viewed it as a dilemma from which ethics cannot ecape. It can be argued that ethical principles are either defended by the appeal to non-ethical principles, which assumes that ethical principles are not ultimate, or by invoking the ethical principles whose validity is at issue, which simply begs the question.

If ethics is essentially the program of providing justification for human conduct, to question either the validity of those principles or, more basically, the necessity for the justification itself is to challenge the ethical enterprise. Why be rational in one's conduct or attempt to be morally responsible for it? Especially so, if it can be evaded or, even if attempted, must culminate in failure? It would be tempting to say that man is by nature a moral being, and hence that he cannot escape the responsibility of attempting to justify his conduct. It might then be argued that even when he does not act for good reasons he must at least rationalize his conduct so as to put a good appearance on it. Unfortunately this answer will not stand up, for some men are a-moral. Standing always at the fringes of the ethical life, they refuse to translate desire into volition, and hence never bring themselves under ethical categories. What we can say effectively is that the man who does not take over the responsibility for his existence in such a way as to regard his actions as properly his own necessarily defaults on the task of becoming a self. The justification for the ethical life must therefore be existential and ontological. If ethics is necessary it can only be because it is a condition for the achievement of man's humanity. It should be apparent, however, that in alluding to the concept of humanity we are introducing a normative concept. And it may appear that we are thereby begging the question by smuggling in an ethical concept in our attempt to provide a warrant for ethics. But whatever term we use, it is impossible to avoid this consequence. Such terms as "man," "self," "person," "individual," etc., serve a dual purpose as both normative and descriptive. It is not, as some philosophers have suggested, that there are really two distinct concepts conveyed by a single expression, but rather a single concept which applies to an essentially telic process. From knowing what a man is we do not know what he should be. That is a problem for each man to determine for himself. But we do know in a general way what conditions must be met if he is to affirm and develop not only as a man but as an individual.

The ethics of existentialism seems to be principally an ethics of self-realization, since the chief ethical category it recommends is "authenticity." The ethics of existentialism would thus appear to be identical with its ontology, proclaiming a single imperative: Be the self that you are in truth. But what is "authenticity" and how can a self that must choose itself follow any rules at all? Must not all rules be after the fact, as it were, and hence of no real usefulness in guiding choice? It may be helpful in answering this question to consider how men do make such choices as whether to get married or become a physician. If a man is contemplating marriage it is easy enough for him to determine that it is a possible way of life for him. He can thus establish his capacity for being married. Moreover, he may consult his desires to see whether or not he has a disposition toward the state of marriage and with the particular person involved. But neither his capacities nor his desires in and of themselves entail that he ought to be married or to this particular woman. If he is at all reflective and wants an antecedent justification for his decision to be married, he simply will not be able to find it. In choosing to be married, if that is the choice he makes, he chooses not only to be wed to the other person and to enjoy the wedded state but to be himself as one who is married. The choice could be only partially justified before the decision is made. The final justification for the choice must derive from the way in which the choice is carried out. It must be, in other words, to a considerable degree self-validating.

It would be clearly impossible for any ethical theory to attempt to provide a schema which could simply be filled in by the individual in answering this sort of question. There is an ethics of marriage, but it presupposes rather than justifies the marriage contract. Yet, the fact that antecedent factors do not fully warrant a choice does not mean that they are not relevant to it nor even that the choice cannot be subsequently justified. Marriage, like the career of a doctor, can only be justified in the way it is carried out. The choice is the beginning rather than the end of the process of justification.

14. Authenticity and Bad Faith

In spite of his skepticism regarding ethical justification, Sartre had recourse to other considerations which play a crucial role in human choice. In his penetrating analysis of the individual's relation to himself and to others, Sartre delineated what he termed "patterns of bad faith" which enter into most if not all human relationships. "Bad faith" is essentially a mode of alienation from oneself and others and assumes an original relatedness which may be distorted through human choice. If "bad faith" is alienation and if alienation is a form of disrelatedness to ourself and others, Sartre's ontology provides at least negative instruction for avoiding deficient forms of existence. Sartre informs us in a footnote to *Being and Nothingness* that "bad faith" can be surpassed, but does not attempt to tell us just how it may be accomplished. If he were to have written the promised sequel to *Being and Nothingness* it would not have been an ethics in the accepted sense, though it doubtless would have suggested alternative patterns of authentic existence. In spite of this limitation, Sartre has set us on the right track, for we cannot assess human love normatively unless we understand its motivations. Only if we know what human love intends and how it seeks to relate persons are we in any position to judge under what circumstances it might accomplish its objective. By the same token, we can understand the full meaning of love only if we comprehend how human beings are actually related to one another. "Bad faith" for Sartre, like despair for Kierkegaard, is what Kierkegaard termed a "disrelationship within a relationship." To understand the structure of such phenomena is already to know in general terms what would be required to surmount them. Adequate norms are thus initially revealed in and through the experience of frustration and failure.

It is a virtual dogma in many philosophical quarters today that the "ought" cannot be derived from the "is." In other words normative rules cannot be derived from the analysis of matters of fact. This proposition is unassailable if matters of fact are conceived of as devoid of all teleological and normative principles. If, in other words, the facts of human experience are value-free, they have no intrinsic normative implications. But neither of these assumptions holds with respect to human action. The notion of matter of fact as it applies to human existence is only a limiting concept. It applies not to a closed and self-complete body of impermeable data, but to a polar dimension of human becoming. We simply cannot divide up the concepts that apply to man into two radically distinct classes, namely those which have pure descriptive import and those which are normative. Such terms as "body," "mind," "sex," "will," etc., serve both a descriptive and a normative function. If they did not perform this dual function they would be inapplicable to a process which is essentially teleological, and hence defines itself as it goes—and partially by the employment of the reflective concept itself.

What the body is in itself and what we think the body is are inextricably linked. To regard the body as something impervious to our thought about it would be to regard thought as disembodied and the body as completely external to consciousness. The body, like all aspects of existence, *is* what it means. What it means is not a result simply of our reflection, else we could make it be anything we liked. It is highly determinate and hence falls under the category of facticity. But its factual and determinate character is never such as to prohibit entry to our reflective consciousness. The body is not simply a thing in itself but a way in which we exist for ourselves. It thus falls under the two primary categories of facticity/transcendence and exhibits themes which are both empirically determinate and ideal. Norms are thus implicit in the very constitution of matters of fact so far as existence is concerned. It is not a question, therefore, of deriving normative rules from a value-free realm of fact like rabbits from a hat. If it is not to be hopelessly abstract and irrelevant, ethical reflection must be seated in facticity. Thus conceived, ethical reflection *participates* in the development of material themes instead of attempting to control them from an external vantage point. Reason can be practical, but only if it is rooted in appetite and inclination.

Moralists have too long assumed that the primary task of ethics is to project an ideal order which might or might not be striven for but which, nonetheless, "ought" in some ideal sense of the term to be incorporated in actuality. Carving out for itself a realm of ideal possibility about which it could presumably become clear through a progressively refined intuition, ethics has relegated matters of fact to empirical science. But in taking such a stance it has defaulted on one of the most important tasks of philosophical ethics, namely, the description of those canons which constitute the imperfect world within which men live. If existential philosophy has made any substantial contribution to contemporary philosophy, it consists in no small part in the attempt to reveal those basic motivations which operate in the often bizarre conduct of human beings. However inadequately, it has attempted to analyze the structure of man's relatedness to himself and to others not simply as it might be ideally, but as it is in fact. It has sought to show, further, that even in those instances of greatest perversion and depravity normative concerns are involved. The difference between this sort of philosophical anthropology and empirical science is that the philosophical account concentrates on those categorial structures which by delimiting possibility illumine actuality. It carries the Freudian type of analysis one step further by asking what kind of being man is that sexuality can be problematic for him, or that he can become neurotic or psychotic.

To understand what a neurosis is is to know what would constitute a healthy response to the problems of one's existence. But this does not entail that there is only one positive alternative to a specific neurotic pattern. Even after the individual becomes aware of the structure of his neurosis and recognizes the defenses that are involved, he is still faced with the problem of choosing a constructive alternative. No psychotherapist can solve that problem for him. The reason is not that the psychotherapist is not a moralist, but rather that there is simply no one constructive alternative. No ethical theory can ever prescribe specific lines of conduct which the individual must follow if he is to lead an adequate life. At most it can formulate the imperatives which define the task and provide the criteria for judgment. Similarly, we can analyze patterns of human alienation, failure, and despair without being able to prescribe specific remedies. We can and must, of course, be able to specify constructive patterns as an alternative to the patterns of bad faith and despair. But they can only be "patterns." No specific line of conduct or manner of existence ever follows as a strict consequence from a situation. To this extent the ideal "ought" never follows from the "is." But the "ought" is nonetheless rooted in the concreteness of the situation. The terms of the situation make both positive and negative demands upon the decision to be made, though within the area framed by these demands there is considerable leeway for untrammeled choice.

With these qualifications it is quite true to say that human choice is not justifiable. It is not justifiable in the sense that there are no sufficient antecedent conditions to certify that one and only one action could properly follow from the situation. Every decision thus carries with it considerable risk and must always be warranted to some extent by what follows from it rather than from what went before. But it would be misleading to say that human action is unjustifiable if we meant to rule out the possibility of a self-justifying choice. There is never any one objectively right career for a man any more than there is an objectively right wife for him to marry. Yet, among the legitimate alternatives available he can, by the way in which he pursues the choice of a career or follows through on his commitment to a marriage, make it the uniquely right choice for him. In the same way there is never a uniquely right novel for the writer, though in the way he writes the book he has elected to write the choice may be completely justified.

15. The Quest
for Meaning

To return at the end of our discussion to an issue that was raised at the beginning, the present situation in American philosophy appears to involve two versions of philosophy that are diametrically opposed to one another. There are genuine issues between them which cannot be dismissed as of no philosophical consequence. But there is also a wide area of agreement which even now facilitates a *rapprochement*. It consists in the fundamental concern about meaning on both sides of the opposition. From the first, the existentialist philosophers have been concerned to describe those meaning structures which are intrinsic to everyday human existence. Heidegger is, perhaps, the most explicit about this concern in stating that the question: What is the meaning of being? is the focal point of his philosophical career. To talk about meaning in this way is, of course, far too speculative and ontological for the linguistic analyst. Still, he too is concerned about the meaning of human existence as it is incorporated in language. If, as with Heidegger and Merleau-Ponty, the analysis of language is counted as of primary importance for a phenomenological analysis of existence, the two schools are in obvious agreement as to the indispensability of ordinary language for the assessment of meaning. The agreement would be virtually complete if the analyst would acknoweldge that language is neither fully self-contained nor self-interpreting. There is, I believe, no intrinsic reason why linguistic analysis should not enlarge its sphere of meaning to include the whole of existence.

The existentialists have concentrated on one dimension of meaning and the linguistic analysts on another. Neither has any confidence in the prospects of a purely speculative metaphysics nor in the creation of an artificial and ideal language that would fulfill the ancient longing for perfect clarity and distinctness. Each after its own manner, they are both empirical and even phenomenological. Insofar as existential philosophy is analytically clumsy it must fail of its objectives. There can be no doubt that existentialist writers have sometimes confused phenomenological description with fairly grandiose speculation and buried phenomena under elaborate conceptual paraphernalia. But on their side the analysts have claimed a transparency for language which it does not possess. If being and existence can be disclosed only through the medium of language, language must show a level of meaning which it cannot express.

Lest what I have said be misunderstood, let me hasten to add that I have not stressed the commonality of interest on the part of the two schools of philosophy in order to recommend frantic efforts at mediation or reconciliation. The philosophical scene is far more interesting and exciting because of the divergence than it would be without it. There is no reason to believe that any philosophical method or perspective can be so complete as legitimately to claim the allegiance of all philosophically minded thinkers. *Viva la différence!* When this opposition is mitigated we shall have to develop another lest we confuse one version of truth with the whole of it. We may still hope, nonetheless, that there will be fruitful communication between the schools so that reflection on each side will be fructified by the exchange. Such communication is the best possible preventative of that dogmatic spirit which deadens the nerve of philosophical inquiry.

CHAPTER TWO

SØREN KIERKEGAARD
THE POETRY OF INWARDNESS

LOUIS MACKEY

LOUIS MACKEY *is professor of philosophy at Rice University. He received his Ph.D. at Yale University and taught at Yale until 1959. His essays on the thought of Kierkegaard have appeared in scholarly journals and other publications. Among these essays are "Kierkegaard and the Problem of Existential Philosophy"* (The Review of Metaphysics, March-June, 1956); *"The Loss of the World in Kierkegaard's Ethics"* (The Review of Metaphysics, June, 1962); *and "The Analysis of the Good in Kierkegaard's* Purity of Heart" *in* Experience, Existence, and the Good *(ed. by I. C. Lieb, Southern Illinois University Press, 1961). Mr. Mackey's present interests center in medieval philosophy and aesthetics, especially in the doctrine of symbol and in the relations between philosophy and poetry. Indicative of this interest is a forthcoming essay in* Thought *entitled "On Philosophical Form: A Tear for Adonais."*

The Man
Without a Present

Infandum me jubes, Regina, renovare dolorem:[1] these words, which
Kierkegaard set as an epigram over the account of his unhappy
betrothal to Regina Olsen, might stand for an epitaph over the man
and his work.[2] The biography of Kierkegaard has been written so
often that it would be tiresome even to recapitulate it here.[3] But it
is worth recalling that his entire life was a retelling—to his journals,
to himself, to God, and to posterity—of a grief inexpressibly out of
proportion to the events that occasioned it. The public circumstances
of Kierkegaard's life were inconsiderable: a troubled devotion to his
father, a broken engagement, a squabble with a tabloid paper, and a
flurry of pamphlets flung at a Church so secure in its Establishment
that it scarcely stirred itself to reprove him. Yet at the bidding of
these—an old man confused by guilt, a guileless girl half in love and
half mesmerized, a brightly irresponsible journalist, and a pair of comfortable bishops—he renewed daily the anguished self-examination
that was his real life. This self-scrutiny appears poetically transformed in the fourteen volumes of his published writings, and lies
pathetically naked before the reader of the eighteen volumes of his
journals.[4]

Kierkegaard's life was spent "in the service of the Idea."[5] Whatever befell
him was reflected and doubly reflected, translated almost before it
happened from experience into idea. His every overt action—and
they are few—had been so prepared and doubly prepared in advance
that the actual performance was but a tired epilogue to the exhausting
ideational drama. In his youth he was told by one of his professors
that he was "too polemical"; in the year before his death he was still
shining this remark into the dark corners of his personality, looking for the goblins.[6] His assault on the Danish Church had deployed
inwardly through persecution and martyrdom before he ever uttered
a critical word; when he did finally "speak out," the proper episcopal
indignation he aroused could not begin to measure up to the epic
crucifixion projected in his journals.[7]

[1] *"Thou biddest me, O Queen, renew an unspeakable grief." Kierkegaard is slightly
misquoting Aeneid II, 3: Infandum, regina, jubes renovare dolorem.*
[2] *Alexander Dru, ed. and tr.,* **The Journals of Søren Kierkegaard,** *Oxford University
Press, London, 1938, no. 367. In another entry (ibid., no. 717) Kierkegaard
writes: "By a strange freemasonry I can make these words of the poet a motto
for part of my life's suffering: Infandum me jubes Regina renovare dolorem."*
[3] *The fullest accounts of Kierkegaard's life in English are Johannes Hohlenberg's
Sören Kierkegaard, Pantheon, New York, 1954, Walter Lowrie's Kierkegaard,
Oxford University Press, London, 1938, and Harper Torchbooks, New York, 1962,
and the same author's A Short Life of Kierkegaard, Princeton University Press,
Princeton, N.J., 1942.*
[4] *The standard Danish editions of Kierkegaard's published and unpublished writings
are listed in the bibliography at the end of this chapter.*
[5] *Cf. Dru, op. cit., nos. 22, 70. Cf. also Søren Kierkegaard,* Repetition, *Princeton University Press, Princeton, N.J., 1946, pp. 145–146.*
[6] *Dru, op. cit., nos. 626, 1191, 1252, 1333, 1334.*
[7] *The journals for the last few years of Kierkegaard's life are filled with this preoccupation. Cf. in particular ibid., nos. 1260 and 1275, as well as numerous notes*

He was, as he himself might have said, infinitely dialectical. Things that move ordinary men to a simple readjustment of their circumstances necessitated in Kierkegaard a total upheaval of the personality. Every event, every action or passion, every concern, required a recasting de novo of his image of himself. The result was that these same events, actions, passions, and concerns, given absolute significance as ideal possibilities, lost all meaning as realities.

For this reason, the substance of his life was a pervasive melancholy formed in the crucible in which he transmuted all experience into reflection.[8] Living as he did in possibility, out beyond the real, there was no one to whom he could express that unutterable grief, the being of which nonetheless was its own everlasting reiteration. He could find no contemporaries, because he was in truth a man without a present. His life was essentially over and done with before it had begun: in the midst of life he was as one already dead. "Periissem nisi periissem," he wrote, "is and always will be the motto of my life. Therefore I have been able to endure what would long ago have killed another who was not already dead."[9]

It is understandable that this motif should thread through his writings. Kierkegaard's melancholy produced and reproduced itself by a kind of superfetation of the spirit; by its own dialectic it destroyed the innocence it mourned and made impossible the "repetition" it yearned for. Virginity, of the spirit as of the flesh, is never loved until it is lost, and by then it cannot—short of a miracle—be restored. So Kierkegaard's "spheres of existence"—the aesthetic, ethical, and religious ways of life which the first part of this chapter will examine— are determined by the round of recollections, pains, and longings that articulate his inner life.

Periissem nisi periissem is the motto affixed to Quidam's diary ("Guilty?/Not Guilty?") in Stages on Life's Way.[10] The anonymous author of "The Unhappiest Man" and other essays in the first volume of Either/Or belongs to a nocturnal society lugubriously and synthetically named symparanekromenoi, "the fellowship of the deceased."[11] All of Kierkegaard's writings lament an immediacy hopelessly lost in reflection, a youth-that-never-was recollected in the impuissance of eternal old age. His vision of Christian consummation is a miraculous and elusive redintegratio in statum pristinum, a new immediacy, a contemporaneity with oneself possible only by virtue of the absurd.

---

from the year 1852 on. Cf. also Kierkegaard, The Point of View, Oxford University Press, London, 1939, and Harper Torchbooks, New York, 1962, pp. 100–102.

[8] Cf. Dru, op. cit., index references to "melancholy," but especially nos. 641, 921, 952, 1299.

[9] Ibid., no. 767. The Latin means, "I had perished, had I not perished."

[10] Kierkegaard, Stages on Life's Way, Princeton University Press, Princeton, N.J., 1945, p. 187.

[11] Kierkegaard, Either/Or, Princeton University Press, Princeton, N.J., 1944, and Doubleday Anchor Books, Garden City, N.Y., 1959, vol. I, pp. 135, 163, 215. I refer here and throughout to the paperback reprint, which is a revised translation.

Between paradise lost and paradise regained he pitches an ethical struggle to fuse the actual and the ideal, a struggle whose desperate issue is the everlasting recollection of guilt.

Immediacy—never possessed but always forfeit, vainly sought and paradoxically bestowed—is the *cantus firmus* about which the polyphonic Kierkegaardian literature shapes its varied and often dissonant counterpoint. In order to hear the strange music ringing from this Phalarian bull,[12] it is necessary to attune oneself first of all to Kierkegaard's understanding of immediacy.

1. Such Stuff
as Dreams Are Made On

The word "immediacy" is a bit of jargon that Kierkegaard picked up from Hegel and the Hegelians. There is no point in pursuing the technical meaning of this term in Hegel's system, but it is important to get the general sense of the word as a way into Kierkegaard's mind. It is common to equate *immediate* experience with *direct* experience, experience *simply given* and *simply had* before the onset of reflection. Life as it is before it doubles back on itself in the "mediation" of self-consciousness is "immediate existence." If nature be opposed to the reflexive operations of freedom, then a man's immediacy is what he is "by nature."

Traditionally "aesthetic" has come to mean "pertaining to beauty and the fine arts," but in Kierkegaard it retains its etymological sense of *aisthesis*, "sense perception." He defines what he calls the "aesthetic," as a dimension of existence and as an overall design for living, by means of the immediate. "The aesthetic in a man is that by which he immediately is what he is."[13] If we could discover what human nature is, then we could catch ourselves in our immediacy, and we would understand what Kierkegaard means by the aesthetic.

But the difficulty with immediacy is that it never *is* where it is asked about. Asking about immediacy is already an act of reflection once removed from the immediate. Just as a man cannot look himself straight in the eye, so immediacy cannot be got at directly; it can only be divined as the prelapsarian origin mirrored but never substantially present in every condition of self-awareness. This alienation of the self from its immediacy infects the philosophical attempt to comprehend human nature categorially, but it is more arresting in the case of the man who tries to *be* his immediacy.

Kierkegaard's "A" is such a man. The anonymous dilettante whose dilations fill *Either/Or* I is a representative aesthetic personality. In view of the identity of the aesthetic with the immediate, one might expect him to be a man whose overriding aim is the direct satisfaction of his wants. It is true that he lives for pleasure. Yet he is disenchanted enough to know that no life is lived on the strength of impulse alone.

---

[12] Cf. *ibid., vol. I, p. 19.*   [13] *Ibid., vol. II, p. 182.*

True to the paradox of immediacy, desire and gratification are presented not as A's life but as the chief *preoccupation* of his life.

A is a perfervid admirer of Mozart's *Don Juan*. In his essay "The Immediate Stages of the Erotic or the Musical Erotic" he praises Mozart's opera as a perfect work of art, "classic and immortal," on the grounds that it realizes a total fusion of form and content.[14] In *Don Juan*, as A hears it, the musical form is so happily wedded to the passional content that together they body forth sexual desire in its immediacy. Don Juan's sensuality is pure undifferentiated desire. He craves *woman*, wholesale and without discrimination of age or beauty: *pur chè porti la gonella, voi sapete quel chè fà.*[15] His passion is a force of nature, unriven by reflection and undisturbed by moral misgivings. Mozart's music is the artistic analogue of this passion, an aural energy not yet articulated into the intelligible forms of speech. There are words, of course, but their very absurdity ("one thousand and three in Spain . . .") negates their significance as language and hurls them back into the floodtide of sound. In Mozart's opera A finds immediacy immediately presented, the content of immediacy interfusing and interfused by immediate form. In this exquisite alchemy art (reflection) *is* nature (the immediate).

Yet there is ambiguity in this achievement. *Don Juan* is after all *art*. It is to art that one must go if he wants to find the immediate given in its immediacy. Don Juan could never happen in real life: one thousand and three in Spain! Global sexuality is a fictive biology of the heroes of imagination. Pure immediacy cannot be experienced as the content of an actual life; it can only be savored as fantasy.

This contradiction is implicitly recognized in A's analysis of *Don Juan*. He is fascinated by the Don because he is a pure type, and by the opera because it is the pure presentation of a pure type. Mozart's masterpiece is the embodiment of the most abstract idea (sensuality) in the most abstract medium (music). Sensuality is "abstraction" because, as immediate, it is not yet parceled out into specific preferences for discrete objects (*pur chè porti la gonella . . .*), and not yet constrained by moral necessity to accept the discipline of a part within an ordered whole. Sensuality *simpliciter* is only the abstract dynamic, the "exuberant joy," of life. Music is similarly abstract. Language— naming, defining, judging, and discoursing—is the spirit's vehicle for the tenor of the concrete. Music with its moving and interacting tonal patterns mimics the syntactic form of language but altogether lacks its semantic commitment: it is the abstract dynamic of spirit without the content of spirit.[16] By A's logic of inversion, that which appears to be most concrete evaporates into the airiest of abstractions.

[14] Ibid., vol. I, pp. 45–134, especially p. 47. In A's interpretation of Don Giovanni, the Commendatore is not part of the unity of the opera, but a voice of divine judgment morally shattering this unity ab extra.
[15] From the libretto of Mozart's Don Giovanni. "If only she wears a petticoat, you know what he does."
[16] Kierkegaard, op. cit., vol. I, pp. 52–55, 63–72, 100.

It is this logic that prompts A's genuflection in the presence of pure types purely enshrined in a pure medium. Too sophisticated to be a sensualist himself, he is reconciled to *admiring*, in its artful and only possible realization, that perfection which he cannot *be*. The man who wishes to be only what he immediately is, will, if he is honest, be driven by the logic of immediacy to the antithesis of immediacy: enthusiasm for a beautiful but impossible ideal. The internal nexus joining "aesthetic" in its etymological sense to "aesthetic" in its traditional connotation is hereby exposed: Art is the transfiguration of nature by self-consciousness.

But A is too thorough a dialectician and too determined an aesthete to *repose* in admiration at the expense of enjoyment. If he cannot make immediacy his life, he will make life itself an art. This reversal takes place already in the essay on *Don Juan*. No sooner has A declared the essential abstractness of the opera and its theme than he turns around to deliver an encomium of the infinite richness of every work of art. In passages reminiscent of Kant's doctrine of Aesthetical Ideas, he speculates: Because the unity of form and content in a consummate work of art precludes any *definitive* critical analysis, no understanding of the work is ever final; but for that very reason the possibilities for understanding it are infinite. His rationale is quasi-Hegelian: That which lacks all determinacy is receptive to any and every determination. If the most concrete, by reason of its density, is the most abstract, then the most abstract, by reason of its emptiness, is potentially the most concrete.

This turn in his theory of art offers A a way out of his personal impasse. The aesthete, knowing that he cannot have his pleasures by instinct, seeks to contrive them by craft. He cannot attain to the condition of nature; he will therefore aspire to the condition of art. A's *diapsalmata* or "refrains," and his paper on "The Rotation Method" are ventures in the art of living.[17] The aphorisms, directed *ad se ipsum*, are the fruits in his own person of the counsel advanced in his "essay in the theory of social prudence."

The burden of A's moods is clearly heard in these typical *diapsalmata:*

I do not care for anything. I do not care to ride, for the exercise is too violent. I do not care to walk, walking is too strenuous. I do not care to lie down, for I should either have to remain lying, and I do not care to do that, or I should have to get up again, and I do not care to do that either. Summa summarum: I do not care at all.[18]

Let others complain that the age is wicked: my complaint is that it is paltry; for it lacks passion. Men's thoughts are thin and flimsy like lace, they are themselves pitiable like the lacemakers. The thoughts of their hearts are too paltry to be sinful. . . . They do their duty, these shopkeeping souls, but they clip the coin a trifle, like the Jews; they think that even if the Lord keeps ever so careful a set of books, they may still cheat Him a little. Out upon them! . . .[19]

[17] Ibid., vol. I, pp. 17–42, 279–296.   [18] Ibid., vol. I, pp. 19–20.
[19] Ibid., vol. I, p. 27.

The essence of pleasure does not lie in the thing enjoyed, but in the accompanying consciousness. If I had a humble spirit in my service who, when I asked for a glass of water, brought me the world's costliest wines blended in a chalice, I should dismiss him, in order to teach him that pleasure consists not in what I enjoy, but in having my own way.[20]

The last of these is the root and reconciliation of the first two. What the aesthete is after—the condition of all subsequent pleasure—is "having his own way." On the one hand he does not care to do anything; for anything he does puts him under the compulsion to do something else. At the same time he despises the paltry caution that shortchanges its vices for the sake of higgled virtues; to balk at *les grandes passions* is to stop short of a full realization of one's possibilities. It is necessary to enjoy everything and to care about nothing.

In an "ecstatic lecture" A defines the "sum and substance of all philosophy" in a series of monotonous dilemmas: If you marry, you will regret it, and if you do not marry, you will regret that; if you trust a woman, you will regret it, and if you do not trust a woman, you will regret that; hang yourself and you will regret it, don't hang yourself and you will likewise regret that, *ad infinitum.* Either/or: for any x, either you do x or you do not do x, and in any case you will be sorry. Every decision and every action entail regret for the alternate possibility concurrently and irrevocably renounced. Therefore, one should so live *aeterno modo* that he abrogates the law of contradiction in advance by—doing nothing. No decisions, no regrets; no actions, no consequences. The path to free enjoyment is the way of *dolce far niente.*[21]

But the sweet life of indolence calls for delicate management. One cannot, for example, *resolutely* do nothing and survive the resolution unscathed. To do nothing in an affirmative way is just as constraining as doing something: If you do something, you will regret it, and if you do nothing, you will regret that. Strictly speaking, one should not even do nothing. But this is also, strictly speaking, impossible: like it or not, one will either lie down or stand up. Some practical expedients are required.

One course that recommends itself is romantic frenzy: Let yourself go. Since it is a matter of indifference what a man does, then anything he goes at is fine and beautiful if he does it with total abandon. But the romantic is a very poor counselor. Wiser by an eternity, A knows that if he lets himself go, he will *certainly* regret that. The secret of enjoyment is neither to do nothing nor to do anything with all one's might. The secret is to do *everything* in such a way that one rigorously *avoids all commitments.* The art of living is neither an impossible self-denial nor a prodigal self-squandering, but the most fastidious self-discipline.

Self-discipline, as a technique for maximizing pleasure and minimizing boredom, is the prescription of A's disquisition on the rotation method. The artful hedonist rotates his pleasures as the farmer rotates his crops. To this end he must be prepared to allow any or all of his desires to lie fallow at any time. The first precept of this *ascesis* is the counsel of despair: *nil admirari.* "It is impossible to live artistically before one has made up one's mind to abandon hope; for hope precludes self-limitation."[22] Hope exposes the hopeful to the possibility of frustration; therefore walk circumspectly that you may forget the unsettling at will and redeem the tedious with recollection. The art of recollection—the imaginative revision of a delightful past—and the art of forgetting—the sidestep by which one diverts himself from the path of a disgruntling present—together compose the dear desperation that can shield the aesthete forever (*aeterno modo*) from the threat of the future, "insure" him "against sticking fast in some relationship of life, and make possible the realization of a complete freedom."[23]

From this synderesis follow the particular maxims of aesthetic praxis: Take fullest advantage of people, but beware the obligations of friendship; enjoy love, but shun marriage; cultivate the arts, but see that you reap no profit therefrom. Whatever the situation, stay in control. Now there is only one way a man can stay in control of every situation, and that is by first assuming complete control of himself. He cannot produce at will the events and environs of his life; he cannot even create his own moods. But he can determine the *meaning* these circumstances will have for him by the practice of systematic *arbitrariness.*[24] Suppose, for example, he goes to church (no experienced aesthete would neglect the charming possibilities offered by the practice of religion): he will so attend to the sermon that he refuses the pastoral edification in order to beatify himself with observations of the pastoral Adam's apple. In an erotic *pas de deux* he will be the curious voyeur of his own athletic lovemaking. By seizing the occasion and turning it to capricious ends, he makes and unmakes his situation as it pleases him. By his hopeless withdrawal from immediacy he perfects his freedom; by his arbitrary return to immediacy he keeps his independence and simultaneously gives his life content. The varied round of pleasures is enabled by the larger "rotation method," the dialectical circle of withdrawal and return.

So the pattern of A's life duplicates the structure of *Don Juan.* As in the aesthetic unity of the opera the most vacuous abstraction is by implication the most teeming concretion, so in the aesthetic unity of A's existence the kenosis implied in his *nil admirari* is the emancipation by which he releases himself for the arbitrary pursuit of every pleasure. The practical dilemma of the hedonist is resolved in the light of the art theorist's analysis of immediacy. However circuitous the route, A comes at last to the land of heart's desire.

Yet the solution is suspect, because it does not match A's character as this is delineated in *Either/Or* I. The discussion so far, intent on the rationale by which A orders his life, has overlooked several aspects of

---

[22] Ibid., *vol. I, p. 288.*   [23] Ibid., *vol. I, p. 291.*   [24] Ibid., *vol. I, pp. 295–296.*

the life itself. It has ignored the heavy sadness that palls the *diapsalmata*, and the fascination with death and dereliction in essays like "Shadowgraphs,"[25] "The Ancient Tragical Motif as Reflected in the Modern,"[26] and "The Unhappiest Man."[27] In particular it has said nothing of A's membership in the *symparanekromenoi*. These are strange themes and strange predilections for a hedonist, and yet they follow irresistibly from the aesthetic presupposition that life consists in enjoyment: "There are well-known insects which die in the moment of fecundation. So it is with all joy; life's supreme and richest moment of pleasure is coupled with death."[28] The familiar connection between sexual consummation and death is the consequence of a less obvious but more intimate and fundamental conjunction of death and delight.

"Death," says A, addressing the *symparanekromenoi*, "is for us the greatest happiness."[29] In his lecture on "The Ancient Tragical Motif," subtitled "an essay in the fragmentary," he outlines the metaphysical and artistic tenets held by the brotherhood of defunct men. Reality, in their view, is a show of accidental events, of which the only thing one can confidently say is: It passes. Reality is essentially *pastness*. But it is a pastness without finality or fulfillment: reality is as desultory as it is fleeting. That which is past without being perfected is dead. Reality aesthetically conceived is death.

Theory of art follows ontology. The literati of the *symparanekromenoi* are dedicated to the production of works marked by a "gleaming transitoriness." Their essays are "anacoluthic," "fragmentary pursuits"; or as A finally sums it up: "Let us then describe our purpose as an attempt . . . in the art of writing posthumous papers."[30] Since for these aesthetes art is not distinct from life, their art of living is an imaginative dying before their death. The fellowship of the deceased are those who have chosen death as a way of life. "The unhappiest man" in the world is the man who absents himself from experience, whose hope and whose memory are equally vain, because his future is already past in anticipation and his past forever imminent in recollection. A man without a present, his life a possibility never tried and never to be overtaken, but ever cherished, he is embalmed before his birth. "But what do I say: the unhappiest, the happiest I ought to say, for this is indeed a gift of the gods which no one can give himself."[31] The unhappiest man, and paradoxically the happiest, the man whose life is death, is the aesthete himself.

The paradox is illumined by a recapitulation of the aesthetic project and its execution. The aesthete wants enjoyment, but enjoyment cannot simply be had, it must be arranged. Life must be made an art, but the art of living requires a total detachment from everything merely given and possibly unpleasant, as well as a disinterested arbitrariness in the concoction of actual pleasures. The perennial threat to this

---

25 Ibid., *vol. I, pp. 163–213.* 26 Ibid., *vol. I, pp. 135–162.*
27 Ibid., *vol. I, pp. 215–228.* 28 Ibid., *vol. I, p. 20.* 29 Ibid., *vol. I, p. 165.*
30 Ibid., *vol. I, pp. 149–151, especially p. 150.* 31 Ibid., *vol. I, p. 228.*

insouciance is misfortune, and the supreme misfortune is death. Fate, in its double role of chance and necessity, and especially death, inevitable in its outcome but inconstant in its choice of time and place and manner, seem to constitute the absolute frustration of aesthetic freedom. The one gift that cannot be refused is death. Suicide will not work: the aesthete could not consistently kill himself unless he could survive to enjoy the event.

Two consequences follow: First, the aesthete worships fate. In the *ultimatum* of death it sets the outer limit to his *nil admirari* and his caprice; it is the one power he cannot transcend or overwhelm. A's devotion to tragic literature is the offering he lays on the altar of his god. But (and this is the second consequence) the tragic corpus itself is the divine liturgy in which death is transubstantiated to art. In the celebration of this liturgy the aesthete receives the bread and wine of his own communion with life. The holy mystery of aestheticism is that everything—even misfortune and death—can be enjoyed. In possibility, Kierkegaard liked to say, everything is possible. In the grace of this possibility the aesthete consumes his god and enters into his beatitude.

But it must not be forgotten that this is a Black Mass. The aesthete's communion is a foretaste of death. His beatitude—prefigured already in his initial retreat from life and now perfected in his tragic necrolatry —is *melancholy*. Melancholy is the ultimate and only consistent form of aesthetic enjoyment. Over the entrance to the aesthetic life burn the prophetic words: *lasciate ogni speranza, voi ch'entrate.*[32] The art of living is the art of enjoying despair.

I say of my sorrow what the Englishman says of his house: my sorrow is my castle.[33]

My life is like an eternal night; when at last I die, then I can say with Achilles:
Du bist vollbracht, Nachtwache meines Daseyns.[34]

But if the prospect is dreary, the achievement is magnificent. A is unequivocally intent on living aesthetically, and he accepts the consequences of his project with matchless consistency. To say that he is effete is no refutation: he embraces his vanity with the enthusiasm of despair. To complain that he is gloomy is beside the point: he savors the wormwood and the gall with bittersweet relish. Seen from inside his skin, any protest against his way of life—in the interests of sanity, sound sense, morals, or piety—is bound to seem philistine. He is, to give him his proper name, the *poet* par excellence. His medium is not words, but himself: he is the living *poiesis*, the root and branch of which all merely verbal making is but the flower.

Unlike Don Juan, who must vanish when the house lights go up, A might really exist, does indeed exist as the father of us all. Like most men most of the time and all men some of the time, he seeks (but with

---

[32] *From Dante's Inferno, III, 9. "All hope abandon, ye who enter here."*
[33] *Kierkegaard, op. cit., vol. I, p. 21.*   [34] Ibid., *vol. I, p. 35.*

exemplary single-mindedness) the richest satisfaction of desire compatible with the widest exercise of freedom. That this involves him
in paradox is a fact he sees and welcomes, because he is more honest
and more thorough than the rest of us. His life is the indefatigable
process of reconciling its own contradictions. Each stage of the
Hegelian dialectic is driven by its inner contradictions into a higher
stage. In the Kierkegaardian dialectic, each of the "stages on life's
way" *contains* its contradictions—is, in fact, the *project* of so containing them. While the typical Hegelian protagonist is the abstraction of an abstraction (*Herrschaft* and *Knechtschaft*), the Kierkegaardian "existence-spheres" come to focus in *dramatis personae*
who struggle to assimilate their problems into the integrity of their
individual personalities.

A then is a real man, or, as he is ensconced in his literary productions, an
"existential possibility." The excellence of his poetic achievement is
validated by the cogency of his *modus vivendi:* he exists his poetry
and poetizes his existence. To call him "aesthete" is to acknowledge
the hypostatic union of immediacy and freedom where art is incarnate
in life and life is redeemed in art.

At the end of the first volume of *Either/Or,* hard on the heels of "The Rotation Method" and balancing in bulk the long essay on *Don Juan* with
which the book opens, stands the "Diary of the Seducer."[35] Apparently alien to the rest of the book—allegedly found among the papers
of A, who in turn claims to have copied it out on the sly, it purports
to be the private journals of the one Johannes nicknamed "the
Seducer"—the Diary is also somewhat deceptive. It is indeed the
record of a seduction, but any salacious expectations raised by the
title are laid in the perusal. The carnal climax occurs in the interval
between the ultimate and penultimate entries, while the remaining
140-odd pages detail the intricate procedure by which the seduction is
accomplished. Having sighted and fancied Cordelia Wahl, Johannes
determines upon her undoing, lays his snares, and takes his prey.
Once he has her he immediately releases her (having introduced her,
as he puts it, into a "higher sphere" of consciousness),[36] for her
interest is gone with her maidenhood.

More interesting than the story itself is Johannes' theory of seduction and
the techniques by which the theory is implemented. Seduction, as
Johannes understands it, is not the act of defloration, nor does it presuppose an excessive concern with sex. To seduce a woman means:
with no force but with much art to secure the free capitulation of her
mind to yours. That sexuality will be the normal context for such an
enterprise is obvious; but it is strictly incidental to the real objective,
which is the conquest of the spirit and not the congress of the flesh.
It is difficult but not impossible to imagine Johannes a eunuch. When
a woman has acknowledged herself captivated, be her body never so

---

35 Ibid., *vol. I, pp. 297–440.*   36 Ibid., *vol. I, p. 432.*

intact, she is possessed more effectively than if she were captured by rape.

The character and the escapades of Johannes the Seducer suggest a comparison with Don Juan. The Don is sensuality pure and simple, to the exclusion of intellect. He is no more a seducer than is the force that through the green fuse drives the flower. Johannes is an intellect that can become sensual at will: "He lived far too intellectually to be a seducer in the common understanding of the word. Sometimes, however, he assumed a parastatic body, and was then sheer sensuality."[37] *Pur chè porti la gonella, voi sapete quel chè fà* describes the amorphous longings of Don Juan; the Seducer's more discriminating desire is presaged in the motto of his Diary, *Sua passion' predominante è la giovin principiante.*[38] The texts are from the same libretto, and it is not surprising to find A, in his commentary on *Don Juan*, imagining another kind of seducer, a seducer who will enjoy not the satisfaction of desire, but the "deception," the "cunning," the "how, the method"[39] of seduction. Johannes is this "reflective Don Juan,"[40] whose pleasure is the seducing and not the rewards of seduction. Don Juan wants women, and for his purposes they are all sisters. His Teutonic namesake wants the excitement of a contest of minds, and for this end he needs a very particular woman: *la giovin principiante*, old enough to have a mind of her own, woman enough to want to give it away, and young enough to be unscarred by previous combats.

Johannes is after Cordelia's mind and the thrill of beguiling it. As he is scrupulous in his choice of victims, so he is ingenious in the selection and use of his weapons. He brings to his task resources of cunning, psychological insight, and patience—especially patience; Cordelia is five months in the making—that would tax and tire the ordinary sensualist. He shifts his moods in Cordelia's presence with calculated randomness: bewilderment begets attraction. He drones for hours with her old aunt about the high price of butter: boredom gives franchise to erotic fancy. He arranges to have her courted by an obliging boor: contempt of Edward becomes a bond that ties Cordelia to Johannes. He is betrothed to Cordelia, and promptly breaks the engagement: transferred from public trust to clandestine adventure, her desire burns sweeter and stronger. Johannes never makes a move to seduce, and by that fact is made more seductive. His strategy, consistent with his theory of seduction, is to make himself an object at once terrifying and fascinating, *mysterium tremendum et fascinans.* He makes himself—to adduce what Kierkegaard sometimes calls *the* aesthetic category—"interesting." Bewitched at last, Cordelia throws herself into his arms, unable any longer to deny him the love he has evoked but never demanded. When she finally succumbs, it is not clear to her just who has done what and to whom.

---

[37] Ibid., *vol. I, pp. 303–304.*
[38] *Again from* Don Giovanni. *"His ruling passion is the fresh young girl." Cf.* Kierkegaard, op. cit., *vol. I, p. 298.*
[39] Ibid., *vol. I, pp. 107, 98.*   [40] Ibid., *vol. I, p. 107.*

It is almost, in retrospect, as if she had seduced him. This, of course, is exactly the effect Johannes has wanted and so faultlessly prepared: that his desire should become hers, that she should freely but help-lessly surrender herself to her destroyer.

His journal gives us primarily Johannes' view of Johannes, and from within he looks very much like A. He is, by his own admission, a poet. Seduction is a kind of *poiesis* worked in the medium of woman's sexuality. If Johannes is careless of Cordelia and her feelings, it is only because he is so painstakingly careful of his artistry. He is faithless with Cordelia the girl, but only because of a higher fidelity to Cordelia "the Idea," who is priveleged to be immortalized in his art. His pact is with the aesthetic, and that involves, as the case of A has already shown, detachment and arbitrariness in relation to actual per-sons and events. All love—poetically viewed—is essentially faithless.[41]

Johannes could if he wished offer justification for his practice, though he is far too pure an aesthete to defend himself morally. The qualities by which he seduces girls are just those qualities of tact, diplomacy, and skill in the handling of people which are universally honored among men of affairs. If from a certain perspective he seems cold, cruel, inhumane, it is only because he does successfully what most men mostly bungle: he uses people exclusively for his own ends. If it be objected that he has deceived Cordelia, he can reply: Yes, but for her own good; I found her a girl, I left her a woman. She is not ruined by her seduction, but made; she has become for the first time free, self-conscious, and mature. Her husband—if she finds one—will be indebted to Johannes for his services. The seducer, by norms and devices commonly approved, but with much greater expertness in the application, is the benefactor of mankind.

Cordelia, however, is differently impressed. Her letters (four of them are incorporated in Johannes' Diary)[42] speak alternately confusion, out-raged innocence, pathos, self-pity, and—preeminently—horror. She shudders at the awareness that she has been possessed by a demon, she has made love to a "parastatic" body! Her lover dwells in splen-did and terrible isolation in a phantom realm behind the real world. In the whimsicality of his moods he appears suddenly out of nowhere and as quickly vanishes again, so that Cordelia has often found herself "embracing a cloud."[43] Because he willed to be her god, Johannes has become her devil. The aesthetic integrity of his personality is, from Cordelia's point of view, the dreadful vacuity of one who does not *practice* deception but *is* deceit itself. Johannes' fidelity in the "service of the Idea" necessitates in principle a betrayal of every real relationship. He declares to the world—and to Cordelia in the very act of making love to her—"What have I to do with thee?"[44]

That Cordelia should feel this way is hardly astounding. More important is the fact that A himself is aghast at Johannes. The account of his

---

41 Ibid., vol. I, p. 432.   42 Ibid., vol. I, pp. 305–306, 308–309.
43 Ibid., vol. I, p. 305.   44 Cf. Matt. 8:28ff.

transcription of the Diary begins in Gothic mystery ("I cannot conceal from myself, scarcely can I master the anxiety which grips me at this moment . . ."),[45] moves to the realization that Johannes is a "depraved personality,"[46] and concludes to a prediction of derangement. A, who is a confidant of Cordelia's and sees the desolation of her virginity, prophesies that Johannes will eventually outsmart himself:

As he has led others astray, so he ends, I think, by going astray himself. . . . He who goes astray inwardly . . . soon discovers that he is going about in a circle from which he cannot escape. I think it will be this way with him later, to a still more terrible extent. I can imagine nothing more excruciating than an intriguing mind, which has lost the thread of its continuity and now turns its whole acumen against itself, when conscience awakens and compels the schemer to extricate himself from this confusion.[47]

Strange to hear A speaking of conscience, and ominous that he does so only in the presence of Johannes the Seducer. He confesses that he is

never quite able to control the anxiety that grips me every time I think about the case. I, too, am carried away into that nebulous realm, that dream world, where every moment one is afraid of his own shadow. Often I seek in vain to tear myself away; I follow along like a menacing shadow, an accuser who is mute. How strange! He has spread the deepest secrecy over everything, and yet there is an even deeper secret, and that is the fact that I am privy to it. . . . There is really nothing else which involves so much seduction and so great a curse as a secret.[48]

A man who wills mystification as an end may wind up caught in the springs and elastics and false bottoms of his own legerdemain; the secrecy that is a condition of seduction may become a solitary confinement in which the seducer goes mad for want of another against whom he can rectify his wild imaginings.

Yet it is not Johannes who is on the brink of madness, but A; it is not Johannes in whom conscience starts, but A. Of Johannes, A says:

Conscience exists for him only as a higher degree of consciousness, which expresses itself in a disquietude that does not, in a more profound sense, accuse him, but which keeps him awake, and gives him no rest in his barren activity. Nor is he mad; for the multitude of finite thoughts are not petrified in the eternity of madness.[49]

Not Johannes' secret life, but A's privy involvement in *l'affaire* Cordelia—as an observer tranced in fascinated terror—is the beginning of insanity. *Johannes is the omen of madness and the awakening of conscience in A.*

Johannes sees himself as an artist, a poetizer of girls. To Cordelia he is an incubus with whom she has lain to her soul's damnation. For A Johannes is just *himself looked at from without.* The demonia of the seducer is the melancholy innocence of the aesthete seen from the

---

[45] *Kierkegaard,* Either/Or, *vol. I, p. 299.*   [46] Ibid., *vol. I, p. 299.*
[47] Ibid., *vol. I, p. 304.*   [48] Ibid., *vol. I, p. 306.*   [49] Ibid., *vol. I, pp. 304–305.*

other side, the side of his relations to other people with whom, willy-nilly, he is involved, and whom, willy-nilly, he draws into the vortex of his own confusion. A, who knows both Johannes and Cordelia, is granted this double recognition of himself and the awful wisdom it brings: the wisdom of fear and of a conscience born in fear.

But the intimacy between A and Johannes goes even deeper. In the general preface to *Either/Or*, Victor Eremita, the pseudonymous editor, argues his conviction that A is the author, and not as he claims the pilferer, of the "Diary of the Seducer." For

the dominant mood in A's preface in a manner betrays the poet. It seems as if A had actually become afraid of his poem, as if it continued to terrify him, like a troubled dream when it is told. If it were an actual occurrence which he had become privy to, then it seems strange that the preface shows no trace of A's joy in seeing the realization of the idea which had so often floated before his mind. . . . [The reference is to the reflective seducer imagined in the essay on Don Juan.] I find no trace of such joy in the preface, but rather, as was said, a certain horror and trembling, which might well have its cause in his poetical relationship to this idea.[50]

The suggestion that Johannes is a possibility projected by A is con-firmed by the latter's remark that the Diary is a "poetic reproduction" of experience, and "therefore neither historically exact nor simply fiction, not indicative but subjunctive."[51] It is written in the mood of "as if"; Johannes looks so much like A because he is a poetic elonga-tion of A's personality. The madness and the moral upheaval on which he is verging are the unfolding of possibilities already latent in A himself. In the "Diary of the Seducer" A has imaginatively pushed his way of life beyond its extreme limit, and he is appalled when he sees where it is leading him.

But Johannes *is* a possibility, not a person. Just as pure sensuality (Don Juan) is possible only in art, so also is pure reflection (Johannes the Seducer). In *Don Juan* the unity of form and content is perfect because the distinction between them has not yet been drawn. In the journals of Johannes the separation between nature and freedom is so complete that it can never be healed. It is no accident that Don Juan and the Seducer have names—indeed the same name—univocal names appropriate to pure types, whereas A is as anonymous and equivocal as immediacy itself. For neither Don Juan nor Johannes is a possibility that can be actualized. They are, rather, the ideal *terminus a quo* and the equally ideal *terminus ad quem* of the aesthetic life, which A alone and ambiguously lives. In Don Juan art is impos-sibly submerged in life; in Johannes life is impossibly lost for the sake of art. Inspired to enthusiasm by the one, recoiling in dread from the other, the aesthete strikes between them the precarious unhappy equilibrium of his own life in art. His existence is such stuff as dreams—bad dreams—are made on, and his little life is rounded with the sleep of unconscious nature. But that is merely to say that he is man—man as he immediately, aesthetically *is*, haunted by memories

50 Ibid., *vol. I, p.* 9.   51 Ibid., *vol. I, p.* 300.

of bestial innocence and nightmares of demonic experience, melancholy in the assumption of his uncertain destiny.

It is therefore to A the man, not to Don Juan the myth or Johannes the menace, that Kierkegaard's champion of the ethical life addresses his solemn admonitions.

2. World Enough and Time

Volume II of *Either/Or* consists of a brace of very long letters and a sermon. The sermon (of which more later) is by an unnamed priest. The author of the letters is called *B*, to distinguish him from *A*, the author of volume I; but his letters tell us that his name is Wilhelm, that he is married and a father, and that he is an Assessor, or judge in the lower courts. The letters are addressed to A, who is a friend of Judge Wilhelm and a frequent visitor in the older man's home. The first letter defends "The Aesthetic Validity of Marriage" against the casual eroticism of the aesthete.[52] The second, to be considered here, bears the formidable title "The Equilibrium between the Aesthetical and the Ethical in the Composition of Personality."[53] Under this head the Judge mounts an attack on A's way of life and constructs a rationale for his own ethical mode of existence.

His approach is in keeping with his status in society and his epistolary form. He writes loosely and at his ease, from the security of an official position and the warmth of an idyllic marriage. His attitude is never argumentative and his concern never theoretical. Though his form permits him occasional digressions into philosophy, he is at bottom always the judge and paterfamilias, and his letter is appropriately compounded of advice and counsel, fireside wisdom, friendly exhortation, and occasionally sharp accusation. His purpose is exclusively practical: to get A to change his way of life.

The whole point of his critique of aestheticism is just that: it is not *practical*. Seizing on the catchword "either/or," which A had used as a pretext for idleness, the Assessor throws it back in his face. For an ethical man this motto epitomizes the utter seriousness with which he confronts a choice between two exclusive alternatives. For A it is a retreat into that eternity of imagination where all contraries are reconciled in a harmony of indifference. For the speculative fancy the opposition of good and evil has no force. The idea of one is no better and no worse than the idea of the other, and there is no choice to be made between them. The aesthete, insofar as he lives *aeterno modo*, makes no choices; and since a man's character is constituted by the choices he makes, the aesthete has no self. But such a stasis cannot be sustained. A recognizes that he must do something; and so he acts, but he acts arbitrarily and without commitments. Ideally he is detached from life; actually he samples everything life has to offer—with the proviso that he is not buying. This means, in ethical

---

[52] *Ibid., vol. II*, pp. 5–157.   [53] *Ibid., vol. II*, pp. 161–338.

terms: ideally his self is a vain imagination, actually it is dissolute in the etymological sense of "dissolved." His virtuosity, his ability to acquit himself in any situation and to play at everything, means that he is nothing but a *poseur*. His life is an endless series of masks in an endless masquerade, dissipated in its own external relations. The aesthete—this is the Assessor's charge—is trying to combine Don Juan (pure immediacy) with Johannes the Seducer (pure reflection), but the project is impossible, and he constantly comes apart at the seams. On the one hand he withdraws to demonic vacuity, on the other he returns in a plenitude of chaos; but never shall the two meet in the identity of a single personality informed by a fixed and steady character. You are impractical, the Judge tells A, in the radical sense that you cannot even be a self on your own terms.[54]

The same futility can be observed in the aesthete's attempts to deal with time. The connection between time and personal identity is clear from a consideration of the nature of choice. A's "choices" do not commit him to anything, which is to say that they are all for the moment. Decisive choosing binds the chooser to the consequences of his choice, either permanently or for a specified period of time. Ethical choice takes the form of vow or public contract; it decides a man's character for the future, it defines him in advance. Only that man has a self whose personality is continuous through time, and this requires that he be willing to put his future in trust by means of his choices. So it is that the Assessor takes marriage (the vow) and vocation (involving contractual obligation) as paradigm cases of ethical choice.

Moreover, it is natural that Judge Wilhelm should adduce the problem of time. As a judge he is daily encountering the necessity of decision. Making a decision requires preliminary deliberation, and in the course of this deliberation there is a moment of indifference, in which several alternatives are present and the will can incline any way. But whereas the aesthete wants to remain poised in this indifference —lest some pleasure elude him—the ethical man knows that the moment of indifference is also the instant of resolution, which must be seized or lost forever. Life moves forward, and this movement prohibits everlasting deliberation about alternatives. At some point one alternative must be chosen to the exclusion of its opposite— Guilty? Not guilty?—else both of them are irrecoverably gone. For the aesthete, a possibility is an everpresent opportunity for enjoyment; for the ethical man, it is the now-or-never demand for decision. Therefore the Judge can say: I am fighting for possibility, for freedom, and for the future.[55]

The aesthete has no future; his existence is a recollection of eternity, never a resolution in time. He loses his possibilities in the attempt to preserve them inviolate, for he never actualizes them, and a possibility unactualized is as profitable as miser's gold. His ideal of noninvolvement is a freedom suspended from decision, not a freedom engaged

54 Ibid., vol. II, pp. 161–164. 55 Ibid., vol. II, p. 180.

to decide, and it is therefore barren.   Yet—the other side of the
paradox returns—the aesthete does face a future, he does actualize
his possibilities, he does choose.   But he does it *malgré lui*.   Lost to
the world in deliberation, he acts on impulse, he vacillates, he chooses
by default or by accident.   But the possibilities he actualizes in this
way are not his own, they are things that happen to him.   And the
actions he arbitrarily elects to perform show by their arbitrariness that
they are actions to negate action, chosen for the purpose of avoiding
the consequences of choice.   By his way of life he assumes an
irresponsibility for his actions, which prevents him from choosing in
an ethical sense.   Judge Wilhelm believes that A is torn in contradiction between the rich but abstract ideality of his imagination and the
pointless hither-and-thither of his actual life.   From an ethical point
of view his anonymity signifies not concreteness, but the extremes of
emptiness and formlessness to which his way of life alternately compels him.   His either/or is at the level of theory an indifferent
both/and, and at the level of action an equally indifferent neither/nor.
The ethical either/or—a resolute choice shaping the personality
through time by reference to an ideal apprehended in the instant of
reflection—exceeds the compass of his aestheticism.

The Judge's accusation can be further generalized: The aesthete confuses
the theoretical and the practical domains.   He takes for the whole of
life what is at best a part of it, the idealizing activity of imagination
and intellect.   There is no doubt, Judge Wilhelm tells him, that "if to
deliberate were the proper task for a human life, you would be pretty
close to perfection."[56]   The Judge acknowledges A's superiority as a
dialectician and for that reason does not question the logic of his
position.   What he questions is the propriety of logic as a way of life.
If a man makes a career of theorizing, he identifies his existence with
the "instant of deliberation," which, however, "like the Platonic
instant, has no existence, least of all in the abstract sense in which
you [A] would hold it fast."[57]   The instant of deliberation is the
momentary withdrawal from existence in which the ethical man surveys his possibilities and gathers his forces for a return via decisive
choice and action.   But the aesthete, striving to hold the moment fast
in contemplation, makes his whole life a withdrawal from the arena of
decision and action.

The man who confuses theory and practice can go mad in his theoretical
isolation, as the case of the Seducer has shown.   But he can also be
tripped up in practice.   Suppose, says the Judge, a charming and
gifted young man, for whom you feel a genuine affection, should come
to you for advice on how to conduct his life.   You initiate him into
the mysteries of your aestheticism, he disappears from your society
for a time, and then reappears older and wiser.   Wiser, however, with
your own wisdom—cynicism, hatred of life, and melancholy.   Is it not
conceivable that you might be taken aback?   Might you not deplore
your own personality reflected in another whom you love?   If you
are able to be affected in this way by another human being, then your

---

[56] *Ibid., vol. II, p. 169.*   [57] *Ibid., vol. II, p. 167.*

aestheticism is not consistent. A perfectly consistent aestheticism would amount to the demonia of the seducer; this is a possibility A has shrunk from in horror. Judge Wilhelm asks him to imagine, not a fanciful extension of his personality, but an actual *alter ego* who might show him what sort of man he really is. And this, the Judge adds, is a consummation devoutly to be wished. The only hope for the aesthete is that he may be caught off guard and moved to acknowledge the extremity of his condition.[58]

The Assessor knows that it will take more than a disturbing personal experience to dislodge A from his aestheticism. But the example of the young friend clears the way for a devastating conclusion. The art of living requires that the aesthete stay in control of himself and his situation. However, the case of the young man suggests that he is not in control at all. His aim is enjoyment. *"But,"* Judge Wilhelm counters, *"he who says that he wants to enjoy life always posits a condition which either lies outside the individual or is in the individual in such a way that it is not posited by the individual himself."*[59] That this is the case with health, beauty, love, wealth, fame, status, talent, pleasure, and the like is obvious.[60] But it is also the case with that view of life which Judge Wilhelm describes as "the most refined and superior"[61] of all aesthetic views, the view of A himself:

Your thought has hurried on ahead, you have seen through the vanity of all things, but you have got no further. Occasionally you plunge into pleasure, and every instant you are devoting yourself to it you make the discovery in your consciousness that it is vanity. So you are constantly beyond yourself, that is, in despair. . . . You are like a dying man, you die daily, not in the serious significance usually attached to this word, but life has lost its reality, and, as you say, you always count your days by the number of times notice is served on you to quit your lodging.[62]

The Assessor perceives that A's melancholy is the most sophisticated form of aestheticism. But it is nevertheless desperate, and it betokens the loss of a world. However consistent it may be in itself, it cannot be made consistent with reality. The aesthete, who thinks to conquer fate by anticipating and transforming in tragedy the worst it can bring, may still be shattered by the best. It does no good to proclaim oneself the unhappiest man:

He who says that sorrow is the meaning of life has joy outside him in the same way that he who would be joyful has sorrow outside him. Joy may take him by surprise in exactly the same way that sorrow may take the other by surprise. His life view thus hinges upon a condition which is not in his power, for it is really just as little in a man's power to give up being joyful as to give up being sorrowful. But every life view which hinges upon a condition outside itself is despair.[63]

If he is surprised by joy, the aesthete has lost the mastery of life on which the success of his aestheticism depends. That he can be so

[58] Ibid., *vol. II, pp. 163–167.*   [59] Ibid., *vol. II, p. 184.*   [60] Ibid., *vol. II, pp. 185–195.*
[61] Ibid., *vol. II, p. 198.*   [62] Ibid., *vol. II, pp. 199, 200.*   [63] Ibid., *vol. II, p. 240.*

surprised is clear. Though he is prepared to transport everything that happens to him into the never-never land of reflection, he must nevertheless wait for it to happen. However effete, he is always liable to be taken unawares by some happenstance that he could not neutralize *a priori* and in the concrete—and that on the terms of his own metaphysic. He may make a garden of his melancholy and water it with poetic tears, but the flowers and the weeds still grow where they list. That his life, even in its most tragic and poignant moments, is only a pose is made evident by the fact—surely disconcerting to a member of the *symparanekromenoi*—that there are days when he is happy in spite of himself.

In his very joy the aesthete is in despair, a despair quite different from the hopelessness which he recommends as a condition of freedom. The despair of which Judge Wilhelm speaks is a consequence of unfreedom, of the aesthete's unconditional dependence upon conditions beyond his control.

So it appears that every aesthetic view of life is despair, and that everyone who lives aesthetically is in despair, whether he knows it or not. But when one knows it (and you indeed know it), a higher form of existence is an imperative requirement.[64]

The words in parentheses are important, for they mark the possibility of a transition to a "higher form of existence." The aesthete knows that he is sick unto death, and still persists in his aestheticism. His choice—the one real choice that he makes—is the election of a way of life whose inevitable end is despair. That is why Judge Wilhelm reminds A of the teaching of the Church that melancholy (*acedia*) is a sin, and adds that "a man may have sorrow and distress, yea, it may be so great that it pursues him throughout his whole life, and this may even be beautiful and true, but a man becomes melancholy only by his own fault."[65] Stifling though it be, *the aesthete's unfreedom is an unfreedom that he has freely undertaken* by choosing to live aesthetically. It is an unfreedom, therefore, from which he can by another free choice emancipate himself. The way of emancipation is the passage from an aesthetic to an ethical mode of existence.

To characterize the ethical life is to move from the Assessor's accusation of A to the advice which he, still judge and husband, has ready to hand. His first admonition, and the first step toward a higher "stage" on life's way, is: Despair! The initial movement toward the ethical is the same as the terminal moment of the aesthetic. The same and yet different; for the despair which Judge Wilhelm recommends is not the despair which the aesthete nurtures as the last end of a life of enjoyment. It is a *despair of the life of enjoyment as such,* and thus *the gateway into a new kind of life.* You can see, says the Judge to A, that your life is desperate. Accept this fact and break with aestheticism altogether, give up without reservation your impossible attempt to achieve freedom and selfhood at the level of immediacy. You will *ipso facto* have elevated yourself to the true freedom and the concrete selfhood of the ethical man. "The aesthetical in a man is that by which he is immediately what he is; the ethical is that whereby he becomes what he becomes."[66] By giving up the vain endeavor to be himself (aesthetic), a man is first enabled to become himself (ethical).

This election of despair is the critical breach with immediacy that distinguishes the aesthetic from the ethical. The aesthete, in spite of all his reflection, remains "in his immediacy." His art of living is an attempt so to arrange the given that it can be (reflectively, to be sure) enjoyed as it is. The ethical man undertakes the wholesale reconstruction of his nature in the light of his duty and in the power of his freedom, to the end that he may thereby make himself what he is obligated to become. "So then," the Judge repeats,

choose despair, for despair is a choice; . . . one cannot despair without choosing. And when a man despairs he chooses again—and what is it he chooses? He chooses himself, not in his immediacy, not as this fortuitous individual, but he chooses himself in his eternal validity.[67]

What the aesthete must do is to abandon his whole way of life. And then he will be in a position to become himself. In fact, by this first authentic act of freedom, he will already have become a real person. By despairing of himself qua aesthetic he will at once have chosen himself qua ethical in his eternal validity. For his eternal validity as a self is nothing other than the freedom by which he chooses himself. The "absolute" self of which Judge Wilhelm speaks, the self which a man becomes by decisively resolving against a life of enjoyment, is just freedom.[68]

The self so chosen both comes into existence with the choice and exists prior to the choice as something to be chosen. What exists before the choice is the self as immediately given. The self that comes to be by the choice is the same self lifted from nature to self-consciousness by means of freedom.

In this case choice performs at one and the same time the two dialectical movements: that which is chosen does not exist and comes into existence with the choice; that which is chosen exists, otherwise there would not be a choice. For in case what I chose did not exist but absolutely came into existence with the choice, I would not be choosing, I would be creating; but I do not create myself, I choose myself. Therefore, while nature is created out of nothing, while I myself as an immediate personality am created out of nothing, as a free spirit I am born of the principle of contradiction [either/or], or born by the fact that I choose myself.[69]

The freedom by which a man chooses himself in his eternal validity is not abstract, like that of the aesthete, but concrete; for the self which is chosen is the self that is given in the whole of its natural and historical determinations. Likewise the choice itself is not a once-for-all bit of derring-do (the sort of thing an aesthete might try off and on), but a daily reengagement of the whole personality in the terms

66 Ibid., vol. II, p. 182.   67 Ibid., vol. II, p. 215.   68 Ibid., vol. II, pp. 217–218.
69 Ibid., vol. II, pp. 219–220.

and consequences of the original decision. Self-choice is not only the entrance to the ethical life; it is also the constitutive principle by which that life is structured. As such it is compounded of the two essential moments of *repentance* and *duty*. In the *present* resolution of self-choice a man takes all of his *past* into his freedom (repentance) and freely programs his entire *future* (duty).

The necessity and the significance of *repentance* in an ethical mode of existence are obvious if it is noted that a man who chooses himself ethically chooses to be absolutely responsible for whatever he is and becomes. But the self for which he assumes responsibility has a spatial and temporal spread; in particular it has a past. This past becomes his when he accepts the liability for it, and he cannot reject it without going back on his self-choice. Yet there is much in any man's past that cannot be affirmed as good. It must therefore be affirmed as guilty. The affirmation of oneself as guilty is repentance. Repentance is the movement of freedom by which a man gets under the whole weight of his past and shoulders it for the future.[70] For "my life does not begin in time with nothing, and if I cannot repent the past, freedom is a dream."[71]

Free self-choice is the choice of oneself as guilty. Any other understanding of freedom is either paltry or abstract, the paltriness which the aesthete despises or the abstraction that he is condemned to remain. Judge Wilhelm wants to make clear to A that any qualifications introduced at this point would be no more than a craven effort to get an easy acquittal for aestheticism. It is easy to see why Kierkegaard entrusts the commendation of the ethical life into the hands of Judge Wilhelm; for to live ethically is to sit in judgment on oneself and hand down the bitter verdict: Guilty.[72]

Repentance, however, is but one moment of the ethical choice; the correlative movement in the opposite direction is *duty*. The aesthetic life was structured by a dialectic of withdrawal and return. The same dialectic repeats itself in the ethical life, but in radically altered form, now concretely temporal rather than abstractly eternal. Having attained the level of freedom by despairing of aestheticism, the ethical man concurrently chooses himself in his eternal validity. The movement of repentance is the element of withdrawal in this self-choice; by repentance he gets all the way outside himself, behind his own past. In the life of duty he returns to himself and advances into his future.

The self that is repented is the past actuality of the individual who chooses; but insofar as he chooses it, it becomes his future possibility. Nature overtaken by freedom and considered in relation to the future becomes task. The task of the ethical man is to take his given nature in hand and make it his responsibility. And to accept oneself as one's own responsibility is to acknowledge the claim of duty. "For as soon as in despair a person has found himself, has absolutely chosen him-

---

[70] Ibid., vol. II, pp. 220–223, 229, 236, 252–253.   [71] Ibid., vol. II, p. 244.
[72] Ibid., vol. II, pp. 221–222.

self, has repented himself, he has himself as a task under an eternal responsibility, and thus duty is posited in its absoluteness."[73]

Duty conceived is abstract. But duty acted on is as concrete as the individual himself. The principle of duty can be stated in a form applicable to every man without exception: Thou shalt become thyself. But particular duties (what a modern moralist might call values) cannot be defined in theory, they can only be discovered in situation. Particular duties arise, for each person, out of the exigencies of his particular nature and the particular circumstances in which he finds himself. Judge Wilhelm, as a married man, a father, and a civil servant, has no difficulty descrying the duties that are appropriate to his station in life. And neither, he suggests, will anyone who is seriously committed to the principle of duty, who has not kept back some little aesthetic reservation by which he hopes to get himself an occasional moral holiday.[74] That is why the Assessor does not represent the primary ethical choice as a choice *between* good and evil, but as a choice *of* good and evil as the constitutive categories for one's life. The distinction between good and evil does not exist for the aesthete; morality is not an immediate qualification of human nature. To choose to lead one's life in terms of the opposition of good and evil is to take the ethical as against the aesthetic mode of self-understanding.[75] But for that reason the choice of the ethical *is* the choice of the good; for the good in an abstract sense is just the free resolution to become oneself by the way of repentance and duty. "As soon as one can get a man to stand at the crossways in such a position that there is no recourse but to choose, he will choose the right."[76] Not that the ethical man does what is right in every case; but even when he does wrong in some particular, his commitment to the principle of good is still primary. The fundamental orientation of his will, which shows itself in his repentance and his recognition of the principle of duty, is right. In this respect he is opposed to the demoniac like Johannes the Seducer, who is imprisoned in evil even though he may incidentally do good.

Ethics, for Judge Wilhelm, is not a matter of values but of being. It is not in the first place a question of following a certain set of moral rules; it is the determination to become a certain kind of person. As over against the aesthete, who drifts through life neutrally occupied with imaginative possibilities and therefore never becomes a self, the ethical man sustains in day-to-day exercise of will the resolution by which he ever consolidates his personality around the either/or: good/evil. If by repenting the past a man can assume the burden of responsibility for himself, and if by daily facing the future in dutiful resolve he can build the integrity of this self, then it may be added that his

eternal dignity consists in the fact that he can have a history, the divine element in him consists in the fact that he himself, if he will, can impart to

---

73 Ibid., vol. II, p. 275.   74 Ibid., vol. II, pp. 258–275.
75 Ibid., vol. II, pp. 171–173, especially p. 173.   76 Ibid., vol. II, p. 172; cf. p. 171.

this history continuity, for this it acquires only when it is not the sum of all that has happened to me or befallen me but is my own work, in such a way that even what has befallen me is by me transformed and translated from necessity to freedom.[77]

Now, however, although the choice of the ethical way of life entails the rejection of the aesthete's way of life, the aesthetic element in existence remains. A man does not eliminate his immediacy by choosing to live his life in other than immediate categories. Therefore it is incumbent on Judge Wilhelm to show that the ethical life does justice to this aesthetic component. And he does so at great length. The ethical choice is so far from negating the aesthetic element of life that it is the necessary condition of genuine aesthetic enjoyment. For example, suppose a man possesses great wealth. So long as he continues to live aesthetically his wealth is his fate. He is dependent upon it for his enjoyment; his wealth owns him, he does not own it. If he then makes the ethical choice of himself, he becomes free with respect to his wealth. His life no longer depends upon it or upon any gift of fortune; good fortune or bad, he is master of himself. He can enjoy his wealth and enjoy it freely—because it has become a matter of indifference to him. This indifference may sound like the aesthete's hopelessness, but there is a new twist. In his hopelessness the aesthete remains enslaved to the fate he flees. In ethical self-choice a man buys his immediacy back out of slavery to nature and fate, and makes it his own. The ethical choice does not destroy the aesthetic, but redeems it.[78]

The transfiguration of the aesthetic by the ethical is the theme of much of Judge Wilhelm's letter, and works itself out in a series of contrasts between the aesthetic and the ethical ways of life. The ethical, he says, is the *universal*, as opposed to the aesthetic, which is *differential*. While the aesthete's personality is always built on his possession of some talent that differentiates him from the mass of men, the ethical man refuses to take any advantage from such gifts. The fact that one is a genius or "the unhappiest man" in the world is ethically irrelevant, and no man devoted to duty would claim any virtue either from his excellence or his wretchedness. The ethical choice equalizes men in a way that most men, their lives aesthetically determined, find it hard to tolerate. It is difficult to resist the temptation to hold back from the universal some little difference, be it only one's misery, that sets one apart from the herd. Yet it is ethically intolerable that a man's character should depend on luck, or that men should be distinguished from each other *as men* by aesthetic accidents. Of course all the aesthetic differences remain within the context of the ethical choice; but there they exist as freely appropriated and ethically neutral.[79]

The ethical universal (duty) is a *concrete* universal as opposed to the *abstract* or poetic universal. Duty works intimately into and through the finite world, while poetry can only retreat from it. The poet may

---

[77] Ibid., vol. II, p. 255.   [78] Ibid., vol. II, pp. 257–258.   [79] Ibid., vol. II, pp. 259–266.

be the child of eternity, but he has not the seriousness of eternity, which is its ability to incarnate itself in time. Mysticism, asceticism, monasticism the Assessor regards as a kind of aesthetic *contemptus mundi* masquerading as religious; intrusive in their relation to God, they take the ethical decision in vain and deceive themselves out of a world. The ethical man takes his place in the world in the midst of the community of men; he knows that it is his duty to reveal himself to others, while the aesthete—whether poet, demon, or mystic— always remains in the concealment of his aesthetic differentia. Though he can conceive of a man who, because of some unique voca- tion, finds it impossible to "realize the universal," the Judge can see nothing in the life of such an "exception" but unrelieved misery. If such a man is "reconciled to the universal" at all, it will only be by remorse over his inability to actualize the universal directly.[80]

In the light of these observations it is easy to see why the Judge exults in the view that every man has a calling and is obliged to work in order to live—whereas the aesthete, for whom the necessity of working would be burdensome, requires (the accident of) opulence in order to carry out his project of enjoyment. The contractual obligation involved in work points up the ethical conviction that there is an order of things in which every man can find a place, a place where he can accomplish the universal (by earning . . .) in his own individuality (. . . his living). Such a man is his own providence, and that is no more than to say that he lives ethically.[81]

Finally, Judge Wilhelm's ardent advocacy of marriage, as against romantic love and seduction, expresses the way in which the ethical self-choice works itself out in time and transfigures a man's immediacy. Bio- logically bound to the bearing and rearing of children, the life of woman is limited and defined by the cycle of conception, gestation, parturition, and maturation. She therefore understands time more intimately than any masculine philosopher; she and not man deserves to be called the lord and master of nature. Her ethical role, conse- quently, is to be man's finitude, and this she achieves only in her capacity as wife and mother. To treat her as an ideal (seduction), or as an occasion (romance), is to defraud her and oneself of destiny. It is only in marriage—where it becomes duty via the solemn vow—that love achieves actuality in time. Any other view of love treats it as an abstraction or as an accident, betrays it or loses it by default. The freedom that is vainly sought in seduction, and the pleasure that is vainly demanded of romance, first become realities in the ethical context of marriage, where immediacy ("falling in love") is taken up in freedom (the vow) and made concrete in the public trust and private devotion of family life.[82]

So Judge Wilhelm concludes—or rather does not conclude, for he is as garrulous as time itself. The length of his letters suggests that his

80 Ibid., *vol. II*, pp. 245–259.   81 Ibid., *vol. II, pp. 281–302, especially pp. 287, 297.*
82 Ibid., *vol. II, pp. 302–321.*

wife's expert management of his finitude leaves him infinite leisure for distributing extra-professional counsel. But that in a way is his point: Only by advancing to an ethical understanding of himself does a man find world enough and time to achieve a stable equilibrium of the aesthetical and the ethical in the constitution of his personality. "What I wanted to do," he writes by way of rounding off A's lesson in morals,

was to show how the ethical, in the regions which border on the aesthetical, is so far from depriving life of its beauty that it bestows beauty upon it. It affords peace, assurance, and security, for it calls to us constantly: Quod petis, hic est.[83]

Judge Wilhelm can address A as he does because they are struck by a common perplexity: the contradiction between nature and freedom in the human self. And they are engaged by a common problem: how to work these conflicting elements into a single personality. A, as aesthete, wants simply to be himself as he is. And the Assessor's reply is that this cannot be done, for what a man is immediately is just this contradiction of immediacy and reflection. The equilibrium which A tries to maintain is worse than precarious, it is impossible. Forever vacillating, losing nature for the sake of freedom, and losing freedom for the sake of nature, he ends by losing himself as the particular worldly and temporal person he is bound to become. The "composition" (*Udarbejdelse*) of personality which the Assessor presses upon him is etymologically a "working-out" or "elaboration" of the self in the temporal order of the world. The victory that Judge Wilhelm wins in the arena of the finite is more than an equilibrium: it is the concrete opportunity—world enough and time—to reconcile what he is and what he can be in the integrity of what he becomes.

3. All
in All

Judge Wilhelm means to be a practical man. Consideration of his theories is fittingly supplemented by a scrutiny of his practice. His extravagant praise of connubial love suggests in particular a closer look at his marriage. That marriage, he boasts, is as nearly perfect as an earthly union can be. "I have never," he says, "experienced any conflict between love and duty, nor for that matter any serious marital conflicts at all."[84] One need not be a cynic (though perhaps one needs to be married) to remark that such an idyllic relationship could only be imagined by a bachelor like Kierkegaard. Even if we allow for nineteenth-century conventions about the place of woman in home and society, Judge Wilhelm's marriage is prima facie suspect.

It is suspect because of its tidiness and its facility. The Assessor's wife has presumably "chosen herself in her eternal validity"; otherwise she would not have been capable of the marriage vow. And yet, by her husband's theory, her reality consists in being his "finitude." She

---

[83] Ibid., vol. II, p. 328.   [84] Ibid., vol. II, p. 155.

organizes the Judge's finitude in a way that is perfectly consonant with his will. Her "absolute" self is identical with her relationship to her man. She is all freedom qua human, and all nature qua woman and wife.

It appears that the Judge has protested too much. At one and the same time he affirms his wife's freedom and the nice compliance of her freedom with his. Is this not, in a very subtle way, just what Johannes did with Cordelia? Judge Wilhelm says that sentimentality, because it is unrealistic, is the same as heartlessness.[85] Is it not sentimental of him to base "the aesthetic validity of marriage" on his wife's docility? Hasn't he handled her rather heartlessly by presuming that her freedom is his nature? To the extent that he makes of his wife's humanity a willing plasticity to his own prerogative the Judge, like the Seducer, is sentimentally calloused. "I cannot blame the Judge," says the voice of another pseudonym,

for his enthusiastic zeal in behalf of marriage; but nevertheless I think that the Judge, supposing I could get hold of him and whisper a little secret in his ear, will concede that there are difficulties he did not take into account.[86]

The suspicion that there is a dishonesty lurking in the upright heart of Judge Wilhelm is borne out by the "Ultimatum" that concludes Either/Or II.[87] As the "Diary of the Seducer" draws the ultimate consequences of aestheticism, so this ultimatum exposes the presuppositions of the ethical life. In form it is a sermon, composed by an old classmate of the Assessor, now priest of a lonely parish on the northern moors of Jutland. The sermon has been sent by its author to Judge Wilhelm, who in turn passes it along to A. The priest in his religious solitude reminds the Judge of his young friend's aesthetic isolation.[88] The sermon says briefly all that Judge Wilhelm said at length in his letters; indeed it says more and says it more felicitously. In the note which accompanies the sermon, the Judge advises A to read it and think of himself, for, he adds, "I have read it and thought of myself."[89] Just as A was unsettled by the vision of his extremity in the Seducer's Diary, so Judge Wilhelm is disturbed by this sermon, which is no more than the last word on his own life. It is an ultimatum issued to the ethicist by a representative of the religious.

The title of the sermon is "The Edification Implied in the Thought that as against God We Are Always in the Wrong." Its text (Luke 19:41–48) describes the prophetic lamentations of Jesus over Jerusalem. From the inclusion of the innocent with the guilty in the sack of Jerusalem, the priest infers: Are we not all guilty as over against God? And is this not the most edifying (opbyggelige, literally "upbuilding" or "constructive") thought a man can have? Trying to calculate one's moral worth by reference to human standards leads to disquietude and doubt of self, never to certainty and self-assurance. But before God

85 Cf. ibid., vol. II, p. 183.
86 Kierkegaard, Concluding Unscientific Postscript, Princeton University Press, Princeton, N.J., 1944, p. 161.
87 Kierkegaard, Either/Or, vol. II, pp. 339–356.
88 Ibid., vol. II, p. 341.   89 Ibid., vol. II, p. 342.

we are always in the wrong, and in this knowledge we find rest and peace.

The words of Jesus to the doomed city of Jerusalem may be an oblique complaint of the fluency of Judge Wilhelm's self-understanding:[90] "If thou hadst known in this thy day, even thou, the things which belong unto thy peace! but now they are hid from thine eyes. . . . Thou knewest not the time of thy visitation." The Judge confidently builds his peace on the conviction of the essential rightness of his life: When a man lives ethically he is always good in principle even though he occasionally does wrong. The Jutland priest counters: Whatever the relative rights and wrongs of a man's conduct, he can find repose only in the understanding that he is always guilty as against the Absolute.

Kierkegaard's priest is suggesting that dogged persistence in an ethical way of life will bring a man to the point where he must either choose to acknowledge himself absolutely in the wrong or lose himself in a maze of casuistries. If he does not reach this point he deceives himself and shortchanges his principles. The sermon strikes at the assumptions that underlie Judge Wilhelm's views, especially his assumption of an easy harmony of freedom and nature in human action. To make his point, the priest examines the case of a relationship between two lovers. Love is the Judge's specialty, but the priest considers a possibility that never arises in the Assessor's life or thought. Suppose, he says, there is a radical conflict between lover and beloved. How can such a conflict be reconciled? Will the lover spend himself computing the rights and wrongs of each party to the relationship? Even if that were not an impossible task, such pettiness would hardly bespeak a deep and sincere love. Will he assert his own rightness as against the beloved? If he does, then it is not the beloved but his rightness that he loves. The true lover will neither defend himself nor bargain for advantages; the true lover will without reservation *choose* to be in the wrong that his beloved may be right and their love secured. Only the thought that he is in the wrong will quiet his anxiety, heal the breach, and preserve their love.[91]

It may be objected that a human relationship is a thing compounded of relativities and appropriately judged by less than absolute standards. No man is absolutely right or absolutely wrong over against another man. There will be a comparative right and a comparative wrong, but no total guilt. This objection would be valid were it not that Judge Wilhelm's ethics makes an absolute claim; he must either make good the claim or relapse into the "paltriness" which both he and the aesthete disdain.

According to Judge Wilhelm a man *chooses himself absolutely* when in repentance he takes his whole past and in duty his whole future under

---

[90] Cf. ibid., vol. II, pp. 243–244, for Judge Wilhelm's use of this same text against the aesthete. It is standard practice for Kierkegaard's pseudonyms to comment on each other, often with the effect of reciprocal or transitive irony. See the last section of this chapter.

[91] Ibid., vol. II, pp. 349–350.

the lordship of his freedom. It is his freedom assuming responsibility for his nature that constitutes his absolute worth as a human being. The priest does not contest the notion that a human being has absolute worth or that it is by his freedom that he has it. His doubts, reflected in the story of the unhappy lovers, concern man's ability to master his own life as completely as the Judge's theory requires. If the Judge supposes that such conflicts are impossible in his own marriage, that marriage is built on an illusion. And when such conflicts occur, they cannot be resolved by moral computation in a way that meets the Judge's ethical demand. No man acquires his "eternal validity" by coming off better in a quarrel with his wife. If the ethical man is in earnest about choosing himself in his eternal validity, he will have to choose himself as he is in relation to the Absolute. And if the true lover would not wish to be right as against his beloved, what man could will to be anything but absolutely in the wrong before God?[92] If Judge Wilhelm means what he says, he will make the leap from an ethical to a religious mode of existence.

Judge Wilhelm thinks that a man can get behind his whole history and push. He claims to do by means of repentance what he finds the aesthete unable to do by means of imagination: to overtake himself and take himself over completely. But he cannot get himself in hand, as the case of his marriage shows. He may try to persuade himself of the malleability of his own—and his wife's!—immediacy. But the slightest discord in their marital harmony will reveal obscurities of nature not illumined by freedom. The attempt to explore these recesses will issue either in the degradation of marriage into moral horse trading, or in the hardening of sentimentality into self-deception. The act of repentance does not solve all the concrete problems to which a man may be exposed in daily life. Nor does devotion to duty guarantee a man against the contingency of future moral impasse: the Judge may yet encounter actual duties he cannot perform and particular obligations he cannot fulfill. He may, for example, find himself presented by his children, for whom he has assumed responsibility by begetting them, with unsurmountable barriers to his own rectitude. If the aesthete can be surprised by unquenchable joy, Judge Wilhelm may be brought up short by unredeemable guilt. He is not his own captain after all. Aesthetic freedom flees from life; ethical freedom takes life as a task. But ethical freedom can no more empower a man to control his destiny than aesthetic freedom can shield him from it.

Of course the Judge is no stranger to guilt. But whereas he takes his guilt as a moral challenge, he would be better advised to see it as moral defeat. The affirmation of guilt does nothing to get rid of it, and herein lies the tragedy of the ethical life. If a man is to achieve selfhood by freedom, he must shoulder responsibility for the past, even for "the sins of the fathers."[93] But he is incapable of eliminating or reforming that past and therefore barred from meeting the absolute demand of duty. The ethical battle is lost before it begins. A man

---

[92] Ibid., vol. II, pp. 350–353.　　[93] Cf. ibid., vol. II, p. 222.

may recognize this and console himself with that "worldly wisdom" which the priest caricatures in the words: One does what one can.[94] But who knows what he can do? He may either assume that he can do all that he should, which is presuming too much; or he may conclude that he only can do what in fact he does, and by this he gets rid of repentance, duty, and his title to absolute worth at one stroke. In any case freedom, which is potent to make a man guilty, is impotent to remove guilt. The evil that a man does is his own doing, and he is answerable for it. But since it has become an ineradicable part of his past, he cannot answer to one in a thousand. A man can no more consolidate his self ethically than he can compose it poetically, for immediacy conspires to righteousness as little as it does to beauty. The ethical man is involved in a complicity with evil and a duplicity in himself from which he can find release nowhere but in religion. When he admits defeat, a man's personality is constituted absolutely (. . . as against God) in the only way it can be (always in the wrong . . .).

So long as he continues to be satisfied with what he ekes out by his own freedom, Judge Wilhelm knows not the things that belong to his peace. In the despair which he commends to A and enacts as the prelude to his own life he is close to apprehending his predicament. But he identifies despair with self-choice, and so reveals that the despair was incomplete. A thoroughgoing despair would exhaust the self and leave it no strength with which to make reprise of itself. Speaking *in persona* Johannes Climacus, Kierkegaard says:

The difficulty is, that the ethical self is supposed to be found immanently in the despair, so that the individual by persisting in his despair at last wins himself. . . . But this avails nothing. When I despair, I use myself to despair, and therefore I can indeed by myself despair of everything; but when I do this, I cannot by myself come back. In this moment of decision it is that the individual needs divine assistance. . . .[95]

But Judge Wilhelm does not discern the time of his visitation and misses the *divinum auxilium* to sink back into the comfortable fiction of his own competence.

To be fair to him, Judge Wilhelm is a pious man. The name of God occurs frequently in his letters; he even speaks of learning about God through pain and distress.[96] But where his piety is not a vague surcharge of feeling, it tends to be a vague support for his self-confidence. He writes, for instance, of his delight that he "can come to the aid of the Deity" by freely appropriating everything that happens to him, the joyful as well as the sorrowful.[97] Yet it is a long way from religion as ethical prop and ethical decor to the knowledge of God of which the Jutland priest is speaking. The God of the religious way of life appears not in ethical victory, but only in the shipwreck of freedom on

[94] Ibid., vol. II, pp. 346–348, 353–354.
[95] Kierkegaard, Concluding Unscientific Postscript, pp. 230–231.
[96] Kierkegaard, Either/Or, vol. II, pp. 241–243.
[97] Ibid., vol. II, p. 255; cf. also p. 125.

the shoals of guilt. Judge Wilhelm's religion is as sentimental as his marriage. It too easily becomes a caviling with God, a will to be always in the right and to have the world on his own terms. His distrust of the people he calls "exceptions," those unfortunate people who cannot put body and soul together in the ethically approved fashion, his satisfaction with his own familial and social life, and his ever-sanguine conscience show that he has not chosen himself with utter honesty. His ethics succeeds aesthetically as well as it does because he cheats a little here and there—which is to say, he cheats absolutely. A serious choice of himself would not automatically bring him to a lovely concord of freedom and nature, man and wife, individual and society. A serious self-choice would isolate him before God in the awareness of his inadequacy to render account of himself. It would leave him no alternatives but God or nothing.

Therefore, the priest tells his hearers, choose yourself. But choose yourself as you are: in the wrong against God. You lose yourself eternally as long as you continue to absolutize your freedom. You gain yourself eternally as soon as you recognize your nothingness. The decision for absolute guilt—and it is a decision, not reached by calculation but taken in freedom—is the only edifying (constructive) decision available. This is the act of freedom by which a man's self acquires absolute worth: the choice of his self as worthless in relation to God. If a man would not deceive himself with a tender notion of himself, let him abandon the hope that he can justify his life, and prefer the sober consolation of guilt. If he would not stultify himself with the thought that he can always do well by doing good, let him inspire himself to action by the thought of guilt, unencumbered by the necessity to be right or to become ever and ever righter. If he would not be reduced to the jejune expedient of making himself up as he goes along ("One does what one can"), let him take the painful but redeeming option of religion.

Summarizing the "stages on life's way," Kierkegaard wrote, "While aesthetic existence is essentially enjoyment, and ethical existence, essentially struggle and victory, religious existence is essentially suffering. . . ."[98] An aesthete's life is organized around pleasure, an ethical life around the opposition of good and evil. The religious life is a life in which God is acknowledged as the sole sufficient point of reference for human existence. Reflection on the nature of God shows that such a life is necessarily a life of suffering.

God may be called Absolute Reality, Absolute Power, *id quo majus cogitari non potest, ipsum esse, Qui est*—or any of an indefinite number of comparable names. And they are all correct. But none of them really defines or describes God. For if God is the *Absolute*, then He is transcendent of everything that can be known by men, all of which is but relative. God is altogether *other* than man and man's world. His existence, therefore, cannot be proven nor His nature conceived. To demonstrate or delineate God would be to bring Him within the

98 *Kierkegaard,* Concluding Unscientific Postscript, *p. 256.*

ambit of finite reason and so to demean His absoluteness. Anything said about God discredits Him, except this confession itself.[99]

Nevertheless God can be experienced. Because He is wholly other than man, He can be encountered as the negation of everything human. This is what happens in the experience of guilt; when a man admits the impossibility of legislating, enacting, and warranting his own conduct, he is exposed to God. God is the infinite nothingness that appears in the failure of the finite. Whenever some finite hope or finite assurance breaks down, there is an access to God. Whenever all human possibilities—aesthetic, intellectual, moral—are exhausted, there God is present. This is true especially of man's religiousness; human attempts to make contact with God must be frustrated before God Himself can break through. For if God is God, then every endeavor to build one's life (edify oneself) on anything less than the recognition of God—be it so crass as pleasure, so respectable as duty, or so sublime as piety—is an idol interposed between man and God. It is only when his idols crumble that a man can know God.

This knowledge of God, attained in the disaster of everything taken for God, but not God, is *identical with* the experience of the nothingness of man. Though He is in Himself the fullness of reality (*ens realissimum*) as the classical theologians said, God is only known to man as man's emptiness. Where there is uncertainty, despair, the consciousness of guilt, suffering without relief—there also is the experience of God. There *is* God, for the meaning of God in human experience is just the suffering of guilt implicit in the renunciation of every idol. God is, from a human point of view, urgently and manifestly at hand only in the dissolution of man and man's idolatry.[100]

Judge Wilhelm's idol is his freedom and his supposed self-mastery. Yet that idol is his way to God. It is an idol because he makes an absolute claim for it; it can lead him to God because it fails to support the weight laid upon it, and in crashing down brings his life to the ground with it. There, his half-gods destroyed, the ethical man is before God. His guilt is the time of his visitation. For any man who entrusts his life to his own or any finite power, it is a terrible thing to fall into the hands of the living God. For such a man God is wrath; as the only Absolute, He is the enemy of man's attempt to be his own destiny. Man is always "against" God insofar as he understands himself in aesthetic or ethical terms, and therefore always guilty.

But God, whom no man can see and live, is also the source of all being, the creator and revivifier of men. The thought of guilt is the edifying thought, because it provides the solid ground on which life can be

---

[99] This theme runs throughout all of Kierkegaard's writings. *For a concise statement of it, cf. Kierkegaard,* Philosophical Fragments, *Princeton University Press, Princeton, N.J., 1962, chap. III, "The Absolute Paradox: A Metaphysical Crotchet."*

[100] *Another persistent Kierkegaardian theme. Cf. Kierkegaard,* Edifying Discourses, *Augsburg, Minneapolis, 1943–1946, vol. IV, pp. 7–47; Kierkegaard,* Thoughts on Crucial Situations in Human Life, *Augsburg, Minneapolis, 1941, pp. 1–41.*

built without fear of ruin. There is, as Kierkegaard says, a necessary misunderstanding between man and God, since they are opposites. But there is also the possibility for man of an enthusiastic endurance of this misunderstanding.[101] This endurance, which Kierkegaard calls "worship," is the other side of the encounter with God.

"Worship," in Kierkegaard's language, means the recognition in practice of the "infinite qualitative difference" between man and God, the everlasting remembering of guilt.[102] Such a worship is entirely private, since God and His relation to man exceed all liturgical representation and devotional expression. Nevertheless it is the reservoir from which the religious man draws the waters of life. When he owns himself guilty, he is not confessing that he broke some of God's rules; the consciousness of inevitable and total guilt could not be arrived at by drawing up a balance sheet. Kierkegaard's word for guilt (*Skyld*) means originally "debt." To know oneself guilty in a religious sense is to know oneself *in debt* to God. The religious man *owes himself* completely to God.[103] He is aware that the self which is reduced to impotence in the presence of God is also upheld by the divine power. In his weakness he is sustained by a power not his own, for he has dried up his sources in despair. Unlike the aesthete, who poetizes himself, and the ethical man, who sits in judgment on himself, the religious man *receives* himself as a gift from God. Outwardly he does not differ from other men: he enjoys life like the aesthete, and he works at his responsibilities like the ethical man. Yet he is inwardly supported neither by fate nor by freedom, but by the consciousness that all he is or does is a divine gratuity.

The difference between the religious man and the ordinary man, Kierkegaard often describes in language like this: The ordinary man gets up in the morning, shaves, dresses, eats breakfast, kisses his wife good-bye, and goes to work; the religious man gets up in the morning, shaves, dresses, eats breakfast, kisses his wife good-bye, and goes to work. The difference, in other words, is invisible. For the ordinary man these things are his life, and if they are taken away his life is over. For the religious man God is his life; wife, work, and the like are concessions with which he is indulged, though he has no stake in them nor they in him. If God were to withdraw them all—well and good. He is prepared to give them up, in fact has already given them up in the suffering with which he detaches his self from the world and commits it to God. And when he finds (unlike the aesthete and the ethical man he is ever mindful of his weakness) that he has not the strength to perfect this resignation, when he clings to that which he should let go of—especially then in the depths of guilt he is restored to himself. He is both given and forgiven his self. God's annihilation is a creation, and the suffering of guilt by man is one with the sufferance of guilt by God.[104] This is the unique "withdrawal and return"

101 *Kierkegaard*, Concluding Unscientific Postscript, *pp. 239–240.*
102 Ibid., *p. 369.*
103 *Kierkegaard*, Edifying Discourses, *vol. II, p. 77.*
104 *Kierkegaard*, Concluding Unscientific Postscript, *pp. 347–493 passim.*

of the religious life, paralleling but transcending like movements in the aesthetic and ethical spheres.

Kierkegaard's edifying discourses, which he published under his own name and in which he speaks directly from the religious point of view, portray this dialectic of annihilation and restoration over and over again from many approaches. One of the simplest is a discourse on the text of St. James, "Every Good and Every Perfect Gift is from Above."[105] The believer acknowledges, he says, that everything comes ultimately from God. Man's opportunity and his task is to receive what God gives. Whatever happens is a good and perfect gift if it is received with the recollection of guilt (total indebtedness) and with thanksgiving to God. Prosperity may tempt a man to the impudence of complacency; adversity can tempt him to the despair of self-rejection. The religious man must remember God and his own guilt and give thanks, in prosperity or adversity, for whatever happens. The aesthete thinks that life owes him a living; the ethical man is proud to earn his own living. The religious man renounces every attempt to get a purchase on life and makes himself nothing before God but a grateful and humble recipient. This is no more than an alternate way of saying that "we are always in the wrong" against God. The religious man has learned the lesson of Job: We "have no rights" (*have altid Uret*) to maintain against God. His claim on us is absolute—He is God—but we have no claim on Him nor on the world nor on ourselves. Our selves and our world, like every good and every perfect gift, come from above.

This discourse, along with many others, makes evident that the religious life is a repetition, but at a higher level, of the aesthetic life. Like the aesthete, the religious man receives rather than makes himself; but whereas the aesthete is at the mercy of a fate which he frantically tries to elude, the religious man is at the mercy of God, which he embraces with enthusiasm. Like the aesthete, the religious man is a spiritual hermit (compare Victor Eremita, editor of *Either/Or*, with the lonely Jutland priest); but whereas the aesthete is demonically shut up in himself, the religious man is alone with God, the giver of all good. Like the aesthete, the religious man suffers; but whereas the aesthete suffers his own vanity, the religious man is oppressed by the excess of divine bounty. The difference and the similarity are due to the fact that the religious man has passed through the crisis of ethical freedom and its demise in guilt. He is able and willing to receive himself because he knows the futility of trying to create himself. He can repose in solitude because he has been disabused of the idea that he can effect a neat consonance of freedom and nature. He can sorrow joyfully, because he knows that his abasement is God's glory.

Yet what Judge Wilhelm said of immediacy—that it is given its rightful place by ethics—can be said of both the aesthetic and the ethical by the religious man. The life that is received from God includes moral

---

[105] *Jas. 1:17ff. Kierkegaard, Edifying Discourses, vol. I, pp. 34–55.*

striving as well as enjoyment; from his private understanding with God the religious man is enabled to return to the life of community. The pleasures of love and the daily responsibilities of marriage—which in his heart he sacrifices to God—are given back to him with the cup of his religious suffering. He knows that he has them as moratoria from God. They are not his fate, but neither must he accrue them out of his own resources. That he is in debt to God means that he is released by God to the possession of his life without concern lest he lose it and without the anxiety of failure; for he has already failed and he has already given up succeeding. Woe to the man, Kierkegaard says, who succeeds against God! Blessed the man who is strong enough to be weak and poor in spirit before God![106]

"A man has only one God," Kierkegaard wrote, "and if he cannot reach an understanding with Him, to whom, then, shall he go?"[107] That he himself is nothing means to the religious man that God is all in all. This is the unfailing certainty that emancipates him from slavery to nature and himself, and delivers him to his beatitude. The self which he could not find in nature or in flight from nature, the self that he could not earn for himself, he first receives—in its eternal and absolute validity—when he abandons it to God. By the decision to be in the wrong as against God he is armed against despair and inspired to action. No longer tormented by the bad dreams of the aesthete nor defeated by the illusions of the ethicist, he knows in his day the things that belong to his peace. In the confidence that God is all and in all he has found the rock on which to edify his life.

4. Naked and Alone
We Came into Exile

On his own allegation Kierkegaard's writing was coerced from him by the press of two urgent questions: What is it to be a man? and What is it to be a Christian? Not that there was in his day a shortage of answers to these questions; he felt there were too many and too facile answers, and not enough understanding of the questions. The voracious Hegelian philosophy had dialectically devoured human existence and Christian faith, and was regurgitating their speculative meaning in compendia predigested for popular consumption. Kierkegaard distrusted the agility with which speculation explained everything, and set himself to make things hard that everyone else was making easy.[108] His program in books like the *Philosophical Fragments* and the *Concluding Unscientific Postscript* was to rehearse the difficulty of the questions by means of a polemic against the ready speculative answers.

Kierkegaard was convinced that the questions—What does it mean to exist? What does it mean to believe?—were so ordered that the latter could not be discussed until the sense of the former had been clarified. It

---

106 Cf. *Kierkegaard*, Repetition, *p. 133; Kierkegaard*, Fear and Trembling *and* The Sickness unto Death, *Doubleday Anchor Books, Garden City, N.Y., 1954, p. 31.*
107 *Kierkegaard*, Thoughts on Crucial Situations in Human Life, *p. 33.*
108 *Kierkegaard*, Concluding Unscientific Postscript, *pp. 164–167.*

is after all a *man* who *believes.* Moreover, the question of the meaning of human existence had to be raised existentially before the attack
on speculation could have its effect.[109] In the stages on life's way
Kierkegaard prepares an existential setting for philosophical consideration of this question. The stages, not described by a disinterested
observer but dramatized by representative *personae,* suggest that
human existence is amenable to a diversity of living interpretations,
each consistent in itself, each provident of a unique perspective on
the others, and each irreducibly distinct from the others. For in spite
of the ascending scale in which he presents them (aesthetic, ethical,
religious), and in spite of his own commitment to the religious,
Kierkegaard never lost sight of the fact that each existence-sphere is
a way of life eligible and enactable by a human being, and that the
only passage from one stage to another is a radically free choice
entailing a wholesale revision of the personality and its world.

To the question: What is man? there are as many existing answers as there
are existing men. The stages on life's way are the larger categories
into which the answers fall, but each man by living his own individual
life works out his own unique solution to the problem of the meaning
of human existence. This fact supplies a motif for Kierkegaard's
critique of speculative philosophy. If life has an indefinite plurality of
meanings in the concrete, then it has no one definitive meaning in the
abstract, and it is perverse of the theorist to "discover" such a meaning and package it for retail distribution.

With this consideration and the previous discussion in mind it is possible
to unravel passages like this:

Man is spirit. But what is spirit? Spirit is the self. But what is the self?
The self is a relation which relates itself to its own self, or it is that in the
relation, that the relation relates itself to its own self; the self is not the
relation, but that the relation relates itself to its own self. Man is a syn-
thesis of infinity and finitude, the temporal and the eternal, freedom and
necessity, in short a synthesis. A synthesis is a relation between two. So
regarded man is not yet a self.

In the relation between two the relation is the third term as a negative
unity, and the two relate themselves to the relation, and in the relation to
the relation; such a relation is that between body and soul, when man is
regarded as soul. If on the contrary the relation relates itself to its own
self, then this relation is the positive third term, and this is the self.[110]

This is not the gobbledygook it seems to be, though there is good
reason why it must seem so.

By classical philosophers the human self was interpreted as a psychophysical duality. Plato takes man to be a synthesis of reason and
appetite. What he calls "spirit" is merely the togetherness that unites
the other two. It is "the third term as a negative unity" of *eros* and
nous, in and to which they are bound. Allied in the good man with

---

[109] Ibid., pp. 223–224.
[110] *Kierkegaard,* Fear and Trembling *and* The Sickness unto Death, *p. 146.*

reason and in the bad man with desire, "spirit" is *nothing but* the ascendancy of one over the other in a given personality.[111] The pagan, Kierkegaard says, always conceives the self as *nature*. For Plato the soul, like any other object or event, is a point of engagement for the cosmic forces of form and dynamic. For Aristotle the human self, like any other entity, is a substantial juncture of form (soul) with matter (body).[112] It is in either case the nature of the universe, writ small in human nature, that determines man to be what he is.

Suppose now the self is understood as *spirit*. According to Kierkegaard, this is the view of Christianity, though its vision has often been skewed by the Greek spectacles through which it has looked at its own revelation. In this version the union of psychic and somatic elements in the self is effected not by the nature of things, but by some "positive third term." This third term that positively joins body and soul ("that in the relation, that the relation relates itself to its own self") is the *self-consciousness* by which the psychophysical synthesis transcends itself as nature and asserts itself as spirit. The self as spirit is the natural synthesis of body and soul become *conscious* of itself and *free* with respect to itself.

Freedom (or self-consciousness: the terms are finally synonymous in Kierkegaard) does not fit the naturalistic understanding of man at all. It is not the substantial essence of man (as such it would be determined), nor an accidental attribute or operation of man (it is the *sine qua non* of selfhood), nor an essential property or power of man (as such it would be causally implicated in his essence and so determined). It cannot be defined, derived, or demonstrated by a study of human nature, for definition, derivation, and demonstration are equivalent to determination, and a freedom determined by nature is a contradiction in terms. Presupposed in every human act, self-consciousness is necessarily inscrutable; it is always behind the thinker and within him, never wholly outside him or before him. Freedom can only be conceived *via remotionis* as the original undemonstrable source, the undefinable insubstantial essence, and the continuing self-initiating act of spirit.[113]

This is the "relation which relates itself to its own self": freedom, self-consciousness, or (which is the same thing) the self understood as spirit. Its reality is indicated by men's moments of ultimate self-surpassing—e.g., suicidal despair and self-sacrificing love—and by the ostensible difference between man and beast—such as the ubiquity of culture among men and its total absence among animals; the fact that the beast never gives himself an image of himself, whereas man is always trying to live up to the self he thinks he is or wants to be; the circumstance that man the adverbial creature lusts shamefully, loves beautifully, and kills cruelly, while the beast can only mate, tend its young, and prey. But though it is everywhere hinted at, the self

---

[111] *Republic, 434D–441C; Phaedrus, 246Aff.*

[112] De Anima, *II, 1, 2.*

[113] *Kierkegaard,* The Concept of Dread, *Princeton University Press, Princeton, N.J., 1957, pp. 20, 96–97, 99–101.*

remains a mystery that eludes the understanding. That is why
Kierkegaard "defines" it in impossibly tortured paradoxes. He is
holding the jargon of his contemporaries against them, to show that
when one tries to grasp human nature categorically, he comes up with
nonsense.

Yet the irony is soberly drawn, and the paradoxes mean just what they say.
Human existence is not a unity of form and matter embedded in
nature. Existence as spirit is the collision in man of nature (the
psychophysical synthesis) and freedom (the self-consciousness of this
synthesis which robs it of substantiality and negates it as nature).[114]
"The self is not the relation, but that the relation relates itself to its
own self."

Kierkegaard often describes human existence as a passion (*Lidenskab,
passio*) inflicted by the straits in which the self is placed: Man must
forge his self by freedom, but the very capacity of transcendence that
makes him a man upsets the stability of any self so achieved. To be
spirit is to forfeit the security of nature; to be free is to lack the
solace of natural determination.[115] Unlike the animal who simply *is*
what he *is*, man suffers as spirit the need and the contradiction of
becoming what he *can be.*

The rationale for the "gobbledygook" is now clear enough: If we try to
understand man as he is, we fail; for by nature man is not. "So
regarded man is not yet a self." The theoretical discussion of immediacy reinforces the conclusion at which the aesthete arrived existentially: Immediately man is nothing but a lack (of a given self), a
prospect (of acquiring himself as spirit), and a friction (between
nature and freedom as the conditions of spiritual selfhood). The
aesthete is described as "an existential possibility that cannot win
through to existence."[116] Answering to the chaotic poetry of the
aesthetic life, the aesthetic element in man ("that by which he immediately is what he is") is limned in contradictions. The force of
Kierkegaard's paradoxes is to define human nature by pointing up the
impossibility of defining it. His existential philosophy—which could
not be written until the inhabitants of the existence-spheres had
exfoliated imaginatively the richness and the poverty, the glory and
the horror of human life—is a ponderous ironic epitaph over every
philosophy of existence.

It is therefore important, when reading Kierkegaard's "philosophical" works,
to respect their avowed fragmentary and unscientific character.
Above all it is necessary to take him at his word when he says he has
no opinions and proposes no doctrines.[117] For the matter under
discussion is human existence, concerning which the point to be made
is that opinions and doctrines are beside the point.

In 1842 and 1843 Kierkegaard made sketches for a book to be called

[114] *Kierkegaard,* Concluding Unscientific Postscript, *pp. 74–86.*
[115] Ibid., *pp. 177–178, 276–278, 313–314.*
[116] Ibid., *p. 226; cf. pp. 262–264.*
[117] Ibid., *pp. 545–550; Kierkegaard,* Philosophical Fragments, *pp. 5–7.*

Johannes Climacus, or De Omnibus Dubitandum Est: A Story.[118] *De omnibus dubitandum est* had been the motto of Descartes, but the Hegelians had interpreted methodological doubt to mean: Philosophy cannot begin by assuming anything; the philosopher must isolate and think through all of his presuppositions so as to get behind them to an absolute starting-point for constructive speculation. The formula of Cartesian doubt became for the Hegelians the charter of philosophical absolutism.

Kierkegaard knew that the program of universal doubt could not be carried through. The philosopher can no more get behind all his presuppositions than Judge Wilhelm could get behind his whole history; to do so he would have to step outside space and time and his own intellectual skin. Reflective thought, generating as many problems as it solves, is potentially infinite. Its momentum is never halted by itself, but by an act of will incalculably arbitrary in relation to the possibilities yet to be considered. The simplest question becomes a hydra of prosyllogisms if one attempts to evoke a completely rational answer: Which girl shall I marry? becomes Shall I marry? What is marriage? What is man? *ad infinitum.* In the end one marries—or does not marry—without sufficient reason. Human deliberations are never final, and there is no absolute beginning for philosophy.[119] If a philosopher says he has doubted everything he is lying, and in fact the windbagging arrogance of the Hegelians proved them charlatans who never meant to practice what they preached. *Johannes Climacus* was to be the story of a young man ingenuously in love with thought, who took the philosophers literally and *did* doubt everything, beginning with common sense and science, moving through history, ethics, and religion, and ending with himself. He doubted himself or rather, despaired of himself—for he was not a philosopher writing about doubt but a man actually doubting—so thoroughly that he lost himself beyond hope of recovery. The thread of his personality was snapped, a victim of the irresponsible gabble of the philosophers.[120]

But the book was never finished. Kierkegaard soon perceived that it was not an excess of doubt, but an excess of certainty that was the real peril. Not skeptical modesty but the grandiloquent self-assurance of speculative thought prevented men from apprehending the paradox of existence and the prerequisites of faith. *Philosophical Fragments* and *Concluding Unscientific Postscript* are devoted to undermining this assurance by exposing the weakness of its foundations.

Philosophical Fragments (ascribed to Johannes Climacus as author) poses the question:

Is an historical point of departure possible for an eternal consciousness; how can such a point of departure have any other than a merely historical

---

[118] *Stanford University Press, Stanford, Calif., 1958.*

[119] *The whole of Johannes Climacus pokes fun at the attempt to find an absolute starting point for philosophy; cf. especially pp. 130–142. Cf. also Kierkegaard, Concluding Unscientific Postscript, pp. 101–106.*

[120] *Kierkegaard, Johannes Climacus, pp. 101–102.*

interest; is it possible to base an eternal happiness upon historical knowledge?[121]

> In effect this is the question: Is Christianity true? though the problem is not dressed in its "historical costume."[122] More significant is the fact that the question is not answered. In his Preface Johannes Climacus warns the reader that he cherishes no opinion in the matter, but only executes a kind of nimble dance with death in the service of thought, to the honor of God, and for his own satisfaction.[123] The question is proposed "in ignorance, by one who does not even know what can have led him to ask it."[124]

What is given in lieu of an answer is two hypotheses: (1) that the temporal moment in which a man glimpses eternal truth is but an insignificant episode in the career of his immortal soul; (2) that the "historical point of departure for an eternal consciousness" is a crucial instant in which the truth first comes to exist for him who learns it. These are the hypotheses, respectively, of Socrates, for whom learning is a recollection, occasionable at any time by any teacher, of truths already latent in the mind of the learner; and of Christ, for whom learning is a conversion of the soul from the willful error of Sin, by a unique Teacher who, in an instant that is the Fullness of Time, imparts both the Truth and the Faith to acknowledge it, a Teacher who is therefore Judge, Saviour, Redeemer, Atoner, God-in-Time.[125]

The opposition of Socrates the midwife to Christ the Mediator is not the opposition of human reason to the irrational, Greek philosophy versus the scandal of the Cross. The Socratic ignorance testifies that human reason is invested with the potency to transcend itself in that which is other than itself. In its passion to think a reality distinct from itself, to immolate itself in sheer transparency to its object, reason is unwittingly at one with the eternal purposes of God in the Paradox of the God-Man. Man's offense at the unreasonableness of Christianity is the self-assertion of reason by which it defrauds itself of its beatitude, while faith is the happy self-surrender of reason to the Mystery of Revelation by which it is fulfilled. Christianity is not the frustration but the paradoxical satisfaction of human reason.[126]

What Climacus is getting at in the *Fragments*—hypothetically in chapter I, poetically in chapter II, metaphysically in chapter III and the Interlude, and epistemologically in chapters IV and V—is that the historicity of human life screws every truth, Greek or Christian, into a paradox, since truth is timeless and the truth seeker temporal.[127] For Socratic recollection the love of wisdom (philosophy) issues in the paradox: One must learn how to die. Rooted in the Miracle of Incarnation, Christian faith incurs a dialectical complication of Socratic recollection by taking the historicity of man to be his reality and not an accident of his eternal essence.

[121] *Kierkegaard, Philosophical Fragments, title page.*
[122] Ibid., *p. 137.*   [123] Ibid., *pp. 5–7.*   [124] Ibid., *p. 9.*
[125] Ibid., *pp. 11–27.*   [126] Ibid., *pp. 46–67.*
[127] Cf. *Kierkegaard, Concluding Unscientific Postscript, pp. 169–210.*

Climacus forces his reader into a corner where he must admit, not that the Christian hypothesis is true, for that "is an entirely different question, which cannot be decided in the same breath,"[128] but that there is no honest way of understanding human existence that can avoid contradiction. The enemy of human integrity is not doubt, as Kierkegaard had thought when he began *Johannes Climacus.* Socratic recollection respects the uncertainty of human knowledge by telling likely stories and ironically postponing all conclusions until the life hereafter; faith, which accepts uncertainty and transcends it in an act of assent, comprehends doubt within itself as a threat that is constantly being overcome.[129] The antagonist is not the man who denies the reality of eternity (the skeptic Sextus Empiricus or the sophist Protagoras), but the man who mitigates the reality of time in the interest of a simplistic doctrine of man. The final battle is pitched between the essentialist philosopher who views life under the aspect of eternity and the existential thinker who grapples daily with the paradoxes of his life and surmounts them in recollection or in faith.[130]

But even this puts the matter much too abstractly and neatly. The character of the *Philosophical Fragments* may suggest a metaphysical reading. But Johannes Climacus—in his Preface, by his hypothetical method, and in the whimsical conversations with an imaginary interlocutor that follow each chapter—has taken pains to disarm such an interpretation in advance. By making light of everything he says, by accusing himself of plagiarizing God,[131] he reneges the conclusions he implies and comes up with no results after all. The book is literally fragmentary, "scrapings and parings of systematic thought."[132] To the philosophical reader who begs his theoretical opinion, Climacus' reply is firm: No, thank you, I will not have this dance.

The motto of the book—a German rendition of Shakespeare's "Many a good hanging has prevented a bad marriage"—is "Better well hung than ill wed."[133] Climacus' intent is to hang his reader on the contradiction—that there is no certainty in human knowledge and that every moment is nevertheless a *kairos* that demands decisive thought —rather than marry him to a systematic "higher synthesis" that is eternally finished with life before life is through with the thinker. At the same time, inasmuch as it formally negates its results and imposes on its reader the necessity of decision, the book is inversely self-justifying. Otherwise, Climacus concludes: "How will we ever come to begin?" Just as the monks never finished telling the history of the world because they started anew each time with Creation, so we shall never get to live if we wait for the philosophers to explain life first.[134] To be hanged on the necessity of decision is the good hanging that prevents a bad marriage.

---

[128] *Kierkegaard,* Philosophical Fragments, *p. 139.*
[129] Ibid., *pp. 97–106.*
[130] Ibid., *pp. 47–48; Kierkegaard,* Concluding Unscientific Postscript, *pp. 267–322.*
[131] *Kierkegaard,* Philosophical Fragments, *pp. 26–27, 43–45, 57–60, 66–67, 81–88, 132–138.*
[132] *Kierkegaard,* Concluding Unscientific Postscript, *p. 2.*
[133] *Kierkegaard,* Philosophical Fragments, *p. 2.*   [134] Ibid., *p. 138.*

The details of the argument in the *Fragments*, as Climacus' interlocutor points out, can all be traced back to standard philosophical and theological sources.[135]   The book is not designed to make a contribution to philosophy or theology—something that "every divinity student would be able to furnish"[136]—but to get the reader to risk his life in the service of understanding, to the glory of God, and for his own good.   Insofar as it necessitates an intensified self-knowledge, it is a book in existential philosophy.   And in view of the total incommensurability between essentialist speculation and Christian belief, the *Fragments* performs the only service any apologetic can render: It nails you to the incommensurability and leaves you hanging.

The *Fragments* approaches the problem of man by contrasting Socrates and Christ with each other and with the philosopher who "goes beyond" both by understanding neither.   The philosopher of course is no "honest" Greek, but a "mendacious" Hegelian who makes bold to domicile human existence in the paragraphs of that "System" of "absolute knowledge" which in its completeness and finality claims to reflect unambiguously the workings of Absolute Mind.   The *Concluding Unscientific Postscript* to the *Philosophical Fragments* (also by Johannes Climacus) affronts the deiform thinker outright by informing him that human life and its problems are nowhere contained in his philosophy.

Climacus remarks in the *Postscript* that Hegel had absentmindedly neglected to include an ethics in his philosophical system.[137]   By this he does not mean that Hegel had forgotten to discuss matters ethical. Hegel's absentmindedness was of a less obvious sort.   In his zeal to exhibit the rationality of history, *der Gang Gottes in der Welt*, he had failed to make provision for the *subject* of ethical concerns, the existing human being.   If we sit in the Hegelian grandstand and look at the human individual, regarding him simply in his particularity, he becomes a perishing irrationality, the litter cast by the Absolute along the freeways of world history.   To be sure he furthers the aims of God, but he does so chiefly in his capacity as cannon fodder.   On the other hand, if we consider him in his "essential reality" and "universal truth," he is at once rapt into dialectical union with God.   The soldier of the *Grande Armée*, who is (personally) splattered by a cannon ball, is (essentially) privileged to suffer the Golgotha of Absolute Spirit.

What Climacus calls "objective thought"—thinking that reifies whatever it thinks about—understands any individual, human or otherwise, only by regarding it as an instance of a universal.   Underscoring *instance*, the individual is as nugatory as the dissected frogs discarded by a college zoology class.   With the accent on *universal*, the individual takes on the dignity of an exemplar Idea in the mind of God.   This kind of analysis may be appropriate for garlic and sapphires, mud and axletrees.   It is inevitable that scientific thought should aspire to the condition of logic and conceive its objects as universals or cases of

135 Ibid., *pp. 26–27, 43–45, 66–67, 132–138.*
136 *Cf. Kierkegaard*, Concluding Unscientific Postscript, *p. 14.*
137 Ibid., *pp. 108, 110.*

universals. But the human person is neither a category nor a statistic. Both dimensions are present in each man—he is at once eternal verity and vanishing trifle—but present as unsettled potentialities which he is obliged to arbitrate in a lifelong process of self-becoming. Because human existence is caught in the toils of time, particularity, and finitude, this process is a perpetual striving, spasmodically illumined by intelligence and fancy, but uncheered by any promise of millenial reconciliation, either in a life after death or in the depths of present existence. No man can give himself apocalyptic surety of immortality, though he may *believe* in it ardently enough to die for it. And no man is helped by the idealist eschatology that asks him to sacrifice his self for a meaning so deeply rooted in being that it is unavailable for his personal comfort. Selfhood is neither given as an antecedent nor guaranteed as a consequent; it is a possibility which may be won or lost, but never enjoyed.[138]

In short, speculative philosophy is of no use if a man wants wisdom to live by. If it does not misconceive human existence naturalistically in the manner of pagan realism, it seeks prematurely to quiet the raging of spirit by recourse to the "fantastic shadow play"[139] of idealism. The philosopher who confuses life with intellection and scribbles paper answers to flesh-and-blood questions is like the poet insofar as he flees to an abstract eternity from the turmoils of time. But he lacks the poet's imaginative virtuosity, the endlessly resourceful ingenuity by which the aesthete lives his withdrawal from life. The philosopher therefore has not the poetic melancholy, and his life is not, like the poet's, tragic. He is a comic or at best a pathetic figure: the self-deceived *Privatdozent* who really believes that he breaks wind *sub specie aeternitatis*, or the drab old professor whose self is but the cast-off walking stick of his system.

For the existing individual there is neither a home in nature nor a place of rest beyond it. Man is "an infinite existing spirit."[140] And there is, as Kierkegaard said, "no such thing as immediate health of the spirit."[141] Immediately man is but the possibility of spirit, a bare "to be able"[142] anxiously placed between ideality (the domain of intellect and imagination) and reality (the spatiotemporal stretch of becoming). As spirit he is neither Platonic Idea nor positivistic fact nor the perfect splice that classical naturalism envisaged. His existence—the subjectivity that Climacus says is truth and reality[143]—is his concern to catch an evanescent possibility in the mesh of fact, and to regiment a scattered actuality under the hegemony of ideal meanings. His "ethical [here = "existential"] reality" is neither inner intent (intentions are as cheap as the aesthete's daydreams) nor outer act (the case of Judge Wilhelm shows the recalcitrance of nature to man's resolutions), but the tension of his will to move creatively from project to performance.[144] In this tension and its pathos he has his life.

---

138 Ibid., *pp. 97–113, 115–147, 267–322.*
139 Ibid., *p. 292.*   140 Ibid., *p. 75.*
141 *Kierkegaard,* Fear and Trembling *and* The Sickness unto Death, *p. 158.*
142 *Kierkegaard,* The Concept of Dread, *pp. 40, 44.*
143 *Kierkegaard,* Concluding Unscientific Postscript, *p. 306.*   144 Ibid., *pp. 267–307.*

The freedom that is essential to selfhood and the skein of contradiction from which this selfhood must be woven proliferate problems that cannot even be programmed by philosophic thought; nor do they admit the kind of solutions that can be appended as a footnote to section 14 of the System, or filed for ready reference on grave occasions. They can only be apprehended by a "subjective thinking"— thinking born in passion rather than in disinterested curiosity, concerned not with the contemplation of life in general but with the conduct of this life in particular—that continually experiences the anguish of the human estate and holds out in its presence by continual resolve. The subjective thinker is like the ethical man in that he is free (the possibility of spirit) and therefore must himself integrate the given elements of personality into the unity of a person (the obligation to become oneself). But he is more dreadfully on his own than Judge Wilhelm ever dreamed of. What he is by nature (say a male American twenty-one years old) is but a cluster of ambiguous possibilities whose eventuality (husband or hermit, patriot or expatriate, believer or blasphemer, success or suicide) is determined by the man himself. In this determination he is guided by no eternal truths (the temporality of his life stains their white radiance with uncertainty and change) and by no hard facts (his self-transcendence dissolves the brutality and dense reality of fact and brings it into the whirl of possibility). Knowledge is either (like logic and metaphysics) true in the abstract but doubtful in its application to existence; or empirically problematic (like natural science and history), its truth a desideratum ever out of reach.[145] "Subjective thinking" must be a "double reflection" that simultaneously sees the insufficiency of knowledge and tenaciously holds to the norm of its decisions.

To be man is to be, without security of nature or knowledge, compelled to make a security, a truth, for oneself. "Only the truth which edifies" —that is, builds up your self—"is truth for you." A human being is a freedom caught in the intersection of time and eternity, there constrained to mold in decision and action the integrity, the existing truth at once actual and ideal, that he does not have by nature and cannot find by taking thought.[146] Human existence is an *interest* (*inter-esse*), a being-between the terms of a contradiction that cannot be resolved but must be resolutely endured, an unrelieved and unceasing concern with the passion, the possibility, and the predicament of becoming oneself.[147]

Neither is the individual supported, in his quest for selfhood, by the solidarity of human society.[148] The freedom which is the franchise of spirit disintegrates every natural community, splintering family, state, and race into a multitude of single human beings, each isolated with the problems, pains, and prospects of his own person. The existence of other men presents him not with a public in which he is firmly set as a part sustained by an organic whole, but only with further possibili-

---

145 Ibid., *pp. 169–171.*   146 Ibid., *pp. 84–85.*   147 Ibid., *p. 279.*
148 Cf. Kierkegaard, The Present Age, *Oxford University Press, London, 1940; also* " 'The Individual': Two 'Notes' concerning My Work as an Author" in *Kierkegaard, The Point of View.*

ties—beckoning, tempting, or threatening—that he must take into the gamut of his inner life.[149]   His own inwardness is the only reality to which he has entrance without trespass, and the only reality with which he is properly occupied.   The reality of others he can only know, and by knowing, distance.[150]   Whatever community of spirit is established among men is strung precariously across the chasm of freedom and made fast at the ends only in the solitude of the self-concern of each person.   Sprung from nature but cut loose from her umbilical, capable of knowledge but deprived of a certainty equal to the demands of action, the existing individual also stands, in the midst of his fellowmen, essentially alone.

But this, as Climacus says whenever the philosophical rhetoric threatens to run away from him and tear through the streets like a town crier of inwardness, sounds a little too much like seriousness.[151]   The *Postscript* is a humorous book.   Its technique is not solemnly to define man (not even with the bizarre solemnities of existentialism), but to destroy by irony and indirection, by lyric and by lampoon, the self-confidence of those thinkers who are so thoughtless as to suppose that man can be solemnly defined.   When Climacus "defines" truth as "subjectivity," "an objective uncertainty held fast in an appropriation process of the most passionate inwardness,"[152] he is writing a satire on definition to recall his reader from the illusory certainties of knowledge to the awareness that every belief and every truth claim has no surer warrant than the freedom and the fervor of him who asserts it.   When he says that every individual is isolated in his inwardness, he is not proposing a theory of human community, but reminding those men who put their trust in the ways of culture and the verdict of history that this commitment is an expression of their personal choice of themselves and not a child of the *Zeitgeist* or a mass product of institutions and conventions.[153]   The *Concluding Unscientific Postscript*, faithful to the paradox of existence and the "dialectics of communication," is a whimsical book with a frighteningly sober purpose: to lead its reader down a path of merriment to the brink of the bottomless pit of freedom and to surprise him with the awful responsibility he bears for his own life.   Read as a philosophical treatise it is nonsense; but the sense of the nonsense is to strip away every veil that covers the gravity of the human condition and thereby to force the reader back on his own resources.   To read the book as Kierkegaard wrote it is to experience that dreadful rebirth by which each of us comes naked and alone into the exile of this extremity of spirit.

5. The Way
of the Cross

The *Concluding Unscientific Postscript* opens with the question: How can I, Johannes Climacus, become a Christian?   How can I or any man avail himself of the eternal blessedness Christianity offers its adher-

---

[149] *Kierkegaard*, Concluding Unscientific Postscript, pp. 67–74, 320–322.
[150] Ibid., pp. 282–292, 305.
[151] Ibid., pp. 163, 210; cf. also p. 71.   [152] Ibid., p. 182.   [153] Ibid., pp. 115–167.

ents?[154]   Its conclusion is apparently irrelevant, largely negative, and certainly unscientific: Man exists in alienation from the world, without the consolations of objective certainty, without the uplifting arm of human community, without the vision of historical destiny, in a chaos of maybes.   For such a being the quasi-aesthetic makeshifts of the philosopher have no valence, the poet's life is but the sigh of a shadow, and the brave self-confidence of the ethical man a whistling among the tombstones.

Yet the result is not negligible, for the man who has come up against his self in the emptiness of its need and the weight of its responsibility has also stood in the terrible presence of God.   The situation of the existing individual which Kierkegaard's philosophical works depict by the tongue in cheek of theoretical indirection is the same as the situation of man presupposed in the edifying discourses: before God.   God is at hand, Climacus writes, whenever the uncertainty of all things is thought without limit.[155]   The uncertainty of all things is the fruition of freedom, which transforms all realities into possibilities.   But he who rubs the wonderful lamp of freedom and invokes the geni of possibility has called up the Spirit that is his Lord.[156]   For

God is that all things are possible, and that all things are possible is God; and only the man whose being has been so shaken that he became spirit by understanding that all things are possible, only he has had dealings with God.[157]

To live in the anxiety of freedom, without finite support or encouragement, is to live by the power of God.

When he describes the human predicament in terms of paradox and insists that human freedom is absolute, Kierkegaard is not recommending an heroic defiance of the absurdity of existence without God.   The bravado of some of his epigoni would strike him as vainglorious rhetoric decorating an aesthetic refusal to face the real absurdity: that in the weakness of the finite the strength of the Infinite is given to man.   His polemic against the philosophers recapitulates the wisdom of the stages: The exploitation of human freedom is the exhaustion of human potency in renunciation (of finite security), suffering (the pain of the excision of finite hope), and guilt (the total indebtedness of the finite to the Infinite).[158]   The *Postscript* is Kierkegaard's "speeches on religion to its cultured despisers," but in a spirit quite unlike that of Schleiermacher the sentimental theologian, the voluble humorist Climacus wants to call the distracted attention of the philosophers to the terse piety of the Jutland priest: There is no greater edification than that implied in the thought that as against God we are always in the wrong.   Its dark humor is comprehended in the realization that the *Concluding Unscientific Postscript* is a systematic destruction of all the idols of System that come between man's want and God's abundance.

154 Ibid., p. 19.   155 Ibid., p. 80.   156 Ibid., p. 124.
157 *Kierkegaard,* Fear and Trembling *and* The Sickness unto Death, *pp. 173–174.*
158 *Cf. Kierkegaard,* Concluding Unscientific Postscript, *pp. 347–493, for an elaborate analysis of these moments of the religious consciousness.*

How, then, does a man become a Christian? Johannes Climacus—"John the Climber"—cannot vouch for the reality. His name and his testimony reveal that he himself is only on the way up, not yet arrived. But the condition—the possibility—of becoming a Christian is well within his bailiwick: First become a man, and when you are driven by this exertion into the narrows of despair, when you have become spirit by the recognition that absolute freedom is identical with absolute dependence, when you are alone in fear and trembling, without sustenance of nature, knowledge, or community, with no recourse but God —then and only then may the threat and the promise of Christianity surge redemptively from the abyss.

The actuality of Christianity, its annihilating word of condemnation and its comfortable word of reconciliation, is the theme of Climacus' opposite number, the "ideal Christian" Anti-Climacus. In the first part of *Training in Christianity*, Anti-Climacus, following the *Fragments*, defines Christian faith as contemporaneity with Christ. He develops this definition in a rhapsody on the text, "Come hither to me, all ye that labor and are heavy laden, I will give you rest."[159] He who issues this invitation is Christ, and in order to appreciate the invitation it is necessary to know more about the identity of the inviter.

The Christian Church has enshrined its dogmatic understanding of Christ in the Nicene Creed:

one Lord Jesus Christ, the only-begotten Son of God; Born of the Father before all ages, God from God, Light from Light, Very God from Very God; Begotten not made; Consubstantial with the Father; Through whom all things were made: Who for us men and for our salvation came down from heaven, And was incarnate by the Holy Ghost of the Virgin Mary, And was made man. . . .

But the symbolic formula sets its object at the distance of cognition. It is in the New Testament that Jesus of Nazareth, His appearance as a man to men, may be more readily approached. The contending attractions and repulsions of His personality compel that "infinite interest" in His *reality* that is forbidden to the "possibility-relations" of ordinary human intercourse.[160]

Anti-Climacus is sensitive to the attractions of Jesus' person. In contrast to human charity, which must insist upon its due if it is not to become condescension, He offers His aid gratuitously to all who labor and are laden. Unlike human sympathy, which must retain its superiority to evil lest it become impotent, His compassion is a self-emptying by which He undertakes the sufferings of the wretched of the earth. Ignoring the distinctions which human affection must make if it is not to become effete, His invitation is extended to all who travail. No man can be the bond of another's peace, but here the Helper is the Help, He is Himself the rest He offers: "Abide with me, for in abiding with me there is rest."

[159] Matt. 11:28. *Kierkegaard*, Training in Christianity, *Princeton University Press, Princeton, N.J., 1947, pp. 5–72.*
[160] *Kierkegaard*, Concluding Unscientific Postscript, *pp. 289–291.*

The mercy of God poured out through the Christ, transcending the inevitable and legitimate limitations of human solicitude, proffers healing and refuge to all men. Wherefore Anti-Climacus' repeated exclamation: Wonderful! That repose of the spirit always longed for and never attained, that ideal of love which in human relations is but a deceitful romance, is here truth and reality. Wonderful![161]

But this very "wonderful!" sows the seed of offense. Approached by another human being with the words: "Come to me, and I will be everything to you, your joy, peace, light, health, and comfort!" who would not draw back in suspicion? What man, disillusioned by his trial of human love, would not smell fraud? All experience warns against the allurement here offered; all experience testifies that the promise cannot be kept. What man, presented with this invitation, would not, sadly no doubt, but wisely and firmly, send his regrets?

This is what men have done.[162] But they have done it dishonestly. The comfortable promise of Christianity is contained in the invitation: "Come hither to me, all ye that labor and are heavy laden, and I will give you rest." The offense of Christianity is that the invitation— which only God has the right and the might to make—was given by one whom his biographers describe as an itinerant teacher of dubious origin and ignominious end. This is the Absolute Paradox of which the *Fragments* speak: that God assumed the unlovely form of a servant, made Himself intimate with every grief and shame that break the human heart, and won beatitude for men by assuming the penalty of their guilt. The comfort of Christianity is promised only to those who can surmount their offense at the Absurdity of Christianity: that the historical son of Mary is the eternal Son of God.

Naturally men wanted the blessedness and the consolation of Christianity, but they wanted it without the offense. Instead of rejecting outright the unpleasant Galilean and His invitation, they pretended to accept Him, but in fact put in His place a set of convenient illusions. The name of this pretense and these illusions is Christendom.

One of the pleasantest of Christendom's self-deceits is the fantasy that Anti-Climacus calls the illusion of "Christ in glory." According to orthodox Christian belief the crucified, risen, and ascended Christ now sits in majesty *ad dexteram patris.* So be it. But it was not the glorified Christ who issued the invitation, "Come hither to me. . . ." Christianity did not enter the world as an authoritatively magnificent communication wafted to earth from realms of heavenly splendor, and to this day Christ has uttered not a word from his celestial throne. The Christ who speaks in the Gospels—the only Christ who has ever spoken to men—is the man of sorrows, mocked, scourged, spit upon, and slaughtered, the repellent Nazarene with no form nor comeliness that men should desire Him.

"Christ in glory" is only a promise and an expectation. He is not and never has been a reality present among men. To ascribe the gospel to the

---

[161] *Kierkegaard, Training in Christianity, pp. 10–15.*
[162] Ibid., *p. 25.*

glorified Christ is a revision of Christianity that misrepresents it as a divinely beautiful poem. It is natural that a militant Church should anticipate its own triumph, natural even that it should be sometimes deceived by its longings. The picture of Christ in glory is theologically correct and aesthetically proper, as an expression of the believer's hope and the groaning of the creation for redemption. But it is a deceit if it puts a fairy-tale prince in place of the sign of offense as the object of faith. Christianity demands no less than a "contemporaneous" meeting of human pride with Christ in his humiliation. It does not flatter men with the lie that they can transcend their terrestrial limitations and aspire to God, but offends them with the good news ("Come hither to me. . . .") that God has condescended to the littleness of their finitude and the pinch of their predicament.[163]

Equally illusive and equally common is the notion that the consequences of the life of Jesus, especially the centuries-long continuity of the Church, demonstrate the truth of the claim that He is divine. But even if perfect knowledge of the "historical Jesus" were not impossible, it would still not amount to a knowledge of the Christ, the subject of Peter's confession and the object of the Christian's trust. Historical research necessarily remains within the framework of the presupposition that men are only men. One may prove—or try to, since historical evidence is never more than approximation to proof—that Caesar was a hero or scoundrel. But no historian would argue that he was a ghost or an angel or an avatar of the Buddha, or even for that matter a man. Reincarnations and free-floating spirits are outside the historian's domain. His province, marked out in advance and so conditioning but never established by the historical method, is human action. Assuming that his subjects are men, he endeavors to show from the consequences of their lives their relative significance within the bounds of that assumption.

By no means then could one demonstrate historically that Caesar (or Jesus) was (or was not) *God*. Because of the absolute difference between God and man, the project would be, from the historian's point of view, vain, and from the believer's perspective, blasphemous. The belief that Jesus of Nazareth is God will not be made less paradoxical by centuries upon centuries of ecclesiastical success. Until the beatific vision it will remain an article of faith to which no historical evidence is even remotely relevant.[164]

When the inherent repugnance of the Christian claim and the limitations of historical knowledge are not respected, men are hoodwinked by the illusion of familiarity, which Anti-Climacus calls the "misfortune of Christendom." The sign of offense (Christ in his humiliation) is replaced by the standard of victory (Christ in triumph) and whittled to the dimensions of human ingenuity (the proof of the centuries). Christianity becomes a culture phenomenon, a folk religion, and a second nature for all who are born in Christendom. The advent of "Christian civilization"—Christendom—is the end of Christianity.

163 Ibid., pp. 26–28.   164 Ibid., pp. 28–34.

Where He is not eclipsed by Santa Claus and the Easter bunny, the man who was numbered among the malefactors has become, for a bourgeois society, the symbol of the *status quo* of those who profess the faith out of the depths of the insecurity of their own privilege, and for the disinherited *illuminati* of that society, the rallying point of social change.   Once His cause is espoused by human intelligence and imagination, Christ becomes whatever men want Him to be by dint of ceasing to be the one thing He is: a scandal and a stone of stumbling.[165]

The contemporaries of Jesus were more consistent: they were offended and they put Him to death, out of human honesty and godly fear.   They could not gloss the absurdity that so plainly declared itself: the son of the carpenter and the maiden, conceived out of wedlock, familiar of whores and tax collectors, says that He is the Son of God.   It was not the riffraff of Judaea, but the pillars of state and church, that crucified Jesus, thinking they did God service.   Humanity essentially and at its best rebels against His person and His profession.   The contradictions may be softened for us by our historical and spiritual distance from A.D.30, but to the men of Jesus' time they were sharp enough.   He promises eternal life (wonderful!), but He cannot keep His own skin. "Cast not your pearls before swine," He warns His disciples, but what are these followers of His if not the most swinish of the vulgar herd? He preaches in the synagogue—in order to damn the Establishment. This undistinguished man, who says that God does not dwell in the temple at Jerusalem, accepts divine honors from the crowd.   He grandly forgives the sins of slatterns and denounces the Pharisees, who of all men honor the law with meticulous observance.   He is immoral (Except a man hate father and mother . . .), imprudent (Take no thought for the morrow . . .), and silly (The meek shall inherit the earth!).

So He came to a bad end, just as anyone with a scrap of sense might have predicted: This is madness and will come to a bad end.   Losing the patronage of the mob, running afoul the authorities, getting Himself executed, He vindicates every negative judgment ever laid against Him, including the consummate accusation: pity.   If He really were the Son of God, He would surely come down from the cross, but He doesn't.   He saved others, Himself He cannot save.   Therefore He was wrong, and now He is lost.   Poor man.[166]

This is the logic of offense.   Once a man is disabused of the trumperies of theological fantasy and the irrelevancies of historical criticism, once he makes himself contemporaneous with Jesus, then offense is his only natural and reasonable response.   Anti-Climacus takes the polemic between man and the God of Christianity to be absolute. There is no passage from the human to the divine, and the divine itself appearing in the human milieu can only fester opposition to itself.   It was no accident that Jesus was crucified; crucifixion would be at any time and in any place the consistent—and from a purely

[165] Ibid., pp. 37–39.   [166] Ibid., pp. 40–60.

human point of view justifiable—rejoinder of men to the claim made by and about the Christ. Man crucifies God: this is the truth about man and about his relationship to Christianity.

But if the logic of offense is unexceptionable, how is *faith* possible? If Golgotha is a necessary truth, what is the sense of Christianity? Let Anti-Climacus reply:

Christianity did not come into the world . . . as an admirable example of the gentle art of consolation—but as the absolute. It is out of love God wills it so, but also it is God who wills it, and He wills what He will. . . . But what, then, is the use of Christianity? It is, then, merely a plague to us! Ah, yes, that too can be said: relatively understood, the absolute is the greatest plague. . . . Christianity seems madness, since it is incommensurable with any finite wherefore. What is the use of it, then? The answer is: Hold thy peace! It is the absolute![167]

To become a Christian demands, in view of the absolute difference between God and man and the absolute impossibility of assimilating the divine to the human, that one "be transformed into likeness with God."[168] But this can happen only if a man has first become contemporary with Christ, the Absolute invading the realm of the relative. "For in relation to the absolute there is only one tense: the present."

Christ is . . . not at all a merely historical person, since as the Paradox [the Eternal-in-time] He is an extremely unhistorical person. . . . What really occurred (the past) is not . . . the real. It lacks the determinant of truth (as inwardness) and of all religiousness, the for thee. The past is not reality— for me: only the contemporary is reality for me. What thou dost live contemporaneous with is reality—for thee.[169]

As "the historical event which on principle could not happen,"[170] Christ is not Himself a homogeneous part of human history. He is the irruption of the Absolute into history, and for that reason the "sign of contradiction"[171] and the signal for offense. But He is also and for the same reason a possible object of faith. Reality is *that which is present for you*. Christ as the Absolute is never past, but perpetually present, so that any man at any time can become His contemporary.

A man becomes the contemporary of Christ and is transformed into the likeness of God only if he participates in the life of Christ. And this he does if, like the God-man Himself, he suffers the offense and the contradiction of God and man in his own person.

If thou canst not endure contemporaneousness, canst not endure the sight in reality, if thou art unable to go out in the street and perceive that it is God in this horrible procession, and that this is thy case wert thou to fall down and worship Him—then thou art not essentially a Christian.[172]

---

[167] Ibid., p. 66.   [168] Ibid., p. 67.   [169] Ibid., pp. 67–68.
[170] Cf. Kierkegaard, Philosophical Fragments, pp. 107–110, 124–126; also Kierkegaard, Concluding Unscientific Postscript, pp. 512–513.
[171] Kierkegaard, Training in Christianity, pp. 124–127.   [172] Ibid., p. 69.

To have faith is like Simon to bend publicly under the cross of Christ in the dead march down the street of sorrows and out to the place of skulls. *Via crucis:* that is the true contemporaneity with Christ, the true participation in his abjection, transformation into the only likeness of God that God has ever vouchsafed us. This is the embarrassment of faith.

And if a man has not faith, then

What thou hast to do . . . is unconditionally to admit this to thyself, so that above all thou mayest preserve humility and fear and trembling with relation to what it means in truth to be a Christian. For that is the way thou must take to learn and to get training in fleeing to grace in such a wise that thou dost not take it in vain.[173]

The "training in Christianity" which Anti-Climacus recommends is simply honesty before God and with oneself about one's inability to be a Christian. The condition for becoming a Christian, said Climacus, is that one first become a man. The practice of Christianity, says Anti-Climacus, begins with the candid confession of offense:

In how far a man may succeed essentially in becoming a Christian, no one can tell him. But dread and fear and despair are of no avail. Candor before God is the first and last. Candidly to admit to oneself where one is, with candor before God holding the task in view—however slowly it goes, though one only creeps forward: yet one thing a man has, he is in the right position. . . .[174]

Offense is the natural human reaction to Christ; the honest avowal that one is offended is the only contribution a man can make toward his own participation in the promises of Christ. Strictly speaking it is not within a man's power to believe; faith is a divine visitation for which the only preparation he can make is the admission of his own unworthiness. The prevenience and the prerogative belong to God.[175] Let a man recognize the absolute claim that God has made in the person of Jesus, and then let him acknowledge without evasion that he cannot meet this claim.

And then no further; then for the rest let him attend to his work, be glad in it, love his wife, be glad in her, bring up his children with joyfulness, love his fellowmen, rejoice in life.[176]

The only power a man has before God is the capacity to admit his impotence; this is what Christianity calls the *consciousness of sin.* The power of God to make good man's failure is grace.[177] "Only the consciousness of sin is the expression of absolute respect" for God (worship), and

only consciousness of sin is the way of entrance, is the vision, which, by being absolute respect, can see the gentleness, lovingkindness, and compassion of Christianity.[178]

---

[173] Ibid., p. 69.   [174] Ibid., pp. 69–70.
[175] *Kierkegaard, Philosophical Fragments,* pp. 17–22, 68–88, 111–132.
[176] *Kierkegaard, Training in Christianity,* p. 71.   [177] Ibid., p. 71.   [178] Ibid., p. 72.

The religion of the edifying discourses Kierkegaard labels "Religion A." Its worship is man's enthusiastic endurance of his alienation from God, renouncing the world, suffering the pain of this severance, and ending in the everlasting recollection of guilt (total indebtedness) against God. The religion of the discourses is the immanent expression of the discrepancy between the finite and the infinite. Christianity ("Religion B") transforms this "religion of immanence" dialectically with its claim that God has entered time in order to reconcile the world to Himself.[179] God gives Himself to men, and men refuse Him; therefore Christianity proclaims that men's alienation from God is self-incurred. Sin is the paradoxical Christian inversion of guilt. In the wake of the originality of sin, the suffering of Religion A is grotesquely malapropos: "dread and fear and despair are of no avail." Not spiritual debauch, but straight-faced confession of sin, is the entry into grace. Nor is the renunciation of the world demanded; the salvation of the Christian (the forgiveness of sin) is God's permission to be—not in "hidden inwardness," but in the publicity of the marketplace—the man he is: to attend to his work, be glad in his wife, bring up his children, love his fellowmen, and enjoy life. Here is the relevance of the Christian Absurdity: that which a man's burning wish and his determined resolution cannot effect, the pearl of price without which all else is vanity, is here granted. His self—the self that is dissipated in aesthetics, dissembled in ethics, and suffered in religion—is restored *in statum pristinum* in the life of faith. To the man racked on the contradictions of existence and worn out in the struggle to become himself, Christianity offers in this world the "new immediacy" of life by grace, and the hope of Paradise in the world beyond.

In his determination not to sell the consolations of Christianity too cheap, Kierkegaard more often dwells on the consciousness of sin than on the emoluments of grace. In his resolution to respect the boundaries of thought, he never allows himself to fancy the wonders of Heaven. But in "three godly discourses" on the lilies of the field and the birds of the air he counters the resignation, suffering, and guilt of Religion A with a meditation on the silence, obedience, and joy in which the Christian relinquishes the project of becoming himself and receives his being from the hand of God. No longer the "unhappiest man" lost in recollection and anticipation, nor the ethical man straining to pull past and future together in resolution, nor the religious man with his Now drained into eternity, the contemporary of Christ who seeks not himself but "God's kingdom and his righteousness" dwells in the power and the glory of the presence of that kindgom, its everlasting Today.[180] Another trio of discourses on the same text celebrates the contentment, the splendor, and the happiness of "common humanity"

---

179 *Kierkegaard*, Concluding Unscientific Postscript, pp. 493–519.
180 *"The Lilies of the Field and the Birds of the Air: Three Godly Discourses"* in *Kierkegaard*, Christian Discourses, Oxford University Press, London, 1940, pp. 311–356.

created and recreated by the grace that is given with faith on the other side of offense through the consciousness of sin.[181]

But it is the consciousness of sin and that alone through which a man may enter into Christianity. The Paradox of Christ—that tormented manhood that nevertheless enjoyed the consubstantial presence of the Father—is the Pattern for the life of the believer, and that life is, for all its joy, a *Via crucis*. *Imitatio Christi* is a Way of the Cross that extends until the *eschaton*, in the hope of a blessedness beyond time and existence and man's ability to conceive, a Resurrection whose reality rests inscrutably in the depths of the divine power and love, a depth which not even faith can fathom, and about which therefore both Kierkegaard and his pseudonyms are silent.

The Poetry
of Inwardness

"Every divinity student" would presumably be able to furnish the information that the Christianity of Anti-Climacus is incomplete and distorted. Its substitution of absurdity for mystery draws a Nestorian cloud over the Incarnation and darkens even a Lutheran understanding of Sacrament. Anti-Climacus' compulsion for a contemporaneity that leaps the centuries all but pushes the history out of sacred history; not the historical Jesus but the historicity of Jesus becomes the sting of the Christian Paradox. The eternal presence of Christ, which makes contemporaneity possible, not unnaturally renders the Church of Christ and all but the barest bones of Scripture embarrassingly superfluous.[182]

To all such proper protest Kierkegaard would reply that *Training in Christianity* was only a "corrective"[183] recommended to the complacent debility of the "present age." The works of Anti-Climacus are a volley of thoughts that wound from behind,[184] aimed at "revival and increase of inwardness"[185] among Christians, not at a theological synthesis for the benefit of the professors of Christianity. Theologians may doubt the apologetic wisdom of mounting Calvary in Tivoli Gardens to shock the merrymakers, but Anti-Climacus will excuse his loud insistence on the Crucifixion and his casual suppression of the Resurrection by reference to his incendiary purpose.

In other words, Anti-Climacus is a pseudonym. He is that "ideal Christian" that never was and never will be. From the aerie of his faith he perceives that what he administers is not the Christianity of the New Testament *toute entière*, but an attack on a Christendom grown prosperously fat and philosophically flatulent. Kierkegaard was not

---

[181] *"What We Learn from the Lilies of the Field and the Birds of the Air: Three Discourses" in Kierkegaard, The Gospel of Suffering*, Augsburg, Minneapolis, 1948, pp. 165–236.

[182] Cf. *Kierkegaard, Philosophical Fragments*, pp. 130–131.

[183] *Dru*, op. cit., no. 1141; Kierkegaard, *The Point of View*, p. 156.

[184] *Kierkegaard, Christian Discourses*, pp. 167ff.

[185] *Kierkegaard, Training in Christainity*, p. 5.

always able to make the distinction; to his own discredit and derangement he often forgot it in the broadsides that he nailed to the doors
of the Establishment in his last days.[186]   But Anti-Climacus is clear:
this is not the New Reformation, it is an outrageous exaggeration "for
edification and awakening."[187]

The pseudonymous extravagance of Anti-Climacus forces into the foreground
the problem of hermeneutics.   Every reader of Kierkegaard's works
knows that he declares them to be "indirect communications"; yet it
is by no means patent what the indirectness consists in and what it
communicates.   It is easy to see what a direct communication is.   A
man with knowledge of certain realities forms concepts that are the
mental symbols of those realities, and expresses what he thinks by
means of words which are the spoken or written signs of his concepts.
When a hearer or reader apprehends the verbal symbols, translates
them into the concepts they stand for, and these in turn into the
realities signified, the process is complete.   The communication is
direct because both communicator and recipient are capable of the
same knowledge of the same realities, and in order to share that
knowledge need avail themselves only of symbolic vehicles the being
of which is exclusively their translucence to the tenor of the knowledge
in question.   The direct route from mind to mind is a segment of
that larger communion in which minds are bound to the intelligible
totality of being.

The centrality of freedom in "human nature" and in Kierkegaard's "message"—the freedom that sets both these classical entities in quotes—
riddles the totality and intelligibility of being, dismembers the community of men with each other and the cosmos, and deflects all
existential discourse into the detour of indirection.   Pseudonymity is
the most striking of the devices by which this diaspora is acknowledged in Kierkegaard's writings.

Kierkegaard's misbegotten attempt to deceive Regina about his real character should not be confused with his literary employment of pseudonyms.   When he signed his books with impossible names like
Johannes de Silentio (John of Silence) and Vigilius Haufniensis
(Watchman of Copenhagen), no one in the gossipy little world of
Danish letters had any doubt about their origin.   Nor did he mean
they should; his purpose was not mystification but distance.   By
refusing to answer for his writings he detached them from his personality so as to let their scheme reinforce the freedom that was their
theme.

The effects of this pseudonymity are many and subtle.   At the first level of
analysis the attribution of the works to representative characters
permits these spokesmen of the existence-spheres a liberty they would
not have as expressions of the opinions of Kierkegaard.   The differ-

---

[186] Cf. Kierkegaard, Attack upon "Christendom," Princeton University Press, Princeton,
N.J., 1946, passim.
[187] Kierkegaard, Fear and Trembling and The Sickness unto Death, p. 141.

ence between *personae* and persons is crucial: the pseudonyms are not mouthpieces through which Kierkegaard hopes to get a hearing for his views, but fictive personalities whose lives are poetically observed and reported. As the poet is silent in his poem, so Kierkegaard is silent in his books. This is the second level of pseudonymity: the disappearance of the poet behind the *persona*. By contemplating his *persona* in the fulguration of imaginative possibility—infinitely ambiguous and dialectical—and creating him in that illustrious shifting light of fancy, the poet guarantees the *persona* objectivity and himself the silence that seals that objectivity.[188]

Because the imagination is dialectically agile to traverse possibilities without end, a third level of pseudonymity discovers itself: the distinction of poet and *persona* not only qualifies the relation of Kierkegaard to his books, but is repeated and complicated within the books themselves. In *Either/Or* Victor Eremita edits the papers of A and Judge Wilhelm; the Judge holds a mirror up to A at the same time that he transcribes and is transfixed by the sermon of the Jutland priest; A examines the complex entanglements of (among many others) Mozart, Don Juan, Leporello, and the Don's victims, while simultaneously he authors his own undoing in the diary of Johannes the Seducer. The writers are interlocked with each other like the pieces in a Chinese puzzle, and the reader is never certain who is being seen through whose eyes— who is poet and who *persona*—at any moment. More intricate because more compressed is the network of *personae* in *Repetition*. Ostensibly the work is a casebook novel in which Constantin Constantius, the experimental psychologist and dilettante author, reports the history of a Kierkegaardian young man who falls in love, realizes that he cannot marry the girl, nearly achieves a religious reconciliation to his sorrow by reading *Job*, but is at last made a poet by the girl's magnanimity in marrying someone else. "Really" the book investigates the possibility of "repetition"—of restoring a personality to integrity after it has been broken by grief and guilt. With an irony appropriate to the investigation the two pseudonyms are diffracted into a series of masks that satirize themselves and each other (several times over) and finally the reader, who is presented at the end with a calling card, bearing a blank space for his name, and an admonition to be reconciled to the flippancy and incoherence of the book.[189] The reader who recovers *himself* from the farcical shadow play of the

---

[188] For an excellent treatment of the relation of poet to persona in Kierkegaard's pseudonymous writings, cf. Aage Henriksen, Kierkegaards Romaner, Glydendalske Boghandel Nordisk Forlag, København, 1954; cf. also the same author's "Kierkegaard's Reviews of Literature" in Symposion Kierkegaardianum, Orbis Litterarum, tome X, fasc. 1–2, Munksgaard, København, 1955, pp. 75–83.

[189] Kierkegaard, Repetition, p. 147, 158–159. For my awareness of the formal complexity of Repetition I am indebted to an unpublished study by a former student, Kathryn Pulley Respess. Her evaluation of the techniques of indirect communication differs from that here proposed; she concludes that Kierkegaard rather than diverting attention from himself only focuses the reader's interest more sharply on his own personality. In her estimation the technique is a failure, and must fail insofar as every communication, however indirect, presupposes an act of direct communication as its basis.

novel will have achieved repetition, and the heretics eager to ascertain the author's position will get nothing to run with.

The use of pseudonyms first severs Kierkegaard's *personae* from Kierkegaard. At the second level pseudonymity obliterates Kierkegaard the poet. Finally the identities of the pseudonyms themselves are so scrambled that they become masks without faces, and their works self-standing objects unbuttressed by human subjects. The blank calling card inserted in *Repetition*, and the concluding exordium of *Either/Or* ("Only the truth which edifies is truth for you"),[190] along with like hints in the other books, direct the reader to supply the necessary personal identity: his own. So the form of Kierkegaard's writings insinuates their content: subjectivity, inwardness, the passionate appropriation of objective uncertainty, is the only truth possible for an existing individual.[191]

Pseudonymity as such is only a gambit, a powerful but not isolated tactic in the overall strategy of indirect communication. Its import is expanded by a consideration of Kierkegaard's discussions of irony and humor. These modes of obliquity are said to be *confinia* bounding the stages on life's way, irony separating the aesthetic from the ethical, humor dividing the ethical from the religious. As such they open halfway houses to people in progress: the aesthete who is disenchanted with aestheticism but not yet gathered for ethical choice will look with ironic duplicity on his own life; the ethicist who is disabused of his moral self-confidence but not yet ready for religion will smile good-humoredly at his eagerness in well-doing. After their respective leaps have been made, the aesthete-turned-ethicist and the ethicist-become-religious will continue to wear irony and humor as incognitos in which to go among their erstwhile peers. Knowing the gulf that parts him from his former friends, the newly arrived ethicist will hide his eternal validity under a bushel of irony when he addresses them. The religious man's converse with his ethical associates will take the form of a jest the humor of which dissembles his own suffering.[192]

Irony and humor are modes of communication secretively arch rather than conventionally sincere. As the ethicist thinks to master existence by resolve, so his irony scrutinizes the contradictions of life through the stern jaundice of the ideal; the religious man, resigned to suffer what he cannot subdue, wrings his humor out of a sympathy with those contradictions. In either case irony and humor disengage the communication from the communicator so as to signalize and to charge the gap between communicator and recipient. Between two freedoms they insert a "doubly-reflected" work of artfulness condensing the

---

190 *Kierkegaard, Either/Or, vol. II, p. 356.*

191 The fact that the edifying discourses are not pseudonymous is significant. They give direct expression to a point of view that is religious, but not distinctively Christian. This is the only point of view for which Kierkegaard felt he could assume personal responsibility.

192 *Kierkegaard, Concluding Unscientific Postscript, pp. 400–404, 446–468, 489–493; cf. Frithiof Brandt, Søren Kierkegaard, Det Danske Selskab in cooperation with the Press and Information Department of the Danish Foreign Office, Copenhagen, 1963, pp. 29–30.*

inwardness of the communicator into an explosive shock of recognition for the recipient.[193]

The meaning of indirect communication emerges as the pattern of existential
distance, personal detachment, and artistic mediation woven into the
motley of Kierkegaard's works and exemplified by such instances as
pseudonymity, irony, and humor. The same pattern is visible in the
superficially argumentative but fundamentally satiric texture of *Philosophical Fragments* and *Concluding Unscientific Postscript*; it could
also be traced in such diverse fabrics as the "dialectical lyric" of *Fear
and Trembling*, the psychological microscopy of *The Sickness unto
Death*, and the pedantic posturing of *The Concept of Dread*. Its
genres are as illimitable as possibility and as devious as imagination.
But the routine is the same throughout all its expressions: to inter-
pose between author and reader an anonymous object so articulated
by the author that it deploys upon contact into a phalanx of possibilities for the reader. Such communication is indirect because it
turns author and reader away from each other toward "some third
thing, something more abstract, which neither of them is."[194] Such
indirection is a communication of subjective truth because the impersonality of the object returns the reader to the arena where the possibilities it displays must be acted on: his inwardness.[195]

The method of indirection is prefigured in the peirastics, anatreptics, and
maieutics of the Socratic dialogues. Kierkegaard discovered it there
and in what he took to be the compassionate cunning of the Incarnation.[196] More immediately he was impelled to wield the Romantic
irony as a weapon against the pretensions of the Romantic philosophers and their theological imitators. His own practice of indirect
communication, which he describes as "elusive and artistic,"[197] is not
unlike the techniques evolved by modern poets and familiar to contemporary literary critics. It is a commonplace of twentieth-century
criticism to distinguish sharply between poetic language and prosaic
discourse. The terms of the distinction are differently defined by
different critics, but the theme is not lost amid their partisan variations on it. In "direct" or prosaic language, words are straightforward
expressions of the writer's meaning; his language is a symbolic extension of his mind, as unambiguous as he can keep it. The speech
of a poet does not utter his inner states, but rather builds meanings
into a freestanding structure of language. Paradox, self-concealment,
plural connotations, distentions of metaphor and the like are shears
by which he clips the umbilical of his fancy's child and sends it out
on its own. His art is not the externalizing of himself, but the objectifying of a work of words: *poiesis*.

What the poet produces is a verbal object (*poiema*) in which meanings,

---

[193] Ibid., pp. 73, 320–322.   [194] Ibid., p. 455.   [195] Ibid., p. 320.
[196] Cf. Dru, op. cit., nos. 427, 1122; Kierkegaard, Philosophical Fragments, pp. 68–88,
     and Training in Christianity, pp. 124–144. Cf. also Kierkegaard, The Concept
     of Irony with Constant Reference to Socrates, Harper & Row, N.Y., 1966.
[197] Kierkegaard, Concluding Unscientific Postscript, p. 73.

released from any personal interest he may vest in them, are neither affirmed nor denied, but simply placed. A poem in this sense does not *mean*—it does not urge the feelings and opinions of the poet on the reader; it *is*—as a thing made it is self-sufficient (*perfectum*) and bears no message not indigenous to its perfection.

But the poetic object, however much it dispatches the poet's words from the poet, is nevertheless an object and as such commands a response. A direct communication (indicative prose utterance) is a request for assent, and the proper response is some degree of belief or disbelief: one swears by a religious dogma, abandons a moral conviction, gives moderate credence to a scientific hypothesis, denies a factual allegation, etc. But it would be out of place to believe in, to doubt, or to disavow a poem, since the poet makes no claim to which such attitudes would be relevant. At the same time a poem is not a bit of mute decor that is adequately appreciated when it is savored. Its locutions embody meanings, and its sensuousness addresses the intelligence. Kierkegaard would say that a poetic object, like any object, but with the preternatural vivacity induced by art, functions as a *possibility* when it is apprehended by a subject. And that in two distinct but related ways: as a term of knowing and as a challenge to action.[198]

A poem calls not for belief but for knowledge, not for admiration but for personal appropriation. A theory, a doctrine, a statement of fact purport to say something about realities, and for that reason must be believed or doubted or rejected. A poem gives insight into possibilities by fashioning them in words; as a symbol that incarnates what it symbolizes such a verbal structure is the avenue and the object of an act of gnosis.

Kierkegaard's correlation of reality with belief and of possibility with knowledge[199] instructs the interpretation of his own poetry of indirect communication. His books, *poiemata* and not statements of his views on human life, are out of the reach of the ordinary distinction of truth and falsity, which strictly applies only to the yeas and nays of the intellect compounding and dividing. Yet they open ways—if A's analysis of *Don Juan* is correct, infinite ways—for understanding; they are seeds of possibility fecund with meanings, buds that flower perennially for the reflective imagination. Because they are works of irony and humor, they deftly evade the kind of evaluation that suits the generalizations of scientists and the theories of theorizing philosophers. Poems like jokes may be refused; they are never refuted. They may be rich or sparse, superficial or penetrating, estimable in a variety of ways, but they are never propositionally right or wrong. As poetry Kierkegaard's works fertilize the seeing intellect and bring to birth the offspring of the visionary fancy; as poetic irony and poetic humor they survive the misplaced and ineffectual assaults of a literal-minded and prosaic critique.

Not to mention the misplaced and impotent embrace of a literal-minded and prosaic espousal. The heresy of paraphrase and the intentional fallacy tempt the reader of Kierkegaard as they tempt readers of poetry generally. The pitfalls of the latter trap those earnest endeavors to determine what Kierkegaard "really means"—which, if they do not conveniently leave out everything that conflicts with what the scholar thinks Kierkegaard ought to mean, conclude either that Kierkegaard is a fool deaf to the most resounding self-contradictions or that he is saying something so precious and so deep that it cannot help sounding silly. Taken as instruments of his intent, his works add up to magnificent nonsense. But the truth is that Kierkegaard the poet of inwardness did not "really mean" anything. His "intent" is to exfoliate existential possibilities, not to offer a systematic appraisal of reality as seen from his point of view; like all poets he is concerned not with mentioning but with making.

That it is heretical to paraphrase Kierkegaard is equally noteworthy. The "arguments" of his pseudonyms on behalf of religion and Christianity, as these are paraphrased in this chapter, make abundantly clear by their unpersuasive formality just how important is the contextual setting of the originals. Any paraphrase of Kierkegaard must carry a disclaimer and an injunction to return to the source. It is for this reason that the influence of Kierkegaard on contemporary existential philosophy and theology is so questionable in spite of its vast publicity value for the Dane. Existential theologians tend to offer in place of the historic faith of the historical Church in the historical Incarnation an abstract of the dialectic of Climacus—an ersatz congenial to a disinherited generation oppressed by life and incapable of supernatural faith.[200] But it was manifestly not part of Kierkegaard's program to found a school of theology on the barren crisis of despair, only to recall men to the divine imperative and to the conditions of faith in their own sufferings and their own freedom.

By the philosophers who follow in his train Kierkegaard has been prolifically pilfered from,[201] his paradoxes have been twisted into doctrinal parodies of themselves, his mischievous recalcitrance to system has been chastised and solemnly invested with systematic dignity. There is no private property in the realm of the spirit, and there is no reason why everyone should not take from Kierkegaard what serves his turn. But it is impossible not to imagine Kierkegaard sharpening his wit and going to hilarious work on those contemporary ontologies of freedom that are determined to make inwardness academically respectable. The mysteries of the epoché and the disdain of the *existentiale* thinker

---

[200] *Paul Tillich is a particularly striking case in point. See his* Systematic Theology, *vol. II,* The University of Chicago Press, Chicago, 1957, *and* The Courage to Be, *Yale University Press, New Haven, Conn., 1952.*

[201] *The largest borrowings are by Martin Heidegger. He has acknowledged the importance for his own work of* The Concept of Dread, *and, in a grudging way, of the edifying discourses.*

for his *existentielle* gaucheries would impress Kierkegaard as so many new attempts—only slightly less honest than Hegel's—to give human existence the dubious prestige of professorial sanction. He would insist—and the form of his insistence would reduplicate the content— that system enslaves and that only poetry can adequately communicate inwardness in such a way as to emancipate the recipient.[202] Only *poiesis*, which cuts the tie that binds words and men and things, joints a verbal framework tough enough to contain the negativity of freedom without breaking; only poetry can crystallize limitless possibilities in an object capable of engaging the understanding and enticing the imagination ("making aware") without seducing or prostituting the spirit.

The theories of the systematic thinker—it was Hegel's genius that he saw this fact and his perversity that he exploited it—inevitably tend to be set up as ends and to usurp the place of the realities they should serve. The poetic object, however, not only rejoices the mind with its objectivity; it also, by its repellent aloofness, challenges its reader to his own activity of actualization. This is the second sense in which it functions as possibility. The success of an indirect communication depends upon its capacity to awaken in the recipient an awareness that the possibilities it objectifies—alluring, exciting, or frightening— are his own. He has not received the communication until he has read the concluding *de te fabula narratur* that can turn him from the wonder of the object to an engagement with the urgency and the unfinality of his own existence.

Kierkegaard's poetic is a rhetoric designed to coerce its reader to freedom. By the impassioned detachment with which it marshals the resources of spirit, it lays on him the necessity to act and deprives him of any warrant for action except his own freedom. The Kierkegaardian corpus can neither be "believed" nor "followed": it is and was meant to be—poetically—the impetus, the occasion, and the demand for the reader's own advance to selfhood and to a solitary meeting with the divine. Not by exhorting him to this or that line of conduct, not by offering him the chance to let knowledge or admiration go proxy for decision, but by vividly summoning before him the richness and the risk ingredient in his freedom, Kierkegaard's works impart to "that individual" who is their true reader the opportunity and the need of achieving himself in the sight of God.[203]

Kierkegaard's writings are public domain, and as such they may and will be made to serve a variety of purposes. But they are most consistently and most rewardingly understood as the poetry of inwardness their author fashioned them to be. Their *poetry* opens to the inquiring intellect and the restless imagination the infinite wealth of possibility that is the material of human selfhood. As the poetry of *inwardness* they drive their reader through the calm of contemplation into the passion of personal appropriation.

---

[202] *Kierkegaard*, Concluding Unscientific Postscript, *p.* 69.
[203] Ibid., *pp.* 320–322.

BIBLIOGRAPHY

Recommended readings for this chapter

The Man without a Present: Alexander Dru, *The Journals of Søren Kierkgaard* (paperback abridgment), Harper & Row, New York, 1959. *Part I:* Kierkegaard, *Either/Or,* Doubleday Anchor Books, Garden City, N.Y., 1959, vol. I, "Diapsalmata," "The Immediate Stages of the Erotic or the Musical Erotic," "The Unhappiest Man," "The Rotation Method," "Diary of the Seducer." *Part II:* Kierkegaard, *Either/Or,* Doubleday Anchor Books, Garden City, N.Y., 1959, vol. II, "Equilibrium between the Aesthetical and the Ethical in the Composition of Personality." *Part III:* Kierkegaard, *Either/Or,* Doubleday Anchor Books, Garden City, N.Y., 1959, vol. II, "Ultimatum." Kierkegaard, *Edifying Discourses,* Augsburg, Minneapolis, 1943–1946, vol. I, "Every Good and Every Perfect Gift is from Above;" vol. IV, "Man's Need of God Constitutes His Highest Perfection." Kierkegaard, *Thoughts on Crucial Situations in Human Life,* Augsburg, Minneapolis, 1941, "What It Means to Seek God." *Part IV:* Kierkegaard, *Philosophical Fragments,* Princeton University Press, Princeton, N.J., 1962. Kierkegaard, *Concluding Unscientific Postscript,* Princeton University Press, Princeton, N.J., 1944, pp. 67–224, 267–322, 345–493. *Part V:* Kierkegaard, *Training in Christianity,* Princeton University Press, Princeton, N.J., 1947, part I, "Come hither, all ye that labor and are heavy laden, I will give you rest." Kierkegaard, *Christian Discourses,* Oxford University Press, London, 1940, "The Lilies of the Field and the Birds of the Air: Three Godly Discourses." *The Poetry of Inwardness:* Kierkegaard, *Concluding Unscientific Postscript,* Princeton University Press, Princeton, N.J., 1944, pp. 67–74, 224–266, 312–322.

Kierkegaard in Danish

1. *Samlede Vaerker,* Ud. af A. B. Drachman, J. L. Heiberg, H. O. Lange, Anden Udgave, Bind I–XV, Gyldendalske Boghandel Nordisk Forlag, København, 1920–1931. (A new printing of this edition is available from the same publisher, 1962–64. The new printing is in 20 volumes, and is supervised by Peter P. Rohde.)

2. *Søren Kierkegaards Papirer,* Ud. af P. A. Heiberg, V. Kuhr, E. Torsting, Bind I–XI i 18 afdelinger, Gyldendalske Boghandel Nordisk Forlag, København, 1909–1948.

3. *Breve og Aktstykker vedrørende Søren Kierkegaard,* Ud. ved Niels Thulstrup, Bind I–II, Ejnar Munksgaard, København, 1953.

Kierkegaard in English

(In the following list only the most recent editions are given. When a paperback reprint incorporates important revisions in the translation, that edition alone is listed.)

1. *Kierkegaard's Attack Upon Christendom*, Princeton University Press, Princeton, N.J., 1946.

2. *Christian Discourses*, Oxford University Press, London, 1940.

3. *The Concept of Dread*, 2d ed., Princeton University Press, Princeton, N.J., 1957.

4. *The Concept of Irony with Constant Reference to Socrates*, Harper & Row, New York, 1966.

5. *Concluding Unscientific Postscript*, Princeton University Press, Princeton, N.J., 1944.

6. *Edifying Discourses*, vols. I–IV, Augsburg, Minneapolis, 1943–1946.

7. *Either/Or*, vols. I–II, Anchor Books, Doubleday & Company, Inc., Garden City, N.Y., 1959.

8. *Fear and Trembling* and *The Sickness Unto Death*, Anchor Books, Doubleday & Company, Inc., Garden City, N.Y., 1954.

9. *For Self-Examination* and *Judge for Yourselves!* Princeton University Press, Princeton, N.J., 1944.

10. *For Self-Examination*, another translation, Augsburg, Minneapolis, 1940.

11. *The Gospel of Suffering*, Augsburg, Minneapolis, 1948.

12. *Johannes Climacus: or De Omnibus Dubitandum Est*, Stanford University Press, Stanford, Calif., 1958.

13. *The Journals of Søren Kierkegaard*, Oxford University Press, London, 1938.

14. *Judge for Yourselves!* (see above, *For Self-Examination*, etc.)

15. *The Last Years* (selections from the Journals, 1853–1855), Harper & Row, New York, 1965.

16. *On Authority and Revelation*, Princeton University Press, Princeton, N.J., 1955.

17. *Philosophical Fragments*, Princeton University Press, Princeton, N.J. 2d ed., 1962.

18. *The Point of View for my Work as an Author*, Harper Torchbooks, Harper & Row, New York, 1962.

19. *The Present Age*, Oxford University Press, London, 1940.

20. *Purity of Heart*, Harper & Row, New York, 1948.

21. *Repetition*, Princeton University Press, Princeton, N.J., 1946.

22. *The Sickness Unto Death*, (see above, *Fear and Trembling*, etc.)

23. *Stages on Life's Way*, Princeton University Press, Princeton, N.J., 1945.

24. *Thoughts on Crucial Situations in Human Life*, Augsburg, Minneapolis, 1941.

25. *Training in Christianity*, Princeton University Press, Princeton, N.J., 1947.

26. *Works of Love*, Harper & Row, New York, 1962.

CHAPTER THREE

KARL JASPERS
COMMUNICATION THROUGH TRANSCENDENCE

RICHARD F. GRABAU

RICHARD F. GRABAU *received his B.A. from Capital University, and his M.A. and Ph.D. from Yale University. The subject of his dissertation was "The Concepts of Existence and Truth in the Philosophy of Karl Jaspers." Presently teaching at Purdue University, he has also taught at Yale, Hanover College, and Williams College. He is author of articles in the* Journal of Philosophy, Review of Metaphysics, *and the* Journal of Religion. *He contributed a chapter, "Existence and Being," to* Experience, Existence and the Good *(ed. Irwin C. Lieb, Southern Illinois University Press, 1961), and one entitled "Existential Universals" to* Invitation to Phenomenology *(ed. J. M. Edie, Quadrangle Books, Inc., 1965).*

For Karl Jaspers philosophy is intimately bound up with life. In order to communicate an adequate understanding of his philosophy to persons in our philosophical tradition one must compare him to such men as William James and John Dewey. To be sure, there are differences between pragmatism and the Existenz philosophy of Jaspers, many of them so large as to make this comparison misleading. It is the men who must be compared. Whatever differences exist between their philosophies, Jaspers, Dewey, and James produced them in the attempt to illuminate human existence in the concreteness with which it is lived by existing men. All three believe that the task of philosophy is not to produce a system of categories which correctly describes an independent reality in universally compelling terms, but to orient men in the midst of their existence. The whole enterprise of philosophy is practical.

Like James, Jaspers came into philosophy from psychology, having written a book on psychopathology which in the German tradition occupies a place similar to James' *Principles of Psychology* in ours.[1] Like James, moreover, Jaspers has sought to ascertain and describe the manifold expressions of human experience that have appeared in history. One thinks of Jaspers' *Psychology of World Views* [2] in relation to James' *Varieties of Religious Experience*. Even the manner of treatment is similar: not to reduce to a formula but to present the richness of religious experience and world views with the intention of appealing to possibilities of comprehension and appreciation in the reader.

Like Dewey, Jaspers is concerned with the problems of men and feels that philosophy, while it cannot solve all these problems (because their solution requires much objective scientific knowledge), it certainly can and must put them into new perspectives by lifting them out of the isolated contexts in which they are often imprisoned by our tendency to fragment life. Thus, like Dewey, Jaspers has written on politics, the present age, history, and religion. Both believe that where reflective thought abdicates the function of clarifying human problems (as it has done in academic philosophy) they will be solved in an irresponsible and arbitrary manner.

Two more points of similarity must be pointed out. Jaspers, like James and Dewey, has formulated a metaphysical or general philosophical position as a framework within which to interpret and give substance to the more special investigations of the human situation. James called his approach radical empiricism: a method and position which refused to place *a priori* restrictions upon the lives and affairs of men. Always the eye is on the concrete lived experience from which conceptual analysis springs and to which it must return for its validation. No element is allowed to fall away ignored because it does not meet an abstract standard. Likewise, Jaspers affirms that no mode

---

[1] Karl Jaspers, Allgemeine Psychopathologie, 6th ed., Springer, Berlin, 1953.

[2] Karl Jaspers, Psychologie der Weltanschauungen, 4th ed. Springer, Berlin, 1954 (hereafter cited as PdW). *All translations of quotations from German titled books are by the author.*

of the encompassing may be left out; reason allows each to have its place and tries to formulate a scheme of existence which will enable us to understand it as men live it.[3]

Consequently Jaspers, as have Dewey and James, has produced a philosophy which has been criticized for being loose, amorphous, obscure, esoteric, nonsystematic, relativistic, unrigorous, etc. In each case these criticisms, while true, are not objections to the philosophy they seek to attack. All three philosophers have often pointed out that the features just noted cannot be helped if one is loyal to human experience, which is spontaneous, loose, amorphous, obscure, fragmented, etc. The criticisms stem from assumptions about philosophy and life which are rejected by all three: that the function of philosophy is to construct theories about existence and that human existence is amenable to this kind of conceptual analysis.

Finally, each of our philosophers is concerned with the problem of communication. Jaspers asserts that from his childhood he noted the frequent failure of men to understand and get through to one another, and that it troubled him and brought the question of the nature and possibility of communication to a central place in his thinking.[4] All three men have complained about being misunderstood by others. James devoted much of his lectures in *Pragmatism* to refuting distortions of pragmatism by its unsympathetic critics. Dewey pointed to an almost willful misunderstanding of his position by some of its critics.[5] Jaspers warns continually that statements in the philosophy of Existenz can be distorted and misunderstood quite easily and that one must always guard against it.[6] In senses which would have to be spelled out more fully in each philosopher's case, Jaspers, James, and Dewey made communication an integral part of what they mean by truth, and would subscribe to Jaspers statement: Truth is that which founds community:[7]

Thus we see the ramifications of the claim that for Jaspers philosophy is in the service of life. To him philosophy is a human—and humane— enterprise in which men become truly themselves by an exercise in self-understanding. Philosophy is concrete, not abstract; a process of thought which never comes to an end because existence never comes to an end, not a conceptual product which describes a static object. Philosophy is a reflective lifting to consciousness of the contours of concrete life, to the end that men shall be more authentically aware and free.

---

[3] *Karl Jaspers, Von der Wahrheit, Piper & Co. Verlag, Munich, 1947, pp. 113ff (hereafter cited as VdW). Cf. Karl Jaspers, Reason and Existenz, tr. William Earle, Noonday Press, Inc., New York, 1955, pp. 67–79 (hereafter cited as RE).*

[4] *Karl Jaspers, "Philosophical Autobiography," in P. A. Schilpp, ed., The Philosophy of Karl Jaspers, Tudor Publishing Company, New York, 1957, pp. 85, 93. Cf. K. Jaspers, "On My Philosophy," in W. Kaufmann, ed., Existentialism from Dostoevsky to Sartre, Meridian Books, Inc., New York, 1957, pp. 145ff.*

[5] *John Dewey, "Experience, Knowledge and Value: A Rejoinder," in P. A. Schilpp, ed., The Philosophy of John Dewey, Northwestern University Press, Evanston, Ill., 1939, pp. 527, 546, 549.*

[6] *Karl Jaspers, Philosophie, 2d ed., Springer, Berlin, 1948, pp. 310–314. Cf. RE 76.*

[7] *Ibid., pp. 348f. Cf. RE 79.*

These features also make Jaspers the most Kierkegaardian of the contemporary existentialists. Although comparison with Dewey and James demonstrates the range of Jaspers' philosophy, it is Kierkegaard (along with Kant) who is the basic source of Jaspers' philosophizing. More than the other existentialists Jaspers uses Kierkegaardian terms to illuminate human existence. Like Kierkegaard, Jaspers insists that the individual person transcends any objective description which can be made of him. He must be communicated with as a free individual, appealed to, and stimulated to an awareness of himself in his situation as an existing person who can never be reduced to the categories of a system.

So fundamental is this view that Jaspers—like Kierkegaard—conceives of his own philosophy as an effort at communication. It is a halfway house in a total communicative situation and comes alive only if it is appropriated by the reader.[8] There can be no neutral and detached descriptions of human existence: what Heidegger calls an ontology of human existence. Such attempts reduce the individual to an object and take away his freedom and personal decision. For Jaspers a philosophy becomes true to the extent that it communicates with and illuminates the existence of the reader. It is false if it fails. Considered out of this relation it is only an empty shell, the bare bones of a philosophy, neither true nor false.

Illumination and communication are fundamental themes which organize Jaspers' philosophy into a meaningful whole. When read in the light of these themes much that is otherwise obscure takes on meaning. Jaspers sees in Kierkegaard (and Nietzsche) the decisive emergence of these themes in modern thought. They are the turning points in our intellectual tradition because they presented the problem of the individual over against the forces which tend to destroy him, whether objective philosophical and scientific conceptions of man, social and economic institutions which force his life into standardized routines, or pressures of public opinion and mass culture. They pointed out brilliantly, often by becoming object-lessons of the doctrines they announced, the alienation of man from man and consequent lapse of communication. Men no longer exist in the midst of a context of shared commitments, goals, values, and world views which facilitate mutuality. In a fragmented world of fragmented men the identity of man is a question and communication is a serious problem.

No one can think in a way relevant to the contemporary situation if he neglects these two men. But we cannot follow them. Their significance is their being exceptions: individuals who break out of every framework and stand alone.[9] No one can ever take the life of another as his model; and no one saw this more clearly than Kierkegaard and Nietzsche, both of whom renounced disciples and wanted each individual to become himself.

Though we cannot follow them we must think in the light of their eruption

---

[8] W. Kaufmann, op. cit., p. 150. Cf. pp. 134, 147; Philosophie, pp. 313, 557, 693; VdW, 5, 846.
[9] RE, Lecture I.

into the world. Our problems are still the ones they faced and could respond to only by personal choices: the questioning of systems, the realization of the endlessness of thought abstracted from existence and its impotence to justify any course of action or value, their theory of masks and interpretation, by which they show that we understand reality only in symbols and that many of these symbolic constructions are frauds and illusions, their suspicion of science as a dehumanizing force (especially in its technological applications), their awareness of the voluntaristic source even of reason itself, and their demonstration of anxiety as the style of life.

Even though Kierkegaard is the source of much of his thought, Jaspers believes that reason has a decisive place in the working of a communicative illumination of human existence.[10] Willful, irrational choices, as exemplified by Kierkegaard's Christianity and Nietzsche's choice of the will to power, are self-destructive for those who make them and blind alleys for others. Jaspers tries to unite reason and will. In his concept of reason he is again—in his way—very close to the pragmatic concept of reason as a structuring and organizing function in life. Reason provides order and keeps one from the arbitrariness and brutality of sheer will. Just as for Dewey reason is intelligence in action, so for Jaspers it is a principle of openness, an effort toward communication, a force which allows all material a hearing and seeks to organize it into a temporal whole. Reason is the binding power which pushes beyond and questions all standard forms and interpretations. It constantly confronts them with other dimensions of man's existence and seeks to establish larger and more adequate wholes in which the various elements of existence are brought into relation.[11]

Yet in this task reason is not an originary function. Life provides reason with its content and keeps it from becoming mere speculative system building. This means, of course, that no longer is a closed system of thought possible in which reality finds an adequate, final, and universally valid articulation. In its place we must rely on the function of reasonableness in life: an existential force which seeks to clarify and bind together (but not finally) the elements which emerge in concrete experience to the end of a truly human life. It is, in fact, only in this philosophic task that the image of a truly human life begins to take shape. For, if reason without existential roots is abstract and hollow, without rational clarity human existence becomes arbitrary, demonic, and self-destructive.

1. The Subject-Object Relation and the Concept of World View

The only way philosophy can provide an illumination of human existence is to reveal its place and station in the scheme of things: that is, by constructing a metaphysics.[12] Aristotle expressed this in his distinc-

---

[10] Ibid., pp. 65ff. Cf. K. Jaspers, Reason and Anti-Reason in Our Time, tr. Stanley Godman, Yale University Press, New Haven, Conn., n.d., p. 63.
[11] RE 64ff. [12] Philosophie, p. 23.

tion between philosophy, which deals with being itself, and the special sciences, which investigate some aspect of particular objects and yield specialized knowledge. Jaspers continues in this main line of Western thought. For him philosophy is the attempt to lay hold of authentic being by means of thought.[13] It does this by constructing a representation of the whole of reality in the endeavor to get answers to such questions as: Why is there anything at all—why not nothing? Who am I? What do I really desire? What is being itself?[14]

The only trouble with questions like these is that there are no direct or permanent answers, as one glance at the history of philosophy will verify. Moreover, it is highly instructive to reflect upon the perennial asking of these ultimate questions to find out why this is the case. The ability to ask such questions is the root of the existentialist concept of the self as an activity of self-reflection and of Jaspers' idea of philosophic thought as a continuous process of transcending.

I find that I always ask questions from the midst of a concrete situation. My asking and the answers I receive are colored by two features of the fact that it is I—an individual human being here and now, in these circumstances—who asks the question of being.[15] The first is that beginnings and endings are obscure. I never push so far back in time, for example, seeking causes and origins, that I come to an obvious stopping point where it is impossible for me to ask further for causes and origins. Neither can I project future states which are finalities.[16] I can always ask: What next? The consequence is that everything seems to lose substance and meaning. There is no answer which gives security and support. Anxiety over the ephemeral character and possible meaninglessness of existence comes over the inquirer, who sees the determinate present trailing off into two obscurities. He seeks a way out.

Second, I never meet being itself as an object. I discover myself in many relations to particular objects which present themselves in my situation.[17] Every time I am aware of something new it turns out to be another thing in the world which can be transcended by asking about it, its origin, its causes, its meaning. Being, it seems, forever eludes the quest. Perhaps there is no being as such. Perhaps there is only a collection of things and people, just absurdly there, as Sartre, for example, maintains. This remains a possibility for Jaspers—that is, it cannot be logically refuted. To refute it would mean to have access to a situation having neither of the features we are discussing. But to maintain it as fact presupposes the same thing. So Jaspers does not accept this possibility, but pushes further in his interrogation of the situation in which we ask the question of being. His refusal is an act of philosophical faith, which holds that being is more than its manifestations; it is the motivating force of the reflective examination which is philosophy.

---

13 Ibid., p. 32.   14 Ibid., p. 1.   15 Ibid., p. 3.   16 Ibid., p. 1. Cf. VdW, 305.
17 Ibid., p. 2. This idea is already developed in Allgemeine Psychopathologie, pp. 468, 632.

All of the features of Jaspers' philosophizing derive from an awareness of the situation-bound character of human thought. The idea of being as transcendence, the encompassing and its modes, philosophy as the illumination of existence, the idea that objective thought is a process of world-orientation, the theory of boundary-situations, the emphasis upon historicity and the appropriation of tradition, and finally the conception of metaphysics as a cipher or hieroglyph of being within the confines of historical situations with their special pasts and expectation: all have the form they do because Jaspers keeps asking: How does being appear to a person in a situation?

Jaspers names this situation the subject-object dichotomy. He developed it early, in his first two books on psychology, and it has been the controlling idea in his thought ever since. Analysis of our situation, Jaspers suggests, must take the form of an analysis of consciousness:

Because existence [18] is consciousness and I exist as consciousness, things exist for me only as objects of consciousness. Anything which exists for me must enter into consciousness. Consciousness as existence is the medium of everything. . . .[19]

But consciousness is not a thing like other entities in the world; it is a being "whose essence is to be directed intentionally toward objects."[20] This being directed towards objects is a "fundamental phenomenon, as self-evident as it is wondrous."[21] To be conscious is to be conscious *of* something, to be oriented toward it, to be concerned and involved with it in some respect, whether it is a sensation, a concept like $\sqrt{-1}$, or the idea of democracy. Since consciousness is my manner of existing I am a concrete subject defined in a situation by the particular relations I have with objects.

Several interesting features are bound up with this subject-object structure, which "cannot be clarified by means of anything else, but is itself the way of becoming clear in the world."[22]

First Jaspers points out that there simply is no subject without an object or object without a subject: they are polarities. This insight alone has tremendous consequences for philosophy. Descartes started with consciousness of self and tried by tortuous routes to achieve similar certainty about the existence of the world. Jaspers shows that to be a subject means to be directed to some object which is built up into a world by categorial relations with other objects. The object is as certainly real as the subject. In fact, I am never aware of myself as

[18] *I shall translate and use Jaspers' term "Dasein" by the English word "existence." Others have used "being-there," justifying this by pointing out that it is a literal translation of "Da-sein." But "being-there" is awkward in English. Since Dasein is the normal German word for existence, I have used the most natural English term. Some (Earle) have translated the term by "empirical existence." I do not see that this adds anything, and it creates the expectation that there is some other kind, namely nonempirical existence, which for Jaspers plainly is not the case. In any case Jaspers' term "Dasein" must be distinguished from Heidegger's. The latter includes what Jaspers refers to as Existenz.*
[19] Philosophie, p. 6.   [20] Idem. Cf. VdW 231.   [21] Idem.   [22] VdW 231.

subject, per se. I am only aware of being a preoccupation with objects; reflectively I consider myself a subject.

Similarly there is no object without a subject. This does not mean that when I no longer exist neither does the world. It means that the object of awareness of any person is a representation in his consciousness. As such it is not just a copy of something "out there" nor is it necessarily the same representation as some other subject has. The reason is that we do not just passively receive objects; we apprehend them against a background of experiences, thoughts, and interests which we bring to the situation and which enable us to build our experiences into a world. This is obvious when it comes to such things as tools. Jaspers argues that this happens with respect to all objects of awareness: They are structured by the intentions of consciousness.

The second feature of the subject-object relationship is that the relation between subject and object is not direct and immediate, but very complex. Human consciousness is different from animal consciousness. The latter seems to be dominated by instincts and other mechanisms which orient it automatically to its environment. The robin builds its nest as have members of its species for eons. It comes into the world equipped with certain ways of responding to its environment. Indeed, its environment is, properly speaking, that part of nature to which it relates by means of its instinctual mechanisms. The animal-environment relation is a totality; there is no environment in the abstract into which an animal is inserted. The animal can be considered as a center of environment-determining activity. Nevertheless in the case of the animal there does not seem to be any culture; the mechanisms of orientation are immediate, and conciousness, when it occurs, is largely confined to these instinctual mechanisms.

With man the case is different. Consciousness is more indeterminate and hence important in the life of the person. Although its general structure is that of a subject being directed toward objects, there is a wide leeway in the ways in which this happens. The relation is neither built into men as members of a species nor is it immediate. It is mediated by means of symbolic instruments: Ideas which determine both the object as a particular object to which certain reactions are appropriate and others not, and a subject in a concrete historical situation. They must be acquired by the individual by participating in a historical community.[23]

The relation between subject and object in situations by means of symbolic ideas is one of the most fascinating and perplexing of all philosophical ideas. It contains the problem of the nature of being and the nature of knowledge. Most philosophies have erred in trying to describe this relationship too objectively. They have tried to make the subject-object relation itself into an outlandish object and describe it in terms derived either from the objective or the subjective side. Positivism and

23 RE, *78f.*

idealism are illustrations of this distortion.[24] The thing to do, however, is to illuminate the relationship while living within it. We cannot escape it and turn it into an object. It is not an object at all, but the context in which we apprehend objects.

Once we have reached the concept of the idea as the mediating agent between subject and object we can see that the relation between them is subject to change and growth, corruption and fulfillment, and exhibits various dimensions or levels.[25] One must therefore turn, as Husserl proposed, "back to the things themselves," and indicate the various ways in which subject and object are related. The result is the concept of world view, one of the central ideas in Jaspers' philosophy.

In defining what he means by world view, Jaspers says:

When we speak of world views, we mean ideas, what is ultimate and complete in man, both subjectively, as experience, power and conviction, and objectively as the formal world of objects.[26]

It is by constructing a world view (or by participating in one through appropriation of their traditions) that men acquire the frames of reference in terms of which they understand themselves. As a frame of reference a world view has a subjective pole, which Jaspers calls an attitude (Einstellung), and an objective referent to which he gives the name world image (Weltbild). Attitude and image constitute a totality of symbols by which persons accommodate themselves in the world. Such a totality is, so to speak, a shell (Gehäuse).

But at best a world view is only a finite articulation of being. It is generated in concrete situations and cannot offer a complete survey of being.[27] Though necessary means of accommodation, world views also must be dissolved or transcended.

The process of living thus includes both a dissolution and formation of shells. Without dissolution rigidity would set in; without shells there would be destruction. Both dissolution and shells can, however, be detached . . . from the living whole; the result is, on the one hand, nihilistic processes, and on the other, an ultimate crawling into one's shell.[28]

A consequence of this is that there are a plurality of world views, both as efforts of different individuals located in different situations and as a developing series in a single individual. Man as conceived in Stoicism is a different subject living in a different situation from one for whom Christianity or Nietzsche's philosophy serves as the dominant idea relating subject and object. Here one can already see the origin of the problem of universality and communication for Jaspers.

Motivating Jaspers' analysis of world views is a loyalty to the concrete person. He does not try to cut him to fit an epistemological or metaphysical theory. Our thinking must be out of the situation of existence.[29] And there we find that there is no one line from subject to object,

---

24 Philosophie, pp. 182–206.   25 PdW 460. Compare p. 21 and RE 80ff.
26 PdW 1.   27 Jaspers contrasts a Weltall with a Weltbild.   28 PdW 423.
29 Philosophie, pp. 21ff.

but countless lines (one could represent them as for example a self-dispersing bundle that in the infinity of subjects and objects unites itself at points, or as a group of parallel lines).[30]

A study of world views can thus only illuminate them. They must be presented in such a way as to allow each to demonstrate its function as a shell in which men represent themselves in a world.[31]

Jaspers is unexcelled among the existentialists (excepting Kierkegaard) in reconstructing the various world views and allowing each to demonstrate its illuminating power in uniting subject and object. And nowhere in his own writing is he more effective than when he is charting out, as Kierkegaard did, the various human worlds in terms of which men have lived and acted. These are not exhaustive analyses of all possible world views. Once one realizes what Jaspers is doing he sees this to be impossible. World views are unique creations of men in historical situations. Jaspers' purpose is the illumination of existence to show how men have related themselves to being in the course of their self-reflection. Man remains a horizon of possibilities which manifest themselves historically in concrete situations. He is what he has become; he is what he will become; but even more he is the transcending origin of still further becomings. All Jaspers can do is to exhibit some of these. Already in the *Psychologie* Jaspers had developed the ideas which were later to become the notions of the encompassing and Existenz.[32]

One last feature of the subject-object relation must be mentioned, for it has large methodological consequences. Jaspers calls it the fragmented character of being.[33] The whole analysis of the subject-object dichotomy leads to this notion; and it is enshrined in the very idea of a world view. There is no total knowledge of any kind, only partial world images, on the part of individuals existing in historically concrete and unique situations. Neither the subject-pole nor the object-pole of the relationship is a finished totality in terms of which being can be finally construed. The subject may try to achieve adequate knowledge of himself. But reflection discovers that every such attempt fails, for there still remains the subject who projects this analysis by turning himself into an object of investigation. And this subject escapes the analysis.[34] Subjectivity exists as partial, fragmented, unique subjects.

Similarly the object-pole remains fragmented into objects for subjects in the empirical contexts of relatedness. We never grasp anything like the

[30] PdW 25.   [31] VdW 235.

[32] *I am not going to translate Jaspers' term "Existenz." There is no adequate English term. Earle does not translate it in RE. Existenz is that primary source of selfhood which always eludes characterization, but which manifests itself in every characterization. It is authentic selfhood and can only be appealed to, awakened, and enacted. Section III deals with Existenz. In the present context Jaspers wants to present the various world views which determine subjects and objects as creative manifestations of Existenz in appropriate historical circumstances.*

[33] "Die Zerissenheit des Seins," Philosophie, p. 676; VdW 703ff.
[34] Philosophie, p. 7.

world as a total object. We know only things in the world, and then only from particular perspectives which may be surpassed in the next awareness. We try to bind these objects and perspectives together into a totality, but this world is present only as a goal, as an idea in Kant's sense of the term. In actuality we have only a world picture as the objective correlate of a subjective "attitude."

Conscious awareness thus fragments being into a subject-pole and an object-pole. Neither can be reduced to the other. Yet neither do they constitute being. Instead they raise the question of a third possibility: being considered not as subject nor as object, but as it is in itself.[35] In a sense this is an impossible idea, for to think about anything is to represent it as an object for a subject. Nevertheless it is a necessary thought: One cannot refrain from asking a question about a primordial being beyond its articulation into subject and object of which the latter may be seen as appearances. Access to this being can be had, if at all, not by cognition in categories, but by an existential awareness we shall come upon later. But it should be pointed out here that it is precisely this sense of being which divides Jaspers from other existentialists, such as Sartre and Camus, who reject such a concept of being.

None of these modes of being can be dispensed with in any adequate philosophy. They are three "inseparable poles of the being in which I find myself."[36] Each needs the other for completion. Existentially catastrophic results follow from trying to maintain one of these poles as being.

Then either I construe being-as-it-is-in-itself as the only being—without noticing that I have already made it into an object for myself—; or I construe being as this object for me—without noticing in this transformation of all being into appearance that this being as object must be an appearance of something for someone—; or I construe selfhood as being in that I make the "I" as subject into the ultimate reality—without noticing that I always am related to objects in a situation, as a consciousness which is intentionally searching toward being-as-it-is-in-itself.[37]

Naïve metaphysics, notes Jaspers, wants an entirely adequate portrayal of being beyond its appearance as subject and object. But alas, "it can only populate it with representations out of the realm of objects."[38] And these objects are always for subjects in situations.

2. The Encompassing and Its Modes

The concept of the encompassing is the culmination of the development of the idea of the subject-object dichotomy. It generalizes that concept into a philosophical doctrine; and since 1935 Jaspers has referred to his own philosophy as the philosophy of the encompassing. The idea is a simple one: Because the subject-object dichotomy makes it im-

---

35 Ibid., p. 4.   36 Idem.   37 Ibid., p. 5.   38 Idem.

possible for being to appear adequately in the structures of subject and object, it can be represented only as an encompassing horizon.[39]

One builds up to the idea of the encompassing. Everything we know is an object within a horizon of objects. Increase in our knowledge merely pushes the horizon further on; still further determination of both subject and object is always possible. I never enter an absolute situation.[40] The horizon is thus a background of potentiality against which all thought and action occurs. The horizon which contains all horizons is the encompassing. It itself is never surveyable and nameable as a horizon, for I cannot leave it to get a perspective on it. It reveals itself only indirectly through a movement of thought playing upon its articulations in subject and object. Not itself manifest, it is that within which all else is manifested.[41]

Awareness of the encompassing is reached by a fundamental operation: transcending. Philosophical thought is transcending thought; where there is no transcending there is no philosophy, only science or calculation on the level of everyday existence.[42] Philosophy lives on the boundary of such knowledge, constantly trying to become clear about what we know and what we do not know by thinking beyond the limits of any particular horizon.

The idea of transcending thought as a method comes from Kant. It was transcending thought which yielded the insight that the world of phenomena is an appearance of a thing in itself to a transcendental unity of apperception.[43] If one explores the process of transcending he discovers that in it no new facts about the world are learned or theories propounded.[44] Information about objects is the exclusive domain of science. What results is a new perspective on our knowing and being in which the world becomes transparent to a ground.

If we say that world is appearance, we also say that that of which it is an appearance is in principle no object and no possible object. It is not at all in itself any kind of determinate being in a categorial sense. World as appearance is only an expression for that act of transcending that as it were, brings the world and me in it into suspension, without leading me to any trans-worldly object. *In the world, therefore, the expression, "the world is appearance," has no meaning.*[45]

Transcending thought exists as an inner process and cannot be objectified.[46] Awareness of it comes only in carrying it through. To communicate it one does not give results to another, but leads him to do it himself. Therefore transcending is easily misunderstood. If one should consider what is said in the process of transcending in isolation one gets the idea that it is a transcendent source of positive knowledge of

---

[39] VdW 37ff. Re, *chap.* 2. Way to Wisdom, tr. *Ralph Manheim, Yale University Press, New Haven, Conn., 1954, chap. 3 (hereafter cited as* Wisdom).

[40] Philosophie, *p. 10.*   [41] RE 52; Wisdom, *p. 31.*

[42] Philosophie, *pp. 34, 675ff. Cf. VdW 40, where Jaspers calls it "ein sich-selbst-überschlagender Gedanke."*

[43] Philosophie, *p. 35.*   [44] Ibid., *p. 36.*   [45] Ibid., *p. 37 (emphasis added).*

[46] Ibid., *p. 34.*

being—as mystics claim. Jaspers rejects this. There is no way to lay hold of being except to think within the subject-object dichotomy in such a way that one renders it transparent to its ground.

One can refuse to transcend. No one can compel another to perform the operation of thought by which one lays hold of being. If transcending fails, being is identified with its appearance in the world. Idealism, materialism, vitalism, voluntarism, positivism, even existentialism,[47] are all instances of the thwarting of transcending thinking. Some of these philosophies are "advances" on others because they have partially transcended; but common to them all is the fact that the process of transcending was stopped.

Transcending is thus an act of freedom, a rational act of openness which is the result of a will to let being manifest itself. Jaspers calls this carrying through of the philosophical act of transcending "faith." For both Jaspers and Kant (who limited knowledge to make room for faith) faith is an intellectual posture in the world. It is not a content or a method of gaining access to realms of being inaccessible to more pedestrian methods. It is a way of thinking beyond subject and object, yet always in relation to them, and where it is successful it eventuates in a sense of the presence of being. Faith thus conceived, far from being opposed to reason, is the attitude of a reason rooted in existence and reflecting upon its situation by daring to go beyond all particular organizations of subject and object.

Since transcending cannot be compelled, the need for it can only be presented by appealing to possibilities of it in others. Jaspers speaks of the dissatisfaction we experience in all forms of being where transcending is omitted.[48] Only when, for example, I become aware of myself in transcending thought do I apprehend myself as origin beyond the roles I play as a subject in various situations. Only then am I open to being as an encompassing. This deepest, transcending appropriation of myself is not a scientific bit of information about myself, but an existential understanding of myself as freedom. This awareness—or lack of it—determines our apprehension and appropriation of everything else: the world, other persons, knowledge, and finally being itself. Philosophical treatment of these topics is a transcending treatment of them.

Where transcending occurs one is already thinking from the encompassing. Still, the illumination of the encompassing must relate it to the subject-object relation in more detailed ways than just to say that it transcends it. Jaspers claims that the encompassing manifests itself as the encompassing that we are and the encompassing that being is: the encompassing of subjectivity and objectivity. Being, however, remains the encompassing beyond both of these lesser horizons: "the encompassing of all encompassings."[49] Like Plato's Good, it is beyond all the categories of being, which are merely its offspring. The movement to the ultimate encompassing by transcending its appear-

[47] VdW 165.   [48] Philosophie, pp. 677–679. VdW 658ff.   [49] VdW 109f.

ances as subject and object is similar to the movement of dialectic through the various levels of forms in Plato to a glimpse of the Good.

Jaspers explores first the encompassing which we are. There are three immanent modes of this encompassing, the structures of which are open to investigation and description: existence, consciousness in general, and spirit. In addition there is the encompassing of man beyond all the immanent modes: Existenz.

Next he moves to the encompassing of objectivity. Here there is an immanent mode: world; and the transcendent mode to which he gives the name "Transcendence." We shall discuss the immanent modes of subjectivity and objectivity in the remainder of this section.

"Existence (*Dasein*) is the encompassing which I am as a living being . . . ; it is the reality in which everything is—myself and that which is object for me."[50] It is the level of being in which I participate because of my "nature": a spatiotemporal organism. At the level of existence I act in order to fulfil the needs and carry out the functions of an organism. I become involved in a world which has existence, too: objects, tools, language, social institutions. The level of existence is the condition upon which all else rests, and Jaspers delineates its main characteristics: (1) "Though it certainly has features which we can illuminate as 'existence in general,' each existence is not a universal, but essentially this fulfilled, single, irreplaceable existence."[51] (2) It is life in the world, a domain of observation, perception, building, ordering. (3) It is a succession of ephemeral states which come and go. (4) It is desire (drive, stress, will) seeking satisfaction. (5) It is unrest and struggle. (6) "Existence is the encompassing reality"[52] of space and time in which anything which becomes real for me must appear.

Because existence is roughly identical with spatiotemporal reality and the needs of organic life, it can be made the object of knowledge and scientifically investigated. History, biology, psychology, sociology, anthropology, economics, politics—all investigate the person as existence, and with right, for he is there as an accomplished objective fact.

But for Jaspers existence is more than the assemblage of facts studied by these objectifying modes of thought. When the special sciences set out objectively to study man and reduce his behavior to law, "this object is no longer the encompassing."[53] What Jaspers means is that although existence is a determinable object, it is more: existence itself is an encompassing horizon of life, thought, and action. If one objectifies it as empirical existence into discrete nameable objects, he loses this transcending character of it. By calling existence an encompassing in its own right Jaspers points out a fundamental feature of human being, even at the empirical level where it is also open to investigation: its nonspecificity, its potentiality, its horizonal character. Desires and drives are themselves encompassing fields out of which

---

[50] VdW 53.   [51] Ibid., p. 54.   [52] Idem.   [53] Ibid., pp. 155, 55; RE 55.

have come a rich assortment of political, social, linguistic, and sexual forms for satisfying them. As existence we are not only these forms, but also an encompassing source which gives rise to them and can break out into novel forms. Such drives at the level of existence are known, of course, only through their fruits. But these fruits do not exhaust them; properly they are encompassing fields, potentiality for further expression.

Implied in this is the thesis that every objective understanding of man at the level of existence is at the same time a falsification, a watering down of a much richer and more spontaneous encompassing of concrete life and action. Man is not exactly definable even at the level at which the sciences properly deal with him. The loss of this insight Jaspers sees as the source of claims to total knowledge of man in the modern world.

The second mode of the encompassing of subjectivity is consciousness in general. Jaspers makes a sharp distinction between existing consciousness and consciousness in general.[54] Existing consciousness is the awareness one has as individual existence by living through life in its concreteness. On this level the hallmark of truth is successful accomplishment of purpose. Existence is interested in satisfactions and results, not universal truths. Relativity and change characterize this level.[55]

On the other hand consciousness in general presses on to compelling truth which is universal. As consciousness in general therefore I am not an existent knower, but an abstract epistemological subject: the impersonal knowing we have come to call "objectivity." It is not so much a subject as a structure of subjectivity, and is Jaspers' version of Kant's transcendental unity of apperception with its categories for ordering the manifold of sense. As such it is the structure of consciousness which is the same in all men.[56] Logic and the sciences are its domain. Where existence is studied scientifically it is studied from the standpoint of consciousness in general.

Because "as consciousness in general we participate in a . . . valid, universal truth,"[57] this level is the condition for the possibility of any community and communication beyond the momentary alliances of convenience into which the pressure of existence forces us.[58] Unless we transcend these pressures and push on to universal consciousness we have no larger context for meeting each other than our own desires and impulses. Everything else is twisted to fit them. Consciousness in general, on the contrary, is the arena in which man can leave the immediacies of existence and begin to build structures which change the quality of life. Here we have the emergence of law, enduring structure, order. Thus, objective knowledge for Jaspers is never merely the instrument of will, but an encompassing in its own right, of universal, public, objective, verifiable truth. Methodological correctness reigns; the urgencies of existence are seen in perspective,

---

54 Philosophie, p. 67; VdW 65. Cf. RE 56.   55 RE 81f.   56 VdW 65.
57 Ibid., p. 66.   58 RE 56–57.

and changed by being thought in categories which universalize them. Jaspers, more than any other existentialist emphasizes the role of this level of the encompassing. He is no voluntarist; there is no route to truth which outflanks objectivity as there was for Kierkegaard. One must carry out this level and transcend it. But to transcend is not to neglect.

Consciousness in general is an encompassing horizon of universal thought. This means that it is a potentiality for further development and cannot be defined in terms of a set of concepts. Those who have drawn the distinction between science as a method of investigation and science as a particular set of results have made this same point. Though it ranges over the whole of existence it never reaches a final interpretation of it.

The third form of the encompassing of subjectivity is spirit, which, says Jaspers, "is the totality of intelligible thought, action and feeling—a totality which is not a closed object for knowledge, but remains idea."[59] If consciousness in general is analogous to Kant's transcendental unity of apperception, spirit is related to Kant's ideas of reason. These latter are not concepts through which objects of experience are determined, but unconditional totalities which regulate the understanding in seeking ever more order and unity in experience. Although Kant first emphasized the regulative function, it was Hegel who pointed out that ideas actually exist only in historical totalities. Spirit becomes that quality of mind which is exhibited in such things as nations, institutions, scientific societies, religions, and moral codes.

Spirit thus represents a concrete whole informed by a content, an idea of some kind which gives order and meaning to the members of the whole. It binds men of science into a scientific community through commitment to a standard of veracity and method. It binds men driven together by the urgencies of existence into communal wholes or nations. One lives at the level of spirit in so far as he participates in the idea which constitutes the whole. One is lifted out of his immediacy into a public world.

Spirit, unlike consciousness in general, is a temporal totality. One might, indeed, imagine it as the synthesis of existence and consciousness in general. The one is a timeless abstraction, merely a form. The other is a tissue of empirical expressions of the encompassing of existence. Together they provide a unity of form and content which is an historical creation: a concrete universal. One first becomes human through membership in a spiritual community. Conviction, commitment, loyalty to the spiritual idea informing the whole are the marks of truth at this level. Tradition is the means by which spirit is sustained and transmitted to others. We participate in existence automatically by virtue of our organic nature. Consciousness in general is the abstract structure of all subjectivity. But spirit is a more tender plant; it must be nurtured in the young by training and opportunity for participation.

59 Ibid., p. 57.

Though spirit unites and gathers what would otherwise be a meaningless welter into a substantial whole, it is an ambiguous blessing. Spirit by its nature is concrete. There is no spirit in general as there is a consciousness in general. Spirituality exists as some actual totality informed by an idea which has come to shape in time and place. This totality demands obedience and loyalty of its members; obligations emerge in the life of one committed to a spiritual whole. But this means that members of one spiritual totality are potentially enemies of members of other units. Though many overlap, so one can at the same time be a Christian, an American, and a Capitalist (*pace* Kierkegaard!), often they exclude each other (and even these can conflict). Then loyalty to one is apt to erupt into hostility to the others. Especially is this the case where the spiritual whole organizes the vital interests of existence into political unities the integrity of which are taken to depend upon supremacy over or unrelenting competion with other totalities. Also, where spiritual wholes lay claim to finality and ultimacy, as religious groups have often done, conflict of a fanatical kind may emerge.

Thus, membership in spiritual wholes, for all its civilizing and form-giving functions, its provision of an area of communication and mutuality, can keep men from communicating with each other. If there were no level at which men could transcend this situation, conflict would be the final word in human relations. But there are possibilities of transcending: there is the stage of Existenz.

In the light of our analysis we can see how subjectivity is an encompassing. It is a structure of many perspectives and levels, each of which is itself an encompassing horizon of thought and action. It can never be possessed as a whole; each perspective is capable of indefinite further development.

The same can be said about the encompassing of objectivity. Although we interpret the object with which we are engaged through concepts on the various levels of subjectivity, we do not create the object. We encounter it. There is a given element about it. In all cases, even the universals of consciousness in general, our concepts refer beyond us.[60] The name we give to the totality of being as it appears to a subject is "world."

Jaspers is more exacting in his description of subjectivity than of world. There he distinguishes carefully between the modes; he does not just put them all together and call it "self." But in the notion of world he lumps all the forms of immanent objectivity together and thus raises some confusion. Are there, for example, different worlds which are objects for existence, spirit, consciousness in general, or is there only one world? And if only one, to which mode of consciousness is it the object-correlate?—for there can be no object without a subject. Finally, I myself can be considered as an entity in the "world" as well as other kinds of object.[61] In spite of these difficulties, certain features of world emerge.

[60] RE *59–60; VdW 81ff.*   [61] Philosophie, *pp. 55, 57–65; VdW 87ff.*

First, world is an encompassing. As such it is a background of potentiality
against which we know and interact with objects. It is always subject
to further interpretation. Consequently no view of the world as such
or as a whole is possible.[62] Only partial organizations of the world
are carved out of the encompassing background.[63] Applied to science
this means that scientific conceptions of the world are never so unified
and complete that we can claim to have a finally true model of it.
Upon inspection any claim to have such a model turns out to absolutize some historically developed theory into an absolute.

Not only is the world an encompassing, it has dimensions which correspond
to the modes of subjectivity. There is the world of ordinary everyday
projects—the world of gross objects of perception which are interpreted by the person involved with them in terms of his intentional
concerns. There is the world of abstract understanding, as represented in the objective categories of the sciences. Finally there is a
world of intentional spiritual meanings.

Investigation of any of these realms shows unique features which exist only
at that level and are lost in a reductionist attempt to bring them all
under one model. Even at the level of science the world seems to
break into four discontinuous realms: inorganic matter, organism, consciousness, and mind.[64] Complete system can be introduced only by
means of a self-closing world view which it can occur to anyone to
accept only if the process of transcending is stopped.[65]

Philosophical thought about the world Jaspers calls world-orientation. Its
aim is not to produce any new knowledge of the world, or to decide
between scientific theories; only the sciences can do that. Instead,
it seeks to discover the limits of world-objectifying thought—not the
temporary limits from which any knowledge suffers, but which will
ultimately be transcended as research continues, but what Jaspers
calls limits in principle "on which investigation stops, but the possibility of philosophical transcending emerges."[66] The chief results
of world-orientation are the disclosure of the world as being-as-
appearance and of thought as a human enterprise whose function is
orientation by constructing interpretations for human purposes rather
than final replicas of the world.

When one reaches this perspective one can see the meaning of myths such
as creation, which have as their purpose not to theorize about causes
of processes in nature, but to express the existential nonfinality and
non-self-sufficiency of the world.[67] Neither the whole of being nor
nothing,[68] world is appearance, and, to Existenz may become a symbol
or cipher of Being itself.[69]

Once one acquires a standpoint from which to view the world and such
attempts to know it as science, one can acknowledge their power
without falling victim to them. More than any of the other existen-

[62] What Jasper calls a "Weltall."   VdW 85f; Philosophie, pp. 68ff.
[63] What Jaspers calls a "Weltbild."   VdW 91; Philosophie, pp. 68ff.
[64] VdW 98.   [65] Philosophie, pp. 182–202.   [66] Philosophie, p. 39.
[67] RE 71; VdW 93.   [68] VdW 86.   [69] Ibid., p. 90.

tialists—with the possible exception of Merleau-Ponty—Jaspers insists that philosophizing must never lose relation to the sciences. It is no accident that the great philosophers of the past have been masters of one or more sciences. Jaspers may put science "in its place," but its place is an important one: the condition upon which serious philosophy can occur.

Science is not an alienating, fracturing, dehumanizing force. It is a means of orientation by which men construct interpretations of the world. Science is thus a method chosen for certain purposes and must be able to pursue them without hindrance from external objection. But neither can it be isolated from its function in human life. What is alienating, fracturing, and dehumanizing is the philosophical position which limits reality to what appears in the forms of scientific understanding. Such a philosophy not only loads science with a burden it was never designed to have, but it fails utterly to see that the apprehension of being is an endless task of trying to think through and relate all the modes of the encompassing.

World thus is an encompassing goal which can be approached from many possible perspectives, but refuses to yield peacefully to any one or any combination. It is as though by its recalcitrance to and transcendence over every objectification the world were giving testimony of an elusive and transcendent being.

3. Existenz

Although each mode of the encompassing of subjectivity is an indefinite horizon, if I consider myself only in these three modes, I experience dissatisfaction and despair, for none of them touches what I really am in the depths of my being.[70] As existence I am present in the world as body, character, past, action—Jaspers calls them aspects of myself[71]—which do not in themselves form a totality or have any meaning.[72] They must be given a meaning by a decision which transcends them and organizes them together as the expression of a self. Only then does existence take on substance and become a place of self-realization rather than an empty desert of desire and satisfaction. Although the self must enter the world in terms of character, body, and action or remain mere possibility, it cannot be nailed down to them. Selfhood supervenes upon these elements and transforms them.

As consciousness in general I am a unity of apperception: an *Ich-überhaupt*.[73] I am replaceable by any other person and am not engaged in my unique selfhood. If not given a center and orientation, consciousness in general disintegrates into an endless series of abstract correctnesses with no relevance to life. Similarly spirit touches my being only as a member of a totality structured by an idea. Where spirit is taken as the highest mode of selfhood, totalitarian modes of thought emerge which reduce the person to his being an instance of an idea

---

70 *Philosophie, p. 324.*   71 *Ibid., pp. 317ff.*   72 *RE 85–87; Philosophie, p. 22.*
73 *Philosophie, p. 316; VdW 79.*

and allow him no authentic self-expression as an individual. (Not only Marxist nations do this; Jaspers sees as one of the great problems of the technological perfection of the West its reduction of the individual to a conforming function in a world dominated by the abstract processes of the machine.)

Beyond all these modes is the authentic mode of selfhood: Existenz. This is my being considered "in itself." As such it is a self which can never become an object of investigation. Nor can it be simply there as a subject, for as concrete subject I am always there as existence, spirit, or consciousness. It is rather an origin, a completely different level of selfhood, where one must speak of freedom and decision rather than objectivity.[74] It is selfhood in the mode of transcending. Therefore it is the self, not as it is at any time and place, but as it can be and ought to be, and must decide its being.[75] It is selfhood as encompassing in its absolutely irreplaceable uniqueness: that which gives ground and meaning to the other modes:

It is not, as are existence, consciousness, spirit, something which could be replaced; as if everything were a playing by means of roles and masks, in which no one really performed; as if to the question: who am I? even at the end the answer must still be wanting because nothing is really behind the roles. Rather is Existenz the self which is unrepresentable in intuition, in which I am one with myself, behind all my roles, a self which supports and carries these roles.[76]

Existenz must be conceived as a process of self-reflection and self-determination. In this the existentialists are unanimous. Consciousness is usually quite unselfconscious in its preoccupation with its objects. When it rises to reflective awareness of itself as Existenz it breaks through the circle of subject and object and comes to an inner awareness of its own irreplaceable individuality. Not an object of knowledge, Existenz is a possibility. Not given as an empirical object, it can only be enacted and then not once for all, but perpetually through choice, decision, and action. It is not so much an entity as it is a quality of subjectivity at the other levels. Certainly it must find expression there; but its essence remains a transcendence over these expressions.

Jaspers tries to bridge the paradox of the absolute individuality of Existenz and the fact that philosophical illumination of it involves conceptual thought in universals with his theory of signa: symbols by which Existenz is brought from the level of inarticulate feeling to conceptual clearness. In the concept of the signum we meet again the idea of transcending thought. Concepts can be used in two ways. One is to take them literally as determining and describing objects of experience. Thus we can know man as existence, spirit, and consciousness. The other is to treat concepts as self-overcoming pointers to something which can never be an object. This transcending type of thought does not end in a complete description of an existential reality, but only throws up the sketch of a possibility for choice to the

---

[74] Philosophie, p. 13.   [75] Ibid., pp. 13, 295; VdW 76ff.   [76] VdW 83.

other (and even to oneself).[77]   The very idea of an illumination of Existenz is communicative in its constitution.   I must think in such a way as always to represent Existenz as a possibility which I then appropriate or fail to appropriate.   Such thinking is a practical matter of inner action rather than a detached one of speculation or objective description:

When I understand myself in these thoughts as one who thinks his own possibility, I appropriate the thoughts in a nontransmissible way; and without such appropriation, Existenz-illuminating thoughts, being reduced to generalities, have no meaning; they remain ununderstandable.[78]

A *signum* of Existenz is thus a universal concept used in a way to call attention to freedom, possibility, the ineluctable individual and personal by putting forth a representation of it which is potentially general.[79]   Both universality and individuality are necessary for the *signa* to work, and there is always the danger of falling into one or the other of the two sides exclusively: "the one untrue (the merely general), the other impossible (speechless Existenz)."[80]   The preservation of the tension in the *signum* is essential; it enables the universal to be used so as to constitute an existential communication to the individual of a schema of Existenz in order to awaken him to an awareness of his own depth:

The illumination of Existenz speaks . . . of many selves as Existenzen.   It cannot mean this, for the many are not exemplars of a universal. . . .   It speaks of communication and means my communication; it means in a similar way my freedom, my historical consciousness, my boundary-situations, and yet can speak of them only as universal.[81]

It is obvious that for the illumination of Existenz thus conceived there can be no objective criteria of truth.   Indeed Jaspers says quite bluntly: "Existenz makes no claim to universal validity."[82]   It cannot be proved to one who questions it that the human person is more than the three immanent modes.   Furthermore, as we saw, one cannot demonstrate that thought must transcend.   Hence, the level of Existenz is proved only by its being lived.[83]   Where it occurs it insists upon itself.   But each Existenz is unique, unrepeatable, irreplaceable. Consequently, there is no guarantee that even at the level of Existenz the conceptual clarification which will prove true for one Existenz will also hold for another.   In fact, in his metaphysics Jaspers asserts that the truth of a symbol derives from its power of illuminating Existenz and securing an awareness of being as transcendence in individual, unique cases.[84]   No limit can be set to the ways being is able to appear in time.   Similarly, Existenz cannot be hemmed in by definitive descriptions.

If there is no proof, no objectivity, there is left only appeal.   All philosophy can do is to chart out the quality of life meant by Existenz as experienced by one person.   I can speak out of Existenz, give expression to

77 Philosophie, p. 302.   78 Idem.   79 Ibid., p. 303.   80 Idem.
81 Ibid., p. 308.   82 Ibid., p. 310.   83 Ibid., pp. 302, 312ff.
84 Ibid., pp. 689, 703, 790, 802.

it in *signa*, and "insofar as another hears me, then both Existenzen exist for each other; but this being-for-each-other is not a matter of knowledge."[85] It is a matter of "the single one speaking to the single one."[86] Consequently there can be no ontology of human existence in a Heideggerian or Sartrean sense. Such attempts either merely succeed in taking one possible expression of Existenz and identifying it with Existenz directly or they make it into a universal structure of which the concrete person is regarded as an instance.[87]

Two dominant *signa* of Existenz are freedom and historicity. Freedom is the name for Existenz in its power of self-determination. It rests upon the fact that the individual transcends the world, including his own immanent modes of being, which are merely raw materials of himself. Hence, one can say that even the attack upon freedom is an act of freedom. Only a being who transcends his situation can raise a question about its meaning. Therefore, "either freedom does not exist at all or it exists in the very questioning of it."[88]

Consequently the old arguments for and against freedom are futile. Both determinists and indeterminists have erred in the way they formulated the problem, for both made the will into an object whose properties can be investigated like those of any empirical object. One party claims to connect it with other events in an endless chain of causation. The other finds it an entity which is its own beginning. Will, however, is not an entity: it is the self as a transcending, self-forming power which supervenes upon the various elements of life. Hence, it is a mode of self-consciousness, "in which I do not observe myself from the outside as spectator, but in which I actively relate myself to myself."[89] More than just a selection of means or even ends, free will is the willing of oneself in an historical situation.[90]

To discuss freedom is not to try to demonstrate it, but, as Kant saw, to defend it. Because it transcends the realm of causal explanation it is incomprehensible at that level, and if one wills to stay at that level, of course nothing more can be said. Freedom exists only in the act of transcendence where the self enacts its own being and thus it can be grasped only in the act of transcending thought. This understanding is not mere observation or contemplation, but a matter of self-constitution. Therefore freedom is never apprehended with detachment as a thing, but through feelings of responsibility and obligation. It is related to and bound up with knowledge and law; but ultimately it is the resolution of the individual to act in the world which results in the eruption of a reality beyond knowledge, idea, law, motives, and causal forces. As such, freedom is the apprehension of the individual as the source of his own being and as responsible for it as he actualizes it in concrete situations. "Insofar as I choose, I am; if I am not, I do not choose."[91]

Consequently freedom is experienced as anxiety and occasions an attempt to flee. I apprehend myself as responsible for myself, able to push

85 Ibid., p. 313.   86 Ibid., p. 27.   87 Ibid., p. 10.   88 Ibid., p. 445.
89 Ibid., p. 425.   90 Ibid., p. 430.   91 Ibid., p. 451.

this responsibility off onto no one else. I shudder before the possibility I confront and am tempted not to actualize myself, but to stay at the level of possibilities where I do not have to stick out my neck. But even this is a choice: I decide not to decide my own being, but to have it decided for me by others, by the pressure of events and circumstances, by my own inclinations.

Finally, freedom is situational. There is no absolute freedom. It is a spontaneous, creative power of self-determination. Therefore it requires necessity. No one can make a choice in a vacuum: if there is nothing given to freedom it is a phantom.[92] But though it can occur only in specific situations it is freedom which determines the meaning of the situations by organizing the elements in them. In this sense, nature and our own motives are the material for our free wills.

Because Existenz must enter into the world in its various modes in order to actualize itself, historicity is an important *signum*. Existenz is historical in its very roots. Freedom is possible only for an historical being. Neither the events of the world nor Transcendence has freedom. Being as such is what it is eternally. Natural phenomena are temporal, but not historical. This means that history is the structure of Existenz, not something which just happens to it.

Jaspers uses two terms to indicate what we in English must designate by the single term "history." In one sense history means the knowledge of objective events in the past. This historical consciousness is one of the manifestations of consciousness in general. In the other meaning, historical consciousness is the self aware of its own being as an enduring self-determining agent. By appropriating the events of objective history within the context of his choices, Existenz turns them into its past and binds them together into a meaningful flow toward an envisaged future. It is this existential historicity which provides whatever reason there is for engaging in objective history.

It is also this kind of history which is involved when Jaspers claims that truth is historical and hence that there can be no universal truth or adequate representation of being in time. It is not simply that truth occurs in time; this is a truism, albeit still the source of most relativistic theories. It is that truth is historical—that is, it occurs in the historical projects of Existenz and must be relevant to them. And since these are the acts of self-creation of unique and irreplaceable persons, truth is fractured in the world through its historical occurrences.

Jaspers delineates historicity as a *signum* of Existenz. First, it is a unity of existence and Existenz.[93] In this unity the features of life as existence acquire a depth and organization. They are not just there, but seized upon, appropriated, and integrated into an historical constellation and directed to a purpose. The interests and struggles and drives of mere existence take on the role of expression: they are made to

92 Ibid., p. 461.   93 Ibid., pp. 400f.

subserve and be parts of a quality of life which supervenes upon them. Thus they acquire meaning.

This deepening of mere existence by being organized within Existenz by appropriation and choice produces constellations which are both absolute and relative. They are relative because bound to materials available at a given time and place. Not all things are possible or desirable at all times. But they are absolute in the sense that they are created by Existenz in its freedom and they thus constitute an historical form which gives significance to life. Historical life is thus a tensional unity of empirical material and existential form. The elements organized into Existenz threaten to break away and pulverize life. And the form can maim the elements instead of organizing them meaningfully—which is what happens every time it becomes wooden and unyielding: that is, when one loses a sense of its historicity.

Second, says Jaspers, historicity is the unity of necessity and freedom. Necessity is the element of givenness, the basis of life. Freedom is the capacity for spontaneous organization of this material in the interest of a supervening quality. Since the latter is never contained in the elements, freedom is secure. But since I never begin at a radical beginning, but always act within a situation which has come to me from a past, even past decisions, necessity is there. Existenz apprehends the historical situation as a given field of action with room for choice, not as states of affairs determined by their elements. But again there is tension. Freedom can try to cut off necessity and in the process it becomes arbitrariness, meaningless randomness. Necessity can threaten to engulf the self as determined product and one loses spontaneity.

In addition historicity is a unity of time and eternity. When Jaspers first introduces the notion of Existenz he speaks about it in language which relates it to eternity.[94] By being brought into an existential quality of life which transcends it, what otherwise would be just another abstract length of time achieves significance beyond itself. It acquires, so to speak, eternity. By this is meant not timelessness nor even an endless series of moments (which would be meaningless), but a fulfilled moment, which is at once a temporal instant and the determination of the meaning of past and future.[95]

Finally historicity is continuity: what Kierkegaard called repetition. Historical man is one who knows his past and communicates with it, builds upon it, and is open to the possibilities which it contains for development and choice. Historical realization is thus a matter of decision in the light of the past. Without continuity there is no meaning. With it, time is fulfilled and Existenz is nourished into a meaningful whole. It is because in the present technological mass society men lack any sense of historical continuity that they can be the easy victims of mass propaganda. A man who knows who he is, that he stands where he is because of the labor of others, and is aware of the price paid is much more invulnerable to propaganda.

[94] VdW 83; Philosophie, p. 14.   [95] Philosophie, p. 404.

Historicity as elucidated in these structures takes on concreteness as the quality of personal life in fidelity or loyalty.[96]   Loyalty is the relationship one has to the past when it is seen as his past, when it is appropriated as the source of his being.   Ahistorical man on the level of mere existence has no loyalties; he is therefore a victim of his present motives and can be exploited by manipulating them, as we have just seen.   A man with fidelity to historical realities can transcend these motives.   In loyalty he loves and takes over his past as the substance of his own being: desertion of it would be desertion and betrayal of self.   Objects of loyalty are: parents, one's childhood, youth, country, home, culture.   These give the ground and basis for action and meaningful choice; even changing them can be a kind of loyalty to them and must be if change is to constitute progress.

Historicity is subject to corruptions and distortions, just because it is an inner awareness, unavailable to consciousness in general.

The world and character of the individual man are neither given nor do they correctly develop according to premeditated plan, but are realized in tension, doing step by step that which I cannot absolutely hold as correct, but which I grasp out of a feeling of my rootedness in my historical situation as my responsibility.[97]

In historical Existenz we are constantly tempted to seek refuge in the constant and the permanent and thus lose ourselves.   We try to find some secure authority: a church, a state, a philosophical doctrine, and fail to see that we have absolutized some historical particular thing.   Or, says Jaspers, we seek to absolutize ourselves: to pursue Existenz without existence.   The requisite conditions of a meaningful life are rejected and one tries to found Existenz on no existential basis.   He may even take up existentialist philosophy and live in its categories rather than becoming a self in the world.   But this way, too, is self-defeating: one can become man only by active participation in the worldly structures of historical life.

4. Communication

The development of Existenz as freedom and responsibility involves the relation of self to self which Jaspers calls communication.   More than any other existentialist he makes it a central theme in his philosophy:

To be a self and to be in the truth are nothing other than unconditionally to be in communication.   Here in the depths any attempt to preserve oneself is to lose oneself.   For Existenz is only accessible to itself and real where it comes to itself with the other Existenz, through it and with it.[98]

Jaspers develops at length the idea that knowledge itself is a kind of communication in that it is bound to the conditions and limits of communicability.[99]   At first consideration it seems that the relation between knowledge and communication is external: that knowledge is something in itself which we later find we can communicate.   Such a

[96] Ibid., p. 412.   [97] Ibid., p. 416.   [98] VdW 377.   [99] Ibid., p. 387.

view is an abstraction.   Knowledge is produced by existing men; it is, as Jaspers says, an encompassing domain[100] in which areas are progressively marked out by the struggling activity of men in communication with each other.   The necessities of communication serve as constituting agents in knowledge: the incommunicable is ruled out of the domain of knowledge.   Finally Jaspers points out that knowledge is possible only in a situation of openness and will to communicate. Where this does not obtain one has a state of "will against will" which corrupts the whole process of knowledge and subordinates it to personal or group interests and desires.[101]

Truth as a philosophical idea is also tied to communication.   Not only does Jaspers replace the traditional theories of truth with one which asserts that truth is that which founds and furthers communication, but the achievement of truth is a communicative process.[102]   Truth makes no sense except in relation to falsehood; where truth exists falsehood could have.[103]   The process by which falsehood is supplanted with truth in human experience is communication.

Finally, even morality is bound up with communication.   Jaspers points out that for Kant and Fichte the moral law is universal and necessary: lying, for example, can never be morally justified.   But such a position is impossible.   "There is no universal law in isolation from the communication of man to man."[104]   Such a law would be one which treated men as instances of a genus.   But there is no such thing; man is defined by his historical freedom and communication.   Therefore, "presupposition of the law is mutuality in communication."[105]   Since communication has a manifold structure according to the level of subjectivity upon which it occurs, there is demanded in each mode a kind of truth appropriate to it, "from the rules of the game of existence to the revealing of Existenz."[106]   Finally, says Jaspers:

If I should obey at all times the general universal law, I would betray communication, because I would look upon my fellowman as man in general, . . . and act toward him in this manner.   I would not stand in a real, historical, open relation to him under factual and unavoidable presuppositions.[107]

Communication occurs on all levels of the encompassing of subjectivity, and takes a different form on each.   At the level of existence men communicate from within the drives and interest of that level, seeking fulfilments and satisfactions.   Gradually standardized ways of thinking, feeling, and acting emerge.[108]   But there is tension, too, for the individual's interests can conflict with the community's.   So communication takes on the form of bargaining, haggling, compromise— and sometimes open hostility.[109]   There is communication in the realm of consciousness in general with its logical structure and rational methodology.   Also there is the communication which occurs

---

[100] *The second part of VdW is called "The Encompassing of Knowledge."*
[101] VdW 320.   [102] VdW 475.   [103] Ibid., p. 484.   [104] Idem.   [105] Idem.
[106] Idem.   [107] Idem.   [108] Philosophie, p. 339.
[109] RE 81ff.   Cf. VdW 579; RE 152.

out of a common participation in an idea: spiritual communication in which the individual finds root and substance. Yet none of these levels suffices. Made into an ultimate, each has a way of breaking limits and usurping the others. Even spiritual communion finds its limits in the free individual, who, though he must be rooted in a community, transcends it.

There is finally the communication between Existenzen. Paradoxically it is this level, which is the communication of the single one with the single one, which for Jaspers provides the ground of the possibility of universal communication between men. The other levels unite but also separate. Members of spiritual wholes are unable to commune with members of other ones if transcendence over spirit is not preserved. It is only free men, at once tied to particular arrangements of existence and spirit and transcending them as Existenzen who form a universal community, and can communicate simply as men. Yet it is a most peculiar kind of community. For one thing, it is not actual, but only possible. For another, membership in it is not on the basis of an idea, but of freedom. And third, it does not have duration and stability, but exists only in fleeting moments when two selves meet each other beyond all conditional concerns. Hence it is not to be forced or produced at will by objective techniques; and its actual accomplishment is restricted to a few face-to-face relationships.[110]

Jaspers characterizes existential communication under several headings which stress its dynamic, dialectical nature: solitude and union, self-revelation and self-realization, loving struggle, communication and content, process, love. Chief among its features is that it is a process in which the participants become what they are as they meet and confront each other in their historical situation. Each self is unique and irreplaceable, not an instance of a universal. The communication therefore is not the transmission of something already in existence, but a bringing of the self into being.[111] Outside the communicative situation there is no self: selfhood comes into being in the give and take of human meeting.

Such a communication is an interplay of solitude and union. Union alone produces only the joiner, the social self which is never quite an individual, a little too much like everyone else, and hence with nothing to communicate to the other. Solitude, which does not dare to go out to the other, produces only the isolation of a "torpid, empty I."[112] Only the one who knows solititude and has individual color can make fruitful contact with the other. But this contact also helps constitute him as an individual. Such a relationship is a risk; one opens himself to the other. Hence, only in a context of absolute confidence and trust can this kind of mutuality occur. Since all the subtle masks by which we hide ourselves from each other (and from ourselves) must drop away, love is the only framework in which existential communication can prosper.[113] In love the individual confronts and affirms the other individual in his uniqueness across wide variations in condition

110 *Philosophie*, p. 346.   111 Ibid., p. 350.   112 Ibid., p. 348.   113 Ibid., p. 355.

of existence, mind, and spirit.   Only love permits each to remain
himself in communication with another.   Hence the process of communication is a loving struggle.   The end is not victory over the other
but mutual selfhood.   Therefore, there can be no reservations or
secret weapons.   "All cards," says Jaspers, "must be shown."[114]

Such a communication is never finished.   It is a process as selfhood itself
is a process.   It must occur in and through the relations of men to
each other as consciousness, existence, and spirit.   It is the depth
and meaning of these relationships, yet it transcends them.   Hence
it is a desideratum.   Results in the form of achievements on which
one is tempted to rest have a way of hardening into burdens which
suppress selfhood rather than continuing as vehicles of communication.   Nor can its course be planned beforehand.   Mutuality of two
selves is a concrete coming together which has ways of going off
into new and unexpected areas.   It lives by adjustments, modifica-
tions, conflicts, syntheses, and agreements which cannot be foreseen
by the most circumspect planning.

Even so, in the momentary occurrences of it in which Existenz leaps up one
realizes that this is what human relationships should be.   It becomes
a standard by which one judges all else: economic and political institutions as well as truth itself.   How do they affect communication?
One apprehends communication existentially therefore, as one apprehends freedom, as an obligation.   One experiences its nonoccurrence
as guilt and the diminution of life.   And even though it must occur
between single ones in historically concrete situations, one realizes
that mankind forms a community of Existenz beyond all the structures which separate them and set them against each other.   Jaspers
ends with a paean to existential communication:

I and thou separated in existence, are one in Transcendence; there not
(subject to the contingencies of) meeting and failing to meet; here, however,
in the becoming of struggling communication which reveals and establishes
(its results) in danger.[115]

Because existential communication is a quality of life which must find
expression in the relations of men to each other in the world yet at
the same time transcends these expressions, it is a vulnerable phenomenon.   It is constantly under pressures which result in what Jaspers
calls a failure of communication and a breach of communication.[116]
Communication may fail because the interests which arise at the
immanent levels of subjectivity present too great an obstacle to
authentic communication.   Instead of being vehicles for it, they
thwart communication.   The demands of empirical existence may
create a gulf between men across which they cannot reach.   The
objective forms of consciousness in general can insulate men from
each other.   Empty silence rather than mutuality results.   But, says
Jaspers, the possibility is there for communication to emerge anew.

Much different is the phenomenon which he details as the severing or breach
of communication.   Here men cut off communication purposefully in

114 Ibid., p. 351.   115 Ibid., p. 356.   116 Ibid., pp. 358, 374.

the interest of something else.   It is not a matter of the mere failing of communication.   Hence there is guilt involved; there is a corruption of one's own selfhood in the breach.   Noncommunication here follows a break with and loss of oneself.[117]   Many things contribute to this breaking down of communication.   Since it is at all times a risk in which one must present himself to the other in openness, so that he has no defenses, anxiety over possible betrayal of oneself can lead one to cut short the communicative process.   One becomes unavailable to the other and unformed to oneself.   The inordinate ambitions of pride and the will to be what Kierkegaard called a world-historical individual lead one to refuse the demands of mutuality.[118]   In all cases Jaspers claims that where communication fails selfhood also fails.[119]

Communication must acquire concrete expression in the world, and thus it involves historicity.   It is not an ethereal relation between two minds.[120]   Hence Jaspers suggests certain "communicative situations" which are the affairs men have with each other in the world: social, political, economic relationships, and dependencies.[121]   They can become the media wherein men meet each other authentically. But they can also become areas for self-aggrandizement and victimization of the other.   They can become deserts in which the self is dispersed in the routines of the daily task.   Even in the mutuality of discussion one can hide behind theoretical proofs and objective ideas and never come into contact with the other.   On the other hand, discussion can be the place where authentic communication occurs:

Possible Existenz enters discussion in order to become clear about the meaning of his own believing and willing. Neither discussant knows upon entering discussion what he really means.   In their discussion they try to . . . obtain a clarity which can be had only in the form of principles articulated in the discussion.[122]

The end of such discussion is communication not of objective content, but as contact of selves.   This means that the participants do not try to convince each other of the truth of their position.   Since what is communicated is oneself in a process which is at the same time the emergence of oneself, truth here is the truth of each Existenz.   Universality would be uniformity.   Each Existenz has his own, but recognizes the truth of the other and values it as such; in communication with it he comes to clarity about his own truth.   Existential truth thus remains multiple and fractured, not universal.   Truth is a becoming-true in time.[123]   As in all existential illumination one must not interpret this remark as an objective theory about truth, but as an illuminative *signum* made from the situation of existential communication.

The most extreme form of existential communication, where men constitute themselves as unique persons beyond their more particular structures, is philosophy.   Philosophy is philosophizing, an endless discussion of free selves with each other.   It is a "sym-philosophizing" through which, in the medium of material content Existenzen touch and open

117 Ibid., p. 365.   118 Ibid., p. 373.   119 Ibid., p. 369.   120 Ibid., p. 374.
121 Ibid., pp. 374–386.   122 Ibid., p. 381.   123 Ibid., p. 387.   Vdw 869 passim.

themselves to each other.[124]   Philosophic truth is a function of this communication.

It is the truth with which I live and not only think, which I, being convinced of it, realize and not only know; of which I ever again convince myself by acting on it, and not only through thought-possibilities.[125]

Such truth can occur only in a dialog in which two authentic selves seek to clarify their being.   Therefore, the ultimate question, before which every other one pales is: What concepts are necessary in order for the deepest communication to become possible?[126]   For beyond all the structures of science and art, politics and self-interest, there remain men with whom I can communicate.

5. Transcendence

The culmination of Jaspers' philosophy is his concept of Transcendence. Philosophy, we saw, is the appropriation of being by means of thought. The thought all along was a transcending treatment of the objects and relationships which emerge in experience.   The end of transcending thinking is an awareness of being as Transcendence.   The attempt to articulate and give expression to this Transcendence systematically and conceptually Jaspers calls metaphysics.[127]

Transcendence is the expression for being in itself within the subject-object dichotomy.   It is the transcendent mode of objectivity just as Existenz is the transcendent mode of subjectivity.   Its description, as well as the term itself, attests to the ubiquity of the subject-object relation in Jaspers' thought.

Transcendence is complicated by the fact that it cannot be simply identified with being, which is always an encompassing.   One must view Transcendence in relation to Existenz in order to see how it can become a representation of being.   Thus, it is at once the mode of objectivity which transcends the world and the object to which Existenz is related. Within the subject-object dichotomy being can only be expressed as a relation between Existenz and Transcendence.   Being "is" Transcendence only for Existence,[128] and unless one transcends to the level of Existenz he cannot experience being as Transcendence.

In its attempt to make Transcendence palpable to Existenz and to communicate it to others, metaphysics proceeds in three ways.   First, Jaspers presents Transcendence as a transcendent mode of objectivity in relation to world.[129]   Second, as the limit of Existenz in existential relations to Transcendence;[130] and third as itself an object in the doctrine of the cipher.[131]   But to think of being at all is to dissimulate it into its various subjective and objective modes.   Consequently beyond all the positive lines of representing Transcendence Jaspers

---

[124] Philosophie, p. 392.   [125] Ibid., p. 396.   [126] Idem.   [127] Ibid., p. 28.
[128] Ibid., p. 42.   [129] Ibid. pp. 38f; bk. III, chap. 2, "Formal Transcending."
[130] Ibid., pp. 40f. bk. III, chap. 3, "Existential Relations to Transcendence."
[131] Ibid., p 29, bk. III, chap. 4, "Reading of Cipher-writing."

expresses the final transcendence of being in his doctrine of foundering.

Transcending thought in world-orientation makes the apparential character of the world developed in Section II yield something more than meaningless fragmentation. We saw in dealing with the world that it was an encompassing which never could be rounded out into a complete system. At best completeness remained an idea. In metaphysical thought the nonfulfilment of the project of world interpretation is taken as a sign of Transcendence. Being is never possessed; it is always sought. To the investigating subject who transcends his knowledge in his self-awareness, the visible islands of clarity which he achieves in that knowledge are seen against a background of Transcending being and thus made transparent. At the same time the failure of thought to complete the synthesis of being is taken by Existenz as revelation of being hovering beyond the network of the subject-object relationship. It is not just that we cannot complete the world. It is rather than the concepts we use lead to antinomies and absurdity when we try, and we are stranded in the labyrinths of our own concepts and cannot ultimately decided between being and nothing, unity and duality, or form and matter. Nor can we give complete determination to the series we call space, time, and causality.[132] It is as though we made contact with being in our very failure to grasp it. We realize in this moment of transcending through our categories to Transcendence that all our concepts are ways of relating subjects to objects in concrete situations. The relation of Jaspers here to Kant's doctrine of appearance and thing-in-itself is striking.[133]

By thinking through the antinomies, by trying to carry through the project of world-orientation, we are forced to the conclusion that "it is thinkable that the unthinkable exists."[134] Formal transcending allows us to take what for existence and consciousness in general are objects of intentional awareness as negative indicators for possible Existenz of Transcendence. Existentially the world has become transparent by being taken up in a new context of the nonobjective encounter of Existenz with Transcendence: it is seen to "hover like a ball" between the two.[135]

Transcendence emerges not only as the transcendent mode of the world. It also comes to realization in the illumination of Existenz as a proper object of Existenz: indeed as the only object in relation to which Existenz can be itself. Transcendence emerges as the condition for the possibility of Existenz. If Existenz did not have this relation to Transcendence it is questionable whether the fragmented and antinomial structure of our knowledge would be a symbol of Transcendence rather than of the absurdity of existence. The fragmentation of the world is merely the condition in which Existenz may awaken.[136] It does not imply it.

132 Ibid., pp. 711–728.
133 Cf. my article, "Kant's Concept of the Thing in Itself," Review of Metaphysics, vol. XVI, pp. 770–779, June, 1963.
134 Philosophie, p. 707.   135 VdW 145ff.   136 Philosophie, p. 723.

The idea is that in the freedom and historicity of Existenz one is both most authentically aware of himself and aware that one is not alone: one is given to oneself, sent to oneself in the world.[137] In one's own free action the self as Existenz comes to an awareness that if the world were all of being Existenz itself would be impossible. Although no cognitive account of this realization is possible, Existenz understands itself in relation to being as Transcendence.

This nonobjective, existential encounter occurs in what Jaspers styles the unconditioned character of Existenz. The chief phenomena involved in this are his concepts of the boundary-situation, absolute consciousness, and unconditioned action.

We have already seen that for Jaspers all thought and action goes on in a horizon. No matter how far I try to extend my knowledge I am always in a context which is the concrete arena in which I work out my interests and projects. This context Jaspers terms a situation.[138] Now, situations are not just neutrally apprehended by a person. They are taken as restrictions or as providing acting space. They augur well or ill, offer opportunity or obstacle.

For the most part situations are changeable. By changing my perspective I can alter my situation and also my prospects. I can look at things in a new light: I can, for example, bring the world of existence into relation to spirit and hence change the way I view my own drives, interests, and passions. Objects and goals which seemed valuable before may be questioned when brought into this new perspective.

One thing I cannot change: the fact that I am always in a situation. Living in a world and being in a situation are identical. Of course, I can naïvely be in a situation without realizing it. Only when my being-in-a-situation comes to conscious awareness does it become a boundary-situation. Thus to exist on the level of Existenz and to experience boundary-situations are identical.[139] This experience of being always in a situation is a limit, a wall against which I collide. I come to see myself in my determinateness as one who must do or refrain in just these circumstances, and also to see that they are not complete enough ever to justify my actions objectively. In such a situation I grasp my freedom, my limit, my unjustifiability. And I see that either there is Transcendence or all is absurdity.[140] We can call this boundary-situation contingency.

Boundary-situations, like all existential references, are not objectively demonstrable. They must be lived through. When this happens one recognizes them to be bound up with one's very being as Existenz. To him they are objective in the sense of being inescapable situations which give life its existential quality and enable one to encounter Transcendence. But this happens only when one accepts and appropriates them and does not try constantly to escape their poignancy by objectifying them.

---

[137] Ibid., pp. 333, 733ff.   [138] Ibid., pp. 467f.   [139] Ibid., p. 469.   [140] Ibid., p. 473.

Besides the general situation of contingency there are specific boundary-situations in which the very meaning of Existenz is put in question. They are: death, suffering, conflict, and guilt. Death, when appropriated existentially as my death or experienced as the death of one with whom I have been in communication, rather than just as an objective event which happens to people, raises the question about the significance of life and the destiny of personal existence. Death points up the finitude of our being. And this finitude occasions decision: We do not have an infinity of chances or an infinity of time to utilize them. We can irretrieveably lose ourselves and die without ever having lived. In the light of an honest appropriation of death rather than self-deceiving attempts to flee it we are stimulated to sort out the important from the trivial and to decide between them.

Consequently death is a limit or boundary to Existenz. As the nonfulfilment of our attempts to unify the world through knowledge forces us to transcend to personal Existenz, the experience of the boundary of death forces us to admit the nonfulfilment of Existenz in the world and to transcend or despair. Thus we are brought to a brink: we must decide how to take it, what to do in the face of a death which points up the fact that we must give our lives meaning and quality, that it is not written objectively in the scheme of things. Death presents a challenge to living: we are called upon in its presence to determine how we shall live considering that we are to die. Yet death is a threat as well as a challenge; hence our decision is in the face of that which possibly negates all meaning. In reaction to death I may fail to bring about the actualization of myself as Existenz. I may instead dissipate my life in redoubled efforts to cover up death and secure my life in the world. Or I can, transcending, recognize myself as transcendent to my own empirical modes and thus in relation to Transcendence which gives life a meaning beyond its immanent structures. It is freedom which comes to the fore in the face of death.

Similarly conflict, suffering, and guilt function as boundary-situations where Existenz is brought to an awareness of its being in situations which limit and reveal the precariousness of life in the world. Suffering reveals the inability to achieve finality in temporal extension. Even Aristotle, whose ethics were based upon happiness, realized that in a real sense no man could be called happy until he was dead. Conflict shows that communication may never quite succeed, that there at least is no objective guarantee in the nature of things that it will succeed in overcoming the hostilities between men which arise on the levels of existence and spirit. They are in competition for the goods of life and they belong to different spiritual totalities. Thus conflict raises the question of authentic communication and the place where it occurs. And finally, argues Jaspers, one must admit guilt as a feature of Existenz. Not only do our actions have unintended consequences (because our knowledge is an encompassing which is never complete), but in existence we are never without corrupting even the purest motives with what Kant called considerations of the "dear self."

The net effect of the boundary-situations is to bring us to the realization of the "questionable character of our existence."[141] We are aware that our footing has been lost in the world, and that any answer must come from beyond the boundary. I may try to escape the boundary-situations by assuming an aesthetic attitude (in Kierkegaard's sense) toward existence, but this itself is a choice not necessitated by the situation. It is a decision to exist in a certain way in the light of it. But, for Jaspers, it is a self-defeating way, something akin to the ever deepening compulsions of neurotic behavior.

Beyond the boundary ultimately means in absolute consciousness and unconditioned action. Absolute consciousness, says Jaspers,

is the most comprehensive signum for the consciousness of Existenz. In it as the consciousness of authentic being out of an unconditioned source, I find support and satisfaction while as empirical existence I am without support and searching; I find rest for the restlessness of existence; reconciliation for the strife and tension; decisive answers to authentic questions.[142]

Absolute consciousness is a sense of fullness of feeling, of peace beyond all the clamorings of existence. Having experienced the boundary-situations, where the impossibility of support in finitude is existentially realized, Existenz in absolute consciousness lays hold of unconditioned being, in a sense of the presence and eternity of being. It is an attitude which can never be an object of investigation. These all exist for consciousness in general. Transcendence is an object only for absolute consciousness. Certainty, rest, fulfilment are its hallmarks. Without it all else is empty; with it there is certainty of the presence of being beyond its worldly articulations. Thus the manifestations of absolute consciousness must be called "nonknowledge" (a state of mind which experiences a depth of being in the fracturing of all positive knowledge), vertigo and shudder (where the apparential character of existence is open to the certainty of transcendent being), existential anxiety (by which freedom experiences itself beyond all objectivity in relation to being in responsibility which at the basis of existence appears as nothingness), and finally conscience (which is the voice of my own authentic self when it is aware of its freedom and responsibility, i.e., its relation to Transcendence).[143]

Absolute consciousness is thus individual consciousness at the level of Existenz, with its own commitments, choices, and the necessity of its own action. It can never be reduced to law or universality. It transcends them as it secures a relation to Transcendence in historically determinate form. Thus, its fulfilment takes place in love and faith and fantasy.[144] Love is the relationship of one individual to another in their modes of transcendence. I love a person (or thing) not when I represent him as only a possible ally or obstacle, as something to be manipulated, but when I see him as open to Transcendence. Likewise, faith and fantasy are modes of absolute consciousness because in them a relation to being is expressed beyond the expectations and

141 Ibid., pp. 508f.   142 Ibid., p. 515.   143 Ibid., pp. 518f, 521, 522f, 534ff.
144 Ibid., pp. 531ff.

assurances of immanent consciousness. By their means one is aware of being as Transcendence and should all worldly being collapse, it is not the end: there is still being beyond any of its modes, clung to in faith, represented in creative fantasy.

It is not surprising that absolute consciousness, by which Existenz grasps authentic being in high moments of awareness, eventuates in unconditional action in the world, beyond all finite purposes and rules.[145] From the standpoint of absolute consciousness all these are limited. Purpose founders on the realization of the noncompletion of all purposing in the finite world, on death and the other boundary-situations. If life has a purpose, it must be given it by a free constituting choice. The establishment of an existentially valid purpose is an unconditioned action, necessitated by and justified by no objective considerations.

Laws and rules cannot specify any ultimate purposes, for they are for the most part limited to specific situations.[146] Where the law transcends them, as in the categorical imperative, it presents itself as the formative principle of Existenz. Thus all the moral law can do is to clarify Existenz. It cannot justify it. And since each Existenz is unique, it can specify no universal which is normative for Existenz as such. Even if one should interpret it as doing so, still moral action (existential action) is unconditioned in the sense that it is action beyond any finite formulation. The only justification for it is that Existenz chooses it as the structure of its own being.[147] Hence it is relative to the individual Existenz, and is not authoritative for others. But it is absolute also, for unconditioned action is the choice by which Existenz determines itself in the presence of Transcendence.

In the concept of unconditioned action we have Jaspers' counterpart to Kierkegaard's suspension of the ethical. In both cases the ethical (universal) is suspended, not in the interest of empirical existence, but of Existenz. Of course, there is no public, objective way to tell them apart. Hence, from the point of view of objective consciousness unconditioned action looks like sheer arbitrariness. Especially so when the necessity to preserve the integrity of Existenz leads not only to an awareness of its nonfulfilment in existence, but to the renunciation of existence, either symbolically in religious action or actually in suicide.[148] But considered from the point of view of Existenz both can be "heroes of the negative" and express the essential relatedness to Transcendence. The voluntary death of Socrates symbolizes the nonaccomplishment of Existenz in existence and the necessity for unconditioned action. But if there is no Transcendence, then unconditioned action is identical with insanity.

In the concepts of boundary-situation, absolute consciousness, and unconditioned action, Jaspers tries to show that Existenz and Transcendence belong together. Though I am free, responsible, transcendent to my elements, I still am not through myself alone. I am given to myself, and in that situation am responsible, under obligation to become

145 Ibid., bk. III, chap. 9.   146 Ibid., p. 578.   147 Ibid., pp. 548, 578.
148 Philosophie, pp. 552ff, 564ff.

myself. This rootedness in being and uniqueness of Existenz gives
rise to dynamic attitudes and postures which Jaspers calls "Existential
Relations to Transcendence."[149]   They are dialectical relations where
Existenz asserts itself, yet comes back to relate itself to Transcen-
dence. The very names suggest this dialectical quality: Defiance and
Surrender,[150] Descent and Ascent,[151] The Law of the Day and the
Passion of the Night,[152] and the Opulence of the Many and the One.[153]
In each set of polarities the singleness, uniqueness, and freedom of
Existenz (defiance, descent, night, many) and the oneness of Tran-
scendence (surrender, ascent, day, one) work themselves out in a
subject-object relationship which reveals concretely the rootedness of
Existenz in Transcendence, yet its accomplishments only in decisive
individual action.

The final note in Jaspers' metaphysics is the doctrine of ciphers and the
idea of foundering.

Although being as Transcendence is hidden and available only to Existenz
in its depth, it must take on objective form: "Being is for us only in
so far as it comes to articulation in Existenz. A pure other-world is
empty and as good as nothing."[154] It becomes materialized, so to
speak, as men in their various cultures at various times endeavor to
represent it to themselves and communicate it to others in ways that
give specific meaning to their situations.[155] This objectification of
that which can only be touched nonobjectively by Existenz produces
symbols of Transcendence or what Jaspers calls ciphers: "the being
which brings Transcendence to presence without making it into being
as subject or being as object."[156] The doctrine of the ciphers manifests in an excellent way Jaspers' concepts of the historicity of truth
and its consequent absoluteness and relativity.

Since a cipher is a symbol of Transcendence in worldly forms and structures Jaspers carefully distinguishes it from a sign. A sign stands for
something which can itself be an object of awareness in a nonsym-
bolic way. Hence one can compare the sign with the object signified
to decide whether the sign is a good sign, is ambiguous or univocal,
etc. But a cipher is unique in that though it stands for and points
beyond itself to Transcendence, that towards which it points is available only in and through the symbol. Moreover, it does this pointing
only for an Existenz who accepts and uses the symbol.

It follows that there is no way objectively or externally to test a symbol. It
follows, second, that there are possibly as many ciphers or symbols of
being as there are Existenzen. Since the latter are historically unique
persons and since they meet Transcendence only in the depths of
their own situations, truth is relative to them and historical. And it
follows, third, that for the Existenz who uses a certain cipher to
represent Transcendence that it is an absolute and final symbol, for
in it the meaning of being is enshrined for him. In communication he
may realize that there is the truth of the other, but it is not his.

[149] Ibid., pp. 733ff.   [150] Ibid., pp. 736ff.   [151] Ibid., pp. 746ff.
[152] Ibid., pp. 762ff.   [153] Ibid., pp. 774ff.   [154] Ibid., p. 792. Cf. 679ff.
[155] On materialization cf. ibid., pp. 684ff and 679ff.   [156] Ibid., p. 793.

Since ciphers are unique, noninterpretable symbols,[157] Jaspers points out that

the understanding of a symbol does not mean to know the meaning of it rationally, to be able to translate the symbol. It means rather as an Existing individual to experience, in the intention of the symbol, this incomparable relation to a Transcendent, on the boundary, in the disappearance of the object.[158]

Consequently the truth of a symbol, which can be assessed only by Existenz, is decided not by logical criteria, but by:

its power of illuminating Existenz in appeals to freedom or of witnessing to Transcendence in the playful breaking through itself as object.[159]

This means, of course, that to Existenz ciphers are self-certifying.

Both of these claims, however, also imply that there cannot be any universal system of ciphers. They have meaning only for individuals in their freedom and uniqueness. They are not external indicators of something which can be an object of direct awareness, but pointers organically bound up with what they symbolize. Thus, the relation of a person with them is not utilitarian; he lives with the ciphers, is involved with them; he images his life in their terms. Because symbols are the unique disclosures of Transcendence in privileged moments to Existenz Jaspers rejects any attempt to certify a set of ciphers as orthodox, a phenomenon he calls catholicity.[160] Thus, the doctrine of ciphers forms the basis of Jaspers' criticism of religion and his differentiation of it from philosophy.[161] If there are any privileged ciphers (objectively) then being is not truly transcendent, but more feasibly manifested in one place or time than another.

Finally for Jaspers anything can become a cipher. There is no limit.[162] All that is requisite to any object's at all becoming a cipher is that through it some Existenz is brought concretely into the presence of Transcendence in absolute consciousness.[163] The cipher is thus the result and expression of the relation of Existenz to Transcendence and is created when an Existenz views any finite object or situation in a transcendent relation. The object thus becomes an "immanent transcendence."[164] But only for Existenz. The most grand and the most trivial aspects of existence can be the bearers of such meaning. But only to authentic selfhood aware of its own freedom and transcendence over its own elements. If one does not approach the ciphers from the perspective of Existenz they are blank and dumb.

Cipher language takes three forms. The first Jaspers calls "the immediate language of Transcendence."[165] Here Jaspers has in mind such experiences as the grandeur, sublimity, and wonder of nature, its fertility and creativity. The beauty and order of nature can lead one

---

157 Ibid., pp. 801. *Jaspers distinguishes between interpretable and intuitional symbols. Ciphers are the latter.*
158 Ibid., p. 688.   159 Ibid., p. 689.   160 VdW 832–869; Philosophie, pp. 816f.
161 Philosophie, pp. 252–272; VdW 916f, 965f.   162 Ibid., p. 820.   163 Ibid., p. 689.
164 Ibid., p. 792.   165 Ibid., pp. 786ff.

to Transcendence. The communication achieved with another person in loving struggle can be a cipher of being. History itself, when seen not as objective events reducible to law, but as the expression of the freedom and transcendence of man, becomes a cipher of Transcendence. This first language, which is the source of the others, is thus an immediate reading of the world and its contents in terms of Transcendence as its ground.[166] To be able to read this language requires living experience (*Erfahrung*):

Not the abstract thought, but the symbol in its historical specificity of presence reveals being. Not a metaphysical hypothesis in which I make conclusions and calculate what being might be, manifests being to me, but the substantiality of the symbol, beyond which I do not think because being shines in it.[167]

Jasper cites the landscapes of Van Gogh as an illustration of this kind of sensing of Transcendence in immanence.

The second language is one men create in order to give utterance to the immediate reading of the first. Without this second language, which Jaspers calls "the language which becomes general in communication,"[168] cipher reading would be ephemeral. As art gives form and permanence to our emotions, so myth and religion give permanence and communicability to our experience of Transcendence. Hence myth and religion become ciphers. In them Transcendence is represented as another world; things in this world are seen to be effects of that transcendent world. The danger is that the myths and rituals and institutions constructed here become substitutes for rather than vehicles of Transcendence.

Third, there is the language of speculation.[169] This is the language of philosophy, which in its metaphysical systems tries to construct theories of reality which relate the world and man to being. The attempt results in an objectification of being and the representation of the world as an expression of this being.[170] But this can never become a science of being. The fact is that philosophical systems are creative representations of being as a whole by Existenz in the attempt to comprehend and illumine his own being. Hence philosophies are not like objective knowledge in universal structures: they are symbol constructions in which being as Transcendence finds existential presence through conceptual formulation.[171] Ultimately philosophy pictures being as the ground of factual existence and takes almost tautologous form: "Being is such that this existence is possible."[172] Objectively this is like saying that opium puts one to sleep because of its dormitive properties. But as philosophizing it serves to show how being is thought behind the immanent forms it takes and how man struggles to find expression for this source, this origin, this ultimate meaning.

Again, this happens only for Existenz. And for this reason there can be no universal philosophy. There can be only the perennial task of philoso-

166 Ibid., p. 787.   167 Ibid., p. 788.   168 Ibid., pp. 788ff.   169 Ibid., pp. 790ff.
170 Idem.   171 Idem. Cf. VdW 412, 269ff.   172 Philosophie, p. 790.

phizing pointing to the encompassing being by transcending thinking in the world. Philosophy is man's freedom and transcendence when it takes rational and conceptual form. It is therefore the task of Existenz.[173] Where man does not reach the level of Existenz, philosophy becomes wooden, dogmatic, a science which purports to capture being in its categories as a knowable object. It becomes, in short, ontology.[174] But we can have no knowledge of being in this sense; hence philosophy is not ontology, but conceptual cipher building.

The ultimate cipher is man himself in his freedom. Although anything can become a cipher, it does so by being viewed by Existenz as mediating Transcendence. But as Existenz man is himself a kind of transcendence, and is thus the final cipher. Man is a true replica of being, a microcosm, or as Jaspers puts it, a *Knotenpunkt* of all the levels of being: nature, consciousness, history, transcendence.[175] This is the meaning of the myths which say man is created in the image of God (God being an objectification of being.) As the transcendence of subjectivity man stands in relation to Transcendence which grounds the possibility of free selfhood. Man's seeking for meaning, for the answers to the question of being with which we started this study, is the locus where the cipher is born. The cipher character of everything else depends upon man's transcending to find his own being.

But no lasting answers are possible. The last cipher of being, and for Jaspers the most adequate one, is the cipher of foundering or shipwreck.[176] Foundering is the realization that all attempts to capture and represent being in the languages of ciphers fail. For they all represent being which is an encompassing as an object within the subject-object relationship. Being forever escapes this objectification and this escape turns up in human cipher language as the foundering and destruction of all ciphers. Amidst the wreckage of all one's attempts to objectify being in the categories of thought and imagination, one is reduced to silence. The last word is therefore silence. Not the silence which comes from the refusal to communicate, but the humble silence which is the result of the attempt to articulate, illuminate, and communicate, but where one experiences in that very attempt the inadequacy of these processes to do justice to their "object." It is the silence of wonder in the presence of being as Transcendence. In the end it is enough that being is.[177] We have reached the end when we come to experience this utter transcendence of being over all its modes in the foundering of all our constructs. And although the will to founder is self-contradictory, the experience of it constitutes our confrontation with being in a living experience.[178]

6. Psychology,
Religion, History

As is well known, Jaspers began his career as a psychiatrist. But in one sense he was in philosophy all the time. Commenting on his *Psy-*

---

173 Ibid., pp. 804ff.   174 Ibid., p. 810.   175 Ibid., p. 835.
176 *The German term is* "Scheitern." Ibid., pp. 863–879.
177 Ibid., p. 878.   178 Ibid., p. 879.

chologie der Weltanschauungen, he says that it was a work with philosophic content.[179] It can be shown that in spite of the fact that his psychological works antedate his philosophical ones, the concepts which later came to expression were already at work informing the earlier writings. Thus, Jaspers' psychological writings may be seen as applications of his philosophical ideas. The early *Psychologie* undertakes to describe possible human attitudes and world pictures, for Jaspers believed even then that Existenz transcends its manifestations.

His writings on religion and history are even more directly related to his philosophical essays. Most of them have appeared since the publication of *Philosophie* in 1932 and are interspersed with his philosophical writings. No less philosophical than his psychological explorations, they too approach the human situation from the standpoint of potential Existenz.

PSYCHOLOGY The *General Psychopathology* is an illumination of psychological thought. It describes the various methodological approaches in psychology, their powers and limits, the results they can obtain, their relations to each other and to Existenz. This feature makes the book a work with philosophical content.

Informing the whole procedure is the subject-object structure of awareness. A psychological method, which consists of assumptions, concepts, and techniques of observation and experimentation, is a way of investigating an object. The object, a human being, is never exhausted by the method. Nor is the investigator merely a methodologist. Because both he and the person he studies are men, they have many relations which transcend the method. Also, the investigator cannot ignore the fact that he has various methods at his disposal which will make his object assume new aspects. Thus, there can be no complete—or even completeable—scientific comprehension of man in psychology. The psychological account of man yields many partial pictures, each of which is the result of the application of a method-determining leading idea. A total view remains an idea in Kant's sense; if it exists at all, it is because the investigator uses it as a regulative idea in building as comprehensive an account as possible.

Psychology thus conceived can never destroy the freedom of man; it is limited to investigating the objective manifestations of human existence within circumscribed categories. Understanding this limitation illuminates the nature of psychological thought. Only a science which is unaware of its own procedure and which forgets its methodological limits, can claim to give a complete account of its object.

Jaspers' chief contribution to psychology is his distinction between "understanding" (*verstehende*) and "explaining" (*erklärende*) psychology. Explaining psychology is bent upon causal explanation of psychological data by establishing laws of their connection. There are levels of particular causal connections which one cannot yet generalize (e.g.,

---

[179] Schilpp, The Philosophy of Karl Jaspers, p. 25.

the connection between diseases of the eye and hallucination), general rules (e.g., heredity), and finally laws proper (e.g., connection between general paralysis and syphilis). Explanation in psychology is more restricted, however, than in physics, for there is no complete quantification in the former: "since these are psychic events, which by their very nature have to remain qualitative, such quantification would as a matter of principle remain impossible without losing the actual object of the inquiry."[180]

Understanding psychology seeks insight into the meaningful structures which connect psychic phenomena, not causally, but intentionally. Personality is represented by Jaspers as an "entirety of meaningful connections;"[181] understanding any material consists in seeing it in relation to this entirety.

In the natural sciences we find causal explanations only, but in psychology our bent for knowledge is satisfied with the comprehension of a quite different sort of connection. Psychic events 'emerge' out of each other in a way which we understand. Attacked people become angry, and spring to the defense, cheated persons grow suspicious. The way in which such an emergence takes place is understood by us, our understanding is genetic. Thus we understand psychic reactions to experience, we understand the development of passion, the growth of an error, the content of delusion and dream; we understand the effects of suggestion, an abnormal personality in its own context, the inner necessities of someone's life. Finally we understand how the patient sees himself, and how this mode of self-understanding becomes a factor in his psychic development.[182]

For Jaspers the difficulty with much psychology is that because it can represent material discovered by understanding to be predictable on the basis of causal analyses, it thinks it thereby reduces intentional relations to causal ones, creating the illusion of a completely adequate method. Although Jaspers insists that the phenomena turned up by *verstehen* must be treated causally,[183] the carrying through of this causal analysis changes the standpoint: "when searching for causes we are always forced to think of something extra-conscious"[184] (e.g., body mechanisms). When this occurs, material which is understood at the level of meaningful intentional connection is related to something ununderstandable at the extra-conscious level.[185] Care must be exercised not to take this reduction as yielding a generally more adequate account because it is more adequate for certain purposes. The fact that intentionally meaningful wholes can be treated causally does not entail that understanding can be reduced to explanation. Exclusive use of explanation is in danger of losing something significant to the knowledge of a human being.

It is at the level of meaningful connection reached by understanding that another perspective first opens: one is able to view the presented material as a manifestation of Existenz.[186] One can see the results

[180] General Psychopathology, tr. J. Hoenig and M. W. Hamilton, Univ. of Chicago Press, 1963, p. 302 (hereafter referred to as GP).
[181] Ibid., p. 305.   [182] Ibid., pp 302f.   [183] Ibid., p. 305.   [184] Idem.
[185] Ibid., p. 311.   [186] Ibid., pp. 308, 311.

of understanding lying "as it were midway between the objective facts, the phenomena of experience and implied extra-conscious mechanisms on the one hand, and the spontaneous freedom of Existenz itself on the other."[187] A denial of understanding, hence of Existenz, is always possible in the interest of the neatness of mechanical explanation. But it would be an example of a self-closing world view. So, "let us try to manage with such a division of the field."[188]

Such is Jaspers' illumination of psychology. It proceeds by unpacking the various methods by throwing their concepts, assumptions, and techniques into relation with each other and with the Existenz of both the psychologist and the patient, who transcend their objective manifestations. Unless existential awareness permeates scientific thought, it becomes inhuman (and inhumane), and investigates only empty shells.

Jaspers' studies of individuals make use of the concept of understanding. His psychological analyses of Nietzsche, Strindberg, and Van Gogh differ from those of Freud in that the latter exhibit personality as the causal product of material, some of which is understandable in Jaspers' sense, some not (e.g., reduction to psychic or physiological drives). Jaspers tries to understand his subjects intentionally, showing the dynamic relation between subject and object. He sees the diseases of his subjects in relation to their life projects. They are not merely subjective or even physiological occurrences, but subjective poles (attitudes) of a world view which has an objective pole as well (world picture). Hence illness has an understandable intentional structure which plays a role in determining the world in which the subject lives.

The attention is always focused upon the mysterious source (Existenz) in his subjects so that one sees not just the psychological material and its connection, but that and how it is a manifestation, an existential element in the shell a person creates in order to live in the world. Thus, Jaspers does not explain the person he is studying, but communicates with the whole person by a transcending consideration of his manifest behavior. It was this need for communication which led Jaspers from psychology into philosophy.

RELIGION Jaspers has been preoccupied with religion. Almost every book contains a discussion of it. Most contain a chapter devoted to it. Two deal with it directly.[189] It is ironic that the very element in his philosophy which relates him to religion also grounds his difference from and attack upon religion. Nowhere has Jaspers been more acrimonious than in his critique of religion, as a reading of his polemical discussion with Bultmann will bear out.

The place where Jaspers' philosophy makes contact with religion is the notion of Transcendence. Philosophy, he says, is a transcending form

---

[187] Ibid., p. 311.   [188] Ibid., p. 312.
[189] Myth and Christianity, (with R. Bultmann), tr. H. Wolff, Noonday Press, Inc., New York, 1958, and Der Philosophische Glaube angesichts der Offenbarung, Piper & Co., Munich, 1962, (hereafter referred to as PGAO).

of thought.   Unless there is Transcendence both Existenz and philosophy are impossible.   But this awareness of Transcendence cannot
be forced; transcending thinking involves risk and requires an act of
faith.   The two features of Transcendence which put philosophy into
relation to religion are: faith and the modes of representing Transcendence.

Religion is characterized by cult, ritual, sacred writings, authority, catholicity,
and orthodoxy.   Religious faith is acceptance of a set of symbols
representing Transcendence as an object.   It produces community
among its members through its doctrines and institutions, but at the
same time tends toward exclusiveness.   It represents Transcendence
in definite manifestations of creed and ritual which it claims are compelling for all.   To defend its faith religion requires authority and
sanctions.   In short, religion makes a claim to total knowledge of the
most obnoxious kind: not merely, as science sometimes does, the
claim to understand the world, but a claim to understand being-itself
as an objectified Transcendence which itself need not be transcended.

Against this claim stand philosophy and philosophical faith, though just what
the latter ultimately consists in is difficult to determine.   Philosophical
faith acknowledges God (or Transcendence), though not as a special
being.   Anything, as we saw, can become a cipher of Transcendence.
Because Transcendence has no features, there is nothing about it
which excludes any object from being a cipher of it.   Only Existenz in
the concreteness of its own situation meets Transcendence in a radical
act of transcending some particular object or situation.   The object
involved, when seen in this transcending movement of thought to
point beyond itself, becomes a cipher.   It is taken as the language in
which Transcendence speaks to Existenz.

This means that philosophical faith can have no creed (other than the empty
ones: God is; there is a categorical imperative, etc.),[190] no sacred
writings (any text can become a cipher), no cult, and especially no
claim to absoluteness, authority, or catholicity.   It rests upon the
freedom of Existenz.   Jesus is a cipher for Jaspers, in that he points
consciously to Transcendence as his ground (God the Father).   But he
is no more a cipher than Bruno, Socrates, or Confucius.   To Jaspers'
philosophical faith nothing is exempt from question and criticism,
whereas for religion there is always a point which is not subject to
question, to transcending.   Where this occurs, a rupture of communication results.   Religious people retreat to dogmatic assertions; one
can only oppose them, though not totally, but only in so far as they
claim totality.

Finally, religion comes under criticism, because after thousands of years
neither Christianity nor any other religion has been able to develop a
basis for world community.[191]   One must transcend religion completely to a more transcending view of Transcendence (philosophy)
from which religions themselves become merely existential ciphers.

---

[190] Wisdom, pp. 82f.; Perennial Scope of Philosophy, tr. R. Manheim, Philosophical
Library, New York, 1949, pp. 34ff.
[191] PGAO p. 7.

Only in this way can one provide a ground for a world community. Especially is this necessary today when for the first time a world-wide community is both a possibility and a necessity if man is to survive on this planet. Hence not only does religion have the defect of total claims; it is also not adequate to provide a context upon which men can communicate across barriers of spirit and everyday existence.

Even so, religion is closer to what is needed than science. It is an illusion to believe that science will bind mankind together; it unites them only at the level of consciousness-in-general, not in the common ground of their lives. Religion makes the effort to go beyond this, but ends in separating men from one another. Only a truly transcending philosophical faith is open to and tolerant of all possibilities, and can build a community of men who at the same time remain loyal to their own traditions.

HISTORY   Jaspers' philosophy of history and culture is an illumination of them in relation to Existenz. He does not treat history as an object or process with laws of its development, as did St. Augustine, Hegel, Marx, Spengler, and even Toynbee. Rather, he represents it as a network of possibilities. Only the past is irrevocable, determined; and even it is not so in its meaning and consequences.[192] These depend upon how it is appropriated by Existenz. Jaspers' philosophy of history is thus an application of philosophical faith.

There can be no one view of history. Men "hear it altogether differently, and yet, is it not, for all of them, meaningful in their own particular ways?"[193] The reason for this is that "in history . . . we are, in the very process of trying to understand it, struggling with the forces that have arisen within it. We appropriate that out of which we live, and we ground ourselves in the history which bears us."[194] Since a view of history grows up in the process of living in history, the tradition in which one lives and his manner of appropriating it are decisive to the outcome and significance of history.

Philosophical faith gives to history its main contours. For Jaspers this is the thesis that mankind has one single origin and one goal. The empirical origins of man are, of course, lost in the darkness of prehistory. But it is clear that it is not to these that Jaspers refers when he speaks of origin, but to man's origin in being or Transcendence. Such an origin is compatible with the future historical discovery that mankind had several empirical origins. In fact, in his discussion of the axial age Jaspers insists both upon pluralistic emergence of historical man and the common ontological origin of man.

Similarly the end of history is contributed by faith: It is a community of Existenzen, each rooted in his own tradition, but because they are open to Transcendence, open also to each other in love and communication. Neither origin nor end is an actual occurrence, but they are

---

192 Schilpp, The Philosophy of Karl Jaspers, p. 766.
193 Idem.
194 Idem.

existential structures in terms of which Jaspers analyzes history and culture.

Although the contours of his view of history are the result of faith, the philosophy of history and culture must include empirical elements. Included under this rubric are not only particular events, but more cosmic phenomena, such as his notion of the axial age—the most illuminating idea in his philosophy of history. The axial period[195] is Jaspers' version of the Christian idea of the center of history. Jaspers rejects the Christian interpretation as being too provincial; it permits history to have meaning only for Christians. A philosophy of history needs at its center some conception with which men can make contact as men. As his candidate for an axial period Jaspers selected the era (800–200 B.C.) when men managed to transcend their animal and prehistoric background and emerged as men. The axial age is characterized by the emergence of reflective self-consciousness. Man became conscious of "Being as a whole, of himself, and his limitations. He asked radical questions."[196] The axial age is the beginning of history, and man as we know him is thus historical man.

During the axial age were formulated in various civilizations the basic notions of what it is to be human. Conceptions of life, values, philosophies and religions, political aims and orders emerged, grew, and founded the traditions which constituted the context of future man. In a spontaneous eruption of spirit, content was given to human life. Only in and after the axial period do the categories of spirit, consciousness, and Existenz emerge, in very different ways in the various cultures. Though they exhibit no common material element, they share some of the same structural characteristics.

Jaspers' theses about the contemporary historical situation are (1) that the Western consciousness, because it developed science and technology, has brought about the conditions of one world and has thrown its conceptions into relation (often hostile) with those of others, and created the problem of world community; and (2) that in producing science and technology we have entered upon at least the threshold of a new or second axial period, in which the very nature of human existence undergoes transition.

The former feature gives rise to the problem of one world, to which Jaspers is committed—but only as a community of men residing in local, historically different traditions. Should a world culture develop by inundating indigenous world views and cultures, it will be a dull, authoritarian, and monolithic culture in which Existenz is destroyed. Hence, Jaspers argues for a world unity which preserves cultural differentiation, yet in which men can communicate across these boundaries. Politically he sees it coming in the form of a system of treaties between nations rather than a world government, which would necessarily be a leviathan crushing everything under it.[197]

---

195 The Origin and Goal of History, tr. M. Bullock, Yale University Press, New Haven, Conn., 1953.
196 Ibid., p. 2.   197 Schilpp, The Philosophy of Karl Jaspers, pp. 751f.

A difficulty in the accomplishment of such a goal of world history is brought about by the dominance of science and technology in our own culture and through it in the world. On the one hand these forces have created tendencies to larger economic and political collectivities which work against the necessary cultural differentiation. On the other, technology is an engine which has so radically altered the conditions of human existence that it is a question whether the style of life Jaspers calls Existenz can endure. One can see this in the emphasis upon the search for identity and the difficulty of finding meaning in literature, social thought, and existential philosophy.

For Jaspers the two main tendencies of modern times—world unity and socialism—are ambiguous. Each has tremendous promise: the possibility of real liberty and humanity for all without the drudgery of brutalizing work. Each has direful portents: the loss of individuality and the dying away of human self-consciousness in a beelike uniformity brought about by the technization of all human functioning. Only if we preserve a philosophical faith can we avoid the latter alternative. Only in this attitude is there the Transcendence by which men assert their freedom, the openness from which a meaningful future is possible. Without faith there is only a new animality.

At this point the question might be raised whether in his analysis of the historical prospects facing us, Jaspers has either taken seriously the enormity of the events which he has described or rightly applied his own doctrine of the historicity of truth and existence. He points out, to be sure, how radically technology has changed the conditions under which men live. But when he comes to an estimate of the situation, instead of calling for or providing new definitions of human existence, he seizes upon the concept of humanity developed between the first and second axial periods as normative. In its light he talks of the promise and threat of the future. One would expect that an appropriation of the historicity of man would require one to ponder the possibility that the new conditions of existence simply render the old conceptions outmoded. Though his accounts of what humanity is in his Existenz illuminations are brilliant, they may be acts of Verstehen of a world-view possible only in the interval between two axial periods, hence inadequate to serve as norms. Jaspers clearly prefers the "humanity" developed in the pretechnological period. His question is always: How can we preserve its salient features in radically altered circumstances?

This is the source, I think, of Levi's comment on the social philosophy of Jaspers' existentialism, that "its only solution is a retreat from the domains of the political altogether, and a dependence (without essential inventiveness) upon the traditional resources of the good man in the bad society."[198] Jaspers' problem is that of the conflict between the demands of the technical mass order and those of authentic human life. But the latter are defined in terms of the actualities of an earlier age. Hence the emphasis is always on how one can keep

[198] A. W. Levi, Philosophy and the Modern World, Indiana University Press, Bloomington, 1959, p. 430.

certain things from happening rather than on exploiting the possibilities of the new.   Finally Jaspers must claim as an act of faith that, although Existenz is headed for rough times, it will remain as a possibility to break out again in some future axial period just as man once emerged from his animality.   Meanwhile one can nurture Existenz in small communicative groups.   In this respect Jaspers is more like the Epicureans and Stoics than more activist philosophers of social reconstruction such as Dewey, Sartre, or even Marx.

Dewey in philosophy and the liberal democrats in politics have noted the revolutionary aspects of science and technology more profoundly than has Jaspers.   They have seen that one must project new forms and styles of human life in the new conditions, and they are trying to invent them.   Thus they are far less concerned about the past than is Jaspers.   Jaspers seems to be more concerned with criticism of the modern age from the standpoint of Existenz than he is in exploring its possibilities for a new humanity.   The consequence is that for him philosophy, instead of providing leadership into the future, has little to say about it; and it almost insures that the future will develop without benefit of the philosophic point of view.

Even to this criticism one could reply on behalf of Jaspers' larger scheme of thought that the need for a new definition of man, a new exploration of human possibilities, instead of conflicting with his basic ideas, illustrates them.   The historicity of man, his transcendence, and the impossibility of total knowledge demand that in new situations new forms of humanity will and must be developed.   There is sufficient insight in Jaspers' position; it simply requires a more positive application to social and political problems than Jaspers has given it.

7. Critical Remarks

1. In one sense it is almost impossible to offer criticisms of Jaspers' philosophy.   For, in his conception philosophy becomes philosophizing.   This consists of inner movements of thought on the part of individual persons in concrete situations.   Its aim is not objective and universal results, but the illumination of the thinker.   Jaspers grants that this is achieved by constructing "conceptual schemes, which make assertions about structures, and which . . . are to be culled out as systematic insights into . . . structures of being human."[199]   Still, he says of them:

It is essential and notable, however, that I do not recite these structures outright, nor as the main point.   True enough, they play a role in the disposition of and offer guidance for changing formulations, but they are not the motors of the movement of thought.   Furthermore, they are without claim to absolute validity.   There are several schemes.   They are tools of communication, not objects of knowledge.[200]

To respond to such a philosophy by saying that one finds in his own existen-

[199] Schilpp, The Philosophy of Karl Jaspers, p. 819.   [200] Idem.

tial reflections structures and conceptual schemes other than those
Jaspers describes is hardly a criticism, at least not one that Jaspers
would recognize as such. For his system of thought not only allows
for this sort of demurrer, but insists that it is the normal state of
affairs. One can only state where he disagrees with Jaspers and go
his own way. But again this is what one is expected to do. For
Jaspers, as for Nietzsche, the idea is to become what you are. Even
in a confrontation which results in rejection, illumination and communication may occur. Appropriation of a philosophy, says Jaspers,
consists in creative interaction with it, not necessarily in agreement or
acceptance; and it does not spoil the exchange when one party
decides that he must reject the presented conceptual schemes, which
are, after all, only tools of communication.

2. Still, in another sense one must criticize Jaspers on exactly this aspect of
his philosophy. Although Jaspers' concrete description of world views
and Existenz are brilliant, his writings also contain a large metaphysical element which one has a difficult time in viewing as more than
the carrying through of his own search for Transcendence. Description of concrete material is replaced by a metaphysics of the encompassing in which philosophy is viewed as a personal quest through the
appearances of the world for the One which lies hidden beyond all
appearance and which alone gives peace. More and more this quest
and its main achievements are represented as identical with philosophy. The result is that although there is plenty of philosophical
insight in Jaspers, it is often difficult to separate it from the items of
his own faith or the peculiarities of his own situation.

Certainly it is a philosophical point that since no ultimate standpoint is
possible, no total knowledge is possible. Consequently one must
always be open to other methods and other possibilities, and never,
as Peirce would say, block the road to inquiry. But it is not necessary
to claim that everyone is engaged in the quest for the One. Such
items as the affirmation that God exists (as a personal faith) or that
one must see things in the world as private ciphers of some deeper
reality are not essential to philosophy. Jaspers does not make clear
distinctions. He characterizes philosophizing in a way so closely
enmeshed with the particulars of his own commitments that he is led
to maintain that one who denies Transcendence or the cipher character of things, is an enemy of philosophy and a partisan of unphiloso-
phy. For Jaspers philosophical faith stands in opposition to the
principles of unfaith. Genuine philosophizing is bound up with the
former.

Some conceptions which Jaspers identifies with philosophy might better be
classed as religion. That he does not do so puts his thinking into
needless conflict with religion and burdens philosophy with the task
of being a surrogate religion for its practitioners. Such a surrogate
either becomes so vacuous that it is difficult to ascertain what it
stands for, or its contents become just as absolute and unconditional
for its holder as religious belief is for the religious man. A philosophi-

cal illumination of religion should illuminate the nature and function of religion instead of turning philosophy itself into a quasi religion.

3. Jaspers hardly ever argues for Transcendence. Where he does the argument is that Existenz is impossible unless there is Transcendence. For otherwise man would be completely described on the levels of empirical existence, consciousness and spirit. Naturalistic modes of thought must fall into denials of Existenz which only Transcendentalism can avoid.

Unfortunately, the facts do not support this argument. In the first place, transcendental styles of thought are not exempt from the same kind of absolute and catholic claims that Jaspers sees as characterizing naturalism. Second, it is not necessary that nontranscendental styles of thought should claim all-comprehensiveness or self-sufficiency. The notions of horizonality and the situational character of thought, which Jaspers describes so well, insure that every level of inquiry is an open one. The burden of proof must be on the one who insists that immanent existence needs to be represented as a cipher of Transcendence in order to be understood properly and to preserve the integrity of Existenz.

Jaspers' transcendentalism is an understandable reaction to the claim made by some naturalists to the effect that immanent existence is not only all there is but that it is exhausted in a given conceptual scheme. But these are two independent claims, and the former does not entail the latter. Only the latter thesis gives rise to a self-closing world view.

None of the features of human existence which Jaspers mentions requires a transcendental approach. Existenz, spirit, and consciousness are indefinitely interpretable levels of finite reality. Spirit is not a new entity which refuses to find a place in it, but a new level, a way of organizing elements under an idea. The same can be said of consciousness. Finally, I think that Existenz turns out to be a way of existing on the other levels which is rewarding, satisfying, and hence said to be authentic. It stands in no need of certification by a Transcendence which cannot be presented in any positive way.

Thus the metaphysics of Jaspers is the least satisfactory part of his philosophizing. It is unclear how his existential analyses require the support he gives them in his ontology. The ideal of human community is not perceptibly furthered by the claim that "you and I, though separated in existence, are one in Transcendence." Nor do discussions which represent the realms of the experienced world as ciphers of Transcendence aid in illuminating the features of our world. As ciphers they have no feature determinate enough to affect the way we relate to them. And one is almost completely at a loss to understand what possibly could be meant by the statement that ultimately Being-itself is such that this existence (*Dasein*) is possible. Ontologizing of this kind does not secure the reality of the world. It gives no answer to the questions which start philosophical thought: Why is there anything at all—why not nothing? or What is being itself? These remain as much a mystery after Jaspers' analyses as they were before. Relating existence to Transcendence in this way gives no new ideas, no solutions to problems and suggests no new and creative schemes by which one can cope with the future. Instead, it seems to demand that we interpret it as a counsel of resignation: When all else fails, one can rest with the statement: Being is.

BIBLIOGRAPHY

**Major works
of Karl Jaspers**

GERMAN

1. *Allgemeine Psychopathologie*, J. Springer, Berlin, 1913; completely rewritten and published as 4th ed., 1946.

2. *Die Atombombe und die Zukunft des Menschen*, R. Piper, Munich, 1958.

3. *Descartes und die Philosophie*, De Gruyter, Berlin, 1937; 2d ed., 1948.

4. *Einführung in die Philosophie*, Artemis Verlag, Zurich, 1950, and R. Piper, Munich, 1953.

5. *Existenzphilosophie*, De Gruyter, Berlin, 1938; 2d ed., 1956.

6. *Die Frage der Entmythologisierung* (with R. Bultmann), R. Piper, Munich, 1954.

7. *Die Geistige Situation der Zeit*, vol. 1000 of Sammlung Göschen, De Gruyter, Berlin, 1931; 5th rev. ed., 1933.

8. *Die Grossen Philosophen*, R. Piper, Munich, 1957.

9. *Die Idee der Universität*, J. Springer, Berlin, 1946.

10. *Max Weber*, G. Stalling, Oldenburg i. O., 1932; 2d ed., J. Storm, Bremen, 1946.

11. *Nietzsche: Einführung in das Verständnis seines Philosophierens*, De Gruyter, Berlin, 1936; 3d ed., 1950.

12. *Nietzsche und das Christentum*, Seifert, Hameln, 1947, and R. Piper, Munich, 1951.

13. *Philosophie*, J. Springer, Berlin, 1932 (in 3 vols.); 2d ed. (in 1 vol.), 1948; 3d ed. (in 3 vols.), 1956.

14. *Philosophie und Welt*, R. Piper, Munich, 1958.

15. *Philosophie und Wissenschaft*, Artemis Verlag, Zürich, 1949.

16. *Der Philosophische Glaube*, Artemis Verlang, Zurich, 1948, and R. Piper, Munich, 1955.

17. *Der Philosophische Glaube angesichts der Offenberung*, Piper & Co., Munich, 1962.

18. *Psychologie der Weltanschauugen*, J. Springer, Berlin, 1919; 2d rev. ed., 1920; 3d ed., 1925; 4th ed. 1954.

19. *Rechenschaft und Ausblick*, R. Piper, Munich, 1951.

20. *Die Schuldfrage*, L. Schneider, Heidelberg, 1946.

21. *Strindberg und Van Gogh*, J. Springer, Berlin, 1926. This is the 2d ed., the first being an essay in a cooperative volume; 3d ed., J. Storm, Bremen, 1949 and 1951.

22. *Schelling. Grösse and Verhängnis*, R. Piper, Munich, 1955.

23. *Unserer Zukunft und Goethe*, J. Storm, Bremen, 1949.

24. *Verunuft und Existenz*, J. W. Wolters, Groningen, 1935; 2d and 3d eds., J. Storm, Bremen, 1947, 1949.

25. *Vernunft und Widervernunft in unserer Zeit*, R. Piper, Munich, 1950; 2d ed., 1952.

26. *Vom Europäischen Geist*, R. Piper, Munich, 1947.

27. *Vom Ursprung und Ziel der Geschichte*, Artemis Verlag, Zürich, 1949, and R. Piper, Munich, 1950; 3d ed., 1952.

28. *Von der Wahrheit*, R. Piper, Munich, 1947.

ENGLISH TRANSLATIONS:

29. *The European Spirit* (tr. of #26 above by R. G. Smith), Macmillan, New York, 1949.

30. *The Future of Mankind* (tr. of #2 above by E. B. Ashton), University of Chicago Press, Chicago, 1961.

31. *General Psychopathology* (tr. of #1 above by J. Hoening and M. W. Hamilton), University of Chicago Press, Chicago, 1963.

32. *The Great Philosophers*, ed. H. Arendt (tr. of #8 above by R. Manheim), Harcourt, Brace & World, New York, 1962.

33. *The Idea of the University*, ed. K. W. Deutsch (tr. of #9 above by H. A. T. Reiche and H. F. Vanderschmidt), Beacon Press, Boston, 1959.

34. *Man in the Modern Age* (tr. of #7 above by E. and C. Paul), Routledge, London, 1933; 2d ed., 1951.

35. *Myth and Christianity* (tr. of #6 above by H. Wolff), Noonday Press, Inc., New York, 1958.

36. *Nietzsche: An Introduction to the Understanding of His Philosophical Activity* (tr. of #11 above by C. F. Wallraff and F. J. Schmitz), University of Arizona Press, Tucson, 1965.

37. *Nietzsche and Christianity* (tr. of #12 above by E. B. Ashton), Regnery Gateway Editions, Chicago, 1961.

38. *The Origin and Goal of History* (tr. of #27 above by M. Bullock), Yale University Press, New Haven, Conn., 1953.

39. *The Perennial Scope of Philosophy* (tr. of #16 above by R. Manheim), Philosophical Library, New York, 1949.

40. *Philosophy and Science* (tr. of #15 above by R. Manheim), *Partisan Review*, New York, vol. XVI, no. 9; also appendix no. 1 in #43 below.

41. *The Question of German Guilt* (tr. of #20 above by E. B. Ashton), Dial Press, New York, 1947.

42. *Reason and Anti-Reason in Our Time* (tr. of #25 above by S. Godman), Yale University Press, New Haven, Conn., 1952.

43. *Reason and Existenz* (tr. of #24 above by William Earle), Noonday Press, Inc., New York, 1955.

44. *Tragedy Is Not Enough* (tr. of pp. 915–961 of #28 above by H. A. T. Reiche, H. T. Moore, and K. W. Deutsch), Beacon Press, Boston, 1952.

45. *Truth and Symbol* (tr. of pp. 1022–1054 of #28 above by Jean T. Wild, Wm. Kluback, and Wm. Kimmel), Twayne, New York, 1959.

46. *Way to Wisdom* (tr. of #4 above by R. Manheim), Yale University Press, New Haven, Conn., 1954.

CHAPTER FOUR

MARTIN HEIDEGGER
THE SEARCH FOR MEANING

KARSTEN HARRIES

KARSTEN HARRIES *is an associate professor of philosophy at Yale University. Born in Jena, Germany, he came to the United States in 1951. He received both his B.A. and his Ph.D. from Yale. Before returning to Yale, he taught at the University of Texas and for a semester at the University of Bonn. Currently he is working on a philosophic interpretation of modern art. Articles related to the present chapter have appeared in* The Personalist, The Review of Metaphysics, *and* The Journal of Existentialism.

1. The Question
of Meaning

The response to Heidegger's philosophy has tended towards extremes: fascination, on one hand, immediate rejection, on the other. Heidegger's
manner of writing has fostered this. His idiosyncratic use of language
—the invention of new words, frequent distortions of accepted meanings, a love of etymological games, and highly condensed, at times
almost poetic formulations—demands a sympathetic reader. If the
reader is not sympathetic, all these devices may appear to be little
more than a veil hiding how little has been said. What, to give just
one example, does Heidegger accomplish when he uses the anti-
quarian *Seyn* instead of *Sein* (Being), or the same word crossed out
(~~Sein~~)? Is this still philosophy? Or is it an esoteric game, perhaps
derived from philosophy, but devoid of philosophic content? The
unsympathetic reader will grant that such play may be mistaken for
wisdom by those who have despaired of giving or receiving answers
which can withstand sober questioning; but in that case, is Heidegger's
considerable popularity more than yet another sign of the decline of
reason?

Sympathy is indeed required if we are to understand Heidegger. Such a
requirement has its dangers; it can too easily make critical understanding impossible. Heidegger, especially the Heidegger encountered
in his most recent works, often seems like a magician, chanting
hermetic formulae, forcing Being to reveal itself. Once the decision
has been made to listen to these incantations, it is difficult not to
succumb. This fascination is difficult to understand. What is it
that causes so many who have hardly exposed themselves to philosophy to listen to lectures and read books which the trained philosopher
has trouble understanding? What explains the popularity of a thinker
who in his way of writing is so determinedly unpopular? What kind of
a philosopher is Heidegger?

Schopenhauer distinguished two philosophic types: those who were made
philosophers by philosophy and those who were made philosophers by
life. Heidegger represents the first type. His works seem curiously
divorced from our everyday concerns. His thinking is not so much a
thinking about life as a thinking about thinking, particularly about
philosophic thinking. His first published works already suggest this.
They are written in the shadow of the struggle between those who,
following Schopenhauer and Herbart, strove to subordinate logic to
psychology (e.g., Wundt, Brentano, and Lipps), and those who, on the
contrary, fought to emancipate logic from the tutelage of psychology.
The Neo-Kantians at Marburg led the battle against the "psychologists"; men such as Rickert, Husserl, and Frege made important contributions. Heidegger's dissertation, *Die Lehre vom Urteil im Psychologismus*, gives rather modest support to the cause of the
logicians. Especially if we tend to think of existentialism as having
little patience with logical investigations, it is interesting to note that
Heidegger's thought has the same source as Wittgenstein's. These
origins are never denied. This, of course, does not mean that the

Dissertation presents us already with the key ideas of Heidegger's maturity; it is, however, the case that these later ideas are developed in answer to certain problems which have their origin in this first logical phase of his thought.

If there were only this logical side to Heidegger, it would be difficult to explain his popularity. But there is another side: the young philosopher who calls himself a "mathematician" in the *Dissertation*,[1] also describes himself as a "Christian theologian."[2] Understood literally this phrase makes little sense. Heidegger's mature works have left the theological studies of his youth far behind. And yet, these studies are not forgotten. Heidegger's thinking retains its roots in theology —where it has to be emphasized that what is retained is not an answer, but a concern. This "theological" concern appears in Heidegger's choice of the term "hermeneutics" to describe his approach to philosophy. Traditionally "hermeneutics" refers to the interpretation of Scripture. More generally it can be used to refer to any kind of interpretative investigation. In interpreting something, we exhibit its meaning. An interest in interpretation shows a concern about meaning. Heidegger's own thinking is governed by such a concern. This finds expression not so much in a discussion of the methodology of interpretation, as in an attempt at interpretation itself.[3] In calling his philosophy "hermeneutic" Heidegger suggests that it is interpretation in search of meaning. Such a search lacks direction unless it is provided with a focus; we must look for meaning somewhere, e.g., in a work of art or in our own life. Heidegger raises the question of meaning in the most fundamental manner possible by asking: What is the meaning of Being? His philosophy may be described as a continued struggle with this question.

But does this justify his choice of the term "hermeneutics" with its theological implications? Heidegger tells us that these were in the back of his mind when he adopted it. He was familiar with the term from the theological studies of his youth; the question which occupied him then was that of the "relationship between the word of Holy Scripture and the speculative thinking of the theologian."[4] Heidegger interprets his later philosophic concern as a metamorphosis of this early interest. The choice of the term "hermeneutics" ascribes thus an almost religious significance to his search for Being. When Heidegger goes so far as to call himself a "Christian theologian" this may be misleading; we do not expect to find the term applied to someone who rarely speaks of God and never as a believer; it does, however, serve to point out the importance of his early theological interests which run like a hidden current through his work to give it a religious tinge. Perhaps this explains the appeal of Heidegger's search for the meaning of Being in an age which has experienced the death of God and

---

[1] Die Lehre vom Urteil im Psychologismus, *Johann Ambrosius Barth, Leipzig,* 1914, p. v *(referred to in text as the* Dissertation*).*

[2] *Karl Löwith, Heidegger: Denker in dürftiger Zeit, 2d ed., Vandenhoeck und Ruprecht,* Göttingen, 1960, p. 106.

[3] Unterwegs zur Sprache, *Neske, Pfullingen,* 1959, p. 120.

[4] Ibid., p. 96.

which yet continues to demand meaning. It is no accident that so much of Heidegger's published work is part of an extended dialogue with Nietzsche, who had predicted the collapse of the traditional structure of values and beliefs and the rise of nihilism. Heidegger wants to exorcise this specter—not by an attempt to patch the broken value system together once more, nor by raising a new one in its stead; he does not follow Hartmann or Scheler in writing yet another ethics out of Platonic fragments, which cannot convince anyone who is not already convinced. Instead he shows the hollowness of the notion of value, but in the hope to replace the lost value dimension with an interpretation of the meaning of Being. Heidegger's hermeneutic philosophy is essentially a search for meaning (*Sinn*).

"What is the meaning of meaning?"[5] Already in his dissertation Heidegger raises this question. A first consideration suggests the ambiguity of the term. On one hand we can speak of a meaningful life, on the other hand of a meaningful sentence. In asking for criteria of a meaningful life, we raise a question of value; in asking for criteria of meaningful sentences we raise a question of logic. Is this ambiguity simply a sign of an unfortunate lack of precision, or does it perhaps point out the way towards a more fundamental analysis which will enable us to escape from the bifurcation of fact and value, of logic and ethics, by exhibiting the common root of both in meaning? Heidegger attempts to show the latter: ethics and logic, as clearly distinguished areas of inquiry, are artificial abstractions if we forget the more fundamental level of meaning. Thus when Heidegger was asked why he had not written a treatise on ethics, he could answer that once the nature of his questioning had been understood, the need for a distinct ethics would be seen to disappear.[6]

If this is the program of Heidegger's philosophy, how is it accomplished? What is the meaning of meaning that it can bend together the seemingly disparate realms of fact and value? An adequate answer to this question can be provided only by an exposition of Heidegger's thought in all its complexity. As an introduction to such an exposition, it may, however, be well to take at least a brief look at Heidegger's discussion of meaning in those works which precede *Being and Time*, particularly in the *Dissertation* and the *Habilitationsschrift*.[7]

Meaning, Heidegger points out in the *Dissertation*, is closely related to thinking, more precisely, to a thinking which is not a mere representing, but rather can be said to be correct or incorrect, true or false.[8] The problem of meaning is related to the problem of truth. But what is truth? Already at this point Heidegger rejects the traditional conception of truth as *adaequatio intellectus et rei*, as a correspondence

---

[5] *Die Lehre vom Urteil*, p. 95. *All translations are my own.*

[6] *Über den Humanismus*, Klostermann, Frankfurt a. M., 1949, p. 39.

[7] *Die Kategorien- und Bedeutungslehre des Duns Scotus*, Mohr, Tübingen, 1916 (referred to in text as *Habilitationsschrift*). *A second dissertation, required before the right to lecture at a German university is granted.*

[8] *Die Lehre vom Urteil*, p. 96.

between our thoughts and the realities which they are supposed to picture.[9] For how can these realities ever be given? Are they not in principle inaccessible and does this not render the definition useless? Instead, Heidegger suggests, an understanding of truth and meaning cannot be divorced from an understanding of judgment. But what is its meaning?

As I look out of the window at the dark blue late afternoon sky, the judgment "the sky is blue" seems like a rather pale, but nevertheless acceptable candidate for a true and meaningful statement. Suppose a blind man were in my place; imagine him making the same statement: The sky is blue. Is it still true? Is it still meaningful? Our first reaction is probably to answer in the affirmative. After all, the sky really is blue and that is what is being asserted. But surely the statement does not mean the same thing to the blind man as it does to me. To be sure, he may have learned that the sky is blue by listening to those who can see; but it would make little difference to him if it were really green or violet. His judgment, if indeed we can call it that, is not a response to the experience of looking at the blue sky, but merely a meaningless repeating of what he has heard others say. The meaningful statement, on the other hand, claims our assent (*gilt*) by exhibiting what is true of an object.[10] Such an exhibition must itself be a response to a claim made by the object encountered which demands to be acknowledged. The sky reveals itself to me as blue; I can shut my eyes, I can simply overlook what is before me by being inattentive; I can turn away from the window; but I cannot change the color of the sky. The sky speaks to me with a clear voice which I cannot mistake. The meaning of an object is what is true of it: the essential characteristics which the object reveals to me. Meaningful thinking is a presentation of the truth; it has to be distinguished from thought which is merely representational, which merely repeats what is already familiar. Such thinking is not a response to a claim received and acknowledged. (This should be remembered when one reads the question: What is the meaning of Being? on the first page of *Being and Time*. Heidegger does not simply ask for a technical discussion; he asks also: What, if anything, is the claim which Being makes on us?) To really see the meaning of something we have to acknowledge its claim. Seeing is more than a mechanical reception of data. We can be blind to the beauties of an evening sky out of laziness, out of a lethargy which prevents us from receiving what nature offers us.

There is another side to meaning which may not be overlooked. In asking the question: What is the meaning of something? Heidegger asks: What is its essential structure? The meaning of an object is its essence, which is brought out into the open when we interpret successfully what the object is. In knowing an object we single it out of the stream of experience, oppose it to that which it is not, and thus isolate it. "Reality can become meaningful only when it is grasped in some way by means of the logical; something is broken out of it,

---

[9] Cf. Kategorienlehre, pp. 86ff.   [10] Cf. Die Lehre vom Urteil, pp. 96ff.

and thus distinguished, limited, and ordered."[11]   Judgment is essentially a positing of an object.   Such a positing is an exhibition of the
essential structures constitutive of the object examined.   Meanings
are essences.   *The meaning of an object may be defined as the*
structure constitutive of that object, discovered in response to a claim
exerted by it, and expressed in a judgment.

Meaning is the *ens logicum;*[12] the essence of logical judgment is meaning.[13]
Logic differs thus from descriptive science, which is concerned with
facts which have their essence in their "real existing."[14]   Logic and
descriptive science possess different ontological status.   This refutes
the claim of those who hope to subordinate logic to psychology.
Logic is a normative discipline dealing with meanings, while psychology cannot do more than exhibit facts.   Its attempts to explain logic
must in principle remain inadequate.   Still, there is not a total lack of
relation between the two.   Insofar as the psychologist himself gives
a meaningful discussion of facts, his thinking exhibits the essence of
logic.   Facts are given "only through and in a context of meanings
which exert their claims."[15]   Every fact appears in a "logical place,"
determining its position in the entire context of meanings.[16]   The
discussion of facts is thus subordinated to a discussion of meaning.
Psychology is subordinated to logic.

The independence of meanings from facts opens up the possibility of a
science which would draw a map indicating the "logical places" of all
possible facts.   Such a science would not be a description of facts;
the entire realm of existence would lie outside its scope.   Instead it
would exhibit the essential meanings presupposed by all human
experience, especially the *categories*, the most general structures constitutive of the things encountered by man.   Husserl's phenomenology
represents an attempt to draw such a map.   Heidegger's *Habilitations-*
schrift may be read as a contribution to that program.

Phenomenology is the exhibition of the structures constitutive of beings.   As
Heidegger points out in *Being and Time*, such an exhibition would be
pointless if it were to exhibit only what is readily apparent.   Phenomenology looks beyond what is familiar to what this familiarity conceals:
"the meaning and ground" of the investigated beings;[17] it seeks to
discover the essence of these beings, their being.   It is thus essentially ontology.[18]   "Ontology," in turn, "is possible only as phenomenology."[19]   To understand something in its being is to understand its meaning.   Such understanding Heidegger terms *ontological;*
it must not be confused with a knowledge of facts, which Heidegger
terms *ontic.*

As an inquiry into meanings, phenomenology is not empty speculation or
repetition of what one has heard elsewhere.   Thinking is phenomenological only so long as it is able to present its credentials

---

[11] *Kategorienlehre, p. 97.*   [12] *Ibid., p. 108.*   [13] **Die Lehre vom Urteil**, *p. 96.*
[14] *Ibid., p. 101.*   [15] *Kategorienlehre, p. 96.*   [16] *Ibid., p. 22.*
[17] *Sein und Zeit, 7th ed., Niemeyer, Tübingen, 1953, p. 35.*
[18] *Ibid., p. 37.*   [19] *Ibid., p. 35.*

(*Ausweisung*), i.e., so long as it is able to show that what it presents are not mere conjectures, but that in thinking about an object, full justice has been done to the claims of that object. Phenomenology is not concerned with making new discoveries, but with freeing our vision from obstructions so as to see in the familiar the concealed meaning.

Heidegger acknowledges his debt to phenomenology by dedicating *Being and Time* to Husserl. Yet, already in the *Habilitationsschrift* there are elements which suggest certain misgivings and which hint at the departure from Husserl's conception of phenomenology which takes place in *Being and Time*. This dissatisfaction is implicit in Heidegger's discussion of meaning. "Objectivity has meaning only for a judging subject."[20] Meaning is essentially for a subject. If this role of the subject is forgotten, it is impossible to provide an adequate discussion of the meaning of meaning. We have to beware of thinking that a logical discussion of meaning can dispense with an account of subjectivity.[21] For too long philosophers have asked the meaning of the objects encountered while forgetting the more fundamental question: What is the meaning of that encounter? Our emphasis on essences may lead us to forget that consciousness is the life of the spirit. The subject which is presupposed by all thought must be understood as "living spirit."[22] Heidegger concludes the *Habilitationsschrift* with a demand for a more satisfactory treatment of the problem of subjectivity: Philosophy confronts the task of a "final metaphysical-teleological interpretation of consciousness."[23] Both terms should be noted. In calling for a *metaphysical* account, Heidegger rejects on one hand all attempts to reduce consciousness to the level of blind fact,[24] on the other an approach which makes it into a lifeless epistemological or transcendental subject.[25] The inadequacy of the former approach is demonstrated in the *Dissertation*. The latter approach is equally mistaken in making the assumption that a particular discipline, be it epistemology, be it logic, be it phenomenology, can be prior to ontology. The epistemologist cannot provide principles or criteria which all meaningful discourse, including that of the ontologist, must obey. To do so is to overlook that these criteria themselves have a certain being which requires ontological clarification. Epistemology presupposes ontology just as much as ontology presupposes epistemology. The attempt to argue for the priority of one over the other overlooks the circle which ties the two inseparably together.

In calling for a *teleological* interpretation of consciousness, Heidegger expresses the belief that consciousness possesses the valuable (*das Werthafte*) within itself. Consciousness is essentially "meaningful activity realizing meaning."[26] It is "meaningful activity" in that it is in response to a claim; the subject is essentially claimed by meaning. It is "activity realizing meaning" in that it is essentially a constituting of objects; such constituting is a revelation of meaning. In calling consciousness teleological, Heidegger wants to point out that meaning

---

[20] Kategorienlehre, *p. 234.*   [21] Ibid., *p. 235.*   [22] Ibid., *pp. 234, 235.*
[23] Ibid., *p. 235.*   [24] Ibid., *p. 236.*   [25] Ibid., *pp. 237, 238.*   [26] Ibid., *p. 235.*

is not something which we just happen to find, but rather dwells within us. Understanding is essentially meaningful. A metaphysical inquiry into the essence of consciousness can therefore be nothing but teleological.

Heidegger hints that such an analysis would cause the difference between what is and what should be, between fact and value to disappear, by exhibiting their common root in a more fundamental level of Being.[27] Philosophy may not rest content to spell out reality, but it must aim at a "break-through into true reality and real truth."[28]

2. Fundamental Ontology

What is true reality? What is the meaning of Being? Heidegger raises this question in the beginning of *Being and Time* only to point out that before an answer can be given, the meaning of the question must be understood. What kind of a question do we raise when we ask for the meaning of something? An adequate understanding of meaning was seen to require an understanding of subjectivity. Our initial question thus gives way to another: What kind of a being is man to ask such a question? Who is this being who, in asking it, shows himself to be concerned about Being? Before we can ask for the meaning of Being, we must ask for the being of the questioner. *Being and Time* answers this question with a thorough examination of the ontological structure of human existence (*Dasein*). Thus it meets the demand for a more adequate treatment of subjectivity voiced in the last pages of the *Habilitationsschrift*. In doing so, it not only prepares us for an investigation of the meaning of Being, but also supplies a foundation for the investigation of the meaning of things, i.e., for ontology. Heidegger has the latter in mind when he calls the phenomenological analysis of *Dasein* fundamental ontology. Traditional ontology differs from fundamental ontology in that it exhibits the structures constitutive of the things man encounters without questioning the meaning of that encounter. Fundamental ontology attempts to meet this deficiency by turning to the structures constitutive of the relation between subject and object. These structures are called *existentials* (*Existenzialien*) in *Being and Time*. One has to guard against an interpretation which sees in Heidegger's existentials a particular kind of categories, i.e., those categories constitutive of the substance man. The fundamental role of the existentials is overlooked by such an interpretation. *Categories are related to existentials as ontology is related to fundamental ontology.*

Fundamental ontology is in need of a still more fundamental questioning: What is the foundation of the encounter between man and things? If we take *Being and Time* to be Heidegger's statement of fundamental ontology, we should expect a further movement which pushes our questioning beyond fundamental ontology to the "fundamental question":   What is the meaning of Being? (It should be noted that the

---

27 Ibid., *pp. 234, 235.*   28 Ibid., *p. 236.*

discussion of the "fundamental question" does not belong to fundamental ontology, but to a thinking more fundamental than fundamental ontology itself.)[29]   Ontology, fundamental ontology, questioning about Being—these are the three stages of Heidegger's
thought.   The latter stages are required to answer the inadequacies of
the former; they themselves require the former as an answer requires
the problem.

Such an approach is by its nature circular.   Fundamental ontology and
thinking about Being can ultimately not be separated.   Thus, while it
is impossible to gain an adequate understanding of the meaning of
man's situation in the world without an understanding of the meaning
of Being, it is equally impossible to gain an adequate understanding
of the meaning of Being without having understood first the meaning
of the question and the questioner.   A similar circle ties ontology and
fundamental ontology together.   In *Being and Time* Heidegger asks
for the meaning of the encounter between man and things; but to
understand that question we must understand the meaning of things.
This in turn, as was suggested above, reveals itself only when we
understand things as encountered by the subject.   In the end the
separation of ontology, fundamental ontology, and thinking about
Being is a somewhat artificial tool which should not lead us to overlook how intimately the three are tied together.   To understand fully
the meaning of anything around us, be it a painting, or a mottled tile
roof, or a plow, is to understand also the meaning of *Dasein* and the
meaning of Being.   To argue that philosophy can avoid the circle just
pointed out is tantamount to saying that philosophy cannot deal with
the problem of meaning.[30]   Once this circle has been discovered,
traditional philosophy must give way to a more fundamental approach
which Heidegger calls "hermeneutic phenomenology" and which finds
its first expression in *Being and Time*.   In choosing this term,
Heidegger emphasizes his debt to Husserl, while at the same time a
movement beyond phenomenology is suggested.

In calling phenomenology "hermeneutic" Heidegger seems at first to add
very little which is not contained in the first word.   Both words refer
to an interpretation of meaning; and although the term "hermeneutic"
possesses a theological significance which is not found in the more
neutral "phenomenology," this hardly suffices to give us a clear idea
of why Heidegger chooses to call phenomenology hermeneutic.
Heidegger's own explanation only emphasizes the proximity of the
two terms: "Hermeneutics indicates in *B. a. T.* neither the doctrine of
the art of interpretation, nor interpretation itself, but rather the
attempt to determine the essence of interpretation by means of the
hermeneutic."[31]   The circularity of this definition is evident.   Heideg-

[29] Was ist Metaphysik?   Einleitung, *8th ed., Klostermann, Frankfurt a. M., 1960,*
pp. 19ff.
[30] *Heidegger is therefore in agreement with Wittgenstein when the latter points out in*
the Tractatus that any discussion which confines itself to the level of facts
must leave the question of meaning untouched.   Only while Wittgenstein argues
that this forces philosophy to leave the dimension of meaning alone, Heidegger
concludes that it must go beyond the dimension of facts.
[31] Unterwegs zur Sprache, *pp. 97, 98.*

ger says little more than that phenomenology has to discover the essence of interpretation in interpretation itself.   But implicit in this formulation is a demand that the essence of interpretation be not taken for granted.   *Hermeneutic phenomenology is phenomenology which questions itself.*   It is interpretation in search of itself.

To interpret is to exhibit essential meaning; to understand the meaning of something is to understand it in its being.   Hermeneutic phenomenology implies thus a recognition of the fact that ontology, the inquiry into the being of things, may not forget the question of its own being, but must be tied to an analysis of man, the being engaged in that inquiry.   Man's inquiry into Being, is itself a manifestation of Being.   Man is not outside Being, but in the midst of it, while it is within him.   The subject cannot be discovered in a realm transcending Being; nor can Being be discovered in a realm divorced from the subject.   Only an ontological approach can do justice to the problem of subjectivity.   Only a subjectivistic approach can do justice to the program of ontology.

3. The Existential Structure of Dasein

Fundamental ontology is the analysis of the existential structure of *Dasein.* Is Heidegger then a subjectivist who, in subordinating ontology to fundamental ontology, founds the world in man?   Heidegger has frequently been accused of giving an undue significance to the subject. The answer to this question depends on the interpretation of *Dasein.* How close is Heidegger's conception of *Dasein* to the traditional view of the subject?   What is man?

Whatever man may be, at least this much seems certain: Man is a being in the world.   But so are other things such as trees or houses.   Is man then one of many other things in the world?   Is man in the world as matches are in a box?   Within limits this is of course correct. Thus it describes the way in which my body is in the room.   But man seems to be more than just another object.   For objects to be given at all there must be a being to which they are given, a subject which perceives and understands them.   The notion of object presupposes that of subject.   Objects can be only for a subject.   Instead of being just another thing in the world, the subject is thus the being to which alone the world, including all the things within it, can reveal itself. Should we then identify *Dasein* with the subject as we find it, let us say, in the philosophy of Descartes?   Such an approach threatens to rob objects of all independent being, making them into mere appearances for a subject.   The subject is given as a substance to which the world just happens to appear.   We are left with an isolated substance, requiring the intervention of God to break out of the circle of its isolation.[32]   But man is more essentially in the world than the Cartesian analysis allows.   It is impossible to give any meaning to the notion of a self which does not find itself in some world.   To be

---

[32] *Cf. Sein und Zeit, pp. 132, 202–208.*

a self is to be in the world. *Dasein* is essentially being-in-the-world (*In-der-Welt-sein*). Such a being cannot be identified with the Cartesian subject. It is not something which happens to be in the world, but something whose essence is to be in the world. Man is essentially a relation, not a substance. Heidegger points this out when he suggests that, if we were to use the language of Descartes, it would be more correct to identify *Dasein* with the relation holding between subject and object than with either subject or object. Man is the gap which separates and at the same time unites subject and object. He is the "in-between" subject and object (*das Zwischen*).[33] The term "in-between" is, however, too neutral to do justice to Heidegger's conception. His own term, being-in (*In-Sein*), is more suggestive in that it interprets the relation between subject and object as a "dwelling in . . ., being familiar with. . . ." Man is essentially a being dwelling in and familiar with the world.[34] As such he stands over against the world while at the same time tied to it.

To make the encounter between man and things possible, there must be a distance separating the two. As the encounter with things, *Dasein* is characterized by distance; it is marked by the opposition of the self and something other than the self. All consciousness is a positing of some object of thought. In understanding the meaning of something I place it before me. This is implied by the German word *Vorstellung*. Such a positing of an object is not a creation *ex nihilo*. Rather it must be a response to a claim if it is to possess any truth. It must arise out of a willingness to let Being be what it is. Meaningful thinking lets objects appear as what they really are. This presupposes that objects can disclose themselves; but they can disclose themselves only as other than the self. The other supplies the dimension in which alone objects can appear. Man must have opposed himself to an other before the encounter with objects is even possible. What is this "other" which is presupposed by experience? Perhaps this is a meaningless question, for to give an answer would seem to make this other into something, into some definite object, while it is the condition of all objectivity. Thus it cannot be anything, it must be nothing. The projection of man into nothingness is another expression for the being-in of *Dasein*.

Even this formulation is misleading in that it gives too much substantiality to *Dasein*. It suggests that *Dasein* is something which then projects itself into nothingness, whatever this may mean. What Heidegger wants to suggest is that *Dasein* is nothing apart from this projection. A questioning which discovers meanings only in facts must find such formulations meaningless. *Dasein* is indeed not a fact, but a nothingness: a relation, a gap, an in-between. But only as such a nothingness can it be the place where Being reveals itself, i.e., understanding. With the appearance of understanding the unity of Being is shattered. *Dasein* is a rift within Being; only the appearance of this rift makes it possible for Being to disclose itself. *Dasein* is the place of this disclosure.

[33] Ibid., p. 132. [34] Ibid., p. 54.

One of Heidegger's favorite images, that of likening *Dasein's* relationship to Being to that of a clearing in the forest, suggests this. A clearing is a gap within the forest which permits light to enter and thus enables the person standing in the clearing to see the things around him with a clarity which the darkness of the forest does not allow. Only as man steps out of the forest into the clearing and pauses to look at the wall of trees surrounding him, does he realize what it means to be in a forest. Similarly, it is only when a rift has opened within Being, when things appear at a distance, that understanding is possible. The image of *Dasein* as a clearing makes its first appearance in *Being and Time;* it recurs in many of Heidegger's later works. These give a somewhat different interpretation, as we should expect from a thinking which has left fundamental ontology behind. In *Being and Time* Heidegger is the surveyor of the clearing which is *Dasein.* The emphasis is on *Dasein* as a gap, a nothingness. The forest, i.e., Being, is present as that without which the clearing, i.e., *Dasein,* could not be, but it is not made itself the subject of investigation. This emphasis on the clearing has led many interpreters to forget the quiet presence of the forest; as if the clearing could be without the forest, as if *Dasein* could be without Being. In Heidegger's later works, what has remained in the background in *Being and Time* is made explicit: We turn our eyes away from the clearing to the forest.

Is such thinking subjectivistic? Can we even apply the terms "subjectivism" and "objectivism" to Heidegger's discussion of *Dasein*? If Heidegger's conception of *Dasein* has been understood, this must be denied. The opposition of subject and object is just another pair of opposites, part and parcel of traditional ontology, which has been put in its place by fundamental ontology.

In his *Habilitationsschrift* Heidegger had pointed out that the Aristotelian discussion of categories had established too narrow a basis for an interpretation of the world;[35] this led subsequent philosophers to overlook the richness and complexities of the encounter between man and things. In the course of this tradition the world was increasingly emptied of meanings. It became a collection of mere facts, objects of detached observation, to be catalogued and classified. But our first, and still most frequent, encounter with the world is not at all a detached observing of the facts around us. Rather such detachment implies a prior involvement. Thus when the philosopher pauses and gropes for an example of what he means by an object and finally comes up with the chalk which he is holding or the blackboard on which he was writing, he easily forgets that chalk and blackboard were given to him in a rather different manner when he was using them, than they are given to him now that he has stopped writing and detached himself from them. Before this act of detachment they were known in their use. They were essentially things to be used, regardless of whether at a particular moment they were actually in use. The act of detachment changes this. Now chalk and black-board become mere objects, brute facts. The use which is made of these objects becomes accidental. In the former case, where an object is given as a thing to be used, *Being and Time* speaks of it as being-to-hand (*zuhanden*); in the latter case, where it has been neu-tralized into a mere thing, Heidegger speaks of it as being-at-hand (*vorhanden*). Traditional philosophy has emphasized the latter at the expense of the former. In so doing it has reduced the meaning of objects to a point where the world threatens to become a collection of mute facts, which in their brute givenness are meaningless.

A second example may help to clarify Heidegger's position. Take an apple tree blooming in some peasant yard. The peasant, anticipating the harvest, looks at it with different eyes from the artist who discovers color values and the excitement of a net of crisscrossing gnarled branches. A botanist will see something else again, interpreting the phenomenon before him in terms of learned classifications. A boy might see yet another thing: perhaps a tree to climb or a branch to swing from; or he may anticipate what the tree will be to him in the fall: not a bearer of the harvest, but a seducer, beckoning him to climb the fence and to pilfer some of the fruit.

What is the real tree? Or is this perhaps a question which already implies a commitment to the scientific attitude? The real tree—that would presumably be the tree freed from subjectivistic interpretations con-tributed by the different individuals. Thus to get at the real tree we would have to detach it from the different contexts of interpretation. This is the program of traditional ontology. As already indicated, Heidegger sees a need to replace such ontology with a more funda-mental approach. If this is granted, the meaninglessness of this ques-tioning for the real tree is apparent. All the different ways in which the tree reveals itself are justified. To elevate one at the expense of the others is to do violence to the richness of human experience. If, on the other hand, we refuse to abandon the program of traditional ontology, Heidegger's interpretation will seem to put an unjustified emphasis on the point of view of the particular subject.

These different interpretations betray the world in which the interpreter finds himself. Just as the question of the real tree is meaningless for Heidegger, so we cannot ask for the real world. For the peasant this tree is not simply one tree among others, just one thing more in the world; rather it is irreplaceable. Perhaps he does not even notice its quiet presence in the backyard; perhaps it is taken so much for granted that it is noticed only on certain occasions when it seems to demand attention. Such attention will not be a detached contemplat-ing, but a caring for the tree: it requires pruning; or the apples have to be picked; or the splintered branches left by the last storm have to be sawed off cleanly. In such care the tree reveals itself to the peasant. The same is true for his animals, his house, his tools, the fields, the church, and his family. Perhaps he never confronts any of these in their brute givenness as mute objects. But that he has an understanding of the word cannot be denied.

A peculiar geography goes along with such a view of the world. We have become so used to number and measurement that distance has become a neutral quantity. It seems obvious that a field three miles away from the village is closer than one five miles away. Similarly it is obvious that Mexico is closer than England. Or is it obvious? Just look at a map, take ruler or compass and measure the distance! we may reply—but there are different ways of measuring the world. And in this world the ruler may not always adequately reflect what is near and what is distant. The fields of some other peasant, although "objectively" much closer, may lie on the periphery of this peasant's world. In his world distance has a qualitative character; it is related to care and concern. His world is a context of care.[36]

The world described by a geographer shows a very different structure. Distance has become quantitative measure. Such a world lacks a center. Depending on his specialty, the geographer may be as at home in New Guinea as he is in New York City. Or is "home" the wrong word? How can one be at home in a world which lacks a center? With the advance of technology the world in which we find ourselves and have to live has tended to an increasing degree to approximate that of the detached scientific world view. Communication ties our world so closely together that a parochial emphasis on the little plot of land where we happen to have been born has become suspect. And yet, there is a price which has to be paid for this. To be at home everywhere is to be at home nowhere. A curiosity about other places has taken the place of the ability to identify oneself with a certain landscape which is home.

The world in which man finds himself possesses not only a spatial, but also a temporal order. Here again it is possible to contrast the time of the detached scientific observer with time as it is discovered in caring for the world. The peasant knows when it is time to get up, time to milk the cows, time to go out to the fields, and time to return; he knows when it is time to sow and time to bring in the harvest; there is the cycle of the year marked by the great religious holidays. We can expand this orbit and speak of a history which possesses the peasant and which he possesses. This history is not learned from history books. It reveals itself in the Sunday afternoon walks to the graves of his ancestors, in the short prayer which is said, in the watering of the pansies on the grave, or in the careful pulling of some weeds. It reveals itself in the walk past the massive renaissance city hall, past the portal of the church where another age had carved the devil dragging frightened evildoers with a huge chain into the gaping, sharklike jaws of hell. In making history into a science this sense of belonging to history is lost. We have removed ourselves too effectively from the past to still belong to it. To the detached observer the time intervening between the present and the events described is no longer a constitutive element of the historic fact. Time has been reduced to a coordinate on which one may move back and forth with equal facility. Again we find that just as the scientific-

36 Cf. *Sein und Zeit*, pp. 63–113.

technological spirit of our age has led us to feel increasingly at home in different parts of the world, so it has acquainted us with different historical periods. A sign of this is the openness of the artist to stimuli from all periods and cultures, an openness which goes hand in hand with a pervasive rootlessness. The rise of history as a science, or perhaps better, the rise of the spirit for which it stands, has led to a loss of the sense of possessing and being possessed by history. History which strives to be a science (*Historie*), robs man of his history (*Geschichte*). That this is done in the name of greater objectivity, is only an invitation to demand that this objectivity present its credentials.[37]

I chose as my example a peasant; and although Heidegger likes to choose similar examples, such a choice may seem somewhat anachronistic in a society where the peasant is doomed to extinction, to be replaced by the farmer who will exploit the soil in the way an engineer forces a river to turn the turbines which will yield electricity. Such an example betrays a certain nostalgia, a desire to find a home in an urban world marked by faceless anonymity. It is indeed not difficult to discover such a longing in Heidegger's works. Heidegger likes to think of himself as of someone who still belongs to the country, who is still more at home in the tavern, talking to other peasants about the weather or the illness of some animal, about these little events which matter in a peasant's world, than amidst the chattering crowd attending professional conferences and social gatherings. Still, one is not quite convinced by this show of earthiness. It seems typical, not so much of a peasant turned thinker, as of a very modern dissatisfaction with the modern world. There is in Heidegger much of the old *Wandervogel* spirit, which led young men and women to escape from the grey cities into the countryside, armed with lute and song, in search of a Germany which already the romantics had failed to find. At times it is very difficult to say when the search for a home in history and landscape becomes an escape from the situation into which the individual has been cast rather than an affirmation of it.[38] This vision of the peasant's serene acceptance of his place in the world may be attractive, but do we not also know that we cannot make it our own, that to do so is not so much an expression of the will to affirm oneself and one's roots as a flight from the present?

I have tried to suggest briefly the role played by landscape and history as constitutive structures of man's understanding of his situation. Throughout this discussion another such structure was present, if not made explicit: *Dasein's* being-in-the-world as a being-with-others (*Mit-Sein*). If we follow Heidegger, the attempt to prove that there are other human beings besides myself must not only remain a failure, but is unnecessary; it shares the futility of all attempts to prove the existence of a real world. In both cases we find a refusal to put the

---

[37] Cf. *Sein und Zeit*, pp. 372–404. Also "Der Zeitbegriff in der Geschichtswissenschaft," Zeitschrift für Philosophie und philosophische Kritik, vol. CLXI, pp. 173–188, 1916.

[38] Cf. "Warum bleiben wir in der Provinz?" Der Alemanne, Zu neuen Ufern, Kulturbeilage, Folge 9 (3. 7, 1934), p. 1.

basis from which the argument proceeds in question. As a consequence a problem is created which disappears when the movement to fundamental ontology is made. Man is not an isolated substance, a being in isolation, who accidentally, nobody knows how, establishes relationships with other equally isolated beings. Rather, being-related-to-others is constitutive of our own being. As human beings we are part of a community. This community is not something which has to be established, but it is given to man as part of his own being. Thus history and landscape are first of all structures of communication. Our peasant would think it silly if we tried to prove to him the meaning of his dead ancestors or the reality of the people encountered in his daily walk through the village. The philosopher expounding a proof of the existence of other minds to more or less attentive students does indeed have a problem; but this problem has been created by bracketing too much of the world—which reveals itself to him, at the very moment he is addressing his students, as richer than his problem allows. But this bracketing makes it impossible for him to do justice to the problem of communication.

If this problem were confined to a small and harmless segment of our population, there would be no reason for concern. But the possibility of an estrangement from self to a point where man is unable to discover a meaningful human context is not so remote as that example might suggest. Man can fail to recognize his fellow human beings; he can become apathetic to them or mistake them for objects to be manipulated and perhaps to be cast away as he sees fit. Where we find such a failure it is senseless to accuse the murderer of murder; where man is not recognized in his humanity the word "murder" has lost all meaning. This might seem a rather farfetched academic discussion, if the events of not too distant years had not demonstrated how far in this direction man can go. Such a failure on the part of the individual to grasp himself in his being-with-others, betrays a lack of strength in the face of the temptation not to be oneself. The discussion of subjectivity, which has become a central strand of the development of modern philosophy, has done its part to further such an estrangement.

4. Truth
and Value

In the daily walk to work, in our care for house and garden, in conversations with our neighbors, we understand the meaning of life. But what is it that we understand? What should we answer to someone who came to ask us about this meaning? Undoubtedly such an itinerant philosopher would be disappointed in his curiosity. We should hardly know what to say to him. The meaning of our place in the world does not disclose itself to us in clear and distinct ideas; there is only a feeling, a mood.

Traditional philosophy, with its stress on objective, sober questioning, has done little justice to the phenomenon of mood. It has regarded moods as little more than confused ideas, hardly worth serious discussion and certainly not reliable guides to an understanding of the world. Heidegger rejects this view. For what do we mean when we say we understand something? Certainly we have to admit that we never understand completely isolated objects; rather whatever is understood is understood as part of a larger context. Our discovery of things in the world always takes place against the background of the situation in which we happen to find ourselves. Our understanding of that situation colors whatever we discover. Heidegger calls such understanding mood (*Stimmung*). Mood discloses the situation (*Befindlichkeit*) of *Dasein* in its entirety. Mood may thus not be regarded as a consequence of some particular experience which causes us to be in that mood; rather, all particular experiences presuppose a mood in Heidegger's sense. Thus to encounter something frightening presupposes the mood of fear; in a particularly frightening situation even the smallest things, which often would hardly be noticed, can suddenly assume frightful significance. Similarly a phrase such as "to look at the world with rose-colored glasses" calls attention to the fact that man discovers the world in a manner governed by mood. Even the detached and apparently so objective understanding of the philosopher presupposes a mood. When this mood gives way to another, when, for example, he permits himself to be distracted by the summer light outside the library window, the philosopher may have little choice but to close his books and to take a walk. He is simply not in the mood to think about the meaning of Being.

One has to beware of interpreting mood merely as an emotional state of the subject which can be made the object of scientific investigation. It must be admitted that all moods are indeed such emotional states and as such can be investigated by psychology; but the possibility of such investigation should not blind us to the fact that the world view which governs such questioning also presupposes a mood. The phenomenon of mood can be interpreted in two rather different ways: on one hand as a psychological state of the subject, on the other, as a constitutive element of the encounter between subject and object, i.e., as part of the existential structure of *Dasein*. The former approach yields a factual, ontic, the latter an ontological analysis of mood. If the scientific point of view is accepted, to look at the world with "rose-colored glasses" has to be considered a too subjective and therefore deficient mode of interpreting the world. The ontological structure of mood must, however, escape such an approach. It can be provided only by an analysis of the existential structure of *Dasein*. For such an analysis we have to turn to fundamental ontology. The two accounts of mood cannot be divorced completely, as both psychology and fundamental ontology contribute to our understanding of man. Man's curious dual nature makes it possible to view him on one hand as a being in the world, and on the other hand, forces us to admit that all attempts to speak of the world presuppose the existential structure of *Dasein*, which can therefore never be found in the world. This ambiguity in man's nature makes it imperative for any study of man to put itself in question and to attempt to gain an understanding of the fundamental concepts under which it is operating.[39]

But what happens to truth when mood is given this much importance? Take the example of the philosopher whom the summer sun entices to leave the library. Does the fact that his mood has changed affect the nature of the truth for which he is searching in any way? Does mood have any relevance to a discussion of what is true? Should it not rather be bracketed to the greatest possible degree as an unfortunate impediment on the path to truth? Heidegger's emphasis on mood does indeed suggest that the search for "the truth" about an object is vain. Such a truth could be discovered only if it were possible to divorce knowledge from all subjective interpretations introduced by the mood of the observer. But is the objectivity demanded by this view of truth even conceivable? Heidegger denies this. His rejection of the traditional view of truth is based on his denial of the underlying assumption that something can be given apart from our understanding of it. Traditionally, our understanding can be said to be true or false depending on its correspondence with some given object. The correspondence theory of truth presupposes thus a polarity of the given and understanding, of real and ideal being. But how is any being given except in understanding? To speak about beings in any way whatsoever is to speak about them as they disclose themselves to man. Thus the polarity of the given and understanding breaks down. There are no objects which are given independently of all understanding. This makes it impossible to demand that understanding be objective; for to do so is to imply the independent reality of objects. Similarly it is impossible to claim that understanding is too subjective. In doing so we presuppose that the subject is given prior to understanding. But *Dasein* does not possess understanding as an accidental attribute; it *is* understanding. As such it is essentially in some mood in which man's situation discloses itself. Such a disclosure cannot be a subjective distortion of truth, as there is nothing outside understanding which could be distorted. Heidegger's fundamental ontology ascribes such a basic role to understanding that it is impossible to find any standard outside it by which it could be measured. Consequently, if truth is not to become a meaningless term it must be discovered in understanding itself. Heidegger does this by arguing that understanding and truth cannot be divorced: understanding *(Verstehen)* reveals to man his situation *(Befindlichkeit)* and the things which make up his world; such disclosure Heidegger calls truth. Truth is the discovery of what is. Something is lifted out of the unknown and made known. Such a discovery implies a willingness to let the discovered being be what it is. To know the truth about an object is to accept the way in which the object reveals itself to me without distorting it. Such knowledge is possible only where there is a willingness to listen to the claim of that object and to respond to it. Thus in caring for his tools or animals, a peasant understands them, and such understanding may

[39] *Sein und Zeit, pp. 134–140.*

be said to be true, if it is not based on mere manipulation which does not care for what it manipulates, but is born out of a willingness to listen to the claim of these things. The will to truth is a will to listen. Only he who is able to listen will succeed in discovering the truth of beings.

Things can be discovered only because *Dasein* is essentially understanding. The truth of beings, which lies in their discovered meaning, has its foundation in the truth of *Dasein* which lies in its being essentially discovering. Heidegger calls the latter the primary sense of truth.[40] It has its ground in the existential structure of *Dasein* as the clearing of Being, i.e., as the place where Being reveals itself. Truth, in this sense, is the disclosure of Being. "Being—not beings—'is given' only in so far as there is truth. And truth *is* only in so far and as long as there is *Dasein*. Being and truth 'are' equally fundamental."[41]

It remains to be shown how this conception of truth is transformed into the correspondence theory of traditional philosophy. Our original understanding of things, as suggested in the last section, is not distinct from our concern for these things. The things encountered are interpreted in terms of a context of use and care. They are beings-to-hand. Traditional philosophy and the scientific world view which is part of that tradition have demanded a more detached view of things. This detachment isolated things from the living context in which they normally appear. The object is reduced to a brute fact confronting me. Knowledge becomes *of* a thing, where the "of" is emphasized to suggest the detachment, the lack of engagement. This conceals the intimate relationship between understanding and what is understood. The discovered is separated from the act of discovery. Having split understanding from its object, both are regarded as beings-at-hand, as *intellectus* and *res*. Truth becomes a correspondence between the two: *adaequatio intellectus et rei*.[42] On this view the phrase "objective truth" makes perfect sense. Take a statement such as "Vaduz is the capital of Liechtenstein." In some sense it is certainly true: Vaduz really is the capital of Liechtenstein. But what is the meaning of this statement? Is it indeed meaningful, if we remember that meaning is discovered only in response to a claim? For most of us a statement such as this is little more than a repetition of something we have heard elsewhere. It is not the expression of an experience. It does not reveal being in its being. To be sure, it does exhibit a fact. But a fact is precisely something which no longer has a place in a living context of care and concern. Heidegger calls such statements "certain." *Certainty (Gewissheit) is truth which has become meaningless*. The demand for "the truth" about an object is a demand for certainty. Certainty does not yield meanings, but facts. The object is reduced to a brute given confronting man, in its muteness defying meaningful understanding. This disengaged way of understanding is not more fundamental than one which is engaged, but derived from it. *Being-at-hand presupposes being-to-hand*. The latter implies that things are part of a living context; the former way

---

of understanding brackets this context. The latter implies that things are discovered as meaningful; the former refers to beings devoid of meaning.

Heidegger's discussion of truth in *Being and Time* represents a significant development over the earlier discussion of truth and meaning in the *Dissertation*. In the *Dissertation* Heidegger had still thought it possible to oppose a realm of *ideal* meanings to a realm of *existing* facts. In accepting the polarity of essence and existence the *Dissertation* still belongs to traditional ontology. This bifurcation is rejected by fundamental ontology. Heidegger now realizes that an essence which does not retain its roots in concrete existence is meaningless. With this the essentialism of the young Heidegger is overcome. Essence cut off from existence is as meaningless as existence cut off from essence.

Traditional ontology with its stress on objective and detached understanding has tended to reduce all reality to being-at-hand. This reduction has fostered an understanding of the world which sees in it little more than a collection of meaningless objects. The world view of traditional metaphysics is nihilistic in that it has lost sight of the dimension of meaning. Heidegger's struggle against traditional ontology is thus at the same time a struggle against nihilism. This suggestion may seem somewhat perplexing. The concern for value seems to have its place at the very center of the philosophic tradition. Again and again philosophers have built elaborate systems of values and thus defied the specter of nihilism. How are we to understand Heidegger's charge that such attempts serve only to disguise the presence of nihilism, throwing over the absence of meaning the veil of value? What is the relationship between meaning and value? What indeed is nihilism?

Nietzsche had summed up the essence of nihilism in the phrase: God is dead.[43]   Nietzsche refers here first of all to the Christian God; but beyond this, the phrase expresses the conviction that the dimension of true being beyond appearances, the realm of ideas and ideals, has lost its power of claiming man. The *nihil* of nihilism suggests that this dimension is nothing. "The word 'God is dead' means: the supersensible world is without effective power. It grants no life. Metaphysics, i.e., for Nietzsche Western philosophy understood as Platonism, has come to an end."[44]   The place which God had occupied has become empty. There are no binding laws. Everything is allowed. We may attempt to disguise the death of God by raising idols in His stead: The belief in social progress may take the place of belief in God; eternal bliss may be transformed into the greatest happiness of the greatest number; religious devotion may give way to a cult of strange cultures and customs. But in the end this dance around the golden calf barely conceals the underlying emptiness.

The rise of nihilism is closely tied to the emphasis placed on the subject-object polarity by traditional ontology. In this polarity the distinction

43 Holzwege, *Klostermann, Frankfurt a. M., 1950*, p. 196.   44 Ibid., p. 200.

of fact and value has its roots. Only when the context of care, in which things are encountered in terms of the projects in which man is engaged, is bracketed, do we confront something as a brute fact. The Cartesian *cogito* is the product of such bracketing. It represents a revolt on the part of the subject against the ties of care which bind it to the world. "With this revolt all beings become objects. As objective, beings are drowned in the immanence of subjectivity. The horizon no longer possesses light of its own."[45] With the trans-formation of *Dasein* into a subject the world loses its meaning. Man is no longer claimed. Nothing matters. But how, if nothing matters, is it possible to act at all? Is not all action rendered pointless? A total lack of things which matter leads to a paralysis in the face of the future. If man is to exist at all there must be things which matter, for to exist is to become, to engage in projects. If man is to affirm him-self in his becoming, if he is not to forsake his "will to power," he has to discover values. In this he can succeed only if besides the realm of facts which simply "are," there is also a realm of values, of beings which confront us with an "ought."[46] "Value," according to Heideg-ger, "is value in so far as it is valid. It is valid in so far as it is posited as what matters."[47] Following Nietzsche, Heidegger interprets value to be an entity which answers man's need to affirm his own being. "The will to power posits values as conditions of its own being."[48] Thus man calls valuable the bread which nourishes him, the law under whose protection he stands, the religion which sanctions his way of life. These objects are not valuable in and of themselves, but only insofar as they enhance man in his being. The demand for values is a demand that there be something without man which can answer his needs, including the need to live and the need to under-stand. A world of facts cannot assure these demands. It is not related to man and his needs. The refusal of the world to heed man's needs constitutes its absurdity. To defeat this absurdity the meta-physician resorts to value. He remedies the lack he discovers in the world of facts by "pasting value labels" on these facts.[49] Value theory, according to Heidegger, is thus essentially an attempted answer to the reduction of reality into being-at-hand. This answer differs from that provided by fundamental ontology in that it takes the factual approach for granted. It remains on the level of traditional ontology. In particular it does not question the subject-object polarity. The acceptance of this polarity dooms value theory to failure; for where should we seek value, in the subject or in the object? That the latter fails to provide an answer is easily shown; for in making values into some kind of objects we force it to share the inability of all objects to exert a claim.[50] In spite of all assertions to the contrary, such an explanation of value in the end reduces value to fact. This leaves only the subject as the source of value: values must be posited by the subject. But what provides the subject with the strength to

---

45 Ibid., p. 241.
46 Cf. Einführung in die Metaphysik, Niemeyer, Tübingen, 1953, p. 151.
47 Holzwege, p. 211.   48 Ibid., p. 213.   49 Sein und Zeit, p. 150.
50 Cf. Über den Humanismus, p. 35.

do so? Will a value, which man knows he has posited arbitrarily, retain its validity? If, on the other hand, this positing is not arbitrary, but for a reason, what provides this reason? One may answer that the very nature of the subject provides us with such a reason: Values are conditions reinforcing the subject in its being. Heidegger does indeed point out that all values are such conditions. But this view of value suggests a critique of value theory, for it presupposes that the subject is given as valuable. But what enables the subject to posit itself as valuable in the first place? What enables man to ascribe a value to his own life? That he does indeed almost always do so cannot be denied. What we must deny is that the subject can do so out of its own volition. Man is not self-sufficient. If he could not discover values in the world, he could not find his own life valuable. The subject lacks the strength to posit values.

The discussion of value rests thus on a rather shaky foundation. And yet, it does have its roots in a legitimate need to restore to the factual interpretation of the world the element which has been left out, the dimension of meaning. Meaning, as was pointed out before, has the double aspect of being a claim and an essential structure. The metaphysician in reducing reality to being-at-hand loses sight of meaning as claiming man. The result is a world which does not matter and a subject to whom nothing matters. To restore what has been lost the metaphysician turns to a discussion of value. *Value is the shadow of meaning preserved by traditional ontology.* Where value is divorced from meaning it loses its power over man. No matter what values are discovered, unless traditional metaphysics abandons its deficient categories it cannot do justice to the phenomenon of man's being confronted by an "ought." Indeed, in substituting a discussion of values for a discussion of meaning it will conceal what really matters, for man's existence can become meaningful only where he discovers the meaning of the things around him and the meaning of Being. But all understanding of meaning presupposes a willingness to listen to the claims of the things around us, a willingness to let Being be what it is. The discovery of meaning presupposes a will to the truth. Value theory lacks this will. In giving something a value we refuse to let it be what it is, but subject it to conditions which we have posited. "All evaluation, even where it is positive, subjectivizes."[51] "It has to be recognized that precisely in marking something a 'value' we rob the thing evaluated of its dignity. This means: in esteeming something as a value, the evaluated is admitted only as an object for the estimation of man."[52] Just as certainty implies a loss of truth, so value implies a loss of meaning. Both are aspects of the failure to confront the meaning of Being, in which the meaning of things and the meaning of *Dasein* have their roots. Hoping to conquer nihilism, value theory only succeeds in intensifying its reign. Nihilism is understood here no longer as the absence of values, but more fundamentally, as the absence of Being. "The truth of Being is forgotten." "The *nihil* of nihilism means that it is nothing with

---

[51] Über den Humanismus, p. 35.   [52] Ibid., p. 34.

Being."[53] Being does not reveal its meaning. It remains silent. In this silence the meaning of our own life and the meaning of the things around us must remain obscured.

5. Dread
and Care

Normally and most of the time man finds himself in meaningful situations. He answers the question: What is the meaning of life? by living. The importance of man's daily cares and concerns is taken for granted. But there are moments when a suspicion seizes man that in the end all his striving and all his good deeds count for nothing, that his life is of no account, that all finite being is but an island in an emptiness which in the end will submerge all. Heidegger, acknowledging his debt to Kierkegaard, calls the mood which discloses the nothingness at the heart of everything dread (Angst). So long as man is able to remain within the domain of the everyday, faithfully following the route prescribed to him, dread remains submerged. But suddenly this may no longer seem possible: a voice makes itself heard within man telling him how little all of this matters. He begins to doubt what were believed to be the very foundations of life. The little sphere which encloses man most of the time disintegrates, leaving only a feeling of emptiness. Thus someone who has spent his life being a loyal employee or a faithful husband may someday realize that all the things which he has taken so seriously have not really touched him at all in his inner being. A curious calm fills him. The world of the everyday fades into insignificance. For a moment, at least, he is free of it, alone with himself and the emptiness surrounding him.

Such a mood is always attended by a certain uneasiness; but this uneasiness has little in common with fear. Fear is part of the everyday world. To fear is to face the possible loss of something that matters. Where nothing matters, fear is no longer possible, for nothing deserves to be taken seriously enough to be feared. Dread precludes fear, as in dread the objects or persons which normally demand care no longer seem worth caring for. In dread there are no projects which can interest the individual; one action is as good as another. A kind of vertigo seizes man: Nothing is stable, nothing offers man a place to stand or a sign by which to orient himself. He is left alone with his limitless freedom, limitless because no claim is made to limit it. In dread man understands his utter homelessness. He is uneasy about the meaning of his own being-in-the-world.

What is the source of dread? What is it that man dreads? The answer to the latter question has already been suggested: Dread has no definite object; man is in dread of that nothingness which pervades his being-in-the-world and from which there is no escape—there cannot be an escape because this nothingness has its origin in the structure of

---

[53] Holzwege, p. 244.

Dasein. Man bears the source of dread within himself. Man is essentially a being which understands. To understand things is to confront them as standing over against us, as "other." This otherness is presupposed by any encounter with finite being. Before anything can be given in understanding, there must be this "otherness" which can only be not-anything, i.e., nothing. To understand anything is to project it against the background of this nothingness. Normally we are too busily engaged in the world to become aware of this background; it is concealed by our activity. Only when the veil of meanings thrown over the world by our daily concerns is torn away is the essence of *Dasein* revealed as transcending all finite beings. The nothingness which man dreads is his own.

In dread man withdraws from his engagement with other things into his own being. It is precisely this withdrawal which makes it possible for man to assume a position over against the world and to encounter beings in their being. Only an awareness of the meaning of nothingness can lead man to understand the meaning of Being. Only where there is a willingness and the strength to endure dread can Being reveal itself. Dread prepares man for the understanding that there is something rather than nothing. This mystery may seize us whenever the concerns of the everyday have been negated. Thus looking at a gnarled tree in the fog we may for a moment lose the myopic vision of the everyday and understand what it means to *be* a tree.[54]

But what if the meaning of Being is nothing? If instead of hearing its mysterious call, dread only lets us stare at the nothingness pervading all things and forces us to turn away in nausea? At this point of the investigation the possibility that "nothing" might possess the last word cannot be excluded. The strength to face dread is thus the strength to face an abyss which in the end may swallow all meaning. Where this strength is lacking all that remains is a flight from dread. Since man is essentially a being in dread, this flight must also be a flight from man himself. Man does not want to know what he really is; he does not dare. In dread of dread he flees back into the world of the everyday. Instead of listening to the voice of the nothingness within him, he lets others tell him what he is. He takes refuge from the burden of having to be himself by escaping into the anonymous safety of the mass (*das Man*). It is reassuring to know that one is part of a whole which is greater than the individual, that one is doing only what everyone is doing. Yet this reassurance is bought at the price of authenticity. To be authentic (*eigentlich*) is to possess oneself as one really is. The escape from dread precludes such possession. And yet, if man is essentially a being in dread, what has he lost in losing his true being except his dread? What is missing in the inauthentic life? After all, does one not do what is expected? One has attended the right schools, married the right girl, and associates with the right people. One is successful, one is loyal to one's friends, one's country; one believes in God. So what is it that one has lost? And we can only answer: *Nothing.*

---

54 Was ist Metaphysik?, *pp. 21, 46ff.*

The possibility of an escape from dread is implicit in the structure of
Dasein. Indeed, the dreadfulness of dread lets us regard inauthenticity as the general mode of human existence. Instead of facing the
nothingness into which man has been cast, we throw the veil of inauthentic understanding over the void. Inauthentic existence disguises
the abyss in a surrender to the world and the anonymous "one." Man,
by his very nature, faces the constant temptation to lose possession
of himself.[55]

Throughout this analysis the terms care and concern were used rather
loosely to suggest that the situation in which man finds himself does
not confront him as a brute given, but rather places him into a context of things to be done and people to be cared for. Such a context
is by its nature meaningful; an understanding which has not divorced
itself from such caring, cannot but discover meanings. The analysis
of dread has cast some doubt on this by raising the specter of a
meaningless world. But is this quite accurate? The finite meanings
of the everyday may indeed collapse in dread; there may be no objects
which demand our care; but this should not lead us to believe that
man is therefore left free of care. If this were so, we could not speak
of dread as filling man with a certain uneasiness—for to be uneasy
is to care. In dread man is uneasy about his own being-in-the-world.
Dread reveals Dasein's care for itself in its nothingness.

A lack of meaning was said to preclude care. Care is possible only where
there is meaning; it is essentially care for the meaningful. It can
therefore not be correct to say that in dread all meaning collapses, if
at the same time, we grant that dread presupposes care. What
collapses can only be the meanings of things or persons encountered
in the world. The meaning of Dasein is not only not denied, but
revealed in dread as transcending all finite meanings. The meaning of
Dasein is care (Sorge). Man is a being concerned in his being about
this being. As care Dasein embraces itself in its nothingness: a being
cast into a situation which it has not chosen and from which there
is no escape, facing an uncertain future which in the end will defeat
all its projects.

To say that dread reveals the essence of Dasein to be care, is not to say that
this meaning is given as a fact. In questioning the meaning of things,
dread also questions the meaning of man's being-in-the-world. But to
question is to be engaged in a project. It is itself an expression of
man's care for his own being. Thus it implies the meaning of man's
being-in-the-world, even as this meaning is put in question. If meaning were altogether absent, dread would leave man absolutely indifferent. Were this indifference to swallow all care, Dasein would have to
cease to be.

We spoke of man as discovering the meaning of his life in discovering the
meaning of the things he encounters. The two, it was argued, cannot
be divorced. But has the preceding analysis not forced us to acknowl-

---

[55] Cf. Sein und Zeit, pp. 184–191; Was ist Metaphysik?, pp. 29–35, 45–47.

edge such a divorce, in exhibiting that the meaning of *Dasein* transcends all finite meanings?   What is the relationship between the
meaning of *Dasein* and the meaning of things?   The meaning of
hammer or saw is understood in our careful handling of these tools.
Such understanding, as all understanding, is possible only because
Dasein is the place where Being reveals itself.   As the "clearing of
Being" *Dasein* is essentially in dread.   Only to man, as the being in
dread, is it given to understand meaning.   *Meaning is founded in
dread.*   This dread need not be explicit.   Indeed, it rarely will be;
dread is too dreadful not to be concealed.   Nevertheless, it runs
through all existence like a "hidden trembling," a suppressed recognition of the nothingness of man.[56]   Dread in turn implies *Dasein's*
care for itself.   It is thus also true to say that *meaning has its foundation in care.*   This is not to be interpreted as a self-centered preoccupation with one's private affairs.   Such an interpretation understands
Dasein in too narrow a fashion.   Man's care for himself is not just
another mode of caring, such as care for others or the care exhibited
in the use of a tool; rather such particular cares presuppose man's
care for himself, the former in his being-with-others, the latter in his
encounter with being-to-hand.   As man can only be in a concrete
situation, his care for himself implies care for the things he encounters in the world.   Dread therefore does not extinguish the meaning of
these things, rather it is its foundation.   It forces man to withdraw
from the world only to let him return.   Such a withdrawal prevents
him, however, from losing himself in the world and from mistaking
such a life for meaningful.   The "meanings" of the inauthentic life,
which has forgotten that *Dasein* transcends the world, are denied.
Dread guards against such inauthenticity.   It returns man to himself,
free to acknowledge the meaning of the world.

The answer to this question only raises another: If this is the case, how
is it possible to speak of a loss of meaning at all?   In the sense in
which we speak of losing a pen or a penny, meaning cannot be lost.
Meaning is not an object which can be misplaced and later found
again.   To understand in what sense it is possible to speak of a loss
of meaning, it is necessary to see dread and care together as constituting the essence of *Dasein*.   Nothingness provides Being with the
place where it can reveal itself; it is the foundation of *Dasein* as the
clearing of Being.   It calls *Dasein* in dread.[57]   But to put too much
emphasis on nothingness is to overlook that *Dasein* is the clearing of
Being.   It belongs to Being, listening to its call.[58]   *Dasein's* care for
itself is a care for Being.   Nothingness and Being, dread and care,
cannot be divorced from each other.   This, however, can become
transparent only when the question of Being has been answered: Does
Being have a meaning, does it claim man, or is Being the veil of
"nothing"?   *Being and Time*, which demands and presupposes, but

---

[56] Kant und das Problem der Metaphysik, 2d ed., Klostermann, Frankfurt a. M., 1951,
    p. 215.
[57] Cf. Sein und Zeit, p. 296.
[58] Cf. Holzwege, p. 321; Erläuterungen zu Hölderlins Dichtung, Klostermann, Frankfurt
    a. M., 1951, pp. 25–28.

does not supply such an answer, is thus apt to be misunderstood as a nihilistic document which places an undue emphasis on nothingness and dread. Such a nihilistic interpretation, Heidegger suggests, is itself founded in the nothingness of *Dasein* which not only makes it possible for the meaning of Being to reveal itself, but also its conceal-ment. Meaning is not given to man as something which cannot be overlooked, but in the quest for meaning which is the struggle of man to be himself. Meaning is given to man as a task, not as a fact. Man can fail in this task, he can lose meaning, either out of weakness or because the meaning of Being conceals itself. This double danger makes man's position precarious. He may find himself in situations where meaning threatens to disappear altogether. Yet it is this very precariousness which alone makes meaning possible.

6. Life as a Task

Dasein was compared to a forest clearing. This image may be misleading because it suggests an open space whose borders can be clearly defined. Thus it favors a static, spatial interpretation of *Dasein*. This interpretation makes it difficult, if not impossible, to make sense of such notions as care, meaning, or being-to-hand. In using such terms we take the temporality (*Zeitlichkeit*) of *Dasein* for granted. The analysis of *Dasein* remains incomplete so long as we fail to make its ground in temporality explicit. The temporality of *Dasein* is sug-gested by those passages which describe the "in-between" of *Dasein* as a walk or journey,[59] or as a coming and going, an appearing and disappearing.[60] To understand *Dasein* as a journey is to understand it as being between that from which the journey comes and that to which it proceeds. This implies that before the journey has begun or once the journey has been completed, *Dasein* cannot be in any way, as its essence is denied. Man stands essentially between birth and death. Life is essentially a journey unto death. *Dasein* is this jour-ney. It should be emphasized that *Dasein* is not *on* a journey, but *is* a journey. If the former were true, an attempt could be made to separate the essence of *Dasein* from the journey and to argue that man just happens to have been cast from eternal being into the flux of time, but that his true essence is only obscured, not destroyed by that fall. Heidegger's analysis forbids such an interpretation. It is fundamentally against Platonism.

The description of *Dasein* as a journey suggests the importance Heidegger gives to the project (*Entwurf*). Journeying, *Dasein* projects itself towards the future. Man confronts himself always as engaged in projects to realize himself in the future. The primary phenomenon of temporality is the future;[61] man's care for himself is first of all care for the future. Man does not confront the future as an openness which makes the realization of all his projects equally possible. This is denied by man's having been cast (*Geworfenheit*) into a particular

59 Hebel—Der Hausfreund, Neske, Pfullingen, 1957, p. 17.
60 Sein und Zeit, p. 79; Holzwege, p. 327.   61 Sein und Zeit, p. 329.

concrete situation. The openness of what is to come is limited by the
facts of what has been. Future is limited by past. Man cannot
escape from the past into the future, for past and future are both
constitutive of his essential being. Such an escape would be possible
only if to possess one's past were like possessing a house which one
could sell or get rid of in some other way. But man carries his past
with him. He can indeed estrange himself from it, he can reject
his past and in this sense he can lose it. But he is so intimately
wedded to it that such a loss of the past implies a loss of self. It is
equally impossible to escape from an unpleasant future into a
pleasant past. Again the price which must be paid is a loss of self.
Man can possess himself only as the journey from past to future.

The present is enclosed by future and past. It discloses itself to man in his
activities born by care for what is to come, governed by a knowledge
of what has been. The flight from past and future into a so-called
concrete present is self-defeating and entails a loss of the present
which was sought. Neither future, nor past, nor present can be understood or affirmed without an understanding and affirmation of the
other two. Man's being-in-the-world is essentially temporal. This
implies the temporality of care, which in turn points to the temporality
of meaning.

Dasein understood in its temporality is seen not to be at one with itself.
Looking towards the future it is ahead of itself, looking towards the
past it is lagging behind itself, and engaged in a present encounter
with persons and things it is with others. Ahead of itself, lagging
behind itself, with others, *Dasein* is essentially outside itself. Future,
past, and present are the *ecstases* of temporality.[62] It is this ecstatic
nature of *Dasein* which prevents us from making it into a fact; it also
enables us to understand in which sense *Dasein* is said to be fundamentally care for itself. The notion of care becomes transparent only
when read in the light of the ecstatic nature of *Dasein*. The meaning
of care is temporality.[63]

To characterize *Dasein* as care is to emphasize the openness of human
existence. Man is never given to himself as a whole. He is always
confronted by the task of having to be himself and is thus incomplete.
This openness is constitutive of *Dasein*. Where this openness has
disappeared man can no longer be; man completes himself only in
death. In contemplating the possibility of its completeness, *Dasein*
faces the possibility of its not-being. The demand to survey the
clearing which *Dasein* is in its entirety, can be answered by man only
in facing himself in his being-unto-death. In the face of death man is
filled with dread of his own nothingness. As ecstatic dwelling-in-the-
world *Dasein* has its ground in nothingness. This was pointed out
before when the notion of the clearing was related to dread and
nothingness. In the light of *Dasein's* temporality this relationship
becomes more explicit: being unto death, *Dasein* is in dread. The
strength to face death frees *Dasein* from inauthenticity. This last

[62] Ibid., p. 329.   [63] Ibid., p. 326.

possibility which cannot be surpassed by further possibilities reveals to man the meaning of his being-in-the-world. The meaning of *Dasein* is its freedom unto death. And yet, this meaning is too dreadful to be readily accepted. In dread of dread man seeks refuge in inauthenticity. Man wants to forget death. Thus funerals, rather than acknowledging the meaning of death, more frequently permit man to forget death: someone has died; but in talking about the dead, in honoring him, in speaking of his great contributions to the welfare of the community this fact is concealed. Are eulogies perhaps veils thrown over the dead which veil us ourselves in our being-unto-death? Of course, we cannot but admit that one dies; we know that we, too, shall have to die some day. But not yet; death is still far away, far enough at any rate to permit us to raise screens to hide this last inescapable possibility, which nobody can take from man, which more than any other reveals to man how inescapably this life is his own, how alone each one of us is in the face of death.

The meaning of *Dasein* is its freedom unto death. It can thus not be divorced from the nothingness which is at the foundation of human existence. This nothingness is revealed in dread. Only through dread is man led to himself; only through dread is man led away from himself. Authenticity as well as inauthenticity have their ground in dread which confronts man with the possibility of either gaining or losing himself. This twofold possibility should not be interpreted as confronting us with a clear decision which can settle the matter of authenticity once and for all. Wherever we are this decision has to be made. In every situation the authenticity of *Dasein* is at stake. Human existence is essentially a tension between authentic and inauthentic *Dasein*. Even when one pole seems to have suppressed the claims of the other, the voice of the latter has not been silenced altogether. It either tempts man to surrender his responsibility and to seek the anonymous safety of the masses, or it recalls man to himself. Man is torn between the voices of temptation and conscience. Both are expressions of the tension in which man stands. Both have their foundation in the "in-between" of *Dasein*.

Who is it that is calling when the voice of conscience (*Gewissen*) calls man? The phenomenon is familiar, and traditional philosophy has made numerous attempts to understand it. The reality of the phenomenon could not be denied. But reality had to be interpreted in terms of being-at-hand. Thus the caller was identified with God.[64] Where such explanations seemed implausible, attempts were made to interpret conscience using the language of the sciences, e.g., the voice of conscience was analyzed as the sediment of the sanctions imposed on the individual by society. A satisfactory starting point for a discussion of conscience is provided only by fundamental ontology which interprets conscience as the voice of *Dasein* calling inauthentic *Dasein* back to itself. As such it is the warning call of man's care for his own being.[65]

---

[64] Ibid., p. 275.   [65] Ibid., pp. 274ff.

What does the voice of conscience tell the individual? What message does it convey? What indeed can *Dasein* tell itself? The voice of conscience is silence.[66] This silence leads us back to our own nothingness. The call of conscience is heard in that silence which prevents us from losing ourselves among the many, which sometimes surrounds us in the midst of an enthusiastic crowd and makes us a stranger. This same silence is the foundation of all genuine communication. Most of the time conversations are little more than meaningless chattering which creates a medium into which we can escape from others and from ourselves. The voice of conscience silences this chatter, denies the medium, and forces us to be ourselves. Strength is required to face another person in silence: the strength to let the other person be himself, coupled with the strength to be ourselves. The compulsive need to talk incessantly, like the need always to be occupied in some way to keep boredom away, is a flight in dread of dread. Boredom is the inauthentic response to the silence in which nothingness speaks to us. The inauthenticity of our age finds its expression in the inability to listen to silence.

It is well to warn here against a too ready identification of the voice of conscience with the voice of the good. Many ethical systems would have to interpret Heidegger's conscience as an evil force. For it is a voice which can poison life by preventing man from finding happiness in being like others, by forbidding community spirit, by killing his enjoyment of the innocent pleasures of the masses. Instead it isolates the individual, bringing him the gift of nothingness. Would it not perhaps be better to exile this messenger of the dark, who only comes to cast man out of comfort into homelessness? This home may indeed represent an inauthentic response to the human situation; but is such a response not perhaps "better" than authenticity? Heidegger would answer that such labels only stand in the way of a more basic understanding. They belong to a thinking which fundamental ontology has left behind.

Conscience calls *Dasein* to acknowledge its guilt (*Schuld*). It is necessary to keep in mind that what Heidegger calls guilt is part of the existential structure of *Dasein* and is therefore not to be understood as a consequence of some action. Usually someone is called guilty when he is the *author* of an action which *should not* have been done, or when he is *not* the *author* of an action which *should* have been done. The notions of authorship and negativity are the two central elements of the common understanding of guilt. Heidegger's own analysis exhibits a similar structure: *Dasein* is guilty in being its own foundation, but in such a way that it is completely in the hands of nothingness. Its guilt is its lack of Being. *Dasein* lacks Being as the clearing of Being, as the "in-between," as care. The call of conscience calls *Dasein* to acknowledge its guilt. This is to say nothing fundamentally new: To call *Dasein* to guilt is to call it to be itself in the face of nothingness.

---

[66] Ibid., p. 273.

Conscience demands to be heard. Such hearing is more than passive
receptivity; it implies a response.   Hearing the voice of conscience,
man can respond by running away in obedience to the call of temptation, or he can summon the strength to place himself under his own
truth which calls in conscience.   The voice of conscience discloses to
man his essential being. The authentic response to such disclosure is
the resolve (*Entschlossenheit*) to be oneself in the face of nothingness,
affirming the future in one's projects, the past in one's facticity, the
present in one's care for the world.   Resolved, *Dasein* possesses itself
in its entirety.   Resolve is thus essentially in the face of death.   It is
born out of dread, out of a will to the truth which is the revelation
of the nothingness engulfing man.   Resolve is the affirmation and
seizure of the meaning of *Dasein*, its being-unto-death.

To identify the meaning of *Dasein* with its freedom-unto-death suggests a
heroic nihilism, a faith in the meaning of life in spite, or, perhaps
better, because of a lucid awareness of the nothingness which
governs human existence and which dooms man to certain defeat.
Perhaps this attempt to salvage victory from defeat, meaning from
nothing, is peculiarly German.   *Being and Time* reads at times as if
Heidegger had written it in the shadow of the *Nibelungenlied*, as if its
hero were dark Hagen, who stands beyond good and evil, whose life is
essentially a life unto death, who possesses the strength to accept the
certainty of defeat and death, responding to it with the affirmation of
the situation into which he has been placed, and who discovers meaning in this decision.   This interpretation of *Being and Time* overlooks
that the work is incomplete, that it was to be supplemented with
an analysis of Being.   Such an analysis cannot be supplied by fundamental ontology, which analyzes the structure of the encounter which
is man's discovery of the world.   For it we must turn to a thinking of
Being which asks for what has constituted this encounter.

7. Language
and Meaning

Being and Time has remained a fragment.   Perhaps the optimism which led
Heidegger to hope that fundamental ontology might uncover the
meaning of human existence was somewhat premature.   The meaning
of man's situation in the world proved to be not nearly so transparent
as the program originally suggested.   The reason for this lay in the
elusive character of the meaning of Being, which had to be uncovered
to exhibit the meaning of human existence.   One sign of this lack of
a conclusive answer to the question of meaning is the possibility of
a nihilistic interpretation of *Being and Time*; another is its fragmentary
nature.   Heidegger failed in *Being and Time* to make the turn from
the meaning of *Dasein* to the meaning of Being; and yet, this turn
had to be made if the meaning of *Dasein* were not to remain clouded
in mystery.

The basic fault of *Being and Time*, Heidegger later suggests, is perhaps that
it was written at a time when the author was not yet in possession of

the equipment necessary for the proposed task. Its failure is the consequence of an attempt to do too much too soon.[67] Heidegger found himself unable to do justice to the question: What is the meaning of Being? Already his attempt to move beyond traditional ontology had been hampered by his proximity to that tradition. This is particularly apparent in the language of *Being and Time*. Heidegger shows some awareness of the difficulties inherent in any attempt to overcome traditional ontology with a language borrowed from it,[68] but the fundamental importance of language is not yet fully realized. There are passages which suggest this importance and which should have led Heidegger to be more careful in his own use of language.[69] In writing the book they seem to have been forgotten. As a consequence of this the general misreading of *Being and Time* in terms of traditional ontology was perhaps inevitable.

If one senses the strain Heidegger placed on the language of traditional ontology in his attempt to force it into the service of fundamental ontology, language failed him altogether in his attempt to think the meaning of Being. This failure taught Heidegger not to take language for granted; it forced him to think about the meaning of language and to be more careful in his own use of it. The later Heidegger is always highly self-conscious in his use of language. At times this self-consciousness lets his writing become bizarre and artificial; more frequently it leads to suggestive, almost poetic formulations.

Why should language not be taken for granted? Is this shift away from thought about thinking to thought about language not a dead alley? How closely allied are understanding and language? In *Being and Time* Heidegger already argues that the two are inseparable. Understanding cannot be divorced from speech (*Rede*). To guard against misunderstanding, the thinker must guard against a misuse of language. He can succeed in this only if he is guided by an understanding of the essential meaning of language.

What is the essence of language? *Being and Time* gives a somewhat puzzling answer: The essence of language is speech.[70] Although the distinction between language and speech is no longer emphasized in the later works, it may serve as an introduction to Heidegger's thinking about language. Its origins go back to Heidegger's first logical phase. At that time Heidegger thought it necessary to draw a sharp distinction between a thinking of meaning and the expressions given to such thinking. The grammatical structure of the overt sentence could not be considered to correspond in an unmistakable fashion to the logical judgment.[71] This distinction was drawn to free logic from a psychologistic understanding basing itself on an examination of spoken language. *Being and Time* softens this distinction somewhat by emphasizing that thinking cannot be divorced from the expression of thought. Speech is as fundamental as thought. Speech, however, does not refer here to overt language as it is discussed in grammars and dictionaries. Rather it refers to an articula-

[67] Unterwegs zur Sprache, p. 93.   [68] Sein und Zeit, p. 39.   [69] Ibid., pp. 160ff.
[70] Ibid., p. 160.   [71] Die Lehre vom Urteil, p. 101.

tion of meaning.[72]   To say that the essential meaning of language is speech is to say that language is essentially an expression of meaning. This formulation suggests how closely allied thinking about language and thinking about meaning must be.   In speech fundamental ontology uncovers the foundation of language.   This distinction is neither entirely abandoned nor rigorously adhered to in the later works. "Language" there refers not only to a factual phenomenon which can be made the object of scientific investigations, but far more frequently to an existential constitutive of *Dasein*.   I shall follow this usage in my own discussion.

The idea that the essence of language is speech is rather empty until its implications have been developed.   Fundamental ontology sees language as one of the basic elements constitutive of the being-in of *Dasein: In language* (i.e., speech) *the understanding of the situation finds expression*.   All understanding is through language.   Thus, when we walk to a fountain or through a forest, we do not first encounter certain objects which are then labeled "fountain" or "forest."   Rather, in discovering fountain and forest the words are already present and presupposed, even if they do not enter explicit awareness.[73]   Language is constitutive of beings.   Where the right words are lacking there cannot be understanding.

Before, we described human existence as a journey.   This journey is essentially a *journey through language*.   Language prescribes the limits of man's world.   All attempts to escape from its tutelage are in vain; such attempts can only lead to total darkness.   Man's dwelling in the world is essentially a dwelling in language.   Heidegger thus likens language to a house in which man lives; walking through this house he discovers the world.[74]   This house, however, is not owned by man —language is the house of Being.   Perhaps we should use the word "temple" instead.[75]   Just as the god is present in the temple, so Being is present in the house of language.   Just as the god is not just one more thing and thus may not be discovered at all by one lacking belief, so Being is not just one more thing, and may therefore be said to be nothing.   Being reveals itself in language in such a way that this revelation is at the same time a concealment.   What we see first of all when we journey through language are things, to be used, to be contemplated, or to be treasured.   Language is a vehicle through which Being reveals itself in finite things.   But in revealing itself in the finite, Being as that which transcends the finite tends to be concealed.   Language poses a threat to Being.   It is, as Heidegger says using one of Hölderlin's phrases, the most dangerous of all possessions.[76]   Language is dangerous because in concealing infinite Being it throws us into the arms of the finite.   It presents the surface and lets us forget the depth.   The danger of language is superficiality.

To speak of the possibility of man's becoming superficial by estranging himself from Being suggests a view of man which furthers the analysis

---

[72] Sein und Zeit, p. 161.   [73] Holzwege, p. 286.   [74] Über den Humanismus, p. 5.
[75] Holzwege, p. 286.   [76] Erläuterungen, pp. 31ff.

given in *Being and Time*. *Being and Time* could account for the transcendence of *Dasein* over finite things, by exhibiting the foundation of the latter in the former.   Based on this, it could give an account of inauthenticity as a loss of self in a surrender to the finite. Authenticity was interpreted in terms of dread and nothingness, rather than in terms of Being, although there are suggestions which point in this direction.   *Being and Time*, as well as Heidegger's later works, may be said to understand *Dasein*'s standing between authenticity and inauthenticity in terms of the *ontologische Differenz* as a standing between the ontic and the ontological dimension.   But what this phrase suggests changes.   In *Being and Time* "ontic" refers to finite beings in the world, "ontological" to the essence of *Dasein* presupposed by and transcending the ontic; this essence, it will be remembered, is a nothingness.   In the later works the ontic pole remains identified with finite beings; the ontological pole, however, is represented by the dimension of Being, constitutive of *Dasein*.   According to the first view man stands between beings and nothingness, according to the second between beings and Being.   These two formulations do not contradict each other.   They may be read together to give a third interpretation which places man between beings and a nothingness which is the veil of Being.[77]

Similarly the image of man dwelling in the house of Being must be understood to complement rather than to deny the image of man as a clearing.   To speak of man's dwelling in a house suggests that man is at home.   Heidegger's thinking about language wants to restore man to this home.   It thus contrasts with the thinking of *Being and Time* which emphasized the homelessness of authentic man.   But again there is no contradiction, as *Being and Time* has *beings*, the later formulation *Being*, in mind.   *Being and Time* represents a necessary stage in the search for home in that it prevents us from losing ourselves in the finite.   The voice of conscience is a voice warning against superficiality.   But the analysis of *Being and Time*, leading to dread and resolve, fails to be convincing unless resolve is not only in the face of nothingness, but also a response to the call of Being.   By itself it is insufficient to give meaning to human existence.

Throughout the later works we find a tendency to deemphasize the role of *Dasein*, while placing a greater emphasis on that of Being.   An example of this is the shift from the call of conscience to the call of Being. This represents a surrender of the earlier optimism concerning man's ability to discover his own meaning.   In the later works the meaning of human existence is seen more clearly to be dependent on the meaning of Being.   The meaningful life is a response to the call of Being.   This is also suggested in *Being and Time*, but, and here we can notice Heidegger's later pessimism, man may wait for the call of Being and yet hear nothing.   Being can withdraw from man and conceal itself, in the case of the individual as well as in that of an entire age.[78]   The ground for nihilism cannot be sought in man alone; it also

---

[77] Cf. Was ist Metaphysik?, p. 45.   [78] Über den Humanismus, pp. 25ff.

is the consequence of a withdrawal of Being.   One senses here a metamorphosis of the theological doctrine of grace and predestination. Man cannot force Being to reveal itself with magical incantations. He can only prepare himself to be ready when it calls him.   In Heidegger's later works a calm willingness to await the call of Being takes the place of resolve.[79]   The hope that philosophy can lead us to meaning has been given up; it can only lead us to its threshold.

The meaning of Being may be obscured.   Not hearing the voice of Being, man is in danger of losing himself amidst the finite objects of the world, losing sight of the infinite which is their ground.   The inauthenticity entailed by such a surrender to the finite is essentially a loss of the whole.   Man's affirmation of himself is only partial; indeed it cannot be more than partial until the meaning of his own being is transparent to him.   Lacking the whole, man is essentially *heil-los*.[80] The German word suggests not only that man has lost sight of the whole in an affirmation of fragments, but that lacking the whole, man lacks salvation.[81] The whole is the Holy.   *The Holy is the meaning of Being*.   Being calls man as the Holy.   The original guilt which governs all human existence is that, in existing, man is witness to the rift pervading Being, a rift which breaks the whole into parts.   As long as this guilt is acknowledged in the call of conscience, man stands in readiness to subordinate himself to the call of the Holy.   But guilt also implies the possibility of closing one's ears in an affirmation of finite splinters and fragments of reality.   The finite may take control of man so completely as to make him incapable of even seeing that the Holy escapes him.

Finite being is posited through language.   The threat posed by language is thus one directed against the dimension of the Holy.   The thinker hopes to circumvent this danger by watching over language, preventing its misuse and guarding against a loss of the meaning of Being. But how is it possible for the thinker to be the guardian of Being, if to think is to use language, and if language is essentially a positing of the finite?   Is this attempt to think the meaning of Being or the Holy not one which must go against the very essence of language? Perhaps silence alone can do justice to Being.   Thus we spoke before of the silence in which conscience calls us.   Such silence is the voice of nothingness.   But how are we to distinguish between a silence which is the voice of a nothingness which is also the call of the Holy, and a silence in which absolutely nothing calls us?   This distinction must be made if Heidegger's search for meaning is not to end in total failure.   Granted that in the end all adequate understanding of Being may be in silence, there must still be a thinking which leads us up to this point.   Such thinking cannot dispense with language.   In other words, how is philosophic thinking about Being possible?   If Heidegger's attempt to think the meaning of Being is to find expression in language, it must be possible to free language from its ties to

---

[79] Cf. Gelassenheit, Neske, Pfullingen, 1957.
[80] Erläuterungen, p. 61.   [81] Cf. ibid., p. 66.

the merely finite. The attempt to think about Being requires an analysis of language which will uncover its possibility.

In his concern for the essential meaning of language, the thinker seeks a dialogue with the poet as one who, in his use of language, can make its essence explicit. At the heart of Heidegger's thinking about Being stands his encounter with the poets, particularly his dialogue with Hölderlin. I chose the word dialogue advisedly. Heidegger's analysis of Hölderlin's hymns is not a dissecting of some given objects, but a response to the call of the poet. Such a thinking presupposes a concern with the meaning of the poet's words. To convey the openness of such thinking, which is first of all a listening, a literary form must be chosen which is itself open, and thus opposed to the scientific essay with its emphasis on fact rather than meaning. This can be said not only of Heidegger's discussions of Hölderlin, but also of the rest of his later works. Heidegger's thinking about Being is aware of its own lack of self-sufficiency and the need to listen to the call of Being. Therefore it tends quite naturally towards the dialogue form; at times this is adopted explicitly, more frequently it appears only in disguise.

Heidegger turns to poetry to learn. But what can the poet teach the thinker? More particularly, what can Hölderlin teach Heidegger? Heidegger's preoccupation with Hölderlin (although there are also essays on Trakl, Rilke, George, and Hebel) suggests that the poet's message finds clearer expression here than in the works of other poets. Hölderlin not only knows how to use language in a way which reveals its essence and thus reveals what it means to be a poet, but he makes this meaning explicit by writing about the vocation of the poet. A high degree of self-consciousness is implicit. As Heidegger is the self-conscious philosopher, so Hölderlin is the self-conscious poet. In both cases this self-consciousness is at heart care for language; this care in turn has its roots in care for the Holy. It is this common care which makes the dialogue between Heidegger and Hölderlin possible. Thinker and poet know themselves to be the guardians of language, the house of Being. Still, there are differences which make the dialogue fruitful. The poet is still closer to the Holy; the poet was raised in the arms of the gods, as Hölderlin writes. The voice of the Holy calls the poet to speak. The poet can reveal its meaning because this meaning has revealed itself to him.

While the poet speaks as one in possession of the Holy, the thinker responds to the call of nothingness. The care for meaning which governs his thinking lets him make the attempt to lift the veil of nothingness and to see past it into the heart of Being. By himself he lacks the strength to do this. His relationship to Being is less immediate than that of the poet. And yet, precisely because he is homeless, and yet filled with the desire to be home, it is given to him not only to understand the call of the poet, but to warn man against a flight from the nothingness into which he has been cast into an existence where the call of the Holy, and thus the call of the poet, not only cannot be heard, but will not even be missed. The thinker teaches man to listen. In this he prepares for the advent of the Holy. The poet listens to the Holy. In this he becomes a mediator between gods and men.

But if, as was pointed out before, language is essentially a positing of the finite, how can poets and thinkers in speaking to us be the guardians of Being? Either this view is mistaken or our description of language is inadequate. The latter is indeed the case: to speak of language positing the finite is misleading. Even if we were to guard against a subjectivistic misinterpretation of such a formulation, it still places too much emphasis on *Dasein* in its finitude, obscuring the meaning of Being. Perhaps it would be more adequate to speak of Being revealing itself in the word as the finite. However, a satisfactory reading is obtained only when the two are read together: the positing of finite being is the self-revelation of Being. The essence of language is tied to the essence of Being. To understand what it means to confront a finite thing in its finitude is to be thrown beyond the finite to its ground. Language may in principle be unable to do complete justice to Being; still, the poet is able to present the finite in such a way that it stands before us revealed in its finitude. In finite objects, made transparent by the word of the poet, we discover the meaning of Being.

How is it possible for the poet to use words in such a way that it is no longer ontic speaking, tied to the finite, but rather ontological, tied to Being? This transformation of language can be understood only if its ontic-ontological character is kept in mind, i.e., if language is understood in terms of the *ontologische Differenz*. It is possible to distinguish between an ontic and an ontological aspect of language, even if such a distinction disrupts the fundamental unity of the language phenomenon. The grammar of language, Heidegger suggests, corresponds to its ontic, the words to its ontological dimension. Language can do justice to Being only if it is possible to free it from the bondage of grammar.[82] Even before the meaning of this statement is understood, it is apparent that Heidegger departs here from his earlier views of grammar. In the *Dissertation* he had demanded that logic be freed from grammar;[83] *Being and Time* reversed this demand by asking for the liberation of grammar from logic;[84] he ends up by asking that language be liberated from logic and grammar.[85] But what at first seems like an obvious reversal of Heidegger's position, becomes part of a progression when seen in the light of the development of his thought. In his first period Heidegger defends logic and ontology against the psychologists. Grammar is understood as an ontic phenomenon. The demand to liberate logic from grammar is a demand to liberate the ontological from the ontic. The demand of *Being and Time* to free grammar from logic interprets logic as inevitably tied to traditional ontology. In overcoming this tradition something more fundamental must take the place of logic. The

---

[82] Über den Humanismus, p. 5.   [83] Die Lehre vom Urteil, p. 101.
[84] Sein und Zeit, p. 165.   [85] Cf. Unterwegs zur Sprache, p. 15.

demand for grammar could be translated as a demand for an existential logic. But such a conception still fails to do justice to language's being the house of Being. Grammar and logic obscure the essential meaning (*Wesen*) of language: to be language of essential meaning.[86] Essential meaning is the call of Being which finds expression in the word. Authentic use of language is in response to such a call.

Grammar and logic place the word into a linguistic or logical space which threatens to obscure its meaning. There is a tendency to interpret the word entirely in terms of the context in which it appears. To learn what a word means, one should, according to this view, ask how it is used, how it operates within a given language. This brings us back to the example of the blind man, making the judgment: The sky is blue. The grammatical approach would have difficulty in finding anything wrong with this judgment. And yet, it is quite clear that the sentence when spoken by a blind man is only repetition rather than response to the call of Being. The grammatical approach fails to do justice to the problem of meaning. The demand to free language from grammar is a demand to free it for its real task of revealing meaning. The context in which a word operates should not be permitted to obscure its essential meaning.

Perhaps it should be pointed out at this point that the word "grammar" is not used here in any technical sense, but simply to refer to the context in which the word operates. We can speak of inauthentic language wherever grammar swallows the word and its meaning. All inauthentic modes of existence develop their peculiar grammars, which provide rules determining how a certain word should be used and in so doing silence its claim. Inauthentic existence demands clichés to guard man against the shock of having to encounter reality. For example, do we still know today how words such as good and evil are used, or is our knowledge simply a repetition of what we were told, liable to give way to a rather different understanding if somebody else should come along to tell us so? Or take a phrase such as "I love you"—what is its meaning?

The character of inauthentic existence can well be discovered by examining the language rules which govern it. It may thus seem possible to reduce ethics and aesthetics to a matter of linguistic conventions. For many, perhaps for the majority, this reduction has become a fact; what should be done is determined by what "one" says should be done. But when philosophy is misled by the fact that such an approach "works," into thinking that it has therefore gained an understanding of morality, it is so caught in the net of its own superficiality as to prevent it from even recognizing that there might be more than the inauthenticity of the surface.

Heidegger's use of language is the expression of his understanding of its essence. Heidegger does not escape from grammar altogether; such an escape, if successful, would only leave us incoherent nonsense. It is, however, possible to use language in such a way that words do

---

[86] Ibid., *pp. 159ff.*

not become completely absorbed by the context in which they appear. Language must not forsake grammar, but it must free itself from its bondage. Heidegger's language does this by alerting us to the essential meaning of certain key words. To assure that the reader will pause to listen to what the word has to say, and wrestle with its message, Heidegger introduces linguistic devices which shock the reader into thought: an otherwise familiar word is made unfamiliar by hyphenating it, calling attention to its roots; familiar roots are used to coin new words; the meaning of a word is developed through an etymological investigation. In his interpretations of the works of others, be they poets or philosophers, the same technique may be seen at work. Key words are singled out and discussed at great length, often at the expense of the context in which they originally appeared. Heidegger has thus opened himself to charges that his interpretations are based on a willful misreading of the texts. I do not wish to deny these charges; in many cases they are supported rather easily. It should, however, be noted that such attacks do not confront what is of central importance in these interpretations. Heidegger does not want to present us with one more interpretation of an often interpreted work which can then be compared to the others. There are no objective criteria which would make such comparison possible. The dialectic nature of his thought forbids such an approach. Instead he hopes that in his dialogues with poets and thinkers the meaning of Being will light up. Perhaps such dialogues will be seen to rest on a misunderstanding when objectively considered; but if such misunderstanding leads to an understanding of the meaning of Being, Heidegger would consider it rather unimportant.

The sceptic may interject at this point that in this vortex of fundamental questioning and thinking not only traditional philosophy, but indeed all possibility of coherent, sober discussion, has been overcome. Heidegger, he may argue, does not even grant his opponents a basis from which an attack could be launched. The only basis which is finally admitted is that represented by thinking about Being. Such thinking may perhaps be meaningful, but there is no way of testing this. Its recognition depends on an act of grace, incomprehensible like all acts of grace. Left are the alternatives of silent wonder and mute bewilderment.

The existence of this danger cannot be denied. It is implicit in a thinking which ends up by obscuring the limit separating thinker and poet. To preserve the possibility of meaningful discussion, it is necessary to see that this last phase of Heidegger's thought is part of a journey rather than a self-contained whole. This journey possesses its own rigor. It is fundamentally the path taken by transcendental questioning which asks for the presuppositions, first of our knowledge of things, then of categories and traditional ontology, and finally of existentials and fundamental ontology. It is here that a critical discussion of Heidegger's thought has to begin. To isolate the last stage of Heidegger's thought from what has preceded it is to preclude the possibility of meaningful discussion. However, we must keep in mind that in the end this transcendental approach negates itself. This negation is the result of the failure of the transcendental approach to clarify the ambiguity of the meaning of Being which results when one asks for the ground of *Dasein:* Is Being mute or does it speak to us as the Holy? This ambiguity is finally resolved in favor of the Holy, as the thinker receives the call of Being in the words of the poets. At this point the transcendental method must be abandoned. Thinking must listen rather than ask for presuppositions. Its speaking must be in response to the call of Being. The distinction between poet and philosopher breaks down, or at least should break down. The later Heidegger tries to be poet as well as thinker, even if his poetry does not let us forget that in the end he belongs to those who seek rather than to those who were raised in the arms of the gods.

In language the meaning of man's situation in the world finds expression. In his use of language a thinker cannot but tell us how he understands the meaning of human existence. In discussing Heidegger's answer to the problem of meaning, attention must be paid not only to what is said, but to how it is said as well. His few attempts to write poetry are thus as relevant to the discussion of meaning as his essays.[87]

Heidegger's demand to liberate the word from the domination of grammar finds expression in his own poems. Many of these are incomplete sentences, ending in silence, e.g., "when the light of early morning grows quietly over the mountains . . . ."[88] This schema is repeated again and again. The word "when" introduces a clause which briefly and very simply sets the stage by raising an image suggestive of the Black Forest: a rainy sky above mountain meadows, torn by scattered sun rays; daffodils blooming in spring; a butterfly sitting on a flower; the light of the evening sun falling golden on the stems of the pines. But the stage remains empty. The spectator waits in silence, a silence which is intended to be and sometimes succeeds in being the language of meaning. Perhaps these poems are too obviously written according to a rule to be entirely successful, perhaps the marriage of thinker and poet is an uneasy one, still we feel at times the touch of the muse, we hear at least an echo of the voice of Being.

Whatever their literary merit, these poems illustrate a danger in Heidegger's discussion of meaning. In *Being and Time* Heidegger seeks meaning in life in its entirety. Very little of this concern is found in the work of the later Heidegger. The everyday world has disappeared. Little is said of man's daily struggle for life and love. The meaning of Being reveals itself in such things as the sound of bells drifting across a summer hillside or a pine tree in the light of late evening. Instead of an acceptance of life we have an acceptance of fragments.

---

[87] *With one exception, all of Heidegger's published poems were written in 1947 and appeared in* Aus der Erfahrung des Denkens, Neske, Pfullingen, 1954. *The exception is* "Abendgang auf der Reichenau," Das Bodenseebuch 1917, Konstanz, 1917, vol. IV, p. 152. *In view of the early date—the poem antedates* Sein und Zeit *by ten years—it is surprising to discover how much its language resembles that of Heidegger's later works.*

[88] Erfahrung des Denkens, p. 6.

As language cannot be divorced from the human situation, the demand to liberate the word from grammar would seem to imply a demand to free the meaning of the moment from the structure of life. The loss of grammar in language seems to imply a loss of grammar in life. Poetry is identified with the meaningful word, authentic life with the meaningful moment. This is an exaggeration; it is suggested by a misunderstanding of the term "word." We cannot identify Heidegger's use of the term with our common understanding of it. Otherwise the ideal poem might be said to consist of just one word. In spite of the fact that his poems show a certain tendency in this direction, Heidegger uses the term "word" to suggest an expression of the meaning of a situation grasped in its unity. G. M. Hopkins has coined the terms "instress" and "inscape" to capture a similar awareness. Every good poem, even one several pages long, is in this sense a word. One can understand Heidegger's stress on the word as a transformation of the classic demand for aesthetic unity. The word assigns everything its rightful place. It demands subordination under a unity. This unity is not to be discovered in formal structure; rather it is the ray of the Holy illuminating the situation. Grammar, on the other hand, demands coordination. Coordinating, grammar levels everything. Everything becomes equally meaningful, and by this token, meaningless.

But while this makes it possible to reconcile *Being and Time* and its stress on human existence in its entirety with the later discussion of the word, it must be admitted that the later Heidegger lacks the strength to capture meaning in the larger context and has to confine himself to detail. Little is to be found which suggests an ability to discover the meaning of life in its entirety, encompassing the meaning of life and death. Perhaps in this age of need, which has experienced the departure of the old gods and has not yet seen the coming of the new, all we can hope for is to catch glimpses of meaning. We must be grateful to see meaning light up in isolated things. However, a warning is in order: Such a fascination with the fragmentary can easily lead us to disregard the structure of our existence and thus to lose the grammar of life. It is no accident that Heidegger's favorite poet, Hölderlin, and his favorite painter, Van Gogh, were schizophrenic.

Man is essentially a being in-between. As such he stands continuously between alternatives. Throughout this discussion we have encountered examples of this. The demand of grammar, on one hand, and that of the word, on the other, present us with another such choice. If instead of having to confront two paths, we were given only one road to follow, there would be no problem. Given two, man is faced by the constant temptation to sacrifice one or the other. "King Oedipus has one eye too many perhaps," writes Hölderlin. Heidegger accepts this formulation, applying it to Hölderlin himself in an allusion to his final insanity.[89] The poet has one eye too many and therefore has to blind himself. He is particularly and painfully aware of man's position in between the ontic and the ontological dimensions. Having

[89] *Erläuterungen*, p. 44.

heard the call of the Holy, the poet is no longer at home in everyday affairs; and yet he cannot escape from them altogether. He is torn between Being and beings. By silencing the claims of either dimension he can put an end to his plight: Thus, he can incur the risk of losing the grammar of life while staying true to his calling; if, on the other hand, in a desire to become just one more member of the community, he seeks refuge in the whirl of the everyday, its busy din will drown out the call of the Holy. Thus Hölderlin's insanity cannot seem accidental. The attempt to lift the veil hiding Being has its price: a surrender of the grammar of life which in the end can only lead to insanity. The commitment to open our being to the call of the Holy shatters life into fragments. Just as such a commitment demands that grammar be sacrificed to the word—Hölderlin's hymns are an example of this—so the grammar of life has to be brought as a sacrifice to the Holy. The poet, or anyone who dares to lift the veil hiding Being, must die or become insane. Expressing the same thought in terms of an analysis of language we can say: The attempt to answer the question of meaning can end only in silence or incoherent, if very meaningful, stammering. Language succeeds ultimately only in suffering shipwreck, returning to that silence in which it had its origin.[90]

One would like to avoid this conclusion, which seems to make sanity the price to be paid for meaning. There is indeed nothing in Heidegger's work which rules out the possibility of a discovery of meaning which would imply an affirmation of life in its entirety. At the same time it must be admitted that Heidegger lacks the strength to move very far in this direction. Indeed, if he is right, his failure to do so is not one which can be remedied by trying once again. A satisfactory analysis of the meaning of Being cannot succeed without submission to the call of the Holy. It requires faith. This cannot be forced; the thinker can only wait.

What is the meaning of Being? The meaning of Being is the Holy. In giving this answer we only point out that in the end this question cannot be answered by the philosopher. He can only lead us to the point where we are prepared to accept an answer should it be offered to us. The answer can be given only by those who have been called by the Holy, by poets and prophets. Insofar as Heidegger makes an attempt to answer it, he turns from philosophy to another, perhaps more fundamental mode of thinking. The step from Heidegger's later philosophy to theology is small. Heidegger is aware of this. Thus when he points out that all thought leads us back to our beginnings he has the theological studies of his own youth in mind.[91] Heidegger's journey leads from theology to theology. This is not to say that in the end philosophy and theology merge so as to become inseparable. Heidegger's philosophy does not provide us with a substitute religion, a philosophic faith. Perhaps it is possible to read *Being and Time*, with its stress on the self-reliance of man, in this way, as a document of faith in the ability of finite man to endow his life with meaning.

[90] *Unterwegs zur Sprache*, p. 216.   [91] Ibid., p. 96.

Heidegger's later works make such an interpretation impossible. Meaning can only be discovered by listening to Being. Man is not so transparent to himself as to permit him to discover the meaning of human existence on his own. In his discovery of meaning he is dependent on an act of grace. With this realization philosophy becomes once more the servant of theology; or, should we say, of poetry? What name we choose matters little: What should be seen is that philosophy cannot give a final answer, it can only provide the strength to wait patiently to be called. It leaves man in that silence in which the call of Being can be heard.

It takes strength and courage to wait. The thinker faces the constant temptation to force open the doors of the Holy before he has been called. He must beware of mistaking the longing to be called for the calling itself. Such impatience makes the thinker a magician or false prophet. Only honesty, the will not to permit oneself to be deceived, can guard us against this. More than any other thinker today, Heidegger demands such honesty from us if he is to lead rather than mislead us.

BIBLIOGRAPHY

The following two works are indispensable aids in the study of Heidegger:

1. Feick, Hildegard, Index zu Heideggers "Sein und Zeit," Niemeyer, Tübingen, 1961.

2. Lübbe, Hermann, Bibliographie der Heidegger-Literatur, 1917–1955, Hain, Meisenheim a. Glahn, 1957.

Works by Heidegger

1. "Das Realitätsproblem in der modernen Philosophie," Philosophisches Jahrbuch, vol. 25, pp. 353–363, Fulda, 1912.

2. "Neuere Forschungen zur Logik," Literarische Rundschau für das katholische Deutschland, vol. 38, pp. 466–472, 517–524, 565–570, Freiburg, 1912.

3. "Kants Briefe in Auswahl, Herausgegeben und erläutert von F. Ohmann," Literarische Rundschau für das katholische Deutschland, vol. 39, p. 74, Freiburg, 1913 (review).

4. "Zeitlichkeit und Zeitlosigkeit, von N. Bubnoff," Literarische Rundschau für das katholische Deutschland, vol. 39, pp. 178–179, Freiburg, 1913 (review).

5. "Von der Klassifikation psychischer Phänomene, von F. Brentano," Literarische Rundschau für das katholische Deutschland, vol. 40, pp. 233–234, Freiburg, 1914 (review).

6. "Kant und Aristoteles, von C. Sentroul," Literarische Rundschau für

das katholische Deutschland, vol. 40, pp. 330–332, Freiburg, 1914 (review).

7. "*Kant*—Laienbrevier, Zusammengestellt von F. Gross," *Literarische Rundschau für das katholische Deutschland,* vol. 40, pp. 370–377, Freiburg, 1914 (review).

8. *Die Lehre vom Urteil im Psychologismus. Ein kritisch-positiver Beitrag zur Logik,* Barth, Leipzig, 1914, dissertation, Freiburg, 1914.

9. "Der Zeitbegriff in der Geisteswissenschaft," *Zeitschrift für Philosophie und philosophische Kritik,* vol. 161, pp. 173–188, Leipzig, 1916 (Heidegger's first lecture, *Probevorlesung,* July 27, 1915).

10. *Die Kategorien- und Bedeutungslehre des Duns Scotus,* Mohr, Tübingen, 1916 (*Habilitationsschrift,* Freiburg, 1915).

11. "Abendgang auf der Reichenau," *Das Bodenseebuch 1917. Ein Buch für Land und Leute,* vol. 4, p. 152, Konstanz, 1917 (poem).

12. "Zur Geschichte des philosophischen Lehrstuhles seit 1866," *Die Philipps-Universität zu Marburg 1575–1927,* pp. 680–687, Marburg, 1927.

13. "Sein und Zeit, Erste Hälfte, *Jahrbuch für Philosophie und phänomenologische Forschung,* vol. 8, pp. 1–438, Halle, 1927. Published simultaneously in a separate edition by Niemeyer, Halle; 7th ed., Niemeyer, Tübingen, 1953. (The pagination is identical for editions 1 through 6; that of later editions shows a slight change, differing by never more than a few lines from that of the earlier editions.)
Being and Time, tr. J. Macquarrie and E. Robinson, Harper & Row, New York, 1962. Simultaneously published by SCM Press, London.

14. "Ernst Cassirer: *Philosophie der symbolischen Formen, z. Teil: Das mythische Denken,*" *Deutsche Literaturzeitung,* vol. 5, pp. 1000–1012, Berlin, 1928 (review).

15. "Vorbemerkungen des Herausgebers," *Jahrbuch für Philosophie und phänomenologische Forschung,* vol. 9, pp. 367–368, Halle, 1928. (Preface to Edmund Husserl's "Vorlesungen zur Phänomenologie des inneren Zeitbewusstseins.")

16. "Vom Wesen des Grundes," *Ergänzungsband zum Jahrbuch für Philosophie und phänomenologische Forschung, Festschrift Edmund Husserl zum 70. Geburtstag gewidmet,* Halle, 1929. Published simultaneously in a separate edition by Niemeyer, Halle (cf. #40).

17. *Kant und das Problem der Metaphysik,* F. Cohen, Bonn, 1929; 2d ed., Klostermann, Frankfurt a. M., 1951.
Kant and the Problem of Metaphysics, tr. J. S. Churchill, intro. T. Langen, Indiana University Press, Bloomington, Ind., 1962.

18. *Was ist Metaphysik?* F. Cohen, Bonn, 1929. (Antrittsvorlesung, Freiburg, July 24, 1929.)

19. *Die Selbstbehauptung der deutschen Universität. Rede, gehalten bei der feierlichen Übernahme des Rektorats der Universität Freiburg i.*

Br. am 27. 5. 1933, Korn, Breslau, 1933 *(Heidelberger Universitätsreden 11)*.

20. Short statements made by Heidegger in his capacity as rector of the university, in *Freiburger Studentenzeitung*, June 20, 1933, Nov. 3, 1933, Nov. 10, 1933, Dec. 18, 1933, Jan. 23, 1934. Reprinted in Guido Schneeberger, *Nachlese zu Heidegger, Dokumente zu seinem Leben und Denken*, Bern, 1962, nos. 57, 114, 129, 144, 145, 158, 159.

21. "Die drei Bindungen," *Freiburger Zeitung*, vol. 150, no. 190, p. 5, July 16, 1933. Reprinted in Schneeberger, no. 79 (excerpt of #19).

22. Lecture given in Leipzig on Nov. 11, 1933, published in *Bekenntnis der Professoren an den deutschen Universitäten und Hochschulen zu Adolf Hitler und dem nationalsozialistischen Staat*, Dresden, 1933, pp. 13f. Reprinted in Schneeberger, no. 132.

23. "Nationalsozialistische Wissensschulung," *Der Alemanne*, Folge 33, p. 9, Feb. 1, 1934. Reprinted in Schneeberger, no. 170.

24. "Ein Schreiben Heideggers an den Reichsführer der deutschen Studentenschaft," Feb. 6, 1934. Reprinted in Schneeberger, no. 176.

25. "Warum bleiben wir in der Provinz?" *Der Alemanne. Zu neuen Ufern. Kulturbeilage*, Folge 9, p. 1, Mar. 7, 1934. Reprinted in Schneeberger, no. 185.

26. "Wege zur Aussprache," *Alemannenland. Ein Buch von Volkstum und Sendung. Jahrbuch der Stadt Freiburg i. Br.*, pp. 135–139, Engelhorns Nachf., Stuttgart, 1937. Reprinted in Schneeberger, no. 207.

27. "Hölderlin und das Wesen der Dichtung," *Das innere Reich*, vol. 3, pp. 1065–1078, Langen und Müller, München, 1937 (cf. #35). "Hölderlin and the Essence of Poetry," tr. D. Scott, in *Existence and Being*, intro. W. Brock, pp. 291–315, Regnery, Chicago, 1949. Simultaneously published by Vision Press, London.

28. "Lettre de M. M. Heidegger à M. J. Wahl," *Subjectivité et Transcendence. Bulletin de la societé francaise de philosophie*, vol. 37, p. 193, Paris, 1937.

29. *Qu'est-ce que la métaphysique?* tr. H. Corbin, pp. 7–8, Paris, 1938 (author's preface).

30. *Hölderlins Hymne "Wie wenn am Feiertage . . . ,"* Niemeyer, Halle, 1941 (cf. #45).

31. "Platons Lehre von der Wahrheit," *Geistige Überlieferung*, vol. 2, pp. 96–124, Berlin, 1942 (cf. #36).

32. *Vom Wesen der Wahrheit*, Klostermann, Frankfurt a. M., 1943 (cf. #39). "On the Essence of Truth," tr. R. F. C. Hull and A. Crick, in *Existence and Being*, pp. 319–351.

33. "Andenken," *Hölderlin. Gedenkschrift zu seinem 100. Todestag*, ed. P. Kluckhohn, pp. 267–324, Mohr, Tübingen, 1943 (cf. #45).

34. *Was ist Metaphysik?* 4th ed., Klostermann, Frankfurt a. M., 1943 (postscript added; cf. #38).
"What is Metaphysics?" tr. R. F. C. Hull and A. Crick, in *Existence and Being,* pp. 353–392.

35. *Erläuterungen zu Hölderlin,* Klostermann, Frankfurt a. M., 1944 (includes #27 and "Heimkunft: An die Verwandten"; cf. #45).
"Remembrance of the Poet," tr. D. Scott, in *Existence and Being,* pp. 251–290 (translation of the latter essay).

36. *Platons Lehre von der Wahrheit. Mit einem Brief über den "Humanismus,"* Francke, Bern, 1947 (includes #31).
"Plato's Doctrine of Truth," tr. J. Barlow, and "Letter on Humanism," tr. E. Lohner, *Philosophy in the Twentieth Century,* vol. 3, ed. and intro. W. Barrett and H. D. Aiken, Random House, New York, 1962, pp. 251–270, 270–302.

37. *Über den Humanismus,* Klostermann, Frankfurt a. M., 1949 (separate edition of the second essay in #36).

38. *Was ist Metaphysik?* 5th ed., Klostermann, Frankfurt a. M., 1949 (introduction added).
"The Way Back into the Ground of Metaphysics," tr. W. Kaufmann, *Existentialism from Dostoevsky to Sartre,* pp. 206–221, Meridian Books, Inc., New York, 1956 (translation of introduction to #38). Reprinted in *Philosophy in the Twentieth Century,* vol. 3, pp. 206–218.

39. *Vom Wesen der Wahrheit,* 2d ed., Klostermann, Frankfurt a. M., 1949 (postscript revised).

40. *Vom Wesen des Grundes,* 3d ed., Klostermann, Frankfurt a. M., 1949 (preface added).

41. "Der Zuspruch des Feldweges," *Sonntagsblatt,* vol. 43, p. 5, Hamburg, Oct. 23, 1949 (cf. #52).

42. Excerpts of a letter to Husserl in Walter Biemel, "Husserls Encyclopedia-Britannica Artikel und Heideggers Anmerkungen dazu," *Tijdschrift voor Philosophie,* vol. 12, pp. 246–280, Louvain, 1950.

43. *Holzwege,* Klostermann, Frankfurt a. M., 1950.

44. Letter to Emil Staiger in Staiger, "Zu einem Vers von Mörike. Ein Briefwechsel mit Martin Heidegger," *Trivium,* vol. 9, pp. 1–16, Zürich, 1951. Reprinted in Staiger, *Die Kunst der Interpretation. Studien zur deutschen Literaturgeschichte,* pp. 34–39, Atlantis, Zürich, 1955.

45. *Erläuterungen zu Hölderlins Dichtung,* Klostermann, Frankfurt a. M., 1951 (includes #30, 33, and 35).

46. "Seinsverlassenheit und Irrnis," *Ernst Barlach. Dramatiker, Bildner, Zeichner,* ed. Kulturverwaltung und Landestheater Darmstadt, pp. 5–12, Darmstadt, 1951 (cf. #60).

47. "Das Ding," *Gestalt und Gedanke. Ein Jahrbuch,* ed. Bayerische Akademie der schönen Künste, pp. 128–148, München, 1951 (cf. #60).

48. "Logos," *Festschrift für Hans Jantzen*, pp. 7–18, Berlin, 1951 (cf. #60).

49. "Bauen, Wohnen, Denken," *Mensch und Raum*, ed. O. Bartning, pp. 72–84, Darmstadt, 1952 (*Darmstädter Gespräche 2*; cf. #60).

50. "Was heisst Denken?" *Merkur*, vol. 6, pp. 602–611, München, 1953.

51. "Georg Trakl. Eine Erörterung seines Gedichts," *Merkur*, vol. 7, pp. 226–258, München, 1953 (cf. #72).

52. *Der Feldweg*, Klostermann, Frankfurt a. M., 1953 (reprint of #41).

53. *Einführung in die Metaphysik*, Niemeyer, Tübingen, 1953.
An Introduction to Metaphysics, tr. R. Manheim, Yale University Press, New Haven, Conn., 1959. Chap. 1 reprinted as "The Fundamental Question of Metaphysics," *Philosophy in the Twentieth Century*, vol. 3, pp. 219–250.

54. "Heidegger über Heidegger," *Die Zeit*, no. 39, Hamburg, Sept. 24, 1953 (letter to the editor).

55. "Die Frage nach der Technik," *Die Künste im technischen Zeitalter. Gestalt und Gedanke III*, pp. 70–108, München, 1954 (cf. #60).

56. "Anmerkungen über die Metaphysik," *Im Umkreis der Kunst. Eine Festschrift für Emil Preetorius*, pp. 117–136, Wiesbaden, 1954 (cf. #60).

57. "Wissenschaft und Besinnung," *Börsenblatt für den deutschen Buchhandel*, vol. 10, no. 29, pp. 203–211, Frankfurter Ausgabe, Apr. 13, 1954.

58. ". . . dichterisch wohnet der Mensch," *Akzente*, vol. 1, pp. 57–71, München, 1954 (cf. #60).

59. "Heraklit," *Festschrift zur Feier des 350 jährigen Bestehens des Heinrich-Suso-Gymnasiums in Konstanz*, pp. 60–76, Konstanz, 1954 (cf. #60).

60. *Vorträge und Aufsätze*, Neske, Pfullingen, 1954 (includes #46–49, 55, 56, 58, 59, and other previously unpublished essays).

61. *Aus der Erfahrung des Denkens*, Neske, Pfullingen, 1954.

62. *Was heisst Denken?* Niemeyer, Tübingen, 1954.

63. "Über 'Die Linie,' " *Festschrift für Ernst Jünger zum 70. Geburtstag*, pp. 9–45, Klostermann, Frankfurt a. M., 1955.

64. *Zur Seinsfrage*, Klostermann, Frankfurt a. M., 1956 (slightly revised edition of #63).
The Question of Being, tr. W. Kluback and J. T. Wilde, Twayne Pub., New York, 1958.

65. *Was ist das—die Philosophie?* Neske, Pfullingen, 1956.
What is philosophy? tr. W. Kluback and J. T. Wilde, Twayne Pub., New York, 1958.

66. Gespräch mit Hebel, no. 4 in Schriftenreihe des Hebelbundes Sitz Lörrach, 1956.

67. Hebel—Der Hausfreund, Neske, Pfullingen, 1957 (reprint of #66).

68. Identität und Differenz, Neske, Pfullingen, 1957.
Essays in Metaphysics: Identity and Difference, tr. K. F. Leidecker, Philosophical Library, New York, 1960.

69. Der Satz vom Grund, Neske, Pfullingen, 1957.

70. Gelassenheit, Neske, Pfullingen, 1959.
Discourse on Thinking, tr. J. M. Anderson and E. H. Freund, Harper & Row, New York, 1966.

71. "Der Weg zur Sprache," Die Sprache. Gestalt und Gedanke IV, pp. 93–114, Darmstadt, 1959 (cf. #72).

72. Unterwegs zur Sprache, Neske, Pfullingen, 1959 (includes #51, 71, and other previously unpublished works).

73. "Aufzeichnungen aus der Werkstatt," Neue Züricher Zeitung, vol. 69, no. 2898, p. 5, Sept. 27, 1959.

74. "Vom Wesen und Begriff der Physis. Aristoteles Physik B 1," il Pensiero, vol. 3, nos. 2–3, pp. 131–156, 265–290, 1958. Reprinted in the Biblioteca "il Pensiero," Istituto Editoriale Cisalpino, Milano—Varese, 1960.

75. Nietzsche, 2 vols., Neske, Pfullingen, 1961.

76. "Sprache und Heimat," Dauer und Wandel. Festschrift zum 70. Geburtstag von Carl J. Burckhardt, ed. H. Rinn and M. Rychner, Callwey, München, 1961, pp. 174–193.

77. "Aus einer Erörterung der Wahrheitsfrage," Zehn Jahre Neske Verlag, Neske, Pfullingen, 1962.

78. Die Technik und die Kehre, Neske, Pfullingen, 1962 (in the series Opuscula, Aus Wissenschaft und Dichtung; includes reprint of #55).

79. Die Frage nach dem Ding. Zu Kants Lehre von den transzendentalen Grundsätzen, Niemeyer, Tübingen, 1962.

80. Kants These über das Sein. Klostermann, Frankfurt a. M., 1963 (Sonderdruck aus der Festschrift für Erik Wolf Existenz und Ordnung, Klostermann, Frankfurt a. M., 1962).

81. Über Abraham a Santa Clara, Stadt Messkirch, 1964.

CHAPTER FIVE

GABRIEL MARCEL
THE MYSTERY OF BEING

EDWARD G. BALLARD

EDWARD G. BALLARD *studied philosophy at Harvard University, the University of Virginia, The Sorbonne, Université d'Aix et Marseilles, and elsewhere, and has taught at the University of Virginia, Virginia Military Institute, The University of Texas, and Yale University. He is now a professor of philosophy at Tulane University. Among his publications are "On Cognition of the Pre-Cognitive"* (The Philosophical Quarterly, *1961);* Art and Analysis (The Hague: Nijhoff, 1957); *and* Socratic Ignorance, a Study in Platonic Self-Knowledge (Nijhoff, 1965). *He, together with Mr. Lester Embree, is currently translating a collection of essays on phenomenology by Paul Ricoeur which will be published by The Northwestern University Press.*

Gabriel Marcel's childhood was strangely marked by ambivalences. He was
an affectionate child, but a lonely one, having been left an orphan by
his mother, whose presence he nevertheless continued to feel throughout his life. Although he was naturally of an artistic and unsystematic
disposition, he was brought up in an atmosphere of strict discipline.
He was an excellent pupil in a school which he detested. His was a
religious temperament, yet he received his early guidance from
agnostics. These contrasts were carried over into adult life, where his
whole career seems to have been marked by a curious combination of
delight in human living and love for art and philosophy and yet at the
same time darkened by basic revulsion from many of the most pervasive characteristics of the world of his time. Accordingly, we find
that his philosophy is both constructive and negative; it expresses
both hope and despair. In this sketch of his philosophy, an attempt
will be made to disentangle these two aspects of his thought and to
exhibit his view of their relationship.[1]

1. Introductory: Marcel's Method
   and Intention

Marcel's way of writing philosophy requires comment. Philosophers have
most frequently used two methods of communication. The first
moves through precise definitions of concepts, linked in orderly arguments, to present a clear-cut theoretical translation of that portion of
experience which the author has elected to explain. The second
method appears on the surface to be informal, even careless, perhaps
poetic. This method is used to perfection by Plato. Its air of care-
lessness derives from the avoidance, sometimes intentional, of an
official, univocal terminology and from an apparently cavalier attitude
toward logic. Its intent, however, is no less designed than the
logician's. Its means are peculiar in that the very rejection of a
technical vocabulary and mathematical form are indispenable to its
end. The reader of Plato's dialogues will probably recall that the lack
of an official vocabulary had the effect of forcing him to an exceptional
intellectual and imaginative effort, with the consequence that his grasp
of the thought, when finally this was achieved, was all the more
secure and, more importantly, had allowed him to participate in
philosophic discovery. This method, then, contrives to share that
most precious of philosophic possessions: discovery and insight.

The reference to Plato is not accidental. Since 1949 Marcel has rejected
the title of existentialist and prefers to be known as a neo-Socratist,[2]
for this term suggests a questioning and anti-dogmatic attitude and a
reliance upon the situation of the dialogue in which one person joins

---

Note: *The works abbreviated by capital letters are identified in the bibliography p. 258.*

[1] *Brief accounts of Marcel's life as related to his philosophy are to be found in Kurt
    Reinhardt, The Existentialist Revolt, New York, 1960, chap. 7, sec. I; and in
    J. Collins, The Existentialists, Chicago, 1952, chap. 4, introductory section. A
    more elaborate account is by Roger Troisfontaines, S.J., De l'existence à l'être,
    Vrin, Paris, 1953, two vols., vol. I, Introduction.*

[2] MJ *xii;* MMS 264.

with another in a common inquiry.[3] Moreover, the particular sort of inquiry which Marcel was interested in pursuing led him naturally to an adaptation of the dialogue form of philosophizing. This adaptation is the diary in which the author invites the reader to accompany him on a journey of philosophic exploration. The route followed is never an easy one; Marcel's thought is anything but systematic and academic. His route is opened piecemeal in the first journal and continues through two others. It offers here a labored bit of reasoning, there a dead end glanced at, again a brilliant suggestion half communicated only to be dropped and picked up again half a hundred pages later. Even his essays continued the unsystematic and personal character of the journal form. Marcel's way is being broken with difficulty over strange yet familiar territory: human life itself. His writings call to mind the windings of a labyrinth and a labyrinth's religious function, both concealing and revealing the secret of life. The association is by no means inappropriate; Marcel himself remarks upon "the hidden identity of the way which leads to holiness and the road which leads the metaphysician to the affirmation of being." He adds, "it is necessary above all for a concrete philosophy to realize that here is one and the same road."[4]

Looking back over twenty years of philosophic activity, Marcel observed a certain regularity in this labyrinthine wandering. He observed his regular recurrence to the same topics but with a continuing increase in profundity of treatment.[5] He referred to this outcome as an orchestration of themes. In this essay some attempt will be made to suggest this recurrence in variety and in particular to disengage and express the pattern in the recurrence of themes.

Many of these themes may be called "existentialist," despite Marcel's dislike of this name, if the term be understood in a wide sense. All the existentialist writers have at least these two points in common: first, they believe the human being is radically unlike any thing or object; second, they hold that this uniqueness is expressed in the telic or oriented character of his concrete being. After these points of agreement, there is mostly difference. Wherein the human uniqueness lies, which experiences best express this human quality, what is or what should be the direction of the human change, what is the proper order and method of study of these matters, all these questions lead to variety in existentialism. But whatever the variety there is a common concern with the individual, actual human being.

Before the First World War Marcel published an article indicating his preoccupation with the themes later to become known as existentialist.[6] There he rejects rationalistic and idealistic philosophies because of their distortion of concrete experience, and he points to the absurdi-

---

[3] *The association with Plato is relevant in other philosophic respects also, cf.* P. Prini, Gabriel Marcel et la méthodologie de l'invérifiable, Paris, 1953, lettre-préface de Marcel, p. 7f.; cf. 123, 126.

[4] BH *84f.*   [5] MB *II*, 3.

[6] "Les conditions dialectiques de la philosophie de l'intuition," Rev. de Méta. et de Morale, *1912, vol. 20, pp. 638–652.*

ties of identifying the concept of being with concrete being. On the positive side he affirmed an intuition which is at once an immediate participation in concrete being and a new creation or transcendence of the world of objectified beings. This article gave expression to many of the themes which Marcel's later philosophic writing was to orchestrate.[7] And not Marcel's alone! It is astonishing how much of existential philosophy is anticipated by this early writing, especially if the first *Metaphysical Journal,* written two years later, is added to this article. It must be recalled that Kierkegaard was totally unknown in France, and that Heidegger's great work was not even published until 1927. Marcel is undoubtedly one of the originators of this type of philosophy.

The concrete and personal nature of this philosopher's interests was first indicated by his absorption in the drama, and he has never lost the conviction that the theater is, as it were, the natural matrix of metaphysics. Marcel himself observes that many of the concepts later developed in his philosophy first appeared quite spontaneously in his plays,[8] a natural sequence since the drama so clearly invites the presentation of just the human change which from the first was the center of his concern. His play, *Le Monde cassé,* illustrates this movement as well as any. Christiane, its dominating personage, a charming and intelligent woman, is like most other persons in his plays, a "soul in exile." She was frustrated in her first love for a young man by his entering a Benedictine monastery. She later married as a matter of course, and soon was reduced to filling her time up with frivolous social engagements and superficial personal attachments in an effort to extract some amusement from a life become meaningless. Her husband was a correct but egoistic government official. She speaks of their life as "broken," like a watch without its spring. Then, after the death of the young Benedictine, she learns that he had known of her love for him, had regarded it as a "mysterious responsibility," and had offered it to God as a sacrifice. She reaches a strange sort of understanding of this sacrificial act and enters into a sort of "communion of souls."

This existential movement of a person from the first state of innocent acceptance, through a wandering dissatisfaction with conventional goods and social pretense to an experience of emptiness, and finally to a fulfillment in communion, is the experience which Marcel has taken as his own and has sought to illuminate. This movement is said to begin in existence, to make its way through the objective world, and to end in being. Marcel's enterprise is to describe these

---

[7] He summarizes his position in this article by proposing a dialectic "which will manifest the transcendence of thought in relation to knowledge. Intuition itself is reduced finally to the act by which thought affirms itself to be transcendent to that in it which is merely pure objectivity. Thus in sum, intuition is an act of faith, and its content would be elaborated only in a practical dialectic of participation by which thought, moving beyond the world of knowledge by successive movements of creation, approaches the center where it ought freely to renounce itself in order to offer a place to Him who is."

[8] MB I, 22; 57; PE 15.

crucial points in life and to develop the concepts through which the nature and orientation of human change may be grasped. We shall follow his meditation through three stages: the first is centered upon existence; the second is critical of an incomplete and inadequate reflection upon existence in the world; and the third attempts to formulate a doctrine concerning an adequate reflection upon being.

Probably it is safe to add that the language in which Marcel seeks to accomplish this task will be taken in the future, as it has been taken in the past, as a target which a scientifically or analytically inclined mind can scarcely miss. This tactic, though, fails to allow for the author's explicit effort to avoid using the language properly susceptible to this sort of analysis.[9] It inevitably fails also to lay hold upon his philosophic intention. Part of the function of this essay will be to indicate the rather exceptional usage to which Marcel turns his philosophic terminology. Its chief purpose, however, will be to communicate Marcel's philosophic intention by way of explicating the structure of his thought while retaining to some degree the sense of its concrete character.

2. Existence
and Reflection

Philosophic concern has been said to have moved from the effort clearly and objectively to see the individual Aristotelian substances, to an apprehension of their empty container, the Cartesian extended substance, thence to the empiricists' preoccupation with sensation—the subject's effort to see—and finally to analysis of the subject's constructs, ideal objects within the subject. Thus its gaze has shifted from the objects seen to the conditions for seeing them. What will be the next move in this progression? Perhaps an effort to apprehend an original unity of the subject and his world. This, at any rate, is the way in which Marcel directs his philosophizing.

Returning in his own manner to beginnings, he seeks to describe pre-reflective existence. The philosopher accepting such an undertaking is in a position not unlike the music critic who is asked to tell what the rendition of a certain Beethoven quartet is like. The obliging critic has only words at his command, but these can never be made into a substitute for the quartet itself. Still the critic can communicate to the musically knowledgeable person something of the sort of experience which might be expected from this music. The terms and metaphors at his disposal help him to allude to the values involved. Similarly, the philosopher may, even at the initial and inchoate point in existence, generate certain terms and meanings which assist in, even if they cannot fully accomplish, the task of communication. These meanings, moreover, can be constructed only upon the philosopher's (or his reader's) prior apprehension of himself, of the world, and of being, which is analogous to the musical sensitivity and knowledgeability presupposed by the music critic. Among

[9] RI *21ff.*

the terms which Marcel chooses at this level of his endeavor are: existence, participation, presence, incarnation, my body, sensation, admiration. The development of the sense of these terms must be undertaken. It must be added that most of them recur with changed meanings at other levels of his reflection. We are interested now in understanding their meaning at the initial level of their usage.

The initial term is "existence." Marcel appears to use the term in three ways. There is, first, the generic and etymological sense in which it is so frequently used today, referring to a "movement out from" a source. The term is used in Marcel's philosophy, as in any philosophy of the existentialist type, to express its opposition to philosophies — which attempt to comprehend the world or man in terms of a general theory analogous to scientific theory. This etymological meaning of "existence" seems to be present as an element in the meaning of the term when used in other senses. A second and basic usage of the word refers us to that in which all thought begins. At this initial level we encounter an obstacle in communicating precisely what the term intends. For existence is immediate, and communication is mediation through language. Hence, not unnaturally, this initial immediate is referred to as "an unnameable and unnamed confusion."[10] In the third place, Marcel uses the term occasionally to refer to the initial phase in a movement of transcendence. In this sense "existence" refers only to that which is relatively first in such a process. Thus existence is said to be the means to being.[11]

Let us consider the sense in which existence refers to that which is first in experience. The etymological meaning of "existence" does not throw much light upon the notion of immediacy, but it does call attention to a natural movement to transcendence. If, Marcel holds, "I exist" were to be interpreted literally, it would mean "I am manifest, or I have something to make known." This sense of the self moving toward self-expression is called an "exclamatory self-awareness."[12] This existential unity of self and expression is prior to the unity in distinction of thought and objective existence expressed by the Cartesian *cogito*. It is prior because the reference is to a stage of experience which precedes the abstraction of self from experience and precedes the establishment of the contrast between the self and objects. At this stage the self lives its events, or—to use Marcel's term—participates in them. Existence, then, is "participation in just the sense in which this is non-objectifiable."[13]

An illustration will be useful. In returning to a house where one has lived intensely and has known others, one involuntarily experiences a strange return of the sense of presence. These recollected presences are not objectively at hand, yet they are effective and cannot be said not to be. The awareness of them may be scarcely expressible, but even in an unconceptualized awareness of them, they are partially

10 MMS *160*; MJ *32.*
11 MB *II, 33.* The term is occasionally, sometimes explicitly, used in a more conventional sense to refer to the routine appearance of things, e.g., MB *I, 139; II, 28.*
12 MB *I, 90f.*   13 RI *36.*

thought.[14]   We exist in these half-thought presences; yet not passively
as an oyster does.   We take them as beginnings for action or reflection.   "Existence," Marcel writes, "is that from which all thought sets
out."[15]   Thus, he looks upon existence not so much as a datum,
thrown into the world, but rather as the initial gift.

Another factor in this initial sense of existence is the global and undifferentiated certainty of the world.[16]   This assured world is not an object
given to a subject, but rather a certainty which is part and parcel of
my self-awareness.   It is the awareness or intuition of an absolute and
indubitable presence involved in my own self-awareness.

This intuitive awareness may be called "infra-objective," for it is not the
grasp of any particular object or of some abstract object in general.
Neither is this awareness attributable to the knowing subject separated from the world which it inspects impersonally.   The self cannot
be abstracted from this world of its experience.[17]   In sum, world, self,
and awareness of their being are one.   "In this sphere everything
seems to go on as if I found myself acting on an intuition which I
possess without immediately knowing myself to possess it—an
intuition which cannot be, strictly speaking, self-conscious and which
can grasp itself only through the modes of experience in which its
image is reflected."[18]   The self involved in its world in this intuitive
manner subtends the distinction of subject from object, and serves
as the point of departure for their analysis and is suggestive of their
final synthesis.[19]

Consider again our musical illustration.   There are some who find the
quartet noisy and tiresome.   Others, however, are absorbed in its
offering.   It exists for them as music.   Clearly there are different ways
and degrees in which the quartet exists for various people.   But for
all, there is an initial level of response to the situation which suggests
the present sense of existence.   Something of it may be apprehended
if it is thought of as the primitive human situation, preceding the
subject-object distinction and expressed instead in terms of immediate
absorbed presence and lived participation.   To be human is to exist in
such situations.   The world is the situation in which all exist and
participate.

Marcel became more and more convinced during the writing of his *Metaphysical Journal* that the question concerning existence was closely
bound to the question of sensation and the problematic relation of
soul and body.   Indeed he once remarked that the latter philosophic
problem was the key to all others.[20]   It will be indispensable, in order
to come more closely to grips with this central notion, to follow the
development of Marcel's thought from his consideration of sense
awareness to his views on bodily incarnation and bodily existence.

Sensation, like existence, is said to be immediate.   A white spot is directly
present, not before my glance, but rather as my glance itself.   Taken

[14] MJ 302.   [15] MJ 32.
[16] *"Existence and Objectivity"* included as an appendix in MJ 319–339, cf. 322f.
[17] MJ 331.   [18] BH 118.   [19] MJ 325.   [20] MJ 277.

alone, it is not a sign of something else present to me, although, it may be so used. Such a usage of sensation is precisely a *usage*, an interpretation of sensation. But the sensation itself—that which may be so interpreted—is rather an affection than a reference.[21] It is rather a way of existing than a cognition of existence, and of itself suggests nothing beyond a sort of continuity between me and whatever might be given to me as a datum.[22] Since one cannot say that sensation spontaneously and in its own nature constitutes a set of signs, one can only conclude that, like any other immediate experience, sensation is without meaning.[23] Thus also, it is without error or the possibility of error.[24] This is the level of pure feeling where nothing is explained, nothing understood, an existential realm of pure chance and sensory confusion. It is, therefore, quite impossible to describe except in the sense that a description may denote or recall a level of indeterminate awareness which all, doubtless, may experience or imagine.

Sensation as immediate, nonrepresentative, infallible awareness is prior to all experience and thought, yet it is precisely that which is subject to the most complex sort of interpretation.

We now encounter the usual movement of thought which leads straight on to the conviction that sensation should be used as a system of signs which, by way of the instrumentality of the body, will provide us with a flow of information concerning the environment. Marcel, however, avoids this movement as philosophically misleading, even absurd and dangerous, except as a fiction temporarily useful in physiology. Sensation cannot be coherently regarded as a message, nor the body as an instrument.[25]

Sensation is quite commonly imagined to be like a vibration or disturbance which is broadcast, so to speak, from a transmitting object, then captured by the sense organs acting like receiving stations. The message is then decoded somehow in the brain. Now this set of metaphors, seriously proffered by scientifically and objectively oriented reflection, becomes upon examination quite meaningless. Consider, as the sensation to be interpreted, the perfume of a flower. The physicist may explain the odor in terms of the movements of small particles operating without intention. At another extreme the panpsychist may regard it as reflecting an analogous activity in the flower, expressing perhaps an obscure vegetable joy in life. Which is correct? Marcel holds that these and other hypotheses supposedly explanatory of the process of decoding sensa in order to recover information communicated from the outside world merely rehearse the various permutations of Cartesian dualism and its derivatives. In particular if sensation is a message from the outside world, what or whom does it inform? A message must, by definition, be received by someone. If the body is, as is usually said, only an intermediate instrument of transmission, a relay, then somewhere within it there must be an end to transmission. There must be an intelligence at the end of a

21 MJ 18.   22 MJ 273f.   23 MJ 3.   24 MJ 131.   25 MJ 256ff.

finite number of relays if there is to be any transmission at all. This receiver cannot be merely another instrument; an infinite series of instruments would be an absurdity.[26]

There is, on the contrary, good reason for not supposing the body to be an instrument.[27] An instrument is an object which serves as a means to some end. It may be thought of as extending the body or bodily senses, as clearly the microscope extends the reach of the eye or the gun the power of the hand. But what of the eye or the hand? Aristotle spoke of the hand as the instrument of instruments. Marcel would add that as such it must be quite unlike any other instrument. Without the body, nothing else could be an instrument. The body, then, is the *condition* for anything else to be an instrument. The body uses all the others. But the body itself, is it an instrument? If so, who uses it? and for what end? Shall we say that the hand is used by certain nerves and muscles and these by still others, and so on without end? Or shall we stop at some arbitrarily posited principle of quite another nature, such as a soul, with all its Cartesian difficulties, or shall we rather endeavor to stop thinking of the body as an instrument, whether for sending or receiving sensory messages from a supposedly external world? Marcel chooses the latter course.[28] If an inquiry is to be made into the way the body exists, the message and instrument analogies must be put aside. Marcel's reflection suggests that the body occupies a unique status. He expresses his decision in the matter by the striking phrase, "I am my body."

The unique status attributed to "my body" is further specified by asking how I can lift my arm. The problem is merely physical if I think of myself as a kind of machine made of levers and connectors. The problem becomes paradoxical in the philosophic context when the lifting is dissociated from its intimate bond with the "I" and regarded as a consequence of some sort of communication between distinct physical and psychic spheres. In fact such a communication is unintelligible. There is no science of the relation between idea and act.[29] Traditional metaphors to the contrary, I cannot think of myself as external to my acts. I find myself submerged in my activity at least in my pre-reflective life. The dissociation of myself from my body must be recognized to be the product of later reflection which interprets my body as an impersonal object and thus precisely *not mine*. It is only after a later reflecting upon this objective reflection that I note the divisive effect of objective thought, correct for this division, and reestablish the unity in which I exist as incarnated.[30] Then I observe that I inform my acts with myself or express myself in them, and for just this reason am responsible for them. I live through and in my body and cannot be separated from it as a pilot from his ship. For such reasons it cannot be said either that my body is merely a machine, or a machine controlled by a sort of spiritual pilot. That this body is mine in my world suggests an entirely unique relation which Marcel terms "participation." Participation is to be apprehended as a pre-objective, lived, dyadic relation,[31] illustrated not only

26 RI 29.   27 MJ 250; MB I, 106ff.   28 MJ 257f.; RI 29.   29 MJ 325.
30 MJ 334; BH 10.   31 MJ 255f.

in the involvement of the self in the body but also in experiences of love, aesthetic appreciation, and faith.

The convenience or necessity of thinking of the person in separation from his body for certain limited purposes cannot be denied. The surgeon who operates on me cannot but regard me, so far as his medical function goes, as an object. As it were, he underlines his abstract view by the use of anesthetic. But after the operation I do not take possession of my body again as I might repossess a rented house. My body could not survive my absence. That is, my body thought of apart from me is only an abstraction. Nor can I think of the relation between me and my body, in actuality, as analogous to the relation of subject and predicate. This relation is no more grammatical or logical than physical or physiological. Indeed one might run the whole gamut of objective and commonsense relationships without finding one which adequately describes the relation of soul or self and one's body. Care must be taken, therefore, in asserting that the "am" in "I am my body" is the "am" of identity. Marcel is explicitly not setting forth a materialistic doctrine of the self.[32] His "I" could not survive in a materialistic world. Others can touch my body in a sense, but I am not literally touched by this contact. One must suspect then that my body is not an object and the "am" in "I am my body" denotes a unique and even mysterious relationship.[33] To be incarnated is to appear "as this particular body, but without being either identified with it or distinguished from it, for identification and distinction are correlative operations which are applicable only within the sphere of objects."[34]

Thus one comes finally to a position which holds initially that my body precisely in the sense in which it is *mine* is not an object and that the copula which expresses my union with it refers to a non-objectifiable participation. What is non-objectifiable is, naturally, difficult to express in ordinary language, designed primarily to symbolize and describe objects. Nevertheless, with care we may use language to "allude to" such non-objectifiable situations. One is aware, for example, of being one's body by virtue of a continual awareness of the body, a feeling-awareness which is the condition of any other feeling.[35] It is misleading to say that I observe and recognize the feeling of my body's presence, for I am not outside of or distinct from this feeling. It encroaches upon my own being. This feeling is the presence of my body; it is an *Urgefühl* to which all other feelings, sensations, and awarenesses are referred as their bench mark, so to speak. This is not a Cartesian recognition of the mental or intellectual self. Marcel uses the expression *sentio ergo sum* to emphasize his separation from Cartesianism. He is affirming what A. N. Whitehead referred to as the "withness of the body." Damage to this sense of my body as the locus of all other feelings and sensations or destruction of it would damage profoundly my relation to my world or would signalize my death.

I am my body, then, in the sense that to feel, to be, or to be identified with

---

[32] RI *30.*   [33] MJ *259.*   [34] RI *31.*   [35] MJ *52f.; 236; 240.*

anything or anyone else, I must first be incarnated in just this body. My body enjoys this absolute priority. It follows that my body cannot without distortion be made the independent object of thought. Rather it is the condition of my thinking of other things.[36] Indeed it is the condition of objectivity. Marcel uses the term "incarnation" to refer to the priority and indispensability of "my body" in this sense. In virtue of this incarnation, this immediate being my body and its sensation, I can participate in situations. Incarnation here is not used in a theological sense, it should be observed, but rather in the sense in which it constitutes a bond between the concrete man and his world. In this sense it aroused Plato's wonder; it recalls the bond which unites members of a family.[37]

I, as incarnated thus, am the fundamental existent, the "central 'given' of metaphysics."[38] Other "things exist for me to the degree that I regard them as extensions of my body."[39] Without this incarnate self the world would be at best only a network of abstractions. That is, it would not exist. Given it, however, experience of other existents becomes possible. To say "Caesar exists" is to say that a series of experiences can be constructed or imagined in consequence of which Caesar becomes copresent to me.[40] This notion of bodily presence in the world or incarnation is, thus, one of the elementary notions of Marcel's existentialist metaphysics. Troisfontaines has described existence as "a situation centered upon a subject."[41] My point here has been to show that this subject is an incarnation, a self whose actuality is his body, and second to show that other things may be said to exist only in the sense that they are interrelated with such a subject.

Marcel is uncompromising in his effort to begin philosophy with the fully actual situation, however puzzling and paradoxical this initial life situation may be. It will not be amiss to emphasize the paradoxical character of this beginning point. The bodily self in situation in the world cannot rightly be called an object. It cannot, therefore, be adequately translated into discursive subject-object terms. To this extent, it must remain opaque to the theoretic intelligence. This opaqueness is further reflected in such puzzles as this one: the non-objective body can indeed be used as an object. The manual worker allows his body to be used as an object or instrument; we have observed that the surgeon uses his patients so. Thus one's body is after all an object.[42] It is both objective and non-objective. Much of Marcel's method consists in isolating paradoxical situations such as these which arise inevitably from the effort to do justice to the concrete while remaining within the limits of everyday prose.

In what experience or attitude is the awareness of existence, of being my body sensitively in the present situation, most clearly recognizable? For the purposes of philosophy, the most ontologically valuable experience of this kind, Marcel writes, is admiration.[43] This is distinctly not the admiration to which Descartes awarded a high place in his

[36] MJ 243.   [37] HV 97.   [38] BH 11.   [39] MJ 273.   [40] RI 28.
[41] Op. cit., vol. I, 188.   [42] RI 31.   [43] RI 167f.

Passions of the Soul, for Descartes failed to see its ontological value.[44] Descartes indicated his evaluation clearly enough by beginning his philosophy with doubt, thus betraying a sort of "ontological mistrust." The wonder of which Marcel speaks is illustrated, he says, in the eyes of a child who is just waking from sleep, or in the adult who sees, with a sense of mystery, his own restless insecurity in contrast to the everlasting repose of nature. This admiration in simplicity, a sort of wondering naïveté, is clearly related to the religious consciousness and is expressed as a filial relation with the cosmos, a sort of natural piety. It acts as a restraint upon one's self-affirmation and self-reverence, attitudes which may so easily degenerate into an exaggerated and egocentric sense of independence. Wonder is the first reaction of the whole self to that which is contemplated. Marcel refers to the peasant who comes gratefully to regard the fruits of the earth as the reward for his labor. He participates thus in the life of the world. This attitude is one of openness to reality or of readiness for a common life. To acquire it, or better to reacquire it—since the child seems to possess this readiness without effort—commonly demands a change of basic attitudes, a conversion. Such a conversion opens one to a new kind of existence which we shall recognize later to be an approach to being. The average man, though, is completely converted to commonsense attitudes and the convictions associated with our scientific and objectively oriented civilization which lull wonder to sleep and close up the primitive openness to the world and to other persons. Nevertheless, it is necessary to recover this wondering assurance. Only thus will one recover access to the existent and take up the pre-objective position which underlies and undergirds the objective world. The philosopher must, in Marcel's phrase, recover the sense of *"la morsure du réel."*[45] It is not suggested, though, that philosophy abjure all abstractions and plunge into the stream of sensation and existence. Rather it must use abstractions with care, recognizing them as means but never as the end of human endeavor.

Inevitably in these remarks about existence as that from which all thought begins, we have reached the sense in which existence stands as the initial phase in any movement of renewed participation. Such a shift was inevitable; the absolutely immediate is not easy to describe. We cannot discuss the "exclamatory awareness" of the world without getting beyond this awareness.[46]

Existence is only the beginning of the human drama. Remaining in the state of existential immediacy is wholly contrary to our inclination and if persisted in would deny the very *élan* which Marcel holds to be at the root of all our activity. He expresses this *élan* as the demand or need for being (*l'exigence de l'être*).[47] This is a demand for movement beyond any given state of existence. It is a strange demand, one never wholly clear to itself.[48] It may be described as a premonition of the possibility of approaching being in the concrete,[49] but it is also an apprehension and an impulse which may be perverted. The

---

[44] BH *217ff.*   [45] RI *89; 140.*   [46] MB *I, 66f.*   [47] MB *I, 39ff.*
[48] *"The Ontological Mystery"* in PE *1–31,* cf. 4.   [49] MJ *x.*

wondering naïveté with which one first views the world manifests this *élan*. Only slowly does it reach conscious awareness, as more of the human power comes into play. Other aspects of the Marcellian view of this need will become evident as we proceed. For the present let us consider how men move in obedience to it beyond the initial state of unreflective existence.

Marcel terms the first inchoate existential state the state of "submerged participation."[50] This is a sort of philosophic state of nature, yet one which carries within it both unrest and the incipient orientation to later development. Existence is open either to being or to atrophy. We are tempted to think of the process as a kind of ontological evolution.[51] The fertility of the initial state is best exhibited through his observations upon truth.

Marcel sides with that part of the Western tradition which holds that "truth" is properly descriptive not only of propositions, where it refers to their claim to adequacy, but also to the reality to which propositions purport to refer.[52] The latter sense of the term he holds to be the important and also the neglected sense. The truth for which one is willing to die is not merely an adjective qualifying certain propositions. It is rather that which is; at the least it is that faith in being to which one is committed. We are willing to die only for a commitment in which our profoundest convictions concerning the nature of reality are at stake. Traditional terms describe truth, regarded as the aspect of reality open to us, in metaphors involving light. In this respect Marcel associates himself with Heidegger's views.[53] The light of truth is not the light cast by a theoretical grasp of factual matters. Perhaps it is rather the light which, originating at least partly within one, determines what the facts are which one will see and value.[54] For facts acquire value only in virtue of their relations to an active self. The self in this respect is, through its body and its insertion in time, a portion of an incomplete structure of which facts also are a part. Facts acquire their identity by being integrated into this incomplete structure. The relation of facts to the self within this structure is described as a kind of obligation of the self to yield to the "dumb pressure" with which the facts press the self to discover and acknowl-

---

[50] MB I, 114.

[51] Marcel's use of the term existence (and of being also) lacks something of clarity. Troisfontaines expresses the distinction, as I have, in relation to reflection. Existence is immediate and unreflective participation (at least relatively unreflective). Being, as we shall observe, is participation mediated by reflection (op. cit., vol. 1, 44f, 188f). Marcel expressly accepts Troisfontaines' study as a faithful interpretation of his thought (ibid., Lettre préface, p. 9). K. I. Gallagher, on the other hand, thinks it more reasonable to follow Jean Wahl's suggestion and interpret the distinction between existence and being as a distinction between realms of experience; the first realm is characterized by bodily incarnation, the second by intersubjectivity (cf. his The Philosophy of Gabriel Marcel, New York, 1962, p. 59 and n. 41). The fact probably is that Marcel sees and expresses the distinction in different ways at different times. The important point, as I understand this philosophy, is that however the distinction between existence and being be drawn, a dramatic movement between them must be recognized which it is the business of philosophy to illuminate.

[52] MB I, 58.   [53] MB I, 57; 70.   [54] MB I, 65.

edge them as they are. It is improper to speak of a struggle against the facts; they are what they are. The struggle is always against oneself or some aspect of the self which prefers the lie or the flight from reality and tends to settle for the infantile pretense of a dream world. Propositional truth reports upon the outcome of this struggle; it presupposes, however, the prior encounter which the existent self has established with reality.

The initial encounter with reality has been described as the inchoate state of existence, a submerged participation. In this state truth is, so to speak, dormant. It is lived or unreflectively expressed. Other possibilities, however, also exist. Truth, for example, might be entertained more critically or denied. How are these possibilities to be developed?

What has been termed the ontological exigence or need for being may be expressed as a response to the pressure of facts to be expressed in truth. This is another manifestation of the appetite for the "bite of the real" which is the hunger after a more complex and significant existence. This urge, natural to human life, develops by way of a reflection upon oneself and one's experience. Reflection may be described generally as an "alert recapitulation."[55] It initially assumes the value and linkage to human life of the object or experience reflected upon and seeks to bring its nature and value into clear awareness. Evidently this reflection destroys the earlier spontaneity and the original unity of experience.[56] Yet it promises, in the end, the reward of a greater good.

Reflection thus is the means to change, and change is the inevitable movement into a life of greater complexity and significance. This change is usually thought to be a development in the sense of cultural and technical progress. Marcel, however, regards the desirable change as an inner and personal development. This latter kind of human change has only rarely been the object of consideration. One difficulty has been that the language for describing it has not been available. An important aspect of Marcel's undertaking is to work out, at least in preliminary fashion, the language and concepts required for describing this kind of change. A first step is to distinguish two different kinds of reflection upon experience.

Reflection, a rough intrusion upon the first fine spontaneity of existence, is often aroused by the malfunctioning of a needed object. Marcel instances a lost watch, which calls one out of the daily activities of existence to reflect upon one's recent whereabouts. Likewise he recalls a Kafka who looks back upon the sinister significance of officialdom's red tape. In a sense an official form which one is asked to fill out appears to be innocent enough. It calls for only a modicum of reflection upon one's past and present and serves, perhaps, to facilitate administration. Its sinister aspect lies not only in the fact that such forms multiply with unnecessary and uncontrollable rapidity, but more especially in the metaphysical fact that the habit of seeing oneself through such a form wrenches one away from one's identity

55 MB I, 78.   56 MB I, 215f.

by categorizing it in a series of checked squares. It separates one from one's bodily incarnation and leaves one only the abstract being of a series of entries in a dossier or of a number assigned to the dossier. This kind of reflection, whether upon the salient facts of one's life or upon the location of a watch, tends to select certain elements and to ignore others. The scientist's reflection is a specialized application of the same habit of mind. His explanations usually proceed reductively by showing that the puzzling datum, which seems to be *this*, is in reality the simpler *that*; his general assumption is that every phenomenon is constituted by a necessary, definite, and reproducible set of conditions. His practical aim is to reconstitute these conditions and so to reproduce the phenomenon. He then dissociates himself, his training, and protracted mental toil, from the phenomenon reproduced and persuades himself that it was reproduced automatically.[57] Thus reflection of this kind breaks the link which unites one, whether scientist or ordinary citizen, with the body and with the world. It dissolves the intuited unity of experience. The thoughtful spectator, searching for a solution to a problem, is noncontemplative and nonparticipating; he is impersonal and remote. He ignores whatever seems to be irrelevant to the solution of his problem. He especially ignores his own personality, except that aspect of himself which entertains the problem and invents and manipulates the means to its solution. The problem solver is an abstract self.

Now these habits of abstract thinking and the techniques which go along with them have proved to be a mixed blessing. They have wrought a rude disturbance in man's primeval Eden. On the other hand they have immeasurably advanced knowledge and technical mastery over the environment and have provided the scientist himself with no small discipline. They have enabled men to organize themselves into the complex social patterns which modern life requires. Indisputably they are responsible for progress toward a more organized and possibly more useful world. On the other hand we have paid for this advance with so much loss and so many evils that Marcel seems sometimes to be disposed to look upon the whole enterprise with contempt. This mood of regret and contempt is, however, a deceptive expression of Marcel's overall philosophic intention. The perspective which his philosophy seeks to take is better illustrated in this remark: "What is given us to start with is a sort of unnamed and unnameable confusion where abstractions, not yet elaborated, are like so many little still unseparated clots of matter. It is only by going through and beyond the process of scientific abstraction that the concrete can be regrasped and reconquered."[58] I think it reasonable to interpret Marcel to mean that this first or objective reflection is a necessary moment in the movement of the human spirit beyond immediate existence, however dangerous this movement may, if uncriticized, become. It will be profitable to examine the effects of this unrestrained primary reflection in some of its details. Thus some notion may be formed of the kinds of excess which Marcel expects his philosophy to expose and to discipline. Afterwards are examined a corrective reflection and the doctrine supporting it which Marcel will offer as a cure to the hybritic and sometimes sacreligious extremes which characterize modern thought and life.

3. Man and Society
in the Broken World

Marcel finds evidence for his diagnosis of the modern sickness on every hand, and he devotes a great many eloquent and bitter pages to detailing this evidence and his inferences from it. I offer only a brief selection of the points from this indictment. His observations tend to support the conviction that the world is in a sense "broken," is, indeed, near the brink of a planetary catastrophe. This condition has arisen, not in consequence of political ineptitude, economic greed, or new military weapons, though these are matters to be reckoned with, but rather owing to some deficiency or disease gradually suffusing and possessing the human personality itself. The presence of this disease is evident over the whole gamut of human activity, and not least in philosophic and intellectual pursuits. We shall first examine evidences of its presence in social and political life and then pass on to its more general expression in philosophy.

One symptom of the ill of our age has already been observed in the governmental demand that one be continually filling out questionnaires concerning one's biography, occupation, and the like. Marcel discerns a connection between this apparently innocent requirement and the conduct of Nazi concentration camps during the last war.

The low point of human degradation for modern times was doubtless reached in these and other similar concentration camps and prisons. Marcel utilizes certain accounts which have issued from former prisoners to essay some generalizations about the personalities involved. He finds that the techniques of degrading prisoners were intended to persuade the prisoners to acquiesce in their own humiliation. Prisoners were brought to the point of wishing to humiliate themselves.[59] The reader is reminded of George Orwell's *1984*, a novel which Marcel regards as prophetic. This systematic degradation, aimed at securing the connivance of the degraded in the denial of their own humanity, he regards as a kind of ultimate in moral sacrilege. Yet the sadists in charge of these camps gave evidence of a kind of awareness of their own weakness, dependence, and human emptiness by their very need to make their presence felt by their prisoners. Their evil is recognizably a human evil and a perversion of the need for relationship to others. Even at this level, in other words, there is evidence for the demand of men for being in a milieu of human responses. Still this minimum of participation in humanity scarcely provides grounds for hope. Clearly, the world in which these events occurred is radically deficient in some essential human ingredient. Moreover, these events were not only tolerated, but the

[59] MMS chap. III.

memory of their toleration has been easily and quickly neutralized and all but forgotten. They are not relived, nor have they taught us any moral or historical lesson. Unlike the few who possess some poetic vision, the greater part of mankind has learned to live "insulated in time."[60] What judgment shall be passed upon this situation?

Another significant symptom of the times is the enormous growth in techniques. Techniques are not said to be an evil in themselves; nevertheless, it is indisputable that they are put to destructive and criminal use. Marcel's view of their destructiveness is characteristic. He sees this effect in the great power which a machine affords a man who has in no way contributed to its invention, development, or building. The man in control of the machine commands that which he does not understand and could not invent. Invention to the man professionally concerned is not a means but an end. It is an adventure in creation. Invention is the means for incarnation of power dormant in the human person; its successful exercise provides a genuine and deep satisfaction. Our society, however, is so organized and its institutions so specialized that most men are prevented as a matter of policy from participating in the human value of discovery and creation.[61] On the contrary, they are treated as appendages to the machine, or else as customers and consumers. They share, therefore, only the superficial function of using products to which they have contributed nothing. The suggestion scarcely dormant here is that their contribution is not worth much. Their mechanical energy is more valued than their imagination. Their cash is more desired than their presence. Marcel recalls the man dulled to the point of being incapable of understanding and appreciating the perfection of the automobile, who nevertheless uses automobiles constantly and develops a childish interest in speed and speed records.

The major effort of the modern world is directed toward the production of commodities. The average man's participation in this effort is limited to a certain determined and precalculated output. The man of objectively calculable output is the archetype of the worker. He is totally in the service of the machine.[62] Does there not exist the immanent danger that the conquest of nature by the machine is also a process of bringing men into servitude to techniques? There is evidence, moreover, that the sciences themselves are being brought within the ambit of this same kind of servitude. They are coming to be looked upon increasingly as accessory to the organization of techniques. Science means power to most people.[63] And the popular belief holds that the scientist's occupation is justified only by its contribution to technical and economic progress. The significant thing is that scientists themselves are coming to accept the same evaluation.

The progress of enslavement to this opinion is evidenced by the degree to which the traditional idea of man is decomposing before our eyes, its place being taken by an idea of man as comparable to a machine.[64] It is essential to any machine that each part perform a certain clearly

[60] MMS 38f.   [61] RI 180.   [62] MMS 179.   [63] MMS 61.   [64] MMS 179.

defined function and no other. Each part is instrumental in some precisely defined sense to the function of the whole and has no other reason for being. This instrumental aspect of the machine is that which Marcel finds to be analogous to modern man. The function of each person is reduced, even in his own eyes, to that of an instrument of production. The man's unity with his body is broken, and his body comes to be regarded merely as a handy instrument. When ill or idle, he is regarded as deficient, an unprofitable burden to society. When dead, he is a broken machine, a useless tool ready for the scrap heap.[65]

These attitudes are expressive of a barbarism based upon reason. One must ask himself how they come to be endured. The answer most immediately at hand refers us to the effectiveness of administration and propaganda.

The mechanization of life is completed by administration. Administration organizes life with technical efficiency for technical operation. If one is to exist in any of the larger modern societies, one must accept the niche and function appointed for him by the bureaucracy. He then *is* this function. Before the administrative machine, a man is no more than a number and a dossier.[66] Seen through his dossier, he appears as no more than a specialized brain or a pair of skilled hands. Neither his human presence nor his creative qualities are manifested through this medium. Indeed, nothing is viewed with so much suspicion by the administrator as originality or individuality, for creativeness is by nature nonadministrable.

Ironically, the administrator himself is caught in his own toils. The value of his daily office routine is anything but evident to him and finally comes to be performed mechanically, merely in order to keep his post. Others are, as Sartre observed, threats to oneself and to one's job.[67] This administrative disease, invigorated by ambitious and dominating individuals, spreads like an infection. Only a national catastrophe could prevent its absorbing the energies of a whole nation. Criticism does not touch it; nothing could be more irrelevant, once this machine has been set going, than its failure to reach stated objectives. It operates automatically to produce an "anthill" society. Marcel refers to C. V. Gheorgiv's *The Twenty-fifth Hour;* this novel relates the story of a family made to suffer one indignity and disgrace after another, first in Nazi Germany, then in America, simply because of the classifications in which they happened to be placed by official rules, no account whatever being taken of what the people themselves were or thought or felt.

We do not accept our administratively organized life simply because there is no alternative. Rather, men are induced by means of propaganda to accept docilely, even joyfully, the administratively assigned function. Propaganda is regarded as the manipulation of the consciences of other people for self-interested ends. Marcel terms it "the spirit of imposture."[68] Propaganda invades one's privacy, cynically denies men's natural love of truth, and by means of all the techniques of

---

[65] MMS 94f.; RI 95.   [66] MB *I,* 31.   [67] MB *I,* 30.   [68] MMS 69.

persuasion, to which all but the most critical must yield, conjures men into embracing their own slavery to techniques and into rejoicing in their own reduction to administratively assigned functions. Psychoanalysis, Marcel believes, must then be employed in the service of propaganda in order to renew and strengthen this enslavement, when its bonds weaken, in the name of adjustment to reality.[69]

The final product of propaganda is mass society itself. Propaganda succeeds, by appealing to the lowest common element among men, in reducing them all to an agglomeration of similars.[70] Marcel quotes with approval Ortega's description of the mass man, adding only that to achieve the state of being a member of the faceless mob, one had first to divest himself of his reality, a reality linked with his genuine participation in the life of others as exemplified, for example, in the family. He observes that the provocation for uniting oneself with the impersonal masses is fear. In this subrational unity a kind of safety and peace is indeed reached, but only by way of the negation of one's own personality. Belonging to a group in this manner offers a kind of nourishment to the unconscious hunger which men feel after being deprived of their own proper reality and freedom by the mechanization of life.[71] It is a perversion of the need for being to which allusion has already been made. Since this hunger for being is not immediately discriminating, it renders the power and appeal of propaganda possible. It thus enables a demagogue to arouse the passion of fanaticism and to lead the masses further into the kind of collective self-worship which has characterized fascist and Communist versions of totalitarianism.[72] The illusion sought and nourished is that the mass of men somehow possesses and imparts to its members something more real and more valuable than that which its members taken separately possess.[73] This illusion is a parody on intersubjectivity.

Now this screed of the world's ills is not a disjoint list, but expresses a tendency and a philosophic principle. The common tendency is—the term is not too strong—the inclination to suicide. This inherent inclination, though generally latent, has become patent in the modern world.[74] Suicide, the denial of being,[75] has now become possible on a worldwide scale. The atom bomb is a particularly forceful symbol of it, but another sign no less evident to the discerning eye is the offering of wages to women in payment for their becoming mothers. Indeed, all the characteristics proper to our troubled times are symptoms of the same disease. Marcel's writings abound with references to an impending doom, to an approaching catastrophe. Ours is a world under condemnation.[76] The full danger of the approaching menace to society becomes evident, he holds, only at the philosophical level. The primary element in the philosophical aspect of our predicament is a progressive shifting of philosophical concern away from concrete life. There is one component common to all these species of human error and danger. This element, which will later provide the clue to the nature of these errors, is abstraction.

---

69 MMS 131; 215.   70 MMS 220.   71 MMS 141.   72 MMS 221.
73 MMS 220f.   74 MMS 14.   75 MB II, 173.   76 MMS 76; 158; MB II, 166ff.

Marcel acknowledges in abstraction or "methodical omission" an important and useful means for accomplishing practical purposes. But in addition to using abstractions, the mind may become fascinated with them. It begins to deceive itself about them and then to develop the habit or "spirit of abstraction." This spirit is a disease of the intellect.[77] It is described as a contempt for the concrete conditions for making abstractions and amounts to a sort of "mental imperialism."[78] This spirit is also expressed in attacks "directed against the integrity of the real," the inclination to make one's neighbor into an abstraction. This is to treat him as "nothing but" a functionary, a party member, or a representative of some "ism." It is also to reduce a man to some function or to some particular role which in reality is only one within the complex organization of roles which he as a concrete person does or should play. This procedure may not always extend so far as the custom in prison camps of regarding a man's identity as nothing more than a number. Yet the principle at work is the same.[79] This treatment of men as valuable only in the performance of some particular role expresses a rejection of them as concrete persons and a fundamental contempt for them. Just this reduction to a role is implicit in the supposition that the important information concerning a person is to be got by having him fill in the blanks of a questionnaire. One may be so often subjected to this process that he becomes estranged from himself and dehumanized; he is persuaded to think of himself as nothing more than what the questionnaire says he is.[80] The same dehumanizing attitude, carried to an extreme, betrayed the implicit lie involved in the role which the Jewish people were forced to play by their Nazi tyrants. This state of affairs is communicated by propaganda and preserved by administration. These processes, Marcel believes, have progressed to an alarming extent over most of the world, but especially in America and Russia. Thus abstraction, a necessary instrument for use in meeting practical problems and explaining natural occurrences, is distorted and converted into a systematic means for destroying one's fellow man.

All these descriptions of modern life, which lend weight and cogency to the conclusion that the world is sick, "broken," and under condemnation, are suggestive of parodies on the more human world which Marcel's constructive philosophy seeks to penetrate. The administrator, the mere functionary, is a pale reflection of a whole self. The propagandist is a takeoff on the philosophically reflective person. Science in the service of techniques is a comic version of science in the service of knowledge; techniques in the service of domination are a tragicomic version of techniques in the service of humanity. Prison camps suggest a hideous distortion of family relationships. And mass man is a grimly humorous version of intersubjectivity. Finally the mass adulation of its own nationality or race is a sacrilegious parody on religion. How the instrument responsible for these distortions turns upon the user becomes evident as some types and aspects of modern philosophy come under examination.

[77] MMS 163.   [78] MMS 155.   [79] MB II, 52ff.   [80] MB I, 183.

4. Philosophy
in the Broken World

Let us now ask why there exists this widespread contempt for the concrete which results in the treatment of men as abstractions. An important part of the answer to this question is to be sought in philosophy itself. For there are types of philosophy which formulate and defend distorted views of the human situation. In various ways these philosophies are the dupes of their own abstractions; some manage to discover additional ways of distorting human values. They are guilty in various fashions of a fallacy which Marcel seeks to disengage and to express generally. Since these philosophies have actually been very persuasive, they may be said to be instruments of propaganda. Philosophy, therefore, does not merely offer one more symptom of the ill of our time; it is by no means without blame for the existence of that ill. Marcel's criticisms are leveled primarily at idealism, the type of philosophy which he earlier espoused, at empiricism, and at Sartre's type of existentialism. We shall consider only a selected few of his criticisms.

Certain criticisms of modern philosophic tendencies are best directed against the Cartesian doctrine in which they are still most clearly expressed.

Marcel observes that the Cartesian doctrine and most of the philosophies which develop out of it take up a supposedly indifferent attitude toward the outcome of inquiry. This very indifference provides the foundation for their claim to objectivity. Is, however, such indifference possible in a philosophy which undertakes to deal with the human situation? The plight of the world today must be at least in part an outcome of these philosophies and would seem to belie their claim to the need for intellectual remoteness. Nevertheless, the claim exists and has led to a strange version of human reality.

The Cartesian doubt and the *cogito* in which it culminates signalize not the discovery of the self so much as its removal from reality. Marcel understands the Cartesian position, which takes the subject-object distinction as fundamental, to be the affirmation of a predicate, "existence," of a mental substance or a "that" which is assumed to be intelligible apart from its existence.[81] Here the "I" is supposed to have substantial or objectlike qualities, among which is an abstract kind of existence.[82] But this complex of assumptions reduces the soul or self, no less than its body, to the status of a thing. Descartes altogether failed to see that the "I exist" affirms one's indubitable presence, the "existential immediate," in which a self is inconceivable apart from its actual existence.[83] Thus he failed to grasp the existence which is prior to the distinction of subject from object.[84]

Descartes' assignment of reality exclusively to certain privileged abstractions can be expected to produce insoluble problems. The affirmation of the lone and separate ego, however clear and distinct the idea of it, elicits all the epistemological difficulties with which philosophy has

---

[81] MJ *182, 288.*   [82] MJ *99.*   [83] MB *I, 89; 94.*   [84] BH *12; 27.*

long been familiar.   More seriously, this affirmation denies one's participation in the being upon which it depends.[85]   Positing the thought
of the *je pense* as the prior reality and the first or founding human act
leads to the impoverishment of human experience, for it evaluates
abstract thought above other activities.   It also leads to a generalization of its opposition to whatever is not intellectually clear and exact.
Thus the distinction of the thought-self from everything else, from its
own body for example, becomes a metaphysical distinction.[86]   In sum,
the Cartesian self is an abstract thing, separated from its own body,
from the world which it is to know, and from the being upon which it
depends.

It is fairly evident that in this restricted definition of man and in the
consequent specialization of his functions, one encounters again, but
in an intellectualized form, the same tendency to vicious abstraction
and functionalization which was observed in identifying prisoners with
their numbers.

When the abstract and universal "I think" became the only center of
thought, philosophy became idealistic.   In his earlier days Marcel
was much interested in this philosophic development and made a pro-
longed study of British and American idealists.[87]   He was then chiefly
interested in the idealistic question concerning perception and its
possible contributions to the perceived.   However, he came to regard
this approach as condemned to failure from the start, for it overesti-
mated the role of subjectivity.   It tended to reduce self to self-
consciousness, experience to knowledge of experience, and finally to
accept knowledge as self-explanatory and transparent.[88]   Consequently idealism eliminated the opaque and irrational aspects of existence and even tended to eliminate existence altogether.[89]   Moreover,
even if knowledge were self-sufficient, the temptation to reduce
experience to knowledge could be disastrous, for thought which generates its content with logical necessity, as some idealists have held,
must operate mechanically.   The more logical, the more necessary,
the more mechanical.[90]   But this reduction of the characteristic human activity to a rational automatism is a reduction to something
extra-human.   Marcel, moreover, came to regard knowledge as not at
all self-explanatory.   In particular, abstract knowledge is not "transparent"; that is, it does not contain the principles of its own intelligibility.   Rather it is derivative from the existential situation.   To
ignore this situation is no more sophisticated, philosophically speaking,
than the decision of the engineer to abstract his computer from the
human environment constituted by its inventor and user, and to call
its action "thinking."

The consequence of recognizing that thinking can be grasped only in experience finally convinced Marcel of the untenability of idealism.   Kant's
antinomies, he observed, compel our admission that thought is in-

[85] BH *11f.*; RI *88l.*   [86] MJ *74.*
[87] Cf. Royce's Metaphysics, tr. *Virginia Ringer and Gordon Ringer, Regnery, Chicago,*
1956.
[88] BH *219.*   [89] MJ *326;* BH *105.*   [90] MJ *746.*

extricably involved with something other than itself, in particular with intuition.[91] Thus abstract thought, if regarded as the essential nature of reality, is a lie which persuades us to accept a part in place of the whole from which it was abstracted and leads its believers to eventual enslavement. The negative function of the philosopher, accordingly, is delineated by contrast with the spirit of abstraction exhibited in these doctrines. The philosopher must help to save man from himself "by a pitiless and unwearying denunciation of the spirit of abstraction,"[92] whether this spirit be exhibited in idealism or in any other metaphysics.

Marcel is no more disposed to accept empiricism with its overemphasis on receptivity. The empiricist generally accepts pure immediate experience as in some sense the primary element in knowledge. But this view is self-defeating inasmuch as this immediacy is precisely what is not yet intelligible.[93] Although intuition at this level may be independent of thought, it still sends us to reason in search of its interpretation. Some empirical philosophers hold to the priority of experienced facts. In opposition to these Marcel points out the obscurity in the notion of fact. Facts are related to the perceiver in complex and subtle ways. For example, facts are searched into only if they have value, but they acquire value only in relation to oneself.[94] Thus there is a sense in which facts as known are dependent upon, even created by, the self. Consequently, a theory of fact presupposes an understanding of the self. The empirical concept of the self, unfortunately, is deficient; accordingly its view of the nature of fact is superficial.

The empirical concept of the self has developed out of a one-sided emphasis within the Cartesian philosophy. The empirical self was supposed to be the object of immediate perception. But the relation of this perceived ego to the enduring, rational (Cartesian) self was most difficult to explain. Marcel sees no way of avoiding this dualism within the self,[95] and holds that this defect of theory is quite sufficient to refute the empirical view of the self.[96]

The difficulties encountered by empiricism in apprehending the nature of fact develop out of its historical situation. For empirical philosophy has grown up in close relation to the sciences and often appears to be nothing more than a generalization from the practice of the sciences. That is to say it has grown up without much questioning of the simple picture of an objective world placed over against a knowing subject. But accepting this sharp-cut distinction of the subject from the object as philosophically final destroys the intimate relation between the self, its body, and its world. The very language of empiricism betrays the reductionist character of this philosophy. This is a language imitative of the exactitude of the sciences.[97] Thus it is a routine language for

---

[91] MJ 75.   [92] MMS 273.   [93] MJ 3.   [94] MB I, 66f.
[95] Unless, that is, the empiricist were willing to regard the relation of the universal to the empirical ego as established by an act of faith in God (MJ 40–46), which the empiricist does not do.
[96] MJ 42ff.   [97] RI 84ff.

which the fresh and intimate contact with the world and with others has lost its force and meaning.[98]   Its use expresses, even enjoins, enslavement to that aspect of objects which standard empirical procedures of the sciences reveal and inculcates a blindness to the remainder.   It does not, therefore, perform the philosophic function of criticizing abstractions, but rather imitates the sciences by continuing to cultivate the spirit of abstraction.

Marcel's criticisms of idealism, rationalism, and empiricism are sharp, but usually not bitter.   They are the criticisms of a philosopher directed against respected, if not always admired, opponents.   A quite different note enters into his objections to the philosophy of Sartre.   These criticisms are bitter indeed, and suggest the animosity which sometimes characterizes relations within a family.   In fact, there is a certain kinship between the two philosophies.   Marcel is no doubt right in looking upon Sartre as situated at the opposite end of the spectrum from himself.   Attention, therefore, to his objections to Sartre's philosophy will be useful for clarifying his own position.

Marcel recalls that after listening once to Sartre read a paper, he suggested that Sartre write on metaphysics of the viscous.   This suggestion, in Marcel's opinion, was accepted.[99]   It seems to Marcel that this philosopher's fundamental intuition, expressed in *La Nausée* by Roquentin's interest in ugly and discarded materials, is centered in excretion. Life appears to him to be a superfluous and useless secretion.   The human being himself seemed to be only a waste product of this nauseating and inconceivable universe.[100]   As purposeless and contingent, yet existing, life could be conceived only as absurd.   Thus Sartre was led to a philosophy of non-being, the exact inverse of Marcel's philosophy of being in overabundance.   Now the really dangerous aspect of this philosophy, as Marcel evidently views it, is that Sartre offers it persuasively as a guide to human living.

Sartre's philosophy is said to be a Cartesianism without the Being upon which Cartesianism depends.   Thus consciousness and all that is not consciousness, i.e., being, are related as contradictories.   Since consciousness of being is diametrically opposed to being, and being is always something, consciousness must be said to be nothing.   It is completely empty of being.   Although, in consequence, one can not be said to be anything in particular, still there is in men the longing for being and the desire to escape from their natural nothingness. Indeed men are haunted by the anxious dread of nothingness.   Marcel perceives in this Sartrean recognition of the desire for being a kind of perversion of his own notion of the ontological need.   Certainly Marcel does not deny the existence of the sense of emptiness or awareness of non-being so common among men, especially in modern times.   But

---

[98] MB *I*, 55.
[99] *"Existence and Human Freedom"* in PE.   *The whole of this essay is given over to the discussion of Sartre, as is chap. 8 of HV.   Sartre's name appears in Marcel's writings probably more frequently than the name of any other contemporary philosopher.*
[100] MMS 68.

unlike Sartre, he holds that the human deficiency in being can be mitigated, although it is not knowledge or power which can fill the void in men, but meaningful action.[101] In accepting the human lack of being as incorrigible, Sartre renders it theoretically impossible to recognize meaningful action.

Since for Sartre it is impossible for a consciousness to *be* anything, the satisfaction of its longing for being can be nothing more than pretense and impersonation. The anxiety which one's recognition of one's own nothingness inspires can be concealed only by petty tasks and business which disguise vacancy. Such pretense is bad faith. Regularity in living, development of habits, behaving in accordance with received custom, all these are poor attempts to imitate the permanence of being. Such imitation exhibits insincerity and bad faith. Here Marcel observes that Sartre has stacked the cards against men, for insincerity cannot in principle be avoided.[102] If so, Marcel asks, how can sincerity be distinguished existentially from insincerity?[103]

Not only individual life but life in common offers paradoxes according to Sartre's philosophy. In fact his view seems to offer no understanding at all of intersubjectivity.[104] People look upon each other as so many things, at best as rivals. When another enters the room with me, he attacks my very subjectivity by holding as his own the scene which I view; then he seeks to confirm his conquest and render me the slave of his own freedom by regarding me as a body, merely a thing or an instrument. The sense of embarrassment and anxiety which many persons feel when surprised by another's look is taken as illustrating this view. Hell is, according to Sartre's often repeated remark, other people. And he views love as a defense against this metaphysical hostility; love employs seduction to transform the rival into the willing captive. Sartre, Marcel believes, can imagine only the most egoistic love relationship. As evidence that Sartre's views are not merely an academic curiosity, he cites Sartre's reputed rejection of family life on the grounds that children might annoy him.[105] The modern tendency to deny the responsibility of parenthood seems to be carried to its logical extreme in this philosophy, where fatherhood both as fact and as value is rejected.[106] The serious consequence for Sartre's philosophy is that intersubjectivity loses its meaning. But, as Marcel views it, intersubjectivity is the perspective within which an ontology is to be founded.[107] It is not extraordinary, therefore, that Sartre's philosophy seems to him to condemn human consciousness to frustration in finding the being which it needs and seeks.

Sartre's self-consciousness is a lack of being. But as a nothing, it cannot be determined by a being outside itself, as if it were a being; hence it is wholly free. Marcel holds, however, that this characteristic human property, freedom, is affirmed by Sartre in an absurdly excessive manner.[108] Sartrean freedom is completely unrestricted choice. Nothing can possibly limit it; *all* one's acts are free. But since the self is a non-being, i.e., nothing, this freedom seems to Marcel to

101 HP *66*.   102 MMS *178*.   103 MJ *xi*.   104 HV *176f*.   105 MB *I*, 41; *199*.
106 MB *I*, *199*.   107 MB *II*, *91*.   108 HV *174*.

be the property of nothing; he finds it difficult to understand how nothing can have such a property. Sartre affirms that this freedom is the power to create oneself. Marcel responds by observing that this conviction denies the natural world, our inheritance from the past, and our participation in a reality not ourselves.[109] Further, freedom is viewed by Sartre as creating value. But since the self is nothing, Marcel sees no way that Sartre can distinguish value from disvalue inasmuch as the standard which measures value can scarcely be nothing, nor can it be being, which is indifferent. Marcel, therefore, terms Sartre's ethic an *"éthique de désinvolture"* (an ethic of unrestraint).[110] Finally the unrestricted freedom posited by Sartre is, like a commodity flooding the market, valueless.

The final end posited by freedom for itself, according to Sartre, is the synthesis of being and consciousness. But this synthesis of disparate elements is impossible, a conclusion which leads Sartre to deny the possibility of the existence of God. This denial carries as its consequence the denial of transcendence except in the sense of moving through time on to basically similar events or tasks. This kind of human change is termed by Marcel a "horizontal" transcendence.[111] But the movement to which the human need for being naturally inclines men is a movement of "vertical transcendence" through conversion toward a new kind of being. This natural desire of man is thus at every turn systematically frustrated by the Sartrean doctrine. Sartre has thus placed men in the absurd position of needing to move toward an end which is unattainable.[112] And thus for Sartre the anxiety (*angoisse*) which is consequent upon recognition of one's nothingness is irremediable; it is, therefore, according to Marcel, a fake anxiety, a mere dizziness which is devoid of piety or of authenticity; it is nothing more than a denatured version of Heidegger's dread.[113]

Marcel's general evaluation of Sartre's philosophy is that it is a move in the same "technique of vilification" which he detected in so many trends of the modern world.[114] It even expresses a kind of sadistic pleasure in self-abasement and contributes with a kind of satanic perfection to the decomposition of man.[115] Thus Marcel seems to suggest that Sartre's philosophy systematizes and defends just those motives and policies which characterize modern peoples and are continuing to lead them further along the way of contempt for others, self-estrangement, and alienation from the world and from being. It is a philosophy which finds consciousness to be an emptiness, associates life with waste, condemns man to bad faith and to solitariness, endows him with an unnatural freedom, and directs him to a self-contradictory goal. Thus man is systematically vilified and abused.

Sartre's philosophy, therefore, is not, like empiricism or idealism, an unemotional presentation of abstractions under the guise of concrete insights into human life and its needs. It appears to Marcel to be far more dangerous in that Sartre is possessed in certain respects of a concrete

[109] HP *151f.*   [110] MB *I, 39.*   [111] HV *183.*   [112] MB *I, 175.*   [113] HP *153.*
[114] MB *I, 175; HV 183.*   [115] MMS *178.*

grasp upon human existence. Nevertheless, his grasp is partial and
his orientation is perverted. Specifically and most damagingly, he
fails to apprehend ontological transcendence. Thus Sartre's philosophy is unable in principle to envisage authentic human existence. It
cannot but turn its adherents in a perverted direction. Still this philosophy is persuasive. Its influence lends weight precisely to those
lamentable trends in the modern world which disintegrate it and urge
it on to self-destruction.

The general character of Marcel's criticism of modern social and philosophical trends can now be summarily expressed. The direction in which
Western man and his technical culture are developing is increasingly
mechanical and abstract. The direction in which much of the influential Western philosophy has developed has been toward the reification
of useful or persuasive abstractions. These two trends have rein-
forced each other. The element common to the two areas criticized
is evident: both ignore the whole and develop a part to excessive pro-
portions. Both, that is, ignore the concrete; they recognize and seek
to utilize only those aspects of the concrete which are translatable
into abstract concepts. That is, they do not merely use certain abstractions, they cultivate the "spirit of abstraction"; thus thought
about concrete human life is distorted as a matter of policy and its
development perverted.

The basic mistake is uncritical confidence, not so much in the abstract concepts which are actually formulated, as in the spirit of abstraction. I
suggest the term *"argumentum ad ratiocinativum"* to name this
fallacy. Marcel expresses it when he remarks upon the tendency of
learned men, especially of scientists, to identify being with truth.
Specifically they identify being with scientific truth. But, Marcel goes
on to observe, the appropriate attitude toward being is *reverence.*
Just here the difference between being and truth becomes evident,
for no one regards scientific truth with reverence. The scientist's love
for truth may be a passionate interest or a humanitarian confidence,
but no one would call it reverence. Thus the scientist or the impersonal investigator indicates by these attitudinal evaluations his recognition of the characteristically abstract and essentially nonphilosophic
nature of his interest.[116]

The identification of truth, which refers to some aspect of being, with being
itself is a fundamental error. The recognition of this kind of error is,
after all, not original with Marcel. Whitehead has expressed much the
same point in his discussions of the fallacy of misplaced concreteness.
Bergson and others in recent years had already made the point
familiar. But Marcel has expressed it in new ways and expressed
it forcibly. In addition, Marcel attempts to carry his analysis a stage
further. Consider again his view of the sadists of Belsen or the
Sartrean philosophy. Here we are faced in different ways not with
mistakes which can be objectively viewed and corrected but with a
much more profound disaffection, namely, a contempt which infects

the outlook of the whole person. It is expressed as a policy directed toward the vilification of man. This attitude is not a collection of particular errors but a fundamental disposition, an existential evaluation, an orientation of life. One may term it, more generally, a hatred of the whole world and all that is in it, including finally oneself. Marcel refers to it as a "contempt for the concrete."[117] This is the break in the world. Nor is it merely a historical fact that the world is broken like a watch whose spring no longer functions; the world *tends* to break in this manner. Sartre has merely given voice to an inclination to self-distrust and to an impulse to self-destruction which is inherent within the human spirit. This evil is somehow a part of life in the world. All men are infected with it. Marcel in the end diagnoses the disease of our time as evil itself.[118] And, like nearly everyone who has been touched by the Greek or Christian traditions, he concludes that evil is finally a mystery. The term "mystery," however, is not intended to be a name for something totally unknowable, nor is it used in a theological sense. The term acquires in the course of Marcel's reflection a meaning which leads directly into his view of philosophy as the whole of experience transmuted into thought.[119] This is his doctrine of "contemplation." He relates the evil which characterizes our own day to the dying out of contemplation.[120] But the effects of contemplation are scarcely less mysterious than the evil which it negates. Moreover, the corrective which it proposes is exceptionally difficult to grasp, for this is not a philosophy already thought out, so much as an invitation to *"la pensée pensante"*; it is an urge to reflect upon one's self in relation to being.[121]

5. The Nature
of Secondary Reflection

It has been remarked that objectivising reflection breaks the link with one's body and with the world. This breakage is not necessarily an evil to be regretted. By isolating one's self from one's body, difficulties associated primarily with the body or with the external world may be treated separately.[122] Marcel does not deny the utility of this kind of isolation and reduction nor does he wish to minimize its intrinsic interest. To the contrary, he recognizes the founding and "enabling acts" of the sciences and mathematics to be among the most creative of human achievements.[123] They contain their own kind of mystery. But when this kind of thinking is accepted as complete and adequate to all possible human needs, the difficulty appears. For the scientific worker, as a necessity of his method, leaves himself out of the picture. The consequence of this abstraction of himself from the situation is

---

[117] MMS 155.   [118] MB I, 35f.; MMS 90f.   [119] RI 39.   [120] MB I, 122.
[121] It is worth noting that Marcel, unlike many existentialists, lays no stress upon taking an active part in events. He refused, for instance, to become involved in the Resistance movement during the Second World War, holding that he participated in a more authentic resistance by writing Homo Viator (1942), which was directed toward discovering the nature of human dignity.
[122] MB I, 93f.   [123] MB I, 214.

that he systematically refuses his own participation and becomes the impersonal and noncontemplative spectator who resembles more and more one of his own instruments.[124]

One consequence of the cultivation of this attitude is the growth of a false humility. Humility, as it is sometimes defined within the scientific world, is only another name for the systematic effacement of the self required in the interests of objectivity. Its immediate end is avoidance of error. Its concomitant, though, is the glorification of applied science and of the self as the Promethean ruler of nature.[125] Another consequence follows from the effort to invent a metaphysical justification for this scientific attitude. This justification has usually proceeded, as we have already noticed, on the assumption that the categories of science or of a scientifically oriented philosophy are the categories of all reality.[126] The concepts, devised for the analysis and study of the external and objective world, are then extended specifically to include the life of men. Man thus comes to be regarded as an object. The question whether this extension is legitimate and defensible can scarcely be decided except by a further reflection which takes this objective thought as its topic. Secondary reflection is, at least in part, reflection upon objective or primary reflection.

Secondary reflection does not conflict with the results of primary and scientific reflection. Indeed, primary reflection may be a necessary stage in the whole reflective process. However, contemplation opposes primary reflection in the sense of refusing to accept it or its results as final.[127] Specifically, it refuses to accept the divisive, and disunifying consequences of primary reflection as final. In this respect, secondary reflection is restorative and recuperative. It seeks to reconquer the unity from which reflection began. Thus it is "the special high instrument of philosophical research."[128] For example, it seeks to restore, but upon a new level of intelligibility, the unity of the self with the body which is ruptured early in the career of primary thought.[129] Also it is opposed to the habit of seeking to explain something by reducing it to something else. Secondary reflection, however, does not end or expect to end with a theory which "solves" its problem or explains experience in the same sense that primary reflection achieves these ends. It must, on the contrary, be content to terminate with taking a matter into account rather than accounting for it: or it may merely recognize a matter as, in a technical sense, a mystery rather than a solvable problem.[130] Still its total effect is to integrate dispersed elements, especially the various aspects and activities of the self, into a totality. Thus its real function is to renew and to change one's way of existing and participating in life. This renewed participation is "contemplation;" it is the emerged participation to which we alluded earlier.[131] Participation, as it comes to be penetrated by thought, undergoes a process of "inner reshaping" which accomplishes a metamorphosis of the person[132] and may finally be

[124] MB I, 122; BH 19.   [125] MB II, 86f.   [126] HP 69f.   [127] MB I, 93.
[128] MB I, 83; cf. RI 34.   [129] RI 34.   [130] MB II, 169.   [131] MB I, 114; 122.
[132] MB II, 182.

viewed as a preparation for faith. In sum, the end of this reflection
is not to change the world, but rather to convert the self who reflects.

The articulation of this contemplative reflection as Marcel practices it is
extremely difficult to discern. It appears, as well as I can determine,
most often to consist in two moments. Usually the first step turns
upon the deficiencies of objective reflection and consists in pointing
out its inadequacies, especially its tendency to mistake the abstract
for the concrete. This stage is illustrated by the criticisms discussed
in the two preceding sections. It performs the valuable service of
indicating the direction in which loss and ultimate failure must be
expected and provides a negative orientation. The next step moves
on by appeal to concrete experience, by use of examples, not infrequently by reference to his plays, and seeks to emerge to a more
complete apprehension of the concrete matter under discussion.
This more complete apprehension inevitably is to include man himself,
understood not as an object but as a unique and self-questioning
being. It seeks, furthermore, to include that upon which the being
of the self depends; and finally it seeks to orient one's change in the
direction of fulfillment. Marcel's description of this new understanding is perforce laborious. He sometimes speaks of it as comprehension in opposition to prehension or taking intellectual possession
of an object. It has been briefly illustrated in this essay by the discussion of "my body." Thus the method proceeds by a characteristic use
of language to a contemplative comprehension of a situation, a person, or a presence. This invocation of a total response compares with
a scientific account rather as an inventory might compare with a
poem[133] or as an official biographical questionnaire might compare
with the life of the person questioned, except that Marcel's interest is
metaphysical. The point is that his interest is, in a literal sense of
the term, *meta*-physical, beyond the physical, i.e., directed toward
participating in the concrete.

The two kinds of reflection may be compared in respect to the mode of
transcendence sought by each. Any sort of movement beyond present
existence represents some effort of transcendence. Primary reflection
expresses the act of transcendence toward a world of definite calculable physical objects which may be classified and manipulated.
Difficulties in manipulating and controlling such objects may be
treated as solvable practical problems and, finally, dominated. Here
the movement of transcendence is always upon the same plane.
Marcel speaks of it, as we noted when discussing Sartre's philosophy,
as a horizontal transcendence, since it envisages no change of oneself through a more complete integration in being. Marcel, however,
proposes a "vertical" transcendence[134] to which secondary reflection
is part of the means. In fact its subordination to this end may be
regarded as defining secondary reflection. Vertical transcendence
is directed toward the experience of being and in the last analysis
toward a relation to transcendent being.[135] It requires not refine-
ments in the techniques of apprehending and measuring objects but

133 MB I, 208.   134 MB I, 39f.   135 MMS 22f.; RI 189f.

rather a change in one's way of being. Marcel illustrates it by reference to a person who cultivates association with another because of
his amusing qualities and serviceableness, yet in the end comes to
appreciate this other person as a being in his own right, as another
self.[136] Secondary reflection, thus, is intended to lead one to a new
modality of experience, one which may properly be described as more
of a whole, more integrated, or inclusive of more being.

Marcel, at such a point as this, customarily warns his readers to be on the
lookout for deception by words, for the terms of ordinary discourse
are formed for usage in the contemporary world of primary reflection
and specialized occupations. For just this reason a characteristic of
secondary reflection must be negative; in fact, it is doubly negative.
It must negate primary reflection, its divisiveness, its abstraction, and
above all its tendency uncritically to include man in its theories as if
he were another thing or object. But primary reflection was already
negative in the sense that its use of abstraction constitutes a negation
or rejection of that from which the abstraction was taken. Thus secondary reflection negates the negations of primary reflection. In this
manner it seeks to return to the concrete experience but without loss
of the value of understanding.

The philosopher, however, does not restrict himself to negative expressions.
Rather, he must seek out non-objective functions of language.[137] To
this end he makes large use of the poetic properties of words, remembering all the while that these powers of words tend to disappear as
they are turned to technical and philosophical use. Marcel sides with
Heidegger in the conviction that a large portion of the philosophic task
is to restore the poetic power of words. The point is crucial for the
understanding of secondary reflection. It indicates its special kind
of difficulty, a difficulty which is quite unlike that of a science. For
one can, if one has taken the appropriate discipline, always repeat
the proof of a mathematical formula and thus recapture the insight.
Likewise one can, at least in principle, repeat the experiments which
substantiate a physical law. However, an existential philosopher
speaks in the name of certain experiences which can not be relived at
will. They are dependent upon the recovery of presences and the
effects of contemplation in which the whole person is engaged.[138]
They are communicable only by way of the evocative power of words
or meaningful actions to awaken a dramatic renewal of similar experiences. The important initial task, then, which this philosophy faces is
the determination of the basic terms which will be useful in achieving
the ends of secondary reflection.

We must, for the sake of understanding this philosophy, admit to the existence of two quite distinct kinds of categories: the categories of objective thought which suffice for primary reflection or for the needs of
common sense and the sciences, and also the non-objective "categories of lived experience," which are the means whereby we may
reach some sort of apprehension of the beings which we ourselves
are.[139] These categories are the terms which serve to express and to

[136] MB *I*, 48.   [137] HP *53f*.   [138] MB *I*, 213.   [139] MB *I*, 41.

direct the urge to "vertical" transcendence. We are dealing in this second instance with what Kierkegaard called the categories of the individual and what Heidegger refers to as existentials. Marcel avers that the major effort of his philosophical life has been directed toward discovering them.[140] These are the categories of drama which are put to use, not to divide, classify, and control the items experienced, but to describe them and evoke a renewed participation in them. They can assist the person to become aware of his own metamorphoses and even to direct them.

Marcel occasionally suggests a relationship between his method and that of phenomenology.[141] At least both strive to respect the phenomenon in all its phases. The further effect which Marcel desires from this respect for the phenomenon is a renewed experience of the unity of himself with phenomena. Marcel speaks in the *Metaphysical Journal* of this reestablishment of the links within himself and with the world as "self-presence."[142] In a later work he refers to this contemplative reflection as the movement toward "fulfillment of participation." It opens the way to a participation in being which is comparable to a plant's fruition, and possesses a mysterious quality inseparable from intersubjectivity.

Already in these last few sentences mention has been made of a number of the categories of lived experience which secondary reflection turns to its use. Let us now attempt to disengage these categories, to describe their properties, and to determine the way in which they direct human change.[143]

6. Categories
of Secondary Reflection

In the earlier discussion of existence certain of these categories were already used—unavoidably—and partly described (e.g., presence, participation, incarnation). Rather than returning to a more elaborate treatment of the same categories, it will be more profitable for the purposes of this essay to proceed to certain others which are necessary for understanding the orientation of human existence toward being. These are mainly self, situation, intersubjectivity, and transcendence. In any case, all the categories are intimately interconnected, and an understanding of any one will throw light upon the others.

It is natural first to think of the self, of him who asks: Who am I? Marcel cites a personage from a play of Corneille's who is brought by the

---

[140] HP *69ff.*

[141] H. Spiegelberg, *however, observes that it is difficult to include Marcel within the phenomenological movement, since his phenomenological descriptions, while perceptive, are clearly subsidiary to his metaphysical interests. He is an ally rather than a protagonist of phenomenology.* The Phenomenological Movement, *The Hague, 1960, vol. II, 442f.*

[142] MJ *284;* MB I, *286.*

[143] Marcel *provides no clear-cut definition of these nonobjective categories nor any list of them. Some of my identifications of these categories and the distinctions which I draw between them and such notions as existence and being are tentative.*

sudden betrayal of his friends to gather up his past and his character, as it were, and to call himself to account. He felt at the least obligated to attempt to take the same view of himself which his former friends had taken. The effect of this self-gathering and self-examination was a profound change in himself. But what can be meant by a change of the self? Does it not have to remain the same in order to recognize its change? At least it is evident that the self is not a thing which alters as if it were an object whose properties change with the passage of time. Nor can it be said to be some sort of duality of transcendental ego and empirical ego in which the real and permanent self is abstract, perhaps identical with pure reason, and the concrete self consists in the contingent, temporary, and even trivial, contents of consciousness. The relation which exists between one's identity and the expressions of this identity in existence must be far closer than such a theory allows. A partial disassociation of oneself from the life situation in which one participates might seem to be necessary before grasping the nature of the self. Nevertheless, this step can be effected only at the risk of losing hold of the subject which constitutes itself through its decisions and its use of its situations.[144]

What, then, of the situation from which it is doubtful that one can separate himself? By situation we do not mean merely the external and objective circumstances in which the self is located. For in an important sense one is where one's affections, interests, and thoughts are, and this may be miles and years away from the immediate external localization in space and time. Nevertheless, one's thoughts and interests are rendered effective at the present location. Probably, then, the actual situation is better described as the junction of the internal and the external.

The situation is not to be abstracted from the human actor for whom it is at once the setting and the limit. Reflection on oneself is, thus, reflection upon oneself in a given situation. "Situation" is just that which enables one to stand off at some distance, so to speak, and see oneself sympathetically or critically. As this description suggests, it is the context in which participation may begin.[145] It is from this self-in-encounter or self-in-situation from which reflection may succeed in evoking a renewed apprehension of the self. For such a reason Marcel concludes that "the essence of man is to be in situation."[146] Through being in situation one comes to be what and who one is. And the way of being wholly and responsively in a situation is through reflection upon it. Thus this kind of reflection is a means to the creative development of oneself. The situation in which this reflective change occurs is not the clearly defined environment of biology or sociology; it can be apprehended only through an obscure but apparently irreducible notion.[147] Some further understanding of this lack of clarity may be gained by reflecting upon the way in which one is in a situation.

Let us approach the matter obliquely and shift back again to consider the

[144] MB *133f.*   [145] RI *119.*   [146] RI *113.*   [147] MB *I, 197.*

self, for only in consequence of the self is there a situation. Again we ask: Who is this strange being who asks himself where and who he is? What sort of being can address such a question to himself? This reflective position carries one beyond the "exclamatory awareness" of mere existence expressed in a "*sentio ergo sum*."[148] After its criticism of objective thought the subject who engages in this reflection will no longer be duped by grammar into taking the self as a thing nor in any sense as a Cartesian substance. Contemplation brings the subject first to the consciousness of his own incarnation which denies, as we have already observed, the fiction of the body-as-instrument. This is the affirmation: I am my body. This possession of one's body is the unique possession without which there is no other. One's noninstrumental communion and unity with one's body is the "sympathetic medium" through which one can be *in* a situation. Situation, bodily presence, participation all go hand in hand.[149]

One's participation occurs at many levels and varies in degree. One is first submerged in a feeling response to the situation, but later upon reflection, elements and possibilities emerge, become distinct, and are reshaped. One may participate objectively in a situation by being present bodily, or one may participate non-objectively, as a bedridden person may share intentionally in the performance of a ceremony which is significant for him.[150] Further, either of the two modes of participation, it would seem, can be either relatively passive or actively creative. Marcel finds this last contrast in the scientist who observes or in the technician who manipulates, both of whom avoid being actively in situation and attempt to discount their own mentality and feeling, as opposed to the artist with his commitment and interest in final perfection. This is the difference between the spectatorlike and the contemplative attitudes.[151] The man who does not contemplate is the mere spectator of the world. He may be the curious investigator, but never the anguished or joyful participant. The contemplator, on the contrary, sure of his grip on reality, takes a unique individual as his object, e.g., himself, and pursues self-discovery through questioning himself and his life situation.[152] By this route he seeks a new "modulation of existence." By gathering himself inward in this manner, he withdraws from the world, not abstractly, but with the intent of undergoing a creative development by means of which he can deal with his situation in a nonroutine manner. In this way he may see some hope of being "true to himself"[153] and of bringing his resources to bear upon his own efforts to increase the depth of his participation in the situations to which he is open.

Is it possible to say who the self is who interrogates himself and thus becomes more aware of his involvement in situations? It has seemed to some thinkers that total commitment would answer this question, for such commitment is equivalent to accepting a given identity. And yet total commitment may quite possibly be total alienation, as in the case of political absolutism. Commitment which is not merely an

---

[148] MB *I, 90f.*   [149] MB *I, 100.*   [150] MB *I, 112f.*   [151] MB *I, 121.*
[152] MB *I, 133.*   [153] MB *I, 144.*

avoidance of the question of identity cannot, therefore, be total; it presupposes some prior self-understanding and self-determination; also it assumes openness to others and to change. At the minimum, one is the being who pursues knowledge and can reflect upon himself in order to participate more effectively in his living. This self is not merely the present subject, for if so he could not interrogate the past. A function of this interrogation, however, is to reabsorb and restructure the past self in the new present and thus to transcend the present. Perhaps, then, one's whole career is the self. Could it be said that Van Gogh's paintings present his whole self-reflective life?[154] But who could read this account? And what of the man who has no achievement behind him, no record at all? Marcel observes that he has still the possibility of self-sacrifice for which to be prepared. Perhaps this sacrifice is the only sort of test which can assure a person that he has found an answer to the question. For surely the crucial test and heroism which self-sacrifice calls forth is to be answered only by one who has a confident grasp of himself and who can in that ultimate moment answer with his actions who he then and finally is. Under these circumstances, a person does not recognize himself as that which is exchanged for a definite somewhat for which, presumably, he might be the equivalent. Self-sacrifice, in answering the question concerning one's identity, does not answer by reducing oneself to something else. It answers concretely in willingness to give the total self in response to an invocation.[155] This is the self-sacrifice which has so often been recognized to be self-fulfilment. To shirk it is less than human, to achieve it is superhuman.[156] Still the question is not provided with an easily communicated answer. Who is such a one? Why did he formerly go on living? Why does he now sacrifice himself? Always, however, like Christiane in Le Monde cassé, one may engage in the secondary reflection which reveals both the emptiness and valuelessness of the life which one had been living and also exercises a recuperative effect by suggesting the nature of fulfilment. And this fulfilment is not exactly a Sein zum Tode, as it is for Heidegger, but rather a readiness for self-sacrifice or the supreme affirmation of one's human nature and value, an affirmation which is at the opposite pole from the despairing withdrawal of the suicide.[157]

Even so, the question of one's identity is not settled. Perhaps no objective answer is possible. One is not transparent to himself,[158] even though commitment and self-sacrifice must be admitted to have meaning. Marcel remarks that happiness is "self-presence," but what this self is which may be present to itself he does not risk saying, except to observe that it has been called a kind of marriage to the self.[159] A significant word upon the matter is uttered by the Protestant pastor, Claude Lemoyne, protagonist of Marcel's play, L'Homme de Dieu. Claude is an anguished soul whose unfaithful wife has rejected his pardon and thereby loosened his confidence in the sincerity of his love

---

154 MB I, 158.   155 RI 106.   156 MB I, 166.   157 MB I, 169.
158 MJ 290.   159 MJ 291; cf. 289.

both for God and for his fellowman. "Who am I?" he asks, "When I try to grasp myself I slip through by own fingers." Man is only a wayfarer, a *homo viator* in search of himself, obscurely aware of a sustaining being within him which could fulfill his need. "I am a situation that surpasses me."[160]

If, then, man is the wayfarer, can he not be placed in a context where his travel and his search may be given an explicit direction? The notion of situation is partly the answer to this question. The situation is the context where this pursuit of his own being can be carried forward. But the non-objective concept of situation itself is not sufficient and requires an additional indication of the direction of motion and self-change. Religions lay claim to a privilege in pointing out this direction, but there are many competing religions, and many of them are not persuasive. There remains a function for philosophy to perform in this respect. Marcel's account of this aspect of human change is given in his doctrine of "intersubjectivity."

The meaning which Marcel attaches to intersubjectivity is at the antipodes from the notion of the human collectivity and the mass man of modern times. It refers rather to the human intimacy which can be developed only in small groups, preeminently in the family.[161] It is participation in the being of another person. This intimacy is, however, another non-objective notion and accordingly difficult to acquire.

The remarks which we have made about the self lead naturally to Marcel's comparison of a person's life to a play in which one knows one's own lines but no others, and does not know whether the play has a point or a structure or even whether it has a producer. In the face of this ignorance, what are the possibilities? The conclusion to absurdity is not uncommon; Sartre develops this conclusion further by adding that one may give the play a point and a direction by means of his own decisions. Marcel responds that this suggestion is incompatible with the fact of his existence prior to his own decisions and suggests further that the effort to organize life around such individual decisions is evidence of a childish egocentrism.[162] The child's aggressive fixation upon his immediately present self is a kind of defense against others and is the reverse of intersubjectivity. In collective labor, on the other hand, there may come to exist the beginnings of intersubjectivity in the sense of common fate and common struggle. More specifically, in the bonds which unify persons into one family is to be discerned the true character of intersubjectivity. But this character is difficult to distinguish clearly in a time when the family is distintegrating and when sonship and fatherhood are being emptied of all but their biological meaning.[163] Nevertheless, its significance may be grasped in the "spiritual act" of giving a child a name, an act symbolic of welcoming its birth and participation in the family unity. One likewise may become aware of it by contrasting "communion" with a distant friend and "communication" with an official of a nearby institution. In the latter instance one may understand what is said if distance and

[160] MJ *137.*   [161] HV *68ff.*   [162] MB *I, 174.*   [163] MB *I, 198;* HV *73.*

language differences do not interfere, whereas in the former, persons understand each other and distance is no barrier and speech no necessity. Thus, in the intersubjective group communion is possible. A characteristic instance of communion is the apprehension of a person's charm. Charm is an unteachable and elusive quality, not an objective content. It is perceived as a presence rather than translated as a message. Yet in spite of its inexpressibleness and non-objectivity, it cannot rightly be said to be merely subjective; rather it is intersubjective.[164] It is not apprehended by sense or intellect but by a magical and poetic act.

A grasp of intersubjectivity is of the utmost importance in this philosophy. This being-together is not, it must be emphasized, merely existence in a group or even existence in a group having a common concern. The unity induced by these and similar bonds would not necessarily distinguish intersubjectivity from the human herd or from businesslike relations not characterized by common subjectivity. Intersubjectivity is a kind of fertile indistinction of persons, the product of a will to mutual participation.[165] The bond which effects this vital union, Marcel writes, is "love."[166] Hence his insistence upon the family as the crucial instance. Love is removed as far as possible from the third-person relation to objects and replaces this latter by the I-thou relationship of personal presence.[167] "Presence" is just the presence of love, and the society whose members are thus mutually present is an intersubjectivity. Marcel uses the term "disposibilité" to name the openness to, or readiness for this mutual participation. Intersubjectivity is diametrically opposed to egocentricity, which is an isolation of the self and a kind of death. It is a commonplace, no doubt, to observe that one cannot know or develop his personality alone or in a social vacuum. Marcel raises this commonplace to the status of a metaphysical principle, and maintains that the self is rightly hetero-centric and that, accordingly, self-knowledge begins in communion with others. The way to one's self lies through another. Against Descartes' initial metaphysical assertion of self-existence, which is a kind of metaphysical isolation, Marcel would affirm "we are."[168] This mysterious "we are" of intersubjectivity is not a datum given to me, for I am part of it. Nor is it a localized and dated fact, for it is a condition for anything else to be present or factually given. It can only be acknowledged and accepted as the basis of communion, of language, of the being of oneself and of one's world. Inevitably, therefore, the effort to understand oneself as fully as possible leads to intersubjectivity as the one thing needful. A situation, however "natural" it may appear, superficially considered, is always a product of common human association, activity, and love. The self becomes highly differentiated as a consequence of activity in such an association, and it may, if mature, enjoy a similar harmonious intersubjectivity even within itself. "I communicate effectively with myself only to the degree that I communicate with others."[169] Thus subjectivity is

[164] MJ 206; MB I, 207.   [165] RI 52.   [166] MB I, 167.   [167] MJ 145f and passim.
[168] MB II, 9f.; BH 104.   [169] RI 150.

basically intersubjectivity.[170] That is, one's self is constituted by relations with others; or again the presence of the self is at the same time the co-presence of the "thou."[171]

Of these existential categories, "presence," "self," "situation," "intersubjectivity," the last named is the most fundamental. But it is clear that they are interrelated in complex and subtle ways. Perhaps their character and interrelations can be rendered more perspicious if some common nature or property can be distinguished within them.

7. Category, Mystery, and Being

Objective thought offers, comparatively speaking, little difficulty. Marcel takes over Royce's view of the object according to which the object is related to the knower by a triadic relation; the situation is as if two subjects conversed with each other about the object, which thereupon becomes an impersonal "it" external to the conversation. The object is characterized by this externality even when only one person attends to it. In this manner objects can be isolated from the self. They can also be isolated from each other, classified, and related in complex ways. Problems concerning objects lie like so many obstacles in one's way, but they can be solved by selecting an appropriate relation among objects from among the many possible ones. The distinguishing characteristic of objective thinking is that it is isolating; it disconnects both objects and problems from the inquirer as well as from irrelevant data.

Again it must be emphasized that the exclusion of the inquirer, the essential of objective thought, ignores or destroys his participation in the situation. This simplification is the price required for rendering the problem solvable. Secondary reflection, however, is concerned with situations from which the inquirer cannot abstract himself. He is involved in them as an element vitally affecting the total state of affairs. To affect this situation is also to affect the self and thus to alter one's grasp of the matter. There is no definite technique by which one can manage or control such a situation unambiguously. Marcel terms such situations "mysteries"; they are "metaproblematic."

A mystery is described as a metaproblematical state of affairs which encroaches on (empiète sur) its own data. Thus in no sense is it given to the thinker; rather, it tends to include the thinker as participant.[172] In approaching a mystery the philosopher uses ambiguous data, neither exactly subjective nor exactly objective, in order to get closer to, or to participate more fully in, a situation which is not exactly distinct from himself.[173] Notions which are mysteries in this fashion are just those which we have been discussing: evil, presence, self, participation, intersubjectivity. These are among the non-objective

170 MB I, 182f.   171 MJ 145; RI 150ff.   172 BH 117ff.; PE 8.   173 MB I, 211.

categories of lived experience, and it is through them and by the contemplative study of them that we may ultimately reach an apprehension of our concrete life experience in just that respect in which it changes us as we have it.   This is a level of concrete experience which is surely prior to the distinction between subject and object, observer and observed, and other abstractions of use in epistemology and the sciences.   These categories are to function as the philosopher's instruments for detecting and evaluating abstractions.

Now it is appropriate to ask just what is approached through these categories designed to apprehend mystery.   We can not consistently say that it is something we understand or can even seek to understand. Perhaps, then, we do not know enough about it to know where and how to direct our search.   And yet we observe that the inquiry constantly makes a turn toward mystery.   Suppose, for illustration, we attempt to understand what is meant by "having."   We speak normally of having objects in the sense that they are external to us, that we possess power over them, and that we may transmit them to others if we so desire.[174]   Having an idea is somewhat different in that an idea is not exactly external, yet it is still communicable.   What, though, about "my body"?   It is a possession?   Certainly not in the senses just distinguished; it is only ambiguously external and not at all transmissible.   Rather it is the condition of having possessions.[175] When we come to reality, it is clear that there is no question of possessing it, not even in the sense that characterizing it with attributes is a kind of intellectual posession.   For in regarding it as characterizable, I have to imagine it as a kind of thing placed over against me.   But the fact is that I am part of that reality and cannot remove myself from it without doing violence to its integrity.[176] Reality, then, is something which seems to resist critical dissolution or reduction to a possession.   There is in reality something which resists transmission.   Reality is a something which one has to be or to participate in rather than to possess.[177]   It manifests the character of presence rather than of objects.   Here Marcel introduces a term, related both to mystery and to the tension in human life, which helps to indicate the direction in which—as this example has just indicated —this tension and his inquiry turn.   The term is "being."   Being is the preeminently mysterious, since we, the beings who inquire, are involved in it no matter what we are or what we do.[178]   One cannot but affirm one's existence, and to affirm individual existence is to affirm being.[179]

Marcel's use of this term is elusive.   The inquiry into being is not quite the same as the attempt to distinguish and describe the categories of lived experience.[180]   The fact is that all the categories are related to being through the natural tension of human existence.   But both exis-

174 BH 159.   175 BH 166.   176 BH 169.   177 MJ 311.   178 MJ vii.
179 BH 120f.
180 This is my interpretation.   But the terminology is not, in this respect, clear.   Being
    is said, at least once, to be a category (MJ 311).   But it is also said not to be a
    genus (MB II, 29).

tence and being exceed the categories,[181] whether these are thought
of in a more usual sense, or in Marcel's quite special sense.   The
point is important for the understanding of his philosophy.

The notion of category is used in the primary or objective sense by those
philosophers who formulate the problem of being as that of finding a
complete system of categories.[182]   Their project is based upon the
assumption that philosophy is an abstract theoretical structure analogous to a science.   Marcel points out that the central thesis of his
Metaphysical Journal as of subsequent writings is that "there is no
objectively valid judgment bearing on being."[183]   To attempt to make
— being the topic of an objective study, and so to possess it intellectually, would be to ignore its mysterious character and the investigator's own status as a being whose vision of being is changed by his
very investigation of it.   Thus being cannot be pointed out as if it
were an object or a universal.   It cannot be possessed but only be
"alluded to."   Guided by the occasions which elicit our "forefeeling"
of the direction of inquiry, we can proceed by showing what is not
being and what, therefore, needs to be excluded.

"Category" in the second and non-objective sense is involved in the human
being's effort to come to terms with his own life: Human life is, first,
— immediate existence.   But this existence manifests an ontological
exigence, it is naturally in tension toward being.   The non-objective
categories enable the philosopher to apprehend and to describe his
existence as a way of being, and the direction and articulation of its
dramatic movement toward the fullness of being.   The character of
self-reference and self-involvement and mystery is clear.   One is himself a being.   Being pervades the categories and stands as the end
toward which the human being directs his change.

Marcel strongly disagrees with those existentialist writers who maintain that
the way to being, or to a more authentic life, lies through those limiting or crucial and extreme situations to which one reacts with dread or
anxiety *(Angst, angoisse)*. He regards the anxiety of Kierkegaard and
Heidegger as an excessive, infertile, and paralyzing mood, rather than
as a necessary stage in the development toward a more authentic
self. The anxiety which they mention does manifest some character
of mystery.   It seems to offer one a dizzy and awful alternative; at
the same time it is oneself which offers it.[184]   Thus it exemplifies
the self-involving property which is the mark of mystery.   Nevertheless, the nature of this alternative is suspect; it not infrequently—for
instance in the writings of Kiergegaard—seems to be pathologically
self-punitive and thus justifiably to invite the efforts of the psychiatrist to remove it.[185] There is, on the other hand, an attitude or mood
which Marcel terms unrest or unquiet *(inquiétude)* which he finds to

---

[181] *Intersubjectivity is not quite on a level with the other categories; it recalls the way
in which substance in the Aristotelian schema is an exceptional category. My
main point is that both existence and being are more basic notions than the
categories. Intersubjectivity is an especially important category only because
through it being is more fully apprehended than through any other.*
[182] *MJ 206.*   [183] *MJ 98; viii; MMS 173.*   [184] *HP 82.*   [185] *HP 186.*

be not subject to the same criticism. Indeed, this is the natural and creative mood which characterizes a person's attitude toward his own possibilities, and toward other persons. Neither one's own human possibilities nor the reality of other persons can be known exhaustively and clearly. Both are mysterious and to be apprehended only with a sense of unquiet and expectancy.[186] In modern times this unquiet has been exaggerated to the point of becoming anxiety. Yet there seems to be no reason why it should always be so. No doubt in such epochs as the thirteenth century, when the faith of Christendom was lively, one's sense of orientation toward being was less anguished than in later times. On the whole, though, this sense of unquiet is the natural complement to the "ontological humility" which accompanies the aspiration toward being. "Ontological humility" is the name for the intense awareness of the fact that being includes and yet forever transcends us;[187] thus it is an apprehension of our finitude in the face of that upon which we depend for the gift of our being.[188] This unquiet humility serves to disengage one from the grip of daily trivialities and reified abstractions and to motivate the desire for a being and a value which transcends the conventional.

The aspiration to being, the "ontological need" or "the bite of the real," may be experienced in many ways; the essential thing is that it be experienced keenly and that readiness for participation in it be not dulled, hidden, or denied. The motive for his condemnation of the American and Russian civilizations is his conviction that the masses in these societies are preoccupied with trivial amusements and desire to conceal or disguise such realities as death.[189] But in general all philosophies have observed a tendency in persons and civilizations to repeat the past, to routinize life, and to reject the use of their liberty, in sum to become "used to reality."[190] This lassitude, this preoccupation with daily problems and contentment with conventional abstractions, is precisely that sleep from which the "bite of the real" should awaken us. The philosopher should be most sensitive to this bite. This is the genuine "ontological hunger" which cannot be assuaged by the attentions of the psychiatrist. The philosopher asks questions and engages in interrogative thinking in order to shock himself and others out of intellectual slumber, not however as being provoked by scientific curiosity, but rather by the wonder and unquiet of one who seeks a reunion or participation in being, even though concern about such participation may run counter to all the currents of our civilization.[191] Part of the mystery of being is that, though it is all-inclusive, it is not compelling, and the need for it may be dulled or perverted. This is to say that one of the mysteries of our life is that our being is constantly in danger. One's salvation is always at issue.[192] Thus it is essential that the vision of being be constantly renewed.

The reflection which might awaken this vision must be directed in some definite direction. There is, however, a difficulty in formulating a

186 HP 182ff.   187 BH 133 n. 1; MJ 290.   188 BH 114; HV 26.   189 HP 174ff.
190 RI 88.   191 MMS 174.   192 BH 199; 120ff.

question about being. Some prior apprehension of being would seem to be necessary if we are to be assured that the question is intelligible. How should such a question be interpreted? Would it assume that being is distinct from phenomena? that it is something present in all objects? that it is a predicate? or that it transcends all logical and grammatical categories? Marcel's concrete approach discards all these ways of considering being. For example, in the initial stages of elucidating the meaning of the term, he shows that its meaning includes and also exceeds the meaning of "existence"; he refers to a garden which no longer exists but which continues to be effective and thus still is in being. Both existence and nonexistence are modalities of being.[193] That is, the immediacy of present existence clearly is not the fullness of being. But occasionally one's action may concentrate the whole of his past and involve his future.[194] This kind of fullness approaches closer to the meaning of being.

Marcel cites a person who is becoming more and more of a voluptuary. His change involves a progressive denial of previous attachments to things and to persons. The denial is the consequence of applying a kind of test for a certain quality or value which he seeks in experience and which comes for him to have almost an ontological significance. Can anything survive this testing? Will not the voluptuary's relation to the world and to others be thinned to the vanishing point and his personality be destroyed?[195] Criticism by such tests tends to dissolve everything except that which is immediately and perceptually present. In respect to being, its effect is impoverishing.

Now this impoverishment runs counter to the appetite for being of which we are obscurely aware. Being, whatever else it may be, must be that which satisfies the ontological need. As the satisfaction of a need, being is value.[196] It operates in Marcel's philosophy as a lure, and the intuition of being, however unverbalized and "blindfolded," operates as a guide indicating the general direction for search.[197] Marcel must assume in his readers the existence of essentially the same need and vague "forefeeling" of presence, identified with this intuition. We, his readers, must see that the voluptuary is becoming an empty, less real, and less valuable person. Unless we do see this and experience something of the appetite for being in ourselves, we cannot expect to understand the question about being.

How, though, is one to be assured that the point has been seen? To devise a test for this non-objective presence, being-value, which cannot be definitely characterized, is scarcely a task to be accomplished within either ordinary or scientific language. A concrete test, however, may be possible, and one is suggested in one of Marcel's plays. This test is death. The protagonist of L'Iconoclaste comes finally to recognize that the death of a beloved person was not an annihilation of the beloved's being; it destroyed only his having or possessing his beloved. Being, though, transcends possession. The testimony to his apprehension of the beloved's being was, thus, the recognition of the

---

193 MB II, 28.   194 MJ 198.   195 MJ 180ff.   196 MJ 129; MB II, 58f.
197 BH 118; 122.

irrelevance of death.   Marcel's philosophic writings repeat the view
that death is the test of presence.[198]   A closely analogous test is
self-sacrifice.   If these tests work—and history does provide testimony
to their working—they indicate that there is something, a presence,
which is not an object and cannot be possessed but which transcends
all objects and events.   Our inquiry into being must be guided by the
forefeeling of this presence.

What occasions elicit this forefeeling and thus exemplify the concrete approach to being?   They are evidently certain events through which we
exist.   Existence in this sense might with some truth be said to be a
means to being.[199]   Being, therefore, is like an end sought.   Yet it
is not an end in the obvious sense of a definable goal.   Marcel terms
it an "appeal."   The activity of the creative artist offers an example
of this appeal.   His activity is directed toward an end; it has a social
function.   But the artist is not striving merely to produce something
which satisfies this social need.   As a genuine artist his creative
activity is not obedient to something outside himself.   He is not a
state functionary.   Rather he is sensitive to the "ontological exigence"
or the appeal of being which is more like a need to be himself.   This
is the need to achieve a certain being and value in his own right; it is
the will to find or create himself.[200]   The suggestion is again that we
may apprehend being in experiences of fulfillment.[201]   "Being is the
culmination of hope, the experience of being is its fulfillment."[202]
Such experiences are the concrete ones through which being is approached.[203]   The sense of the term "concrete" as used by Marcel
now becomes apparent.   Concrete fulfillment is not merely the performance of some assigned function, however socially desirable this
may be.   Discharging a function successfully satisfies only a portion of
one's need.   The mere functionary, therefore, leaves the greater part
of his need unsatisfied, a condition of which he is aware as a sense
of emptiness.   But the condition which Marcel is seeking to describe
is a condition which is the opposite of emptiness, especially the emptiness experienced as despondency, depression, the sense of the worth-
lessness of living.   Metaphysics is "a means of exorcising despair."[204]
It is the source of joy.[205]   Marcel hastens to add that he is not seeking
to define being in terms of a hedonistic enjoyment.   The distinction
must continually be kept in mind between partial enjoyment and
satisfaction of the whole of one's existence.[206]   The former may be
consequent upon success in the discharge of various specialized functions; the latter, though, is to be identified with "happiness, love, and
inspiration."[207]

The concrete approaches to being lie through *fidelity, love,* and *hope.*[208]
Faithfulness to something not one's self can be traced through
several kinds of phenomena; it becomes fidelity only at the point
where it is transformed to "active perpetuation of a presence" which
is a sort of continuous participation.   As such it is a mystery.[209]

---

[198] PE 23.   [199] MB *II, 33.*   [200] MJ *183.*   [201] MJ *117.*   [202] MB *II, 44.*
[203] BH *119.*   [204] BH *87.*   [205] MJ *206.*   [206] MMS *158;* MJ *290f.*
[207] MJ *206;* MB *II, 49.*   [208] BH *119.*   [209] PE *22.*

Fidelity of this kind—the opposite of despair—enters into one's own being and is creative of the self.[210]   Finally it is described as a response to an appeal which expresses the assurance that the being from which the appeal issues will be that which satisfies the need which the appeal generates.[211]   Hope may likewise be discovered on a scale which stretches from the egocentric to assurance of a supreme Presence.[212]   Although these three, fidelity, hope, and love, are interdependent, love is primary, since it is the bond which establishes intersubjectivity.

Love is to be discerned in the sense of presence as the means by which one is united with another. We are thus led again to glimpse what Marcel means by his conviction that being is experienced as intersubjectivity,[213] and that intersubjectivity is the "cornerstone of a concrete ontology."[214] This view is first of all a denial of solipsistic and subjectivistic philosophies which attempt to generate the world out of the individual ego. Conversely, however, it certainly is not intended to extend a metaphysical privilege to any sort of magnification of collectivity or to baptize a sentimental attitude toward "groupiness." His doctrine is intended rather to direct attention to the tie always apprehended to some degree which relates one to others. This tie is that sensed community without which one's own existence would be unintelligible. One's existence, as the etymology of the terms suggests, is that which manifests itself in the present, that which rises up and moves forward. But this self is not merely the immediate existence which entails only a minimum of community. The self has continued to receive from others and has made this acquisition into his own being. There is, then, a depth to one's person which renders any present self-manifestation possible. The past, accessible through recollection, is the gift, as it were, of communion with others, a "living communication" from which the ego has emerged "like an island rising from the waves."[215] This living communication, reflecting the intersubjectivity in which one has his individual being, is constitutive of the self. One's own being is received from another.

Others thus come to be reflected in one's own being. In this I-thou relationship the ontological need is most clearly grasped and most fully satisfied. At the same time, this relationship most clearly illustrates the impossibility of understanding other persons through objective categories which reduce the "thou" to an object or an idea.[216] The "thou" who is loved cannot be regarded as an object (a "him" or an "it") and inventoried as a collection of properties. Nor is the "I" who participates in this relation the epistemological subject—although any move to stand off from the situation and understand or describe it can be executed only by use of just these distinctions.[217] Evidently, then, the only way of communicating one's experience of this pre-object-subject situation is by a careful use of objective language, corrected by secondary reflection. This reflection recognizes finally a presence which, as being and not as a perishable object, transcends

210 RI 223f.   211 BH 111; RI 48; 80.   212 BH 91, n. 1; 93f.   213 MB II, 16.
214 MB II, 170.   215 BM II, 13f.   216 MJ 231–234.   217 MJ 302ff.

death.[218] Finally it may come to be directed toward the absolute Presence.[219]

These presences, which through the intersubjective bond enter into the self, are constitutive of the self. This is Marcel's version of the common conviction that personality is developed only in society. Others come to be reflected within one's own being in complex ways. In describing this complex yet unified self Marcel refers to the marriage of the soul to itself, to the "inner city,"[220] and to piety toward one's self.[221] Intersubjectivity is, evidently, a complicated web of common experiences and intercommunication. Moreover, communion among persons may go on in ways as yet unfathomed and which if better known, might radically alter the conventional notions of the formation of the self, its independence, and its relative isolation from others.[222] One can scarcely anticipate in what one will eventuate through the mediation of the relationships involving mystery.

8. Transcendence

The categories which have been examined do not allow us to specify exactly what the mystery of being is. They are designed, rather, to convince us that a human change directed toward increased participation in intersubjective life is also directed toward participation in being. This change is properly termed "transcendence."[223]

Transcendence, generally speaking, is participation in mystery. Its negative sense is the rejection of the "objectivizing" thought which would lead one to regard himself or another impersonally.[224] The positive sense of the term refers us to "vertical" or "authentic" human change which is directed toward the universal. This direction, Marcel holds, is quite generally envisaged by classic philosophical thought and by the highest religions. Marcel names this direction "le révérenciel" (the "holy," the "noumenous"). The term "transcendence" is intended to indicate a universal which is not an abstraction, but rather a whole of harmoniously functioning parts, a "polyphonic universality." The illustration of this kind of wholeness which comes naturally to his mind is a musical one: the common effort by people of divergent temperaments to produce music.[225] Again, an apprehension of this kind of superrational unity with others is conveyed better by the drama than by the elaboration of philosophic doctrines.[226] His final illustration is the Christian doctrine of the Mystical Body.[227] He combines the musical and the religious illustration in a climactic passage of his Gifford Lectures to characterize the brotherly and musical communion

---

[218] MB II, 62; BH 95.   [219] RI 179.   [220] MJ 201.   [221] BH 225.

[222] MB 1, 181f. Marcel, it should be added, has shown a lively interest in psychic phenomena and extrasensory perception throughout much of his life, cf. "The Influence of Psychic Phenomena on my Philosophy," Journal of the Society for Psychical Research, London, 1955.

[223] Although the term sometimes refers to an orientation toward objects (RI 217), and sometimes it names that to which the act of transcending is directed (RI 217).

[224] MB I, 39f.   [225] Cf. BH 136.   [226] "Essays in Autobiography" in PE 79.

[227] MB II, 183.

of all human spirits uniting them all in a symphony of which God is not so much the director as the theme.[228]   Earlier in these lectures Marcel asked whether, metaphysically speaking, God is to be identified ⸺as being, and pointedly left the question unanswered.   But in the analogy last cited, we have an intimation of the sort of answer which might be forthcoming.   Elsewhere Marcel does affirm an "absolute thou" with whom the human personal relation can be completed.[229] Hope is the direct tie with this absolute and transcendent Presence. This "thou" is absolute in the sense that, unlike a human being, his being is unambiguous.   He can not become objectified nor will he regard another individual in the third-person sense.   Thus he is unconditionally a "thou,"[230] communion with whom offers fulfillment.   Transcendence, when referred to this absolute Presence, points to that which gives human change its orientation and saves it from perversion.

Inclusion in the orchestra of spirits, though this may be the vocation of every man, is achieved only after an ordeal leading to the change which marks an increase in participation in being.   By way of this kind of change one comes into possession of human powers and achieves freedom.[231]   But at no stage is this transcendence necessitated.   One may choose contemplation and the common life but also its opposite.[232]   Human existence is ambiguous.   The free and self-productive response to possibilities is not always easy to see nor easy to make once seen, a fact which Marcel recognizes when he terms the world the place of betrayal and contrasts it with being, which is the motive for fidelity.[233]   The creative response is quite opposite to that offered by the egocentric person or the person whose being is imprisoned in a social function and who can offer only the routine responses of an official.   It is of the essence of the human situation that both kinds of responses are always possible: the objectivizing and the participating.   Just as the fact of one's incarnation renders suicide a constant possibility, so the fact of one's being a participating self renders continuously relevant the possibility of the denial of self, or ⸺what amounts to the same⸺its demoniac assertion, or finally its total perversion.[234]

The intent of Marcel's philosophy has by now, I think, become abundantly evident.   The transcendence which completes the reflective or con-

---

228 Cf. BH 136; MB II, 187.

229 MJ 283f.; RI 53.   He holds that the Thomist philosophers who emphasize the causal relation of God to the world tend to reduce God to a thing, although a supreme thing; such a concept of God is completely inadequate where personal relationships are concerned (HP 63f.; BH 200; MJ 64; 98).   He offers instead the assurance of God by way of appeal (RI 192f), and terms God the absolute Presence (BH 212; 147).

230 MJ 73, 137.   The atheist who speaks of God in the third person and denies him existence is quite logical and quite correct.   God does not exist in this sense (MJ 58, 65f, 207).   But then neither can the atheist exist in respect of this relation (MJ 132).

231 MB II, 183.   232 MB II, 187.   233 BH 41.

234 "It does appear that our structure allows of what must be regarded as a total perversion, since it can happen that a human being should consecrate himself as if to a positive principle but to what is in reality only its radical negation" (RI 64).

templative action is a conversion.[235] In his own words "we are fated to undergo a metamorphosis whose nature we can foresee only very imperfectly."[236] The intent of this philosophy, then, is to subordinate objective thought and the technical activity which it informs to a *dramatic* view of man and his situation. Man's end lies not in the production of commodities, but in his conversion to being.

9. Pro and Con

Can some estimate of Marcel's philosophy now be assayed? Can some final questions be addressed to it? It has been called a philosophy of life. This is true if by philosophy of life is meant an effort to bring the concrete data of human life into philosophy and to find or to forge new philosophic concepts which are able to deal with this data with appropriate subtlety and with a minimum of distortion. Obviously this undertaking is enormously difficult. If Marcel's efforts to accomplish it sometimes appear to be elusive, we have only to recall what the poets and dramatists have always known, namely, that this subject himself is the most paradoxical and mysterious of creatures. Now there is certainly no suggestion that Marcel avoids any paradoxes or mysteries by accepting the notion of existence as a gift, by embodying this notion in a doctrine of incarnation, by his account of moving under provocation of an ontological need to participate in the being of others and in his own being. It is of the essence of contemplative reflection to attempt to apprehend such notions as these in the concrete fullness of their meaning. Also the standard which this philosophy has set for itself requires its fidelity to being, whatever the mystery that results from rejecting the tempting successes of abstract methods.

The corollary of this standpoint is the negative evaluation of the greater portion of modern life along with its beliefs and values. It is apparent that modern life as a whole is incompatible with Marcel's vision of human fulfillment. It is, however, difficult to know just how Marcel would have our social arrangements altered in order to avoid the suicide which he predicts and in order to achieve the intersubjective being for which he is convinced men hunger. One feels in him a strong emotional rejection of organized life, planned economy, and all the multitudinous mechanizations of modern times. He breathes a nostalgia for simple family living. Neither urbania nor suburbia are on his horizon. He explicitly emphasizes his conviction that genuine human life is to be lived only in small groups,[237] for only there may creativity come to fruition and charity link men in the intersubjective bond.

Now it is easy to sympathize with this preference. Nevertheless, large—

[235] MB I, 82. Marcel is explicitly not attempting to make Roman Catholics of his readers, although he recognizes the effectiveness of cult in eliciting participation (MJ 47f.), and he recognizes in Christianity a religion peculiarly appropriate to the human need.
[236] MB I, 182.   [237] MB I, 200ff.: MMS 267.

very large—masses of people do exist. Surely it is the part of charity to see at least to their survival and the continued possibility of their freedom. But under the circumstances it is more than difficult to see how the task merely of survival is to be accomplished without modern techniques and complex social organizations. And we know Marcel's evaluation of life under techniques and organization: contemplation, charity, intersubjectivity are rendered all but impossible in this milieu. Can it be, then, that the human predicament is more complex than had first appeared? Can it be that an important, perhaps a necessary, expression of charity requires our developing a technical society in which the growth and expression of charity become impossible? If so, then the world is indeed the place of betrayal. One can only hope that technical society and technical man, as Marcel has pictured them, are abstractions from actuality.

A further question might well be directed toward Marcel's view of the objective thinker, e.g., the scientist, as nonparticipating. Is objective thought radically opposed to participation? It seems to me that Marcel hesitates on this matter. Verbally he acknowledges the importance of objective and abstract methods, but in spirit he seems to deny them value. He seems to grant some participation in being to the great originators of the sciences but none to lesser practitioners. Marcel is disturbed not merely by the fact that the sciences are sometimes misused, but rather by the suspicion that their methods are dehumanizing.

It is difficult to know whether this suspicion follows from his philosophical doctrines or from his predisposition. A Marcellian type of illustration will be helpful: an average physician called upon in an emergency to perform surgery on his loved son. Here we have an instance of objective thinking about an object and technical skill together with the intersubjective participation of father and son. Is this combination—"objective participation"—contradictory? I myself can not think so. Only a long apprenticeship in objective thinking could enable the physician to preserve the coolness, impersonality, and "distance" which the personal relation demanded in this situation. Furthermore, this situation is anything but exceptional. Such long apprenticeship could be motivated only by intensely personal motives, not excluding wonder at organic nature and at the effectiveness of his own skill. It seems reasonable to believe that training in objective thought and technical skill, wherever found, presume as their prior condition some degree of intersubjectivity and some contemplative awareness of the condition of humanity. Personality under the mask and restraint of impersonality is no doubt an everyday occurrence. "Objective participation," if I may so name it, probably involves a paradox; nevertheless, its sympathetic analysis within Marcel's philosophy would seem to be desirable and even necessary. Marcel's failure to perform this analysis and to integrate objective thought more explicitly within his philosophy may be another evidence of ambivalence toward the world. Existence in the world is both a gift and the possibility of betrayal; it offers grounds both for hope and for despair; accordingly, the thinking which can deal with its particular problems holds out both a promise and a threat. Like human life, its value is ambiguous.[238]

It will be appropriate to attempt to formulate a final opinion on the question of the validation of this philosophy, for I do not doubt but that many readers of Marcel are likely to conclude that his philosophy sounds very poetic but also exceedingly subjective. To affirm that the individual existent is dependent upon his human being, and that human being depends upon intersubjective being formed into a whole by the bond of love whose direction of authentic transcendence is toward the holy, is to make an assertion which, so far as intersubjective meaning can be given it, is in no sense objectively verifiable. Indeed, to describe being in terms of presence, feeling, communion, seems to be the extreme of subjectivism. Marcel would be the first to agree that intersubjectivity is not objectively verifiable; it is not a thing which can be got into a laboratory.[239] That his doctrine is, in consequence, merely a subjectivism and a relativism, he rejects with vehemence. Enough has surely been said in this essay to make the point that secondary reflection can under no circumstances achieve its end by replacing the whole which it would contemplate by an abstraction. It cannot, therefore, achieve its end by means of explanation or, indeed, by any sort of theoretical formulation. The objective tests, therefore, of explanation or of theory are irrelevant. This reflection reaches its end only by actually bringing about the contemplation and intersubjective participation in being to which its metaphors and descriptions point. To be a metaphysician is, in Marcel's sense—in the non-objective sense—to be a certain kind of person and to enter into certain concrete relations with others. Thus its author can observe that the inability to experience admiration for another is a metaphysical fault.[240] The question, therefore, whether this philosophy is verifiable or not would seem to be largely meaningless, a "category mistake." Its topic is mystery; and its means is the production of a kind of secular faith whose end is participation in being. The more appropriate question from its own point of view is the question whether it does in fact illuminate a person's way to being himself. This is the question whether or not it has retained fidelity to being. Is it, as one critic has supposed, just a long sermon expressing the personal sentiments of the author?

Marcel has sought to retain fidelity to the concrete by means of the notion of mystery in which the human being is essentially involved, by recognition of the ontological exigence for transcendence, and by an attempt to communicate the noumenous character of being which will satisfy the human need. An essential aspect of being in Marcel's intersubjective sense is the recognition of love and charity as that by which persons are united in communion. Now he rejects describing this bond as sentimental or subjective. He points to those who have

---

[238] Cf. HV 119; PE 14. Cf. P. Ricoeur, Gabriel Marcel et Karl Jaspers, Paris, 1947, pp. 403ff.
[239] MB II, 15.   [240] RI 67ff.

had the experience of love and to their resistance to evaluating it as merely nugatory or illusory. He regards love, rather, as involving an act of faith whose claim to validity may be substantiated by those qualified for the experience of it. Secondary reflection, seeking to do justice to the whole man, tends to treat the question of being as the question of salvation. Both love and salvation depend upon achieving a certain orientation of one's existence. But questions concerning this orientation, like questions concerning love, are reduced finally not to verified theories but to faith.

Our author regards faith as a special sort of belief. It is not the "belief that" a certain fact is the case, but rather it is more like "belief in" a person. This belief in a person is only remotely like that of the banker who allows a client credit for a loan. The banker has various services at his disposal which allow him to categorize the client and to estimate the probability of repayment even without acquaintance with the client. Quite different is the case of the mother who persists in crediting her worthless son and giving him money, although she is well aware that his assurances of repayment are mere words. The difference between the two is not only psychological; it concerns the bond of intersubjective being. The mother is involved with the son on a different level and expresses this by her action and her sacrifice which embody a tacit faith in the son's ultimate intrinsic worth.[241] Secondary reflection does not constitute acts of faith of this kind, though it uncovers them and observes that there are many of them, that they are interrelated, and that they embody the being and value of the life which we lead. Furthermore, among such acts of faith are no doubt the very "enabling acts" which establish the sciences and our social life and lend the hope essential to carrying them on. These acts of faith provide the "proof"—so far as this word retains meaning in this context—that our transcendence is not merely illusory nor merely arbitrary but achieves fidelity to concrete being.

BIBLIOGRAPHY

Selected philosophical writings of Gabriel Marcel

The abbreviations which precede the first eight entries are those used in the footnotes.

BH Being and Having, tr. Katherine Farrer, Beacon Press, Boston, Mass., 1951. First published in London, 1949.

HP L'Homme problématique, Aubier, Paris, 1955.

HV Homo Viator, tr. Emma Cranfurd, Regnery, Chicago, 1951.

MB The Mystery of Being, 2 vols.: vol. I, tr. G. S. Fraser, The Harvill

241 MB II, 86ff.: RI 179.

Press Ltd., London, 1960; vol. II, tr. Rene Hague, The Harvill Press, Ltd., London, 1951.

MJ *Metaphysical Journal*, tr. Bernard Wall, Regnery, Chicago, 1950.

MMS *Man against Mass Society*, tr. G. S. Fraser, of *Les Hommes contre l'humain*, Regnery, Chicago, 1962. First published in Great Britain, 1952.

PE *The Philosophy of Existence*, tr. Manya Harari, of *Positions et approaches concrètes du mystère ontologique*, etc., Philosophical Library, New York, 1949.

RI *Du Refus à l'invocation*, Gallimard, Paris, 1940.

1. *Fragments Philosophiques 1909–1914*, Editions Nauwelaerts, Louvain, undated.

2. *Les Hommes contre l'humain*, La Colombe, Paris, 1951.

3. *Homo Viator*, Aubier, Paris, 1945.

4. *Journal Métaphysique*, Gallimard, Paris, 1927.

5. *La Métaphysique de Royce*, Aubier, Paris, 1945.

6. *Le Mystère de l'être*, 2 vols., Aubier, Paris, 1951.

7. *Positions et approaches concrètes du mystère ontologique*, published with *Le Monde cassé*, Desclée de Brower et cie., Paris, 1933, pp. 255–301.

For a more extensive listing, see Gerald G. Wenning, "Works by and about Gabriel Marcel," *The Southern Journal of Philosophy*, vol. 4, no. 2, pp. 82–96, summer, 1966.

CHAPTER SIX

JEAN-PAUL SARTRE
MAN, FREEDOM, AND *PRAXIS*

WILLIAM LEON McBRIDE

WILLIAM LEON McBRIDE *is an assistant professor of philosophy at Yale University. He received his A.B. from Georgetown University and his M.A. and Ph.D. from Yale University. In addition, he spent a year studying philosophy in Lille, France. His areas of special interest are political philosophy and recent French philosophical thought. The second half of his dissertation "The Concept of Fundamental Change in Law and Society" centered on the concept of fundamental social change in the perspective of Sartre's* Critique de la raison dialectique. *Mr. McBride has contributed articles to* The Monist *and* Natural Law Forum. *His review of Wilfred Desan's book* The Marxism of Jean-Paul Sartre *is soon to appear in* The Journal of Existentialism.

Enormous success has given Jean-Paul Sartre an extraordinary prominence
among philosophers and intellectuals of every sort. A torrent of
literature concerning his work as philosopher, dramatist, literary critic,
and political pundit is constantly pouring forth; this torrent is matched
only by the continued feverish productivity of the author himself.
Sartre has many ardent admirers, of course, but he also has his share
of vigorous critics and detractors. Recently, he has become particularly unpopular with political activists of all stripes, from the self-styled
orthodox Marxists, whom he accuses of betraying Marx, to conserva-
tives and reactionaries, for whom he reserves his deepest contempt
and authentic hatred. But the politically inactive fare no better with
Sartre: passivity, he consistently maintains, only plays into the hands
of reaction. The pure litterateurs, who rightly consider the tortuous
style of his philosophical treatises to smack more of Alsace than of
Descartes' Touraine, and who often find philosophical ideas a bit too
complicated anyway, have further reason to be outraged at Sartre's
politically motivated refusal of the Nobel Prize: his collateral rejection
in advance of a possible, but in fact scarcely conceivable, Lenin Prize
was not calculated to assuage the feelings of literary experts either in
Stockholm or in Moscow. The pure philosophers are apt to be less
distressed by Sartre's extensive dabbling in literature, which they have
learned to live with, than by his attempt to accommodate philosophy
to the inconstant, everchanging exigencies of practical politics. The
list of sources of such more or less superficial criticisms of Sartre
could be expanded almost indefinitely.

The greatest danger is that the more searching questions about Sartre's
philosophy may eventually be buried beneath the mass of petty
criticisms. We are all familiar with infamous transformations of a
philosopher's ideas into Idols—blessed or demonic—of the Theater:
the invoking of Aristotle's name by Galileo's fellow astronomers at
Pisa, the flaunting of Rousseau by the incorruptible Robespierre, the
lip service paid to Marx by the Stalinists, and the role played by
Sartre's philosophy, in its post-Second World War popularization, in
giving rise to the disapproving epithet, *"espèce d'existentialiste!"* What
particularly complicates the situation in Sartre's case (as also, no
doubt, in Marx's) is the fact that, as we shall see later, the activist
thrust of his entire conception of man demands either that that philosophy be idolized—with all the misunderstandings and misuses
running counter to the author's own purposes which must inevitably
ensue and which Sartre himself has analyzed so brilliantly in his discussions of "counter-finalities"—or else that it be discarded as
irrelevant. The intellectualist analysis which pretends to come to
grips with the whole world, and not simply with the world of the
Academy, must leave room in its scheme for the nonintellectual and
even for the anti-intellectual; in the technical language of Sartre's

Note: *The works abbreviated by capital letters are identified in the bibliography p. 328.
Wherever possible, page references to Sartre's works are made first to the French
editions, and then the corresponding pages from the English translations listed in the
bibliography are noted in parentheses. All translations from French texts are by this
writer.*

later philosophy, there must always be an anti-dialectical moment in
the evolution of the dialectic. But the inhabitants of the nonintellectual world may exact a heavy price of the previously aloof mandarin
who has intruded into it. And their own existential situations may
provide them with justifications for doing so.

Amid all the chorus of criticisms on various levels, the one infinitely simple
question that must be raised concerning any philosophical theory is
one which stands in greatest jeopardy of being forgotten, namely: Is it
true? No one can disregard the fact that, often enough in the past,
raising this question and attempting to apply it have released an over-
whelming deluge of naïveté. Sartre himself has contributed as much
as most thinkers of the past century and a half to a deeper understanding of the truth, in some sense or other, of relativism. But the
abstractness of these terms and the need immediately to qualify them
fortify the impression that everything still remains to be said and that
the original, simple question does indeed demand an answer. It is
evident that the claims that the truth of a philosophical theory is to
be judged solely by a "correspondence" between its basic elements
and human experience, or solely by the logical, rational consistency
of its component parts, or solely by its usefulness in solving certain
fundamental problems confronted by man in understanding and
recreating his world, are mutually incompatible and already contain
ontological presuppositions. This frequently gives rise to despair on
the part of the would-be critic, who thenceforth turns to the more
manageable questions of, for example, whether there is unity or dis-
unity among the various periods of Sartre's development, or whether
there is, in Sartre's writings, some basis for an ethics, or even whether
—to return, as one eventually must, to the more superficial level of
criticism which always threatens to submerge the rest—there may be
something about the style and attitude of the existential, living Sartre
which puts into question his philosophical conclusions. We shall deal
with all these questions, too. But we must first make the effort, however great the obstacles, to raise anew the issue of truth.

1. The Ontological Starting Points and Some Problems of Truth

The assumption made here is that Sartre as a philosopher is, above all,
an ontologist—or, if one prefers, a metaphysician.[1] The priority
which he comes to place on *human* existence is logically based on the
fact that he views man as a unique and central kind of being in the
universe. *Being and Nothingness* (*L'Etre et le néant*) is the central
work of the Sartrean philosophical *corpus*, and his well-known subtitle

---

[1] *Sartre himself carefully distinguishes between ontology, which is what he claims to
be doing in* Being and Nothingness, *and metaphysics, a study which would
pose questions about the origins of our particular world as we find it and as the
ontologist has shown it most fundamentally to be. Metaphysics in this sense
would be to ontology, he says, as history is to sociology.* L'Etre et le néant,
*Gallimard, Paris, 1943, 713 (BN 619). Needless to say, "metaphysics" as it is
more commonly thought of by philosophers, and as I use it here, does not
coincide with this technical Sartrean definition.*

of that book denominates it an "essay in phenomenological ontology." His second major philosophical work, *Critique de la raison dialectique*, may best be viewed as an application of a certain ontological framework (however greatly or little it may be altered from that of his earlier period) to the area of social structure, the region of intersubjectivity. His first published philosophical efforts, dealing with imagination, the emotions, and other aspects of human consciousness, lay the groundwork for the theory of *Being and Nothingness*. His novels, plays, and literary and political essays serve to provide concrete verification for the necessarily abstract ontological account of existential man which he has constructed in his more strictly philosophical writings; *La Nausée* and *Baudelaire* are particularly apt illustrations of this. To adopt this assumption is not to imply that Sartre as an ontologist is more interesting than Sartre as a person, or that Sartre's literary essays may not survive better than his books of philosophy; it does entail the view that Sartre, unlike at least some other existentialist thinkers, is consciously propounding a theory about ultimate existents, and that he therefore invites attempts to verify or to falsify that theory.

BEING-IN-ITSELF AND BEING-FOR-ITSELF

Despite the enormous length and complexity of Sartre's writings, the core of his ontology is, as one might expect and hope for it to be, essentially very simple. By means of Husserl's phenomenological method, he comes to the intuition of a "trans-phenomenal" phenomenon (one that is not simply identifiable with any particular phenomenon, though it is also not to be thought of as a distinct entity over and above phenomena).[2] This is, precisely, the phenomenon of being. He then proceeds to reflect upon being as it must appear when considered in itself, without reference as yet to the radically different reality of consciousness; to being-in-itself, he concludes, we can attribute massive, undifferentiated existence and nothing else—neither activity nor passivity, neither self-creation nor creation from without, neither necessity nor derivation from some potentiality, for all such concepts represent the illegitimate introduction of human standards into the realm of the radically non-human. Sartre's strikingly Parmenidean summary of all that can be said, strictly speaking, about being-in-itself (*être-en-soi*) has become famous: "Being is. Being is in itself. Being is what it is."[3]

Extreme positivists have sometimes taken the position that statements of this sort are meaningless. Such an objection, as applied to the above-cited conclusions, is invalid: the statements are logically flawless, and anyone who reads in good faith the first several pages of *Being and Nothingness* will be able to come to some understanding of what Sartre is saying. A certain type of Wittgensteinian, let us say, might deny the possibility of speaking meaningfully about being as a whole, but this denial would itself be predicated on a certain alternative

---

[2] Ibid., p. 16 (BN 1).   [3] Ibid., p. 34 (BN lxvi).

ontology. More to the point, however, might be the comment that the information contained in these statements is useless. But this, in a sense, is exactly Sartre's own view! There is nothing sacred, nothing inspiring, nothing divine about the phenomenon of being-in-itself as Sartre, in fundamental opposition to Martin Heidegger's vision of transcendent Being, perceives it; unlike the "Being" of most of Sartre's predecessors in the ontological tradition, being-in-itself is radically contingent, "superfluous for eternity." If the Sartrean concept of being-in-itself has any "useful" function, it is primarily as a point of contrast. The very terminology of "uselessness," by which one might seek to criticize Sartre's intuition, implies a reference to the activity (or "praxis") of one peculiar kind of being, man, to whom a special ontological status has thereby, in the formulation of the criticism itself, been accorded.

Thus, rather surprisingly, the existentialist humanism of Sartre's ontology has its origin in the rigorous, stark, and seemingly sterile investigation of the phenomenon of being-in-itself with which *Being and Nothingness* opens; that is because the analysis of being as it is without reference to consciousness reveals the necessity, for the ontologist, of finding within human reality some fundamentally *contrasting* type of being. We must now turn to a consideration of human reality in its most distinctive aspect, as *"être-pour-soi"*—being-for-itself.

It would be paradoxical and somewhat confusing, but not incorrect from a point of view external to Sartre's systematic terminology, to say that "being-for-itself" is Sartre's way of characterizing the essence of man. The paradoxicality (which is not at all the same as "contradictoriness") stems from the fact that Sartre flatly denies the alleged reality of any fixed and stable qualities which might be pointed to as constituting a "human nature,"[4] and it is just such a congeries of salient qualities that the word "essence" traditionally suggests. But man, in Sartre's view, is distinct from all other kinds of entities in the universe precisely because of his ability to differentiate, to put into question. Human consciousness is never completely reducible to the massive, undifferentiated self-identity of being-in-itself. In the case of man, there always remains some distance or gap between the elusive reality that is consciousness, on the one hand, and the product of any attempt that might be made to capture what it is in some definitive formula, on the other. Never completely self-identical, human reality is always characterized by some possibility of self-reference or "presence to self," and by the denial that the being who is performing the act of differentiating or questioning is the same as the undifferentiated, the en-*soi*. Thus it may be said that Sartrean man is, first and foremost, "being *for* itself," and thus it comes about that Sartre introduces his account of being-for-itself by pointing to the activity of *negation* as particularly significant. But if it is man alone who is capable of negating and thus distinguishing and differentiating, then being-for-itself must be fundamentally negative. And so the way is

---

[4] L'existentialisme est un humanisme, *Editions Nagel, Paris, 1965, p. 22* (Existentialism, p. 18).

opened for the various dramatic formulations of man's nothingness for which Sartre has become understandably famous.

AN EVALUATION OF THE CLAIMS

These, then, are the core claims of Sartre's ontology. From the intuitions of being-in-itself and being-for-itself, follow all the further ramifications of Sartre's existentialist insight into man in his relations with the world. A fully sympathetic appraisal of these basic claims and of their value as mirroring some aspects of the truth about human reality can only be made after it has been seen how Sartre applies them to concrete phenomena and situations; Sartrean man is never pure being-for-itself, but always a "being in situation," an "être-là." Let us suppose for a moment, however, that these starting points themselves were false, that is, the wrong starting points to use for coming to understand human existence. In that case, all that followed, though no doubt interesting, would be in some sense incorrect, for Sartre's philosophy is an essentially rationalistic one which is coherently constructed on the basis of its starting points. But what means would ever be found for testing these starting points? How could a skeptic be convinced of their correctness? And, in fact, exactly what is the nature or "status" of these Sartrean concepts, being-in-itself and being-for-itself, when considered as the two fundamental types of being? We must address ourselves to these preliminary questions before considering some of the more concrete applications of the Sartrean ontology to the human life-world that is familiar to all of us.

The problem is not, or should not be thought to be: Why ontology? The advantages of such an enterprise, if successfully undertaken, would be considerable. A new insight into the underlying nature or structure (or whatever more neutral word can be found) of existence is an obvious boon to man both as knower and as doer. Now, such an insight will need, by definition, to be something other than a mere cataloguing of outstanding experiences shared and objects encountered by all men in their daily existence. In other words, the slogan that "everything is what it is and not another thing" is not a useful one for ontology. But therein lies the real problem, at least in Sartre's case. For the basic elements upon which he founds his entire philosophy, and which I have now briefly introduced, do not at first sight appear to be familiar objects of experience. And yet use of the phenomenological method of analysis, to which Sartre explicitly adheres in *Being and Nothingness*, entails the rigorous investigation and description of phenomena as they are present to consciousness, thus ruling out, at the very minimum, the speculative postulation of entities that have not been experienced. Since Sartre admits, as we have seen, that the phenomenon of being itself is *trans*-phenomenal, and since he also goes on to insist that the distinctly human is always a being *in situation* (a body, an object to other human beings, etc.), one may be led to wonder whether these ontological starting points are not, after all, illegitimate postulates rather than the stuff of actual conscious experience.

The same question about the correspondence of ontological starting points with experience can be posed with regard to the fundamental concepts, *praxis* and inert matter, of Sartre's later *Critique of Dialectical Reason*, in which he no longer makes any explicit claim to be following the method of phenomenology. In this book, he lays greater stress than in his earlier writings on a distinction which may help to explain in a preliminary way the status of his fundamental concepts—to wit, the distinction between the concrete (defined in the *Critique* as the milieu of history in which we are all actors) and the abstract. Being-in-itself and being-for-itself, then, are abstract referents—a statement that will permit of further elucidation after the concepts themselves have been more thoroughly examined. But the abstractness or formalism which can in a sense, Sartre admits, be attributed to him[5] is not to be thought of as the process of "abstraction" by which certain philosophers claim to have arrived at general laws or facts about the world which somehow exist on a level of reality different from that of the world in which we exist; rather, Sartre would maintain that his starting-points of being-in-itself and being-for-itself, inert matter and *praxis*, are abstract only inasmuch as they are incomplete. They are the most fundamental points from which to begin to comprehend what is. But how does Sartre propose to justify this claim? Ultimately, he can only invite his readers to follow his lead in consciously experiencing "the revelatory intuition of the phenomenon."[6] And what more can any phenomenologist or any philosopher, in attempting to validate the basic elements of his theory on the grounds of their correspondence with experience, be expected to do?

Let us, for the moment, accept Sartre's invitation to reexamine our own experience in the light of his "revelatory intuition." Are there any human experiences which might reveal the *ultimacy* of being-in-itself and being-for-itself? Does the duality of these two concepts make sense as a fundamental way of understanding existence? To what general alternative types of ontological framework is the Sartrean ontology opposed? These are the questions that we must now try to answer. Some of the characters in Sartre's novels, plays, and essays live lives and undergo changes which serve brilliantly to corroborate certain facets of his ontology, but we cannot rely exclusively on their examples; we shall have to consider whether Sartre's existentialist ontology illuminates not just the peculiar personal experiences of Mathieu (in *The Age of Reason*) or Roquentin (in *Nausea*) or Baudelaire, but experiences possible for any and every man.

It will be recalled that Sartre's being-in-itself is characterized by massiveness, self-identity, lack of differentiation: it is, it is in-itself, and it is what it is. Only human reality, by contrast, *makes a difference* in being. Now, it is obvious that the everyday experiences of most people are not dominated by any such intuition of being-in-itself; true, we are constantly aware of many inert, nonhuman objects—tables, chairs, trees, etc.—but we usually become aware of them singly and

---

5 Critique de la raison dialectique, *Gallimard, Paris, 1961, Tome I, p. 179.*
6 EN 16 (BN *xlix*).

as already related to human activity.   Even to call them "inert" is already to have begun to speak of them anthropomorphically.   But it is certainly possible, at least on rare occasions, to perceive the funda- mental "arbitrariness" of the various humanly ordained relationships which we hold to exist among inert objects, the contingency of the very names with which we have endowed them, and their total depen- dence on men for their meaning.   On such occasions, putting every- thing possible into question, we may search desperately for some rela- tionship, some aspect of the reality that we perceive, which cannot in any way be negated or conceived as being other than it is.   But no such distinct reality is discernible; only some notion akin to Sartre's being-in-itself, indeterminate and beyond even the categories of necessity and possibility, remains untouched by our radical question- ing.   This epitomizes, in very brief and general terms, the experience of Antoine Roquentin in *La Nausée:* a psychosomatic condition which at first seems pathological, even to the hero himself, is eventually explained and resolved by his new insight into the massiveness, the contingency, and even the absurdity of all of being.[7]   Roquentin's experience is intelligible, I think, to any reader of the novel, and can thus to some extent be shared by everyone.   It is not difficult to con- ceive of experiences analogous to his that could lead others to the same fundamental insight.

There are, however, at least two grounds for doubting the validity of this allegedly revelatory experience of being-in-itself that deserve mention here.   The first stems from the fact that Sartre frequently uses a variety of metaphors in endeavoring to help his readers to accept his account of being-in-itself.   Two such metaphors are especially promi- nent throughout much of his philosophical writing: the visual metaphor of opacity (with which the "transparency" of pure consciousness and the "translucency" of consciousness regarded as situated in a world and as structured by a human body[8] are contrasted), and the viscosity metaphor employed in *Nausea.*   Surely the peculiar metaphors through which Roquentin and/or Sartre see the world are unlikely to be the common experiences of everyone—indeed, they could hardly be so if the primacy of Sartre's ontological account of human freedom is to be maintained.   Therefore, to rely on these metaphors as heavily as Sartre does throughout his earlier writings (the *Critique of Dialecti- cal Reason* is much less flawed in this regard[9]) is a fault, attributable to his strong literary bent.   Since Sartre never makes the mistake of identifying the metaphors with the phenomenon of being-in-itself, this difficulty is not a sufficient ground for rejecting the concept.   The second source of doubt lies in the disquieting realization that the various experiences by which any of us may arrive at the Sartrean

---

[7] *La Nausée, Gallimard, Paris, 1938, especially pp. 161–168 (Nausea, tr. Lloyd Alex- ander, New Directions, New York, 1964, especially pp. 170–177).*

[8] EN 398 (BN 333).   *In this particular passage, Sartre is discussing the consciousness of pain in terms of his metaphor of translucency.*

[9] *In the* Critique, *Sartre seems to renounce metaphor as a valid philosophical method. Especially enlightening is his attack on Friedrich Engels for using "non- dialectical procedures: comparisons, analogies, abstraction, induction"* (CRD 130).

intuition of the massiveness, superfluousness, and uniformity of being-in-itself are as likely as not to be pathological, as was Roquentin's, or the products of extreme fatigue, rather than the results of careful reflection.   But this circumstance by itself is not sufficient to cast doubt on the truth of the intuition; for, as Sartre's analyses of masochism and sadism show especially well, the anomalous psychological attitude or action is often more revelatory of being than are the routine experiences of ordinary "bourgeois" existence.   One cannot, therefore, simply reject out of hand the Sartrean intuition of being-in-itself in all its stark, totally unattractive indeterminateness; one retains the right, however, to withhold judgment as to its ultimacy until one can examine it more fully in relation to being-for-itself.

A Sartrean essay (a study of the materialist poet, Francis Ponge) bears the title, *L'Homme et les choses (Man and Things);*[10] this is the view of the world, most simply stated, which the ontology of *Being and Nothingness* expresses in more technical language.   Just as being-in-itself, however, is a different concept from that of inert objects ("things") considered in their diversity and in their relations to men, so "man" is not quite identical, in Sartre's ontology, with "being-for-itself."   If the two were identical it would be foolish and unnecessary to look for instances of human experiences to support Sartre's contention that being-for-itself is an ultimate type of being.   But being-for-itself, as we have already noted, is what might paradoxically be called the "essence" of man for Sartre, and it is characterized by the capacity to put into question and to negate.   Every individual person is placed in a particular situation, so that his consciousness is pervaded by what Sartre calls "facticity": he occupies a specific perspective because of his body, he is engaged in a particular occupation which might just as well have been an entirely different one, etc.   It is with "pure" being-for-itself, considered apart from those elements of facticity with which it is always surrounded in concrete experience, that we are concerned at present.   It should be clear, from the outset, that Sartre's concept constitutes a denial of traditional views of the human "self" as an entity, an object, a substance, possessed of certain definable qualities; in this negative sense, at least, Sartre's approach to the notion of "self" follows lines first traced by David Hume.   The reified self of traditional philosophy is an illegitimate abstraction, as Sartre stressed even in his earliest works, and any introspective experience purporting to disclose such a "self" can only be the result of a misunderstanding.   In *The Transcendence of the Ego,* he argued against the Husserlian conception of an absolute consciousness which would serve as a unifying "pole" of experience; an "ego" of this sort, he insists within the new ontological perspective of *Being and Nothingness,* is an in-itself rather than a for-itself.[11]   In his still later writings, Sartre seems to be moving further and further away from the intellectualist tendency to identify being-for-itself with consciousness understood even in a broad sense.

The experiences which might help us to corroborate Sartre's intuition of

10 *L'Homme et les choses, Seghers, Paris, 1947.*   11 EN 147 (BN, 103).

being-for-itself are probably more familiar to most of us than are those which serve as evidence for the reality of being-in-itself. Some of the illustrations provided in *Being and Nothingness*, beginning with simple examples of interrogation and negation in everyday circumstances, are among the most powerful pieces of evidence in favor of the former conception. One of the best-known of these is the case of the perfect, polished café waiter.[12] In his every gesture, he tries to play a part, to make himself into something approximating an automaton. But the reason why such a great effort needs to be made, and also why it can never completely succeed, is that the human person is never reducible to the fixed, exhaustively definable entity that a truly "perfect" waiter, a man become a pure thing, would be. The Sartrean insight into "being-for-itself," then, is open to anyone who will simply engage in self-reflection to the extent of asking whether his occupation, the group into which he was born or has entered, the fragments of specialized knowledge which he happens to possess, or any other set of qualities or attributes is sufficient adequately to define what he himself *is*. There is, of course, one's biological nature, but by definition this cannot be the essentially human. Where is the essential self? The thoughtful person who attempts to find some ultimate answer to this question without resorting to mere speculation or falling back on antecedent commitments to some particular system of thought is likely to settle upon a paradoxical answer along the lines of Sartre's own: The self is, at base, nothing but a capacity to put into question all that is alleged to be unalterable, "given," foreordained, to *create* itself in various guises, and to do this by *acting* on the world outside of itself. Already implied in this brief characterization are many of the important further concepts connected with being-for-itself that are developed by Sartre throughout the remainder of *Being and Nothingness*: the for-itself as lack or desire which demands satisfaction through *possession*; the for-itself as capacity to transcend itself, or to *project* states of affairs or situations different from those at present in existence; and, most of all, the for-itself as *free* agent. These salient, nondeterminate characteristics are the logical concomitants of the Sartrean view of specifically *human* existence as being-for-itself.

We have now begun, however, to see the enormity of the basic paradox that this concept of being-for-itself involves. The essence of man is, literally, nothing; and yet it is out of this nothingness that all that is of interest and of value in the world is created. Can nothing *do* anything at all? This criticism of Sartre is already so stale that one would hesitate to repeat it if it were not so central and, at least superficially, so well warranted. It should be noted, to begin with, that this objection is based primarily on grounds of consistency or of logical coherence rather than of experience. If Sartre were indeed guilty of a logical howler in treating nothingness as if it were a sort of thing capable of creating a world—in fact, as if it were a thing of any sort—all further questions about the truth or falsehood of his intuition

---

[12] Ibid., pp. 98–100 (BN 59–60). Sartre raises this famous example as an illustration of the "inauthentic" mode of existence which he calls "bad faith"; we shall return to this concept later in the chapter.

of the for-itself would be resolved in his disfavor. The experiences of human contingency and of the fundamental elusiveness of the self would not be sufficient to overrule such an elementary logical point. But a sympathetic and sensitive reading of Sartre, as of any serious philosopher, must try to get beyond the skeletal slogans in which such important aspects of the philosophy as the treatment of being-for-itself tend to be epitomized. In claiming to discover in the fundamental indeterminateness of human consciousness the source of negation in the phenomenological world, Sartre is making the strongest and most logically consistent effort possible to *avoid* just the sort of thinking that would make of consciousness a *thing* of any kind. But then, the critic of Sartre's logic may reply, how is he entitled to say anything at all about being-for-itself? Ought he not, rather, to take refuge in the mystic's silence when confronted with the ineffable? How, in particular, is he able to devote the better part of 700 pages in *Being and Nothingness* to a discussion of various aspects of being-for-itself and its relation to others?

The critic who raises such questions may in turn be questioned on his understanding of a certain kind of logic, the logic of freedom. An enormous number of pages throughout the history of philosophy have been filled with considerations of the vexing problem of human freedom, but very few philosophers, with the notable exception of strict determinists, have brought to their investigations the same degree of intellectual rigor and logical consistency as has Sartre. The position of the strict determinist is undoubtedly consistent; its drawbacks, especially its flouting of human experience, are too well known to need repeating. But the usual attempt at compromise, the seemingly commonsensical assertion that we are partly free and partly determined, or free from our point of view but determined from the point of view of God or of a God-surrogate, fails to meet the test of consistency when a more probing analysis of the ontological meaning of freedom is undertaken. This was the conclusion reached by Jules Lequier, the now almost forgotten "father of French existentialism," who devoted all his intellectual life to an analysis of freedom,[13] and it

---

[13] Lequier (1814–1862) was a contemporary of Kierkegaard's, a native of Brittany, who became convinced that almost the entire past philosophical tradition, with the notable exceptions of Aristotle (in his analysis of future contingent possibilities) and of Fichte, in effect opposed the hypothesis of real human freedom, usually while pretending to reaffirm it. A Catholic, Lequier found this to be the case especially with the Scholastic philosophers, for whom he reserved some of his most bitter and often amusing satire. After Lequier's death by apparent suicide, small excerpts from his unpublished manuscripts were published by his friend, Charles Renouvier, who was a dominant figure in late nineteenth-century French philosophy, and who was also to be an important influence on the American philosopher, William James. Interest in Lequier was revived with the publication of a Sorbonne Doctoral thesis, La Philosophie de J. Lequier, Société d'Edition "Les Belles Lettres," Paris, 1936, by Jean Grenier, Camus' early teacher and an acquaintance of Sartre's. Jean Wahl, in his book entitled Jules Lequier, Editions des Trois Collines, Paris-Genéve, 1948, claims (p. 56) that Sartre has found no better formula "for affirming his existentialism" than the following one, devised by Lequier: "FAIRE, non pas *devenir*, mais faire, et, en faisant, SE FAIRE" (TO CREATE, *not* to become, *but* to create, and, *in* creating, TO CREATE ONESELF). Cf. Jules Lequier, Oeuvres Complètes, ed. J. Grenier, Editions de la Baconnière, Neuchâtel, 1952, p. 58.

is a conclusion that his successor has borne in mind. Sartre has seen very well that whatever is held to be free cannot be something possessed of determinate characteristics, because in the very statement of such a possibility the contradiction becomes manifest. To say that the free is determinate is not, as is the claim that being-for-itself is nothing in itself, simply a great paradox; it is an ineluctable contradiction. Between paradox and contradiction, it should be repeated, there is an enormous difference.

Thus, the charge of logical inconsistency may be leveled with equal force against the Sartrean opponent who attributes the quality of freedom to things or "substances." Of course, if we continue to accept the frame of reference of the classical Aristotelean logic, which takes it for granted that qualities or characteristics are predicable only of substances and of no other conceptualizable referent,[14] Sartre's entire effort to characterize being-for-itself in meaningful and important ways, the effort that occupies him throughout almost the whole of *Being and Nothingness*, is inadmissible. But it is essential for the philosopher, as the most radically negating and questioning of men, to put into question any previously accepted frame of reference. In developing his highly radical notion of the freedom of the for-itself, therefore, Sartre is self-referentially exemplifying one of the central insights of his entire existentialist ontology. In doing so, he claims both to have avoided contradiction and to be rendering intelligible, for the first time, some very fundamental human experiences.

Before terminating this phase of our inquiry into the plausibility of Sartre's claims concerning the ontological ultimacy of being-in-itself and being-for-itself, we ought to take note of one obvious and important fact. The Sartrean ontology answered, and continues to answer, particularly well to the experiences of our own historical era. The ever-increasing sense of *contingency* which all the new forms of greater mobility—in social organization, in transportation, in weapons of massive destruction, etc.—have introduced into modern life make the Sartrean accounts both of the self and of being-in-itself more plausible now than they would have been in any previous time. Historically oriented philosophers, including most Marxists, would claim that this was more than a mere accident, and that the particular form taken by Sartre's ontology could be at least partly explained as the complex product of certain twentieth-century cultural and political phenomena. As we shall see later, Sartre has tended increasingly in recent years to sympathize with appraisals of this sort, though not to the extent of accepting total historical determinism or of denigrating all claims to philosophic truth.

We are now in a position to advance, as Sartre himself does in *Being and Nothingness*, beyond our abstract ontological points of departure, the dual concepts of being-in-itself and being-for-itself considered in isolation from each other. In most ordinary human experience, as I have

---

[14] Cf. especially the beginning of the Aristotelean corpus, the first five chapters of the Categoriae, for a brief and illuminating glimpse at the clear-cut but very undialectical world of subjects, predicates, and substances.

already noted, these two "types of being" are not encountered in isolation; the ultimate test of the truth of Sartrean existentialism consists in ascertaining whether human experience can be better understood if considered in light of the various complex interrelationships between being-in-itself and being-for-itself. By way of introduction to the Sartrean picture of concrete existence, however, we ought to reconsider briefly a question that was raised earlier and that has been lurking in the background of the entire discussion thus far, namely, what is the nature or *status* of these two concepts? The answer to this question is by no means pellucid, and yet some tentative clarification is in order. I have already suggested that both being-in-itself and being-for-itself, like the closely parallel concepts of inert matter and *praxis* in Sartre's *Critique*, are in some sense abstractions. Sartre himself somewhat hesitatingly admits this with regard to the for-itself, while denying it with respect to the in-itself, in the following passage:

But if, in a sense, consciousness considered in its isolation is an abstraction, if phenomena—and even the phenomenon of being—are similarly abstract inasmuch as they cannot exist as phenomena without appearing to a consciousness, the being of phenomena, as in-itself which is what it is, could not be regarded as an abstraction.[15]

Although, contrary to what Sartre says here, there seems clearly to be a sense in which the in-itself is also an "abstraction," he is basically justified in pointing out the difference in kind that exists between his two concepts. Being in-itself simply *"is"*; the for-itself must always be found "in situation."

The history of ontological world views is filled with examples of alleged cosmic dualisms, to which Sartre's ontology has already been assimilated often enough by his critics. Whether such an assimilation is regarded as a tribute to Sartre's thought (because it shows Sartre to be the heir of a great tradition that has captivated popular and philosophical imaginations throughout man's history) or the denigration of it (because the critic regards all such world views as little better than sophisticated superstition), it is in either case unfair to the Sartrean position itself. The duality of being-in-itself and being-for-itself is not a dualism in the paradigmatic, Cartesian sense, because the two Sartrean types of being are in no way on a level with one another. For Descartes, there are essentially two different kinds of objects or things in the world, material and spiritual, although there clearly exists a hierarchical ordering between them; Sartre's being-for-itself, on the other hand, is in no sense substance—whether "spiritual" or any other sort.[16] Sartre is basically a *monist* rather than a dualist, as he affirms very strikingly in the following passage in his *Critique of Dialectical Reason*:

Are we returning, then, to dualism? By no means: we locate man in the world, and we simply note that this world for and by man can only be

---

15 EN 219 (BN 171).
16 He experiments with spiritual substance in several of his literary works, notably in Huis clos (No Exit) and in Les Jeux sont faits (The Chips are Down).

human. But the dialectic is a monism precisely to the extent to which oppositions appear to it as moments that are presented, at one instant, for itself . . .[17]

> Some of the terminology of the above passage occurs only infrequently in *Being and Nothingness,* but it is quite in keeping with the spirit of the latter. For Sartre, there exists only being, rather than two or more basic world stuffs; and Sartrean being, as we shall see shortly, is material. It is the constantly recurring temptation to regard being-for-itself as a *thing* that is at the basis of the tendency to misrepresent Sartre's ontology as dualistic.

If being-in-itself and being-for-itself are as truly ultimate as Sartre claims them to be, any attempt to characterize them in terms of less ultimate concepts must result in some distortion of them. Nevertheless, it may be helpful to suggest a certain interpretation of their status from a logical perspective, since this may shed light on the use to which Sartre puts them without requiring us to adopt a dogmatic stance on the desperately vexing issue of the exact significance of ontological concepts and of ontology itself. Let us say, then, that the Sartrean in-itself and for-itself are limiting concepts, systematic developments of extreme or paradigmatic types of existence, the more profound understanding of which will enhance our comprehension of the intermediate forms of existence that mark our daily lives. This is by no means to say that all such pairs of limiting concepts are equally useful or equally "correct," or to deny that the contrast between in-itself and for-itself may in fact be uniquely excellent and "true." But it helps to explain why the Sartrean concepts, though there are indeed human experiences which point to and provide evidence for them, must both necessarily be somehow abstract, and why no single formula or word (such as "consciousness," "freedom," "activity," or "negativity" in the case of the *pour-soi* or *praxis*) can ever capture them with complete precision. It also explains why the major portion of *Being and Nothingness* is devoted to analyzing being-in-itself and being-for-itself in certain of their possible interrelationships, rather than in isolation.

HUMAN REALITY

"Human reality," as Sartre usually designates man, is obviously never pure being-for-itself. Rather, the tension between in-itself and for-itself is the means by which Sartre seeks to explain the individual's relation to himself, to his environment, and to other men. The human being is not his own *raison d'être,* his own ground of existence. He might have been other than he is, and "this perpetually disappearing contingency of the in-itself which pervades the for-itself and attaches it to being-in-itself without ever letting itself be captured is what we shall call the *facticity* of the for-itself."[18] The facticity of the for-itself has many facets, the most basic of which is the fact that the essentially free self must always occupy a particular position and a particular perspective because the human being is always a *body.* The body,

---

[17] CRD 247.   [18] EN 125 (BN 82–83).

according to Sartre, is always an essential characteristic of being-for-itself, but the latter must not be *identified* with body. Similarly, the existing human being always has a past; if he did not, a projection towards a new future objective would be inconceivable, because change always presupposes some being or state away from which the change is taking place.[19] The past, then, is another aspect of one's facticity; Sartre's analysis of the past as one of the three temporal dimensions of being-for-itself[20] rejects the enticing path of extreme relativism and skepticism, which would allege that the past can be somehow "unmade," but shows that the *significance* of the past depends on one's free choice as being-for-itself in the present. And this is the way in which, in general, Sartre deals with all the various sorts of facticity—one's occupation, the absurd future inevitability of one's death, the scarcity of one's tools and other resources, etc.—that he subjects to his fascinating analyses throughout *Being and Nothingness*. The phenomena of facticity will inevitably surround every human being with enormous "co-efficients of adversity" or other unalterable forms of being-in-itself, but none of these facts will ever be sufficient to contradict or overcome the central reality of the self-creative *freedom* of man as being-for-itself; it is, rather, the human reality that freely endows the in-itself of facticity with whatever meaning or significance it may come to have.

The tension between in-itself and for-itself is also the starting point for Sartre's analyses of one's relations with others. His discussion of "*le pour autrui*," being for others, is based on the now famous concept of "the look," *le regard*: the primordial revelation that another person is, like myself, a subject rather than simply one more object comes about, according to Sartre, through my realization of the permanent possibility of my being seen, being looked at, by that Other.[21] Here, once again, the interplay between human reality as for-itself (free subjectivity) and as in-itself (a being that is reducible to an object, though never entirely so) is the leitmotif. The whole conception of man as being-for-itself would lose its meaning if man were not also capable of being regarded, simultaneously, as a mere thing.

This very brief, schematic indication of the way in which the ontological duality of in-itself and for-itself serves to illuminate our world of concrete relationships will have to be supplemented by several specific examples before a reasoned judgment as to the success or failure of Sartre's ontology is possible. However, enough has now been said about it to enable us to reconsider one question that was raised earlier, namely, to what general alternative types of ontological framework is the Sartrean ontology opposed? It would be a hopeless undertaking, of course, to attempt to compile an exhaustive list of such alternatives, but a few examples might usefully be cited. Dualism of the Cartesian type has already been mentioned as one rival ontology to Sartre's own. On the same level of generality, most varieties of idealism and materialism are similarly incompatible with the frame-

19 Ibid., *pp. 577–578* (BN 496).   20 Ibid., *pp. 150–164* (BN 107–120).
21 Ibid., *pp. 434–435* (BN 367).

work of *Being and Nothingness*. From other, more specific, ontological perspectives, Sartre's position is seen to be clearly opposed, for example, to theism and to organicist forms of social philosophy. Reference to his atheism will be reserved for treatment under the heading of "religion," and the problem of applying the Sartrean ontology to the region of intersubjectivity will dominate much of the later discussions in this chapter. The issue of materialism versus idealism, however, requires some further exploration at this point.

Is Sartre a materialist? The apparent simplicity of the question masks an issue of tremendous complexity; two equally competent interpreters of Sartre's thought might, with considerable justification, give opposite answers to the same question. The *locus classicus* of the issue in Sartre's writings is a long essay, "Materialism and Revolution," written in 1946.[22] Here Sartre takes the position that materialism is false, because it denies freedom, but that it has historically been a most useful myth, serving as the most radical instrument of man's liberation. He calls for the construction of a *true* philosophy which can exert the same liberating influence. In *Existentialism and Humanism*, he again underlines his opposition to "every materialism," because, he says, materialism results in treating men as objects.[23] Even in the *Critique of Dialectical Reason*, in which Sartre affirms his adherence to Marx's *dialectical* materialism (distinguishable as this is, both in Sartre and in the writings of Marx himself, from mere *mechanistic* materialism), "inert matter" is designated as the object on which free human *praxis* works; in a struggle which at times takes on the character of a contest between good and evil, *praxis* acts as a contrasting principle to matter. Thus, there are the best textual grounds for denying that Sartre's ontology is a materialist one. But what, then, is the alternative? Is he an idealist? His rejection of this "bourgeois" variety of metaphysics is often as vitriolic as that of any Communist writer. He finds traces of the vice of idealism even in the thought of Edmund Husserl, and this is one of the basic motivations for his critique of Husserl in *The Transcendence of the Ego* and in later writings. In fact, Sartre's eagerness to avoid idealism becomes so intense at times as to obscure the meaning of the word. The paradox of Sartre's ontology reaches its culmination, therefore, precisely in the attempt to answer the question whether he is a materialist. Of course, Sartrean man—the being-for-itself of *Being and Nothingness*, or the practical agent working to change the face of the earth in the *Critique*—is material, and as a thing, as a substance, nothing else can be said about him; but this is just what it is not important to say about him. The same man considered in terms of what *is* important is a free, superfluous *néant*, a nothingness, engaged in a perpetual effort to liberate himself, by means of his capacity to project, from the inertness of matter. Especially in his later work, Sartre comes very close to identifying matter with "Being"; matter is all that there *is*, in the sense of being quantifiable,

---

[22] *"Matérialisme et Révolution,"* in Situations, *III*, Gallimard, Paris, 1949, pp. 135–225 (Literary and Philosophical Essays, pp. 198–256).

[23] L'existentialisme est un humanisme, p. 65 (Existentialism, p. 43).

analyzable, statable in clear concepts which have the ring of eternal truths, and, in short, capable of being subjected to those limited methodological techniques which are often styled "positivistic" and associated with the natural and even with the so-called social sciences.   For Sartre, however, it is that sort of being which is *more* than mere Being, and which is not definable as matter is definable, that is of paramount importance.   But this still leaves him a materialist in terms of the traditional philosophical controversy among idealists, dualists, and materialists.   Later in the same previously cited passage from the *Critique* in which Sartre asserts that his philosophy is monistic, he adds the following clarification:

The only monism which starts from the human world and which situates man in Nature is the monism of materiality . . . . It is the only one which makes of man neither a molecular dispersion nor a being apart.[24]

It is important to emphasize Sartre's rejection of the ontological position that man is "a molecular dispersion," because it shows how completely he rejects the alleged ultimacy of natural scientific explanations.   He regards them as being often true, of course, but never ultimate. Although it might have been possible for Sartre, as an existentialist, humanist thinker primarily interested in "men and relations among men," simply to *ignore* the question how his view of man is related to the conclusions of natural scientific theory, this attitude was not possible for Sartre as an ontologist.   Thus, scattered throughout his philosophical works, one may find numerous defenses of the position that even a very sophisticated theoretical physics would not yield an adequate explanation of reality.   As early as his *L'Imaginaire*, he lays great stress on the view that a cause-effect relationship, measurable by the methods of behavioral science, does not hold between two consciousnesses.[25]   His later turn towards Marxism places in a new perspective his quarrel with those who see in the constructs of natural science the basis of an ultimate ontology, but Sartre's own point of view has remained essentially the same.   Of special interest in this regard are his polemic with Pierre Naville, a French Communist behavioral psychologist, and his contempt for Friedrich Engels' conception of a "dialectics of nature."[26]   Behind the entire Sartrean view-

---

[24] CRD 248.

[25] L'Imaginaire, Gallimard, Paris, 1940, p. 41 (The Psychology of Imagination, p. 35).

[26] The high point of the controversy with Naville is Sartre's denunciation of his opponent for having no sense of dialectical method, and for reducing the dialectical account of change to the naïve and non-Marxist belief in continual progress— "Réponse à Pierre Naville," Situations, VII, Gallimard, Paris, 1965, p. 134. If one follows Sartre's suggestion to reread some of Naville's behaviorist treatises, one will be forced, I think, to agree at least with Sartre's appraisal of Naville's sense for dialectics.
As for the Sartrean polemic against Engels, this is one of the most interesting undercurrents in the early pages of the Critique of Dialectical Reason, especially for the purpose of establishing Sartre's own interpretation of Marxism. Engels attempted, in The Dialectics of Nature, to graft Marxian insights onto Darwinism, and to show that the dialectics of man was only a special case of the dialectics of nature. Sartre berates Engels for the externalism and reductionism involved in this, and especially for Engels' amusing suggestion that the dialectic is

point on this question is, in the last analysis, the phenomenologist's appeal to what is directly revealed in conscious reflection as yielding greater certitude than any set, however internally consistent, of theoretical hypotheses.[27] In other words, it is in *experience* that Sartre finds his most convincing justification for the ontological claim that the most fundamental truth about being is not that it is made up of an inconceivably large number of energy-charged particles, but that it is "in itself"—massive, inert. If all of reality were explicable in terms of the interaction of such particles, as certain materialist ontologists maintain, then clearly Sartre's ontology would be a falsification; it is his deepest conviction, however, that any such explanation would be unable to deal with the essentially human.

CONCRETE SITUATIONS

Sartre himself is, in a broad sense of the word, a pragmatist, as anyone must be who is so firmly committed to the ontological superiority of doing over being. He is not like the doctrinaire pragmatist (or like the popular breed of modern government official who applies to himself the pragmatist label as a means of excusing and even of glorifying his contempt for reason and his own disastrous inability to engage in rigorous thinking about political problems), who holds that success and truth are somehow identical, and that the other traditional criteria of validity are mere irrelevancies: Sartre's previously mentioned distinction, in "Materialism and Revolution," between a mere myth which has been successful historically in encouraging desirable revolutionary activity, and a true philosophy which would have the same effect, is a crystal-clear illustration of the vital difference here. But it remains true that the arenas of practical applicability and of action must be the places where, for Sartre, the most important and ultimate judgment on his ontology, both with respect to its validity and to its value, is to be passed. This very conviction as to the ultimacy of *praxis* already entails, of course, a certain general commitment to an existential way of thinking; it is thus clearly in opposition to the several still extant strains of a venerable intellectualist tradition in philosophy, which insists on the primacy of theoretical over practical

---

reducible to three "most general laws of natural history and of social history" (the transformation of quality into quantity and the reverse, the interpenetration of opposites, and the negation of the negation). Cf. both the Critique (pp. 127–128, pp. 667 ff., etc.) and the memorable academic debate among Jean Orcel, Sartre, Roger Garaudy, Jean Hyppolite, and J.-P. Vigier, entitled Marxisme et Existentialisme: "La dialectique est-elle seulement une loi de l'histoire ou est-elle aussi une loi de la nature?" Tribune Libre, Plon, Paris, 1962.

[27] With reference to this methodological conviction of Sartre's, the plan of his L'Imaginaire is especially interesting. He begins by leaving aside all theories about images, as he says, in order to undertake "a 'phenomenology' of the image. The method is simple: producing images in ourselves, reflecting on these images, describing them, that is, trying to determine and to classify their distinctive characteristics."—L'Imaginaire, p. 14 (The Psychology of Imagination, p. 4). This procedure occupies the section of his book entitled "The Certain." Hypotheses and theories are reintroduced in later sections on the less certain, beginning with that on "The Probable."

reason. It would be far too ambitious an undertaking to attempt to adjudicate here between two such all-pervasive commitments; I shall merely note my own agreement, to the extent to which one must choose between them, with the Sartrean alternative on this issue.

There is, however, a further complication. The arenas of practical applicability and of action, mentioned above, are themselves to some extent distinct. To ask whether the applications which Sartre makes or we ourselves can derive on the basis of his abstract ontological starting points help to clarify our world for us is one question; to ask whether and in what ways, as a result of the influence that the understanding (or even the misunderstanding) of the Sartrean account of the world by his readers may have on their actions, the world as it existed before the publication of Sartre's philosophy has been or may be altered is quite another, though related, question. A brilliant exposition of the nature of the universe, potentially capable of reshaping the thinking and even of altering the actions of large segments of humanity, may never fall into the hands of a single reader; literary creation is as radically affected by contingency as is any other sort of human activity, as Sartre, in reflecting on his childhood illusion that the work of art was "a metaphysical event whose birth interested the universe,"[28] rather sadly remarks. But if a work of philosophical literature such as Sartre's major tomes can be shown (by someone not so over delicate about the issue of historical causation as to refuse to make any statements of this sort) to have had an "impact" on certain individuals or societies, the nature of that impact will have some bearing on our final judgment about the truth of the philosophical theory in question. I mention this final (and never finished) phase of the judgment of a philosophy's truth, the most difficult and the least capable of yielding certitude of all the possible criteria, in order to distinguish it from the more modest criterion of practical applicability with which we are to be concerned at present. A consideration of Sartre's philosophy as a potentially world-changing force—i.e., tritely, of "Sartre before the bar of history"—can be more conveniently and appropriately undertaken at the conclusion of this essay, in the section on "La Belle âme."

Sartre has aptly entitled the series of volumes (seven in number, as of this writing) in which he has collected many of his shorter, more occasional articles, *Situations*. It is precisely to some sample kinds of situations that we must now turn in order to test Sartre's ontology on the grounds of usefulness and applicability. Most of the actual subjects dealt with in the series, however, are inappropriate for our purposes. Some of them, for example, are *too* occasional, so narrowly topical that their interest has already diminished greatly during the intervening years; for instance, some of the outrages and trickeries perpetrated by French governments and the military during the Algerian War, against which a number of Sartrean essays are directed,[29] have already—alas!—faded from the consciousness of

---

[28] Les Mots, *Gallimard, Paris, 1964, p. 148 (The Words, p. 179).*
[29] Cf. especially Situations, V, *Gallimard, Paris, 1964, pp. 25–88.*

people even in France, and no doubt even to some extent in Algeria. In other cases, Sartre's emotionally charged conviction of the moment is so strong as to cause one to wonder seriously whether he has not temporarily abandoned his fidelity even to the deepest currents of his own philosophical thought. To examine any particular essay as a candidate for such censure would take us too far afield, but "Les Communistes et la paix"[30] is a good possibility; it was the all but immediate cause of the temporary rupture of friendship between Sartre and Merleau-Ponty, and while Sartre still maintains that the "objective reasons" for the extremely euphorialike view taken of the Communist Party in this essay were valid for the period,[31] he at least admits to the possibility of there having been some excess in expression and emotion attendant on the conversion of political perspective which he had just then undergone. Moreover, some of the most universal and important of human situations are dealt with in *Being and Nothingness* or in the *Critique*, rather than in the *Situations* series iself. Consequently, I propose to examine briefly three somewhat arbitrarily selected types of human situations with a view to testing whether Sartre's existential ontology is able adequately to deal with them and to shed light on them for Sartre's readers. Common to all three are the following facts: they have all been dealt with in depth by other writers within the existentialist and/or phenomenological traditions, they all hold considerable interest for someone who is engaged in reflection within the humanist framework of Sartre's thought, and Sartre's treatment of (or comparative failure to treat) each of them has drawn considerable criticism. They are: love, play, and religion.

LOVE

Everyone knows that Sartre, like any writer, has dealt with love themes in his plays and novels; on the other hand, the mind boggles at attempting to imagine how many times, and under how many different circumstances, people have quoted Garcin's line from *No Exit*, "L'enfer, c'est les Autres"[32]—Hell is other people. Sartre deals explicitly with love in *Being and Nothingness*; the subject arises in a relatively short section on "The first attitude towards others: love, language, masochism."[33] Perhaps it is the close linking of the last topic with the first that first arouses a certain antagonism among critics towards Sartre's treatment of love. The Sartrean account itself is an exciting *jeu d'esprit*: it is a logical development out of his initial treatment of being-for-itself and, more immediately, out of his discussion of oneself in relation to others. In love, according to Sartre, I as free being-for-itself have it as my basic project to act on the liberty of the other person who is the object of my love; I wish to possess that person as an object while at the same time requiring, for my pur-

---

[30] *Situations, VI*, Gallimard, Paris, 1964, pp. 80–384.
[31] "Merleau-Ponty," *Situations, IV*, Gallimard, Paris, 1964, p. 251 (*Situations*, p. 290).
[32] *Huis clos*, in *Théâtre, I*, Gallimard, Paris, 1947, p. 182 (*No Exit and The Flies*, tr. Stuart Gilbert, Knopf, New York, 1965, p. 61).
[33] EN *431–447* (BN *364–379*).

poses, that he or she remain as much a free subject as before. The lover wishes to possess the beloved neither as a mere thing nor as a completely free agent in a merely voluntary arrangement: what he desires in the other is "a freedom which *plays* at being a determinism of the passions and which is caught in its own game."[34] This account, which is of course developed in considerably greater complexity by Sartre as he unfolds the various kinds of reciprocity possible between two persons in a love relationship, enables him to explain such familiar phenomena in the literature and in the actual experience of love as the lover's oath, the surrender of all one's other values to the beloved, seduction, etc. The *fascination* which is the essential technique of seduction is a certain kind of self-expression and hence of language; masochism is the kind of seduction, doomed to failure, in which one struggles to make oneself completely an object or an instrument in the hands of the Other.

Thus it may be seen, in outline, how Sartre comes to treat together the three topics mentioned under his general heading of "the first attitude towards others." But this schematic explanation is hardly likely to satisfy his critics. Some might even find a certain fitting symbolism in the fact that Sartre's treatment of love leads directly to his treatment of language, for it has long been a commonplace among unfriendly drama critics that Sartre's plays, especially some of the later ones such as *The Condemned of Altona*, suffer from the intellectual's sin of overemphasizing talk at the expense of action. Moreover, Sartre explicitly acknowledges[35] the debt that he owes in his analysis of love to the famous Hegelian dialectic of master and slave, and he insists throughout on the importance of viewing the entire series of possible relationships under the rubric of "conflict." In his *Critique of Dialectical Reason*, the only point in which any phenomenon closely connected with love plays an important role is in his discussion of "the oath," the range of possible actions whereby social groups first begin to introduce into themselves the *permanence* characteristic of institutions; here, Sartre views the lovelike attitude of "fraternity" as one aspect of the two-sided phenomenon whereby the group attempts to enforce upon its members the oath that they have taken,[36] but Sartre characteristically designates the other, complementary aspect as "terror."[37] In many of his plays and literary essays, it is safe to generalize, Sartre shows considerably greater interest in what are commonly called *abnormal* manifestations of love and of sex (*Saint Genet* is a particularly blatant example of this) than what the good bourgeois—and this designation may easily be extended to cover Sartre himself, *malgré lui*—would regard as normal. So runs the gamut of objections, from the technical to the *ad hominem*, that may be assembled in support of the contention that

---

34 Ibid., pp. 434–435 (BN 367).   35 Ibid., p. 438 (BN 370).   36 CRD 453ff.

37 The combination often assumes bizarre and frightening forms. For example, a small group, bound by oath, discovers a traitor in its midst: "In other words, anger and violence are at one and the same time lived through as Terror exerted upon the traitor and (in the case where the circumstances have produced this feeling) as practical bond of love among the [executioners]."—Ibid., p. 455. It is a chilling picture, of course, but is it inaccurate?

Sartre's treatment of love is unsatisfactory, and—to recall the basis of our own particular interest in this topic at this point—that this may be the product of a false ontological foundation.

It is undeniable that Sartre's account of love, whether adjudged satisfactory or unsatisfactory, is directly related to the dialectic of being-in-itself and being-for-itself. The impossibility of the latter's ever reducing itself to the former while still remaining itself, the essential incompleteness of every human project, is the Sartrean ontological groundwork which foreordains the outcome of his discussion of love. An acceptance of Sartre's account would obviously necessitate the dismissal of all idealistic hopes that a perfect concord of two souls could ever be established; in fact, Sartre would also claim to have accounted for the existence of such vain hopes. But the only relevant question is whether or not his account is *true*. Centuries of human experience provide considerable evidence in his favor. For if we analyze the relationship between any two people thought to have lived in the most complete harmony for however long a period of time, we find abundant proof that they have never succeeded in achieving the no doubt desired goal of merging their identities. This explains, for example, just as Sartre claims, the fact that the element of *game* or play continues to be an essential element in any so-called "successful" love relationship. Sartre is by no means contending that every attempt at love or friendship must end immediately in total failure; his own long-standing relationship with Simone de Beauvoir serves as an *ad hominem* rebuttal to his critics on this point. What Sartre's analysis is meant to show is the underlying tension, or dialectic, that may be submerged but can never be erased from any instance of human love. That is why the abnormal and the perverse cases, in which the tension comes more clearly into view, are generally the best illustrations of his theme.

The development of analytic tools with which to deal with the phenomenon of love as it is found in actual human situations, rather than artificially *sub specie aeternitatis*, is one of the great achievements of existential philosophy, and Sartre is especially worthy of praise for this. On the other hand, however, it is disturbing that Sartre's social and political analyses, both in his occasional essays and in his *Critique*, leave so little room for the possibility of love, friendship, or other comparable phenomena in inter- (as distinguished from intra-) group relations. A too literal interpretation of the Marxist concept of class struggle has perhaps exerted a baneful influence on Sartre's thought here, even though the actual analysis that he provides of "class" is a strong argument against all simplistic definitions of class membership and thus of the conflicts resulting from rival memberships. Interpersonal love is said by Sartre always to be envisaged in a perspective of conflict, for "conflict is the basic meaning of being-for-others."[38] But Sartre cannot and does not intend "conflict" here to signify overt, violent opposition, for if he did, he would indeed have made it impossible to account for the phenomenon of love within the framework of

[38] EN *431* (BN *364*).

his philosophy. Similarly, by analogy, the assertion that an atmosphere of violence, whether suppressed or overt, must remain an inevitable feature of the relations of men in society so long as men continue to live in a "world of scarcity" (which characterizes our world but which could conceivably be replaced in the future by a regime of abundance),[39] should not make it as impossible as it seems to for Sartre to envisage some genuine accord, however temporary and partial, between and among groups, nations, etc. But in his critique of the expression, "*l'accord des esprits entre eux,*" he finds fault not only with the idealist notion of "spirits" or "minds," but also with the idea that any agreement is possible so long as we are speaking of two people who, as members of truly different groups, are genuinely Other to one another.[40] The actual prevalence of violence between nations and between smaller social units in the contemporary world argues strongly in favor of the truth of Sartre's picture. But there still remains the suspicion that the strongly pessimistic picture drawn of our world in the *Critique* lacks a necessary balancing element; and the fact that this picture can be regarded as the logical consequence of ontological positions long held by Sartre must leave us with a certain uneasiness, after all, concerning the adequacy of that earlier treatment of love (in *Being and Nothingness*) which received a somewhat parallel development on the basis of the same fundamental ontology.

PLAY

The second test area that I proposed for a consideration of the truth of Sartre's ontology as measured by its practical applicability was what I have called "play." It is perhaps more convenient to think of the French word, "*le jeu,*" which signifies both "play" and "game." A contemporary French Christian philosopher, Régis Jolivet, has written a small book entitled *Les activités de l'homme et la sagesse,*[41] in which he argues that all human activity, or *praxis* if one prefers, can be divided into the three basic varieties of work, play, and contemplation. One need not accept Jolivet's schematism or be concerned with his detailed points in order to appreciate the sort of challenge that his approach presents to one attempting to defend the adequacy of Sartre's humanist philosophy. The question now before us is: can that philosophy deal satisfactorily with the kind of human activity that involves no serious "project" in the sense of an objective outside itself, the achievement of which would somehow alter its world? This question needs to be distinguished, at least initially, from the issue whether Sartre as a person possesses a sense of humor that is exhibited in his writings, though the answer to the second question may help determine and explain the answer to be given to the first.

George Alfred Schrader has already made the remark in his introduction (page 25) that Sartre is "too tense to enjoy the comedy of existence." The shaft is well aimed. Audiences do laugh at lines in Sartre's plays,

[39] CRD 201.   [40] Ibid., p. 527.   [41] *Editions Emmanuel Vitte, Lyon, 1963.*

it is true, but generally "their laughter has an echo that is grim."
His humor, such as it is, is almost invariably deeply ironical and
cynical. Two of his more amusing dramas are fantasies about an
afterlife, *Huis clos* and *Les Jeux sont faits;* he manages, however, to
render heavy with moral purpose even his treatment of that, to him,
most absurd of conceptions, hell, and the word *"jeu"* in the second
title is only part of a gambling idiom used to show the inconceivability
of suddenly altering a way of life, centered around one's social class,
to which one has become committed. *Commitment* is, indeed, the
key to understanding Sartre's way of viewing all his writing. In the
broadest sense, this might be understood as a fairly vague moral
commitment to resist "bad faith" in all its possible forms, but in fact
Sartre has come to place a more and more strictly political interpretation on this commitment in the years since the Second World War, as
his long essay "What Is Literature?" (1947) already shows with
utmost clarity. Now, if we view even Sartre's ontology, to say nothing
of all the rest of his thought, as both leading to and supporting his
commitment to the Marxist (but non- —though not "anti-" —Communist) left, it is a serious question whether he could permit himself
the luxury of being humorous in public. One might, perhaps, be
frivolous about an assumedly nonexistent place, such as hell, but can
one in good faith be frivolous about those aspects of reality—which
in a fully "committed" literature would presumably include practically all the subjects of one's literary endeavors—towards which
one has assumed an attitude of commitment?

The above constitutes, I think, a more immediately relevant consideration
concerning the problem of play in Sartre's thought than would any
one of a number of possible accounts referring to circumstances in
his life—the somewhat precocious childhood that he describes in
The Words, the tragedy of world events through which all members of
his generation have lived, but which no doubt he has felt more keenly
than most persons, the peril of his existence as a participant in the
Resistance during the War—that might also have contributed to a
somber disposition. The difficulty with the latter sort of nonphilosophical explanation, however valid it may be shown to be in some
cases,[42] is that one can usually point to individuals who have lived
through roughly similar or even more trying circumstances but who
display a quite different public disposition: in contrast with Sartre, for
example, one might point to Henri Lefebvre, whose political commitment took the even more radical and at times much more personally
anguishing form of Communist Party membership over a period of
approximately three decades, but whose own later works include some
of the most brilliantly witty passages in the literature of contem-

---

[42] *Sartre himself resorts in an interesting way to such a method of explanation in the
course of recounting his break with Merleau-Ponty: "Underneath our intellectual
divergences of 1941, so calmly accepted when Husserl alone was in dispute, we
were soon astounded to discover conflicts that had their origin in our infancies,
. . . our organisms. . . . In the one, a mad activism, covering up his aberrations; in the other, emotional withdrawals, an extreme quietism."—"Merleau-
Ponty," Situations, IV, p. 258 (Situations, p. 296).*

porary philosophy.[43]   From a certain moral philosophical point of
view, however, one may question the good faith of someone like
Lefebvre—as the French Communist Party itself eventually did, in its
own way, when it expelled him for his severe critique of the current
status of Marxism in that country.   In a world still rent with the
alienations of whole classes of individuals, let play be the concern
of the *bourgeoisie* in its decadence!   Perhaps some such line of reasoning as this could be used to excuse the otherwise surprising dearth
of references to play in a philosophy which is supposed to center
around existential man.

It should be admitted that we have deliberately overdrawn our critique of
Sartre on this issue.   The picture of him as a personality that emerges
from the pages of Simone de Beauvoir's three autobiographical works
is by no means that of a completely joyless individual.   More importantly, there is a kind of play, it seems to me, that often characterizes
the form if not the content especially of Sartre's most serious philosophical works.   For instance, there is some element of arrogance,
some element of a desire to hasten production, but perhaps most of
all an odd spirit of play involved in his having published the *Critique*,
a book of 755 pages, with only a four-line table of contents.   He
appears *fascinated* (it will be recalled, from our discussion of love,
that the phenomenon of fascination has a special importance within
the framework of Sartre's account of being-for-others) by the possibilities of the brilliant dialectical turn of phrase (e.g., the conceivable
configurations of being-in-itself with being-for-itself) or of the apt
neologism (e.g., "totalization" and "detotalization" in the *Critique*).
The peculiar attraction that language has always exerted upon Sartre
is the principal theme of his self-analytic autobiography, *The Words*;
he tells us that he long lived under the illusion that language was the
world.[44]   But it is not so, and even the most precise author, writing
the lengthiest and most carefully phrased of analyses, could never
hope entirely to close the gap still separating that analysis from its
object.   Such seems to be the lesson that Sartre has learned.   It is
completely in accord with the most basic themes of his ontology, and
it puts into a new light the whole issue of the committed writer and
of the permissibility of his concerning himself with play.

Sartre's philosophical world has always been one of approachable but never
wholly bridgeable gaps; the negative, free, elusive, or "fleeting" character of being-for-itself made this outcome inevitable from the start.
It is in terms of this omnipresent gap that, as we have seen, Sartre's
account of love as one attitude of being-for-others is developed.
Similarly, as we shall see in more detail later, it is just such a gap that
makes it impossible for Sartre's self-styled Marxism ever to escape
from the individualistic starting point of his ontology and to become

---

43 Sections of Lefebvre's philosophical, sociological, and literary autobiography, La
    Somme et le reste, La Nef de Paris Editions, Paris, 1959, are especially note-
    worthy in this regard.   His concluding soliloquies with Khrushchev and with
    John Foster Dulles are masterpieces of philosophically inspired satire.
44 Les Mots, p. 151 (The Words, p. 182).

collectivistic in a way which would meet with the approval of present-day Communist guardians of orthodoxy. The gap between the written word and the world is another, and enables us to see perhaps more clearly than any other example just why the charge that Sartre's philosophy cannot account for the phenomenon of play will have to be entirely revised or dropped: in an important sense, an acceptance of the Sartrean ontology entails a view of all literature and indeed of all human action as containing an element of play. Earlier, I defined play as that kind of human activity which involves no *serious* "project," no effort at any self-objectification which, if successful, would somehow alter one's world. In clearest contrast with play as thus defined is the phenomenon of "work" or "labor." Within the Marxist framework that pervades Sartre's later *Critique*, man is viewed as *praxis*, human sensuous activity, with the obvious connotation that *praxis* means work on the inert matter of the world, the outcome of which is an alteration, or "reworking," of that matter. But if we take seriously the inevitability of the gap between the individual's projects and their accomplishment, which is itself the result of the gap that Sartre has discerned between being-in-itself and being-for-itself, *all* labor must have about it something of the futility, the non-seriousness, that we have described as the essential characteristic of play. And this comes as no surprise whatever if we recall to ourselves the famous Sartrean epigram with which he terminates the main body of the text of *Being and Nothingness*, just prior to the conclusion: Man is a useless passion.[45]

It could still be argued, however, that the traces of irresponsibility and of *bourgeois* individualism suggested by that famous phrase are a vestige of Sartre's pre-Marxist past, and that he would be very chary of invoking the same epigram today. After all, it might be said, the view that man is a "useless passion" more or less summarizes the philosophy of the absurd that has been most unflinchingly stated by Albert Camus, with whom Sartre once found considerable agreement, but with whom he later broke precisely on the issue of the "*engagement*" of political commitment. We ought, perhaps, to review the outline of that quarrel. In his vitriolic "*Réponse à Albert Camus*," Sartre in effect supported the charge of *aestheticism* that had been leveled against his former friend in a review of Camus' The Rebel by Francis Jeanson, a member of the staff of Sartre's revue, Les Temps Modernes,[46] and claimed that Camus had changed since the wartime days when he had played such an important role in the Paris Resistance and when his Myth of Sisyphus had evoked widespread admiration. Now, according to Sartre, Camus, in refusing to be a political activist and in denying all possible efficacy to political revolutions as distinguished from personal rebellions, was adopting a *literary* in place of his former *moral* attitude. Camus' attitude, Sartre con-

---

[45] EN 708 (BN 615). *It is also interesting to note that, within the Conclusion itself, Sartre attacks the "spirit of seriousness" said to characterize the bourgeois moral belief in the "givenness" of allegedly transcendent values.*

[46] *Francis Jeanson, "Albert Camus ou l'Ame Révoltée," Les Temps Modernes, May, 1952, vol. 79, pp. 2070–2090.*

cluded, might soon become plainly *immoral.*[47]   One might question
which of the two men had in fact changed more over the years, or
whether it was perhaps more a change of events and circumstances
rather than of characters and philosophies which brought about this
rift, but the gist of the dispute at least makes clear the difference in
viewpoint between them on the issue of commitment, seriousness,
and play with which we have been concerned.   Sartre seems to have
relegated Camus to the status of Kierkegaard's aesthetic man, who
does indeed live his life strictly in terms of the category of play as we
have defined it.   But Sartre himself now claims to be different. I can
only reply that, as I have already begun to show, and as I shall attempt to show in greater detail in the following section of this essay,
Sartre's own philosophy has not altered so greatly as to deprive it of
the essential element of play which has been built into his ontological
account of the "nature" of man.   Though Sartre and Camus did
come to be at odds over questions of political morality and commitment, man has in some sense remained for both a "useless passion"
and thus capable of play and comedy.[48]

Finally, it must be pointed out that this is only as it should be if Sartre
now genuinely considers Marxism to be the dominant philosophy of
our epoch.   For Marx's own vision of man's nature, as it will come to
be expressed when the alienations of present society have been overcome, is also a vision of man as *player*; with what other sort of
vision could a writer have described an ideal society in which the
individual could, if he wished, "hunt in the morning, fish in the
afternoon, rear cattle in the evening, criticize after dinner"?[49]   Marx's
own tremendous moral seriousness is mitigated by this gamelike conception of fully developed communist society, the "realm of freedom,"
which he seems always to have preserved but which is best expressed
in some of the pages of the *1844 Manuscripts*,[50] and which commentators have not hesitated to label, in the broadest sense, as
"aesthetic."   One might complete the parallel between Marx and
Sartre by noting the following consideration: the problem of the role
of the artist in the Soviet Union today, the issue of freedom of artistic
expression versus the demands of "socialist realism," is a serious one
in part because Marx himself never wrote much on the subject, and
it was left for successors of different temperaments, such as Plek-
hanov, to do so.   But no one who has read the section of the *1844
Manuscripts* alluded to above could ever dispute the depth of Marx's
aesthetic sensibility.   Similarly, even though Sartre, largely for rea-

---

47 "*Réponse à Albert Camus*," Situations, IV, p. 125 (Situations, p. 104).

48 *In fact, if one compares Sartre's reply with the indignant letter addressed to him
by Camus ("Lettre au Directeur des Temps Modernes," Les Temps Modernes,
Aug. 1952, vol. 82, pp. 317–333), it is the latter which is more pompous and
devoid of the sense of man's comic absurdity.*

49 *Karl Marx and Friedrich Engels, The German Ideology, ed. R. Pascal, International
Publishers, New York, 1947, p. 22.*

50 *Cf. Karl Marx: Early Writings, tr. and ed. T. B. Bottomore, McGraw-Hill, New York,
1964, especially pp. 152–167. This is the part of the Third Manuscript entitled
"Private Property and Communism," and it is here that Marx envisions a new,
more creative role even for the human senses in Communist society.*

sons similar to those that could be alleged in Marx's own case, says very little that is explicit about the related phenomenon of play, and even though his major essay on literature is a plea for the highest moral and political seriousness, it would be a great mistake to think that his philosophy allows no room for dealing with play and thus demonstrates an irreparable weakness invalidating his entire system. On the contrary, a conception of play is so central to the elementary components of his ontology that any more specific treatment of the phenomenon of play might appear, from a certain point of view, to be as "superfluous" as is Sartrean man himself.

RELIGION

A reconsideration of man's contingency, or superfluousness, which within a Sartrean ontological framework must serve as the basis of any account of *play*, leads us to reflect on the third and final phenomenon which I have suggested as a testing ground for the truth of Sartre's ontology in terms of its applicability to the *Lebenswelt*, namely, religion; for religion is usually defined by its practitioners as man's relation to That Which is *non*-contingent. This is the way in which Kierkegaard, for example, who in this respect was not especially original, regarded the attitude of religiousness around which all of his later writing centered. But Sartre is an atheist, as all those who have even a vague conception about his thought must be aware, and thus cannot regard the alleged relationship supposedly central to the religious phenomenon as being real.

The problem concerning Sartre's treatment of religion is more like that with which we were confronted in the case of love than like that posed with respect to play, since Sartre by no means disregards religious phenomena. He refers quite frequently to the hypothesis of God and to religious practice (although he does not devote to it a special section in one of his major works, as he did in the case of love), but he regards the hypothesis in question as illusory and the consequent practice as unjustifiable. We have already seen that the analogies often drawn by lovers between their beloveds and God make considerable sense within the framework of the Sartrean ontology and serve, in turn, to demonstrate its applicability. Yet, as I have suggested, it is understandable why some readers are left with an uneasiness about Sartre's treatment of love and of related phenomena, such as friendship and cooperation—especially, perhaps, after reading his later, more politically oriented writings. The religious man is bound, of course, to be left with similar feelings of dissatisfaction about Sartre's treatment of religion.

Very early in *Being and Nothingness*, in a short section entitled "The Ontological Proof," Sartre deliberately draws a parallel between the place of God in many traditional ontologies and the role of being-in-itself in his own ontology. Sartre's "proof" makes sense primarily within the context of his use of the phenomenological method and his announced intention of constructing a phenomenological *ontology*. In the classical ontological proof of the existence of God, the consciousness of a Being than which no more perfect being can be thought is held to entail the actual existence of such a supremely perfect Being external to one's own consciousness. Just so, the fact that the consciousness of the human individual, prior even to his having reflected upon it, is always a consciousness of some phenomenal object is said by Sartre to entail the actual existence of objective being external to consciousness.[51] This "proof" serves at once several functions within Sartre's theory of knowledge; most notably, it reinforces his conception of a "pre-reflexive *cogito*" in opposition to the ultrarationalism and intellectualism which characterize the intuition of the thinking subject in Descartes, and it gives Sartre a firm basis for formally anathematizing the element of subjectivism and of idealism that he claims to find lurking in the phenomenology of Husserl, despite the latter's laudable efforts to give philosophy a new foundation in which idealism would have no place.[52] For our purposes here, however, what is most interesting about Sartre's "ontological proof" is the comparison that it enables us to make between the being-in-itself of his philosophy and the God of traditional Western religions. First of all, whereas God is said, as we noted earlier, to be Necessary (non-contingent) Being, Sartre's being-in-itself can by no means be said to exist by any logical necessity; it is as contingent as is being-for-itself, and thus Sartre places himself squarely on the side of those who argue that, rather than there being something, there *could* be nothing at all.[53] Furthermore, although the God of tradition is endowed with personality, nothing could be further removed from the conception of being-in-itself that has been drawn by Sartre. Being-in-itself is the source of no values, either, for whatever values there are in the Sartrean universe have been created by man as being-for-itself. The contrast, then, between the object of the classical ontological proof and the object of Sartre's "proof" is in most respects as absolute as our imaginations will allow a contrast to be.

Religious persons have criticized Sartre's philosophy on the grounds that he nowhere furnishes a proof of his atheism, but seems complacently to take it for granted. As a matter of fact, Sartre makes it clear throughout *Being and Nothingness* that he regards the concept of God as self-contradictory. Now it must be obvious that just as the Sartrean ontology with respect to the all-important question of human freedom will have to be rejected, as we have seen, by anyone who remains convinced that his concept of freedom involves a logical

51 EN 28 (BN lxiii).

52 The beginning of Sartre's break with Husserl, under whom he had studied for a year in Germany, was marked by the publication of the essay, The Transcendence of the Ego, in which Sartre criticized the Husserlian conception of an absolute consciousness because of its idealistic overtones. Sartre here applied the general principle that all consciousness must be consciousness of something, to the self as one more possible object alongside other objects (rather than an absolute subject). His theory of a transcendental field of consciousness, not definable as a personal "I," but completely "transparent" and in itself literally nothing, anticipates his later conception of being-for-itself.

53 A good short presentation of this argument for contingency in a strong sense is Robert Ehman's article, "On the Possibility of Nothing," The Review of Metaphysics, Dec. 1963, vol. xvii, 2, pp. 205–213.

inconsistency, the conviction that there is a real, ineluctable self-contradiction about the idea of God will necessitate a similar rejection of that idea by the person who is so convinced; there will be no need for further argument in such a case.   Towards the end of *Being and Nothingness*, Sartre defines God as the "ideal" of a being-in-itself-for-itself, that is, of a consciousness which, by a sheer act of self-consciousness, would serve as the foundation of its own being.[54] Since every human being, as being-for-itself, can be regarded as being engaged in forming "projects" to objectify and solidify itself and thus overcome its essential "nothingness" or contingency, Sartre can now say that, in this sense, every person aspires to be like that ideal, to be God.   But, Sartre would say, an analysis of the essential characteristics of being-in-itself and of being-for-itself shows the self-contradictory nature of such a concept as that which he has named "God."   At the same time, of course, it serves to explain why that concept—a bit like that idea of a perfect, perpetual concord of two souls which we examined in our discussion of love—has enjoyed such enormous popularity and seems so reasonable.

So much for Sartre's basic position on the supposed object of religion; in his negative way, as we have seen, he is something of a philosophical theologian.   We are now in a position to return to the phenomenon of religion itself, the adequacy of Sartre's treatment of which is the primary issue of this stage of our inquiry.   In *The Words*, Sartre points to those elements in his upbringing—a split between Protestantism and Catholicism in the branches of his mother's family, lukewarmness towards religion within his immediate household, etc.—to which a religious person might want to attribute his "loss of faith." The actual beginning of that disbelief occurred, according to Sartre's own account, very easily and without anguish;[55] the details of his early childhood are there, recorded with an apparent effort at fidelity to the facts, for those who are interested in reading them.   In many of his other writings, Sartre manifests indifference towards religion, but seldom if ever the crusading spirit of the total iconoclast.   He is very much aware, of course, as anyone who is acquainted with the history and traditions of France must be aware, of the potential role of religion in forming political beliefs.   In "The Childhood of a Leader" (a short story), for example, his principal character is a product of that pernicious combination of Catholicism, anti-Semitism, and conservatism which underlay much of French fascism during the period before the Second World War; on the other hand, Sartre is unwontedly warm in his praise of a pamphlet during the Algerian War by a group of Christian draftees—priests, chaplains, and others—in protest against the inhuman way in which the war was being prosecuted.[56]   But it is not simply from this more or less external sort of perspective that religion interests Sartre, for the religious community is a very noteworthy kind of institutionalized group, and this type of phenomenon occupies the center of attention in Sartre's *Critique of*

---

[54] EN 653 (BN 567).   [55] Les Mots, p. 209 (The Words, pp. 250–251).
[56] "Vous êtes formidables," Situations, V, pp. 57–67.

Dialectical Reason. In a footnote in this book that is significant as much for the light that it sheds on Sartre's conception of liberty as for its reference to the religious community, Sartre discusses the meaning of baptism from the point of view of the group into which the infant is baptized. He once thought, he says, that "total indetermination was the real basis of choice," and was therefore astonished by the practice of some religious skeptics, born Catholic, who nevertheless had their children baptized. He now understands that from the group's point of view, the initiation ceremony actually results in an increase in the child's capacity for free choice, because it gives him a share in the common freedom of the group itself; although Sartre regards as fallacious the reasoning of the skeptical parents who have their children baptized, he now finds it necessary to accept the hard truth that a prejudgment (though not an irrevocable one, nor one which obviates the ultimate need for the individual to make a decisive free choice of his own) is made for every child, no matter what the milieu into which he is born and initiated. Even atheists, he has concluded, form a kind of group.[57] There is no question that this *social* dimension of the phenomenon of religion is one with which the Sartre of *Being and Nothingness* was rather ill equipped to deal, and which anyone who claims to understand religion must be able to explain.

Religious people ought to be pleased, or at least intrigued, by this new Sartrean attempt to explain, within the context of his whole elaborate theory of social structures, the apparent paradox involved in a church's asking a newborn infant to make a "free" renunciation of Satan and thus to become a member in good standing. Sartre's new understanding of the processes of initiation and group membership helps to refute certain seemingly obvious kinds of criticisms that can be made of such procedures and thus could, to some extent, be useful to the defenders of religion. But the "common *praxis*"—to use the Sartrean terminology of the *Critique*—that characterizes the *religious* group is likely to be radically different from that of political and all other social groups, regardless of structural similarities. Sartre will, of course, admit that various groups may have an infinite diversity of possible objectives—he would regard as simplistic the Marxist reductionism which views all supposedly nonpolitical goals at the present stage of history as illusory[58]—but he cannot admit that the difference between the religious group and other kinds is so "radical" as the religious person wishes to claim. Surely, historically speaking, Sartre is on very good grounds here: one would be hard put to find an organized church which, however strictly it may (according to its spokesmen) have intended to concentrate on the single objective of ordering its members' relationships of worship to a Transcendent Being, has not found itself deeply engaged in political activities, as well as in many other kinds of nonreligious social action. Such activities may often be useful, rather than objectionable, from the viewpoint of an outsider like Sartre, but they do cast some doubt on

---

[57] CRD *491–492.*

[58] This attitude may be regarded as the focal problem, for example, in Sartre's drama, Les Mains sales (Dirty Hands).

the churchman's claims concerning the radical difference between his group and all other kinds of groups. I can only conclude by noting that Sartre's later philosophy, far more than the earlier, is applicable to the study of religion and religious phenomena in a more sophisticated and satisfactory way than that suggested by such words as "illusion," "opiate," and "mystification," which religious people have become accustomed to hearing bandied about. On the other hand, those who are convinced by Sartre's logic that the concept of being-in-itself-for-itself is indeed self-contradictory, but who still consider it meaningful to talk about the existence of God, will be exceedingly hard put to find some alternative basis for such talk within the framework of Sartre's ontology.

CONCLUSION

In examining the applicability of Sartre's existentialist ontology to the three crucial kinds of human situations—love, play, and religion—dealt with above, we have brought the discussion of truth in Sartre from its necessary starting point, namely, the initial abstract constituents of the system with which Sartre himself began, to its logical terminus, in the life-world upon which Sartre's existentialism is usually thought to offer its most provocative insights. The three phenomena chosen, of course, are only samples of the sorts of phenomena which a really exhaustive analysis of Sartre's philosophy from this perspective would have to take up; in the following two sections of this essay, we shall have occasion to examine at least two other very broad areas, politics and ethics, about which the question of "truth as practical applicability" in Sartre's thought also especially needs to be raised. A purely literary criticism of several of Sartre's novels and plays might well pose *some* of the same kinds of questions as those with which I have just dealt; it might inquire, for example, whether such and such a love relationship, as Sartre has depicted it in such and such a story, is *believable*. But the philosophically oriented reader will realize that Sartre's descriptions and analyses of love relationships and other concrete phenomena are "informed" or guided by a systematic ontology that has its fullest expression in the early pages of *Being and Nothingness*. Furthermore, he will realize that the issue of the truth or the "believability" of Sartre's thought depends very little on whether or not the author has managed to "bring off" a particular description with the proper literary *élan*, and very much on whether Sartre's initial intuitions and subsequent developments meet rigorous philosophical standards.

Now that I have attempted, throughout my entire discussion up to this point, to indicate some important ways of applying these standards, it may seem legitimate to expect the critic to formulate his definitive conclusion: Is Sartre's philosophy, in its essentials, true or false? After such a relatively lengthy discussion, only a short answer to this question is appropriate. I have tried to suggest some of the most difficult central problems that a defender of Sartre's philosophy would need to meet, and I have been generally sympathetic in indicating possible answers or resolutions. I have done so not only because of my own comparative admiration for Sartre's philosophical achievement, but more importantly because I consider it useful for a critical study to indicate weaknesses, naturally enough, but particularly to emphasize strengths. There is, of course, a gap, which may be a considerable one, between having "comparative admiration" for a system of thought and fully accepting it; failure to maintain such a gap would in fact be somehow contrary to the general tone of Sartre's own philosophy as I have discerned it in the preceding pages. But questions of truth and falsehood must never be reduced to the level of any individual's likes or dislikes, and the philosopher must always preserve a tension between the dogmatism which declares that the discovery of fundamental truths is a meaningful goal and indeed the most important possible undertaking for human intelligence, and the openness which acknowledges the "fleeting," illusory, and questionable character of every attempted final formulation even of the most trivial truth. Once again, it should be noted that the spirit of Sartre's philosophy is very much in keeping with this tension. He has recognized more openly and boldly than most of his fellow philosophers, including some of his fellow existentialists, the importance of venturing into the area of ontology and of discussing what are sometimes called "ultimate existents" and considering questions about truth in a manner that frightens many of our contemporaries. But a detailed analysis of some of the claims that he has made shows how very far he is from the naïve self-assurance of many of the philosophers of the past who ventured into similar depths. Sartre's very ontology, in short, shows how complex the whole matter of truth becomes when it is seen that the arbiter of truth is existential man. This makes Sartre sound like a latter-day Protagoras, whereas at the beginning of this section I presented him as a latter-day Parmenides. He is, of course, both.

The individual student of philosophy, then, will have to decide for himself whether and to what extent the philosophy of Jean-Paul Sartre is true. The individual may also decide to suspend judgment on the issue. In any case, the critic may properly only give indications of some of the most important and troublesome questions to be raised. This is as it must always be in philosophy, and it does not mean that a philosophy's truth-value is purely "subjective," in the sense that there are no recognized objective standards for testing it; it means, rather, that philosophy in general, and existential philosophy in particular, encourages a profound respect for the comparative autonomy of the human subject. If such a respect is one of Sartre's most central philosophical themes, this is one more important element of evidence in its favor. I have suggested many other such elements throughout the course of the preceding discussion; to try to summarize them in a phrase or two, and on the basis of such sloganizing to pronounce canonization or damnation on Sartre's entire philosophy, would of course be to make a mockery of the very theme, truth, the honest and careful reconsideration of which I have been urging.

Some proponents of Sartre's thought might argue, however, that I have ensured a biased and unfair appraisal of his work by the very fact that I have applied to it traditional, shopworn standards from earlier philosophies—philosophies that would themselves be discredited if Sartre's philosophy turned out to be a more satisfactory account of existence. There are hints in Sartre's own writing, I admit, of somewhat the same sort of attitude as that which would motivate such a criticism. In the *Critique of Dialectical Reason*, for example, he insists on the superiority of dialectical reason over positivistic and analytic methods inasmuch as the former permits of "the absolute intelligibility of an irreducible novelty *insofar as* that novelty is irreducible."[59] In other words, Sartre is affirming that genuinely new phenomena can come into existence in the world; perhaps his own philosophy is also a genuine novelty. In that case, are not the categories that we have attempted to apply in dealing with it somewhat too analytic, too rigid and conservative, even to allow us to understand it fully, much less to evaluate it? I shall return at the end of the chapter to this very serious problem. For the moment, I shall be content with a *tu quoque*. For, during the course of its evolution, Sartre's philosophy appears to have taken several rather novel turns, especially in the development from *Being and Nothingness* to the *Critique*. If any of the views expressed in the *Critique* are radically new, and if the interdiction against applying old standards to new philosophies were interpreted strictly enough, the earlier Sartre would have to be regarded as totally inadequate as a basis for judging the later Sartre; similarly, the standards formulable in terms of Sartre's present thought would be inapplicable to whatever he might write in the future. But this suggests a much more chaotic philosophical world than Sartre, who is a rationalist beneath the skin despite all the anarchy that he sees and helps us to see around us, intends to create or to portray. The possibility of *complete* discontinuity in philosophical development would imply a radical unintelligibility that no form of thought, dialectical reason included, could hope to overcome.

2. Sartre's Evolution
and the Issue of Unity

What I wish to suggest in this section is, first, that there is a significant problem whether a basic identity is discernible between Sartre's earlier and later philosophical writings, and second, that a resolution of this problem should favor the thesis of unity over that of discontinuity. Perhaps an apology is in order for the excruciating triteness of this issue as a general sort of issue raised about any writer or philosopher who has exhibited freshness of approach over a period of time, that is, about any major writer or philosopher; but there are certain aspects about the problem as it applies to Sartre's case which make it more than usually interesting.

The problem is obvious enough. In the mid-1930s, we find Sartre the philosopher (as distinguished from Sartre the short-story writer and

[59] CRD 147.

novelist) writing exclusively on problems in the area of philosophical psychology and attempting to sort out the true from the false in past and current theories about imagining, partly as a clue to questions about reflection and to wider questions about thought in general. We note, during the same period, the rising importance of Husserl in Sartre's philosophical thinking. In *The Transcendence of the Ego* (1937), Sartre expressed some basic dissatisfactions with Husserl's treatment of the "I." In 1943, *Being and Nothingness* was published. It was the result of the investigations in philosophical psychology begun by Sartre in the thirties, as he himself points out in refuting the contention by Lukacs that this first major Sartrean work was simply the product of the historical situation of the French intellectual *bourgeoisie* under the German Occupation;[60] and it is also something very new. In *Being and Nothingness*, the influence of Heidegger is at least as prominent as that of Husserl. Not only has Heidegger influenced Sartre in many important details of his thinking—as Simone de Beauvoir's frequent references to Sartre's enthusiasm about Heidegger in *The Prime of Life* serve to corroborate—but also, most significantly, Sartre has been transformed from a dutifully Husserlian *"psychologue"* to an ontologist in the full sense of the word, the sense that has already been discussed here.

All of Sartre's philosophical productions up to this point, however, can be regarded as having followed a more or less natural course of evolution. As a beginner in philosophy, it may be said, one is well advised to wrestle with smaller issues and to rest one's case largely, though not exclusively, on analyses of previous thinkers; after a few years, a tendency to greater originality and to dealing with larger questions will then become more permissible. Whether or not this is sound as advice, it appears applicable to an account of Sartre's development up to and including *Being and Nothingness*. Thereafter, however, it is much more easily arguable that the course of development takes a very different turn. The antiunitarian may not wish to point to a precise place in Sartre's interim philosophical essays at which there occurred a change, not simply in Sartre's personal *interests* (from ontology to social philosophy, or something of that sort), but also in his philosophy itself; he *will* argue, however, that the end product achieved by Sartre in his *Critique of Dialectical Reason* is so very different in influences, in tone, in interests, *and* in substance from *Being and Nothingness* that a radical break, or a series of smaller breaks amounting to a radical one, must have taken place in the interim.

To assist the proponent of discontinuity, I shall adduce three significant passages, already the objects of frequent citations, from Sartre's own writings. The first two occur in his eulogistic essay in memory of Maurice Merleau-Ponty, in which Sartre gives his account of their postwar collaboration in founding and directing the revue, *Les Temps Modernes*, and of their subsequent break in friendship and later reconciliation. Both philosophers held political positions characterizable as

---

[60] Ibid. (*"Question de méthode"*), pp. 34–35 (Search for a Method, pp. 37–38).

"non-Communist left wing."   But in the period immediately after the
war, as Sartre admits, his views had been somewhat to the right of
his colleague's. A reading of Merleau-Ponty's *Humanisme et terreur*
(1947), together with personal discussions with its author, resulted in
a change on Sartre's part:

*In a word, it was Merleau who converted me [qui me convertit]: at the
bottom of my heart, I was a relic of anarchism, I posed an abyss between
the vague phantasms of collectivities and the precise ethics of my private
life. . . .   He revealed to me that I made history just as M. Jourdain made
prose.*[61]

The use of the word "conversion" is interesting, and it seems quite
deliberate.   Moreover, the explanation that follows suggests something more serious and more philosophically important than a mere
slight slide leftward on the political continuum might be under the
particular circumstances of a given moment and series of events.
Nor is this the last occasion on which Sartre uses the word "conversion" in the same article.   The outbreak of the Korean War (1950),
he maintains, was the turning point in Merleau-Ponty's own beliefs
about politics and political philosophy: Sartre's colleague held Moscow
primarily responsible for this tragic sequence of events, whereas
Sartre was more inclined to place greater blame on the West and to
suspend final judgment.   The definitive change in Sartre's own attitudes, however, was brought about by a couple of headline-producing
incidents, relatively minor from our own perspective almost fifteen
years later, involving the French government and the Communist
Party.   These were the Henri Martin affair and the arrest of Jacques
Duclos:

*These sordid bits of childishness touched me to the quick: there existed
more ignoble cases, but none more revealing.   The last links were severed,
my vision was transformed: an anti-communist is a dog, I do not retreat
from that position, I shall never again do so. . . .   In ecclesiastical language,
it was a conversion.*[62]

Simone de Beauvoir considers this incident important enough to refer
to it, as well as to make a citation from the same article in *The Force
of Circumstance.*[63]   Of course, Sartre's definitive break with all forms
of anti-communism is by no means equivalent to a blind adherence to
whatever "the" Communist Party (if this expression retains any
rigorous meaning at all in the new era of the Communist diaspora!)
decrees to be right.   Merleau-Ponty, basing his criticisms primarily on
the previously mentioned series of articles by Sartre, *Les Communistes
et la paix*, which were written in testimony to this 1952 "conversion"
and issued in the rupture of friendship between Sartre and Merleau-
Ponty, in effect charges his former colleague with assuming such an

61 *"Merleau-Ponty," Situations, IV, pp. 216–217 (Situations, pp. 255–256).*
62 Ibid., *pp. 248–249 (Situations, p. 287).*
63 *Simone de Beauvoir, La Force des choses, Gallimard, Paris, 1963, p. 281 (The Force
of Circumstance, tr. Richard Howard, Putnam, New York, 1965, p. 262).*

equivalence in his chapter on "Sartre and ultra-Bolshevism."[64]   But much of Sartre's more recent writing, notably his attack on Khrushchev's actions in suppressing the Budapest rebellion[65] and certain sections of the *Critique of Dialectical Reason* itself, serves to indicate that this is too simplistic a version of the matter.

The third passage is even more damaging to the case for unity.   It comes at the end of Sartre's first volume of autobiography, *The Words*, underlines the theme of conversion even more forcefully, and promises more detailed revelations in further volumes.   What Sartre contends here is that although his youthful conversion from Catholicism, from organized religion, and from explicit theism (to which I have already referred in discussing the applicability of Sartre's philosophy to religious phenomena) was a quite simple and untraumatic affair, there continued to be a pseudo-religious attitude of mystification concerning his philosophical mission as "the Elected of doubt" that underlay his thought until "about ten years ago."   (*Les Mots* was published in 1964).   He states:

I have changed.   Later, I shall recount . . . when and how I did my apprenticeship in violence, discovered my ugliness . . . by what reasoning I was led to think systematically against myself to the point of measuring the obviousness of an idea by the displeasure that it caused me.   The retrospective illusion is in smithereens; martyrdom, salvation, immortality all crumble, the building is in ruins . . . ; atheism is a cruel undertaking requiring long effort; I think that I have pursued it to the end.[66]

Even after one makes allowances for literary hyperbole, the claim to have changed and the intimations of the respects in which the change has supposedly been effected are strong pieces of evidence for the view that there are at least two radically different Sartres.   Because of their strength, I have deemed it best to cite the passages verbatim.

Some change has taken place; no one contests this.   Sartre is no longer so interested as he once was in writing about Husserl, for example.   He is constantly making reference to issues with political implications, and the tone of his writing has undergone a considerable alteration from the time, let us say, of *L'Imaginaire*.   Some may welcome the change, but such persons are likely to be in a minority.   As I mentioned at the outset of this essay, many professional philosophers, especially in the West, are apt to regard much of Sartre's later work as an illegitimate attempt to accommodate their discipline to the passing exigencies of practical politics; Sartre might retort, with very good reason in some instances, that such antipathy to political commitment is simply a useful pose for the defender of the political *status quo* to adopt.   At the other end of the spectrum, the faithful adherents of any Communist Party which still requires a high degree of

---

64 *Maurice Merleau-Ponty, Les Aventures de la dialectique, Gallimard, Paris, 1955,* pp. 131–271.

65 "Le Fantôme de Staline," Situations, VII, pp. 144–307.

66 Les Mots, pp. 210–211 (The Words, pp. 252–253).

doctrinal rigidity tend to be most intolerant of those unorthodox positions, such as Sartre's, which pretend to some measure of intellectual allegiance to Marxism. A wide range of other reasons for dissatisfaction with Sartre's change of interests and perspectives also exists. But all such personal preferences and prejudices are irrelevant for our present purposes. The only important question here is whether there has been a fundamental change in Sartre's philosophy with regard to the understanding of reality, and especially of human reality, with which it provides us. The partisan of discontinuity in Sartre's thought must prove that such a change has taken place, and nothing yet alleged can serve as a definitive proof of the sort required.

In fact, it is on the basis of the opposite assumption, namely, the assumption of underlying unity, that I have been writing up to this point. At the beginning of the section on "the ontological starting points and some problems of truth," I indicated my belief that Sartre's *Critique* was an *extension* of the ontology of *Being and Nothingness* into a new area of investigation, the social sphere, and I have consistently reaffirmed that assumption by using illustrations drawn from the *Critique* as well as from the earlier work in my analysis thus far. The assumption has fared relatively well in light of the pragmatic test of truth, but it now needs to be examined more closely. In the process of this examination, some of the equivalences and differences between the frameworks of the two major books, hitherto only suggested in passing as the need arose, will have to be made more explicit. *Being and Nothingness* has served as our point of departure and primary model; now it is the *Critique* which, for the moment, must occupy the center of our attention.

The large volume usually referred to as the *Critique* is imprecisely so named for two reasons, first, because it contains a long introductory essay ("*Question de méthode*") which is not a part of the *Critique* proper, though it deals less systematically with some of the same issues, and second, because the *Critique* as it has thus far appeared in print is intended to be only the first of two volumes. "*Question de méthode*" (*Search for a Method*)[67] is interesting especially because it explains Sartre's present views on the historical relationship between Marxism and existentialism; in brief, he sees Marxism as the single dominant philosophical movement of our entire epoch, whereas he regards existentialism as a "parasite system," an "ideology" rather than a full-fledged philosophy. Existentialism began by opposing Marxism, he maintains, for such legitimate reasons as the stunting of Marxism's growth in the early part of our century and the neglect of the human *individual* by so many of the self-styled "orthodox" Communist thinkers, but it now seeks to become reintegrated with Marxism proper.[68] There is, however, a certain aura of label-mongering

---

[67] "*Question de méthode*" originally appeared, under the title, "*Existentialisme et Marxisme*," in an edition (in 1957) of a Polish journal which was devoted to problems of contemporary French culture. It occupies the first 110 pages of vol. I of the Critique, and has been translated into English as a complete book with the title, Search for a Method.

[68] CRD ("*Question de méthode*") 17–18 (Search for a Method, p. 8).

about this passage, and inevitably also about all attempts by commentators to explain and/or criticize it, which renders it in fact less significant, in the long run, than might at first be thought; it may provide some insight into the nature of Marxism, especially of Sartre's Marxism, but it is not very helpful from the viewpoint of the student of existentialism. At any rate, the *Critique* proper is written on a very different level of discourse—more difficult, technical, and "abstract" in the sense already discussed—from that of "*Question de méthode.*" In the *Critique*, it is a question of establishing a basic framework of thought for understanding all of social reality, that is, men as *acting together.* These two concepts, "action" and "collectivity," are captured in Sartre's subtitle of the published first volume of the *Critique*, "*Théorie des ensembles pratiques.*" What the author proposes to do is to begin his analysis of social man at its most abstract conceivable starting point (something which Marx himself admittedly never undertook in quite the same way) and to proceed in the direction of greater complexity of social organization until, at the end of the volume, he will have arrived at the level of concrete history in which we are all actors. At this final level, presumably, the phenomena to which Sartre refers (which are primarily, as it turns out, the phenomena of class conflict, especially as it has unfolded over the past century in France) will be immediately familiar to all of us in the way in which Sartre's starting points, either here or in *Being and Nothingness*, were not before we came to read Sartre's writings. None of the analysis of the first volume of the *Critique* is intended to be chronological, or "historical"; Sartre has chosen the particular order of development simply for the sake of convenience of systematic exposition. The awaited *second* volume, however, is to be an application of the social structures discerned in the first volume to a Sartrean philosophy of history.

The starting point of the *Critique*, simply put, is man considered as abstract, individual *praxis*, which Sartre defines, much further on in the book, as "organizing project going beyond material conditions towards an objective, and imprinting itself through labor in inorganic matter as a reworking of the practical field and a reunification of the means with a view to attaining the end."[69] A duality is thus established between man, as agent, and the inert, inorganic *matter* upon which he works in order to bring about some change. *Praxis* originates in *need*; it is characterized as dialectical and free, and in this way also it is distinguished from radically undialectical matter. Through relationships of reciprocity, men work together on matter, and it frequently happens that the roles of the two (man and matter) become reversed, the producer becoming his product. Thus, in a world of scarcity, such as our world has always been up to the present time, it is quite possible for men's originally free activity to become passive and inert, like matter; the social structure of men in such a condition is denominated "seriality" by Sartre. In this condition, men regard the structure as being externally imposed, and make no effort to alter their status. By

69 Ibid., p. 687.

contrast to the "series," Sartre discerns a type of social organization which he calls "the group"; aggregations of this type represent men's salvation, for it is through the common *praxis* of the group that social man can "totalize," that is, act to achieve a certain common objective which involves going beyond one's present, serial state of existence and internalizing one's relationships with one's fellows.   Totalization in its most ideal form would be devoid of all formal structure whatever; it would be common activity unanimously agreed to by all, requiring no hierarchy or leader, perhaps best approximated by the example developed in detail by Sartre himself, the group of residents of the Faubourg Saint Antoine storming the Bastille.   Opposed to totalization is the concept of a "totality," a group considered as a completed whole—a perspective that is possible for an external observer of a group other than his own, or that would be possible for a God, if there were a God, looking at human history in its entirety, but that is not characteristic of the active participant in an ongoing movement of totalization.   Sartre maintains that there will always remain an unbridgeable gap, as was noted before, between individual and common *praxis*.   Moreover, the dialectical movement from series to group is quite capable of being reversed in various ways, the most significant of which concerns possibilities of *institutionalizing* groups. A group cannot long remain *à chaud*, in a state of most complete totalization, and so the apportionment of tasks and functions begins; it is in the context of this movement of institutionalization that Sartre analyzes the phenomenon of "the oath," with its dual aspects of fraternity and terror, already mentioned in the discussion of love in Sartre's philosophy.   The complexity of the structures of our daily social life results from the fact that serialities and groups of all sorts, frequently changing and interacting with one another, are the stuff of which those structures are composed.   Sartre's analyses in the *Critique* sometimes reach extremes of complicated detail never attained in *Being and Nothingness*, but I have now summarized most of the principal concepts which are basic to his social philosophy.

The terminology is different, the phenomena under investigation are different, and the methodological emphasis has shifted from phenomenology, which plays no explicit role at all in the *Critique*, to dialectics. How is it possible, under the circumstances, even to begin to draw a comparison?   Sartre himself provides one important clue in a footnote in the *Critique*.   He suggests that "for the persons who have read *Being and Nothingness*," there are functional similarities between *praxis* and being-for-itself, on the one hand, and inert matter and being-in-itself on the other hand.   He goes even further by identifying *praxis* with "consciousness (of) self," an expression frequently employed in his earlier work.   But he concludes the same footnote with the cautionary note that *Being and Nothingness* might wrongly have led one to believe that the fundamental alienation of self-consciousness comes "from a prenatal choice," whereas in fact he has now indicated that it results from the relationship of man to his environment.[70]   At

---

70 Ibid. p. 286.

a very minimum, this leaves one with the impression that Sartre does not regard his later work as constituting a complete rejection of the earlier framework.

But what Sartre himself feels or does not feel in this regard cannot, in any case, be our ultimate ground for deciding the issue. In other words, if Sartre, in later installments of his autobiography, should maintain that the philosophical positions developed in the *Critique* represent a very radical departure from those of *Being and Nothingness*, we should have to consider such testimony interesting and important, but it would not dispense us from having ourselves to ask, from our perspective of greater distance, whether or not this was true. Let us briefly reconsider a few strands of the philosophically relevant evidence which might presumably support the thesis of discontinuity.

First, there is the remarkable shift in language. If it were simply a question of changing certain words on a one-to-one basis, so that "*praxis*" referred to nothing more dissimilar to "being-for-itself" than does the French translation of the latter, "*être-pour-soi*," there could of course be no doubt about the unity between the phases of Sartre's thought. But the connotations of "*praxis*" also seem different, in many respects, from those of "being-for-itself." We may pass over two important differences in connotations, first, the different historical overtones that have been introduced by the use of a word so closely associated with the writings of Karl Marx, and second, the fact that "*praxis*" is a word native to neither the French nor the English language, requiring constant underlining throughout any text, and thus tinged with a certain capacity for mystification.[71] But the word itself, as contrasted with "being-for-itself," provides sufficient material for indicating, at the very least, an important shift in emphasis. "*Praxis*" (considered, for the moment, without reference to its particular use by Sartre) signifies sensuous activity, whereas "being-for-itself" suggests far more exclusively the activities of consciousness. And this is certainly one of the shifts in his thought that Sartre has effected: he now attempts, even more thoroughly than in the past, to avoid an excessively intellectualist analysis of human action and of human reality in general. Thus, for example, the revolutionary change from serial to group forms of social activity need not be, for Sartre, the outcome of a carefully preconceived plan on the part of the participants; changes occur, first of all, as the result of pressures from external material circumstances, and there is very little of reflective thought behind the first stages of such events as the French Revolution. The atmosphere of *Being and Nothingness*, on the other hand, seems far more cerebral; even while rejecting the charge of idealism, for example, Sartre affirms "the identity of being-for-itself and knowl-

---

71 This was a significant point of criticism raised by Roger Garaudy during the intellectual auto-da-fé organized by the French Communist Party in opposition to Merleau-Ponty's Les Aventures de la dialectique. Cf. R. Garaudy, G. Cogniot, et al., Mésaventures de l'anti-marxisme, *Editions Sociales*, Paris, 1956. It is confusing, says Garaudy (p. 66), to use a foreign word like "praxis" when a good French equivalent, "la pratique," is available.

edge."[72]   A complementary change in emphasis could also be noted
with respect to nonhuman reality: Sartre constantly equates materiality
with inertness in the *Critique*, and yet, as I have already had occasion
to point out, matter's inertness seems sometimes capable of imposing
itself on human activity to an extent never suggested in *Being and
Nothingness* even in the analyses of such phenomena as masochism,
in which the human being vainly endeavors to reduce himself to being-
in-itself.   In general, then, the non-conscious elements in reality
would seem to have gained power at the expense of the conscious
elements in the evolution of Sartre's thought.   And this observation
can be confirmed by comparing the language in which Sartre characterizes the basic elements of his earlier and later philosophical works.

Second, quite in keeping with the increased emphasis on what I have very
broadly labeled "the non-conscious elements in reality," the later
Sartre deals with a very different set of phenomena from those with
which he was formerly most concerned.   It is not simply as if Sartre
had set to work to deal with divergent specific areas of investigation
in each of his two major books, and had deliberately "bracketed out"
all the irrelevant areas in each case; the underlying differences are far
more serious than this.   The very universe in which Sartre lives and
sees us all as living seems to have changed radically from the first
period to the second.   It would be impossible to portray this change
adequately in a few sentences, but it is obviously related very closely
to Sartre's previously quoted remark that, in the immediate postwar
period, he discovered that he made "history" just as M. Jourdain
made prose.   Although history is not the explicit topic of any part of
the *Critique* thus far published (since history is to be the focus of the
second volume), the reader constantly feels its brooding presence, in
the sense that Sartre regards history as a vast, extremely complex
movement of totalization, to which all significant lesser human collectivities, the objects of Sartre's first-volume analyses, will eventually
be seen to contribute.[73]   There is no similar impression to be derived
from *Being and Nothingness*, a clue to the relatively individualistic,
unhistorical character of which is Sartre's excessively celebrated remark that man is a useless passion.   To explain away such an enormous difference in world outlook by insisting on the obvious fact that
Sartre is investigating disparate areas of phenomena in his two works
is an inadequate response.   If future history, according to the later
Sartre, is to provide some sort of basis for making judgments about
the attitudes of commitment or noncommitment adopted by us all in
the present, then, to say the least, the "free project" of the individual
which serves as the source of action in both books will now have
taken on a new dimension in addition to those which it had at any
point in Sartre's earlier writing.

Third, there is a difference in philosophical *method* between the earlier and
the later Sartre.   It is true that in "*Question de méthode*," he advo-

---

[72] EN *268* (BN *216*).
[73] Cf. CRD *152*. *Sartre alludes to this view at several points throughout the* Critique.

cates a "progressive-regressive method," which entails investigating underlying structures of social reality as well as the lines of historical development; but the principal methodological emphasis in the *Critique of Dialectical Reason* is, of course, dialectical. Phenomenology, the method employed in *Being and Nothingness*, does not require either the confrontation and reconciliation of equipollent opposites or the synthetic, progressive movement essential to dialectics. There is a short section in *Being and Nothingness* concerning "The Dialectical Conception of Nothingness," in which Sartre finds fault with Hegel for, among other things, seeming to put nothingness on the same ontological level with being; it is only in this erroneous way, Sartre seems to be suggesting, that nothingness can be made to appear somehow to play a role equal to that of being in dialectical development.[74] Sartre's brief criticism here is not exceptionally well pointed, and he does not seem to have a clearly thought out conception of the possible differences between dialectics and phenomenology.[75] Even in light of his later discussions, it is very difficult to characterize briefly, with any degree of rigor, the nature of those allegedly important methodological differences that separate *Being and Nothingness* from the *Critique of Dialectical Reason*. But it would probably be useful to indicate at least one area in Sartre's philosophy, an area that is among the most crucial for his whole thought, in which the new reliance on the dialectical method seems to account in large measure for a certain shift in theoretical conceptions: the question of human freedom. The previously cited passage in the *Critique*, in which Sartre both suggests terminological parallels between his two major writings and also indicates the necessity for rejecting a possible interpretation of his earlier treatment of the source of alienation of self-consciousness which would root it in some "prenatal choice" rather than in the relationship of man to environment, is very significant in this respect. Sartre does limit the range of freedom in the *Critique*: freedom is no longer equated with purely indeterminate choice. In *Being and Nothingness*, it would be difficult to conceive of a chapter heading comparable to the following one, which is located at approximately the halfway point in the *Critique*: "Of the Group. The Equivalence of Freedom as Necessity and of Necessity as Freedom. Limits and Significance of Every Realistic Dialectic."[76] The "equivalence" of which Sartre speaks here suggests at once a certain determinacy that was not present in his earlier treatment of freedom, and an ac-

[74] EN 47–52 (BN 12–16).

[75] On the other hand, it does not seem to me that the idea of dialectics provided by Merleau-Ponty in his book on the subject, Les Aventures de la dialectique, is much more precise than that indicated in Sartre's earlier writings. It is Les Aventures, it will be recalled, which contains Merleau-Ponty's criticism of Sartre's "ultra-Bolshevism." In his concluding chapter, Merleau-Ponty writes: "The adventures of the dialectic, the most recent of which we have retraced, are the self-referential errors by which it must necessarily pass, because it is by definition a thought with many centers and many points of entry, and it needs time to explore them all" (p. 274). A less ambiguous notion of "dialectics" than this one is obtainable, I think, from Sartre's Critique.

[76] CRD 381.

ceptance of the same dialectical principle of placing contradictories on a level with one another for which Sartre had criticized Hegel in his earlier work.

These are some of the most serious philosophical considerations that can be raised in opposing the view that a systematic unity is traceable across the development of Sartre's thought. But it is interesting to note that none of these allegedly radical changes can be established with the *precision* that one would wish. Of course, the *words* are different, but to what extent do such differences, once terminological equivalences have been settled, point to genuine discrepancies in philosophical referents or even in connotations? Of course, the phenomena of the region of intersubjectivity, of social structures, are not identical with the basic ontological phenomena examined in *Being and Nothingness*, but to decide to what extent the divergencies in world view between the latter book and the *Critique* depend merely on such differences in the phenomena under investigation, and to what extent they represent definitive changes in ontological framework, is an almost hopeless undertaking. By the same token, to *name* an acknowledged change in philosophical methodology is not the same thing as to decide that a truly substantive change has occurred as a result; for example, does the different understanding of human freedom, with which we are left after having read the later Sartre, point to a real doctrinal reversal or merely to a needed further clarification? Sartrean freedom has become more and more limited, as Sartre himself is said to have admitted to an interlocutor,[77] and yet man's *capacity* for radically free action has never been denied. A parallel situation will be found to hold in the cases of most other allegedly substantive changes in Sartre's later thought. In short, the contrary evidence is not strong enough to warrant abandoning our earlier assumption of a fundamental, underlying unity.

One very noteworthy fact is that Marxists of many different stripes, both from among those subject to Communist Party discipline and from among those who abjure all party affiliations, have generally found the self-proclaimed Marxism of the later Sartre to be less than completely familiar. At best, Sartre's "Marxism" is *highly* revisionist, even though Sartre appears to have become relatively well acquainted with Marx's writings. This implies that there remains a strong admixture of other elements, and those other elements are, of course, most of the basic components of the more familiar Sartrean existentialism. *Praxis*, like being-for-itself, remains essentially free, indeterminate, and creative, the elusive agent that formulates projects and that is never entirely reducible to inert being-in-itself. The reciprocal relationships between oneself and "the Other" play as pervasive a role in the *Critique* as they did in Sartre's earlier writing. The *Critique* introduces no additional, secondary agent besides the individual human person into Sartre's universe, because group *praxis* is said always to be the product of the *praxis* of individuals, itself constituted and never

---

[77] *Wilfrid Desan, The Tragic Finale, Harper Torchbooks, New York, 1960, p. xvi. This interview took place in 1956.*

constitutive, and thus the group can never, contrary to organicist political theory and even to many collectivist versions of Marxism, have "a life of its own" independent of its members.   Sartre's continued rejection of the contention, discussed earlier in this chapter, that an ontology supplied by natural science might provide a satisfactory account of human reality becomes even more meaningful and clear in terms of his new attack on Friedrich Engels' conception of a larger "dialectics of nature," of which human history would be simply one episode.   Sartre makes no more concession than before to the notion that human nature is in any way definable in terms of fixed "essences," and on this point he is on the soundest possible grounds in believing that Marxism and existentialism are at one.   The "unbridgeable gaps" which prevented the achievement of totalities, whether in love or in any other human endeavor, and left all of human existence with a certain playlike quality in *Being and Nothingness* are as omnipresent as ever in Sartre's social universe, even though they may no longer be taken to justify a slightly "aesthetic" attitude on the part of the philosopher.   And lengthy descriptions of a wide range of concrete situations, even though the adjective "phenomenological" is no longer explicitly attached to them by their author, continue to grace the pages of Sartre's recent writing, as well as to clarify its potential obscurities, just as they did in the earlier stage of his philosophy.

On the other hand, some of the elements that at first seemed most novel about the later Sartre have, in reality, solid roots in the pages of *Being and Nothingness*.   The greater emphasis on the human being as active ("*praxis*"), rather than as conscious, will seem less radical if we simply recall that Sartre's conception of being-for-itself, and even of the imagination in his earliest writings, has always been ongoing and creative as opposed to static and contemplative; being-for-itself could at no time have been thought of as pure, immutable intellect. Nor is the sense of history quite so new to Sartre as he claims in the short passage cited from his eulogy of Merleau-Ponty: his analyses, in *Being and Nothingness*, of the three aspects of *time* (past, present, future) as "*ek-stases*" of being-for-itself (that is, as dimensions of the self which it can only grasp by reference to an ultimately elusive external reality) serve as a possible starting point for an interpretation of history which, while extremely individualistic, could be made viable. The conception of "commitment," albeit in a less definitive form than that held by Sartre at present, plays a very important role both in *Being and Nothingness* and especially in the brief but pointed essay, "Existentialism and Humanism."   Finally, it is Sartre's flair for a dialectical way of thinking and writing, for vivid oppositions and brilliant syntheses, even in a book in which he does not yet claim to be a dialectician, that gives *Being and Nothingness* a stylistic and methodological character which sharply distinguishes it from comparable phenomenological writings of Husserl or Heidegger.

As we have now seen in some detail, the question of unity within the *corpus* of Sartre's philosophical productions is hardly more susceptible of a brief, summary resolution than was the issue of truth.   If we accept the truth of one prominent aspect of Sartre's own thought, we could hardly expect a living philosophy to exhibit anything but an incomplete, fleeting, changing unity; to have attempted to look at Sartre's work as if it were a completed totality is already to have distorted it. Perhaps this brief excursus into a few of the themes of the *Critique of Dialectical Reason*, which is a less polished, less well structured, and generally more forbidding book than *Being and Nothingness*, has had the major advantage of illustrating the *elusiveness* of any meaningful conception of unity, other than the mathematical one, in a complex universe.

The *Critique*, of course, also raises many new questions about the *truth* of Sartre's philosophy, especially in terms of the applicability of that philosophy to the entire domain of social life which so dominates contemporary human existence. These questions hold much greater philosophical interest if my assumption concerning an underlying unity is accepted, because on that assumption Sartre's *Critique* is a very welcome rarity—to wit, a systematic, existentialist philosophy applied to the whole range of social and political problems—instead of being simply the semijournalistic reflections on society and politics of one more intelligent person who happens also to be an existentialist philosopher. Some years ago, John Wild called for the development of a new Western theory about man which could successfully compete, on the level of ideas, with Marxism; he saw existentialism as the best candidate.[78] It is, of course, ironic from this point of view that the most exhaustive existentialist plunge into social theory thus far has been Sartre's, and that it has been blatantly Marxist in direction. But it seems to me that the existentialist, exceedingly anti-Stalinist Marxism of Sartre serves as a more adequate explanation of some of the fundamental social phenomena of our contemporary world than do most of the older, more traditional political philosophies of liberal democracy. Sartre's account, for example, of the "serial" impotence experienced by millions of listeners as, in the isolated solitudes of their own homes, they hear their government's policy line being presented smoothly and unquestioningly in a radio broadcast seems much more immediately relevant to the central social facts of our own time than do abstract theories about representative governments' serving as the "trustees" of a majority "will." His detailed, plausible analysis of what current sociological jargon labels, mysteriously, as "rising social consciousness" gives much more meaning to revolutionary phenomena, both political (overthrows of governments) and other (e.g., protest movements), than do the many well-intentioned attempts to enumerate either certain basic "rights" or certain naked "interests" said to inhere eternally and irrevocably in individual human natures or in sovereign states; Sartre's analysis, once again, deals *existentially* with the concrete individual in social structures rather than with abstract qualities imposed on all persons by a philosopher's fiat. His explanation of the basis of violence and of class and other social struggles, traceable partly to his early investiga-

[78] *John Wild,* The Challenge of Existentialism, *Indiana University Press, Bloomington, Ind., 1959, p. 267.*

tions of "being-for-another" and partly to his new insistence on the role of material *scarcity* in our world, renders intelligible those ugly and monstrous aspects of the same world which we should prefer to exclude from our consciousness, but the deliberate neglect of which can only lead to even greater violence in the long run; at the same time, Sartre so qualifies and clarifies Marx's excessively simplistic conception of "class" as to overcome some of the most obvious historical and philosophical objections to the latter. Finally, Sartre's description of the successive steps in a group's institutionalization gives more insight into the rise of Communist bureaucracy and the rigidifying of "official" Marxism under Stalin than do those all too facile cold war generalizations, especially popular fifteen or twenty years ago before the so-called "thaw" showed how quickly history can outdate facile generalizations, about the inevitable gestalt of all systems of "totalitarianism."

It should certainly be admitted that Sartre's own deep sympathies for this social philosophy, strongly influenced both by other existentialist philosophers and by Marx, but ultimately and inevitably very much his own, has sometimes led him to make political pronouncements of a kind equally as careless and facile as those of the anti-Communist ideologues to whom he is so much opposed; this is especially true, as I have already mentioned, in the case of some of his *Situations* essays, such as "*Les Communistes et la paix.*" He knows much better than most people that Marxism and the Communist Party are not identical, but he occasionally writes as if he had momentarily forgotten this. At such moments in Sartre's writings, the truth is obscured. But there must, on the whole, be a great deal of truth in a philosophy that is applicable in so many ways to the social phenomena which loom largest in the contemporary consciousness, and which most rival social philosophies and nonphilosophical theories are either totally unable to deal with or else unable to explain beyond the level of sheer empirical description. Some classical philosophies, however, are in a better position than purely descriptive theories to contest Sartre's claims, for their adherents may with good reason assert that their aims are primarily normative rather than descriptive. This serves to emphasize the need, at this point, for an explicit consideration of that most tantalizing and already much-debated subject, the Sartrean ethic.

3. Sartre
on Value

Questions about ethics, "how to live," are at once the most central and elusive of all major areas in existential philosophy. Sartre has undoubtedly devoted as much thought to such issues as any professional philosopher of his age could have devoted. Probably for this very reason, it would be foolish to begin by asking, within a Sartrean context, any of the more traditional questions which were supposedly, at one time or another, the keys to ethical philosophy—e.g., What is the good for Sartre? or How, according to Sartre, ought one to live? or

What is Sartre's highest value? or What does Sartre consider the basic principle(s) of morality?—and to expect a direct, partisan answer in terms of traditional categories. George Alfred Schrader's introductory essay in this volume has already indicated, in large measure, why this is so: the questions themselves are badly put, the traditional categories misleading. Existentialism, as exemplified here in Sartre's thought, brings with it a revolutionary outlook on the subject of moral philosophy.

There are, however, a few preliminary remarks that can be made by way of showing the basis of any Sartrean ethic and the reason why that ethic, if such a thing is to exist at all, cannot be expressed in terms of traditional categories. For Sartre, there must be some ontological basis for the subjects that moral philosophers discuss, and the only such basis possible within the framework of his ontology is, of course, being-for-itself, man. In *Being and Nothingness*, he devotes one section of the chapter on "The Immediate Structures of the For-itself" to a treatment of "the For-itself and the Being of Value." It is here that he makes a very simple, unambiguous statement to which he would still subscribe without reservation: "These considerations suffice to make us admit that the human reality is that by which value arrives in the world."[79] Sartre will reject totally, as unprovable, ontologically impossible, and unjustifiable because of the potential limitations that it imposes on man's freedom, the suggestion that values exist in any way prior to man himself, or that any particular values *are* inevitably "imposed" on all men by some alleged essential nature of things. This is completely in keeping with his contention that there is no essential human nature. It can immediately be seen, by anyone who is familiar with the history of moral philosophy or even with ordinary, unreflective conceptions about the meaning of values, to what extent Sartre's position is an audacious departure. One possible critical reaction to this Sartrean starting point on the subject of values might be that it is reducible to a total moral relativism, which, while perhaps theoretically respectable, is neither useful nor morally defensible; nor would relativism be in keeping, it should be added, with the very forceful positions taken by Sartre on many of the critical moral issues of his own lifetime. This is one way of approaching the central problem concerning Sartre's pronouncements on the subject of goodness.

It is not altogether false to say that the Sartrean approach to ethics points to one supreme goal, namely, freedom. But to call this a value on a level with other values would be very misleading. In addition, the mere positing of "freedom" as a goal is sufficiently abstract and ambiguous to be acceptable to a very wide range of persons—even, for example, to some of the "bourgeois" ideologists of American neo-conservatism! There is also a further complication about this way of speaking, inasmuch as freedom has, quite rightly, been said to characterize being-for-itself in Sartre's thought, and must therefore be a starting point as well as a goal. If freedom is the ultimate objective and we are all *already* fundamentally free, we might expect a Sartrean ethic to exhibit the complacency of a Leibnzian world view. But we know, on other grounds, how absurd such an expectation would be.

There is at least one other attractively simple way of attempting to summarize Sartre's views on ethics in a single word; this time, the word is "authenticity." Innumerable are the occasions on which someone has written that the Sartrean saint (e.g., Genet, the playwright) is the person who exists authentically, that is, in accordance with his own deepest values, however radically they may differ from the values of his society. This, too, is important and not incorrect, but it is only a beginning in understanding Sartre's ethical outlook. The further problem with which we are still faced is perhaps best seen if we reflect on a mode of life which Sartre's philosophy most explicitly opposes to that of authenticity, namely, "bad faith." George Alfred Schrader, in his introduction, points to the difficulty here when he notes (page 40) that Sartre never indicates just *how* it might be possible to escape from living in the mode of bad faith, or, in terminology which has gained even more prominence in Sartre's later writings, to escape from all forms of "alienation." In short, although authenticity can rightly be pointed to as a Sartrean ethical ideal, it is not at all easy to see how anyone could ever really be said fully to have attained it. This is why a certain aura of pessimism surrounds Sartre's discussions of ethical issues.

The Sartrean pessimism should not be exaggerated, however, for it is very far indeed from the radical pessimism of a Schopenhauer which issues in a counsel of total inactivity. It is nothing new, in the history of thought, for a moral philosophy to hold out as an ideal some state or condition, such as "happiness," "virtue," or a "holy will," which is admitted to be unattainable in the fullest sense by any human being; if Sartre's existentialist approach to ethics is, as I have said, revolutionary, it must be so for reasons other than the seemingly impossible perfectionism suggested by his treatments of bad faith and authenticity. Crucial to Sartre's treatment of "bad faith" is the notion of the negativity and freedom of human consciousness—the fact, for Sartre, that the principle of identity is not constitutive of man. Bad faith comes about when the individual pretends to himself that he is something which in fact he is not. But, according to Sartre's view of consciousness, consciousness is *never* simply or fundamentally "what it is," since the human being always has the possibility of negating what may at present appear to another and even to himself as being definitive about his character. Consequently, the *possibility* of lapsing into the mode of bad faith can never be lacking, and the impossibility of the ideal of "sincerity" as Sartre eventually defines it ("to act so that I admit what I am in order that I may finally coincide with my being; in a word, to act so that I may exist in the mode of the in-itself"[80]) becomes evident. It might seem that Sartre is leaving us, at least in matters of ethics, with the caution to be aware of the almost infinite possibilities of lapsing into the mode of bad faith, and with the advice to do our best. This could be a challenging, exciting moral world in

[80] Ibid., p. 106 (BN 65–66).

which to live—a world in which we are thrown back on ourselves in the creation of values, and in which we are constantly subjected to the most rigorous scrutiny possible, not the scrutiny of some imaginary moral conscience "programmed" with values that have been imposed from without, but rather the scrutiny of our own most reflective selves.[81]   On the other hand, it could be a blind alley, for we must again inquire what "our best" could conceivably be in such a world, and whether the imperative to escape the snares of bad faith is meaningful if no indication is given as to the direction in which escape lies.   We are left, at the end of the chapter on "Bad Faith" in *Being and Nothingness*, with the tantalizing footnote alluded to in George Alfred Schrader's introduction, in which Sartre says, "This does not mean that one cannot radically escape bad faith.   But that supposes [what] we shall call authenticity, . . . the description of which has no place here."[82]

With this much as philosophical background, we are now in a better position to describe the principal pieces of evidence that have gone into creating what some historians of contemporary philosophy regard as a great enigma, the problem of the unwritten Sartrean text on moral philosophy.   The very last sentence of all in *Being and Nothingness* promises just such a forthcoming publication, and the fact that it was the final sentence ensured its attracting greater attention from more readers than a similar sentence buried on page 400 or 500 would have attracted.   Of course, no such book has ever come into existence. In 1947, Sartre's close colleague, Simone de Beauvoir, wrote a comparatively lightweight though not entirely valueless work entitled, in its English translation, *The Ethics of Ambiguity*.   This book was explicitly intended to meet the growing demand for a full treatment of ethical problems from an existentialist perspective, especially in light of the continuing failure of Sartre to fulfill his promise.   During the same year, 1947, Francis Jeanson wrote an excellent full-length study of Sartre's philosophy viewed as ultimately ethical in import; entitled *Le problème moral et la pensée de Sartre*, it drew the warmest praise from its subject himself, who again adverted to the unfinished character of his own reflections about ethics.[83]   So the situation has stood until very recently . The publication of the *Critique of Dialectical Reason*, volume I, has provided the occasion for another series of questions: Can the *Critique* itself, perhaps, be regarded as the fulfillment of Sartre's pledge?   One reviewer answers that question very

---

[81] *This seems to be Sartre's principal point about an existentialist ethics in* L'Existentialisme est un humanisme. *He discusses the moral dilemma of a former student of his whose only brother had been killed by the Germans and whose father, a collaborator, had become separated from the young man's mother. The former student was debating between remaining with his mother and joining the Free French forces in exile.   Such a dilemma, Sartre contends, cannot be resolved by any of the more traditional value systems.*

[82] EN *111* (BN *70*).

[83] *Sartre's remarks appear in a brief prefatory letter.   A new edition of* Le problème moral et la pensée de Sartre, *long out of print, has recently been published, together with a postscript on Sartre's later thought (Editions du Seuil, Paris, 1965).*

judiciously, by saying "Both yes and no,"[84] and I am afraid that this highly unsatisfactory answer will have to be the one to which we must all subscribe in the final analysis. The reason is twofold: not only does Sartre's existentialist perspective on ethical issues put into question the meaningfulness of some traditional ways of discussing ethical problems, as I have already indicated, but also there has been a considerable change in Sartre's own perspective on this particular matter since 1943. One of the most revealing indications of this comes in one passage of Simone de Beauvoir's most recent autobiography:

[As regards] his ethics properly speaking, Sartre abandoned it that year [1949] because he was convinced that " 'the moral attitude' appears when the technical and social conditions make positive ways of conduct impossible. Ethics is a combination of idealistic tricks to help you live through what the scarcity of resources and the lack of techniques imposes upon you."

A footnote reference here indicates that the passage is taken from Sartre's unedited notes.[85]

It should now be perfectly obvious why, given the views expressed here, a Sartrean text on ethics has become inconceivable. Nevertheless, the individual who holds this highly Marxian conception of ethics is hardly dispensed, thereby, from all further explanation. Ultimately, he will have to try to make somehow credible his vision of a kind of society in which both moral philosophy and even "the moral attitude" would be completely superfluous. More immediately, he will have to explain the basis upon which he can pretend to make consistent judgments about ethical issues during the present period, when, even if we allow his claim to have "seen through" the false facade of all traditional ethics, the scarcity of resources continues, and "positive ways of conduct" are therefore, presumably, not yet universally possible; in other words, he will have to outline a sort of "provisional morality," structurally reminiscent of Descartes' conception. First, however, even before he does these things, he will have to elaborate upon his view of ethics as idealistic trickery, in order to give even a potentially sympathetic audience, most of whom have been accustomed to thinking in quite different ways about "goodness," some feeling for what he means.

Sartre's most significant recent statement on ethical questions is undoubtedly that contained in a lengthy footnote on the subject of value ("in the *ethical* sense of the term and not in the economic sense, although the former has its basis in the latter")[86] in the middle of the *Critique of Dialectical Reason*. I think it best to reproduce here the gist of the main points made in this footnote. First of all, Sartre begins by denying that ethics is his concern in the *Critique*, thus apparently still leaving open the possibility that he may deal with the

---

[84] *Michel Dufrenne, review, Esprit, April, 1961, vol. 19, no. 294, p. 678.*
[85] *Simone de Beauvoir, La Force des choses, p. 218 (The Force of Circumstance, p. 199).*
[86] CRD 301.

subject at greater length in the future; such a study would not be a *text* on ethics, of course, but it would presumably go further in answering some of the questions that his position raises. Second, Sartre defines value as one form of alienation ("that of *praxis* itself," as distinguished from the more external alienation of the *objective* of one's activity which occurs, for example, in the case of material need); the phenomenon of value is the means by which, in all freedom, one imposes a certain inertness on one's own actions. But values are not at all entirely negative: they are at once several seemingly incompatible things, to wit, the *products* "of exploitation and oppression" (since they are developed as means of opposing what is inhuman in the existing state of society), the *denial* of exploitation and oppression ("even the aristocratic systems [of value], if not explicitly, at least by their internal logic"), and the *confirmation* of exploitation and oppression (even in the cases of value-systems developed by oppressed peoples, because these systems are a means of acceding to the alleged inevitability of their creators' lot). At times of revolutionary change, Sartre further contends, the values of the past, which have contributed, by their peculiar characters, to the revolution, now cease to have the meanings that they previously had and become mere history. Finally, he expresses an important disagreement with Marxism and, by implication, with Marx himself, by demanding a closer analysis of the familiar Marxist dictum, with which Sartre's own position may at first have appeared to be identical, that morality is simply a part of the "idealistic superstructure" of any precommunist form of society; Sartre points out the unresolved confusion of meanings between "morality" considered as the explicit ethical systems of the intellectuals of a given epoch, to which the dictum might fairly straightforwardly be applied, and "morality" considered as those implicit systems of values embodied in the activities and languages of whole given societies at given times, the denomination of which as "superstructures" is dangerously misleading. The rampant "moralism" of contemporary Soviet society, he believes, is part of the legacy of this very ambiguity.

The preceding synopsis of parts of Sartre's long footnote on value is useful, I think, in making more understandable his initially startling rejection of moral philosophy; one begins to realize that Sartre is fully aware of many of the nuances of the problem of "goodness," and to catch some glimpse of the intellectual perspective from which he regards ethical phenomena. It is important to note, for one thing, that Sartre regards ethics first of all in terms of free choices that define actions and only secondarily in terms of mere tabus that prohibit certain categories of actions. Systems of value perform the latter function, of course, and it is precisely for this reason that Sartre considers them to be forms of alienation. But the focus of his interest in ethical issues is very different from that of so many traditional moralists and legal theorists whose primary concern often appears to be simply to reaffirm, in systematic form, the prohibition against certain obviously inhuman acts such as murder. The very idea of needing to express the undesirability of murder as a systematic prohibition, a restriction of freedom, Sartre seems to feel, can only come about in a society in which alienated individuals have some good reasons for seeing countervailing "values" in the act of murder itself. In a society in which alienations had been abolished and in which objectives could be chosen in complete freedom, there would be no necessity whatever for the individual to "check" his project, so to speak, against an established system of values in order to see whether or not it was allowable. This suggests a still further clarification of Sartre's views, notably of his reasons for considering "morality" to be idealist trickery and ultimately dispensable. Whenever a value or a system of values is regarded as being "established," that is, as defining the limits of "permissible" action, it is always possible for the free human being to conceive of a system of values that would somehow go beyond or transcend the present one in the direction of what, if it were not for the idealist connotations that are by now irrevocably attached to the expression, we might call "the better." But no limit, except the empty one of infinity, could possibly be set to this process; any given value or set of values can always be transcended in this way. These considerations at once support the Sartrean critique of the concepts of "values" and "morality" as they have been regarded in most traditional types of ethical theory, as well as by ordinary individuals in their daily lives, and also suggest that there is a very positive side to Sartre's scattered but intensely penetrating and thorough remarks about ethical issues. They could be made, in short, to serve as the basis of a positive Sartrean theory about "ethics," whether or not the word itself, with all the connotations that it has come to acquire, would be completely acceptable to him. In any case, we must not allow a philosophical analysis to become totally incapacitated through an excessive concern about certain words.

The concepts of "choice" and of "free project" are central to Sartre's understanding of human activity in general, and thus of human activity considered in the light of ethical categories in particular. We may at least tentatively concede that in a world in which "the moral attitude" and values restrictive of freedom no longer existed, there would be no need to ask, for example, whether racism was "wrong" and, if so, why; choices made and projects formed would *ipso facto* be directed towards objectives that were in some way desirable or constructive. Moral relativism would not be a potentially dangerous position at all in a society which had succeeded in totally eliminating the need for systematic morality. But ours is not yet such a society, and we do, therefore, crave some sense of direction as a basis for making our choices and passing our judgments. Sartre himself, for example, is constantly contending that certain social and/or political movements are good and others bad or undesirable, and he clearly does not regard his preferences as being purely "subjective" in the sense of being totally undemonstrable. This is the problem of what I have, in an intentionally provocative way, termed "provisional morality" in Sartre: What can be the basis for our choices in the alienated world in which we still live? As a matter of fact, Sartre's answer to this question is already contained in the reflections which have led us to ask it; it is also the key answer in Simone de Beauvoir's *Ethics of Ambiguity*. The answer is, quite simply: The future:

it is in the light of the future, which is the meaning and the very substance of action, that a choice will become possible. The men of today will be sacrificed to those of tomorrow, because the present appears as the facticity that must be transcended towards freedom. No action is conceivable without this sovereign affirmation of the future.[87]

In other words, the very concept of a "project" suggests not merely a going outside of or beyond one's present self as it is at the present time, but also a movement in a *temporal* direction, towards a future self which one is not yet. This fact, when placed in the context of a completed social philosophy and of a contemplated philosophy of history, can serve as a meaningful basis for the value choices and judgments which are still required of all of us in an alienated world.

There is no doubt that the Sartrean approach to ethics, at least as it has evolved in recent years, is very much dominated by the considerations of his social philosophy. But it is easy to draw improper conclusions from this. Sartre's social philosophy, like that of Marx, in no way downgrades the importance of the individual in favor of some mystical higher good that is alleged to be discoverable in social collectives, as has sometimes been charged. Quite the contrary, for the whole purpose of this philosophy's vision of the future is to promote, through the *means* of common social action, an ultimate liberation of the individual and an opening up of possibilities to him to an extent never previously achieved. In other words, the social dimension now dominates Sartre's approach to ethics precisely *because* he has become so acutely aware of the need to liquidate all the alienating features of social structures for the sake of the *individual*. On the other hand, the social emphasis also implies that problems of the sorts depicted in Sartre's plays about Communist Party members caught in ethical crises, *Dirty Hands* and *Nekrassov*, become *serious* problems, to which the answer is nothing so simple as the automatic decision in favor of the individual over the social movement which would be more likely to be made, for example, by Albert Camus (who broke with Sartre in part over this very issue) or by a total devotee of the Kantian ethic. In short, the ethical concept of "objective meaning"—of a responsibility attaching to one's actions in light of their possible effect of the course of history, rather than simply on the basis of one's subjective intentions (e.g., "*meaning* well") in performing those actions—becomes a very important one in Sartre's thought, even though the particular phrase that I have used for it does not have any special status in his technical vocabulary. This is just another way of characterizing the lesson that Sartre learned from Merleau-Ponty's *Humanisme et terreur*, where the problem of historical responsibility

---

[87] Simone de Beauvoir, Pour une morale de l'ambiguïté, Gallimard, Paris, 1947, p. 161.

is treated very explicitly.[88]   Sartre does not, of course, maintain, as Merleau-Ponty more or less charged him with maintaining after the reversal of political positions on the part of both of them,[89] that the Communist Party is at present the sole judge of whether one has acted well or badly in the light of one's historical responsibility; this would be an impossible position for Sartre, in any case, since he has been so severely criticized so often by the Party in France.   But it is important to note that the orientation of Sartre's approach to ethical issues in the light of a certain vision of the historical future has this important consequence: even though the individual is the *goal* of social action, he cannot by himself, in isolation from all his circumstances, be its ultimate standard.

What remains to be discussed on the subject of Sartre and value is what might be called the "substantive" question, the most difficult of all. In short, what *is* the vision of the historical future to which I have so frequently been referring?   The word "substantive" must be employed in a more or less honorary sense, because, in fact, it is not possible to say a great deal of a positive nature by way of characterizing or detailing the envisaged future society on the basis of anything that Sartre has yet published.   Marx is notorious for having experienced the same difficulty in trying to talk about the full-fledged communist society of the future in his *1844 Manuscripts*.   To draw the seemingly obvious conclusion from Marx's historical failure would, I think—as is usually the case with seemingly obvious conclusions—be precipitate and erroneous.   The conclusion in question is that the paucity of details about the future society shows the whole conception of it to be hopelessly utopian in the most pejorative sense of the word; the really confirmed bourgeois thinker, as Marx and Sartre would both regard him, might at this point even offer his reason why such futurism as theirs is hopelessly utopian: Because you can't change human nature. This shows that the issue can be joined even at the level of ontology, at which our discussion began.   If, however, one agrees with Marx and

---

[88] Humanisme et terreur, Gallimard, Paris, 1947, is Merleau-Ponty's attempt to understand better some of the more disturbing events in the then-recent history of the Communist Party, such as the Moscow purge trials of the 1930s, in the light of "the stern Marxist rule which insists that a man be defined, not by his intentions, but by what he does, and an action not by its subjective meaning, but by its objective meaning" (p. 9). This makes all the more strange Merleau-Ponty's later renunciation of the Marxism of his earlier years as having been "Kant in disguise," a moral a priorism (Les Aventures de la dialectique, p. 312); one would have thought that Kant's position was, if anything, closer to the "definition of a man by his intentions" which Merleau-Ponty had denounced. The only reply from the Sartrean camp to Merleau-Ponty's attack on Sartre in Les Aventures was that undertaken by Simone de Beauvoir in an article entitled "Merleau-Ponty et le pseudo-sartrisme" (Les Temps Modernes, pp. 114–115, June–July 1955; here, she used her antagonist's strange allusion to Kant in order to set the tone of her polemic in the opening sentence: "When, in the light of the Korean War, Merleau-Ponty discovered that he had up to that time confused Marx with Kant, he realized that he must renounce the Hegelian idea of the end of history and concluded to the necessity of destroying the Marxist dialectic" (p. 2072).

[89] Merleau-Ponty, Les Aventures de la dialectique, p. 175.

Sartre to the extent of accepting the possibility that what is improperly labeled "human nature" is somehow alterable, and if one further admits that the most important single characteristic of the most desirable society of the future would be the maintenance of a level of individual freedom never before achieved, then a pellucidly logical reason for our futurists' failure to specify many details about that society begins to emerge almost of itself: if that society is to be genuinely *free*, then the details of its development cannot be predicted.

What can legitimately be done, however, is to talk about the future society in more or less structural terms, first and foremost in terms of the achievement of a reign of freedom. It is now possible to see better why "freedom" can be called the supreme goal of Sartrean ethics, as noted near the beginning of this section, even though the ambiguity of this statement made it seem almost completely valueless at the time. Other formulations, following from this first one, are also possible within the framework of Sartre's philosophy. For example, the future society would be one in which all alienations, or at least all alienations of a harmful and avoidable sort (since Sartre has never fully resolved the question, mentioned earlier, of whether *all* forms of alienation and of bad faith are avoidable by anyone), had been abolished; Sartre ponders, and asks his readers to ponder, the feasibility of this:

To what extent will a socialist society banish atomism in all its forms? To what extent will collective objects, signs of our alienation, be dissolved in a true intersubjective community where the only real relations will be those of men with one another? . . .[90]

Furthermore, the future society would be one in which, in the technical terminology of Sartre's *Critique*, the *serial* form of existence had been ended and "group *praxis*" could prevail "forever."[91] This suggestion indeed approaches the limits of conceivability. Finally, Sartre often speaks of the future society, in a way curiously analogous to some defenders of contemporary American capitalism, as one in which "the regime of scarcity" would also have been abolished. However, given the commonly accepted fact that "scarcity" is such a historically relative concept, we stand in need of a more careful explanation than any as yet provided by Sartre of what would constitute its abolition. "Scarcity" is a purely material phenomenon, and its elimination is therefore conceivable only as a result of certain technological advances. It is important to point out that Sartre's structural description of the desirable free society of the future, by reference to which our actions in the present can be given a direction, looks to a time at which the entire Marxist philosophy itself, including, presumably, its Sartrean variant, will be outmoded. The reason is obvious enough: insofar as Sartre is writing during a period in which alienation and inhumanity are still the order of the day and in which, consequently, treatments of ethical issues are still required of those philosophers who look to the future possibility of abolishing "the moral attitude"

[90] *CRD 349.*   [91] *Ibid.*, p. 351.

entirely, much of what he says in this area will have a merely historical interest if and when the future is ever reached:

*As soon as there will exist for all a margin of real freedom beyond the pro-
duction of life, Marxism will have had its day: a philosophy of freedom will
take its place. But we have no means, no intellectual tool, no concrete
experience which might permit us to conceive either of that freedom or of
that philosophy.*[92]

Many of Sartre's basic philosophical conclusions in the area of
ontology, however, on which I have shown the framework of his social
philosophy to depend in large part, would presumably continue to be
valid and relevant at such a time. The reign of freedom must remain
something of an enigma within Sartre's Marxist-influenced thought
about ethical problems, both because of the very nature of the concept itself, and also because Sartre has thus far only alluded to it
rather than attempted to deal with it in detail. Perhaps the second
volume of the *Critique*, as a discussion of Sartre's social philosophy
in the new context of a theory of historical development, will contain
a more adequate account of this vision. It seems quite apparent, in
any case, that any attempt to understand what "goodness" might
possibly mean for Sartre, that is, on what basis it might become possible within his philosophy to *evaluate* individual or social actions, will
eventually have to come to grips with the problem of the significance
of just such a vision. All the categories employed by Sartre in dealing
with ethical questions, both in the earlier and in the later phases of
his thought—freedom, authenticity, bad faith, alienation, choice, responsibility, group *praxis*, and so on—must finally be referred back
to the kind of conceivable, possible world which, despite the much
more obvious veneer of pessimism and biting criticism that overlies
Sartre's discussions of ethical and social phenomena, remains the
objective basis on which all such criticism can be justified.

In conclusion, our consideration of the Sartrean ethic—or perhaps, more
properly speaking, of the attempted Sartrean transcendence of ethics
—leads us back with a vengeance to the two main questions which
occupied us in the preceding sections of this chapter: Is there unity
between the earlier and later stages of Sartre's discussion of the subject? and Is his analysis of value true? I have already attempted to
answer the first question, and my answer here is clearly in the affirmative. The Sartrean social philosophy seems to me to be a needed
complement, rather than a contradiction, of what was said in *Being
and Nothingness* about bad faith, value, and free choice. The fact
that Simone de Beauvoir's short study, supposedly based as it was on
the existentialist philosophy of *Being and Nothingness*, pointed accurately to some of the principal conclusions of Sartre's later writing on
the subject helps to sustain my point here. It is true that there has
been some change in Sartre's perspective, for he could not now write
the book on ethics that he once promised. But the change is rather
one in his view of the nature of ethics, or of moral philosophy, than
in his more substantial conceptions either of man or of "goodness"

---

[92] Ibid. (*"Question de méthode"*), p. 32 (Search for a Method, p. 34).

and its opposite. There is an understandable fear on the part of *some* philosophers who are sympathetic to existentialism that Sartre has surrendered his earlier existentialist insights to the allurements of Marxism; what I have said in this section may seem to them a confirmation of their fears. On the contrary, it seems to me that the evolution of Sartre's thinking has served to show, among other things, how very much of a protoexistentialist "the early Marx," as distinguished from Marx as popularized in the late nineteenth century and as interpreted by most of his followers, was in his ways of approaching ethical problems. The achievement of Sartre's new social orientation is to give, as I have expressed it, a certain "direction" to the many brilliant but extremely inconclusive insights about values and moral action contained in *Being and Nothingness*. The Sartre of the same period, in his famous little essay, insisted that "existentialism is a humanism." But there were critics who continued to wonder *why* this could be said to be so: Sartre had analyzed well the sorts of possible choices open to human beings, but he had made no serious attempt to explain how "humanity" could serve as a value or an ideal. His own later writing, uniting as it does both his earlier existentialist conceptions and the often forgotten humanist strain in Marxism, is a first step towards delineating in a positive way the humanist goal for man.

Our final question is the extremely baffling one whether Sartre's analysis of ethical phenomena is true or valid. In a sense, his analysis never leaves the descriptive level, to which alone judgments of truth and falsehood can be applied; it never prescribes "what ought to be." Initially, to ask whether Sartre's approach to ethics is correct or not is to ask whether his ontology is correct, for it is on the basis of the view of man as being-for-itself, creator of values, capable of projecting himself into a vast variety of inauthentic modes of existence, that Sartre is able to analyze the more specifically ethical problems. In fact, there is no hiatus between Sartre's ontology and his ethical insights, and this is what has led some to complain in Sartre's case, as in Hegel's, Marx's, and those of many of Sartre's fellow existentialists, that his philosophy "has no ethics." There is an undoubted brilliance about the ease with which Sartre is able to discuss self-deception, race hatred, sadism—in short, the whole gamut of what used to be dismissed as the aberrant human "vices"—in terms of a unified and concrete view of man as we in fact find him to be, rather than as an imposed theoretical construct would make him. The very fact that Sartre's approach to ethics has enabled him to make more intelligible certain types of actions that most past philosophers writing on moral subjects were content simply to dismiss as either wickedness or madness, thinking this to be an adequate explanation, speaks favorably for the validity of the Sartrean approach. It is impossible for us at this point to retrace our steps over the whole ground of Sartre's ontological conception of existential man and to ask again whether this conception is true, in order to ascertain whether what he says, for example, about the freely created and yet restrictive character of value systems is valid. But there are a few serious difficulties that may at least be mentioned concerning the final aspect of the Sartrean approach to ethics with which I dealt above, namely, his vision of the future possibilities open to man. Must systems of values or rules of conduct always retain the restrictive or alienating aspect of which Sartre speaks? Can there not be freely chosen values which serve as guides to action, as rules for achieving the objectives of human "projects," and yet which do not in any way narrow freedom by eliminating alternative possibilities? If so, then could the abolition of "ethics" ever, in any society, be as absolute as Sartre suggests? If not, then is a society without rules and therefore without some forms of "alienation" a really, concretely (as opposed to ideally) conceivable society at all? And, finally, even if the material condition of scarcity were at last somehow eliminated together with the residue of in-humanity which apparently must remain in all of us until such time, how could there be any guarantee of the *permanence* of the ensuing reign of freedom? In other words, would the possibility not always remain of men's freely choosing to return to a less desirable social state very much like our own? It is highly likely that Sartre will eventually attempt to deal with some of these dilemmas. I suspect that when he does so, he will in effect be forced to concede that there still remains a considerable future for anyone who wishes to pursue the career of moral philosopher. This would not, however, reverse the revolutionary change of perspective which Sartre, as both existentialist and Marxist at once, has achieved in approaching questions about "goodness." The fact that one can descriptively analyze, from this perspective, the phenomena traditionally dealt with by ethicists as well as other important kinds of human activity about which the literature in ethics has almost nothing to say, and that one can do so without either resorting to prescriptive preaching or becoming caught, as was once feared, in the morass of moral relativism, argues strongly in favor of the explanatory power and hence of the greater validity of the perspective in question.

"These are high-sounding words," it may be said, "and they serve to endow the Sartrean 'moral attitude' (for such it is and must be, despite all efforts to avoid this label) with a high degree of credibility and of respectability. But we must take to heart the lesson of Sartre's own autobiography, and not allow ourselves to become too fascinated with words. As for the naked reality behind the words, is it not something like this: a philosophy which ridicules and tries to destroy our existing institutions and beliefs in the name of, in earlier years, ethical nihil-ism, and, in later years, political totalitarianism?" The person who raises such brutal objections as these need not be wont to carry about with him either the jawbone of an ass or a thick sheaf of stock cer-tificates; almost all of us have, at one time or another and in one degree or another, felt some such reservations as these about the theories of any thinker who has exerted some real effect on our world, through his influence on ourselves and on others. There is always a large element of non-rational emotion about such a reaction, inas-much as it rejects calm philosophical analysis in favor of a sweeping, scarcely reflected overview. But, even though it cannot be delineated or discussed with the amount of precision that one would wish, it is not wholly beyond the scope of philosophy, either. It is important to make an effort to deal with a few vague but bothersome questions of this kind by way of concluding our discussion of Sartre's philosophy.

4. La Belle Ame

We return now to the superficial level of criticism from which, at the beginning of this chapter, we attempted to depart. Sartre must be placed back on the stage of the Baconian theater, where the strength, coherence, and explanatory power of his existentialist philosophical ideas are no longer very relevant by contrast with some more or less vague, general impressions of those ideas and of their place in the contemporary cultural spectrum. Here, we shall be more concerned with vague, *unfavorable* impressions than with vague, favorable ones, though of course we would find many of the latter to be equally as ungrounded as many of the former. Four general types of accusations, not all of them completely consistent with one another, seem to me to be particularly common among those who are critical or contemptuous of some basic feature or features of the entire Sartrean intellectual "project" and way of life, rather than simply of individual tenets of Sartre's philosophy. These are: that he is a moral nihilist; that he is an incorrigible romantic, a mythmonger, and at heart a terrorist; that he is a totalitarian in his demand for absolute commitments; and that he is too radical an innovator, devoid of respect for *philosophia perennis*. In each case, not surprisingly, we shall find that the precisely opposite accusation has also enjoyed some measure of popularity among critics. And although it is in dealing with accusations such as these that we begin to approach the sphere of relatively uninformed public opinion and mere hearsay, it will not be difficult for us to find philosophers and other intellectuals who have rendered final judgments on Sartre of much the same sweeping sort, sometimes after careful reflection and sometimes not.

The accusation of moral nihilism stems partly, of course, from the Sartrean theoretical stands that were noted in the preceding section of this chapter, but partly also from the cultural climate that prevailed in liberated France, or more accurately in liberated Paris, immediately after the war. The Occupation had been a period of great austerity, pervaded by a sense of personal and national humiliation. The liberation endowed Sartre's philosophy of freedom, in the extremely simplified form in which theories occasionally do become parts of the consciousnesses of large groups of people, with an aura of appropriateness that abetted his already growing reputation. But that reputation was not an altogether desirable one, for—to express it, as we must, in the imprecise generalities which typify this level of thinking—Sartre's insistence on the autonomy of the individual was widely regarded as a call to abdicate, rather than to acquire, moral responsibility. As Sartre points out, existentialism was connected, in the popular imagination of 1945, with lurid tales of "existentialist suicides" and of extreme eccentrics who applied to themselves the label of Sartre's philosophy; *Samedi Soir*, for example, ran the story of a prostitute who had allegedly accepted Sartre's invitation to come to his rooms, where he had shown her a cheese.[93]   Harsh charges of immoralism were not confined to the purely popular press, either; certain articles and small books by Communists and by right-wing Catholics, among others, made the same point in slightly more intellectual ways.   Within a couple of years, the conception of existentialism, the very name of which probably owed more to Sartre than to any other single thinker for its currency, as being essentially immoral was so widespread that a preeminently respectable press authorized publication of a study by a well-known, gifted European philosopher of law which bore the title, The Philosophy of Decadentism—A Study in Existentialism.   The book includes a long chapter on "The Decadentism of Sartre."[94]

Our previous discussions have made it quite unnecessary to reappraise this charge of immoralism, or of moral nihilism, as it relates to Sartre's philosophy.   Its application to his private life, which would be absurd, is in any case ruled out as a topic for discussion here.   But it has not been unknown for critics also to invoke the exactly opposite epithet, "moralist," in a derogatory way in speaking of Sartre's philosophical accomplishments.   The derogatory meaning that can be given to this term is best illustrated by Sartre himself, in his biting attack on Camus: "Your ethics [morale] changed first into moralism, today it is nothing more than literature, tomorrow it will perhaps be immorality."[95]   A "moralist," understood in this sense, is someone who merely preaches, who subordinates the search for truth, in approaching moral issues, to the zeal for converts.   There is, in fact, a tone of pompous moralism about Camus' "Letter to the Director of Temps Modernes," i.e., to Sartre, and a somewhat similar tone (though in support of a very different political orientation) seems to me detectable in some of Sartre's more occasional essays—for example, in parts of his series of newspaper articles on the Cuba of Fidel Castro.   In his more serious philosophical works, Sartre seems most of the time, by dint of what must be continual self-discipline, to avoid such unattractive "moralism," but it is surely a greater potential pitfall in his writings than is the moral nihilism so frequently alleged by his earlier critics.

Second, is Sartre a romantic?   We must first try to establish what this word might mean when used, as critics often tend to use it, in a pejorative sense.   At base, the romantic is one who substitutes feeling or sentimentality for substantial argument.   Romanticism in philosophy may appear in many subtle forms, most of which must, in some way or other, involve a misuse of language for the purpose of emphasizing drama and rhetoric at the expense of truth.   It is in this sense, I think, that Sartre can most plausibly be accused of romanticism in his philosophical writings.   Do not the extreme contrasts between being-in-itself and being-for-itself and between praxis and inert matter, to

93 "Merleau-Ponty," Situations, IV, p. 211 (Situations, p. 249).
94 Norberto Bobbio, The Philosophy of Decadentism—A Study in Existentialism, tr. D. Moore, Blackwell, Oxford, 1951.
95 "Réponse à Albert Camus," Situations, IV, p. 125 (Situations, p. 104).

take the most obvious examples, excessively accentuate the drama of struggle in human existence? Do not Sartre's concepts themselves— "the for-itself," "the look," "totalization," "the oath"—either originally possess or else come to acquire emotive connotations that make them seem to have lives of their own, far removed from the roles in explaining reality that they were originally supposed to play? In short, is Sartre not preeminently guilty of the romantic ploy of "mystification" that he himself has analyzed so well? We are concerned here not so much with the justice or injustice of such a charge as leveled against any specific term or concept in Sartre's technical vocabulary, but rather with the more sweeping dismissal of Sartre's entire thought as mere romanticism that receives from such charges whatever justification it may have. This sort of dismissal is rather commonplace, of course, among the more narrow-minded philosophers of ordinary language, but it also received strident and memorable expression in the most authoritative early Communist attack on French existentialism, Henri Lefebvre's *L'Existentialisme*. Despite the fact that *L'Existentialisme* is probably its author's poorest, most Stalinist-influenced work, it is still interesting inasmuch as it also shows the genuine concern of a reputable French philosopher, who had been influenced very little by Anglo-Saxon philosophical currents and who himself later led a movement among French Communist intellectuals in favor of "revolutionary romanticism" as opposed to "socialist realism" in literature, about a possible lack of rigor stemming from romanticism in Sartre's thought. Lefebvre's conclusion, from which his later, freer studies represent something of a retreat in the direction of moderation, was that Sartre was a philosopher for litterateurs and a litterateur for philosophers.[96] As crude as it may sound, this point of view has been shared by many other critics whose philosophical perspectives have nothing else in common with Lefebvre's.

The charge of undesirable romanticism is abetted even by some critics whose attitude is either indifferent or actually sympathetic. There are students of philosophy who are always more interested in a system's excitement quotient than its possible approximation to truth. Many of Sartre's ideas are undoubtedly exciting, and such students fasten on this excitement and neglect the substance. But perhaps the most significant commentary of all on Sartre's alleged romanticism is that contained in the concluding pages, previously referred to, of *The Words*, in which Sartre admits to having for a long time retained towards his early philosophy some of the attitudes of a religious person without the dogmas of a religious faith: "I was religious. A militant, I wanted to be saved by works; a mystic, I tried to unveil the silence of being by a vexed murmur of words, and, above all, I confused things with their names: that's belief."[97] This is again, of course, deliberate exaggeration, but it is the sort of comment in which critics who dismiss Sartre as a romantic can surely take delight. Most of the same critics, however, will say that the resolution mentioned by Sartre himself, and previously cited here, of "measuring the obvious-

96 Henri Lefebvre, L'Existentialisme, Editions du Sagittaire, Paris, 1946, p. 65.
97 Les Mots, p. 209 (The Words, p. 251).

ness of an idea by the displeasure that it caused" him is itself a romantic one; it is the sort of romanticism, they will contend, which issues in the often infernal machinery of the *Critique of Dialectical Reason*, with its tragic scenes of man dehumanized by the condition of scarcity, and with its insistence on the necessity of violence and even of "terror" for the achievement of any progress in a world cursed with such a condition. It does sound like a desperately romantic vision, does it not? A romanticism focusing on terror is no doubt self-contradictory and eventually self-annihilating, but, in a way, it is simply the ultimate form of the vice. Has Sartre not spoken his own condemnation of his romanticism, then, both in *The Words* and in his attempted later remedy for earlier aberrations?

Once again, as in the case of the charge of moral nihilism, there is no possibility of attempting a thorough examination at this juncture. A sweeping charge of this sort can only be substantiated or rejected by a detailed analysis of the philosophy in question. My comments must be confined to a few obvious points. First of all, if romance and romantic terror are notable characteristics of reality itself, an adequate philosophy will have to mirror those qualities, among others. Second, the coining of neologisms or the addition of new nuances to established words may as easily lead to the clarification as to the obscuring of phenomena, depending upon the manner in which such language reform is carried out; otherwise, neither philosophical nor ordinary language ought ever to be changed. Third, the writing of good philosophy is not incompatible with the maintenance of high literary standards; in fact, the style of Sartre's strictly philosophical efforts may more easily be faulted for its heaviness than for being excessively rhetorical, the quality that is usually associated with the charge of romanticism. Fourth, Sartre has also come under very heavy criticism for exactly the opposite reasons to those advanced against his alleged romanticism; the effort to apply systematic categories to human phenomena that defy systematization, it is sometimes said, is the height of *rationalism*, and there are critics to whom this label is considerably more pejorative than its putative opposite, romanticism. Sartre is indeed a rationalist who philosophizes about the romantic aspects of existence as well as its colorless aspects. He does so in works of high technical proficiency and of considerable rigor, which may be more easily faulted for excessive complexity than for the opposite. Nevertheless, his world is one of struggle more than of placidity, of violence more than of charity. Is this a romanticized illusion, or is this the world in which, whether or not we have always been aware of it, we live? That is a matter for the careful, thoughtful reader to decide.

The third accusation is that Sartre is an intellectual totalitarian in his demand for absolute commitments. His existentialism became associated very early with the idea of the necessity of commitment, and I reviewed some aspects of the development of this idea in my discussion of whether he could deal with the phenomenon of play. The most famous *locus* of this charge of total commitment is the long chapter by Merleau-Ponty on "Sartre and ultra-Bolshevism," in which Sartre is said to hold that the spontaneous decisions of the Communist Party "translate *as a matter of principle* the movement of history."[98] There is more substance to this accusation by Sartre's erstwhile colleague than might at first appear likely, because Sartre is impressed by the need to link theory to action, and he is aware of the inevitability of group action's assuming organizational form in order to continue to be effective; the Communist Party may well be the most effective organization for achieving desirable social objectives in a given country at the present time, as Sartre realizes. However, it should go almost without saying that Sartre is not committed to approving in advance of every decision or of most decisions taken by any Communist Party, and so Merleau-Ponty's characterization of his position here is essentially false. But many critics are far less concerned with the specific details of Sartre's commitments to this or that activity or group than they are with the more fundamental question of commitment in general. Philosophers especially wonder whether a committed philosophy, unlike a committed literature, may not be a contradiction in terms. Philosophy is supposed to be reflective wisdom, acquired through contemplation of the world or of a facet of it; this presupposes the establishment of a certain distance between the philosopher and his world, whereas the idea of a committed philosophy seems to permit no such distance.

It is apparent that this line of criticism, whether of Sartre or of any other philosopher who espouses a "cause," is at once persuasive and yet, when pushed to its limits, self-defeating. The philosopher must not allow his immediate concerns to narrow the range of his more fundamental ones, but he would not be intellectually honest if he denied that his systematic observations about existence had implications for his own and others' "*praxis*" in the present. Eloquent abstention from commitment, as Sartre has not been alone among existentialist thinkers in pointing out, is simply another form of commitment; it was Merleau-Ponty himself who once remarked, speaking of the problem of compromise in politics, that "We do not have the choice between purity and violence, but between different sorts of violence."[99] A certain vision of man, such as Sartre's, may *demand* action by the holder of that vision, within the limits of his own capabilities, to bring about its more complete realization. Commitment *per se* cannot, therefore, serve as a basis for condemnation; one may only be condemned or praised for the specific kind of commitment which one holds, and for the strength of the reasons behind this particular commitment. It would be rather difficult to demonstrate that the writer of *Being and Nothingness* and of the *Critique of Dialectical Reason* has sacrificed breadth of intellectual vision to his commitments. As for the further charge that Sartre insists upon these commitments in too dogmatic, absolute, or totalitarian a fashion, this may be largely a matter of personal style. Sartre is a forceful polemicist, quicker to condemn than to praise, especially in his more literary works; this fact, however, is relatively peripheral to the substance of

[98] *Merleau-Ponty, Les Aventures de la dialectique, p. 175.*
[99] *Merleau-Ponty, Humanisme et terreur, p. 117.*

the commitments themselves. It should also be pointed out that any commitment, however limited in scope and however subject to change it may be, must by definition be somehow absolute; otherwise, it would not be a genuine commitment.

One further reason for certain persons' reading of totalitarian implications into Sartre's insistence on the union of theory and practice and on the necessity for commitment is that the linking of the concept of "totalitarianism" with Sartre's Marxist political orientation can be used by interested parties to serve the contrary "cause" of anti-communism. It is just in reflecting on this point, however, that one suddenly realizes the profound paradox of Sartre's personal political position. He has not joined the French Communist Party and apparently does not intend to do so, nor would he be likely to receive a very warm welcome if he did. His political influence has not been entirely negligible—his protests, together with those of many other intellectuals, during the Algerian War undoubtedly had a certain effect on public opinion and ultimately on government policy, for example—but neither Sartre himself nor his journal, *Les Temps Modernes*, has ever served as a rallying point for any sizable "group" movement of the sort envisaged in his social philosophy. Despite all the seemingly clear-cut stands that Sartre has taken on matters of conscience, then, there in fact remains a certain elusiveness about the nature of his commitments.

Sartre has remained free—and in many senses *uncommitted*, unbound by any institutional discipline. His "soul," therefore, remains his own: perhaps, or so certain critics would say, its contents remain uncommunicated despite the almost endless flood of Sartre's published words. This attitude of consciousness, which has been attributed to Sartre, bears some interesting resemblances to the romantic posture analyzed by Hegel in his *Phenomenology* under the rubric of "The Beautiful Soul"; I have used this as the title of the concluding section of the present chapter, though we need not accept either Hegel's interpretation of the notion or the negative judgment that he passes on such an attitude. At any rate, the somehow elusive and never completely definable character of Sartre's personal "commitments," such as they are, is very much in keeping with the elusive and always changing character of reality as it is discerned in Sartre's philosophy, a point to which we have had occasion to return many times. The subtlety and complexity of Sartre's analysis of existence will continue to render ultimate noncommitment a more deeply significant feature and problem of both his life and thought than its opposite, temporary and partial commitment. In attempting to grasp definitively the nature of Sartre's commitments or indeed of his philosophy as a whole, one is constantly reminded of Aeneas' experience in vainly trying to touch the elusive shade of his wife, Creüsa: "*Ter frustra comprensa manus effugit imago,/par levibus ventis volucrique simillima somno.*"[100] But human existence itself is of this sort in Sartre's world!

The ultimate measure of this elusiveness is to be found in the last of the four accusations selected from among those which hostile critics,

---

[100] *Vergil, Aeneid, Bk. II, lines 793–794.*

both of the superficial and of the more thoughtful varieties, are wont to level against the entire Sartrean enterprise: that he is too radical an innovator in philosophy. At the same time, there also exists a vociferous chorus of critics who raise the opposite objection, that there is nothing really very new about Sartre's philosophy. Sartre has always emphasized freedom, creativity, and the revolutionary possibilities within man; this frightens many of those who are profiting from the present state of things and who therefore fear change. Few truly distinguished past philosophers or philosophies have been so consistently hostile as Sartre to established orders; Marx is a poor exception to this rule, because it is only recently that he has begun to be taken very seriously *as a philosopher.* If there exists anything like a popular conception of the nature of *philosophia perennis,* involving a few specific notions to which bona fide philosophers are supposed to adhere, Sartre's philosophy will be found to jar with this conception on several of its most crucial points—God, soul, eternal values, human nature, etc. We can only discuss popular conceptions of this sort hazily and in terms of vague impressions, for even a public opinion poll on the subject would alter attitudes by raising questions about them; nevertheless, I think it safe to say that Sartre is widely regarded as a philosophical radical, and, of course, this is the manner in which he regards himself. It should be added, for the sake of completeness, that popular conceptions of "radicalism" are more often unfavorable than favorable.

But professional philosophers and historians of philosophy are more apt to see behind Sartre's surface radicalism a parade of familiar historical figures and problems. Sartre himself acknowledges these influences, especially in *Being and Nothingness* and in his earlier psychological works. Besides Heidegger and Husserl among twentieth-century philosophers, there are Descartes, Spinoza ("*Omnis determinatio est negatio*"[101]), Hegel (who, of course, employed the terminology of in-itself and for-itself as well as many other almost equally fundamental Sartrean conceptions), Rousseau (whose preeminent contribution especially to Sartre's social philosophy has not yet been fully recognized), and, obviously, Marx. These names are only beginnings towards a complete list; all the other existentialist philosophers treated in the present volume, for example, could be added without hesitation. As for the problems, they are essentially the perennial ones concerning man's place in a nonhuman universe; common to all philosophers, including Sartre, are certain grounds that cannot be eliminated without abolishing philosophy itself. This is why we could readily compare Sartre both to the pre-Socratic monist, Parmenides, and to the pre-Socratic sophist, Protagoras. And this is also why it seemed worthwhile to raise some *perennial* sorts of philosophical questions about the philosophy of the leading existentialist radical— a procedure symbolized by the so-called "transcendental" categories which I have used to epitomize the themes of each section of this chapter.

101 EN 50 (BN 15).

As I have already noted, some basis for criticizing my procedure may be found within Sartre's own philosophy. It might be said that radical novelty can and does break through the stultifying frameworks of all such past categories, and that any attempt to deal with Sartre's thought in terms of those categories entails infidelity to what are precisely the novel aspects of Sartre's thought. I deny this. Sartre, as we saw, employed what he called an "ontological proof" for the autonomous existence of being-in-itself, rather than for that of God. His use of the traditional phrase was highly suggestive, but it by no means shattered the (comparative) novelty of Sartre's conception. Similarly, the Sartrean philosophy may exhibit its novelty even more clearly if we occasionally try to reconsider it in light of a very different thought framework, such as that suggested by the classical notion of eternal truth.

The question underlying these final considerations concerning the alleged radicalness or non-novelty of Sartre's existentialism is, of course, that of its ultimate historical significance. Two hundred years from now, for example, will it be regarded simply as a curious witness to the intellectual anarchy of our times? (This is the sort of terminology often used today by those who claim possession of solider truths than Sartre's, in order to justify to themselves the study of his philosophy.) Or will it be remembered as the characteristic and even necessary philosophy of our epoch (a designation which Sartre himself would now modestly reserve for Marxism), later become just as necessarily outmoded? Or will it continue to be studied as one of the most important milestones in the history of modern philosophy, still rich in relevant verities? Only in history, in the configuration of the future, can a relatively final judgment, one that could be accepted within the thought framework of Sartre himself, be passed on Sartre.

But we are all parts of the "totalizing" movement that is creating the future. If so, then Sartre's recognizable achievements in the present must point in the direction of history's verdict. The qualities for which Sartre is best known in the spectrum of contemporary thought are not necessarily, in every case, those of which he is proudest; such is, as I noted in the introduction to this chapter, the fate of every mandarin who ventures into the world outside the Academy. He is famous for having insisted on the fundamental sovereignty of the individual against the claims of every collectivity, though he also has few rivals in analyzing the terrifying powers of modern group pressures and prejudices. He has always argued that man rather than a personal God or an impersonal Being is the center of the universe, and yet he makes common cause with the opponents of materialism in asserting the impossibility of explaining the characteristically human in exclusively scientific terms. He is known to have held that men are the only possible creators of values, and at the same time he makes the most rigorous demands on us as moral agents. He stands for activism and commitment in literature, while belonging to an angry but practically impotent wing of French politics. In philosophy, he is at once an heir of the old metaphysics and the strongest debunker of every alleged transcendent reality. In his way of life, he epitomizes the twentieth-century Western intellectual: staid but nonconformist, at once capable of highly esoteric thinking, and yet eager to join in common action to change the world.   In the confluence of these and various other salient qualities lie numerous potential contradictions; as anyone who is familiar with the workings of dialectical reason will realize, it is these latent, practical (rather than theoretical) contradictions that give Sartre's thought its power.   When that thought unfolds further in the course of Sartre's later years and across the writings of those thousands whom he has profoundly influenced, it will no doubt spawn some very bizarre, unpredictable offspring.   So long as Sartre's philosophy continues to grow and to exert influences even of this kind, however, it will continue to exhibit the living, humanly relevant, existential character that is the best evidence of its own deepest wisdom.

BIBLIOGRAPHY

The following list consists of selected nonfiction works by Sartre which are deemed to have substantial philosophical importance.   At least one English translation has been listed, wherever appropriate, below each French title.

1 Baudelaire, Gallimard, Paris, 1947.
Baudelaire, tr. Martin Turnell, New Directions, Norfolk, Conn., 1950.

CRD *2 Critique de la raison dialectique*, Tome I, précédé de "Question de Méthode," Gallimard, Paris, 1961.
Search for a Method ("Question de Méthode" only), tr. Hazel E. Barnes, Knopf, New York, 1963.

3 Esquisse d'une théorie des émotions, Hermann & Cie, Paris, 1939.
The Emotions, Outline of a Theory, tr. Bernard Frechtman, Philosophical Library, New York, 1948.

EN *4 L'Etre et le néant: essai d'ontologie phénoménologique*, Gallimard, Paris, 1943.

BN *Being and Nothingness*, tr. Hazel E. Barnes, Philosophical Library, New York, 1956.

5 L'Existentialisme est un humanisme (first published 1946), Editions Nagel, Paris, 1965.
Existentialism, tr. Bernard Frechtman, Philosophical Library, New York, 1947.
Existentialism and Humanism, tr. Philip Mairet, Methuen, London, 1960.

6 L'Imaginaire: psychologie phénoménologique de l'imagination, Gallimard, Paris, 1940.
The Psychology of Imagination, tr. anonymously, Philosophical Library, New York, 1948.

7 *L'Imagination*, Gallimard, Paris, 1936.
Imagination: A Psychological Critique, tr. Forrest Williams, University of Michigan Press, Ann Arbor, Mich., 1962.

8 *Les Mots*, Gallimard, Paris, 1964.
The Words, tr. Bernard Frechtman, George Braziller, Inc., New York, 1964.

9 *Réflexions sur la question juive*, Gallimard, Paris, 1946.
Anti-Semite and Jew, tr. George J. Becker, Schocken Books, New York, 1948.

10 *Saint Genêt, comédien et martyr, Gallimard*, Paris, 1952.
Saint Genet, Actor and Martyr, tr. Bernard Frechtman, George Braziller, Inc., New York, 1963.

11 *Situations*, I, Gallimard, Paris, 1947.

12 *Situations*, II, Gallimard, Paris, 1948.
What Is Literature? (from *Situations*, II), tr. Bernard Frechtman, Philosophical Library, New York, 1949.

13 *Situations*, III, Gallimard, Paris, 1949.
Literary and Philosophical Essays (from *Situations*, I and III), tr. Annette Michelson, Collier, New York, 1962.

14 *Situations*, IV, Gallimard, Paris, 1964.
Situations, tr. B. Eisler, George Braziller, Inc., New York, 1965.

15 *Situations*, V, Gallimard, Paris, 1964.

16 *Situations*, VI, Gallimard, Paris, 1964.

17 *Situations*, VII, Gallimard, Paris, 1965.

18 *La Transcendance de l'Ego: esquisse d'une description phénoménologique* (first published 1936–37), Librairie Philosophique J. Vrin, Paris, 1965.
The Transcendence of the Ego, tr. Forrest Williams and Robert Kirkpatrick, Noonday Press, Inc., New York, 1957.

CHAPTER SEVEN

ALBERT CAMUS
MAN IN REVOLT

THOMAS HANNA

THOMAS HANNA, *Chairman of the Department of Philosophy at the University of Florida, was previously departmental chairman at Hollins College. He studied philosophy at Texas Christian University and the University of Chicago, where he received his B.A. and Ph.D. For five years he has lived part of the time in Europe where he has been director of a club for refugee students at the University of Paris, supervisor in a Brussels, Belgium, orphanage, student in Mainz, Germany, and director of an overseas study program in France. During the period 1964–65 he was a writer-in-residence at Chapel Hill under the Cooperative Program in the Humanities, sponsored jointly by Duke University and the University of North Carolina. Mr. Hanna's publications include* The Thought and Art of Albert Camus *(Regnery, 1958);* The Bergsonian Heritage *(Columbia University Press, 1963); and* The Lyrical Existentialists *(Atheneum, 1963).*

PART ONE
GYMNOSOPHY

Customarily, philosophy and modesty have gone their separate ways. When, as may sometimes happen, a modest philosophy makes its appearance, the trained philosopher is put on his guard; naturally, he is suspicious. His instincts tell him that somehow this is not really philosophy.

This, of course, is understandable. Rather than modesty, it is pretentious- ness that most frequently characterizes philosophizing. When the professional philosopher puts pen to paper, his prose becomes garbed with a choice of words, syntax, jargon, and allusions which clearly mark him as a philosopher. The knight, before the battle, shrugs and clanks his way into plumed helmet, mail, breastplate, gauntlets, and pointed shoes—not to be more effective, surely, but because his opponents expect it of him and will be garbed the same way. Nor- mally, the professional philosopher goes to battle in his own regalia, letting his potential opponents know that in terms of plumes, bucklers, and historical insignia he is equipped with the best.

This is clanking good fun; it is also pretension. And often it is wise not to be overawed by the weight of the armor, forgetting the conscious sinew inside. It is the man inside who counts and must not be forgotten. Readers of philosophy must often experience the extreme of this: the suspicion that if they open the visor and peer inside they will find no one there.

This is why a modest philosopher appears suspect, and Albert Camus seems naked and defenseless in the midst of the clanking knights of philosophy. This, also, is why Albert Camus—despite much evidence to the contrary—resolutely maintained that he was an artist and not a philosopher. But the fact that Camus' graduate studies were in philosophy, that he published two long philosophical essays and numerous short articles on moral and political philosophy, and that his literary production is permeated with philosophical concerns—all this suggests that he was not merely an artist. Camus was a moral and metaphysical thinker of considerable force and excitement, and the modesty of his philosophy should not blind us to this. For all his lack of armor Camus is not less than a philosopher; being an artist too, he becomes a philosopher and something more; it is this peculiar amalgamation of thought and art that characterizes Camus as such a striking thinker and human being. In his works the frail and incon- stant groping that is authentic philosophy recreates itself beneath our eyes, and we see philosophizing in its simplicity and nakedness. Alexander the Great in one of his excursions of conquest into India was startled to see men of the Jainist religious sect wandering about, as was their custom, unclothed. He called them "gymnosophists," the "naked wise men." Such a one was Camus: the unpretentious and deliberate nakedness of his thought is a sign of his wisdom, not of the lack of it.

Witness: "One goes through life with a few ideas that are one's own. Two or three. As one encounters other men and other realms they are polished and transformed. It takes ten years to have an idea that is really one's own—one about which you can talk. Naturally, this is a little discouraging."[1] This is Camus, the gymnosophist, speaking, and the final sentence is said with a slight grimace and shrug. But it is also said with a clear irony—with one eye on his own barrenness and another on the pretentious clanking of the knights of philosophy.

From the novel, *The Stranger*, notice the same attitude, directed this time not toward philosophy but toward Christian theology. The prisoner, Meursault, says of the prison chaplain, "He seemed so certain, didn't he? But not one of his certainties was worth a single strand of a woman's hair. . . . Of course, it looked like my hands were empty, but I was sure of myself, sure of everything, more sure than he, sure of all I had, but I held on to this truth even as it held on to me. I had been right, I was still right, I would always be right."[2]

With "two or three" ideas "it looked like my hands were empty," but "I was still right"—these words sketch out an attitude toward the Western traditions of philosophy and theology that is, in fact, the attitude of a man in full revolt against the intellectual past. It is a revolt which seems to have empty hands, but which proclaims that the pittance which these rebellious hands hold is, in the balance, far weightier, far truer than the cumulative mass of two millennia of philosophy and theology. Such a claim is patently absurd, but if it be absurd, Camus is not alone in affirming it; for this is the basic affirmation explicitly or implicitly proclaimed throughout existential philosophy.

In his philosophy of revolt Albert Camus has in a simple and lucid manner expressed the basic attitude uniting all the many thinkers who are identified with the movement called "existentialism." To understand Camus' modest but fundamental place in this movement, we should view him in three stages. First, we must make clear his attitude toward the Hellenic and Judaic-Christian heritage of Western civilization; second, we must understand the positive meaning of what he calls "revolt," and third, we should examine the effective critical use which Camus makes of his positive philosophy of revolt.

First, then, let us come to terms with that rebellious attitude which stands before the past with empty hands, and yet is persuaded that these hands are fuller than the massive body of Western civilization.

PART TWO
THE EXISTENTIAL REFLEX

If one understands Nietzsche's pronouncement, "God is dead," in the way Nietzsche intended it to be understood, one is aware that this is the most important single event in the course of Western culture. But as Nietzsche himself knew, the event "God is dead" is so fundamental

[1] *Albert Camus, Noces, Gallimard, Paris, 1947, p. 35.*
[2] *Albert Camus, L'Etranger, Gallimard, Paris, 1942, p. 169.*

and intimate a happening that the pronouncement of it falls on deaf ears; even those who nod in agreement with it do not necessarily realize what it means. The intervening three-quarters of a century have hardly made this observation less true, for, as Camus has noted, even our most militant atheists secretly believe in God without being conscious of it.

In pronouncing the death of God, Nietzsche made a complex judgment which was at once historical and psychological; that is, it had to do with the basic intellectual transformation brought about by modern history, and it also had to do with a specific psychological tendency of Western men. Obviously, Nietzsche is not making an objective historical judgment—as if there once had been a God which has now ceased to exist. Moreover, Nietzsche is not proclaiming atheism in the sense of a rebellion against a *theos*; neither negation nor denial are implied: if there be no God, then there is nothing against which to rebel. The dramatic statement, "God is dead," has nothing to do with a god; it has everything to do with men.

The "God" about which Nietzsche is speaking is the presumed absolute power center, wholly or partially transcendent of human history, which in some fashion is the source of, preservation of, and destiny of this world and its history. This "God," visible or invisible, miraculously intervening or impassively aloof, personally active or impersonally quiescent—this "God," Christian and Hellenic, does not exist. Indeed, this "God" never existed, but, notwithstanding, men have until recent centuries been capable of believing in this "God" without any serious intellectual blocks. The fact that since the renaissance of human inquiry serious intellectual barriers have arisen is testimony that something has happened to men in their ability to believe. Thus, it is a transformation of man, not God, that Nietzsche points to, and, putting precision in the place of drama in Nietzsche's pronouncement, we should not say that "God is dead," but rather that "the foundations for belief are dead." This is what Nietzsche meant. And it is the awareness of this transformation which is at the heart of the existentialist attitude.

So, then, the intellectual event involved in this pronouncement is an old and familiar story. But old as it may be, it is the story of modern history itself in its still-continuing struggle to come to terms with its disillusionment. In the Renaissance it was not hope that the new Pandora's box released into modern history, it was freedom, specifically the freedom to shrug off all previous answers, all authoritarian tradition, and to inquire anew into the nature of men and their world. The result of this new inquiry was men's rediscovery of the world, a world whose origin, nature, and destiny showed itself to be radically different from that world which previous philosophy and theology had depicted. The complex "God" which the Judaic-Christian and Hellenic traditions had posited and Whose transcendent existence was believed attested to by His immanent activities in the world—this "God" was bit by bit divested of the immanent proofs of His existence. His inexplicable miraculous acts were now explicable not as the miracles of God, but as the illusions, conceits, and deceits of men. And the inexplicable functions of the universe were now explicable not as the cosmic actions of a transcendent power, but as the predictable actions of natural laws which were autonomous and had no reference to some supporting transcendent power.

The old and familiar story of modern history is, then, an intellectual discovery: that the evidences supporting belief in a transcendent substance or power have disappeared, and that as these props were gradually removed, the "God" which they were supposed to support was also removed. When, through free inquiry and the development of scientific criticism and research, the intellectual props disappeared, the foundation for belief disappeared. It is in this sense that "God died."

The obvious result of this intellectual transformation would, one might think, be a generalized atheism, that is, a total lack of belief in any transcendent substances or powers. But this has not been the result, and the fact that it has not is a perplexing question, most of all, perhaps, for the innocent-minded atheists of our century. Clearly, the event of "God's death" is more complex than it appears. As an event which concerns men and not "God," there is yet something more which this event should reveal about the nature of men. For if Nietzsche was simply pointing out the intellectual consequences of free scientific criticism, then his pronouncement is, indeed, banal.

The points is this: "The foundations for belief are dead," *but men go on believing*, even those who are aware that the foundations for belief no longer exist. This is why Nietzsche observes that although God is dead, even those who agree to this do not understand what is said; the news has not yet hit home. This is the complex situation which Nietzsche has delineated: that men cannot exist in terms of what they know. This is the unresolved paradox which inheres in modern history, and it is this inner conflict which Albert Camus, more than any other thinker since Nietzsche, has understood and deftly elaborated against the background of recent history.

As Nietzsche remarks in *The Genealogy of Morals*, man will even believe in nothingness rather than not believe at all. In Western men, in ourselves, there is a reflex of believing which is so deep-rooted that it goes on functioning even though the intellectual warrant for believing is no longer there. Washed in the wake of modern science, the world is transformed; it is scoured free of its old transcendent ties and stands out as a barren, self-sufficient cosmos. But men, clearly seeing this barren cosmos and assenting to it, cannot help believing in something, no matter what; the reflex is still there, undiminished. The reflex tells man that there *must* be something "out there" apart from him, a centrum of absolute meaning, to which he can give himself. The extraordinary Jean-Baptiste Clamence puts the matter clearly in Camus' novel, *The Fall*:

Ah, dear sir, for someone who is alone, without God and without a master, the weight of the days is awful. One simply must find himself a master,

*God no longer being in style. The word, after all, doesn't even make sense
any more; no sense to risk shocking somebody. Look. Our moralists—
so serious, loving their neighbors and all that—nothing, really, distinguishes
them from Christians, unless it's that they don't preach in churches. . . .*

*Oh! The little sneaks, actors, hypocrites, so touching in that fashion.
Believe me, it's the same with all of them, even when they're setting fire to
heaven. Whether they're atheists or churchgoers, Muscovites or Bostonians,
all Christians from father to son. But that's just it: there isn't any father
any longer, no more rules! Everyone's free, so you have to get along as
best as you can, but since they definitely don't want anything to do with
freedom, they want their hand slapped by somebody, they invent frightening
rules, they rush out to build funeral pyres to replace the churches.*[3]

> The paradox is that men have accepted intellectual freedom and are
> saturated with it, but they have rejected the final consequence of
> existential freedom and are frightened of it. They cannot exist in
> terms of what they know: that there is no absolute value or authority
> outside them to which they can give themselves. There is no au-
> thority, no longer any father, no longer any rules, and the existential
> consequence of this is to exist lucidly in terms of this lack of given
> values, to exist freely, supplying one's own authority, one's own rules.
> There is no longer anyone else to supply them.

But the reflex of belief, the deep-seated posture of dependence on some
center of value external to oneself, is too fixed to be disturbed. For
the Western individual, freedom does not feel "right," it does not
seem "natural" to him—life cannot be lived in that fashion. And
so, "God no longer being in style," one gives oneself to the same
thing under a different name. God goes underground to reemerge in
different guise. Intellectually, one knows that God is dead; existentially, one cannot accept this discovery, and the *modus vivendi* is the
modern solution of giving oneself to some other "master" or authority
than "God," thus satisfying the Western existential reflex, while not
offending the Western intellectual structure. It should be clear now
why Nietzsche could say that God is dead, but that the news has not
yet reached the men who actually perpetrated the murder.

Let us pause a moment and recontemplate the image we had of the rebel
who stood facing the colossus of Western culture, holding a few ideas
in hands that, to his opponents, seemed empty, but which the rebel
knows to be fuller than the pretentious facade which stands behind
him in the past. This rebel who is in revolt against the now futile
pretense of the past is for Camus (as for the "free spirit" of
Nietzsche) a man who has not only accepted the intellectual consequences of freedom, but has accepted its existential consequences.
To understand Camus' "rebel" is to understand the kind of hero
projected in the writings of all the existentialistic or phenomenological
thinkers. Even at second glance this rebel is difficult to understand,
one focuses on him with difficulty; but when it becomes clear that the
rebel not only intellectualizes his freedom but exists freely, then the

[3] *Albert Camus, La Chute, Gallimard, Paris, 1956, pp. 154–5, 156.*

focus becomes exact.   Then it is understandable how the rebel in the
mid-twentieth century can stand in opposition not only to the ostensible
atheists, but to most of the rebellious intellectuals of recent history,
with the accusation that they are not yet whole or complete, they are
not yet fully and integrally men.   The frightening freedom which has
been discovered in recent centuries is not a cause for a retreat to the
futile nostalgia of the intellectual past; the courageous action invoked
by the existential thinkers is the full affirmation—existential as well
as intellectual—of the freedom which we have wrenched painfully
from our own earlier authoritarian civilization.   To retreat to the intellectual past is sickness.   To risk a total commitment to freedom is an
impulsion toward health.   To contrive the *modus vivendi* of a God-in-
disguise, an idol, is the desperate self-deception which, according to
Camus as well as Nietzsche, has been the favorite gambit employed
by troubled intellectual rebels during the past century or more.   As
will be explained in Part Four, it is precisely this gambit which underlies the social convulsions of modern history and accounts for its
unsurpassed destructiveness.

Albert Camus and Friedrich Nietzsche have supplied us with several examples of these *modi vivendi.*   Nietzsche, in *The Geneology of Morals*
and elsewhere, notes how those hard atheists, the scientists, are really
not atheists at all.   Why?   Because they believe in truth.   Nietzsche
asks: Why do they believe in truth?   What is the value in truth?   The
question is apt.   Not only should one ask: What is "truth?" but also
What is good about it?   The modern answer is that "truth" is an
absolute, and that is why it is good.   This is the implicit conviction
of all scientism, and Nietzsche cites this as an example of a God-
substitute.   In *The Twilight of the Idols* Nietzsche is again concerned
to indicate the many God-substitutes that philosophy has historically
inserted into the thinking of European civilization: "reason," "morality," "ego," "spirit," "motivation"—these are but a few of the many
false entities which philosophy has posited.   Obviously they do not
exist, but to the minds of Westerners, these power centers outside
and inside the individual *must* exist.   Why must they exist?   The
answer is that one's deep-seated reflex declares that they must.
Otherwise life does not make sense.

The same trait of intellectual-but-not-existential rebellion is found by Camus
in the French Revolution.   Here God was destroyed through the
destruction of His earthly representatives: the divinely ruling king and
the sanctified Church.   This was a metaphysical as well as political
revolution.   But if God and His rule were destroyed, it was in the
name of something *more sovereign* than this oppressive God: Reason.
Reason—that sovereign reality inevitably expressed through the free
votes of citizens—was the higher justification for the events of the
Revolution.   But, one asks, what is this sovereign, universal Reason?
Is it a concrete reality, a palpable entity in contrast to the scorned
superstition of a God?   No, it is an abstraction.   And Camus wryly
notes that the accomplishment of the French Revolution was to pull
God down from the heavens while simultaneously sending up Reason
to fill that emptiness which had been created.   And once it was dis-

covered that the "will of the people," rather than unanimously expressing the single dictate of Reason, expressed instead division of
sentiment, there was no way of knowing which voice of the populace
was the voice of Reason. The myth broke down and the Terror com-
menced; the one way to guarantee unanimity was to enforce it with
authority. And thus it was. The Revolution, which was to escape
from authority and oppression, eventuated in authority and oppression
because, without realizing it, men had replaced God with an idol.
Nothing had changed: a new tryranny had replaced the old.

Camus sees this pattern constantly repeated throughout the social convulsions of the nineteenth century and the revolutionary destruction of
the twentieth. The reflex is there, fabricating in various ways new
absolutes in lieu of the God who is out of style. Whether the center
of authority and value be the Nation, the Classless Society, the Führer,
Il Duce—these variations do not matter. They are all varying ways to
fill the emptiness of the heavens which intellectual freedom has
brought about. The emptiness is intolerable; the reflex says that
there must be a master, a final authority "out there," separate from
my own individual groping and confusion. And in its desperate fabrication of new absolutes, and thus new tyrannies, Camus sees the
twentieth century as a time of historical frenzy. And the reason for
it lies within each individual: an existential malaise festers beneath
one's intellectual vision of a valueless and self-explanatory cosmos.

Camus has carried on the sociohistorical critique begun by Nietzsche; and
the sensitive, compassionate manner in which he has done it has
won him a unique position among the existential thinkers of this
century. He is much less formidable "philosophically" than Heidegger, Jaspers, Sartre, or Merleau-Ponty. His concerns are not with the
ontological and epistemological ramifications of this point of view;
rather, his concerns are much more basic: How can one exist in a
world without God? Can one accept the modern vision of the world
and then exist in terms of it? This is the fundamental question, and
Camus has answered it affirmatively. From his earliest writings he
has said: Yes, it is possible, and it is the impassioned, deeply human
way in which he has expressed this Yes that has made such a mark
on his contemporaries.

Camus, himself, does not say that God is dead; he puts the matter differently. He says that there are no absolute values, that absolute values
are foreign to men and their history, and that once they enter, murder
and destruction follow. *L'Homme révolté*, the rebel, is a man who
has revolted against the authoritative absolutes of the past and has
not panicked at the results; he exists in terms of them. He is a man
who can *exist* freely as well as *think* freely. Such a one is fragile
and without the protection of pretension. He lives without hope,
without any ultimate certainty, knowing his mortality. His hands
seem empty. But what he possesses is the knowledge of what he is, of
what the world is, and of his ability to live in terms of this knowledge.
No matter how barren it may first seem, it is better to exist in terms
of truth, rather than in pretension and hope; it is better to exist in

terms of reality, rather than in the unreality of "another world"; it is better to exist in lucid consciousness rather than in self-deception. It is "better" because in each case something fundamental is involved: honesty. And this is the honor of the rebel.

PART THREE
REVOLT AND VALUE

1. The Nature of Revolt

That revolt is particularly a problem of the present age is due simply to the fact that whole societies today have chosen to estrange themselves from the sacred. We are living in a de-religionized history. Certainly, rebellious opposition is not the sum total of human nature, but today's history, by its violent oppositions, leads us to say that revolt is one of the essential dimensions of man. It is our own historical reality. Unless we choose to flee from reality, we will have to find our values within it. Can one, estranged from religion and its absolute values, find a code of ethics? This is the question posed by revolt. [4]

In the light of what was said in the previous section, this citation aptly sums up the special contemporaneity of what Camus calls revolt. To understand the basic content of this word "revolt" is to find the key to understanding both the positive and critical thought of Camus, whether it be in his essays or his literary works. Although the concept of revolt is found in all of his works, the principal expositions of it are in the three works, *L'Homme révolté, Actuelles II,* and—with careful reading—*Le Mythe de Sisyphe.* [5]

First of all, an important distinction: revolt is not revolution. Revolution is a social phenomenon, but by "revolt" Camus is referring to a purely individual experience. Certainly a political revolution might eventually follow from an individual's revolt, but the two are not to be confused. Not only is revolt an individual rather than a societal event, but it has a further basic distinction from revolution. Revolutions begin with a clear idea of what the revolution is to accomplish; in advance, a political or economic scheme is formulated as the goal to be achieved. Revolt does not begin with an idea; it is a personal rebellion that is groping and uncertain. Revolution is initially an intellectual event, whereas revolt is an existential event.

A second general remark is that revolt is an event characteristic only of certain societies, specifically those societies in which a theoretical state of affairs is in contrast to an actual state of affairs—where a supposed equality stands in contrast to an actual inequality, where a theoretical social justice stands against an actual state of social

---

[4] *Albert Camus, L'Homme révolté, Gallimard, Paris, 1951, p. 35.*
[5] *The essay. "Remarque sur la révolte" (see bibliography, p. 367), is an earlier discussion of revolt, roughly identical with that found in the opening section of L'Homme révolté.*

injustice, where a proclaimed freedom is belied by the fact of slavery.
Such contradictions are the seedbed of a society of revolt. Obviously,
there are inequalities in all societies, but in some cases these inequalities are interpreted as ultimately right, as the eternal order of things.
Camus points out that this is a prime social distinction between the
Orient and Occident. Oriental cultures are religious cultures which
understand that traditional inequality, injustice, or slavery are sacred;
the mythology and metaphysics of the culture affirm this state of
affairs as sanctified and immutable, and thus the theoretical state of
affairs is not in contradiction to the actual situation. Theory and
practice are one, and men are at peace with themselves, not questioning. But the West has now produced societies of revolt; this is a
basic Occidental social characteristic, and we are reminded once again
of Camus' and Nietzsche's thesis that in recent centuries the West
has emerged as a civilization without absolute values, without a God
which can explain away and justify the sufferings of men.

With this initial characterization of revolt as a phenomenon of Western
civilization and as a nonintellectual personal event, quite distinct from
the intellectualized social event of revolution, one has the perspective
needed in order to come to closer terms with the idea of revolt.
Revolt is a dialectical event. It involves not only a refusal but an
affirmation, not only a No but also a Yes. When a man revolts he
says No to a situation which he finds unendurable. Up until the
moment of revolt it was not unendurable; his condition may have been
unhappy or painful, but it had not yet reached the point of intolerability.
One accepts, one endures, one tolerates up to a certain point, and
then abruptly one revolts. Without knowing it, each man within himself has drawn a line and says: "Up to this point I can endure it, but
beyond that I cannot: I will revolt." What Camus is saying is that
there are limits within all men. He is affirming that there is a human
nature common to all men, and that given certain conditions, the
limits within a man's nature will become clear; they will suddenly
define themselves. What is the limit past which a man will not be
pushed? It varies even as the conditions against which a man revolts
vary. This is the impreciseness about revolt. But what *is* precise is
that for each man there is a limit: he will wait just so long, and then
the limit is passed: he is in revolt.

But if at a certain point a man shouts out the No of revolt, this means that
up to that limit he was not ultimately threatened by his external condition, and that past that limit, something within him was ultimately
threatened. Past this limit a man discovers that there is something
within him which cannot be sacrificed, which must be preserved at all
costs, otherwise life would not be worth living. It is in this way that
revolt reveals a value which must be defended, a positive demand
within oneself which one clings to and affirms in revolting against that
which would destroy this value. Revolt, then, in analysis shows itself
to be positive as well as negative. Implicit in the revolt is a value
which must be preserved. Thus, behind the No there is a Yes; the
fact that one revolts is made possible only by that positive value which
lies at the base of revolt. Revolt is dialectical: it is as positive as it is

negative, it affirms as much as it denies, it says Yes to something within man that is irreducible, and it says No to something outside man which is unacceptable.

But there is still more to be said about this dialectical experience of revolt: in its unqualified refusal of external oppression, revolt affirms that life itself cannot be lived without this value, that the rebel will forsake life itself in the desperate effort to preserve the value he has discovered as irreducible within himself. This means that the value revealed by revolt is not identical with the individual himself; although it is of absolute importance to him, it is not only *his* value. It is something he has discovered within himself which transcends his own person and unites him with other men. Revolt, says Camus, carries man toward all men, revealing a "metaphysical solidarity."

Revolt is a way of existing, creative of values. Camus underlines the trans-individual quality of revolt by pointing out that revolt is not necessarily a reaction against one's own oppression but can, as well, be the reaction of one who is unoppressed, but in seeing oppression, identifies himself with the afflicted. Or, again, the non-egocentric quality of revolt is in the possibility of revolting against a system of things that actually guarantees one's own social or material welfare.

Revolt is initially a dialectical experience of a single individual, but its impetus immediately throws one into solidarity with other men. These two themes—the individual dialectic of revolt, and the solidarity of men affirmed by revolt—are fundamental in Camus' thought. They go together with equal balance and cannot be played off against one another. Although implicit in the works of all major existential thinkers other than Sartre, this theme of the fellow feeling consequent upon revolt finds its strongest emphasis in the writings of Camus. Camus is, in this regard, expressing a paradox of which Jaspers and Heidegger were well aware: to the degree that the individual, in lonely revolt, asserts some personal value of his own against that oppressive environment outside his person, to that degree does he discover a commonality between himself and other men which he could not have had otherwise. This is one of the many rational paradoxes of existential thought, but to the gymnosophist this need not be a cause for concern; he realizes that revolt inevitably creates logical paradoxes, for revolt is not an intellectual exercise but a way of existence.

2. Revolt and a Common Value

For Camus, the two are inseparable. Revolt is predicated on a threatened value within the individual, and this value shows itself to be transcendent to the individual himself—as Camus puts it, "horizontally transcendent," i.e., shared on this earth with other men.

One must understand that in his affirmation of a common human nature and of common human values, Camus is not reverting to a more traditional philosophical world (e.g., souls, egos, eternal natural laws), nor is he suggesting that there is an essence implanted in human

existence. To affirm a human nature is to affirm a fundamental structure or tendency identical in all men, whatever be their differences; all
existential thinkers are at pains to affirm this identical structure—
even Sartre. Moreover, to affirm the possibility of a common value
is not to posit an essence in man; there are no given "essences," no
eternal and absolute values in the human creature. But even so,
Camus is saying, men find reasons for living; they discover that life is
worthwhile; they discover relative values, values which are born of a
certain moment in history under specific conditions which bring these
values to life. Such values are relative, mortal; they are shifting.
But nonetheless, despite their variety and despite the historical situations that condition them, they are paramount values which can be
common to all men, and thus are creative of society. To say that
there is no God who creates absolute values for us does not leave us
without values. The Hellenic and Judaic-Christian intellectual traditions tell us that otherwise we have no values, but this is not the
case. All is not lost after all. Camus, in pointing to revolt, is simply
saying that a certain way of human existence is creative of values—
relative, changing, groping, deeply human guides for human action
and thought. "Essences" are created out of existence. The intellectual traditions of the West claim that the only possible values are
those which are given to men, given either in the very nature of the
cosmos or given by God. But the "empty hands" of revolt suggest
otherwise: they suggest quite simply that human life is worth living
for those human beings who discover that life is worth living, or, put
in a stricter formulation: The only authentic values are those relative
values created by a way of human existence. Lurking just beneath
this contention is another thought which has vast importance in the
critical writings of existentialism: Throughout history all values have
come not from God or nature, but only from men existing in a certain
way; therefore, if we set ourselves against certain absolute values,
this simply means we are opposing one way of existing to another.

3. Metaphysical
Revolt

As Camus sees it, modern European history is a history of revolt—this is its
dominant characteristic. In his longest philosophical essay, L'Homme
révolté (The Rebel), he has analyzed some of the milestones of rebel
thought, which, he says, begins in earnest during the latter decades
of the eighteenth century. If, in its initial fury, revolt has posited an
authentic value, the question Camus raises is whether the rebel has
maintained this value from that point onward. If modern rebels,
revolting against a tyranny, have affirmed some vision of justice or
freedom as their value, have they been able to maintain this value
and at the same time not forget the tyranny against which they
originally revolted? Have the great rebels since the close of the
eighteenth century been able to maintain the inseparable No and Yes
of revolt, not trading an old slavery for a new slavery or an old injustice for a new form of injustice? Unfortunately, answers Camus, they
have only rarely done so. More often the balance of revolt has been

lost: men have either lived their protest at the expense of the value they had affirmed, thus ending in violence and destruction, or they have affirmed their inner demand so much more passionately than their external denial that their revolt has become a kind of madness, having drifted away from the reality it originally hoped to transform. If revolt be "one of the essential dimensions of man," revolt gone astray and betrayed has been one of the essential features of recent history. As Camus, in *L'Homme révolté*, begins his survey of rebel thought, he reminds us that the solidarity of men is the common value posited by revolt.

But, let us note before going ahead, the foundation of this value is revolt itself. The solidarity of men is founded on the movement of revolt which, in its turn, finds its justification only in this complicity. We shall, then, have the right to say that all revolt which denies or destroys this solidarity, loses at the same moment the name of revolt and actually coincides with a murderous consentment. In the same way, this solidarity, separated from the sacred, takes life only on the level of revolt. The true drama of rebel thought is thus announced. In order to be, man must revolt, but his revolt must respect the limit that it reveals in itself and where men, joining themselves with it, begin to be. Rebel thought cannot do without memory: it is a perpetual tension. In following it in its works and in its acts, we shall be able to say each time if it remains faithful to its original nobility, or if, through weariness and madness, it forgets it in a drunkenness of tyranny or slavery.[6]

Before the impetus of revolt carried men into the revolutions, anarchies, and political convulsions of the last two centuries it appeared in a more general form, not historical but metaphysical. Rather than fixing itself on a particular historical protest, metaphysical revolt includes all meaning and existence in its protest, rejecting the moral and intellectual principles of God Himself in the name of a value of freedom or justice, held to in defiance of God. Metaphysical revolt permeates the past two centuries in varying ways, marking out the broader context in which the specific historical convulsions will be worked out. In its questioning of the ultimate ends of creation, metaphysical revolt has supplied a fertile field in which historical revolt has engendered and grown.

This ultimate form of revolt is simply a personal rebellion against God and God's order. As such, the great prototype of metaphysical revolt is Cain. An even more remote prototype is Prometheus, who defied the gods for the sake of men; but Cain approximates more to the modern rebel in that his is a revolt against a personal God. When one is conscious of being directly accountable to a single God for one's actions, revolt against this God takes on a personal furiousness that is unique. Cain is our mentor because Cain is at the beginning of the same metaphysical vision which has become our heritage.

Camus points to the Marquis de Sade as the first great rebel to launch an assault against heaven. Sade's revolt is unbridled: it roars out an

6 Camus, L'Homme révolté, pp. 35–36.

absolute negation and demands an absolute freedom. Sade's reasoning is that if there is a God and this God permits the obvious suffering
and injustice which we see on earth, this is a criminal deity. And it
follows that if God denies men the justice and ethical order which
they expect, why should not man himself forget about justice and all
ethics and follow the impulses of his own nature? Specifically, why
should not man follow that most imperative summons of his own
nature, his sexual instinct? It is a force of nature, sexuality, which
Sade clings to in his rebellion against God in His heaven and God's
order on earth.

But twenty-seven years in the dank tower of Vincennes prison severed the
marquis's thoughts from reality, and his revolt soared outward into
an absolute demand for the freedom of human passion. If lack of
justice and personal liberty was the original value affirmed by Sade,
his unbridled revolt ended by affirming an insane will to domination
and a terrifying libertinism. Sade's revolt, with its original explosive
authenticity, was pent up too long; in its eventual explosion, it forgot
its origins; the limits implicit in revolt were sundered, and Sade has
in the human experiments of his isolated castles created a microcosm
of the totalitarian societies which were eventually to follow in the
twentieth century.

The pervasive movement of romanticism is also an example of metaphysical
revolt, but like a milder example of the Sadist imbalance, its emphasis
was on defiance at the expense of its initial affirmation of freedom.
The hero to emerge from romanticism was not the revolutionary,
rather it was the dandy—the man who demonstrates his break with
God by creating his own personal order and manner. The dandy thus
became a *personnage*, defining himself by the degree to which he
violates the conventional life of men. In this way the dandy creates
his own solitude, but this solitude is directly dependent upon the
contrasting conventionality of other men. And because of this dependence upon society, the lonely romantic hero is confused about
the positive values he may be affirming. His is a life of defiance, of
self-conscious contrast. Revolting from God's law, he ends, per-
versely, by requiring the laws of man in order that he may define himself negatively.

It is in Dostoevski, according to Camus, that rebel thought makes marked
progress. Specifically, it is Ivan of *The Brothers Karamazov* who sets
la pensée révolté on a higher plane. Here, the revolt against God is
emphatically in the name of a principle which is held to be higher
than God: justice. For Ivan, the suffering and innocent death of
children is a fact which no theology can explain away. It is an unjustifiable fact of this earth, and the doctrine of a loving, mysterious
God who will, in the end, make all things come out right does not
justify the death of an innocent. Ivan asks his Christian brother,
Alyosha, whether the ultimate reign of God's kingdom would be justified if it were founded on the death of a single child. Alyosha replies
that it would not. All the knowledge in the world, says Ivan, is not
worth the tears of children. In the name of a human justice and for

the sake of all men, Ivan refuses the promised salvation of God, even if it be true. It is this "even if" that Camus finds to mark a new stage in rebel thought. It is not simply a matter of disbelieving in God and his order; rather, even if this order exists, still it is unacceptable because it allows unjustified suffering here below. In Ivan we find a man in full metaphysical revolt, shouting an accusation against God in the name of the value of justice.

But if the clarity and balance of Ivan's revolt is a progress, it is a limited progress. In the end, Ivan cannot live in terms of his revolt. Ivan, in refusing God and in denying immortality in God, leaves himself with no ultimate foundation for distinguishing good and evil. If there is no immortality where all is set right, goodness finally rewarded, and evil finally punished, there is no ultimate basis for good and evil. Whatever one does ultimately makes no difference: it comes to the same thing. Thus, Ivan announces that everything is permitted, all acts are equally lawful. With this announcement metaphysical revolt has simultaneously moved into action and into nihilism. The type of thought represented in Ivan prepares the way for the frenetic efforts in the twentieth century to bring about a reign of absolute justice for men even though injustice is the primary means for accomplishing it.

One must understand the aberration that is at the heart of Ivan's revolt. It is this, says Camus: Although Ivan has denied God in the name of a moral value, how can this value of justice be made sense of unless there is a God who ultimately guarantees it? Ivan has taken justice as an *absolute value*, existing sovereignly apart from men and God, and in doing this he has simply opposed one God to another God. Ivan has not followed through in the logic of his revolt, and this logic declares that Ivan can resolve the contradiction between an impossible absolute justice and an unacceptable absolute God only by realizing that the idea of justice, like all absolute moral ideas, is only a last vestige of that dying God whom Ivan has denied. Ivan could not live in terms of the relative imperative of justice which his revolt brought to light; the fact that he demanded absolute justice means that he still believed in an aspect of God: absolute morality. If one denies God then one must deny the kind of morality that God represents. It is this final step which was taken by Nietzsche, who carried metaphysical revolt beyond nihilism into a transformed vision of the world.

A persistent theme in the thought of Camus is whether one can maintain oneself in this tense dialectic of revolt, whether one can both *exist* in it and *think* in it—without abandoning oneself to the temptation of embracing only the positive or negative poles of one's revolt, whereby one assumes the posture of tyranny or slavery. In the *Myth of Sisyphus* as well as *The Rebel*, this theme is dominant. Camus, for his part, answers Yes to the question, but immediately points out how few are those who have actually experienced revolt and held to it. In the earlier work, *The Myth*, Camus surveys several existential philosophers whose thinking has been formed by a metaphysical revolt but who, in the end, have not "held to it." In Jaspers, Shestov, Kierkegaard, and Husserl we find men who have rejected the traditional intellectual vision of a meaningful, rational universe. But Camus points out that with each of these men the dialectical tension created by this intellectual revolt is finally abandoned; each man, in his own way, makes a "leap" into some kind of absolute, some kind of transcendence—the tense anguish revealed in metaphysical revolt is eventually resolved into some higher harmony. Whereas Husserl's phenomenological approach emerges with a doctrine of eternal essences revealed to consciousness, Jaspers, Shestov, and Kierkegaard, in varying ways, point out the irrational fragmentation and ultimate absurdity of this universe and then deify it, declaring that it is just this absurdity which is the ultimate and which should be accepted. This leap into the transcendent is a denial of the original absurdity which triggered their thought and against which they were protesting. Here again it is a question of the old existential "reflex," which asserts itself under a new intellectual guise.

In the case of Nietzsche, we have the metaphysical rebel *par excellence.* Nietzsche accepted a universe devoid of God and devoid of any absolute values; he could both exist in such a universe and think in terms of it. Can one live in this world without believing in anything? Nietzsche says Yes, provided we push our revolt to its logical limits. These limits entail accepting the world *as it is,* with no higher explanation or justification. Reality itself, in its *isness* is paramount; there is no *ought* to contradict that which *is.* This is the basic and thoroughgoing atheism which Camus sees as implicit in Nietzsche's thought. And Nietzsche's bombastic attack on all forms of idealism—philosophical or theological—is that idealism negates this world, this reality, and takes refuge in a nonexistent realm of "truth" or "God." Idealism is, then, essentially a belief in nothing, in nonexistence. Nietzsche sees in this a fundamental immorality: the immorality of denying the one reality given men to know.

But Nietzsche carried the logic of rebel thought far beyond this initial atheism. In Camus' estimate, Nietzsche's great discovery was that true freedom can only be founded on a law. It is all very well to say that God is dead and that there are no longer any moral laws; but this is not a freedom. Ivan had thought that if there were no God then everything was permitted. To the contrary, says Nietzsche, if there is no moral law of any kind, then *nothing is permitted.* If there is a total absence of any guides, freedom becomes meaningless, for there is no reason to do or not do anything. All action becomes groundless and meaningless. It is with this discovery that Nietzsche carries metaphysical revolt beyond the halting point of nihilism and into a positive attempt to come to terms with the world as it is. If the old tablets of the law are broken, we must build new ones, otherwise there is no basis for human freedom—this was Nietzsche's breakthrough.

But in the absence of an immutable deity and an absolute morality, what kind of laws are possible? Nietzsche's answer is that the only laws possible are those mutable and relative laws which men create out of themselves in struggle with a reality which they now recognize as their one reality, their one source of truth. Camus finds Nietzsche faithful to revolt; he has respected its internal limits, maintaining himself in a constant tension, the constant balance between the Yes and No which is alone creative of human values. If there was an implicit injustice and slavery of man under the old absolute God and His laws, Nietzsche, in his protest, has kept in mind the oppressiveness of this old order and will not allow it to reappear in any new guise. And if there was a moral and intellectual demand for justice and freedom at the base of Nietzsche's revolt, Nietzsche, in the fluid, far-ranging vitality of his thought, ever affirmed these values in the relative, changing forms that such values take on in human history.

Metaphysical revolt reaches its greatest clarity and balance in Nietzsche. It is just this clarity and balance which other rebel thinkers have approached but not always equaled. These several examples of rebel thought should have helped to draw clearer the notion of revolt and the kind of thinking which can emerge from it. Camus orients himself within that tense, lucid balance that Nietzsche achieved, although he has drawn the defining lines of this state of existence much more sharply than did Nietzsche. Rebel thought begins in the experience of revolt, in an uncertain, nonintellectual groping. If rebel thought is to reflect this tense and passionate dialectic, it will itself have to be fluid, adaptable, and open to surprising transformations. In a universe without ultimate meaning or absolute end, rebel thought will never have finality. In *The Myth* Camus remarks that

profound thinking is in a state of continual becoming; it weds itself to one's experience and there takes shape. In the same way, the single creation of a man strengthens itself through the successive and multiple visages of his works. Each one complements the others, corrects them or overtakes them, and contradicts them as well.[7]

In his *Notebooks* Camus notes that "feelings and images multiply philosophy by ten."[8] This is the justification for the extension of thought into art, and Camus has, of course, been singularly successful in this —more so than any other existential thinker. To round out this survey of metaphysical rebels we should look at two fictional personnages who—one should note carefully—are not positive examples of authentic thought, but rather are limping examples of a revolt whose limits have been betrayed and which has ended in destruction. Martha, in the play *The Misunderstanding*, and Caligula, in the play bearing his name, are two rebels who, like so many others, revolted but did not "hold to it."

The revolt of Martha is simple. Economically trapped by the life of running a wretched inn in the provinces of Czechoslovakia, knowing no solace or pleasure now and seeing no escape from this in the future, she rebels against a pattern of life which is not worth living. Others might accept their moral and economic duties and bear them hopelessly until death ends their travail, but not Martha. She knows that all the

[7] *Albert Camus, Le Mythe de Sisyphe, Gallimard, Paris, 1942, pp. 154–155.*
[8] *Albert Camus, Carnets, Mai 1935–Février 1942, Gallimard, Paris, 1962, p. 250.*

ultimate reasons one can muster to justify a stultifying existence are patently false; they are ways in which men blind themselves to the misery and hopelessness of their existence. In her revolt she knows that life can be much more than this, that men should be happy, free to live their lives with some beauty and love. But in the backwash of her protest, she ignores this discovered value of freedom to happiness which she and all men should possess. In her blind protest against her condition she forgets the happiness of others and persuades her aged mother to aid her in murdering certain of their unfortunate guests, so that they might have enough money to escape from the interior of Europe to the sea. From time to time they poison solitary travelers whom they discover to have no family or special attachments in the world.

The "misunderstanding" involves the return of Martha's brother, who years earlier had gone away and found his wealth in another country. He returns to the inn incognito, preparing to surprise them with the news that with his wealth he will take them away with him to the sea. Thus, the thing Martha desires has come to her, but it has come for the moment disguised. The brother's wife has come with him and stays in a neighboring inn, waiting for the secret to be revealed. The inevitable irony transpires: the brother is poisoned and his body dumped in a river. Immediately afterward, going through his pocketbook, they discover his identity. The mother is grief-stricken, but Martha, in the desperate fury of her revolt, clings to her protest with obstinate self-justification:

He was given everything that life can give to a man. He got out of this country. He knew other places, the sea, free individuals. But me, I stayed here. I stayed, petty, gloomy, bored, stuck in the middle of the continent, and I grew up with the dullness of the land. No one has kissed my mouth, and even you have never seen my body unclothed. I swear to you, Mother, such things must be paid for. With the silly pretext that a man is dead, you cannot back out just when I was about to receive what is owed me.[9]

Martha has not held to her revolt; her existence is a pure protest against her condition. By her acts she had denied the right of others to happiness, and by the murder of her brother, she has destroyed the possibility of it for herself. She is stripped of everything except her vehement protest against the world that created her condition.

Oh! I hate this world in which we are reduced to God. But I have suffered an injustice, I have been wronged, and I will not bow down. And deprived of my place on this earth, rejected by my mother, alone in the midst of my crimes, I shall leave this world unreconciled.[10]

Unreconciled, Martha goes to her death, following her mother, who has already committed suicide.

If The Misunderstanding is dourly pathetic, the play, Caligula, is dourly comic, indeed monstrously comic. But if the styles of the two plays

[9] Albert Camus, Le Malentendu, suivi de Caligula, Gallimard, Paris, 1944, pp. 81–82.
[10] Ibid., p. 85.

are strongly contrasting, the basic situation is not; it is the same: it concerns a man who, in revolt, has lived the negative pole of his rebellion, betraying the value which originally he felt he and all men had a right to.

Caligula, the young Caesar, desired happiness like any man, and the bit of happiness he had found centered fragilely in the love he had for his sister. His sister lived with him as his wife. But this contentment vanished when his sister and lover suddenly became ill and died. Without reason, without warning, the world took her away; Caligula held that there could be no excuse for this, no extenuating solace. Like Ivan Karamazov he recognized that there is suffering and death in this world without justification. He discovered, he says, the simple truth that "men die and they are not happy."[11]

From the outset, Caligula's revolt miscarries: having felt the common right of himself or any man to happiness, he has been stunned to learn that this world is not a place where providential hands guide and pro-tect us; the world is brutal and irrational: it is absurd. And the conse-quence of this for Caligula is to despair of the possibility of happiness; this value can no longer be a reality for him. But the one reality which *is* left is the absurdity of the world. He reasons that if life in this world is nothing but unreason and unjustified suffering, then one must adjust to this reality. People must learn about this. "It's simply that everything around me is a lie, and I intend for everyone to live in the truth. And, by God, I have the means to make them live in the truth. . . . They are ignorant, and they need a professor who knows what he is talking about."[12] Caligula's gambado is simple: if the one reality is this world which rules the lives of men unjustly and irrationally, then I, as Caesar, will take over this rule and assume the function of the world.

And so the madness follows: arbitrary famines, arbitrary executions, capricious rapes, brutal humiliations. The fault of the world? No, the fault of Caligula; but it amounts to the same thing. The mute presence of the world no longer takes the blame for the absurdity of human life; the prancing, loquacious Caligula gaily takes the blame.

This is, then, the situation. Naturally, rebellion stirs among the patricians, and Caligula's death is quietly plotted. Caligula, quite aware of this, watches with interest, amused that they wish to kill him for quite the wrong reason: they think that life does have meaning, and that with the disappearance of Caligula the absurdity and injustice of life will also disappear. The Caesar scorns such unenlightened reasoning. But there is one plotter, Cherea, who reasons otherwise. Cherea, a former friend of Caligula, is a man in revolt—revolt against any injustice, whether it be that of Caligula or that of the world. Cherea shares the same negative protest which Caligula thrusts out against the world, but he has, as well, a positive demand for freedom and justice for himself and other men, and it is this balancing passion which Caligula lacks. Cherea's reasons are not those of the idealist

who clings to some higher realm of meaning; they are the reasons of
the rebel. When Caligula cannot understand why Cherea disapproves
of the inescapable logic of his manner of ruling, Cherea replies:

*Because I want to live and be happy. I believe that no one can do either
the one or the other by pushing absurdity out to its utmost consequences.
I am like everyone else. Sometimes, in order to feel free, I wish for the
death of some loved one, I covet women whom the laws of family or
friendship forbid me to covet. If I were logical, I would either have to kill
or seduce, but I don't think that these vague ideas are important. If everyone tried to carry them out, we could neither live nor be happy. And once
again, that's the important thing.*
Caligula: *Then you must believe in some higher idea.*
Cherea: *I believe that some actions are more beautiful than others.*
Caligula: *I believe that they are all equivalent.*
Cherea: *I know that, Caesar, and that is why I do not hate you. But you are
a disturbance, and it is necessary that you disappear.*[13]

There is the world. There is the individual. The former is mute and
fortuitously unjust; the latter is suffering and demanding. Both
Cherea and Caligula understand the world for what it is; but only
Cherea has not forgotten man and what he is—Caligula, for his part,
has given in completely to the world.

That his revolt—logical as it seemed—had gone astray, is what Caligula
painfully realizes just before his death. Waiting for his assassins, he
kneels before a mirror, speaking to it, seeing there only an individual
staring back. And Caligula sobs out his frenzied disappointment with
the world, which somehow forgot the human being who still goes on
desiring happiness in this world.

*The impossible! I have sought it to the limits of the world and in the con-
fines of my being. I reached out my hands, I reach them out and it is you
that I meet, always you in face of me, and to you I am filled with hatred.
The path I took was not the right one; I ended with nothing. My kind of
freedom is not good.*[14]

Caligula, Martha, le Marquis de Sade, the romantic dandies, and the others
—all fictional or historical characters whose revolts have aborted.
Their revolt itself was authentic, the limits were there in the dialectical
Yes and No. But one of the poles was abandoned. There were other
rebels who respected the tense balance of their revolt and "held to
it," but these are fewer in number. Camus sees modern history as a
time of revolt, but the misfortune is that most of the revolts have
betrayed themselves—those who revolted could not exist in terms
of this new tension. The old "reflex" reasserted itself. But despite
these betrayals, revolt remains "one of the essential dimensions of
human experience." Camus understands that it is a difficult task;
one must wait while the reflex fades. As he sees it, the mid-
twentieth century has two great alternatives: frenzy or patience. Only
in the latter is there the possibility for a future.

[13] Ibid., p. 179.   [14] Ibid., pp. 210–211.

4. Revolt
and the Absurd

It was observed in Part One that Albert Camus in his philosophy of revolt has given a lucid and simple expression of that basic attitude which characterizes existential philosophy. This dialectical experience with its existential and intellectual aspects is a touchstone for each of the existentialists, no matter what their many differences and special preoccupations. In the dialectic of revolt two things are revealed: what the individual man *is* in relation to what the world *is*. This relation between the individual and his world is one of conflict in which the individual is acutely conscious of those categorical differences which separate his being from that of the world.

In his early writings, specifically *The Myth of Sisyphus*, Camus called this dialectical experience "the Absurd," and not "Revolt," but, nevertheless, in the earlier essay we have a description of this experience which is all the more enlightening because it is boiled down to its purest expression. It was only later that Camus clarified his thinking about the Absurd, emphasizing the new idea of a common value being born in this experience; but, except for this addition which makes for the full-blown notion of revolt, he was dealing with the same thing.

One other difference between the earlier conception of the Absurd and the later notion of revolt is rather interesting. The dialectical experience of the Absurd "happened" to a man, whereas revolt does not "happen" to man, passively, but is initiated by man. If one is thoughtful about these active and passive conceptions of revolt, I think one will conclude that the complex dialectic of revolt in effect includes both factors: this is both something man "does" and something "done to" man—the outer pressure of the world and the inner pressures of the individual are both necessary if revolt is to take place.

Even so, it is interesting to find this shifting distinction within the works of Camus, because it reveals an uncertainty which is also reflected in a lack of accord among many other existential thinkers on this question. For Sartre it is something that "happens." For Heidegger it is something that can both "happen" and be initiated by the individual. For Kierkegaard it is something which the individual initiates, and likewise for Nietzsche. Jaspers also feels that this dialectic is something which the individual must initiate. This is a fascinating discord, because it betrays two distinct attitudes about this experience: analytical or evangelistic. Is revolt simply a disturbance increasingly characteristic of our age, a disturbance which will eventually happen to men when, for each individual, one's time is ripe? Or is revolt something any man can do, which all men must do? Some existential thinkers dispassionately analyze this as a contemporary malaise which cannot be helped; others passionately exhort their readers to cultivate this inner disturbance. As said above, this curious discord is not disagreement so much as a difference of emphasis—both the external condition and the active inner response are necessary to the dialectic. But whatever be these variations of emphasis, it is worthwhile noting that what Camus has described as "Revolt" and the "Absurd" is the same experience described by these other thinkers but named differently. Sartre calls it "nausea." Heidegger calls it "dread." For Kierkegaard it is the action of "despair." Nietzsche calls it quite simply the life of "freedom," and Jaspers sees it in the solitude/communication of "authentic Existenz." In each case it is the same dialectical experience of the individual related to his world, and it is this experience, this way of existing, that is the rallying point of existential thought.

In an effort to put a definitive clarity into this dialectic, it will be worthwhile briefly to examine the simpler garb into which Camus has put his conception of the Absurd. The experience of the Absurd, he says, is a common feature of our times; it is all about us, in the very atmosphere of the twentieth century. The patterns of our urban-industrial life easily engender the feeling of the absurdity of life. It is first of all that, says Camus: a feeling—later it can develop its ideas. In the following famous passage Camus describes the birth of this frequent feeling:

What happens is that the scenery crumbles, Get up, streetcar, four hours at the office or factory, eat, streetcar, four hours of work, eat, sleep, and Monday, Tuesday, Wednesday, Thursday, Friday, and Saturday with the same rhythm—for the most part this cycle goes along smoothly. But one day the "why" arises and everything begins with this fatigue colored by surprise. "Begins" is very important here. The fatigue is the final moment of the activities of a machinelike life, but at the same time it touches off the stirring of consciousness. It awakens it and provokes what follows. What follows is either the unconscious return to the cycle or the final awakening. Eventually, there comes at the terminus of this awakening the consequence: suicide or readjustment.[15]

When, after a gradual attrition, the ritual scenery of the urban-industrial life cycle crumbles, the individual suddenly asks himself; Why go on living? I work, buy food and rest, so that I can go on working, buying food and resting, and so on and so on until I cease to exist. And what will have been the point of it? Ultimately, there is no sense to it. Whether I work or not, eat or not, live or not, ultimately it comes to the same thing.

In The Myth, Camus situates his philosophical concerns squarely in the twentieth century by asserting that the preeminent question of our times is whether life is worth living. "The rest, if the world has three dimensions, if the mind has nine or twelve categories, comes afterward. These are games: first one must answer."[16]

Suicide or readjustment: there are three alternatives here, and not just two. How one readjusts is the question. One can unconsciously "return to the cycle" or one can undergo a "final awakening." Failing either of these there is the finality of suicide. Which of these three seems indicated is discovered through Camus' analysis of the experience of

[15] Camus, Le Mythe de Sisyphe, p. 27.   [16] Ibid., p. 15.

the Absurd. Camus takes this experience as a primary datum which must not be denied; and if one adheres to the reality of the Absurd, the options of suicide or a return to the old cycle do not follow. Suicide does not, because it simply ends the question without answering its challenge. Reimmersion in the cycle does not, because this is possible only through the self-deception of hope that somehow things may be different tomorrow, a self-deception that seeks to escape the primary datum of the Absurd.

Specifically, the Absurd is a confrontation between the individual and his world. It is not the world which is absurd, nor is it man; the Absurd is the lack of correspondence between the two. It is an anxious consciousness of the divorce between the individual and his world. The individual is not absurd; he simply is what he is in his longing for clarity, for a meaningful response to his existence. The world is not absurd; it is what it is in its irrationality, in its ultimate lack of unity and coherency. Man and his world are what they are each in its own right; one cannot be ignored or reduced to the reality of the other, and in this confrontation of two realities the Absurd emerges as the divorce which exists between these two.

Camus enumerates some of the situations which give birth to the Absurd experience, both on the level of existence and on the level of intellect. Already, in mentioning the cyclical meaninglessness of day-to-day urban life, we have touched upon one. Another is a man's discovery at a certain moment in his life—perhaps in his thirties—that he is caught in time; without wanting or intending to he sees that he is ineluctably being carried along on a tide of aging that will soon make him look and feel and act middle-aged and will just as inescapably make him look and feel and act old. There is no sense to this. This is not what he desires; yet he is caught in it. That this ruthless movement is inevitable does not make it right; it simply is what it is, senseless—and here again, man discovers the divorce between himself and his worldly fate.

Another discovery is the unhappy experience of seeing nature, the world about oneself, as it really is, stripped of the normal, workaday, practical myths with which we invest it. One discovers that this landscape, this towering forest, or this heaving ocean is not in itself a beautiful or beneficent reality; it is something utterly indifferent to man, another realm, unwelcoming and hostile in character. When, suddenly, the veils of poetical and practical illusion are wrenched away from one's eyes, says Camus, the "dense," "foreign" reality of nature surges up to us in all its inhumanity. One abruptly knows one's isolation, one's estrangement from this brute pulsing reality before one's eyes.

Even our awareness of others can undergo this same wrenching away of the veil. One looks up, distractedly, and sees mouths moving, hands gesturing, staccato gibberish filling the air, and one realizes the infinite distance, the strangeness separating oneself from these creatures who are the "others." And this applies not only to others, but even to oneself, in that stunned moment when one gazes at the face of a stranger in the mirror, the face of one who is familiar but is somehow unknown, just as unknown as the faces of those "others" whom one has just left.

These are the experiences that increasingly strike men of this century. And we have not mentioned that simplest of all discoveries: the oncoming rush of one's death. It is all very well to study the obituaries and reflect on the death of "others"; it is a categorically different situation when we ourselves have this same certainty that is as inescapable as it is inexplicable and senseless. No man in existence desires non-existence; this is not what existence is for. Men want fulfillment, destiny, duration; but the certainty of one's death is a supreme contradiction to these demands. Before his approaching death, a man realizes the futility of life in this world; his demands on the world and the world's replies are irreconcilable.

These are six examples offered by Camus of the feeling of the Absurd as it meets us on the level of existence: the cyclical meaninglessness, the despair of being trapped in the curve of time, the discovery of the "denseness" of nature, the discovery of one's alienation from others, from oneself, and finally the realization of one's approaching death.

If these are the feelings that evoke the Absurd, there are also corresponding intellectual walls which encircle us in a world of hopeless fragmentation and uncertainty. Camus mentions the logical impossibility of making universal judgments about anything without ending in contradiction; on the level of logic, any effort to grasp absoluteness always leads into paradox. On the same level of logic the mind cannot posit unity in this universe; the mind which asserts the unity of all, sets its judging activity apart from the thing judged, thus negating the unity it is asserting. But not only does the intellectual apparatus itself fail to give us ultimacy; our very knowledge of the world is equally limping in its pretense. None of us, says Camus, knows this world that is about us; we know only fragments of it. And men have never been so ignorant of their environment as they are at the present time. All of us have a practical familiarity with innumerable things in our quotidian world, but we *know* almost nothing about the workings of the cars and airplanes and television sets we use, or even why there is light when we push a switch. On the stricter level of science itself, absolute knowledge eludes us; whether the focus be nuclear or astronomical, science ultimately finds itself groping with indeterminateness and uncertainty. Science always faces the unknown, armed with only hypotheses and curiosity; by its nature it cannot achieve finality. And so, the mind's desire to fully grasp, fully know its world is a hopeless desire. Whether on the level of existence or of the intellect, men of the twentieth century look about them and discover a world where the traditional certainties, patterns, and rituals appear to have been rent asunder by a barren, undeterminable, fragmented world which had always been lurking underneath. With our intellects ordered by science and our lives ordered by our urban-industrial rhythms, the Absurd experience multiplies with greater rapidity throughout Europe and the Americas; the breakdown seems to be in full swing, so that

it is no longer uncommon for a man to ask himself with cold seriousness: Is it worth while to go on living in this world? As Camus insists,
for the present age this is the one question which we must answer.

Camus, we know, says Yes, life is worth living, even if it must be lived
within the contradiction of the Absurd. He says Yes to the Absurd
even as he has said Yes to Revolt; the experiences are the same.
The dialectical divorce between the individual and his world is identical, whether it be called the Absurd or Revolt—the only distinction is
in the passive quality of the former. But even with the Absurd, the
passive quality fades when Camus exhorts the victim of the absurd
revelation to live aggressively in terms of this dialectic, for it is the
one basic truth given to him to know and hold on to. If one lives the
Absurd aggressively, one is in revolt; there is no difference. In both
we have a dialectical divorce between the individual and his environing
world—the individual asserting his indigenous demand against a
world which is unresponsive and threatening to this authentic demand.

Life can be lived in the Absurd/Revolt, because man has discovered, in this
experience, a value which is genuinely his own and which can justify
his life. It is this value—whatever it may specifically be—which is at
stake. It is this value which makes life worthwhile, *his* life worthwhile,
and it is this which he must not surrender. The fact that the world
may not respond to this value, may not ever allow it to be realized—
this does not detract from the basic importance of the value. If one
only demanded those things he was certain of having, then it would be
better to be a stone and not a man. And even though the cosmos
may be intractable before our fragile human demands, human history
is not; it may be unwieldy but it is not intractable. If there is tyranny
in history, one can revolt and struggle against it, realizing a partial
success. "Partial" is the important word here. If one rebels against
slavery and demands freedom, it cannot be absolute freedom one
demands; there are no absolutes left in this universe of ours and in
this history of ours—only relativities. Relative values are maintained
only by a constant tension, a constant revolt which "never forgets";
this is why revolt is, for Camus and other existential thinkers, the only
viable way of existing—personally or socially—in our present age.
Unless there be the constant tension of a human revolt whose values
hold the world at bay and correct it, there will be no human values at
all. If one forgets the tense discipline of revolt and seeks intellectually
or historically to found permanent absolute values, one ceases to
have any values at all; one may have certainty, one may have peace,
one may be anguish-free, but one has also betrayed one's authentic
humanity. Absolutism in all its forms leads to the peaceful stricture
of tyranny or slavery, both in one's intellect and in one's life.

5. Aesthetic Theory
and Practice

Existential philosophers are all drawn toward art. This is not coincidental;
it is inevitable and has a reason. Art, in its communication of static
or dramatic patterns, portrays some aspect of human existence. Art

is not intellectual in substance; it is existential. Consequently, those thinkers who are concerned with existence first, and with intellectuality as a complement to existence, are inevitably concerned about art. Some existential thinkers are concerned with artistic expression only indirectly, that is, they are passionately interested critics and analysts of art works. Others, such as Sartre, Marcel, Nietzsche, and Kierke- gaard, drift wholly or partially into artistic expression as an integral part of their vocation as an existential thinker. Certainly among those who have actively engaged in artistic writing, Albert Camus is the man who has succeeded most brilliantly in this dual function. As a stylist he is one of the great prose writers of modern France, and as a writer of novels, short stories, and drama he is an extraordinary presence in twentieth-century European letters.

One suspects that all existential thinkers would like to have the dual literary- philosophical talent of Camus—their vocation demands it in much the same way that everyone knows that all literary critics would really rather be successful writers. Camus, then, is exemplary in his fulfill- ment of the broader imperatives of communication which an existen- tial vocation involves. Such thinkers know that much of what they wish to say about existence cannot be said directly, but can be said only indirectly and artistically through the re-creation in their readers of the same existential awareness which they themselves have found important. When Camus said that "feelings and images multiply philosophy by ten," he was quite right so far as existential philosophy is concerned: one short story is more likely to get over to the reader what a lengthy, carefully argued philosophical essay might never make existentially cogent.

So then, art is not something on the side for Camus or any existential thinker; it is integral to his task. And the existentialist need have no apology to himself or to the traditional practitioners of philosophy for this dual activity. If a way of existence must come first and then, gradually, thought arises out of it, Camus' interesting way of "feeling" himself into philosophy appears to be an authentic procedure. Camus' insistence that he is an artist is, in this light, completely un- derstandable. In the chronology of Camus' writings there is a sequence of dramatic expressions of a certain existential idea leading up to the culminating philosophical expression of it. Both before *The Myth of Sisyphus* and before *The Rebel*, Camus' literary pieces already fully contain the ideas that are later to be expressed in the rhetoric of the philosophical essay. It is not surprising then, that when he turns to some of the traditional philosophical concerns, one of his prime interests is aesthetics. And the aesthetic theory which he draws from his philosophy of revolt is both lucid and forceful.

As should be clear, revolt is a way of life, a special dialectical way of existing which is creative of value. As a matrix for the creation of value, not only sociopolitical values are affirmed by revolt but aesthetic values as well. The authentic artist is a man who is in revolt, who exists constantly in the tension of revolt; it is this which makes his creation

possible.   The dialectic tension involved in artistic creation is suggested in Camus' observation that

*Art also is this movement which exalts and denies at the same time.   "No
artist tolerates reality," says Nietzsche.   This is true; but no artist can do
without reality.   Creation is demand for unity and refusal of the world.
But it refuses the world because of what it lacks and in the name of what it
sometimes is.   Revolt can be observed here, outside of history, in a pure
state with its original complication.   Art, then, should give us a final perspective of the content of revolt.*[17]

The key phrase in this statement is that creation is a "demand for unity and
refusal of the world."   One refuses the world as it is because of its
lack of conformity to the desire for unification which the individual
artist bears within himself.   Both the Yes and the No of Revolt are
here, balanced and in tension.   Authentic art can come only from this
balance and tension.   Even as, intellectually, man demands unity and
coherence in his universe, so also in art this same demand is implicit.
If, historically, revolt struggles to create a special universe reflecting
common human values, so also in art does revolt create its own
universe.

Camus points out in *The Rebel* that all of the rebel philosophies of the past
two centuries have attempted in various ways to create a substitute
universe which possesses the unity which they demand of the world.
Whether it be the isolated castles of de Sade, the islands and bare
rocks of the romantics, Nietzsche's lonely climes or, in later historical
corruptions, the prisons, concentration camps, and the closed empires
of modern politics—in every case there is expressed in some fashion
the modern rebel's demand for unity in a world which otherwise
appears fragmentary and insufficient.

The artist, says Camus, does not create in total isolation from the unacceptable world which is before him, nor does he turn outward to the
world in total imitation of it.   Authentic art is neither subjective fantasy nor imitation of reality; rather, authentic art is the individual's
transformation of given reality in terms of the demands which he
places on it.   The artist respects the reality of the world, but does not
surrender to it; the artist clings to his demands for unity, but he does
not thrust them out absolutely in total defiance of reality.   Art, like
all revolt, is a tension between man and his world in which both, to a
degree, maintain their genuine identity.   Creation, then, is a correction of the face of the world in terms of the image of man himself.
The work of art is not an exact reflection of its subject—this would be
photography.   Indeed, the subject is there, respected and recognized,
but it is not the same subject that is "really" there; it has been corrected, transformed in the image of the individual artist.

The greater one's revolt, says Camus, the greater is the artist's correction
of reality.   In every such correction, the particular artist is assert-

---

[17] Camus, *L'Homme révolté*, p. 313.

ing his own style on reality; the greater the revolt, the more extreme will be the stylization worked on the subject. It is for this reason that in a period of extreme revolt such as the present age, stylization of reality moves toward distortion and even mutilation of reality. This is, in art as in all revolt, the razor's edge of temptation where the rebel artist is lured toward a total affirmation of his inner demand and a total denial of external reality. At this point we no longer have revolt, nor, according to Camus, do we have authentic art.

The two great temptations in art are the extremes of formalism and realism; in either case there is a betrayal of the rebel existence necessary to art. Formalism is this total denial of one's given reality so that one can emptily, fleshlessly assert the personal demand that burns within. This almost mystical extreme found in contemporary art may be interesting, rational, and geometrical, but it is not engaged with reality. It is not art, but desperation. In the same way, the strong contemporary trend toward realism, in which the artist lies in the dust before the minutiae of reality, lending nothing of himself or his vision to this reality—this abdication of man to the world is not authentic human art, it is a dehumanizing surrender. Revolt as an essential dimension of human reality has its own implicit limits, and art cannot except itself from these limits. Art demands much of a man: an ongoing tension and passion which the artist sustains from his own being. With the passionate integrity discovered in revolt, the artist confronts the world, sees its insufficiency in the light of his own vision, and then proceeds to transform this world.

This thoroughly humanistic and dialectical aesthetics is much the same as that of Nietzsche, and Camus has, in the spirit of this theory, moved into the arts and created a world which bears the marks of his own unique style. His literary pieces have been effective vehicles for the expression of the way of existence which he calls "Revolt" and for the criticism of those ways of existence which he finds to be dehumanizing or murderously destructive of humanity.

In the allegorical play, *State of Siege*, he depicts the Spanish city of Cadiz, suddenly, inexplicably stricken with the plague. But the plague in this instance is not a furtive disease; rather, it is personified. The Plague, a man, moves into the city, takes command, closes the gates of the town and begins his reign. This, a satire on the desperate attempts of totalitarian governments to create unity and justice by brute force, portrays the Plague as possessed of absolute power of life and death. The Plague organizes things so that men shall die orderly and rationally—not according to their chaotic, ill-timed natural span of life, but according to their efficiency and contribution to the community. He rightly claims that he has thus brought order out of chaos, justice out of injustice in the lives of men. The tyranny of the Plague descends upon the people of Cadiz and presses them until they can bear it no longer, and eventually the No of revolt is pronounced. It finds its first voice in the central figure, Diego, who says to the Plague:

I have come to understand your system quite well. You have given them pain, and hunger, and separation to distract them from their revolt. You exhaust them, swallow up their time and their strength, so that they will have neither the leisure nor force for fury. Don't worry, they are really cowed! They are alone in spite of their mass, as I too am alone. Each of us is alone because of the cowardice of others. . . . Don't laugh, don't laugh, fool. You are defeated, I tell you. In the midst of your most evident victories, you are already defeated, because there is in man . . . a force which you shall not reduce, a lucid madness, mixed with fear, unknowing and yet victorious for all times.[18]

Diego's words are not so much a description of revolt as an evidence of it, taken from a moment in human drama. The finitude, the weakness, the cowardice and exhaustion of men are taken fully into account, but at the same time the Plague is told that this oppression can be borne only within certain limits; past these limits men will revolt and the Plague will no longer have its power over them. The reign will be at an end.

In the long novel, *The Plague*, Camus deals realistically with an historical situation and not with one which is allegorical. The Algerian city of Oran is stricken with the plague, and, the city quarantined within its own walls, its people are left to struggle in their various ways with the creeping death which haunts them. This situation, of course, is symbolical of the rebel idea that men must assert themselves in struggle against a world which ever threatens them. In the course of the novel, many of the citizens of Oran betray their humanity in the desperation of their struggle; there are others who do not, and these few are examples of *l'homme révolté*. Two such men are Dr. Rieux and his friend, Tarrou. In the midst of their medical services to the city, the two men, exhausted, find a moment of respite. They stand on a balcony overlooking the city, and a moment comes when they reflect upon their own vocations as men.

"In the end," said Tarrou with simplicity, "what interests me is knowing how to become a saint."
"But you don't believe in God."
"Exactly. Can one be a saint without God? That's the only real problem I know of today."

A few moments later, this further thought is added:

"Perhaps," replied the doctor, "but, you know, I have much more feeling of solidarity with the defeated than I have with saints. I don't think that I have a taste for heroism and sainthood. What I am concerned with is being a man."
"Yes, we're both looking for the same thing, except that I am less ambitious."[19]

Dr. Rieux, in going beneath the peace and fulfillment implied in sainthood, has touched something fundamental and "ambitious"—simply being a man, authentically and honestly a man, this is the final goal which

---

[18] *Albert Camus, L'Etat de siège, Gallimard, Paris, 1948, pp. 175–176.*
[19] *Albert Camus, La Peste, Gallimard, Paris, 1947, p. 210.*

is not a goal at all, because it is a way of existence: it is the life of Revolt.

In Camus' simple and classic work, *The Stranger*, we find one of the finest expressions of the dialectic of Revolt to be found anywhere in the literature of Camus. "Finest," because of the simple lyricism with which it is expressed. In this story we trace the life of the young Algerian office worker, Meursault, through a series of innocent, nonchalant, and meandering events; the final event in this series is his unpremeditated shooting of an Arab on a beach at midday. Meursault, whose eyes are hypersensitive to light, is blinded and confused by the dazzling light and heat of the beach, and when he encounters the Arab, with whom he had already had an altercation, the Arab draws a knife, catching the sun, and the already distraught Meursault, blinded by the flash of steel, thinks he is being attacked and fires the gun that he happens to be carrying.

When Meursault is brought to trial, the prosecution is not concerned to prove homicide, for this is already admitted; instead the prosecution attempts to sum up the various innocent and meandering events of his life in such a way that it becomes clear that Meursault has a depraved, criminal mentality and has cold-bloodedly murdered the Arab. The fascinating transformation is that these events which we have already seen in the light of drifting innocence are now seen, through the charge of the prosecutor, in the light of absolute moral values. A strict moral judgment is placed upon each act of Meursault, and once these judgments are summed up, a convincing case is made that Meursault is a criminal monster. He is condemned to death. The simple contrast here is between the judgment of a man's life in terms of its chartless, day-to-day unpretentiousness or the judging of that life in terms of moral legalism. When legislatic morality descends upon a man, he is crushed, because absolute moral values have no direct correspondence with the life of the human creature.

Meursault, waiting in his prison cell, attempts in his fumbling way to come to terms with the death that awaits him and the strange courtroom scene that somehow brought him to this point. As he says, "It was as if familiar paths, traced under summer skies, could lead just as well to prison as to innocent sleep."[20] Meursault was not ashamed of the life he had lived; unspectacular as it was, he was happy with it. His few good friends, the feeling of evening coming over the city, moments of love, the wash of the Mediterranean's water about his body—these things gave an irreplaceable sweetness to an unambitious but happy life. He did not want to abandon these things; such as it was, this was life for him, and he would not have it any other way. And so, when the prison chaplain visits his cell, and urges him to repent of his former life, renounce it in the expectation of that other life which awaits him after death, Meursault, after patient listening, explodes into revolt against this demand to deny the one happy reality he had known in favor of an imaginary world which he knows

[20] *Camus, L'Etranger, p. 138.*

nothing about. The one thing he knew was that this life which he had loved was to be taken away from him by men who had, in the light of their moral ideals, condemned him as monstrous. It was enough that his life should be demanded for the sake of an ideal system of values, but it was too much to demand that he renounce the quiet happiness of his own life for the sake of an ideal kingdom. This reality was all he had left, and during the short time that he still possessed it, he intended to hold to it as something precious and irreplaceable. With death awaiting not only Meursault, but also the priest, Meursault's sweetheart, and his friends, all men were suddenly seen on the same level; all men were condemned to death in some fashion, and before they dropped into that oblivion, each of them had this life, however incomplete it might be—they had *this* life, flowing away moment by moment, which no deceitfulness, no ideal vision could deny or disparage. Meursault accepted existence as it was, imperfect but sufficient; and he accepted his fellowmen as they were, imperfect but sufficient, who were equally capable of being his friends or in other circumstances of being the easily swayed jury which could condemn him. This was the fragile and pathetic stuff of which men were made, and Meursault understood and accepted it, because he too was like this, and he too, confused and used, might have voted to condemn a man. No one is to be condemned, no one is to be saddled down with a judgment that comes from "above." As Meursault, goaded by the priest, pours out his revolt, he realizes that he has accepted his futile but happy life as well as the meandering lives of others for what they are: fitful struggles against nature and history to find a modicum of happiness in a strange and indifferent world. The nearness of death and the predication of the priest brought forth from him the same fresh reaffirmation of life that he had seen his mother, now dead, experience during her last days.

The priest departed.

With him gone, I was calm once again. Exhausted, I threw myself down on the bunk. I think I must have fallen asleep, because I awoke with stars above my head. Sounds of the countryside came into me. Odors of the night, of earth and salt cooled my temples. The marvelous peace of this slumbering summer poured into me like a tide. . . . So near to death, Mama must have felt herself free and ready to live everything over again. No one, no one at all had the right to weep over her. And I too felt myself ready to live everything over. As if this great anger had left me purged of evil, empty of hope, before this night teeming with signs and stars, for the first time in my life I gave myself up to the tender indifference of the world. Feeling that it was so much like me, so fraternal, I knew that I had been happy and that I still was.[21]

All of it is here. Meursault has come to terms with the world as it is and with himself as he is. The hopeless, inevitable, wonderful dialectic is there; it is the only way life can be lived with lucid honesty—shunning both illusions and escape. In revolt he has come to know the world,

---

[21] *Ibid., pp. 171–172.*

himself, and all the others who like himself seek the same limping happiness. The Yes to himself, the No to the indifferent world, the solidarity with others: all is here. But one more thing is here which is distinctively Camusian. The world may be indifferent, but this is a tender indifference. However strange, however incomprehensible and however hostile it might be, this world, this one reality given us, has beauty for those who are able to see it. The revolt of the modern soul, in shaking loose from the futile illusions of the past, has not triumphed in a lucid but barren honesty. It has gained more than this: in opening himself to honesty, honesty has opened him to the beauty of the world.

PART FOUR
REVOLT AND HISTORY

If revolt affirms the solidarity of men, revolt can never give sanction to murder. But modern revolt, as it has assumed the task of transforming history, has created political systems which spawn murder, which constitutionally affirm murder as a normal operation of the body politic. This being true, the revolutionary frenzy which has increasingly gripped the earth since the explosion of the French Revolution has been a betrayal of the values of revolt. Modern revolutions have failed to achieve that unity or solidarity or freedom which, with the initial passion of revolt, they set out to accomplish. From the French *Terreur* of the 1790s to the Soviet purges of the 1930s and the Chinese purges of the 1960s, modern history has been a series of disastrous failures to achieve those human and social values which revolutions pretended to establish. Camus' thesis is that the twentieth century, as the climax of this growing revolutionary frenzy, has become an age of legalized murder.

Camus' philosophy of revolt has not only its personal and aesthetic aspects, but it also has clear political ramifications. These ramifications come from the fundamental idea that revolt has its own limits, its own balance, which never denies more than it affrms. Revolt is an ongoing struggle to correct and transform the world, but this No of correction can never go so far as to destroy in the world the very values which feed this protest; if this happens, then we no longer have the groping tension of revolt but rather the murderous aggression of certain and absolute values.

When the end is absolute, i.e., historically speaking, when one believes it to be certain, then one can go to the point of sacrificing others. When it is not, one can sacrifice only oneself in the battle for common dignity. Does the end justify the means? This is possible. But what will justify the end? To this question, which historical revolt leaves hanging, revolt replies: the means.[22]

If a man or a party or a nation or an empire is in possession of truths which are certain and admit of no doubt, it is inevitable that those who

[22] *Camus, L'Homme révolté, p. 361.*

stand in the way of the realization of these truths must be eliminated. This is logical, moral, and in the nature of things when men believe in political absolutes. And it is in the nature of things, says Camus, that ours is the century of legalized murder. A fixed, certain ideal is paramount over any human demurral; the ideal cannot be wrong, therefore it is the intractable human who is wrong and must be disposed of. In this atmosphere, constructive criticism becomes deviationism and dissent becomes treason. Concentration camps and mass executions are the striking symbols of modern politics, and the irony of it is that these inhuman institutions have been developed by regimes in the name of human freedom and justice.

Again, it is the "reflex." In politics, absolute values have come to replace that void left by the absolute Lawgiver, God, now that men have ceased to believe in the efficacy of this God. Men must still believe in something other than themselves, they still must believe that values are somehow permanently "given" in the very structure of nature or history, and not that values are the difficult creations of men themselves. As Camus sees it, the great metaphysical revolt against God has been accompanied by the historical revolt against the God whose name sanctioned the oppression by the Church and the injustice of kings over the burghers and peasants of Europe. In revolting against this Godhead of oppression, men were affirming a common need for a world of solidarity, of innocence, of justice, and of freedom. But the balance of revolt was not maintained for long, and soon men and societies veered toward the extremes, affirming one pole of their revolt to the exclusion of the other.

The betrayal of revolt has, historically, led to two murderous extremes. One extreme is the despair of nihilism, when the No of revolt is totally affirmed with a destructiveness that has lost all memory of why it needs to destroy. The other extreme is formalism, which clings to its own absolute values with such tenacity that it has no correspondence to the reality of the world; political formalism is the reactionary frenzy which chops down with an immutable cookie cutter, brutally forcing everything beneath it into its mold. Both political nihilism and formalism are murderous extremes, and it is just such extremes which ferment in modern political life.

Camus has developed his political philosophy in *The Rebel*, the three volumes of *Chroniques* and also in the brief *Letters to a German Friend*. We have already spoken of the sharp distinction which Camus makes between revolt as an uncertain way of existence and revolution as the attempt to force a clear idea into historical reality. Revolutions, Camus observes, are by definition destined to fail in their designs, simply because the ideal system which they have conceived to correct a present injustice turns out not to fit the new reality that has been created by the act of revolution itself. The problem is that fixed, ideal political patterns are inflexible, while human history is fluid. Absolute values have no place in human history; when they do take a place, there is destruction. This is where the ongoing, ever-adjusting protest of revolt is asserted, by Camus, to be the only humanly acceptable way of transforming political structures.

But even though transcendent values may not be efficacious in political reform, Camus points out that, at least, they are efficient—brutally so. Beginning with the French Revolution, which we have already discussed in Part Two, men have taken the place of God in ordering the affairs of society. With the death of God, the ideal kingdom was no longer separate from human history; it was declared to be a part of history, waiting at the end of a long series of revolutionary transformations. If the theorists of the French Revolution replaced the transcendent God with an ideal of Reason which was supposed to be operative in history, this theoretical tendency was fulfilled in the political thought of Hegel, whom Camus calls "the Napoleonic philosopher." With Hegel the ideals of reason, justice, and truth were seen to be integral with history, but in historicizing these values Hegel asserted that they were not something that men could possess and enjoy now, at this historical moment, but rather that they were final goals which were to be realized at the end of history. With this transmutation of values, the foundation is laid for what Camus calls the rational and irrational state terrorism of the twentieth century—political systems where no values guide and limit the actions of the state, where ideal values are placed at the end of an historical development, thus delivering the state into a frenzy of activity moving relentlessly toward this ideal goal. This is a philosophy of efficacity where there is no limit to actions in the present; any and all actions in the present moment are justified in the light of that ultimate goal which they are designed to accomplish. Given this political attitude, injustice may be used to create an eventual state of ideal justice; slavery may be sanctioned as one of the means necessary to create an eventual social freedom.

The irrational terror of the fascist states of Germany and Italy were made possible by this philosophy of efficacity. In Nazism, all of Germany moved toward a vague, anti-Christian empire of soldier-workers, following the *Führer* who was the immanent God, embodying this ultimate, promised reality. In fascism, tribal, provincially oriented urges are elevated to the level of a political religion. In the impassioned movement toward the promised kingdom, the enemy became anyone who was not part of the nation, and any means of destroying the enemy were justified by the sanctity of this mission. Camus argues powerfully that it is the force of belief in absolute historical values that made possible the mass cold-blooded slaughters, the inhuman tortures, the concentration camps, and slave labor of the Nazi state. When one is controlled by nonhuman values beyond history, one's actions in history will be inhuman.

The same analysis is applied to Marxist-Leninism in its prophecy of a predestined classless society which awaits all men and which all men must aid in realizing. When such a kingdom is ultimately right and ultimately necessary, deceit, brutality, injustice, and slavery are all absolutely justified as means for its realization. In Marxist-Leninism we have, says Camus, the philosophy of rational state terrorism where human life is reduced to historical activity, an activity where one sacrifices oneself and others for the sake of a future goal.

This is the murderous visage of this century's political life, and Camus, though he hoped otherwise, did not see an end in sight for this frenzy of destruction in the name of exalted values. In applying his philosophy of revolt to this inescapable modern movement toward reform and revolution, he points out the necessary limits that are involved in any such activity. He sees two antinomies which relentlessly haunt political change: the antinomy of violence/nonviolence, and that of justice/freedom. A state may seek to refrain from violence, but in many cases this nonviolence may indirectly create the even greater, widespread violence of slavery or injustice. But if violence becomes necessary to correct this, it must be performed for the sake of those political institutions which seek to preserve nonviolence. The antinomy is that, politically, both are necessary yet they are contradictory; a politics of rationality would insist that we choose one or the other; a politics of revolt insists that we recognize both as in constant tension according to the fluid nature of a society. In the same way, if a revolution, protesting a traditional injustice, attempts to establish a regime of total justice, it may succeed, but it will also succeed in totally destroying all freedom. And if, on the other hand, the attempt is made to create a society of total freedom, it is just this freedom which will allow the strong to dominate the weak, creating social injustice. Both justice and freedom are essential political desiderata, but they are in conflict; to desire either of them as if they were absolute values for society is to destroy the other. A realistic politics knows that one can never have more than a relative justice and relative freedom; they must be constantly in tension, constantly in adjustment as men, faithful to the life of revolt, respond to the political reality about them. If a revolution seeks to correct social injustice, its first act, when power is seized, should be to guarantee a certain freedom in the midst of its efforts to establish a new justice—otherwise the creation of a new and equally intolerable tyranny becomes inevitable.

Absolutism or limited struggle: this is the choice held out by Camus.

There are two kinds of efficacity, that of the typhoon and that of the sap. Historical absolutism is not efficacious, it is efficient; it has taken and held on to power. Once in possession of power it destroys the one creative reality. Intransigent and limited action, which is the expression of revolt, maintains this reality and attempts only to extend it more and more. It is not said that this line of action cannot conquer. It is said that it runs the risk of not conquering and dying. But revolution will either take this risk or else it will confess that it is nothing more than an undertaking of new masters, meriting the same contempt."[23]

Whether the "efficacity of the sap" can be affirmed, Camus does not know. He felt it his duty to state the alternatives, clarify them and let men choose. Beyond this he can only hope; he has "done his job," as he says. He has also remarked that although he is pessimistic about history he is optimistic about man—this in contrast to Christianity

which, he says, affirms the reverse.   Historically, the last great instance of authentic political revolt that Camus can point to is that of
the young Russian terrorists, the "fastidious murders," whose activities during the first decade of this century have been dramatized in
his play, *The Righteous (Les Justes)*.[24]

Camus' quiet pessimism about the future is founded in his understanding
of the confusion and anguish of the modern individual trying to live
in a world that he sees bereft of God.   Easily the most penetrating
analysis of this confusion and anguish is the strange confessional
narrative, *The Fall (La Chute)*,[25] which concerns a man who has discovered the freedom consequent of the death of God, but who at the
same time is afraid of it.   He cannot go back to traditional morality,
nor can he go forward to that creative personal revolt wherein a man
creates his own relative, groping values.   The time is not yet ripe.
The age is not yet ripe; the "reflex" is weakened but not dead.

Caught in a century of individual anxiety and political convulsion, Camus
nevertheless holds out hope for the individual, at least the individual
who lives the tension of revolt.   In the short story, "The Guest"
("*L'Hôte*"),[26] we have an exceptional example of how an individual
can live the life of revolt in the midst of warring ideologies.   When
the Algerian schoolmaster, Daru, has an Arab prisoner handed over to
him by the French authorities and is asked to deliver the Arab to a
nearby prison, Daru does not guarantee that he will do so.   Even the
gun left him by the policeman, who was rushing back to help battle a
group of Algerian rebels, is useless to Daru.   Even though he knows
the Arab is a murderer, he puts the gun away in a desk drawer.
Later he prepares supper for the young Arab, makes a cot for him,
and sleeps through the night in the same room with the "prisoner."
The following morning he prepares a bag lunch, leaves the isolated
schoolhouse where he lives in the plateaux of Algeria, and motions
for the Arab to follow him.   They walk until they come to a high
level, where the path divides; one path goes toward the state prison,
the other goes downward back to the Arab village which is the young
prisoner's home.   Daru stops at the fork, gives the Arab a thousand-
franc note and the bag lunch, then turns around and walks back.
After walking for a few minutes, he stops, turns, and goes back up
to the fork.   When he reaches it, he looks down the long path leading
to the prison and sees the Arab moving slowly in that direction.
Later, when he returns to the schoolhouse, he finds that Arab terrorists have broken in, scrawling across the blackboard the threat that
he would pay for having delivered their compatriot to the authorities.

Trapped between the demands of two murderous authorities, Daru has
served neither and has sinned against both.   But he possesses the
honor of being in the truth.   Such a story "multiplies philosophy by

---

[24] *Albert Camus, Les Justes, Gallimard, Paris, 1950.*
[25] *Camus, La Chute.*
[26] *"L'Hôte" is from the collection of short stories of Albert Camus, L'Exil et le royaume,
Gallimard, Paris, 1957, pp. 101–124.*

ten." It is a concrete example of an individual standing alone, with apparently empty hands, in proud and confident defiance of all those who have forgotten what it is to be a man.

BIBLIOGRAPHY

Works of Albert Camus (in the original chronological order)

1 *L'Envers et l'endroit,* Charlot, Algiers, 1937; Gallimard, Paris, 1958.

2 *Noces,* Charlot, Algiers, 1938; Gallimard, Paris, 1947.

3 *L'Etranger,* Gallimard, Paris, 1942.

4 *Le Mythe de Sisyphe,* Gallimard, Paris, 1942.

5 *Le Malentendu, suivi de Caligula,* Gallimard, Paris, 1944.

6 *Lettres à un ami allemand,* Gallimard, Paris, 1945.

7 "Remarque sur la révolte," *L'Existence,* ed. Jean Greiner, Gallimard, Paris, 1945.

8 *La Peste,* Gallimard, Paris, 1947.

9 *L'Etat de siège,* Gallimard, Paris, 1948.

10 *Actuelles,* Gallimard, Paris, 1950.

11 *Les Justes,* Gallimard, Paris, 1950.

12 *L'Homme révolté,* Gallimard, Paris, 1951.

13 *Actuelles II,* Gallimard, Paris, 1953.

14 *L'Eté,* Gallimard, Paris, 1954.

15 *La Chute,* Gallimard, Paris, 1956.

16 *L'Exil et le royaume,* Gallimard, Paris, 1957.

17 *Actuelles III,* Gallimard, Paris, 1958.

18 *Carnets, mai 1935–février 1942,* Gallimard, Paris, 1962.

CHAPTER EIGHT

MAURICE MERLEAU-PONTY
INCARNATE CONSCIOUSNESS

DAVID CARR

DAVID CARR *is an assistant professor of philosophy at Yale University, where he received his B.A., M.A., and Ph.D. He also spent two years in Europe, studying at the Universities of Heidelberg and Paris. He is presently preparing an English translation of Husserl's Die Krisis der europäischen Wissenschaften.*

Maurice Merleau-Ponty was one of the youngest of the twentieth-century
philosophers of existence, and perhaps the least known, especially
outside France.   But his philosophy has a unique and important place
among the works of his contemporaries, and his untimely death
interrupted a productive career of highly original writings.[1]   As one
surveys his published work, one has the feeling of being witness to
the "first stage" of a philosopher's thought without knowing exactly
what the second stage is to be.   Merleau-Ponty's most recent essays
give evidence of an important reevaluation, one which, though still
occupied with the same themes, recognizes new significance in them.

While it is difficult to guess the precise direction Merleau-Ponty's philosophy
might have taken, it is quite possible to grasp the fundamental unity
of the many writings which were published during his lifetime.
Merleau-Ponty's essays, whether on literature or science, politics or
art, are but variations on a unified philosophical conception of man,
experience, the world, and being.   This unity does not imply simplicity, nor does the appearance of being a "first stage" indicate
immaturity.   On the contrary, the central conception itself is developed in reflections of considerable richness and complexity.   It is to
the elucidation of these reflections that I hope to contribute in the
following pages.

1. *Existence* *and Dialectic*

Merleau-Ponty can be called an "existentialist" if this term is understood
not as an indication of pessimism, irrationalism, or the tragic view
of life, but rather in the sense that philosophical issues are referred
ultimately to man's concrete situation in his physical, social, and
historical *milieu*.   Concentrating on man's relation to the world,
Merleau-Ponty finds that man himself has been misunderstood by
philosophers, and must be reconsidered.   Philosophy, in turn,
becomes more than a series of propositions which can be true or
false; since it is reflection by man about man, it takes up one of the
earliest conceptions of philosophy, that of a philosophical ethics based
on self-knowledge.

Merleau-Ponty shares this view of philosophy with his European contemporaries, and the result of his reconsideration of man is similar to
theirs, though not always the same.   Naturally he objects to the

Note: *The works abbreviated by capital letters are identified in the bibliography p. 428.*
Page references to the Phénoménologie de la perception and Eloge de la
Philosophie are to the published translations, although the exposition here
often requires the substitution of my own translation; more recent translations,
mentioned in the bibliography, were not available for use in these references.

[1] *Maurice Merleau-Ponty was born at Rochefort-sur-Mer in 1908.   He was professor of*
philosophy at Lyon, later at the Sorbonne and finally at the Collège de France.
He died in 1961 in Paris.

classical notions of spiritual substance, the *res cogitans* of Descartes; he conceives of man as a project, a happening, or what Sartre has called a "being-event."[2]   For Merleau-Ponty, the word "existence" designates a conception of man for which traditional philosophical anthropology had no name.   It is not a magic word for him; in fact, it does not occur very often in his writings.   More frequent and more important is the term "being-in-the-world" (*être au monde*).   Yet these are both borrowed from Jaspers and Heidegger and do not do justice to the originality of his own approach.   The most striking and most significant of Merleau-Ponty's expressions sounds, paradoxically, the most traditional: man is the "incarnate spirit."   It is largely in the conception of incarnation that the difference between Merleau-Ponty and his colleagues is best expressed, as we shall see.

The notion of the incarnate spirit—this union of the two substances which philosophers kept apart for centuries—brings up an important preliminary remark.   Merleau-Ponty's philosophy, perhaps more than that of any of his contemporaries, is *dialectical* in nature.   This is true not only because he often speaks of dialectic and because he is sympathetic toward Hegel and Marx.   It is also because dialectic, with its central notions of negation and mediation, seems to animate his approach to almost every philosophical problem.   One attitude is criticized and rejected, and gives rise to its opposite as the natural alternative.   The latter is in turn rejected as too extreme—the negation of the negation occurs—and the result is a mediation between the two which, in the true spirit of the Hegelian *Aufhebung*, preserves that which has been surpassed.

Now there is a sense in which, as Alphonse de Waelhens has pointed out, (Cf. SC vi–xi) Merleau-Ponty provides an important mediation between the philosophies of Heidegger and Sartre, both of which influenced him a great deal.   It is not, however, in debate with these thinkers that Merleau-Ponty presents his ideas.   In order to arrive at the "fundamental conception of existence" of which I spoke, let us leave the others aside and follow the particular dialectic which is the form of Merleau-Ponty's main work, the *Phenomenology of Perception*, and its companion piece, *The Structure of Behavior*.   This dialectic will be found in the tension between two views of perception and perceiving, one common to objectivist psychology and physiology, the other typical of classical epistemology.   The mediation between these two doctrines is found in phenomenology, and the resulting conception of experience is the way to the understanding of man.

But why "perception," and what is "phenomenology"?   The convergence of these two ideas is the very birthplace of Merleau-Ponty's reflection; and in order to understand it, the discussion of his works must be prefaced with a word on Husserl.

---

[2] *Jean-Paul Sartre, "Merleau-Ponty vivant," Les Temps Modernes, 1961, nos. 184–185 (special issue), p. 308.*

2. Husserl
and Merleau-Ponty

Husserl, the founder of the phenomenological movement, has rightly been
called (because of the importance, not because of the content of his
philosophy) the "Kant of the twentieth century." It is impossible to
understand almost any contemporary European philosopher without
understanding him. But the relation of Merleau-Ponty to Husserl is a
special one. Even though he knew "neither the daily conversation nor
even the instruction of Husserl" (S 202f.), it is obvious that Merleau-
Ponty considers his own philosophy the necessary fulfillment of Husserl's phenomenology. The latter is quoted and discussed from the
earliest to the very latest of Merleau-Ponty's writings, and is the
object of considerable admiration.

Husserl began with an effort to clarify the sciences, starting with the science
of logic, by examining and describing the "essence" of the "experiences" (*Erlebnisse*)[3] on which they are based. It soon became clear
to him that such an examination, if treated with sufficient rigor, was
a fruitful approach to the theory of knowledge in general. In order to
preserve the purity of the investigation, nothing was to be assumed in
advance about the elements of experience: whether its objects "really"
exist; what the effect of natural forces on consciousness might be;
what is *a priori* and what is "*a posteriori*," etc.—all the problems
and solutions of traditional epistemology, psychology and science were
put aside in an effort to get "to the things themselves." If science
was to be understood from the ground up, then the conceptions resulting from science could not be used in order to understand it.

While all presuppositions *about* the elements of experience are suspended,
however, these elements themselves remain. The entire range of
consciousness with all its possible objects—in short, all being—
becomes the subject matter of Husserl's investigation, but in a new
mode. Since all presuppositions as to what it is "in itself" are
suspended, it becomes "the universe of phenomena,"[4] the world *as*
experienced. Husserl compares the elimination of presuppositions
about the world with the Cartesian systematic doubt, calling this transformation of the world-as-existing to the world-as-experienced the
"phenomenological reduction." What remains after the reduction,
it must be remembered, is not only the Cartesian *cogito*, but the
inseparable combination *ego-cogito-cogitatum*.[5]

At this point the stage has only been set for the description of experience,
consciousness, and objectivity in general. At the center of this
description is the conception of the "intentionality" of consciousness,
that is, that "all consciousness is consciousness *of* something." The
world, as the ultimate horizon of this "something," becomes the

[3] *Cf. E. Husserl,* Logische Untersuchungen, *2d ed., M. Niemeyer, Halle, 1913, vol. 2,
p. 2.*
[4] *E. Husserl,* Cartesian Meditations, *tr. D. Cairns, M. Nijhoff, The Hague, 1960, p. 20.*
[5] *Ibid., p. 33.*

intentional correlate of conscious activity. The necessary unity of consciousness and the world in the *cogitationes* becomes the field of phenomenological investigation to which Husserl devoted his life, and which I cannot, of course, begin to recount in detail.

But one important turning point in Husserl's phenomenology is crucial for the understanding of Merleau-Ponty. This is the notion of the genesis of meaning (*Sinngenesis*). Husserl had originally rejected the genetic question—that of where experience and knowledge "come from" in any causal or historical sense—in favor of the study of the pure essence of experience. Once the idea of phenomenology had matured, he turned his efforts toward the experiences which underlay the sciences: those of physical objects, "psychophysical" beings, mathematical concepts, etc. He sought to discover the essential constitution of the various regions as objects of experience, and the theoretical-conscious attitudes of which they are the correlates. Alongside the theoretical attitudes of science was the more general "natural attitude," the correlate of which is simply "reality." " 'The' world is as fact-world always there," as Husserl put it. The natural attitude is the affirmation of the world that "exists out there," from which we distinguish "mere appearance" and hallucination.[6]

Yet Husserl recognized that the "natural attitude" is itself a theoretical attitude[7] in the sense that it is thetic or predicative of existence. It is, in fact, the philosophic attitude of naïve realism, which is not necessarily "natural," but rather what one might say if one "stopped to think" for the first time about the world. All other theoretic attitudes, from that of physical science to that of the most abstract ideality, were seen to derive by a process of discrimination from this basic thetic activity of consciousness. Now it is clear that in speaking of the "origin," e.g. of the physical-scientific attitude with its correlate range of objects, *in* the natural attitude, we have introduced the notion of "genesis" without any implication of causality or temporal history.

But what, in turn, is the origin of the natural theoretical attitude and its world of natural "reality"? To answer this question, Husserl is directed toward an even more "natural world concept" (*natürlicher Weltbegriff*) which is the "field of all possible sciences of the world" (*Weltwissenschaften*). This he calls the "life-world" (*Lebenswelt*), which is the sphere not of scientific "objects," but of values, cultural goods, desires, etc.[8] Once this turn is made, Husserl's undertaking becomes a truly genetic phenomenology, and the "first task," even of a theory of logic or doctrine of judgments, becomes "the genetic tracing of predicative self-evidence back to non-predicative self-evidence, which is called experience (*Erfahrung*)."[9] Toward the end of his life

6 E. Husserl, Ideas, General Introduction to Pure Phenomenology, tr. W. R. Boyce Gibson, Macmillan, New York, 1958, p. 106.

7 Ibid., p. 51.

8 E. Husserl, Ideen zu einer reinen Phänomenologie, etc., M. Nijhoff, The Hague, 1952, vol. II (Husserliana, vol. IV), pp. 375ff.

9 E. Husserl, Formale und transzendentale Logik, M. Niemeyer, Halle, 1929, p. 186.

he designated the understanding of the *Lebenswelt*, this pre-predicative sphere of "*praxis*," not as a partial problem but as the "most universal" problem of philosophy.[10]

It is this last point that Merleau-Ponty takes up as he enters the phenomenological enterprise and focuses his attention on perception. Husserl himself had indicated the "field of perception"[11] as the heart of the *Lebenswelt*. In Husserlian terminology, Merleau-Ponty takes the "life-world"—or, as he calls it, the "lived world" (*monde vécu*)—as the "intentional object" of this sphere of experience, while perception is the conscious activity in which this "object" is "constituted."[12]

This is of course to put Merleau-Ponty's phenomenology in terms which are not his own. In fact, it is precisely in his revision of the phenomenological program that one of the main characteristics of his philosophy is found. But the indication of the way in which his thought "follows" Husserl's has been in order to emphasize the first and most important fact about Merleau-Ponty's major work: when it discusses "perception," it is not referring to an isolated psychological phenomenon which occurs "in" the world. Rather, perception is the "origin" in the Husserlian sense, of the world in all the complexity it can have for the human subject. The "world" is not a given "place" in which experience occurs, but is that toward which one is turned in experience.

3. The Primacy of Perception

This view is most clearly expressed in the preface to the *Phenomenology of Perception*, which begins with the question: What is phenomenology? Here Merleau-Ponty takes up several Husserlian themes and comments upon them, placing much emphasis on the phenomenology of the lived world. After repeating Husserl's call for a descriptive, rather than explicative or analytical philosophy, Merleau-Ponty equates this with the suspension of the acquisitions of science:

The whole universe of science is built upon the lived world, and if we want to subject science itself to rigorous scrutiny and arrive at a precise assessment of its meaning and scope, we must begin by reawakening the basic experience of the world of which science is the second-order expression.

What Husserl had called the return "to the things themselves," is the return to

that world which precedes knowledge, of which knowledge always speaks, and in relation to which every scientific schematization is an abstract and derivative sign-language, as is geography in relation to the countryside in

---

[10] E. Husserl, *Die Krisis der europäischen Wissenschaften und die transzendentale Phänomenologie*, 2d ed., M. Nijhoff, The Hague, 1962, (Husserliana, vol. VI), p. 137.

[11] "*Wahrnehmungsfeld*," Ibid., p. 108.

[12] Cf. A. de Waelhens, *Une Philosophie de l'ambiguïté: L'Existentialisme de Maurice Merleau-Ponty, Publications universitaires de Louvain*, 1951, p. 92.

which we have learnt beforehand what a forest, a prairie, or a river is (PP viiif.).

For Merleau-Ponty, however, the return to the lived world becomes an even more urgent and important task than it was for Husserl. For the latter the world of perception, while perhaps the most "original" level of consciousness, was nevertheless but one stage in the range of phenomenological investigations which led from the lowest to the highest levels of conscious activity. The return to this world was the obligation of philosophy to discover its forgotten origins. Merleau-Ponty's position is that while Husserl pointed the way toward the *Lebenswelt*, he did not observe it closely enough to discover its real significance. If he had, he would have seen the necessity to revise his other conceptions of experience. For according to Merleau-Ponty, "the philosopher learns to know, in contact with perception, a relation with being which makes necessary and possible a new analysis of the understanding (*entendement*)"[13] (the latter being taken in the Kantian sense as the rational faculty). "The certitude of the idea does not found the certitude of perception, but rests upon it. . . ." The primary example of this is that perception "teaches us the passage from one moment to another and procures the unity of time" (Pr 120). The primordial structures of perception pervade and influence the entire range of reflective and scientific experience to such an extent that the investigation of perception embraces the problem of consciousness in general.

This indicates what Merleau-Ponty calls the "primacy of perception" for the philosophical concern. The phenomenology of perception becomes not only an important task within phenomenology, but practically the definition of phenomenology. Previous philosophy's concentration on the knowing situation alone, its definition of the world as that which is discovered by science, and its neglect of the problem of perception have led to grave epistemological misconceptions. Most important of all, philosophy has misunderstood man himself, the perceiving being.

Yet this is to move ahead to what might be called the "results" and "conclusions" of the study of perception; it is impossible to understand these results without knowing first what Merleau-Ponty means by perception. It will be found that he understands it in a sense quite different from the traditional one. After the discussion of the motivations which lead Merleau-Ponty back to the "lived world," it is worthwhile to follow him as he turns to its investigation.

4. From Consciousness to Behavior

Merleau-Ponty, unlike Husserl, is not one to start from scratch, and it is here that one joins the critical-dialectical approach mentioned earlier. It has been seen how phenomenology leads the philosopher to the

---

[13] Annuaire du Collège de France, *Imprimerie Nationale, Paris, 1953, p. 145.*

problem of perception; but in another sense, perception leads him to phenomenology. This is, in fact, the order in which Merleau-Ponty presents his work. Seeing in traditional philosophy either the misunderstanding or the complete neglect of the problem of perception, Merleau-Ponty turns first to the area in which it has been treated, at least in name, the most thoroughly: physiology and experimental psychology.

Merleau-Ponty began his philosophic career with the publication of La Structure du comportement, a book which seems far removed indeed from the phenomenological "re-awakening of the experience of the world." He admits in fact that during most of the book he has "pretended to know nothing about man through reflection," and that he has limited himself to developing "that which was implicit in the scientific representation of his behavior" (SC 199). The work deals with some of the most technical aspects of physiological psychology and seems at first glance to be nothing but the critique of a certain branch of science. In reality, it is directly concerned with the problems treated up to now: that is, the understanding of the "consciousness of something" at its most elementary level. It acts as a kind of introduction to the Phenomenology of Perception by undertaking a sharp critique of preconceived notions on the subject.

Thus, typically, Merleau-Ponty places himself in the thick of a historical-intellectual situation which he feels is full of misconceptions and inner contradictions. These contradictions are to be found in prevalent opinions on the relation between consciousness and nature (or more specifically between "mind and body") and it is to this relation that the author addresses himself. The very distinction between the two "realms" is characteristic of the problem, according to Merleau-Ponty. For in spite of all efforts to overcome Cartesian "metaphysical dualism," the division remains the same: consciousness is the pure transparency of the cogito to itself, the principle activity of which is judgment; nature, including the body, is that of which we are conscious, "a multiplicity of events which are exterior to one another and joined by relations of causality," a "material mass partes extra partes" (SC 1). Such, at least, is the situation in philosophy; as for psychology, it simply takes the "psychic" as a specialized section of the material world which is related to the organism through cause and effect. Consciousness is "distinguished from the beings of nature as one thing is from another thing, by a certain number of characteristics" (SC 2).

It is the psychological notion of consciousness which Merleau-Ponty takes up in his study. Consciousness is approached from the "outside" as a part of reality, just as it is in the psychology which attempts to be a natural science. For purposes of such a treatment the notion of "behavior" (comportement) is found useful, since it is neutral in regard to the distinction between the "psychic" and the "physiological." Even the notion of "consciousness" itself is suppressed, as it was by the behaviorists from whom Merleau-Ponty takes the term.

For the time being, he enters into the world of experimental psychology to see whether it is really consistent with itself.

5. The Theory of Reflexes
and the Notion of "Gestalt"

The classic expression of the objective or mechanistic conception of behavior is the theory of reflexes. Merleau-Ponty first asks what this theory is and what it presupposes. Its "objectivity" is found in the rejection of all naïve notions of purposeful action which one uses to characterize daily activities. For first, it accepts only that which all can see and verify, such as movement or a series of movements; and one cannot see a purpose as such, one can only attribute it to the behavior in question by "analogy" from one's own experience. Second, understanding behavior in terms of physical reality alone excludes purpose by definition: the organism can no more be considered "purposeful" than a stone falling off a log. All conceptions of intention, utility, or value are automatically discarded as subjective or "anthropomorphic," even when it is the behavior of a human being which is in question.

Furthermore, the theory requires the atomistic rejection of formal properties. Just as the horizontal motion of a wave in the sea is the subjective "interpretation" of that which is "in reality" only a succession of vertical displacements: so the form, for example, of the patches of light excitation on the retina is reduced to a multiude of individual processes exterior to one another. It is the material rather than formal properties of both stimulus and organism which are responsible for the reaction which is behavior.

All "anthropomorphisms" are opposed in the materialistic conception as "appearances" are to "reality": and the reality is the collection of "preestablished correlations (often conceived as anatomical mechanisms) between certain receptive organs or apparatus and certain executory muscles" (SC 6f.). Given the preestablished circuit, a like stimulus applied at a like position must produce a like reaction. So much seems required for a thoroughly scientific study of behavior. So far as the appearances are concerned, it is assumed that they will all be accounted for by the facts seen in the light of scientific method.

Now it is well known that this hypothesis has undergone considerable revision on the basis of experimental evidence, and Merleau-Ponty asks what the significance of such a revision is for the original conception as a whole.

Citing many experiments on animals, Merleau-Ponty notes that variations of reaction occur not according to variations of elementary properties of the stimulus but according to its spatial distribution, its rhythm, etc. Moreover, the "effect of a complex stimulus is not predictable on the basis of the elements which make it up" (SC 9). Now since it is not only the form or intensity of the stimulus which determines its spatial distribution upon application, but also the way in which

the organism "accepts" the stimulus, one is involved in a circle: the
resulting behavior is "caused" not only by the applied stimulus, but
also by the organism's own behavior which conditions the way in
which the stimulus is received. "Before any systematic interpretation,
the description of the known facts shows that the fate of an excitation is determined by its relation to the total organic state and to
previous or simultaneous excitations, and that the relations between
the organism and its milieu are not of linear but of circular causality"
(SC 13).

Similar difficulties arise with the notion of the "point of excitation" variable.
Some experiments indicate that the same "reflexogenic field" can
produce a wide variety of reactions with the same stimulus depending
on the day, the circumstances, the intensity, and the frequency of
the excitants. If visual perception is taken as a "reaction," it is
impossible to assign a "spatial value" to a point on the retina; how
the object is seen by the subject varies according to the relation of the
eye to its socket, the relation of the head of the body, etc.

The model of the reflex arc, the linear causal process from stimulus to
response, is the most important and most vulnerable aspect of the
classical theory. It has been found, for example, that the function of
a normal stimulus-reflex series depends on internal conditions which
seem far removed from the possible circuit itself. In both animals
and man, physical alteration of a part of the organism can produce a
total change in reflex behavior. Reflexes also depend on the total
physical disposition of the organism at the time of stimulation and on
reflexes which might have preceded the process in question.

Obviously, the behaviorists have been able to provide themselves with
subsidiary hypotheses which can account for these facts without
changing the nature of the theory. In addition to the linear nervous
trajectory which is supposed to exist between stimulus and response,
one can assume circuits which link the circuits, so long as these, too,
are conceived according to the same linear model. This might account for the appearance of a "form" variable in the application of the
stimulus. Also, conditions which affect the efficacy of the stimulus
can be supposed to activate other reflex arcs which have the effect of
"inhibition" on the circuit in question. If enough circuits, and enough
kinds of circuits, are assumed, one can maintain the notion of behavior as the reaction of a set of preestablished mechanisms to a
"mosaic" of mutually exterior stimuli from outside the organism.

Merleau-Ponty asks, however, how satisfactory such a theory can be if it
requires so many ad hoc hypotheses to keep it in accord with the
facts. As has been seen, the notions of stimulus, receptor, arc, etc.
"melt into one another" (SC 31)—the stimulus must share its status
as "cause" with the receptors, the reflex arc itself becomes a sort of
stimulus for other arcs, etc. Even the notion of "response" or "reaction" is equivocal, since it depends on the previous position of the
part of the organism which is moved. In the case of a scratching
reflex, for example, the muscular contractions required to bring the
hand to the place scratched vary considerably according to the posi-

tion of the arm at the beginning of the motion. "Does one imagine
as many preestablished circuits at the scratched point as there are
possible initial positions of my hand?" (SC 28). When a reflex circuit
does not function as it did before, another circuit is assumed to have
intervened in its activity; "but what would one think of a physicist
who, at each new observation, would be obliged to add to his theory a
sort of safety clause which postponed its application?" (SC 22).

Into this confused theoretical situation, Merleau-Ponty introduces the notion
of "form," and joins the psychologists of the "gestalt" school. It is,
in fact, largely from Koffka, Koehler, Goldstein, and other original
theorists of this school that he borrows much of his critique of the
reflex theory. "Just as a figure owes its characteristic appearance to
the background on which it stands out," he says, adopting the key
formula of the gestaltists, "so each movement supposes positive or
negative conditions in the nervous system as a whole" (SC 22). The
notion of behavior as a structure or form adds to the understanding
of behavior even if it is at the cost of causal explanation. But as
shown before, there are difficulties which are inherent in any causal
explanation of behavior which is to be consistent, i.e., which is not to
introduce an undefined *deus ex machina* of "intelligence" or "vital
force" as a subsidiary cause when all others fail. What is "new"
about the notion of form is that it is always more than the sum of its
parts. As Merleau-Ponty puts it, "one can speak of form when the
properties of a system change for any modification of one of its parts,
but remain the same if all the parts change while maintaining the same
mutual relations" (SC 50). This notion is applicable to a temporal
development as well as a spatial configuration, the best example of
this being a melody in relation to the notes which make it up. Referring again to the figure-background analogy, one can say that the
receptive sector of the nervous system, from which behavior might be
said to "result," is like "a field of forces which express concurrently
the intraorganic state and the influence of external agents" (SC 48).

Such a conception makes it possible to account for—though not to explain
causally—the phenomena of "adaptation" which seem so remarkable
within the framework of the theory of reflexes. An animal, for example, which has lost the use of its right member through partial
removal of the appropriate cerebral region, is able to use the right
member to procure its food if the left has been amputated. If the
excision of the cerebral region controlling the right member is completed, the animal is still capable of using it if the situation demands
it, for example, if the food is within reach outside its cage (SC 40). In
human beings, it is noted that amputees of the right hand do not
really have to "learn" to write with the left, and that the handwriting
of the normal subject maintains its characteristics whether the subject
writes with the finger muscles on a piece of paper or with the whole
arm on a blackboard (SC 41n.). The organism seems to have a certain equilibrium of functions which it seeks to maintain under the
most varied conditions.

If the notion of structure is taken as the norm, the constant reflex arcs
which can be obtained—such as the extension of the knee under

the doctor's hammer—can be considered as isolated aspects of the structure produced under artificial conditions. It is precisely the controlled experiment of the laboratory which is "anthropomorphic," while such subjective terms as "adaptation" and "coherent" behavior on the part of the organism are the best expressions of the natural state for which the theory of reflexes seems so improbable. The notion of "form" is only "anthropomorphic," or at least unsuited to the behavior in question, if it is treated as a cause acting with other causes to produce the final effect. "It is not a question of risking one hypothesis among others, but of introducing a new category . . ." (SC 49), one which expresses the "descriptive properties" of certain natural events (SC 54).

6. Conditioned Reflexes

Merleau-Ponty takes these considerations on the classical theory of reflex and applies them to the traditional theories of more complex behavior, thus bringing his investigation closer to the realm of human perception. The analysis of higher aspects of behavior, especially in Pavlov's theory of conditioned reflexes, is merely an extension of the former approach. Behavior is still to be accounted for by the totality of the stimulants present and their preestablished effects; but through the process of conditioning, the stimuli come to set off reactions which are different from their own original effects. "The essence of nervous activity remains the same: it is a process which is decomposable into material parts" (SC 55).

First, Merleau-Ponty shows the extent to which Pavlov has to alter his theory in order to keep it in accord with its basic model of the conditioned reflex. The nonfunction of a conditioned reflex, when the stimulus is presented with a second stimulus, indicates that the latter is an inhibitory stimulus. If a third stimulus, accompanying the second, partly restores the reflex action, it is considered disinhibitory. The presentation of all three together, however, does not result in the expected combination of their functions, and Pavlov is obliged to introduce "a sort of equilibrium" of the nervous system which saves the day. The result of the combination of the stimuli is qualitatively different from the total effect of the stimuli taken separately, but the theory of conditioned reflex must account for this difference by introducing further stimulant or inhibitory factors, etc. Yet this is only necessary because of the original model of the theory. In describing the stimuli as positive or negative (inhibitory), Pavlov has already gone beyond the facts to the theory, since he treats "a total excitation as the sum of the excitations which each of the stimuli produces" (SC 58). "Far from being a faithful description of behavior, the theory of conditioned reflexes is a construction inspired by the atomistic postulates of material (*réelle*) analysis" (SC 59). It lays claim to greater "objectivity" because it bases behavior on "physiological facts." Yet these facts, rather than phenomena directly observable in the brain or nervous system, are more often the supposed physical processes which the theory must invent in order to explain the facts on its own terms. The central nervous system is never considered as an autonomous process of distribution, but as a mosaic of excited or inhibited points, each corresponding to an individual external stimulus and an individual reaction.

This conception ideally rests on the theory of localized function in the cerebral cortex, and Merleau-Ponty now turns his attention to experimental work in this field. Here the evidence seems to demand revision of both the behaviorism of "physiological facts" and the older psychology of "psychic facts." The former, with its notions of isolated function, and the latter, with its isolated powers or faculties, both seem contradicted by the phenomena. Isolated cerebral lesions, for example, rarely produce simply the loss of certain movements or simple indifference to certain sectors of the physicochemical *milieu*. Aphasiacs do not lose their "power of speech"; rather their ability to use words depends on the context of the situation. Most can speak in an automatic way, but lack a certain "categorical" or "symbolic" ability which applies language to new situations. A single lesion can produce disturbances which extend from tactile perception through motor activity to memory, intelligence, and language. On the other hand, the same structural disturbances can be found to result from lesions situated in different regions of the cortex.

Still, localization is obviously not without importance. Although a function lost through cerebral lesion may be partially regained through certain compensations, it is never restored in its original form. While it cannot be said that individual regions exclusively command individual functions or parts of the body, it seems that different sections correspond to different elements of the total structure. At any rate, the very meaning of "place" in regard to nervous substance is equivocal. In one famous case, for example, a single injury had given rise to inhibition of both sexual initiative and the ability to use numbers. These two activities "have no elementary movement in common, no material (*réelle*) part, they can only be compared or even defined by the use of certain 'anthropomorphic' predicates; one could say, for example, that these two behaviors are 'adaptations to the virtual'" (SC 79). Thus the cerebral region in question can hardly be understood as the activation of certain mechanisms, each of which corresponds to a movement in space. Higher behavior is not "contained" in the brain in this sense; physiologically speaking the "brain" becomes a functional rather than a spatial entity. The same is true for the "parallelism" which the older psychology had assumed to hold between consciousness and the brain: this may be considered a functional parallelism, not the kind in which each perception, each image, or inference corresponds to its tiny mechanism or set of mechanisms in the brain.

But what is the significance of these facts? Does it suffice to correct the atomistic conception with notions of the automatic integration and coordination by the nervous system of the stimuli which are presented to it? Referring to experiments on spatial and color vision, as well as the physiology of language, Merleau-Ponty shows that the higher the behavior involved, the more difficult it is to understand the coordinating mechanism without going beyond the causal reference of physical activity.   If one breaks the understanding of words down into the response set off by the individual phonemes, plus a certain coordination and integration along preestablished lines, one has not accounted for the fact that a phoneme can have many different meanings depending on its position in the words.   The best model is that of a dial telephone system in which each unit in the number has a different meaning according to its place in the whole.   But the telephone "central," in order to connect the numbers with their destination, would have to be able to "understand" an indefinite number of units and combinations of units for which it had not yet been set up in advance.   And the idea of a machine which could complete operations for which it was not constructed is a contradiction.

The necessity of using a term like "understand" here is evidence of the difficulty of reducing consciousness to a combination of objective events.   Behavior and perception always involve all the material elements which are objectively observable about them; but they are always qualitatively more than and different from these elements. "The real world," as Merleau-Ponty puts it (SC 97), "does not make the perceived world"; for in order to understand the perceived world we are, in the last analysis, forced to revert to terms taken from the perceived world itself—like the "understanding of a phrase" or the notion of figure and background, used by the gestaltists to describe behavior in general.

This is nowhere more in evidence than in experiments on training.   Behaviorist theory conceived of the training process along the lines of the conditioned reflex, using the basic notion of "trial and error."   An animal in a cage, for example, executes the movement which makes available its food by opening a door, etc.   This movement, after a number of trials, becomes fixed, while the unsuccessful movements are eliminated.   To view the process in this way, Merleau-Ponty argues, is to leave several aspects of the situation unaccounted for. The goal, for example, acts precisely as a "goal" in the human sense, i.e., as a prospective value to be attained—a relationship which it is most difficult to explain in terms of physical causality.   Whence the fact that the actions of the animal are "trials" and not simply random motion.   Furthermore, unessential motions which accompany the first successful trials often do not remain fixed in the animal's conduct.   What becomes fixed in the traininig processes is not so much the content of the various acts but, anthropomorphically speaking, their "significance," i.e., their orientation toward the goal. There is a wide difference in the conduct of the animal depending on whether the movement it is trained to execute has what we call a "logical" relation to the goal.   Some animals, especially the "higher" animals, seem capable of responding, not in an automatic way, but to "the essence of the problem."

Behaviorism must object to such terminology on principle, of course, because of its anthropomorphism. Such notions as "the essence of the problem" attribute to the behavior in question characteristics which come only from our way of perceiving and interpreting them. But, Merleau-Ponty notes, "it remains to be explained why this interpretation called anthropomorphic is possible in regard to some behavior and impossible in regard to others." Whether anthropomorphic words are used or not, there is a statistical difference between "an organism which, after training, has acquired the power to respond to a definite stimulus and an organism which, after training, accomplishes varied adaptations to situations which are themselves varied" (SC 112). Rather than reducing all types of behavior, regardless of these differences, to the supposed causal process which makes them up, Merleau-Ponty again introduces the notion of form or structure as a means of understanding them. Starting with the notion of structure, then, he suggests that behavior can be classed not according to the "elementary" and the "complex" but "according to whether its structure is submerged (noyée) in the content or whether, on the contrary, it emerges from the content to become, at the limit, the actual theme of the activity" (SC 113).

7. The Forms of Behavior and the Orders of Signification

This criterion leads Merleau-Ponty to suggest three classes of behavioral "forms," the "syncretic," the "detachable," (amovible) and the "symbolic."

The syncretic form includes behavior, common among invertebrates for example, which is "imprisoned in the framework of its natural conditions and which treats novel (inédit) situations only as allusions to the vital situations which are prescribed for it" (SC 114). Here Merleau-Ponty points to the difficulty of obtaining conditioned reflexes in certain invertebrates unless the conditions of the experiment approach the natural ones of the organism.

The "detachable" forms mark the emergence in behavior of adaptibility to new situations, to what Merleau-Ponty calls " 'signals' which are not determined by the instinctive equipment of the species." Here behavior is based on structures which are "relatively independent of the materials in which they are realized" (SC 115). Adaptation to conditioned reflexes is really possible, here, through the juxtaposition of a natural and an unnatural stimulus. What must be remembered, Merleau-Ponty insists, is that the "juxtaposition" is not an objectively spatial or temporal one, but a contiguity "for the organism," i.e., for the structure of its behavior. The theoretical danger at this level is twofold. On one hand, one must not follow the behaviorist tendency to reduce behavior to its material parts; but on the other hand one must not interpret such behavior in terms of the rationality which is peculiar to most of man's conscious activity. Merleau-Ponty refers, for example, to certain experimental work done with chimpanzees which regards their behavior in terms of its "intelligence." From this point of view, description of the actual behavior tends to treat as "deficient" any faculty or ability which does not measure up to human potential in an analogous situation.

The level of symbolic forms is confined to human beings. "In animal behavior, signs always remain signals and never become symbols" (SC 130). It is of the essence of symbolic behavior that its structure is applicable in a wide variety of situations and material contexts. And it is not only in having language that the structure of man's behavior transcends its situation: even in the motor activity of habits, the structure becomes autonomous, separable from its parts. People trained in typing, for example, sometimes cannot find an individual key on the keyboard when asked specifically; yet they are capable of executing combinations never before seen, applying their ability to ever-new situations. It is this possibility of the varied expression of the same theme, this "perspective multiplicity," "which introduces cognitive conduct and free conduct. . . . Here, behavior does not merely *have* signification, it *is* itself signification" (SC 133).

This frame of reference throws a new light on the conditioned reflex as a model for explaining complex behavior. It is known, for example, that the higher the cerebral development of the animal in question is, the more perfect the conditioned reflexes will be to an absolute or objective stimulus, that is, rather than to a complex of relations. In terms of the "forms" of behavior, the conditioned reflex could be seen as evidence of a superior level of activity which is able to dissociate the aspects of its environment from their context. A man, needless to say, gives the best performance of all in a conditioned reflex experiment. Otherwise, the conditioned reflex must be considered a pathological phenomenon. In either case it can hardly be called the explicative principle of behavior.

On a more general plane, the possibility of classing behavior according to form raises the question of the "philosophical significance" of this division and the concept of form itself. Merleau-Ponty has shown the impossibility of understanding behavior if it is reduced to mere causal processes in the sense of classical physics. Here, as we have said, he goes hand in hand with the gestalt psychologists; but he takes sharp issue with them when they say[14] that form is only a means of understanding, and that "in our ultimate explanations" behavior must belong to the very same reality about which physics teaches us. On the contrary, Merleau-Ponty states that

above the physical field . . . we must recognize the original character of a physiological field. . . . If in addition we take account of symbolic behavior and its own characteristics, there is occasion to introduce a third field which we shall call, by nominal definition, the mental field" (SC 141).

Thus one is drawn to the distinction between matter, life, and spirit, or "the physical order, the vital order, and the human order" (SC 139). Rather than reducing these three realms to one, it is precisely the

---

[14] K. Koffka, *Principles of Gestalt Psychology*, Harcourt, Brace, New York, 1935, pp. 48–49; *cited in* SC 144.

task of the "ultimate" analysis—which is philosophy—to keep them separate and realize the distinct structural character of each.

For even the isolable physical law, taken in the positivistic sense as a constant process of linear causality, is unthinkable apart from a system of oriented forces in which it is effective. Modern physics, above all, teaches the impossibility of making statements without reference to the particular framework in which the statement is presented. Thus it, too, deals in a special sort of form which is not finally decomposable into material parts. "The physical form is an equilibrium obtained in regard to certain given exterior conditions" (SC 157), and, no less than the forms of behavior, consists in dialectic, not linear relations. Rather than "explaining" matter in terms of laws, modern physics tends to understand the laws in terms of structures.

But precisely because the world of physics, as well as that of "life" and "spirit," can be understood in terms of form, it is impossible to collapse the second two "orders" into the first. Each order consists in a qualitatively unique set of structural relations; and qualitatively different sets of relations do not admit of reduction to any one set.

This sharp distinction of the three orders does not, however, revert to the classical opposition between the material and the spiritual, the physical and the psychic, that is, the division of reality into substances which act upon one another. Nor does it have anything to do, Merleau-Ponty insists, with the vitalism of the Bergsonians. The latter, finding physical causality insufficient to explain life, introduce the "vital force" into reality-in-itself as another cause. But "the relation of the vital force to that which it produces is not thinkable, it is magic" (SC 171). For Merleau-Ponty, it is the very idea of reality-in-itself which must be eliminated. The notion of form, just like the causal framework of classical science, is a means of understanding what is not an in-itself, but a phenomenon. The sciences, even physics, are not "realistic" in the philosophical sense. "What is required by physics is in no case the affirmation of a 'physis'. . . . The form is not an element of the world, but a limit toward which physical knowledge tends and which it itself defines" (SC 153). The world which is determined scientifically, whether by physical sciences, life sciences, or the sciences of man, is a known world, a world unthinkable apart from the scientist who studies it. Matter, life, and spirit are not three orders of reality, but "three orders of signification" (SC 147).

8. From Behavior
to Perception

But signification in regard to what? Are they, like Kant's a priori, subjective forms which are applied to a manifold of undifferentiated matter? Actually, Merleau-Ponty is far from advocating a Kantian transcendental idealism. The structures which he calls "significations" are the scientific determinations of a world which is already rich in structure: the perceived world. Just as the key notion "figure and background"

is borrowed from the perceived world, so is any conception of structure which enters into physical, biological, or psychological description. Merleau-Ponty's whole critique of behaviorism has shown that
it is impossible, in the end, to account for behavior and consciousness
without resorting to terms which are naïve or anthropomorphic. "The
science of life can only be constructed with notions made on the
measure of and borrowed from our experience of the living being"
(SC 161). The specifically symbolic forms of man's behavior require
the corresponding faithfulness to our experience of man. And the
physical "order," including its causal reference and its amenability to
atomistic interpretation, is derived from our experience of the physical
object.

The world of the sciences, then, is not one of things-in-themselves; but
   neither is it a world of ideas, the multiplicity of which is unified in
   the epistemological subject. If there is a unity to Merleau-Ponty's
   three "orders," it is to be found in the perceived world, a world not
   of things-in-themselves and not of mere appearances, but of *phenomena*. With the three orders of signification one does indeed have
   to do with an *a priori*, but it is an *a priori* to be found in the world,
   the "material *a priori*" of the phenomenologist which distinguishes
   "sectors of experience which are not reducible to one another" (SC
   186).

Thus Merleau-Ponty's treatment of the physical, vital, and human "orders,"
   far from being a "philosophy of nature" or "full-fledged metaphysics,"[15] is a phenomenological critique of scientific experience. It
   corresponds, in fact, to one of Husserl's own investigations into the
   foundation of the sciences.[16] As such, it places before us a remarkable turn in the argument of *La Structure du comportement*, in many
   ways Merleau-Ponty's most brilliant and complex work. The examination of objectivist physiology and psychology has given rise to three
   separate theses, each corresponding to a different task which the book
   fulfills.

1. Within the framework of behavioral science itself, whose task it is to "go
   to the object" and understand it on its own terms, Merleau-Ponty
   offers a critique of purely causal hypotheses, basing his critique on
   the experimental facts. The attempt to reduce behavior to a series
   of linear causal processes is shown to be less scientific rigor than a
   sort of blind belief in a certain concept of nature. Following the
   gestaltists, he introduces the notion of form, a totality which is more
   than the sum of its parts, as the best means of understanding behavior. Furthermore, he suggests a classification system of behavioral forms according to observable criteria.

2. The possibility of the division of behavior into formal groupings, when
   added to new conceptions of physical science, gives rise to the three

---

[15] As suggested by H. Spiegelberg, The Phenomenological Movement, M. Nijhoff, The
   Hague, 1960, vol. II, p. 543.
[16] Cf. vol. II of Husserl's Ideen zu einer reinen Phänomenologie, etc., the divisions of
   which deal with "material nature," "animal nature" and the "spiritual (geistige)
   world."

"orders." Thus, as just seen, Merleau-Ponty moves into the sphere of the philosophy of science in general. The impossibility of reducing the vital and human orders to the physical, and the formal character of the latter, combine to support the thesis we mentioned much earlier: that the scientifically determined world, rather than being the correction or revision of the naïvely perceived world, is, on the contrary, founded and dependent upon it. Science begins with the difference between the physical, the vital and the human, a difference to be found in naïve experience; in the end, it cannot escape this difference or try to overcome it without betraying its objects.

3. Thus one is confronted with two theses, one objective or scientific and the other critical or philosophical; but they both point in the same direction when considering the original question: that of the nature of consciousness. The attempt to understand behavior and perception in an "objective" way ultimately leads back to the "naïve" experience used to characterize them; the examination of objective science in general leads us to the same place. Not only in order to understand consciousness as a particular problem, but also to understand the entire world of which science teaches, one is led to examine consciousness on its own naïve terms. The net result is a sort of victory for subjectivity, and objective observation must be replaced by reflection.

It is from the latter point of view that the *Phenomenology of Perception* begins. As a phenomenology, it is aimed at the essence of experience taken as it is, not as interpreted by those who attempt to found an "objective science of subjectivity" (PP 11). On the other hand, Merleau-Ponty asks, to what extent do the investigations of *La Structure du comportement* justify an "unconditioned reflection"? (SC 199). Does the characterization of behavior as a *structure* find its application only in the positive science of psychology, which, in itself, is ignorant of critical philosophical pronouncements on its objective value? Or can these notions help to correct misconceptions which are common to reflexive or subjective treatments of consciousness? For the answer to these questions, let us turn now to the *Phenomenology* itself.

9. Empiricism, Intellectualism, Phenomenology

Like Husserl's, Merleau-Ponty's phenomenological method is best understood and fully realized, not in definitions and introductions, but in practice. Turning attention to the *Phenomenology of Perception* one will see not only the emergence of a theory of experience and a conception of man and existence, but also the growth of the phenomenological method from the status of a philosophical tool to a conception of philosophy as a whole. Instead of dealing at length with phenomenological method, then, it is better to follow the argument of Merleau-Ponty's major work.

The purist phenomenologist will object to the word "argument" here, and with good reason. Phenomenology does not proceed by argument or proof; it relies on intuition, and its task is to point out, to show, to evoke, to uncover. Still, the *Phenomenology of Perception* (not unlike Heidegger's *Sein und Zeit*) is constructed in a fashion which resembles a kind of deduction. It begins in the world, treating of the body, space, physical things, and other human beings. From these investigations it *derives* its understanding of the subject of perception, human "being-in-the-world." Almost in the manner of a Kantian "transcendental deduction," it seems to develop its conception of existence as the necessary condition for the world's being as it is. There is, of course, no question of deduction, even in the Kantian sense. There are no premises which justify the conclusion of a certain view of subjectivity from a phenomenological description of the world. But the "reawakening of the experience of the world," the examination and description of perception and the perceived—besides providing the basis of an epistemology—serve in turn to reawaken our experience of ourselves by discovering the milieu in which we exist. The world is, in a very literal sense, the *definition* of our being-in-the-world.

Merleau-Ponty's first task is to bring about a "return to the phenomena." As has been seen, he has begun with the modern behaviorist attempt to do away with the notion of consciousness altogether, to explain the interior by the exterior. Having shown the impossibility of this sort of reduction, he is now in a position where the notion of consciousness is taken very seriously indeed. Having criticized the materialistic or realistic presuppositions which mislead behaviorist *and* gestalt theory, he finds himself in the camp of traditional introspective psychology and epistemology, the battleground of the old rationalisms and empiricisms. The unjustified presuppositions are no less rife on this side, and the return to the phenomena cannot be effected without their elimination. While the assumptions and arguments of classical empiricism differ greatly from those of rationalism and the later critical schools, the whole conflict between them has its source in a series of misconceptions, beginning with the notion of "sensation."

While "sensation" is only one of many terms traditionally used to characterize perception, Merleau-Ponty finds it at the root of most theoretical difficulties. The idea "seems immediate and obvious: I have a sensation of redness, of blueness, of hot or cold. It will, however, be seen that nothing could in fact be more confused, and that because they accepted it readily, traditional analyses have missed the phenomenon of perception" (PP 3). This emphatic denial of the notion of sensation is directed first at any theory which attempts to make of the pure sense "datum'" or "impression" the building block of perception. What could such an impression be like? If it is a mere datum, rather than something constructed of data, it must be undifferentiated and instantaneous. Like the effect of the behaviorist's stimulus, the sense impression is an atom of perception, but not itself a perception. If one had the perception of a sense datum, it would lose its value as an explicative factor of perception. It must be "sensed"; nothing more. Yet pure sensing, as most authors agree, is nowhere to be found in experience. The most isolated excitation of one sense takes place within a total field of perception and is in a certain relation—spatial, temporal, etc.—to other aspects of this field. If the "pure" sense datum is not to be found in experience, what, Merleau-Ponty asks, justifies the assumption of its basic role in the makeup of perception as a whole? Surely one has senses which can be said to supply certain data. The perceived world is full of colors, sounds, surfaces, and smells—in short, qualities—but it is a mistake to assert that perceptive consciousness *consists* in such qualities and that perception is thereby accounted for. "Red and green are not sensations, but sensibles, and quality is not an element of consciousness, but a property of the object" (PP 4). Sensed quality is an aspect of the perceived world which is only distinguished and isolated by careful reflection, by the scientifically observant consciousness. The error of traditional theories, especially empiricism, has been to take this single aspect and make of it the explicative factor. But quality can only be found in a world of objects which is rich in spatial and temporal structures: the experience of a sensible seems to presuppose rather than explain perception.

The notion of the pure sensation has long been recognized as inadequate to account for perceptive and cognitive experience as we know it. But how to compensate for its inadequacy? Merleau-Ponty's objection is that, instead of rejecting it and returning to the examination of sensible experience, epistemologists and psychologists have kept it intact and added various "powers," "faculties," etc. which instead of rendering experience understandable, move further and further into the realm of conjecture. Where behaviorism introduces hypotheses of a mechanical sort, psychology and philosophy deal in mental apparatus. Since the mosaic of sensations impressed upon us from the outside world does not account for our continuous experience, we are led to suppose the existence of the faculty of "association" and the "projection of memories." These assure the recognition of similar sensations and the perception, for example, of motion occurring through time. But the association of like sensations can never account for the identity through difference of objects in our experience. Nor can projection or memory render understandable the meaning inherent in a perceptive event. Again, the theory presupposes what it is meant to explain: "recognition" through "memory" requires a world of objects perceived as such, not a mass of meaningless impressions. The addition of association and memory to sensation does not succeed in making sense of the nonsense which is the jumble of sense data we supposedly receive. It merely adds more sensations, or quasi sensations, to those imposed upon us by the environment. These do not account for the coherent experience out of which cognition and science grow.

This critique of traditional empiricism, of course, is not new. But Merleau-Ponty rehearses the demonstration of empiricism's inadequacies in order to set the stage for what he considers to be its classic philosophical alternative, intellectualism. While traditional empiricism has long been rejected by most philosophers, it lives on in modified form in behaviorism, as has been seen in the discussion of *La Structure du comportement.* The only real difference between behaviorism and empiricism is that the first makes its task easy by rejecting the notion of consciousness altogether, and only needs to account for "behavior" as observed from the outside; while traditional empiricism advances its theory as the explanation of consciousness as subjectively experienced. The latter is a much more difficult task, and its failure is the more obvious.

It is the failure of empiricism which, historically, has given rise to its "intellectualistic" antithesis, a movement which for Merleau-Ponty is seen roughly in the transition from Hume to Kant. The conscious subject must be accorded some initiative; the structures of experience must be potentially in consciousness, rather than the result of a series of outwardly related events. For as anyone can see, perceptive experience is always more than the totality of sense information which can be present to consciousness. The world is coherently related in terms of identity and difference, cause and effect, etc., and is, in fact, anything but a chaos of isolated sensations. The notion of "judgment" is introduced as that which is required if sensation is to become perception (PP 32). Experience thus requires the "categories of the understanding" and especially the unity of a subject which judges. The mosaic of sensations needs to be "read" and "interpreted" by "someone"—namely the Kantian epistemological subject. But the fate of the notion of sensation, at least in the Kantian scheme, is well known. It is impossible to find meaning in the passively received sensations, and all structures of experience, including time and space, pass to the subjective side. Sensation becomes the pure "matter" (as opposed to the "form") of experience, which is but "a limiting concept posed by consciousness in its reflection on itself and not a component of the act of knowledge. But from this point on, perception is a variety of intellection, and, as far as its positive content is concerned, a judgment" (SC 216f.).

For Merleau-Ponty, such a turn of thought leads us to a position hardly different from that of Descartes.[17] Whether the subject is the Cartesian *cogito* or the Kantian *ich denke*, knowledge becomes the absolute correlation between it and the scientifically known world. The world has not lost its "in-itself" characteristics; it is still defined by the "absolute exteriority" of its parts (PP 39); but its being is determined through its relation to the *ego* which is pure relation and coincidence with itself. It is that "for which" the world is—the world is "for it" and it is *for-itself.* What was purely objective for the

[17] *Throughout his writings, Merleau-Ponty too often places the Kantian and Cartesian views, at least of subjectivity, together under the title "intellectualism." There are strong grounds, both historical and philosophical, for disputing this near identification. Even Husserl's transcendental subjectivity is sometimes apparently included in this category. One is left with the feeling that in order to facilitate the triadic movement from "empiricism" to "intellectualism" to "existentialism" he has actually weakened his case. For he does not do justice to the strong phenomenological critique which can be addressed to each of these concepts of subjectivity if they are treated separately.*

empiricist becomes constituted in the relation between subject and object, between the for-itself (*pour soi*) and the in-itself (*en soi*).

This, then, is the result of "unconditioned reflection" once empiricist notions are examined closely and the idea of subjectivity is admitted in its own right. There is no doubt that Merleau-Ponty feels some advance has been made over empiricism, and himself feels the force of the intellectualist argument. The notion of the epistemological subject and that of judgment are much more successful in accounting for at least some areas of experiences—notably scientific knowledge—than is the "bundle of impressions" which constitutes the empiricist's consciousness. But how comprehensive is such an account, and how true is it to our experience?

Merleau-Ponty's objection is that while empiricism cannot account for knowledge, intellectualism cannot account for lack of knowledge. The first is overcome because experience is always more than what is supposedly present to the senses. But the second does not explain how experience can be less than completely clear and distinct.

Empiricism cannot see that we need to know what we are looking for, otherwise we would not be looking for it, and intellectualism fails to see that we need to be ignorant of what we are looking for, or equally again we should not be searching (PP 28).

All perception is taken as judgment; illusion, too, must be judgment, and nothing renders account of the progress from error to truth. This very progress was the original sense of the word "judgment"; but for intellectualism, "judgment loses its constitutive function and becomes an explanatory principle," while "the words 'see,' 'hear,' 'smell,' lose all signification, since the slightest vision surpasses the pure impression and thus comes under the general rubric of 'judgment' " (PP 34).

It is easy to see how the language of the "impression" and the "sense datum" is at the bottom of this entire philosophical transformation. The notion seems so clear that it is never really questioned, only added to and at best revised. Between the chaos of sensation and the clarity of scientific propositions about the world there can be no middle ground, no sphere of illusion, of trial and error—in short, no world of perception. The "opacity of the fact" (PP 61), the resistance of the world, melt away before the absolute subject; even the plurality of human beings becomes "empirical" and thus relativized in the face of the knower. The introduction of subjectivity into the empirical world, then, turns out to be an improvement at considerable cost. While it gains in form it loses in matter; what it clarifies in essence it obscures in fact.

But the complementary errors of rationalism and empiricism are more deeply rooted than in the notion of sensation alone. They both stem from what Merleau-Ponty, taking up a Husserlian notion, calls the "prejudice of the world" (PP 5). *The Structure of Behavior* has taught what happens when science tries to understand consciousness on the basis of the atomistic, causally determined world of classical physics alone. Intellectualism realizes that such a world must be placed over against consciousness if both terms are to have any meaning. Yet it attains its definition of consciousness merely by supplying what is missing from the empirical notion in order to obtain that very same world. Kant is the best example of this in his attempt to show the "possibility" of our knowing a world which is defined in terms of Newtonian physics and Euclidian geometry. Merleau-Ponty's point is that consciousness is not always involved in science, and perception is not always geometrical. If intellectualism can relativize the world of science in regard to consciousness, then it should also relativize its conception of the world. While the scientifically constituted world may be one terminus of conscious activity, it is not all of experience; and instead of "deriving" or "deducing" subjectivity from that world, philosophy should turn to the world in its totality and see the "geneology of being" (PP 54), the process through which such a world takes shape.

The "prejudice of the world" is borne by the "mute thesis of perception" itself (PP 54), the orientation which moves from indeterminacy to determinacy, from appearance to reality-in-itself. This movement defines science, and it has also characterized much of modern philosophy. But the world of science cannot be understood until it is traced back to this thesis; and the thesis, in turn, cannot be understood unless we try to *disengage* it. This is Merleau-Ponty's version of the "phenomenological reduction" of Husserl:

It is because we are through and through compounded of relationships with the world that for us the only way to become aware of the fact is to suspend the resultant activity, to refuse it our complicity. . . . In order to see the world . . . we must break our familiar acceptance of it . . . (PP xiiif.).

The mere perception of the "figure and background" is infinitely more than the sense impressions which can reach my eye. It is charged with meaning; yet to call it a series of geometric judgments addressed to a senseless material is pure conjecture. The task of phenomenology, rather than moving backwards toward consciousness from the scientific determination of the figure, is to see how perception starts from the irreducible meaning of the figure and arrives at a scientific, in this case geometrical, determination. This is "why phenomenology is a phenomenology, that is, a study of the *advent* of being into consciousness . . ." (PP 61).

10 The Body

Merleau-Ponty's phenomenology of the body is the centerpiece of his entire analysis. The problem arises immediately from the foregoing critique of the "prejudice of the world." Perhaps nothing in man's experience is more slighted than the body when the world is divided into being-in-itself and being-for-itself. For both empiricism and intellectualism, the body is a physical being belonging to the objective world, whether it is supposed to be moved by the spirit, to move the spirit, or to move only according to laws. It is treated thus by the empiricist, as has been seen—and by itself cannot make perception understandable; and the intellectualist's reduction of sense to undifferentiated "matter" seems to leave the body out of perception altogether and place it among the rest of the objects of the known world. This, it will be recalled, was the situation Merleau-Ponty criticized at the beginning of the *Structure of Behavior* before he began his critique of the objectivist side. In either case the body is not a perceiving being, it cannot in itself be the bearer or even, strictly speaking, the transmitter of meaning. Its objective status allows it no subjectivity at all.

Nothing, according to Merleau-Ponty, is more contrary to experience, and it becomes his task to show the role and the significance of the body in the realm of perception. (In doing this, as will be seen, he gives a measure of credit back to empiricism, and, to a certain extent, to empirical methods. For empiricism at least recognizes the facticity or finitude of man's relation to the world, and its roots in the body.) The main point of his investigation is illustrated briefly in the example of the visual perception of a house. In the manner of Husserl's analyses of perception, he points out the essential difference between "the house," as the fully determined objective terminus of our perception, on the one hand; and the "real content" of the perception, i.e., the perspective we have of the house, on the other. Intellectualism and even Husserl's phenomenology are preoccupied with the former aspect —what Husserl calls the "intentional content"—of perception and knowledge in general: the wonder of the conscious attainment of transcendence, objectivity, and science. Merleau-Ponty wishes to stress the other side. While perception always goes *through* perspective *to* the object, it cannot have the object without perspective—itself always less than the object. The house cannot be seen at all unless it is seen *somehow* and *from somewhere.*

This limitation or finitude which is characteristic of all experience *is* the body. It is "my point of view upon the world" (PP 70)—not, of course, as the objective piece of machinery it is sometimes considered to be, but as the lived body of perceptive experience. As our concrete, existing relation to the world, our "means" to the world, it is more easily taken for granted, more easily ignored by philosophical reflection. If we are able, however, to suspend the thesis of perception, to reawaken and discover the experience of the body, Merleau-Ponty tells us, we shall understand the vital link in the nature of consciousness. "The body, by withdrawing from the objective world, will carry with it the intentional threads which link it to its surroundings and finally reveal to us the perceiving subject as well as the perceived world" (PP 72).

The "experience of the body" which is the subject of Merleau-Ponty's study is, of course, primarily the experience of one's *own* body. The criticism of the behaviorists treated the body as an object of "observation from the outside," and in the end arrived at the notion of "gestalt" as the best characterization of it. Here, however, the situation seems quite different. Speaking of the experience of one's own body would seem to involve the peculiar characteristics of one's body as an object of experience for the subject.

Yet here the first mistake has already been made. The older psychology, too, had described the experience of the body by saying, for example, that it was always perceived, while one could turn away from other things. It was, then, merely another object in the world, distinguished from other beings by a certain number of properties. But Merleau-Ponty asks, if the body is thus experienced, can it truly be called an object? Can it ever completely take its place in the world of physical things and be perceived by its owner? The perceived thing is a permanence which is maintained through a variety of perspective variations; but the body is always encountered from the same angle. Even to the extent that I do "perceive" my body, I do it with my body. Rather than being an object in my world, my body is the "condition" of the perception of that world.

In other words, I observe external objects with my body, I handle them, examine them, walk around them, but my body itself is a thing which I do not observe: in order to be able to do so, I should need the use of a second body which itself would be unobservable (PP 91).

When I "perceive" my body with my body, all I achieve is a kind of reflexive awareness; when I *think* of my body as an independent physical object in the world, I do not perceive it, but rather take the position of another person perceiving it "from the outside."

Superficially, then, the "introspective" psychologist is no more wrong in this description of the body as experienced than is the behaviorist in noting down the data of an experiment. What is wrong in both cases is the ontological presupposition as to the status of the being in question. The mistake is in placing the body in a world of fully constituted objects. One might argue that such a mistake is of little importance so long as the description is accurate. But this misplacement leads to misconceptions concerning the nature of consciousness, perception, and knowledge in general.

This is nowhere more in evidence than in the *spatiality* of the lived body. Psychology has given us a useful concept in its description of the motor activity of the body. "My whole body for me is not an assemblage of organs juxtaposed in space. I am in undivided possession of it and I know where each of my limbs is through a *body image* in which all are included" (PP 98). Yet such an image can be, and most often is, conceived as a system moving in space which informs the mind what is going on in the body. The "prejudice of the world" is seen here in placing the system "in" space, by making it subordinate to the abstract geometry of the intellect. Phenomenologically, this schema, the "coordination" of the body, is its orientation toward the world and the origin of objective space. Instead of moving backward from Euclidian space to that of the body, phenomenology traces the development of the former out of the latter. The words "here" and "there," "up" and "down," "left" and "right," for example, can have only a relative signification for the intellect. For perception they have an absolute meaning.   Yet they bear the roots of the dimensionality of geometrical space and need not presuppose it.

With this reserve, both the observations and some of the conceptions of empirical psychology are extremely useful.   The body schema, for example, if taken without theoretical prejudice, is an aspect of the experience of the body which must not be ignored.   Merleau-Ponty puts to particularly good use the studies of the psychologists Gelb and Goldstein on patients with brain injuries.   He points to a case (the same one mentioned in connection with the earlier book) in which a war injury to a part of the brain had produced symptoms throughout the entire range of behavior.   The most striking disturbances were precisely in the realm of body coordination and movement. The patient could talk fairly intelligently; he could go about his habitual daily tasks (which included making leather wallets by hand) with no problems of coordination.   But he could not carry out a simple movement which the experimenter indicated to him verbally without repeating the order to himself several times and finding a position in which the movement seemed the most "natural."   "What he lacks is neither motility nor thought, and we are brought to the recognition of something between movement as a third person process and thought as a representation of the movement—something which is an anticipation of, or arrival at, the objective and is ensured by the body itself as a motor power, a 'motor project' (*Bewegungsentwurf*), a 'motor intentionality' in the absence of which the order remains a dead letter" (PP 110).   The abnormal, then, can enlighten us about the normal, and aid in the discovery of this "third realm" between "mind" and "body."   This, for Merleau-Ponty, is the basic revelation of the phenomenology of the lived body.

The essence of this "third realm" is the "motor intentionality" through which the body is directed at the world.   It is not the intentionality of intellectual consciousness, but rather what Merleau-Ponty, again borrowing from Husserl, calls "operative intentionality" (*intentionalité opérante, fungierende Intentionalität*) (PP xviii).   It is found in the look, the reach, the walk, the mutual corroboration of the senses in the perception of an object, the general orientation of the body, which, like pure consciousness, is always "of something," always in relation to its world.   The body is never a fully constituted object in the world; it is kept from objective status by its inherent subjectivity, the impossibility of its simply being *in-itself*.   To be sure, it has limits toward which it tends, in the carrying out of its "biological functions," for example, in which it seems to exist independently of "me."   It is not an instrument completely at the disposal of a free subject.   But even these functions link it to its environment in a way which is not purely mechanical.   In its sexual behavior, the body is the perfect example of "functioning intentionality."   It is not an objective physical process, but the meaningful direction toward a definite goal.   And the awareness which goes with sexual activity can never be an intellectual awareness.   "Erotic perception is not a *cogitatio* which aims at a *cogitatum*; through one body, it aims at another body, and takes place in the world, not in a consciousness" (PP 157).   Also, through the gesture, the body becomes expression, the bearer of meaning into the world. The upper limit of this expression is speech, and the body becomes an essential condition of language rather than the merely instrumental transmitter of pure thoughts.

Thus the body, in the dual philosophical world of the in-itself and the for-itself, has an ambiguous status. It is not before me as another object in my world; "I am in my body, or rather I am my body" (PP 150)—not as a process "in the third person" but as a "natural subject" (PP 198). The phenomenology of the lived body, then, far from present-ing a variety of representations and significations, discloses a pattern not unlike that of the organism observed from the "outside": the body reveals itself primarily as a form, which, though more than the sum of its parts, is never completely separable from its content. It is a structure which is defined by its relation to that which is not itself; and, as the medium of perception, it seeks its equilibrium in the per-ceived world.

11. The
Perceived World

The phenomenological investigation of the body brings with it a rediscovery of the world. The body is in the world, says Merleau-Ponty, "as the heart is in the organism: it keeps the visible spectacle constantly alive; it breathes life into it and sustains it inwardly, and with it forms a sys-tem" (PP 203). The natural intentionality of the body is the condition of the appearance of beings in the world and these cannot be under-stood apart from this condition. Thus objectivist thought must again be overcome. Instead of treating the world as a transparent ideality which consciousness possesses, philosophy must recognize the modes of its appearance to consciousness. Just as the spatiality of the body and the intentionality of the look are the conditions of the appearance of the house; so the perspective incompleteness of this appearance, the side of the house I see, is the condition of the house as a fully constituted object. Putting aside again the "prejudice of the world" and not assuming this fully constituted object in advance, one can trace it through perception and reveal its genesis in ex-perience.

In this way, one can see beyond the mythology of the "sense datum" and understand what it is to "sense" (sentir) and to have a world which is sensible. Rather than the isolated impression which is forced on the body mechanism by the stimulus of the outside world, or the undifferentiated matter of consciousness, sense is a distinguishable but inseparable element of the perceived world which has its own structures and is rich in meaning. It extends far beyond the individ-ual, sensed qualities; certain colors are known to produce reactions throughout the body akin to the feelings normally associated with them: violence for red, repose for green, etc. To understand such phenomena one cannot ask "why" the body finds these meanings in colors, one can only learn to relive the qualities themselves as they are part of our experience.

Only such a method can make understandable the fact that one has not merely "sensation" or "sensibility," but *different* senses. This is the kind of "material *a priori*" of experience which is meaningless in the framework of intellectualism. Each sense is "thought subordinated to a certain field" (PP 217), each opens upon its "separate world" (PP 230); but *the* sensed world is the coordination and combination of these worlds, a texture which refers to the senses separately and together. Not only do the senses "corroborate" each other in the perception of an object, they "communicate among themselves" (PP 229), and language bears witness to this when one speaks of "loud colors," "bitter smells," "sharp sounds," etc. "The senses translate each other without any need of an interpreter, and are mutually comprehensible without the intervention of any idea" (PP 235).

The sensible world, then, is in a way the "intentional object" of sensing; and the latter, no less than any other element of perception, is nothing without its relation to the world. But it is the "most rudimentary of perceptions" (PP 241) and its "object" is correlatively the least objective aspect of the world. The intentionality of sense is non-thetic or pre-objective: it does not "pass through the idea" or the ego. It does not pose qualities as objects, but "enters into a sympathetic relation with them, makes them its own and finds in them its momentary law" (PP 214). While it cannot be said that sensations are "given" or "passively received," it must be recognized that they mark a given *situation*, an anonymity which, while rich in meaning, is not in the realm of explicit signification. Insofar as knowledge is the polarization of the self-conscious subject and the intellectually articulated object, then sense is the "matter" of knowledge—but not of perception. It is at the heart of perception and, rather than being posed as a limit by reflective consciousness, is to be found in the phenomenological rediscovery of the world.

Merleau-Ponty now moves from the sensed character of the lived world to the consideration of its *space*. The spatiality of the lived body and Merleau-Ponty's assertion of its original relation to geometrical space have already been mentioned. But he must face up to the strong Kantian argument which places pure space, as the "form of outer sense," in a position of priority over sensation. Does not every movement of the body or anything else, every sensed object in the world, presuppose space as its *milieu*? Again, the question cannot be solved by argument but only by observation. The phenomenology of perception, Merleau-Ponty holds, reveals a spatiality which is basically not geometrical—or at least not of the Euclidian sort, normally assumed to be the space of "our world." Can it be assumed that perceived space presupposes Euclidian space? Can perceived space be derived from it? Or, if its rudiments are found in perception, must not Euclidian space be considered as the intellectual determination of one of the aspects of the lived world?

But what are the peculiarities of perceived space? First, it is "oriented." Its dimensions ("up," "down," etc.) are absolute rather than interchangeable. And the relation of orientation carries over into the perceived objects. A well-known object which is presented "upside down" is not recognizable unless I add to the perception by imagining it "right side up" or in its "natural" position. One cannot account for the orientation of perceived space by calling it a "*milieu.*" It helps to reveal the object, it is the "means" (PP 243) which makes possible the position of things, and is rooted in the experience of the body. Objectively speaking, one is tempted to say that the "up" and the "down," for example, are defined always by the axis of the body. But the body is not always in an "up"-right position, the "up" does not move with it. What counts for the spatial orientation of the perceived world is not the body "as a thing in objective space, but my body as a system of possible actions, a virtual body, with its phenomenal 'place' defined by its task and situation" (PP 250).

The dimensions of lived space, being irreducible to one another, are qualitatively different from one another. Only by considering depth in an objectivizing fashion as "breadth seen from the side" (PP 255), can one agree with Berkeley that depth is not visible, and that it is "inferred" from the apparent size of the objects. If we are not trying to explain it but to grasp its essence, we can see its peculiar visibility, which, it is true, is not in the objects but "belongs to the perspective and not to things" (PP 256). Perspective itself, however, defies what the draftsman can condense into geometric "laws." Objects at different distances do not have their objectively determinable "apparent sizes," but rather, from the objective point of view, seem to "compensate" for their distance as they move toward and away from the beholder. As for the perception of motion, Zeno is forever witness to the confusing constructions of position, time, object, memory, and space with which both intellectualism and empiricism attempt to account for it; while a Bergson can only render it comprehensible by absolutizing it.[18] The phenomenology of motion must

[18] *The reader may wonder why so few references have been made to Bergson, Merleau-Ponty's most famous predecessor at the Collège de France. The fact is that the works in question make little mention of Bergson and when they do, as has been seen, it is in a negative way. Merleau-Ponty holds that Bergson, instead of elucidating the world of objective space, time, and motion, simply opposed and finally reduced it to the durée, which in the end has nothing to do with it. "If . . . the past still belongs to the present and the present already to the past, there is no longer any past or present. . . . If the phases of movement gradually merge into one another, nothing is anywhere in motion" (PP 276n.). Thus Merleau-Ponty's sternest reproach is that Bergson's durée renders no account of the experience of the world, but is merely substituted for it. And instead of being an "immediate datum of consciousness," the durée is abstracted from experience and is no more temporal than the objective world itself: "If consciousness snowballs upon itself it is, like the snowball and everything else, wholly in the present" (Ibid.). Bergson's realism opposes the multiplicity of space to the "multiplicity of fusion and interpenetration," and supplies no unity, no synthesis to either multiplicity.—In later essays, however, Merleau-Ponty shows considerable admiration, not only for Bergson the man, but also to some extent for his philosophy. He praises Bergson as an innovator in his discovery and articulation of the present, and speaks highly of his faithfulness to intuition and the intuitional method (cf. S 240f.). Furthermore, he finds in Bergson's writings the notion of a dialectical relationship between consciousness and being through expression (cf. EP 9–33).*

recognize that there is a single object which does not "change"; but neither does it "occupy" different positions in succession. It is perceived *moving* and motion itself is perceived. This realization is one of the means of access to the perceptive experience of time and its position in the whole of consciousness, a subject which will be taken up later in greater detail.

Through dimensionality, through perspective and through motion, space is a "means" to the object. It is in this sense, and not as a real or logical "*milieu*," that space is a condition of the perceived; and through it perception reaches its terminus in reality, the world of things.

Here again, Merleau-Ponty attempts to steer a middle course between a philosophy which gives appearances but no object, and one which gives the object only to the neglect of appearance. As intellectualism shows, there is and must be a unity of the object which goes beyond "mere" appearance. But phenomenology asks how the object can "show itself" (PP 300) to me and thus how the fluctuation of the appearances is related to the unity of the phenomenon. The main point of Merleau-Ponty's analysis of the world of things is that the object, rather than being a "transcendental object = X" posited by the epistemological subject, "establishes itself" in a logic of appearances which is part of the perceived world and which includes the body. It is more than a plurality of appearances, more even than a privileged set of appearances, but is not an idea which transcends its manifestations.

The coordinated role of the various senses in perception has already been mentioned. There is even a kind of "establishment" operative in each sense taken separately. Color, even before it is intellectualized by science, always "presupposes" light in the sense that it changes in accord with it. Perception knows the differences in color which light brings into the world. But as it becomes familiar, the object acquires "its" color which no longer changes from morning to evening. A similar transformation takes place in the "communication" of the senses. There is a "system" of the object which includes not only its color but its texture and the sound it makes when I rap on it with my knuckles. Only for the intellect and for language is it the "bearer" of these "properties." For perception it *is* them "all the way through."

Still, does not the "establishment" of the object presuppose the notion of object in general? No more, argues Merleau-Ponty, than the latter "presupposes" the former. Only a philosophy which sees this "genesis" of objectivity can account not only for perception and reality, but also for imagination, hallucination, and illusion—their similarities as well as their differences. While perception above all seems to present the object "in person," "in the flesh" (PP 320), it is always open to revision and "verification." The world of things is both reality and the unrealized (*inachevé*); its certainty is never apodictic, not because I cannot prove its existence, but because it is forever revealing itself anew to me. Rather than being posited by consciousness, it is the object of what Husserl calls "faith" or "primordial opinion." "The sun 'rises' for the scientist in the same way it does for the uneducated person, and our scientific representations of the solar system remain matters of hearsay, like lunar landscapes, and we never believe in them in the sense in which we believe in the sunrise" (PP 344).

Merleau-Ponty maintains further that the perceived world contains the irreducible distinction between natural things and cultural objects, a distinction bound up with the primordially perceived difference—indicated already in the "three orders of signification"—between the physical, animal, and human realms. Persons and animals are not constituted in the manner of physical things; nor do I "project" consciousness by "analogy" to my own into an object which I find in my perceptive field. For how could I thus "project" if I did not have the awareness of a *behavior* of the being in question—indeed of a particular *form* of behavior? If studies on children can be taken as indicative, the recognition of other people, and even the understanding of their facial expressions, does not follow the consciousness of self. The awareness of the other person is coincident with the awareness of the self, and the other is not merely in the world but transforms it for my perception: it becomes a world for "you," for "them," for "us."

It is in this way, too, that the perceived world is at the origin of science. For the "objective" world is in essence a world for all, for anyone who cares to look. And, no less than is the case for science, it is to the perceived world that one must look, according to Merleau-Ponty, for the origin of the problems of intersubjectivity, society, and ethics. The presence and the importance of physical, animal, and human reality in unreflected experience indicates the origin of the entire range of knowledge, culture, and even ideality (number, etc.) in the lived world. The rudimentary character of these sources—the body, the physical thing, the other person—does not alter their status as the foundation of all more reflective levels of experience, even though it is of the essence of these higher levels to try to transform them by objective determination.

It is one task of Merleau-Ponty's genetic phenomenology, after it has suspended these objective determinations and reentered the perceived world, to trace further the basic elements of experience as they develop in reflective awareness to the status of the constituted world in which men, as cultural and "rational" human beings, live with one another, form societies, and carry on such activities as science and technology. Before considering this, however, it is necessary to take up the most important result of the phenomenology of perception, that which is the prerequisite for the understanding of all other traditional philosophical problems. This is the elucidation of the nature of man, the perceiving being. The phenomenological "reawakening," Merleau-Ponty argues, reveals man in a new and important way, one which underlies and founds all the traditional conceptualizations he makes of himself. What is this new conception of man, and how does it relate to what has gone before?

12. Time
and Subjectivity

The world of perception, as has been seen, tends towards its own determination in objectivity and transcendence. The move towards objectivity, even if it is never consummated, raises the question of the nature of the subjectivity "for which" this move occurs. The most immediate access to the nature of subjectivity is the consideration of the primary problem still outstanding in what has been treated thus far: that of time.

Any attempt at a completely objective representation of time, according to Merleau-Ponty, is doomed to failure from the beginning. Both the atomistic conception of pure succession and the Heraclitean pure flow, when closely examined, can only refer to an observer *for whom* the events in question can be perceived to succeed or interpenetrate each other. Without the observer, the notions of event and flow bear nothing of the temporal in them, and one is left only with an undifferentiated present, an eternal "now." Even more difficulty is encountered when, as is the case with the empiricists, an objective succession of events is presupposed and the attempt is made, within it, to explain the experience of such a succession by the subject. Even the most intricate hypothetical combination of memory, projection, and impression is unable to transform a succession of perceptions into a perception of succession without becoming involved in a circular argument of some sort. Any perception which is "conserved" in memory, however weak and vague it might be, is still a perception unless it is perceived *as past;* pastness thus becomes not a property of the perception, but a form into which perceptions necessarily fit. Time becomes the *a priori* structure of a multiplicity of cognitions, or, as Kant called it, the "form of inner sense." And such a form is itself meaningless without the introduction of a subjective unity which dominates the multiplicity of temporally related events.

This is, in Merleau-Ponty's view, but another version of the classical transition from empiricism to intellectualism previously mentioned, and is no less based on the abstract presupposition of the discrete, formless sensation or impression. In it is implied not only a theory of experience, already discussed, and a theory of time, but also a characterization of the subject of experience. Time is not perceived within experience, but is the order in which experience is given. Consciousness is not itself subjected to this order, but stands above it as the agent of a general synthesis in which temporal multiplicity is unified in continuous experience. Thus the theory endows the subject with several characteristics: its main activity is synthesis or judgment; it is absolutely subjective or indeclinable, being necessary to any experience, even of itself; it is nonetheless aware of itself or "for-itself," being, as Kant said, a unity of self-consciousness or apperception; and it is atemporal.

Thus the self is either immersed in the time of the objective world, being itself merely a sequence of psychic events; or it stands outside the

world, constituting time in the synthesis through which it unifies experience. In the latter theory, the more persuasive of the two, one
is left with the pure *cogito*. Merleau-Ponty asks whether the investigations of his phenomenology make room for such a theory of time,
and whether, in fact, the traditional *cogito* is the last word to be said
about human subjectivity.

His attack on intellectualist notions of perception already involves, of course,
a strong criticism of the pure *cogito*, and this criticism can be developed without direct reference to the problem of time. Merleau-Ponty
goes far enough with Kant to agree that it must be "possible" for the
"I think" to accompany all our representations; but the synthesis thus
defined does not exhaust the experience, nor is the "I think" constitutive of the self. Because of the limitations imposed on perception by the body, because of the perspectivity and incompleteness of
the lived world, one's knowledge can never be absolutely coextensive
with reality or even with the objects it intends. Because these objects
are unrealized, experience is itself unrealized, and even the most
precise mathematization of knowledge cannot free it from the perspective finitude which lies like a millstone upon its aspirations. The
essence of the triangle may be beyond any concrete example; but my
access to this essence is doomed always to take a perceptive or
imaginative form. This is but another way of saying that sciences are
constructed upon the lived world. And this is true, then, not only for
empirical but also for mathematical sciences. "That which is called
an idea is necessarily linked to an expression, and owes to it its appearance of autonomy" (PP 390). Because of the intentionality of
consciousness, the idea can be achieved in the expression, but never
without it. To say that consciousness is intentional is to say that
it is dialectical: the synthesis "I-think-X" is always more and less than
it is: more because X always implies something beyond itself; less
because the evidence of X is bound to its finite expression or perspective representation.

The most important point for this discussion is that the indeterminacy
which applies to the objective knowledge of X also applies to the "I"
in its "subjective" determination. If we can speak of a pure ego,
Merleau-Ponty insists, it is not because the *ego cogito* is a primitive
self-evidence, in the sense of Descartes; nor because it is a necessary
postulate, as for Kant; but because we are aware of a personal unity
in the acts through which the world is constituted for us. The *cogito*
is not completely transparent to itself; if this is not obvious in the
activity of thought, it can easily be seen in what earlier philosophers
called "acts of the will." Is one always sure what one desires? As
Merleau-Ponty asks: Can the love for a person not reveal itself to be
a false love? Can an expression made in sincerity not be discovered
to *have been* insincere? So long as I can perform acts, cognitive or
otherwise, "without knowing it," there is a possible lack of clarity and
distinctness to both the acts and the subject which is at their source.
I can be aware of my acts of thought, but this awareness is never
wholly coincident with the original act itself. The fact that "I am" is

not a consequence of the fact that I think, or will, or doubt that I am. Rather the assertion of the *cogito* is validated by the awareness of my actual existence and my relation to the world.

Thus the ego can only become a "necessary" presupposition of experience through the awareness of the "functioning intentionality" of perception. Yet I am not merely passively aware of this intentional relationship through a Kantian "inner sense." For, as Kant himself asked, how could I identify this particular sensation with "myself"? The evidence of the *ego cogito* results from the *appropriation* of this personal unity into my actual experience. Such appropriation is not necessary but contingent. The self as a factor in experience is as unrealized, as necessarily unrealized, as is the objective X. Thus it

is true neither that my existence is in full possession of itself, nor that it is entirely estranged from itself, because it is action or doing. I can effect the cogito *and be assured of genuinely willing, loving, believing, provided that in the first place I actually do will, love, or believe and thus fulfill my own existence (PP 382).*

These considerations disclose, as Merleau-Ponty says, a "much more intimate relationship" (PP 410) between time and subjectivity than the intellectualist theory allows. The subject can no more be considered atemporal than it can be wholly integrated into objective time. In a manner similar to previous analyses, Merleau-Ponty wishes to show that the notion of the pure subject is made necessary only by maintaining the objective conception of time and supplying what is needed to make up for the inadequacies of the theory; and that, as usual, such a procedure runs counter to our actual experience. It leads, in fact, to an intolerable paradox. The atemporal subject, as seen above, is opposed to the temporal multiplicity of events in order to make possible the consciousness of succession. But if the subject stands outside the "multiplicity" in order to constitute its arrangement, how can it be anything but eternal? The philosopher can introduce the "empirical" self which adheres to the world, but this, too, is constituted and is not the "real" self. Since the subject is outside time, it is impossible for him to be born and to die. Religious interpretations welcome the possibility of the immortality of the soul, but whence comes the finitude of man? It is hard to see, Merleau-Ponty argues, how such a being really differs from God. In the end, it is impossible for it even to inhabit the finite body which is the human condition of all experience. Its aloofness from time calls into question its ability to be engaged in any temporal event.

But is the consciousness of objective succession the essence of our experience of time? The "prejudice of the world" is operative in this assumption, says Merleau-Ponty, especially the prejudice of physical science. The notion of a temporal succession of events which is useful in classical physics is itself an abstraction, built upon the experience of time by removal of the limitations inherent in that experience. A man does not hover with complete freedom over an infinite succession of "nows," viewing them all with equal transparency; he is rooted to a vantage point, that of the present moment. The experience of time is not ordered in a one-dimensional linear succession, but according to the three dimensions of past, present, and future. The limitations on this experience include the qualitative differences between the recent past and the long past, the near and the distant future. Following an indication of Husserl, Merleau-Ponty likens these qualitative differences to the perspectives of a perceived object: a given moment or actual experience changes aspect as it moves further into the past and is replaced by new actual experiences. It does not merely become more vague; rather, it is seen from an ever new perspective, its horizons now including the present moments with which it has been replaced. The same structure can be seen in the "approach" of a possible future moment or experience. As an "intentional object" the moment is the same throughout the flux of experience in which it is presented to me. But like the physical object, it is accessible to me only through its perspectives, through aspects of itself which are less than itself. One cannot say, however, that different moments succeed each other, thus presupposing the notion of succession. Moments "*differentiate* themselves from each other" (PP 419), and succession is founded in the order of perspectives in which they relate to each other. Rather than a line, then, time is "a network of intentionalities" (PP 417).

The present moment is not a dimensionless "instant" entertained by the intellect, but the glimpse of a totality of being to which the moment's approach and passing point like signs. The presentness of an event, Merleau-Ponty maintains, is the nearest we come to its reality, while its other temporal perspectives only elaborate on its meaning for us. Yet "by becoming past, the event does not cease to be," for "in time being and passing are synonymous" (PP 420). The presence and passing of an event establish it "for all time" while its future is the necessary preparation for this establishment.

There is no need for an active synthesis to bring together the dimensions of time, as if they were related only in an exterior fashion. But just as the perspective of an object presupposes a perceiver to whom it appears, so the passage of time requires subjectivity in order to fulfill itself through the perspectives of past, present, and future. Subjectivity is at the heart of time, but not in the sense that I pose or think the passage of time; rather, as Merleau-Ponty says, "I perform it" ("*je l'effectue*") (PP 421) simply by being. He does not wish to say, therefore, that time is "for someone": events, objects, other people exist for someone, but "time *is* someone" (PP 422), an existence which temporalizes the world through its being as subjectivity. One can hardly say, metaphysically, that without subjectivity the world would be timeless: without subjectivity "world" would have no meaning at all. One can say, however, with Bergson, that the "de-subjectification" of the world for purposes of science robs it of its temporality, translates its time into a spatialized eternal present. Man does not come into a spatial world and create time; but he sustains time insofar as he exists, he is the point on which past, present, and future turn.

13. The
Incarnate Spirit

The various dimensions of perception—such as the body, spatiality, perspectivity, etc.—have been discussed as the conditions of the possibility
of experience in a very special sense: that is, they are the "means"
to the world.   Human subjectivity does not merely have these dimensions as properties, so that one could say that it is spatial, or has a
body; as being-in-the-world it *is* or "exists" these dimensions; it *is*
spatiality through its spatialization, it is its body through what might
be called the "corporalization" of the world.   It is in the same sense
that we can now say with Merleau-Ponty that subjectivity *is* temporality
or temporalization.   There is a preeminence in this dimension, however: it surmounts the dimensions of existence which lead subjectivity
to the world, and, through the world, is the "means" of the self to
itself.

Temporality, then, is the meaning of the appropriation of the self by itself in
the *cogito*.   It is only through the temporality of experience of the
world that a man acquires the "cohesion of a life" (PP 421).[19]   But
does this not give a certain eternal status to his being-in-the-world?
The subject is certainly not *in* time; by *being* temporality man does
not "pass" like an event; and if he grasps the world, a multiplicity of
events, *and* himself, man seems to approach the ubiquity of the
traditional absolute subject.   Merleau-Ponty replies that this is to
forget man's vantage point, the limitation of his grasp of time.   I am
in posession of the immediate past and the immediate future, but the
rest slips away in a movement which I cannot arrest.   The act of
memory, which voluntarily recalls a past moment, must not be confused with the horizon of pastness which delimits my experience; for
this act takes place in the present and attempts to turn a past event
into a present one.   Like spatiality, temporality is a means to something which cannot be achieved; thus it is an inefficient means, but,
Merleau-Ponty argues, it is all one has.   It does present one with at
least an intentional unity in multiplicity and can be called a synthesis.
But it must paradoxically be called a "passive synthesis," since it is
a fact of my existence which I cannot undo.   If there is an eternity in
subjectivity, it is that of the *present*; that in terms of which the horizons of pastness and futurity have their meaning.   But this, too,
must be paradoxical, for it is an eternity rooted in time, finite, by its
very nature.

Up to this decisive point, Merleau-Ponty's analysis of time and subjectivity
is similar to Heidegger's, indeed draws largely upon it.   Here, however, Merleau-Ponty makes an important departure.   For unlike
Heidegger, he considers the present as the "privileged" dimension of
temporality, "because it is the zone in which being and consciousness
coincide" (PP 424).   For Heidegger, human subjectivity can take
over its own future through the resolute decision, overcoming its own

19 *Merleau-Ponty quotes from Heidegger ("Zusammenhang des Lebens"), Sein und*
Zeit, *p. 373.*

dispersion in the world of presentness. For Merleau-Ponty even such resolution starts in the present and can never completely obliterate or even transform it. It is true that subjectivity is not coincident with itself in the present; its attempts to grasp itself go through the past and the future. But they can never suspend the anonymity of the subject at the root of this attempt, the "natural subject" of perception. Man is confronted with his own "facticity," his own concrete existence in a much more intimate way than merely as a particular object in his world. But his facticity is also more than his birth and "thrown-ness" into a world, as it is for Heidegger; it is also the functioning intentionality of perceptive consciousness, the necessary relation to the world in the present.[20]

The privileged status of the present indicates for Merleau-Ponty the most important characteristics of human subjectivity: spatially and temporally, to be in the world is to be *in situation*. And both the spatially and temporally present are defined by the body. His treatment of perception and the perceived has shown us the significance of the body in relation to the world: it is at once the movement away from itself toward the object and the limitation on the attainment of that very goal. As such, the body fulfills the same role in terms of time: by insuring the absolute engagement of the subject in the world of space, feeling, objectivity, it is a limitation on any attempt to escape or to overcome that world, to withdraw into the self. Yet by bearing the living conditions of the possibility of the perceived world, by possessing and coinciding with the passing of an event, the body opens the horizons of past and future to consciousness. In both these directions it leads to the self: the past is that which I am, the habits, given characteristics of my body with which I must begin; the future is action, existence, that which is to be done.

Thus human existence is in the most profound sense ambiguous. The body, as a structure which is inexorably engaged in the world, carries in it the notion of the pure intention, the movement toward that which is beyond itself. It is thus the foundation of the spirit, the intention to encompass itself and everything else. Human being *is* this spirit, this intention, just as surely as it is temporality, spatiality, etc. But the spirit is in turn incarnate; that is to say that the bodily foundation of the spirit is also its limitation, its finitude.

It is the notion of the incarnate spirit which is slowly revealed throughout

---

[20] In keeping with his notion of the privilege of the present rather than the future, Merleau-Ponty places less emphasis than Heidegger on the phenomenon of death. He admits that it is a factor in experience, that it is an essential part of the finitude of the subject, that it is involved with "dread" (angoisse) (PP 404). But it is reduced in experience to the appearance of a limiting contingency, almost an unreality beside the being of the present. In an essay on Hegel, he quotes Simone de Beauvoir (Pyrrhus et Cinéas, Gallimard, Paris, 1944, p. 61): "Ma mort n'arrête ma vie qu'une fois que je suis mort, et pour le regard d'autrui. Mais, pour moi vivant, ma mort n'est pas. . . ." He adds: "I live then, not in order to die, but forever. . . ." (SN 120–1) meaning by "forever," of course, just the finite "eternity" of our engagement in the present—thus the appearance of "forever."

the detailed investigations of both *La Structure du comportement* and the *Phénoménologie de la perception*, and which Merleau-Ponty continuously elaborates throughout his other writings.   The traditional problems of knowledge and the world lead to the problem of perception.   Perception leads us to subjectivity, not as an absolutely free ego over against the world, a "hole" in the plenitude of being-in-itself; but merely as a "hollow" or "fold" in being (PP 215), a structure which is as much a part of and dependent on being as it is distinguishable from it.   The ambiguity of being-in-the-world is the ambiguity of an intention which cannot be entirely fulfilled, but which nonetheless cannot be withdrawn.

14. The Ambiguity of Conditioned Freedom

Is man free?   It is clear that Merleau-Ponty's interpretation of existence rules out any naïve determinism of the naturalistic sort.   There is no cause-effect relation between consciousness and nature.   But at the same time he always leads his discussion back to the primordial intentionality of the body, the relation of life to the life-world which is prior to conscious activity.   Is man's existence any different from the structure of animal behavior, which can be described in roughly the same terms, and which we can hardly characterize as "free"?

The answer is that the recognition of man's bodily nature does not entail the denial of his free action but only its limitation.   And it is only in respect to limitations, Merleau-Ponty argues, that the notion of freedom can have any sense.   This is to say, first of all, that in order to act man must start somewhere, must "be somewhere," must act in regard to "something."   We cannot think of man or even consciousness as being nowhere, when "where" is taken in the broadest sense.   Even the intellectualist position "places" consciousness in regard to the world, i.e., outside it, and thus draws upon our own notion of situation, just as any talk of eternity is based, if only by negation, on the experience of time.   Second, it is only in the face of real obstacles that free action is meaningful.   Obstacles are to be overcome if the situation is to be transformed, and freedom is as dependent upon them as change is dependent on that which was before.   If freedom is to involve choice, choice must be made in regard to given alternatives arising out of the situation.   Thus the conditions on freedom become the conditions of the possibility of freedom.   Freedom is the ability to act under certain conditions; and the ever present condition is that of the body and its relation to the world.   Only the notion of unconditioned or "radical" freedom is impossible, according to Merleau-Ponty.[21]   Action without conditions, alternatives, or "situa-

---

21 *The denial of "radical freedom" is only one of Merleau-Ponty's disagreements with his sometime friend, Jean-Paul Sartre. Other disagreements involve the place of the body in the structure of temporality, the possibility of relations with others and social action, the notion of dialectic and the attitude toward communism. Ultimately, all these are based on Merleau-Ponty's denial of the insurmountable division of the en soi and the pour soi, maintained vigorously by*

tion" is not chosen but arbitrary.   And the notion of "arbitrary"
action is, when examined, a living impossibility, a fabrication of the
intellect.

Thus, while it is true that there can be no causal influence on the conscious
self by the world, there is influence in terms of meaning: any project
undertaken by the self is a structure which stands out from the
background of the lived world and temporality.   There is, then, a
"reaction" to this influence—not a causal reaction, but one of
motivation.   The world, myself, and other people present me with
the indeterminacies and possibilities, the alternatives which require
decision.   I may be hunchbacked, blind, ugly, proletariat, or intellectual, and my possibilities arise at least partially from these conditions.
They, as much as my own desires and ideals, point the way to my
action, motivate my undertaking.   The decision is no less mine, and
can change both my world and myself.   But it does not free me from
the conditions of existence; on the contrary, it is part of the ambiguity
of action that it binds me anew: each action commits me, becomes a
part of me and thus of the situation with which I am faced from then
on.   Freedom does not assure the transition from indeterminacy to
determinacy, but only to a new indeterminacy.

Merleau-Ponty's philosophy of existence is thus very much one of "engagement" and its essential ambiguity:

*Existence . . . is the movement by which man is in the world, engaged in a
physical and social situation which becomes his point of view on the world.
All engagement is ambiguous, because it is at once the affirmation and the
restriction of a freedom: if I decide to render a service, this means both that
I might not render it and that I decide to exclude this possibility (SN 125).*

He insists, however, that such ambiguity does not define existence as
tragic or absurd.   It is true that the intentions of consciousness can
never be completely fulfilled: the perceived world is ever unrealized,
while the engagement of the self in this world precludes the possibility
of its complete grasp of itself.   The object of experience is never
apodictically given, never absolutely self-evident.   But, to use a
Husserlian term, there are degrees of "adequacy" in the evidence of
the self and the world which make possible not only the "cohesion of
a life," but much more besides.   I can take possession of myself to
the extent that I can form projects, make plans, live according to a
pattern suggested by the factual conditions of my existence.   I can
"know myself," if only to be aware, like Socrates, of my own ignorance.   Turning toward the world, I can appropriate the appearance
of objects into expression through language, move from the realm of
phenomena to that of truth.   Our sciences are evidence of this possi-

*Sartre. According to A. de Waelhens (cf. op. cit., p. 3 and note), Merleau-Ponty's
major accomplishment is to have surpassed, like Heidegger, such dogmatic
metaphysical doctrines as those of Sartre, while discovering in the phenomenon
of the body a primordial level of existence neglected by Heidegger's investigations.*

bility. Furthermore, they are the evidence of intersubjective experience and communication, the tentative bridge which is possible
between different individuals. This does not alter their essential
individuality, for only through its assertion can a bridge be attempted.
Nor can such communication ever be fully accomplished. But it can
be achieved for purposes of common projects, tasks, desires.

Thus ambiguity is an expression not of absurdity but of dialectic. The
necessarily unfulfilled intentions which hold between subject and
object, subject and other subject, subject and itself are the conditions
of the operative syntheses of which life is made. There is a mediation
which takes place in all these oppositions, but only in order to place
one on another level of ambiguity—while each level reflects the fundamental ambiguity of perception. The possibility of the "cohesion of a
life" through temporality is the foundation of the historicity of subjectivity, and history is carried from the subject to the community.
Communication through language is the foundation of the "eternal"
ideas, but these are linked to history and the community by the means
of expression through which they are available to us. History, the
acquisition of a past, becomes the situation of the present with which
the individual and society are faced. There is a possible transition
from what Hegel called "subjective spirit" (the individual) to "objective spirit" (the community), but the latter, rather than a newly autonomous being which moves through history, is a project which is
continually made, dissolved, to be remade.

If dialectic is to express human existence, then, it is not in the traditional
triad thesis–antithesis–synthesis, but in the notion of negation—
unfulfilled intentionality—and the negation of the negation—the
move to a new intention through the transformation of the old. This
is, in Merleau-Ponty's view, the essence of dialectic, and he reproaches
Hegel for turning it into "speculation" and "system" through the
introduction of the definitive synthesis.[22] Rather than an explicative
principle of all being, dialectic is the sense which is discovered
phenomenologically in one's own experience, one's relations with oneself, others, and the world. Like the body itself, it is the intention of
that which is not itself, the movement toward the fulfillment of its
intention and the very impossibility of its own accomplishment, resolution and repose.

Thus Merleau-Ponty's reflections on man place him at the threshold of an
ascending dialectic, moving from the individual to the world, to
science, to society, to history. It should be borne in mind that in
order to arrive at a basic notion of the nature of consciousness and
experience, Merleau-Ponty has made a determined effort to put aside

22 Cf. Annuaire du Collège de France, Imprimerie Nationale, Paris, 1956, p. 178. Cf.
    also Le Visible et l'invisible, Gallimard, Paris, 1964, pp. 125–130, for a critique
    of dialectical thought: dialectic is "in a sense, what we are looking for" (p. 125)
    as a solution to the false separation of the en soi and the pour soi, but it con-
    tains a "trap": "as soon as one talks about it instead of practicing it," it be-
    comes "a power of being, an explicative principle," a "someone."

prejudices which reduce man to a network of causalities, whether physical, social or historical. At the same time he has refused to "deduce" the notion of subjectivity from the analysis of our knowledge in these fields. Instead, he turns to perception in the broad sense which we can now understand, applying to it a descriptive, or phenomenological method. The results of this undertaking have been seen, and the question arises how they apply to the very problems which were suspended at the beginning of the project. Merleau-Ponty holds, as has been noted, that each of the "higher" aspects of consciousness has its roots in lived experience, and that the investigation of lived experience necessitates a revision of one's views about them. The possible beginnings of such a revision in the notions of engagement and dialectic have just been seen, and it should now be considered in more detail.

15. Expression:
Art and Language

If there is a beginning to the ascending dialectic of freedom, it is to be found at the point where new meanings are elicited by man from the world of perception and a superstructure of "signification" appears. This, for Merleau-Ponty, is the phenomenon of expression. With its origins in the body and its ramifications in art, language, and all phenomena which somehow depend on these, expression is essential to the understanding of all that comes after.

The point of the phenomenology of perception has been to lead back to a realm of being which is prior to cognitive activity and judgment, but which is nonetheless rich in structure and meaning. Sciences do not result from the meeting of consciousness and meaningless data, Merleau-Ponty holds, but are secondary meanings (*significations*) derived from primary meaning (*sens* or *structure*). The realm of "primary meaning," however, is not a static array of objects, or even structures, which is given to the subject. On the contrary, as we have seen in our discussion of being-in-the-world, it is a sort of open-ended project, sustained in being by the spatialization, corporalization, and temporalization of subjectivity. The difference is simply that we do not undertake the activity as if it were a science, self-consciously proceeding by rules of induction or deduction. Our bodily existence carries on this project according to its own rules, and it is not in our intellectual power to refrain from its execution.

Now if expression is taken as "letting meaning appear," the perceiving body is already expression *par excellence*. Merleau-Ponty's entire discussion of the body was centered on its intentionality, its spatial and sensory orientation, as "means" toward the appearance of the phenomena. But the meanings of perception form the situation in which subjectivity is rooted, while its structure permits the supplementation of these meanings with new ones. The gesture, for Merleau-Ponty, is the elementary form of expression, the purely bodily sign of something beyond itself.[23]   While the gesture, as indicating an object, a person or some feeling, *has* a meaning (as its intentional object), it can also be said to *be* a meaning, a new phenomenon on the horizon of the world which is an expression of the peculiar nature of its user.   The gesture draws upon that which it means and creates for it a new status, not reproducing it, but subsuming it into a new event.

This can be recognized as the original sense of all art, according to Merleau-Ponty, without any speculation about primitive scratches in sand or cave drawings.[24]   "Art is neither an imitation, nor a fabrication following the wishes of instinct or of good taste.   It is an operation of expression" (SN 30).   Working through the body, perhaps through utensils and materials, it is a comment upon some aspect of the lived world, a creation based upon something beyond itself, a concretization and consolidation of a fleeting, sometimes confused meaning. Most of Merleau-Ponty's examples are drawn from painting, which has been largely representational throughout its history.   Painters express their world in many ways, only one of which is the geometrical realism originating in the Renaissance.   The geometric approach to the lived world does not exhaust its possibilities, as later schools attempted to show.   And in an artist like Cezanne (to whom Merleau-Ponty devotes a whole essay in *Sens et non-sens*), who attempted to express the peculiar spatial and intersensory structures of the perceived world, painting can become a sort of phenomenology of perception itself.

This theory is no less valid, of course, for abstract painting, music, and other art forms as well.   Whether through representation or abstraction, art expresses something beyond itself; yet its being is determined less by that "something" than by the particular "system of equivalences" which the artist "constitutes for this work of manifestation, the universal index of 'coherent deformation' through which he concentrates the still scattered meaning in his perception and makes it exist expressly" (S 68).   Such a system of equivalences is first of all the chosen art form, and, within that, the *style* peculiar to the artist and his work.   Thus there is a triple intentionality of expression in the work of art: it expresses its object; any element in it expresses the style or "system of equivalences" of the whole; and through the latter, in a very different way from that in which it expresses its object, the work of art is an expression of the artist.

There is a similar approach to language, mediating between an "objective" linguistic or philological interpretation, treating particular languages

---

23 The fore-going discussion of expression naturally presupposes intersubjectivity as the milieu in which new meanings are perceived.   But other persons are, as has been seen, part of the lived world.   While they give validity to expression, they can, like the rest of the world, also be transformed by it.

24 It is to be remembered that Merleau-Ponty is not speaking of the actual historical beginnings of these phenomena when he discusses their "original sense."   He is speaking, rather, of the "genesis of meaning" which is involved in each instance of the phenomenon whether at its first occurrence or not.

and their development according to their own laws, and a logical approach which considers language the imperfect vehicle of pure thought. This is possible through a return to the matrix from which both aspects arise, namely lived language or speech. The name, the phrase, the verbal expression are sounds created by bodily gestures, and they exhibit the same triple intentionality as the work of art. They refer to and make explicit an object beyond themselves; they express a "system of equivalences" in their own composition, etc.

Yet, without withdrawing this account of language, Merleau-Ponty realizes that it is a much more complicated phenomenon. The "system of equivalences" of our language is never completely created as it is used; language comes with its own system, its own possibilities, its own combinations of the expressible and the understood. As such, it is the property of the community "before" its use, while the work of art achieves this status only upon creation. There are always limits, then, to the extent to which it can be said that the use of language is an expression of its user. It is true, of course, that each person uses language in a different way, and a person can often best be recognized by his pronunciation, intonation, and employment of words. But this is less a matter of ways of creation than of ways of re-creating meanings which are already to be found in the language. Rather than a means for the expression of thoughts, Merleau-Ponty says, "language is something like a being" (S 54), one which bears within itself both its relations to that which it expresses and the ways it can be used to express them. Thus it is possible to have historical and comparative linguistic sciences which treat of language without direct reference to its users, as well as dictionaries and rules of grammar.

Instead of following up this sort of "objective" approach, however, the phenomenology of language must reconcile the quasi-autonomous status of the phenomenon with the experience we have in using it, seeking in the latter the original sense of language. As has been noted, there is an "empirical use of already made language . . . that is to say, the opportune calling-in (*rappel*) of a pre-established sign," which characterizes most daily speech. But this must be distinguished from the "creative use" (alive in the poet, for example, and at times in the philosopher) which establishes meaning in the world. The poet may use empirical language, of course, but only in the sense that the artist uses the materials of his art: in order to transform it into something new. Such language does not represent its object like the proper noun, but "means" it indirectly, like the work of art. Creative language, then, is indirect language, and if speech comes "to signify directly a thought or an object, this is only a secondary power, derived from its interior life" (S 56). All empirical use of language presupposes creative language, according to Merleau-Ponty, as the prior establishment of meaning through speech. Thus, two important questions arise: How does language in its original sense come to signify "directly," making possible all forms of exact language, as in science? And how does it become "empirical," capable of being

used again and again?   These are the two most important senses in
which language, comparable in its creative form to the work of art,
differs from it most radically.

The first question raises a variety of problems.   Drawing upon modern
studies (particularly by the French linguist Saussure), Merleau-Ponty
notes that it is necessary to revise the conception of language as
individual words, representing objects, connected according to certain
rules of grammar and syntax.   A term has its meaning less in its
object than in the difference between it and other terms, its relation
to its context and to language as a whole.   Yet language claims a
closer relation to that which it expresses than this model would imply.
Particularly in science, it attempts to render "in the flesh," the meaning of the state of affairs to which it refers.   "Here we have not
merely the replacement of one meaning with another," which occurs
in the work of art, "but the substitution of equivalent meanings, the
new structure being given as already present in the old" (S 102).
In this very claim, one must recognize in language a much more
direct relation to the perceived world of objects, made possible by the
fact that it can be broken down, to an extent, into components which
stand for distinguishable elements and events of our world   A certain
precision and consistency is possible in both our means of expression
and the experienced events or objects they signify.   But even granted
this, one can comment with adequate preciseness on any state of
affairs in an infinite variety of ways.   There is always more to a perceptive event, Merleau-Ponty says, no matter how carefully it is
observed, than any proposition or finite set of propositions can account for.   Expression is never complete, and is necessarily surpassed by that which it signifies (S 112).

It is wrong to conclude from this, however, that language merely expresses
imperfectly the "thought" or "representation" of the object which is
itself perfect.   As Merleau-Ponty has shown, no object or event is
ever completely self-given, even in perception.   Now language does
not place one a step farther away from the fleeting "object = X" of
experience.   On the contrary, it can impose a unity to the object
which perception cannot provide (for example, if the object is a class
of individuals), revealing the object, again like art, in a new garb.
By thus rendering more explicit that which it signifies, the expression
is the very possibility that the object signified can surpass the expression of it.   For without expression we might not be aware of its
particular being.

If language is to be precise, then, it is not in the total possession of objective meaning.   It is precise only "to the extent that it is understood
without equivocacy" (S 112) in regard to the state of affairs it has
brought to light.   This brings up the second question,—that of the
"empirical" nature of language.   For, in order to be understood, language must somehow be on hand, given to the other.   In the elaboration of this notion is to be discovered the central role of language
in the theory of truth, intersubjectivity and history.

16. Truth,
Communication, Community

"Language is understood": This can be treated first without any reference
to other people. As the gesture which indicates, and thus generates
meaning, says Merleau-Ponty, expression is but an extension of the
spatialization and temporalization of bodily perception. Like the
perceived thing, the meaning in question is "established" within the
temporal flow first by being made present—that is, by coming to
light, appearing. But to say that it is "established" means also that
"by becoming past, it does not cease to be." Like the perceptual
event, it is established "for all time" or destined "ever to have been."
It is "acquired," says Merleau-Ponty, so that I can return to it,
reawaken its presence in me. The meaning of expression appears by
being expressed, but it is only established to the extent that it is
understood or acquired. Like the object or even the *ego cogito*, it
becomes given (or empirical) because I give it to myself—first by
effecting its appearance, then by taking up what has been revealed.
It is possible to refer to these two acts respectively as the "speaking"
and the "understanding" of language, so that even in the individual,
language involves a "de-presentation" of the self by itself (cf. PP 363),
as well as a synthesis of the two resulting "selves": "To the extent
that what I say has meaning, I am for myself, when I speak, another
'other'; and to the extent that I understand, I no longer know who
speaks and who listens" (S 121).

In taking up and carrying on the function of "establishment," language contributes to a process in experience which Husserl called "sedimentation" and which, for Merleau-Ponty, is another name for truth (S 120).
While the establishment of the perceptual object is dependent on its
perspective aspects, the established linguistic meaning intends its
object independently of perception. In it, a perceptual meaning can
be acquired in an even more permanent fashion than perception
allows. Expressions are not simply stored up, however, as a collection
of propositions called "true." Rather, an expression is true to the
extent that it can be used again and enlarged upon by new expressions. There is a temporal dialectic, then, to the process of de-
presentation which is the *becoming* of truth. Like everything else,
truth has its origins in perception as the "place" of meaning in
general. "We are in the truth" (PP xvi) in perception, as being
appears to consciousness; we carry on the truth of perception in
language by a movement which seems to leave perception behind, or
to elevate its self-evidence to a new sphere.

It is through a similar process of de-presentation, according to Merleau-
Ponty, that language plays an essential role in intersubjective experience, in communication, and thus in the possibility of community
in general. Language is "given"; but it may also be given by another,
and in the original act of de-presentation a decisive move occurs.
In perception the appearance of the other person generates a paradox.
The other is a being in my world, but as a "behavior," or consciousness, his meaning is to be a "subject" and thus to reduce me to the

status of "object" for him. While a dogmatic philosophy of the *pour soi* and the *en soi* cannot deal with this paradox, actual experience overcomes it, at least in part. In the recognition of the expression of another, I recognize him as a subject in his own right and relieve him of his ambiguous status. In the *understanding* of another's expression, I effect with him the same synthesis which occurs in myself: I become one with him insofar as I am witness to the same meaning. Again, such a synthesis does not "correct" or replace perception; for limited communication is possible even without language, insofar as different individuals deal with the same world. But language offers a provisional solution to a problem inherent in perception, realizing at the same time a possibility founded in perception. That the synthesis is only provisional is evident, for it applies directly only to certain patterns of communication and their meanings. It is a continual project which must be done and redone, and in this sense it never definitely overcomes the paradox of the other. Communication is forever a problem, as we all know, even once it has been established on a limited scale: for then it must be maintained.

But it is maintained, such that the "understanding" which bridges the gap between persons can itself take on a temporal form. The community of subjects united by common meanings also acquires its sedimentation, the common "truths" which carry the historicity of the individual to the historicity of the community. By consolidating in language the fleeting appearance of its common perceptions, a community acquires a history. It is essential to language to be historical, that is, to remain available to the intersubjective milieu in which it appears. This is also true of art, especially if the work of art, like a statue, has an enduring physical status (as opposed, for example, to the bodily expression of the dance). In the same manner, the written document elevates to an even higher degree of permanence the linguistic expression. For Merleau-Ponty, then, it is impossible to separate art from the history of art, or any types of linguistic expression, including those of isolated "domains" such as science, from their history. The truths which make up our sciences, including the exact or ideal sciences, are carried through time by the written propositions in which they are embodied. They are constantly tested and reformulated according to their appropriateness to present experience. Thus, paradoxically, it is only through repeated temporalization or "presentation" that any expression can acquire the status of an "eternal" truth. It is the essence of all these phenomena of expression, following perception, to found and continue a *tradition*—which Merleau-Ponty, borrowing from Husserl, defines as "the power to forget the origins" (S 74).[25] It is the work of art or the scientific propositions, then, rather than the perceptive origins of these expressions, which become the temporal and cultural "situation" in which any new endeavor is undertaken. The lived world of perception is thus not the only background of man's actions; through expression, he is just as inexorably

25 Cf. *Husserl's paper "Der Ursprung der Geometrie," in* Husserliana, Bd. VI, 2. Aufl., *M. Nijhoff, The Hague, 1962, pp. 365ff.*

"engaged" in his society and in the system of truths with which his culture is laden. In order now to grasp the implications of these considerations, let us turn in more detail to Merleau-Ponty's writings on historical and political subjects.

17. History and Politics

After the philosophy of perception, discussions of history and politics form the largest part of Merleau-Ponty's published writings. Many of these deal with postwar current affairs, written for the magazine *Les Temps Modernes* (directed by Sartre) and later *L'Express*, and need not concern us here directly. They reflect, however, a conception of history and social action, laid out more explicitly in *Humanisme et terreur*, and *Les Aventures de la dialectique*, which is important to the understanding of Merleau-Ponty's philosophy as a whole. This conception is based throughout on an encounter with and an interpretation of Marxism.

There is a "general" and a "specific" level to Merleau-Ponty's acceptance of Marx's theories. In general, Marx is seen as the major political thinker to have discovered man's "incarnation" in the social sphere, and to have overcome the subjective-objective division in the interpretation of history. Characteristically, Merleau-Ponty's defense of Marx is framed in the dialectical criticism of idealistic and realistic views of man and society. The conception of man as the undetermined, free ego which constitutes his world is expressed as well by the liberal tradition of the Western democracies as it is by the epistemology and ethics of Kant. Such a view is essentially nonhistorical, making of history the objective result of our constitution. Man is not *in* history, nor is he determined by any of the social and historical categories he has made for himself. He is a free subject, and society, rather than an intersubjectivity, is the mere plurality of such subjects—equal, transparent to themselves and to each other, judged not by their actions, but by their intentions.

For Marx, man does not have an essence which is distinguishable from the material conditions of his existence. According to Merleau-Ponty, the merit of Marx's critique is to have recognized in man's relation to others and to what he produces a primary dimension of his existence. The Marxian critique of the idealistic view, like Merleau-Ponty's own critique, points to its inherent contradictions, contradictions not of logic but of fact. Modern industrial society cannot construct states based on the notion of subjective freedom without denying to sizable groups the exercise of the very freedom it professes. Since the relation of men to each other is not one of direct transparency, but is mediated by their common relation to the world which they inhabit and transform through production, an imbalance in the control of such production is expressed by an imbalance in the relations between men. The subjectivist view of freedom is a fiction sponsored by those who control—not deliberately concocted, perhaps, but expressive of their own circumstances and necessary to the continuation of their control. The attitudes of men, their philosophies as well as their actions, cannot be understood apart from their "situation" in an economic system of production.

But Marx's denial of the subjectivistic conception, Merleau-Ponty insists, does not imply an objectivistic or deterministic view of society and its development. Basing his interpretation largely on Marx's early writings, Merleau-Ponty attacks the standpoint represented by many modern Communists which sees in dialectical materialism the "laws" governing historical events, a process in which man's freedom plays no role. This, says Merleau-Ponty, is to forget the sense of dialectic. It is not nature which is dialectical, but the relation between man and nature in concrete existence. Marxism does not "reduce" the life of a community to its economic factors, or explain it in terms of them, but shows how the intellectual, the religious, the moral, and the economic reflect and express each other reciprocally. The community and its particular characteristics are partly chosen by, partly forced upon the individuals, and all their action is rooted in the resulting situation. Society is historical in that it begins in situation, acts, and creates a new situation for itself, thus setting the stage for further action. Like the individual, society forges its future through a reading of its past and present, finding in the "is" of its situation the "ought" of its common norms.

This is equal to denying the possibility of a "philosophy of history" in any traditional sense. The philosopher cannot describe the events and ideas of the past as an incomplete expression of his own thought, as did Hegel, without robbing them of their actual indeterminacy for those who were involved. Nor can he discover objective "laws" which will enable him to predict the future. He can only elucidate the general structures of historicity in regard to man and society. Further, he can do his part in assessing the past and present of his own culture, seeking there the possibility or necessity of certain patterns of action. This task is well carried out by Marx, according to Merleau-Ponty. There is in Marx, of course, a deterministic and even teleological strain (from which Merleau-Ponty dissociates himself) which speaks of dialectic as a natural process and points to an end of history (or "pre-history") in its final resolution. For the most part, however, Marx's work is devoted to the analysis of his own times— primarily from an economic point of view—and the outline of certain problems calling for resolution. The future is a matter not for philosophers to speculate upon, but for the people and their leaders to create. The point is not to interpret the world, as Marx said, but to change it. Here is the contingency in his theory; for while the class struggle may be a fact, it is a long way from class to class consciousness and from there to revolutionary action.

This brings us to the "specific" level of Merleau-Ponty's encounter with the Marxist view of history—a level which has its own history in Merleau-Ponty's development. If history is man's action in face of a given situation, what is our situation, and what lines of action does it open up? Are the concrete analyses offered by Marx and his followers—

especially modern Communists—valid for our day? And is their solution, the proletarian revolution, together with its one present-day result, the U.S.S.R., the example we should follow? As we have seen, Merleau-Ponty considers these issues more political than philosophical, and he writes of them as a political commentator.

In his early essays, Merleau-Ponty is sympathetic with Marx's critique of capitalist society. Marx and his successors, up to and including present-day Communists, judge capitalism not on what it says, but on what it does, Merleau-Ponty says, thus revealing its basic contradictions. The modern Communist critique of Western society, with its focus on colonialism, economic imperialism, racism, and militarism, is as telling in our day as Marx's critique was in his. Furthermore, the traditional notion of the class struggle was considered valid by Merleau-Ponty in the immediate postwar years, when major strikes spread throughout Europe and America, and when thousands of workers gravitated toward the Communist parties. The proletariat was still the actual producer and supporter of society, as well as its majority, and its discontent, as in Marx's day, gave evidence enough for the only immediate direction a change of society could take. Finally, a real proletarian revolution had to be considered possible (although it was never predicted) because, as Merleau-Ponty thought, it had happened at least once—in Russia in 1917. The October Revolution was for him the fortuitous case *par excellence* of the convergence of ideas and actions, immediate means and immediate ends, peasants and workers in a spontaneous movement which lowered the barriers between particular individuals and interests.

Yet from the beginning[26] Merleau-Ponty was unable to give wholehearted support to the Communist Party. Naturally he objected to the theoretical treatment of dialectical materialism as a kind of sociological determinism. But there was the more important question of what the Revolution in Russia had become. Like many others, he was troubled by the Moscow trials of the late thirties and (to a lesser extent) by the Hitler-Stalin pact, although his objections took an unusual form. Realistic policies of deception and violence are necessary to every country, according to Merleau-Ponty, and the question is whether they are rationalized, hidden, and thus maintained, as in the Western democracies, or whether they are acknowledged and used at a minimum in order to accomplish the revolution and eliminate their own necessity. Also, deviationists must be disciplined for greater solidarity —deviationists with good intentions as well as deliberate traitors. Yet Moscow presented its trials under the guise of civil law, and its deviationists were not disciplined through discussion, as in Lenin's day—they were shot. In *Humanisme et terreur*, at a time when the

[26] Here reference is made only to what is evident in Merleau-Ponty's published writings, as adequate sources are not available to present his prewar political adherences and activities. By his "early" political writings, is meant parts of the Phénoménologie de la perception, the essays in Sens et nonsens and particularly Humanisme et terreur (1947). The later views are expressed mainly in Les Aventures de la dialectique (1955). Also, the last section of Signes ("Propos"), includes articles on politics written for various periodicals from 1948 to 1958.

turmoil of war was receding and the Soviets' plans for Eastern Europe were uncertain, Merleau-Ponty was unable to decide whether Stalin's tactics were necessary for the furtherance of the revolution or whether the Soviet Union had passed certain undefinable limits to become something quite different from its original conception. For the moment, the "homeland of the revolution" was the underdog, and deserved the benefit of the doubt. "If, tomorrow, the U.S.S.R. threatened to invade Europe and to establish in all the countries a regime of its choice," he wrote (HT 202), "another question would be posed. . . . It is not posed today."

As the years passed and more information on Russia became available, Merleau-Ponty became increasingly disillusioned by the internal and external appearance of the Bolshevik Revolution. "The U.S.S.R. has not invaded Europe," he wrote in the mid-fifties (AD 308), "but the Korean war has posed that 'other question' which was not posed in 1947. . . . We do not claim that the U.S.S.R. wanted or started the Korean war: but since she put an end to it, she probably could have prevented it. . . ." Reports of forced labor in the Soviet Union, of vast economic differences between workers and the new bureaucratic class, of the Hungarian revolt and other facts known well to the Western world, served to heighten his opposition. Always his objections were based on a comparison not with the West, but with what the Revolution should have become, with what it claimed it was. Thus the coming of the Khrushchev era, while welcome in respect to some reforms, only consolidated the position of the U.S.S.R., not as a world leader of revolution, but as one superpower matching its interests with those of another, the United States. It was the "either-or" opposition of the two—communism or anti-communism—which Merleau-Ponty considered the major evil, especially for middle powers like France. His final proposal was for a "non-communist left" (AD 302), a refusal to join either camp which was at the same time the "strict condition" for understanding both.

These developments brought with them a limitation on Merleau-Ponty's allegiance to Marx himself, even on what we have called the "general" level. Severe criticism from many sides seemed to make him aware that he had drawn only from the early Marx, and that one could not honestly separate the early from the late. There is no evidence that Merleau-Ponty's own notion of historicity changed, but he no longer linked it to Marxism. Regardless of the extent to which later politicians distorted the major prophet, one is not able to treat his philosophy, Merleau-Ponty says, as if it "got away intact" (AD 124) when the revolution failed. Furthermore, the present state of world communism makes questionable even its criticism of the West: "It is . . . impossible to cut Communism in two, to agree with its denials and disagree with its affirmations: for concretely, in its way of denying, its way of affirming is already present" (AD 311). Its criticism of the capitalist class struggle is based on the idea of overcoming all classes; if the society operating with that criticism has developed a class system even more intricate and vicious than that of its adversary, the criticism itself is implicated. Finally, Merleau-Ponty calls the notion of revolution itself into question in a way which reflects his basic philosophical temperament. Violent revolution cannot be undertaken, he maintains, unless it "takes itself for an absolute" (AD 278), believes itself to be the solution of all problems. Thus it cannot simply occur, but must maintain itself and believe itself "permanent" (in Trotsky's word). In this it can only succeed through the power of an elite, the very condition it sought to overcome. It must be the annihilation, not the realization of its original intention, thus being not dialectical but merely contradictory and equivocal. "Revolutions are true as movements but false as regimes," he writes (AD 279). "From this arises the question whether there is not more future in a regime which does not claim to remake history from the ground up, but simply to change it, and whether it is not this regime we should seek, instead of entering once again into the circle of revolution."

18. Philosophy
and the Philosopher

This is quite a change, needless to say, from his earlier writings on the subject. But there is a certain consistency: at neither time is Merleau-Ponty able to believe wholeheartedly in the claims of a political movement. He sees in it not only its absoluteness for itself, but also its limitations, the situation which prevents it from being absolute. His thinking on historical action thus joins the pattern we have found in his discussions of perception, language, and science: each phenomenon is seen as an intentional movement toward a sort of resolution or determination on its own terms; but each is prevented by its very nature from thus accomplishing itself. This is no doubt the "new analysis" of man's activities which is made "possible and necessary" by the phenomenology of perception. For the basic problems of perception—our being in space and time, our relation to the physical world, our recognition of other people—run through all forms of human endeavor. Merleau-Ponty's central insight is man's incarnation in the physical, social, and temporal world: man is limited by the very vantage point which allows him to move beyond himself.

This leads us to what must be considered the highest level of the "ascending dialectic"—philosophy itself. Is it not precisely the calling of philosophy to do what Merleau-Ponty says cannot be done: to encompass and understand all that is, if not as the truth of being itself (as for Hegel), then, at least, as an intellectual discipline which expresses that truth? Is not Merleau-Ponty's own discovery and expression of man's bodily situation the proof that philosophy can take a standpoint outside it? Or, on the other hand, if philosophy is not free from the bonds of man's finitude, must we not question the validity of Merleau-Ponty's own philosophy, answering the sceptic with scepticism?

Merleau-Ponty is sensitive and sympathetic to the high aspirations of philosophy. He believes, too, that thought is unable to embody or even express for all time the truth of all that is. But these two notions are not contradictory. It is in their meeting, in fact, that philosophy takes shape. "The philosopher is marked by the distinguishing trait," he writes, "that he possesses *inseparably* the taste for self-evidence and the feeling for ambiguity. When he limits himself to accepting ambiguity, it is called equivocation. But among the great it becomes a theme: it contributes to establishing certitudes rather than menacing them" (EP 4f.). Now Merleau-Ponty's own philosophy is a repeated expression of the ambiguity of being-in-the-world; and we have seen that he refuses to draw from his observations any sort of pessimism. He speaks of a "bad existentialism" (referring, no doubt, to certain of his colleagues) "which exhausts itself in describing the shock of reason against the contradictions of experience, and ends in the consciousness of failure. This is but a renewal of classical scepticism—and an incomplete description" (HT 205). For, as he says, among those very contradictions, "perspectives blend, perceptions confirm each other, a meaning emerges." "Rationality" takes shape in the world (PP xix).

Philosophy is, of course, itself experience, and above all expression. As such, it is limited to its point of view, its means of expression. Philosophy is no more able than the philosopher himself to achieve a position outside the world from which it can view it all in a glance. But as the expression and the thought of an individual or of a community of thinkers, philosophy is capable of as much—and as little—rationality as any other mode of existence. And since its aspirations are higher than those of any other endeavor, its subject matter unlimited, its possibilities are also greater. If it comes—as it must, according to Merleau-Ponty—to the awareness of the ambiguity of all human undertakings including its own, it has not proved itself impossible, but has given expression to a truth as valid as any other, one which lies somehow beyond all realms but its own. As for the recognition of its own limits, this is no less a recognition, an understanding, an advance. From the philosopher's "feeling for ambiguity" can come the constant reminder to others—such as political revolutionaries—of the problems their single-mindedness may overlook. The philosopher is, then, a critic.

This does not relieve him of the duty—a duty which is at the same time a necessity—to act. One can no more refrain from political involvement than one can cease to perceive, use language, or think scientifically. As a human being one is "condemned" (in a word Merleau-Ponty often employs) to exist in these ways, such that even an attempt to withdraw from any of them is but a move within them. In grasping the limitations of scientific or political endeavor, the philosopher is not precluding the possibility of action, but broadening the grounds upon which he can act. The critical "distance" of philosophy is the condition of action which, through understanding its own limits, understands itself. The naïveté of the enthusiast is replaced not by inert, sceptical relativism, but by action which can be as dedicated as it is often reserved and critical. Merleau-Ponty's own career of political writing is evidence that the philosopher can be concerned with action without accepting the "final solutions" offered by absolutists on all sides.

Merleau-Ponty's mistrust of "final solutions" is largely responsible for his attitude toward religion. He came from a Christian background, and his works reveal a sympathetic understanding of the problems of religious faith. At one point he even likens his own meaning of "incarnation" to the Christian notion of the descent of the Absolute into the world (cf. Pr. 135). But the idea of a "beyond," of an Absolute Being in which the paradoxes of existence are resolved, is inimical to his way of thinking. Christianity is praised for its recognition of man's infirmities, but accused of doing so only in order to affirm the perfection of God and put aside the problems of man. Merleau-Ponty's basic position is an a-theism in the literal sense— that is, a refusal both to affirm the existence of God and to deny it— the latter being merely an "inverted theology" (EP 43). He is true to this position in that he devotes very little discussion, on the whole, to religion. But he reserves for the philosopher the right to unmask the false gods of our society, including those which organized religion may often thrust upon us.

Above all, Merleau-Ponty is opposed to any reductionism which seeks to remove man from the open, often paradoxical texture of being which he is privileged to know through existing in the world. His two major books, as we have seen, are in part a criticism of reductionism in the form of empiricism and intellectualism. Throughout his works, he denies such final solutions as the Absolute, because of its dependence on man; history, because of its dependence on man; man himself (in the form of "humanism") because of his dependence on the world; and the world because of its dependence on man's experience.

But the philosopher is not merely a critic, his expression not merely concerned with other positions. His opposition to simple solutions, his "feeling for ambiguity" can only be based upon an acquaintance with the irreducibility of the phenomena themselves. For Merleau-Ponty, phenomenology itself is the "positive" content of philosophy: that is, the peculiar combination of detachment and intensity in "reawakening the experience of the world." The philosopher need not stop with the announcement of ambiguity, but can deepen himself in the experience of it, describing, however inadequately, its structures. Phenomenology is not new in philosophy; it is not a doctrine but a "manner or style" which has been "long on the way" (PP viii). The phenomenological "reduction" is but an expression of man's philosophical "wonder" at the world (PP xiii). If it leads him primarily to perception, it is not in order to deny the reality of other modes of existence, but in order to discover in perception the matrix of his openness to the world, the structures of which are basic to all experience. Properly understood, phenomenology is not even a philosophical method which leads to the enunciation of a doctrine (as it was even for Husserl, who distinguished "phenomenology" and "phenomenological philosophy," the latter being a sort of idealism). For if one traces the meanings of experience back to their origins in the lived world, discovering there the interrelation of consciousness and being, one must become aware of the impossibility of detaching and viewing in complete clarity the totality of experience. "The most important lessons which the [phenomenological] reduction teaches us is the impossibility of a complete reduction" (PP xiv).   At the roots of experience we find not a final answer, but an infinite task of description and expression. Above all we find ourselves, so completely involved in the world that even our philosophical reflection is rooted there.   In a sense, then, phenomenology is either "all or nothing" (S 118): either we continue the expression of our wonder at the world, realizing that it never reveals itself fully to us, or we pass the phenomena by in an attempt at a "final solution."

19. The Visible
and the Invisible

These are the considerations which draw Merleau-Ponty back, toward the end of his life, to the problems with which he began. Since the publication of the *Phenomenology of Perception*, it had been his plan to put in comprehensive form his theory of truth and his philosophy of language, society, and history. These subjects, presented here as they were developed in essays and lectures throughout the late 1940s and 1950s, were always approached with "primacy of perception" in mind: while the more "complex" modes of existence "are, in regard to the life of perception, original formations," they nonetheless "continue and conserve" perception as they transform it; they "sublimate" rather than "suppress" our incarnation (I 405).   But when it came time to bring together his ideas on truth, language, and society, he found he could not merely build upon his earlier work, but had to reformulate his conception of the basis of his theory. This reformulation, on which Merleau-Ponty was at work when he died, became the occasion for a highly original change in emphasis.

Merleau-Ponty's interests are, in the last period, still genetic; indeed he is seeking more intently than ever before for the "birth" of meaning in experience. But two questions converge to alter the direction of his search. The first concerns the source of our perceptive "openness to the world" and its character. Does the analysis of perception and the perceived world go deep enough? If not, is it possible for philosophy to go any deeper? The second question is the "question of being," in Heidegger's sense. Had not the earlier works suppressed the question, replacing being, in the Husserlian fashion, with the signification "Being" or with beings? Is *ontology* possible on the basis of the phenomenology of perception?

The first of these questions leads Merleau-Ponty to return to his exploration of lived experience with renewed intensity. He turns towards the lowest levels of awareness, areas of "passivity" ("sleep, unconsciousness, memory,")[27] in which consciousness approaches its own negation. Like many of those under the influence of Husserl's phenomenology, he had earlier mistrusted the Freudian notion of the "unconscious mind" as a contradiction in terms, and had sought to interpret neurosis as a confusion of intentionalities; but he now recognizes the

[27] Annuaire du Collège de France, *Imprinerie Nationale, Paris, 1955, pp. 161ff.*

validity of a level of complete anonymity which underlies explicit consciousness, even the "operative intentionality" of the body. He speaks of a phenomenology which is obliged to "descend into its own cellar" and which, in doing so, comes closer than ever to psychoanalysis.[28]

But what can one say of these "unconscious" or nonsubjective aspects of human existence? Are they discovered merely as properties of another object in the world? Or are they not rather related to our being as a necessary complement to consciousness, sustaining it from below? Now the idea of the "necessary complement" is close to another of Merleau-Ponty's notions, one that had been his from the beginning and which he now emphasizes: that perception consists as much in what is not perceived as in what is perceived, that "the present, the visible, only counts or has an absolute prestige for me by reason of the immense latent content of past, of future, and of elsewhere that it announces and conceals" (V 153). Similarly, the subjectivity of another person is merely the "other side" of the being he presents to the world in his body, his gestures, and his speech. But this, Merleau-Ponty reflects, is not merely a function of the appearance *to* consciousness of the perceived world of things and other persons. Consciousness itself, as the condition of all appearance and meaning, is dependent on its own "other side" a side which is not at all conscious in the subjective sense. The "unconscious" of Freud is part of this, but another part is the body itself, not as perceiving but as *perceived*.

Following this train of thought, Merleau-Ponty arrives at a new and radical understanding of incarnation. In the *Phenomenology of Perception* the body was singled out as the origin of all subjectivity because it is the "natural subject" of the "operative intentionality" of perception. Now the body is seen in a different light. It is true that in seeing my limbs or touching my hand as it touches something else, I do not perceive my own body in the full sense. Yet this quasi perception reveals in the body a character which is proper to it, that is, its character of being perceived by others and its membership in the perceived world. This aspect of the body is as necessary to perception as is its subjectivity, precisely in the sense of being the complement of subjectivity. The complementarity of the body is the link between human existence and the world of things, for 'the things and my body are made of the same material" (*étoffe*) (OE 21). The body can only be witness to the world by being, at the same time, *of the world, flesh of its flesh*.

This is a new interpretation of the body as the guarantor of our "insertion" in the world. One's own consciousness, that of another, the world of language and ideas are all invisible, like the hidden side of a tree. But they are bound to the visible, for us, through the body which is both seeing and seen. Thus, Merleau-Ponty concludes, "rather than

---

[28] A. Hesnard, *L'oeuvre de Freud et son importance pour le monde moderne*, *Préface de M. Merleau-Ponty*, Payot, Paris, 1960, p. 8.

of being and nothingness" as the principles of the encounter of subjectivity with the world, "one should speak of the visible and the invisible. . . ." (S 30), recognizing these terms not as contradictory but as complementary. Their combination in the body, its "reversibility" (V 317), is the key to the foundation of all human endeavor in perception. But it is also the foundation of perception itself. The unity of the visible and the invisible is not peculiar to man; it is characteristic of the world as well, as the other side belongs to the tree. It is the sense of that "immense latent content" through which the visible takes shape. The relation of the visible to the invisible is not the index of the dependence of the world on perception; it is a sign of something in which both perception and the world share, the sign of their common origin.

This is Merleau-Ponty's response, then, to the "question of being." The "flesh" of the world, of which man partakes through perception, is not matter; it is its very being. Man as a being and the world of object-beings take shape and encounter each other in virtue of the establishment of a relationship between the visible and the invisible. This is the basis of "there being" anything in the sense of the primordial faith of perception that "there is . . . ." The being of the objects of science and of human consciousness "for-itself" both derive from the "brute" or "raw being" (être brut, S 31) which announces itself in perception.

In approaching being through the relation between the visible and the invisible, Merleau-Ponty is not merely making use of a "visual metaphor." Vision itself is the unique occasion of the full revelation of being, it is "the meeting, as at an intersection, of all the aspects of Being"[29] (OE 86). Yet being is not *seen*. It is not an object of perception, much less an object of thought. But vision participates in it, while objective thought can only turn it into a being or pass it by. Painting, according to Merleau-Ponty, which does nothing but celebrate the "enigma of visibility" (OE 26) is the most authentic ontology. The painter uses his body to express the body of the world; his understanding of depth, color, form, movement is an ontological understanding which does not need thought.

But what does this mean for philosophy, which must make use of language and must speak *about* something? It cannot speak about being directly without turning it into an object and risking the loss of its meaning altogether. Is it, then, to be replaced by the silence of merely seeing or, at most, the activity of painting? Merleau-Ponty thinks not, because, as he has mentioned before, language can be indirect as well as direct; as creative language it can reveal something without speaking it. "For one speaks not only of what one knows, as if to display it—but also of what one does not know, in order to know it" (V 139). But this is none other than the operation of asking a question, and it is precisely the view of philosophy

---

[29] In his later writings, Merleau-Ponty sometimes capitalizes the word "être" to distinguish, in Heideggerian fashion, between "being" (Sein) and "that which is" (Seiendes) or "beings."

Merleau-Ponty has in mind. Furthermore it is the philosophy of which his last works, particularly Le Visible et l'invisible, are perfect examples. Phenomenology is not given up; perception and the perceived world are still subjected to intense description. Philosophical discourse still speaks of things and of people, of colors, sounds, and ideas. But the description has a new *intent*. What is described is also *interrogated*; that which is asked after is being. But the philosopher cannot expect the answer to his question in the form of words. Such phrases as the "visible and the invisible" are not descriptions of being, but expressions which put the question of being to the world. In the manner of "negative theology," Merleau-Ponty says, one must conceive of a "negative philosophy" (V 233), the ontological content of which is to be found in what is *not* expressed.

20. Conclusion

There is a sense in which Merleau-Ponty's philosophy as it stands makes a full circle, returning in the end to the place at which it began. But as we have seen, the return is more than a return, since it enlarges upon its original treatment in a way which puts it in a new and different light. Nor was Merleau-Ponty's philosophy intended to stop at the point we have reached. The ontology of Le Visible et l'invisible on which we have touched was to form the basis of a larger work. According to the latest plan the author drew up (cf. V 328), it was to include a consideration of "nature"—which Merleau-Ponty treated in lectures not as the object of our physical and chemical sciences, but as something of which we are primordially aware as that "from which we have arisen" and which continues to furnish our existence with its materials.[30] Finally, under the title "the logos," it was to incorporate the philosophy of truth and of language, of history and of social phenomena.

It is impossible to determine the changes Merleau-Ponty's philosophy might have undergone had this work been completed. But even taking the latest developments into account, it is possible to recognize a fundamental unity in its approach to philosophical problems. This unity of approach is not expressible, by way of a summary in any one of the important themes we have encountered, such as "ambiguity," "the primacy of perception," "phenomenology," or even "incarnation." "Incarnation" is an expression of man's situation, and man plays a vital role. But for Merleau-Ponty, as for most "existentialists," man is not the measure of all things. It is true that metaphysics in the traditional sense is ignored: if there is metaphysics, he says, it is "in man" (SN 145). But man, in turn, is in the world. And it is the elucidation of this last "in" to which Merleau-Ponty's philosophy is devoted. Its unity of approach, then, is one of *direction*: that is, the orientation of each problem toward its origin in the relation between man and the world. Most important, "man" and "the world" are themselves not prior to this relation, but arise out of it. They are incomprehensible without it and each other.

[30] Annuaire du Collège de France, Imprimerie Nationale, Paris, 1957, p. 202.

In the execution of his philosophical program, Merleau-Ponty can himself be accused of a certain reductionism, at least in regard to some points. His treatment of the ideal entities of the exact sciences, for example, as cultural objects limited to concrete means of expression, in one way misses the point. These objects surpass their temporal exemplifications, as Husserl emphasized, in an *essential* way. The whole range of man's "*a priori*," or "universal and necessary" knowledge presents a phenomenological problem which is by no means without its wonder, and which Merleau-Ponty tends to pass over in silence. Also, his dismissal of the problem of God is puzzling. If, as he admits, "it is of the nature of man to think of God," (Pr 151) why is God not treated as a valid, if indeterminate, intentional object of our experience? As a phenomenologist, Merleau-Ponty denies the possibility and the necessity of "proving" the existence of any being. A being is validated rather by its meaning in experience, individual or common. Merleau-Ponty does not adequately concern himself with what the meaning of God might be——whether, for example, God is less a "final solution" than the unattained object of certain intentions, not only of thought, but also of action.

On a more general plane, Merleau-Ponty may be thought to have relied heavily on an oversimplied problem, that is, his constant opposition of "intellectualism" and "empiricism." A historical acquaintance with philosophy makes one wonder what these positions are. And it could be argued that the positive content of his work is but an imprecisely expressed compromise between the two. But this criticism is itself oversimplified, and Merleau-Ponty has already provided an answer to it. For him, philosophy is far from a privileged looking, seeing, and describing what is there. The philosopher's own *situation* requires that he approach being with a point of view. Philosophy is "not only the invention of solutions but the invention of its own problems," he says (EP 14). Problems are motivated by one's situation, whether personal, historical, or intellectual, but they must be elicited from it and made explicit. In this task, simplification is perhaps inevitable, and the history of philosophy abounds with examples: Kant's Hume, Hegel's Kant, Kierkegaard's Hegel. For Merleau-Ponty, "empiricism" and "intellectualism" are characteristics of the intellectual and even social situation in which we live, and his constant reference to them is his recognition of the fact that philosophy consists as much in *negation* as it does in *position*. Furthermore, these schools of thought are not held to be false, but only abstract. The "purely objective" and the "purely subjective," "causal explanation" and "unlimited reflexion" are not errors, but aspects of the world and of ourselves toward which experience tends and to which philosophers have given expression. For Merleau-Ponty, the very recognition of these two aspects, and of their polar opposition, is the suggestion of a middle ground or common origin to be discovered.

In seeking out this common origin, Merleau-Ponty is remarkably equal to his task. His search leads him into the realm of perceptive experience, the structures of which are elusive by their very nature. Their elusiveness is the source, for him, not of frustration but of inspiration. His writing attempts not to dispel ambiguity but to capture and express it. Perhaps more extensively than any of his contemporaries, he reveals to us the meanings which lie hidden, because they are so obvious, in our everyday experience.

BIBLIOGRAPHY

Merleau-Ponty's most important publications (in chronological order)

1 "Christianisme et ressentiment," *La Vie Intellectuelle,* vol. 36, pp. 278–306, 1935.

SC *2* La *Structure du comportement* (précédé d'Une *Philosophie de l'ambiguïte* par Alphonse de Waelhens), 4th ed., Presses Universitaires de France, Paris, 1960. Originally published in 1942.
The Structure of Behavior, tr. Alden L. Fisher, Beacon Press, Boston, 1963.

PP *3* Phénoménologie de la perception, Gallimard, Paris, 1945.
Phenomenology of Perception, tr. Colin Smith, Humanities Press, New York, 1962.

Pr *4* "Le Primat de la perception et ses conséquences philosophiques," *Bulletin de la Société Française de Philosophie,* December 1947, pp. 119–153 (séance du 23 novembre, 1946).
In *The Primacy of Perception,* tr. and ed. with an introduction by James M. Edie, Northwestern University Press, Evanston, Ill., 1964.

HT *5* Humanisme et terreur, Gallimard, Paris, 1947.
Part II, chap. 2, "The Yogi and the Proletarian," tr. Nancy Metzel and John Flodstrom, in *The Primacy of Perception* (cf. #4 above).

SN *6* Sens et non-sens, Nagel, Paris, 1948.
Sense and Non-Sense, tr. Hubert L. Dreyfus and Patricia Allen Dreyfus, Northwestern University Press, Evanston, Ill., 1964.

7 Les Sciences de l'homme et la phénoménologie, Centre de Documentation Universitaire, Paris, 1951.
"Phenomenology and the Sciences of Man," tr. John Wild, in *The Primacy of Perception* (cf. #4 above).

I *8* "Un Inédit de Maurice Merleau-Ponty," *Revenue de Metaphysique et de Morale,* no. 4; pp. 401–409, 1962 (A statement of his projects written shortly before 1953).
"An Unpublished Text by Maurice Merleau-Ponty: A Prospectus of his Work," tr. Arleen B. Dallery, in *The Primacy of Perception* (cf. #4 above).

EP *9* Eloge de la philosophie, Gallimard, Paris, 1953
In *Praise of Philosophy,* tr. with a preface by John Wild and James M. Edie, Northwestern University Press, Evanston, Ill., 1963.

10 *Les Relations avec autrui chez l'enfant*, Centre de Documentation Universitaire, Paris, 1953.
"The Child's Relations with Others," tr. William Cobb, in *The Primacy of Perception* (cf. #4 above).

AD **11** *Les Aventures de la Dialectique*, Gallimard, Paris, 1955.
chap. 1. "The Crisis of the Understanding," tr. Nacy Metzel and John Flodstrom, in *The Primacy of Perception* (cf. #4 above).

12 *Les Philosophes célèbres*, a collective work, with brief introductory sections by Merleau-Ponty, L. Mazenod, Paris, 1956.

S **13** *Signes*, Gallimard, Paris, 1960.
Signs, tr. Richard C. McCleary, Northwestern University Press, Evanston, Ill., 1964.

14 *L'Oeil et l'esprit*, Gallimard, Paris, 1964.
"Eye and Mind," tr. Carleton Dallery, in *The Primacy of Perception* (cf. #4 above).

16 *Le Visible et l'invisible*, suivi de notes de travail. Texte établi par Claude Lefort, accompagné d'un avertissement et d'une postface (posthumous), Gallimard, Paris, 1964.

17 *Annuaire du Collège de France*, Imprimerie Nationale, Paris. (Issues from 1953–1961 contain brief summaries by Merleau-Ponty of his lectures at the Collège).